Notable
Black
American
Scientists

ISBN 0-7876-2789-5

Notable
Black
American
Scientists

Kristine Krapp, editor

GALE

DETROIT • LONDON

STAFF

Kristine M. Krapp, *Editor*

Pamela Proffitt, *Contributing Editor*

James Edwards, *Editorial Technical Consultant*

Christine B. Jeryan, *Managing Editor*

Susan Trosky, *Permissions Manager*
Margaret Chamberlain, *Permissions Specialist*
Jessica Ulrich, *Permissions Associate*

Mary Beth Trimper, *Production Director*
Evi Seoud, *Assistant Production Manager*

Cynthia D. Baldwin, *Product Design Manager*
Barbara Yarrow, *Graphic Services Manager*
Randy Bassett, *Image Database Supervisor*
Robert Duncan, *Imaging Specialist*
Pamela A. Reed, *Photography Coordinator*

Eric Johnson, *Cover Designer*

Library of Congress Cataloging-in-Publication Data

Notable black American scientists / Kristine M. Krapp, editor.
     p. cm.
   Includes bibliographical references and index
   Summary: Profiles approximately 250 black Americans who have made contributions to the sciences, including inventors, researchers, award winners, and educators.
   ISBN 0-7876-2789-5
   1. Afro-American Scientists—United States—Biography—Juvenile literature. [1. Scientists. 2. Afro-Americans—Biography.]
I. Krapp, Kristine M., 1971- .
Q141.N726 1990
509.2 ' 273—dc21
[B]
              94-5263
              CIP
              AC

ISBN 0-7876-2789-5

10 9 8 7 6 5 4 3 2

Contents

Foreword

Why a foreword to *Notable Black American Scientists?* Certainly, this literary device is not essential to the effective utilization of this compendium of biographical vignettes: The foreword should be of interest to potential users, but not essential. Indeed, in my own consultation of encyclopedias and other compendia, I rarely, if ever, pause to read the foreword or preface. It is my opinion that contemporary users of this resource will behave similarly: One is seeking rather specific information; if this information is available, fine; if not, one is generally not disposed to scan the text to see what else might be of interest.

Nonetheless, there are those occasions when I and others eagerly consult the foreword: What makes these occasions special? Such occasions arise, *inter alia*, when one is consulting sources that are mainly of historical significance and there is as much interest, if not more, in the socio-cultural context of the biographical data as in the data themselves: What purpose did the authors envision the compilation serving; how do the times of the earlier writings compare with today, and what progress has been made? It is in such a context as this that I would base the significance of a foreword for *Notable Black American Scientists*. What are the socio-cultural dynamics that warrant its publication?

The sparse coverage, in general, of African Americans in biographical compendia has been commented upon in several publications. There is an unquestionable bias, unwitting or not, in the coverage of African American scientists in standard compendia. This "alleged" bias does not occasion "corrective measures." Any biographical dictionaries such as this one should not be construed as "correcting the record." Rather, they are providing a different kind of record: One that would be as useful in chronicling individual achievement as in laying an informational and motivational foundation for a group's progress. There is a need for African Americans to chronicle and be informed of the progress of their fellow African Americans. This need is not intrinsic to the development of a self-concept that is simultaneously capable of full participation in American scientific enterprise and of transcending it. It is wholly a socially-constructed one. Therefore, appropriate biographical dictionaries might be compiled and oriented in their foci by criteria that exhibit little or no overlap with those employed in constructing standard compendia.

For a set of criteria that may differ from those of other "standard" works, we need offer no apology; it is only necessary that we scrupulously observe the criteria that will constitute the metric for the work in question. Given the fragmented coverage of biographies of African American scientists and the absence of any metric that conjoins their ethnic heritages with their scientific achievements, criteria that ensure inclusiveness and detailed information on the lives of the individuals covered would appear to be appropriate to the socio-cultural dynamics of our times: Times in which there is a rapid dispersion of African Americans in the larger American society and scientific enterprises, a malignant decay of informed senses of community and group solidarity that provide a context and memory for individual contributions that nurture the *informed* aspirations of future generations.

The format of the vignettes in this compilation certainly provides many dimensions of the scientists' careers that can form the basis for further inquiries. In addition to chronicling the scientific achievements of the scientists, personal accounts are given of significant events and persons and of motivating and limiting societal influences. Because a number of scientists are included for a given time period, it is possible for the interested reader to construct a composite image of the humanistic side of the careers of successful black scientists over time, across disciplines, and by gender. Such an undertaking should prove to be particularly interesting and useful to African Americans youths as they seek role models and vicarious experiences that resonate with their own aspirations and situations, as well as helping non-African Americans to learn about, identify with, and appreciate the achievements of a poorly documented segment of their society.

The approximately 250 biographical vignettes in *Notable Black American Scientists*, when melded with those in other compilations, will go a long way in providing the base of information that would be the starting point of a biographical dictionary of African American scientists in which merit and impact of the contributions of individual scientists may be given critical scholarly consideration.

B. J. Evans
Professor of Chemistry
University of Michigan/Morehouse College

Introduction

Students and researchers are always eager for accessible biographical information. Gale has published many collections of biographical sketches of notable people in many disciplines, including the sciences. Similarly, we have published many multicultural titles highlighting the progress and history of blacks and other ethnic minorities in the United States. *Notable Black American Scientists*, though, fills a special niche, since it addresses those blacks who contributed to science in the United States. It is relatively easy to locate biographical information on black civil rights activists and literary figures who have played a more visible role in American society and within the African American community. However, it is much more difficult to find out about the lives of those who struggled against poverty, racism, and other obstacles to earn advanced degrees and build careers in the sciences. Black American scientists fought their battles outside of the limelight, and frequently left little in the way of public record. The further back in time the scientist lived, the higher the possibility that his or her accomplishments were never recorded at all, or worse, covered up or co-opted by someone else.

Notable Black American Scientists highlights the accomplishments of 254 black scientists and physicians, from colonial times to the present. The editors do not claim that those listed are the "most notable"; that would be an impossible goal. Included here are the biographies of men and women who have contributed to their society through scientific endeavors. Many are the "first" to accomplish a specific goal; others have trod the paths cleared by these pioneers to achieve their own successes. *Notable Black American Scientists* includes well-known scientists such as George Washington Carver and Charles R. Drew, as well as lesser known figures like Evelyn Boyd Granville and Marjorie Lee Browne, who were the first African American women to receive doctorates in mathematics, and Keith Black, a contemporary innovator in brain surgery. For many of the scientists featured here, almost no information has previously been published about their lives or their scientific achievements. Similarly, images of most of the entrants were extremely difficult to obtain.

Selection Process and Criteria

A preliminary list of scientists was compiled from a wide variety of sources, including science indices, other biographical collections, and periodical articles. The list was reviewed by an advisory board, and final selection was made by the editor. An effort was made to include as many female scientists as possible, and there are 59 women featured here. Coverage includes those in all of the natural, physical, social, and applied sciences. Entrants are anthropologists, astronomists, biologists, botanists, chemists, computer scientists, engineers, geologists, inventors, mathematicians, physicians and medical researchers, physicists, psychologists, and zoologists. Selection criteria include:

• Discoveries, inventions, overall contributions, influence, and/or impact on scientific progress in the Unites States and abroad

• Involvement or influence in education, organizational leadership, or public policy

• Familiarity to the general public

• Notable "first" achievements, including degrees earned, positions held, or organizations founded

Features of this product

• **Entry head**—lists basic information on each scientist, including name, birth and death dates, and field of specialty.

• **Biographical essay**—offers 400 to 2000 words on the scientist's life and professional accomplishments. Scientific principles are explained in terminology that readers without a scientific background can understand. **Bold-faced** names within entries refer the reader to an essay on that person.

• **Selected Writings** by the Scientist section— lists publications written or edited by the entrant, including important papers, textbooks, autobiographies, etc.

• **Further Reading** section—provides a list of resources the reader may access to seek additional information on the scientist.

• **Timeline**—includes scientific milestones of the book's entrants, as well as significant events in African American history.

• **Indices**—allow the reader to access the entrants by gender or field of specialization. A general subject index with cross references offers additional access.

For easy access, entries are arranged alphabetically according to the entrant's last name.

Acknowledgments

The editor would like to thank the contributing writers of this book for their outstanding job in locating information about the entrants. Many of the entrants who were still living at the time of publication were personally interviewed by our contributors. To obtain information on those who had died, several writers talked to family members, colleagues, or archivists who had access to unpublished personal information. As many thanks are due to those entrants, friends, or family members who answered questions, provided written information, and generously contributed photos for the book. Without their kind assistance, this book could not have been written.

Advisory Board

Barbara Hull
Librarian
Queens Gateway to Health Science Secondary School
Jamaica, New York

Charles Payne
Professor of Multicultural Education
Ball State University
Muncie, Indiana

Mary Purucker
Science Librarian
Santa Monica High School
Santa Monica, California

Contributors

Matthew A. Bille

Maurice Bleifeld

Barbara A. Branca

Leonard C. Bruno

Virginia Canton

Jill Carpenter

Kenneth Chiacchia

Mijoko Chu

Sally Cole-Misch

Jane Stewart Cooke

Ellen Cothran

Rose Estioco

Marianne Fedunkiw

Martin R. Feldman

George A. Ferrance

Jerome Ferrance

William T. Fletcher

David Fontes

Ronie Garcia-Johnson

Loretta Hall

Paul Heckert

Thomas Heppenheimer

Roger Jaffe

J. Sydney Jones

Mark J. Kaiser

Judson Knight

Geeta Kothari

Marc Kusinitz

Penelope Lawbaugh

Linda Lewin

John E. Little

Patrick J. Longe

Gail B.C. Marsella

Kimberlyn McGrail

George Milite

Sally M. Moite

E. Patrick Moore

Angie Mullig

M.C. Nagel

Laura Newman

David E. Newton

F.C. Nicholson

Donál O'Mathúna

Devera Pine

Annette Petrusso

Karl Preuss

Barbara Proujan

Terrie M. Romano

Neeraja Sankaran

Sharon F. Suer

Robert Teitler

Alison Wellford

Photo Credits

Photographs for *Notable Black American Scientists* were received from the following sources:

Alcorn, George. Reproduced by permission of George Alcorn; **Amos, Harold.** Corbis. Reproduced by permission; **Anderson, Gloria L.** AP/Wide World Photos, Inc. Reproduced by permission; **Banneker, Benjamin.** Fisk University Library. Reproduced by permission; **Blackwell, David.** Photograph by Jean Libby. Reproduced by permission of David Blackwell; **Bluford, Guion S., Jr.** U.S. National Aeronautics Space Administration (NASA); **Bolden, Charles F.** Corbis-Bettmann. Reproduced by permission; **Bolden, T. E.** The Meharry Medical College Archives. Reproduced by permission; **Bragg, Robert H.** Reproduced by permission of Robert H. Bragg; **Brown, Dorothy Lavinia.** AP/Wide World Photos, Inc. Reproduced by permission; **Browne, Marjorie Lee.** Reproduced by permission of Patricia Kenschaft; **Brown, Russell.** Corbis. Reproduced by permission; **Callender, Clive.** AP/Wide World Photos, Inc. Reproduced by permission; **Cannon, Thomas C.** Reproduced by permission of Thomas C. Cannon; **Carver, George Washington.** The Library of Congress; **Carruthers, George.** Archive Photos, Inc. Reproduced by permission; **Chappelle, Emmet W.** Corbis. Reproduced by permission; **Clark, Kenneth B.** Bettmann Archives/Newsphotos Inc.; **Cobb, Jewel Plummer.** AP/Wide World Photos, Inc. Reproduced by permission; **Cobb, W. Montague.** Corbis. Reproduced by permission; **Cobbs, Price M.** Reproduced by permission of Price M. Cobbs; **Cole, Johnnetta.** AP/Wide World Photos, Inc. Reproduced by permission; **Comer, James P.** AP/Wide World Photos, Inc. Reproduced by permission; **Cooke, Lloyd M.** Corbis. Reproduced by permission; **Cooper, Edward S.** The Meharry Medical College Archives. Reproduced by permission; **Cornely, Paul B.** AP/Wide World Photos, Inc. Reproduced by permission; **Davis, Stephen H.** Reproduced by permission of Stephen H. Davis; **Drew, Charles Richard.** AP/Wide World Photos, Inc. Reproduced by permission; **Dunham, Katherine.** AP/Wide World Photos, Inc. Reproduced by permission; **Emeagwali, Philip.** Reproduced by permission of Philip Emeagwali; **Elders, Joycelyn.** AP/Wide World Photos, Inc. Reproduced by permission; **Elliott, Irwin W. Jr.** Reproduced by permission of Irwin W. Elliott; **Ellis, Effie O.** AP/Wide World Photos, Inc. Reproduced by permission; **Ferguson, Lloyd.** Reproduced by permission of Lloyd Ferguson; **Forde, Evan.** Reproduced by permission of Evan Forde; **Gourdine, Meredith.** AP/Wide World Photos, Inc. Reproduced by permission; **Granville, Evelyn.** The University of Texas at Tyler. Reproduced by permission; **Gregory, Frederick D.** U.S. National Aeronautics and Space Administration (NASA); **Gunning, Lucille.** Reproduced by permission of Lucille Gunning; **Harris, Don Navarro.** Reproduced by permission of Dr. Harris; **Harris, James Andrew.** Lawrence Berkeley National Laboratory. Reproduced by permission; **Harris, Wesley L.** AP/Wide World Photos, Inc. Reproduced by permission; **Hill, Henry A.** AP/Wide World Photos, Inc. Reproduced by permission; **Hinton, William A.** AP/Wide World Photos, Inc. Reproduced by permission; **Hudson, Roy D.** Reproduced by permission of Roy D. Hudson; **Imes, Elmer.** Fisk University Library. Reproduced by permission; **Jackson, Shirley Ann.** AP/Wide World Photos, Inc. Reproduced by permission; **Jay, James M.** Reproduced by permission of James M. Jay; **Jemison, Mae C.** UPI/Corbis-Bettmann. Reproduced by permission; **Julian, Percy L.** AP/Wide World Photos, Inc. Reproduced by permission; **Just, Ernest E.** AP/Wide World Photos, Inc. Reproduced by permission; **Langford, George M.** Reproduced by permission of Dr. Langford; **Latimer, Lewis.** Schomburg Center. Reproduced by permission; **Lawless, Theodore Kenneth.** Dillard University Library. Reproduced by permission; **Lawrence, Robert H. Jr.** AP/Wide World Photos, Inc. Reproduced by permission; **Lawson, James R.** Special Collections, Fisk University. Reproduced by permission; **Leffall, Lasalle D. Jr.** AP/Wide World Photos, Inc. Reproduced by permission; **Leevy, Carroll M.** Reproduced by permission of Carroll Leevy; **Majors, Monroe A.** The Meharry Medical College Archives. Reproduced by permission; **Massie, Samuel P.** Reproduced by permission of Samuel P. Massie; **Matzeliger, Jan.** Fisk University Library. Reproduced by permission; **McAfee, Walter S.** UPI/Corbis-Bettmann. Reproduced by permission; **McCoy, Elijah.** Fisk University Library. Reproduced by permission; **McNair, Ronald E.** AP/Wide World Photos, Inc. Reproduced by permission; **Mishoe, Luna I.** Reproduced by permission of Luna I. Mishoe II; **Morgan, Garrett A.** Schomburg Center. Reproduced by permission; **Nabrit, S. Milton.** AP/Wide World Photos, Inc. Reproduced by permission; **Owens, Joan Murrell.** Reproduced by permission of Joan Murrell Owens; **Patterson, Frederick D.** Reproduced by permission of Frederick D. Patterson; **Patton, Georgia E. L.** The Meharry Medical College Archives. Reproduced by permission; **Poussaint, Alvin.** AP/Wide World Photos, Inc. Reproduced by permission; **Robeson, Eslanda Goode.** The Granger Collection. Reproduced by permission; **Shaw, Earl D.** Reproduced by permission of Earl D. Shaw; **Sinkford, Jeanne C.** Reproduced by permission of Jeanne C. Sinkford; **Steele, Claude M.** Stanford University. Reproduced by permission; **Sullivan, Louis W.** Reproduced by permission of Louis W. Sullivan; **Velez-Rodriguez, Argelia.** Reproduced by permission of Argelia Velez-Rodriguez; **Wattleton, Faye.** AP/Wide World Photos, Inc. Reproduced by permission; **West, Harold D.** AP/Wide World Photos, Inc. Reproduced by permission; **Wheeler, Emma Rochelle.** The Meharry Medical College Archives. Reproduced by permission; **Wilkins, J. Ernest.**

AP/Wide World Photos, Inc. Reproduced by permission; **Williams, Daniel Hale**. Corbis-Bettmann. Reproduced by permission; **Williams, Theodore**. Photograph by Matt Dilyard. Reproduced by permission of Theodore Williams; **Woods, Granville T.** AP/Wide World Photos, Inc. Reproduced by permission; **Wright, Jane C.** AP/Wide World Photos, Inc. Reproduced by permission; **Wyche, James H.** Reproduced by permission of James H. Wyche.

Entry List

Timeline

1619 *A Dutch ship with 20 Negroes arrived in Jamestown, Virginia. They had been kidnapped from Africa and were sold to the highest bidder.*

1783 **James Durham** purchased his freedom and began work as the first black physician in the United States. Durham was a slave owned by two doctors and an apothecary and bought his freedom with money made by working as a medical assistant.

1794 **Benjamin Banneker** was born in Ellicott, Maryland. Between 1791 and 1802, he published the yearly *Almanac*, which was widely read. He was also the first black man to publish astronomical materials in the United States.

1834 **Henry Blair** was awarded a patent for his design for a corn seed planter. He is the first black on record to be so designated.

1843 **Norbert Rillieux**, an engineer, received his first of two patents (the second one was awarded three years later) for an evaporation mechanism that transformed the sugar industry. By devising a mechanism for controlling how sugar was extracted from beet and cane juice, he was able to cut labor and fuel costs and make high-quality sugar readily available.

1848 **Lewis Temple** invented the Temple Toggle, also known as the Temple Iron or Temple's Iron, used in whaling. Temple's toggle had a barbed head that could pivot and a pin that broke upon entering the whale's body, securing the harpoon within it. The invention was responsible for doubling the number of whales caught in the United States and became the standard around the world.

1857 *The Supreme Court rendered its decision in the case of* Dred Scott v. Sandford. *The justices declared that Negroes were not citizens of the United States, and denied Congress the power to prohibit slavery in any federal territory. The decision fueled the fires that led to the Civil War.*

1863 Abraham Lincoln issued a presidential commission to **Alexander Thomas Augusta**, naming him to the rank of major. Augusta was the first black physician to be granted a commission with the U.S. Army's colored divisions, and his service throughout the Civil War earned him the distinction of becoming first black to be promoted to breveted lieutenant-colonel, U.S. Volunteers.

President Abraham Lincoln signed the Emancipation Proclamation. It declared slaves free in all states and territories then in rebellion against the United States.

1864 **Rebecca Lee Crumpler** became the first black woman to earn a medical degree in the United States.

1868 *The Fourteenth Amendment to the Constitution was adopted. The legislation made blacks American citizens and gave them constitutional guarantees.*

1872 **Elijah McCoy** received a U. S. patent for an invention for train engines that became known as the lubricating cup. It relied on a piston set within an oil-filled container; steam pressure pushed on the piston and thereby drove the oil into channels that carried this oil to the engine's operating parts. The patent for the device, number 129,843, was granted on June 23.

1876 **Edward Bouchet** became the first black to earn a Ph.D. in the United States, when he earned his degree in physics from Yale University.

1881 On July 2, a disappointed office-seeker named Charles Guiteau shot President James A. Garfield at a Washington railroad station. **Charles Burleigh Purvis** was the first physician to treat the President, and though Garfield's wounds proved too severe to save him, Garfield's successor, Chester A. Arthur, recognized Purvis's efforts by appointing him to the head surgical position at the Freedmen's Hospital. He thus became the first black physician to head a civilian hospital.

1884   **Granville T. Woods** submitted his design for an improved steam-boiler furnace to the U.S. patent Office. Between 1884 and his death in 1910, he was awarded more than 60 patents, contributing significantly to railway speed, efficiency, and safety.

1885   **Jan Earnst Matzeliger** publicly demonstrated his shoe lasting machine. The machine could last the leather, arrange it over the sole, and drive in the nails, finishing the shoe in about one minute's time. Before Matzeliger's lasting machine, an average skilled worker could last about 35-50 shoes per day. With adjustments, Matzeliger's machine could make between 150 to 700 pairs a day, depending on the leather's quality.

1888   **Arnold Hamilton Maloney** was born. This preacher-turned-pharmacologist discovered that picrotoxin, a compound obtained from the seeds of a particular scrub (*Anamirta cocculus*), can reverse these effects and protect animals and humans from barbiturate poisoning.

1889   **Monroe Alpheus Majors** became the first black man to pass the California medical boards. He was also the first black physician to practice medicine west of the Rocky Mountains.

1890   **Lewis H. Latimer** wrote a groundbreaking book on electric lighting, *Incandescent Electric Lighting: A Practical Description of the Edison System.* Despite his lack of any formal education, this son of an escaped slave became a member of Thomas Alva Edison's research team and made several outstanding contributions to the development and commercialization of the electric light.

Ida Gray graduated from University of Michigan with a doctor of dental surgery degree, becoming the first black female dentist in the United States.

1891   **Daniel Hale Williams** founded Provident Hospital in Chicago. It was here that he performed the first recorded heart surgery by suturing a tear in a stabbing victim's pericardium (the membrane that encloses the heart); the patient completely recovered from the risky operation.

1892   **Miles Vandahurst Lynk**, fresh out of medical school, began publishing *The Medical and Surgical Observer,* the first black medical journal in the nation. Through his long career, Lynk founded, edited, and published the first black medical journal and served as one of the prime movers in creating the National Medical Association for black physicians.

1894   **George Washington Murray** received his first three of eight patents, for a furrow opener, stalk-knocker-cultivator, and marker. A farmer-turned-politician, Murray also served in the United States House of Representatives for South Carolina.

1895   Largely through his own efforts, **Nathan Francis Mossell** established Frederick Douglass Memorial Hospital and Training School for Nurses, Philadelphia's first health-care facility for black patients. The building opened on October 31.

1896   **George Washington Carver** begins work at the Tuskegee Institute. Carver devised and promoted scores of uses for peanuts and sweet potatoes, and he had a significant effect on the diversification of southern agricultural practices.

The Supreme Court decision in Plessy v. Ferguson *held that the establishment of separate schools for blacks and whites—as long as the schools were of equal quality—did not violate the concept of equal protection under the law guaranteed by the Fourteenth Amendment to the Constitution.*

1907   **Charles Henry Turner** earned his Ph.D. in zoology from the University of Chicago, graduating *summa cum laude.* He was the first to demonstrate that insects have hearing, and further, could discern pitch. Turner was also the first to describe a particular ant movement that was named "Turner's circling" in his honor.

1912   **Ernest Everett Just**, renowned zoologist, published his first paper, describing the results of research which showed what happens when the fertilized egg of the sandworm *Nereis* undergoes its first cleavage division.

1914   **Garrett A. Morgan** received a patent for the "safety hood," the precursor to the modern-day gas mask. The device, which consisted of a hood with an inlet for fresh air and an outlet for exhaled air, drew a number of awards, including the First Grand Prize from the Second International Exposition of Safety and Sanitation in New York City.

1915   *The Supreme Court outlawed "Grandfather Clauses" used by Southern states to deny blacks the right to vote.*

1917   **Charles Herbert Garvin**, a physician, became the first black to be commissioned as a First Lieutenant in the U.S. Army and enters World War I.

1920   **William Samuel Quinland** became the first black member to be elected to the American Association of Pathologists and Bacteriologists. He was a distinguished pathologist and educator who contributed 28 studies to medical journals, including pioneering research on pathology in African Americans.

1925   **Elbert Frank Cox** became the first black to earn a doctoral degree in pure mathematics when he graduated from Cornell with his Ph.D.

1926   **Louis Tompkins Wright** was granted a permanent appointment at Harlem Hospital, after being one of the first black doctors on staff. During his prolonged affiliation with the hospital, he became the hospital's surgical director and founded its Cancer Research Center.

1927   **William Harry Barnes** invented the hypophyscope, an instrument used to visualize the pituitary gland through the sphenoid sinus. The invention would make the physician famous.

William Augustus Hinton developed a test—subsequently known as the Hinton test—to diagnose syphilis. Because it was easier, less expensive, and more accurate than previously used tests, the Hinton test was adopted as standard procedure for diagnosing syphilis.

1930   **Roscoe Lewis McKinney** became the first African American to earn a doctorate in anatomy. He established the anatomy department within the Medical College of Howard University and served as its chairman for 17 years.

1932   **William Montague Cobb**, anatomist, earned his Ph.D. from Western Reserve (now Case Western) University in Cleveland. His investigations of skeletons of different races convinced him of the erroneous and worthless arguments of white supremacists who contended that African Americans were mentally inferior, supposedly based on anatomical studies. He published his observations and conclusions in a number of professional journals and in popular magazines.

1935   **Percy Lavon Julian** accomplished the first synthesis of physostigmine, which was used to treat glaucoma, an eye disease that eventually leads to blindness by slowly damaging the retina. Although many of his peers disagreed with his methods, this success proved Julian correct.

1936   **Herman George Canady** published a well-known article titled, "The Effect of 'Rapport' on the IQ: A New Approach to the Problem of Racial Psychology." The article, which was based on his master's thesis written eight years earlier, showed that the social situation of the I.Q. test had an impact on a person's test performance.

1939   **Charles R. Drew** developed a method to process and preserve blood plasma so that it could be stored and shipped great distances. Because red blood cells contain the substance that determines blood type, their absence in plasma means that a match between donor and recipient is not necessary, which makes it ideal for emergencies.

Chemist **Lloyd Augustus Hall** cofounded the Institute of Food Technologists, establishing a new branch of industrial chemistry. Hall developed processes to cure and preserve meat, prevent rancidity in fats, and sterilize spices.

1941   **Ruth Smith Lloyd** became the first African American woman to earn a Ph.D. in anatomy. Lloyd, who spent a large portion of her teaching career at Howard University, specialized in issues surrounding fertility as well as research on the female sex cycle and the relation of sex hormones to growth.

1942   **Julian Herman Lewis** published *The Biology of the Negro*, based on his research into the history of African Americans in relationship to their anatomy, their physiological characteristics, and their responses to a variety of diseases.

1943   **Frederick Douglass Patterson** proposed that a group of African American colleges form a consortium to raise funds for their mutual benefit. Called the United Negro College Fund (UNCF), the organization had 27 original members who amassed an endowment of $765,000.

1943-6 **Lloyd Albert Quarterman, Edwin Roberts Russell, Moddie Taylor,** and **J. Ernest Wilkins, Jr.** worked on the "Manhattan Project" at the University of Chicago. The World War II project was responsible for developing the first atom bomb.

1946   The U.S. Army's Project Diana sends a radar signal to make the first human contact with the moon. As the mathematician for the project, **Walter S. McAfee** made the essential calculations.

1947   **David Blackwell** published what is perhaps his most significant contribution to modern statistics, "Conditional Expectation and Unbiased Sequential Estimation." Blackwell was the first black mathematician to be elected to the National Academy of Sciences.

1948   **Marie Maynard Daly** made history at Columbia University, becoming the first African American woman to earn a Ph.D. in chemistry.

1949   **Evelyn Boyd Granville** and **Marjorie Lee Browne** earned doctoral degrees in mathematics from Yale University and the University of Michigan, respectively, becoming the first African American women to receive that degree; it would be more than a dozen years before another black woman would duplicate this effort.

1951   **Philip G. Hubbard** formed the Hubbard Instrument Company to manufacture and market hot wire anemometers and related measuring devices. Hubbard developed the hot wire anemometer while at the University of Iowa. The device, which measures fluid turbulence, had become so popular with industry that while in the university environment, Hubbard could not make enough to satisfy the demand.

1952   **Jane Cooke Wright** became director of the Cancer Foundation of Harlem Hospital after her father's death. Her father, **Louis Tompkins Wright**, founded the Foundation.

1953   **Solomon Carter Fuller**, neurologist, died. In this same year medical researchers confirmed the lack of any linkage between arteriosclerosis (hardening of the arteries) and Alzheimer's disease. This had been the prevailing belief at the time of Fuller's work nearly 40 years earlier, but he had disgreed.

1954   *The Supreme Court ruled in* Brown v. Board of Education of Topeka, Kansas, *that racial segregation in public schools was unconstitutional. The Court cited the research of psychologist* **Kenneth Bancroft Clark**, *and described him as a "modern authority" on the psychological effects of segregation.*

1955   **Leonidas Harris Berry** invented the gastrobiopsyscope, a first-of-its-kind instrument for exploring the digestive tract, now part of the medical collection at the Smithsonian Institution.

1957   *President Dwight D. Eisenhower ordered federal troops into a Little Rock, Arkansas high school to enforce school desegregation.*

     Carroll Moton Leevy wrote his first textbook on liver disease. Leevy developed a new and simple method of diagnosing liver disease, for which he holds the patent. He also developed an almost painless method for obtaining liver biopsy samples for microscopic analysis.

     The American Institute of Architects (AIA) elected **Paul Revere Williams** to its College of Fellows, making him the first African American to be accorded this, the AIA's highest honor.

1964   *Congress passed the Civil Rights Act, whose sweeping provisions prohibited discrimination in public accommodations and employment.*

1965   *Thurgood Marshall, the first black justice on the Supreme Court, is named Solicitor General by President Lyndon B. Johnson.*

1968   Psychiatrist **James P. Comer** established his first CSDP schools in New Haven, Connecticut. The Comer School Development Program (CSDP), a visionary approach to improving troubled schools, is based on Comer's belief in the importance of providing children with experiences that promote their social, emotional, cognitive, and moral development. By 1998, about 600 schools in the United States had adopted CSDP.

1969 Embryologist **Geraldine Pittman Woods** was asked to be a special consultant at the National Institute of Health, where she helped develop the Minority Biomedical Research Support (MBRS) program and the Minority Access to Research Careers (MARC) program.

1969-70 **James Andrew Harris** led a group of investigators at Lawrence Berkeley Laboratory in California in the discovery of two new chemical elements: element 104, rutherfordium, and element 105, now called dubnium.

1971 **James M. Jay** published *Negroes in Science: Natural Science Doctorates 1876-1969*, a compilation of names, along with the scholars' regional origins and educational background. The study separated the data into demographic tables arranged and summarized by Jay.

Earl D. Shaw is granted a patent for the spin-flip laser. The spin-flip laser was the first laser that could be adjusted by the user. For example, biologists who are studying a cell, but know that the laser frequency they need to explore the interior of that cell would destroy the cell wall, can alter the adjustments to modify the laser's strength.

Psychiatrist **Alvin Francis Poussaint** published *Why Blacks Kill Blacks*. The book explored the effect of racism on the mental health of blacks, individually and as a community.

1972 *Representative Shirley Chisholm from New York, the first black woman to serve in Congress, also became the first black woman to seek a presidential nomination. She won 151 votes of over 2,000 cast at the Democratic convention.*

A team of NASA engineers built a camera and spectrograph according to the design of **George R. Carruthers** for use during the *Apollo 16* mission. Carruthers's invention is an imaging device which uses ultraviolet light to capture images of both Earth and space from the surface of the moon.

1975 *Congress voted to extend the Voting Rights Act of 1965 for an additional seven years. The act allowed federal registrars and the Department of Justice to assist blacks in registering and voting in the South.*

1977 **Waverly J. Person** became the first black American to hold the prominent position of Director of the United States Geological Survey's National Earthquake Information Center. A respected geophysicist and seismologist, he was also one of the first black Americans in his field.

President Jimmy Carter appointed **John Brooks Slaughter** assistant director of the National Science Foundation (NSF), where he was responsible for coordinating studies in astronomy, geology, meteorology, and related subjects. Slaughter is an engineer who performed early work in the field of computer science and made important contributions to computerized control systems.

1978 **LaSalle D. Leffall, Jr.** became the first black president of the American Cancer Society. An educator at Howard University, Leffall used this national forum to emphasize the problems of cancer in minorities, holding the first conference on cancer among black Americans.

1983 **Guion S. Bluford** became as the first black U.S. astronaut in space when he flew on the shuttle *Challenger*, on August 30.

1984 *Robert N.C. Nix was inaugurated as Chief Justice of the Pennsylvania Supreme Court, becoming the first African American to sit on a state Supreme Court bench since the Reconstruction Era.*

1985 **Frederick Drew Gregory** became only the second black astronaut in space. Gregory, who flew the space shuttle *Challenger*, was also the first black space shuttle pilot.

1992 **Edward S. Cooper** was elected to his year-term as president of the American Heart Association. As the organization's first black president, he used his position to advocate for health education and a national health care system.

W. Lincoln Hawkins was awarded the National Medal of Technology, not only for his work in chemical engineering, but also for his labors in attempting to bring minorities into the sciences.

Mae Jemison became the United States' first female African American space traveler with her eight-day space flight aboard the space shuttle *Endeavour*.

1993   **M. Joycelyn Elders** was confirmed as U.S. Surgeon General by the Senate. President Bill Clinton nominated Elders to replace Antonia Novello. Elders was the second woman, and the first black, to serve in that office. She was pressured for her controversial views, though, and resigned after a year of service.

1995   **Shirley Ann Jackson**, a theoretical physicist, was appointed chair of the Nuclear Regulatory Commission. Under Jackson's direction, the commission has become more aggressive about inspections and even forced top NRC officials (ones who had looked the other way when whistle-blowers spoke up) to resign or retire. She also reorganized the commission to enable inspectors to detect problems early and allow managers to order changes more quickly.

Harold Amos won the National Academy of Science's highest honor, the Public Welfare Medal, for his success in mentoring and providing funds for minority students pursuing biomedicine.

Numa Pompilius Garfield Adams
1885-1940
Physician

Born during the latter years of the nineteenth century, Numa P. G. Adams helped determine the quality of education for African American doctors in the twentieth century. Adams was the first African American to be named Dean of Medicine at Howard University in 1929. As dean, Adams not only recruited and inspired outstanding students, he strove to reform the curriculum and to improve the quality of doctors' training. Adams worked, as **Joseph L. Johnson** later reported in the *Journal of the National Medical Association*, to put the Howard University School of Medicine "on a par with the best medical schools." Although Adams was not well appreciated by his contemporaries for his efforts, he is remembered for his tremendous influence at Howard and on various African American physicians.

Numa Pompilius Garfield Adams was born to Martha E. Mathews in Delaplane, Virginia, on February 26, 1885. His grandmother, a midwife, taught Adams about medicinal herbs, and he attended a country school led by his uncle. Just before the turn of the century, Adams's family moved to Steelton, Pennsylvania, where Adams excelled in high school. He graduated in 1905 and worked as a substitute teacher and seventh-grade teacher in Carlisle. Adams earned a bachelor's degree, *summa cum laude* (some sources say *magna cum laude*), from Howard University in 1911, and went on to earn an M.A. in chemistry at Columbia University in 1912. He taught chemistry at Howard University for the next two years, and became an assistant professor there in 1914. In 1915, Adams married the former Osceola Marie Macarthy, and eventually, they had a son, Charles. Adams continued his career at Howard with a promotion to associate professor in 1919, and he also served as the chair of the chemistry department.

Despite his success in the chemistry department, Adams left Howard in 1919 to begin studies at the Rush Medical School at the University of Chicago. Adams worked his way through school by playing the cornet and then the saxophone with the Lyric Orchestra, a dance band. Adams earned an M.D. in 1924 and was initiated into the Alpha Omega Alpha Fraternity, in the Rush Chapter. Adams began work as an intern that same year at St. Louis City Hospital no. 2 (the Homer G. Phillips Hospital). He practiced medicine from 1925 to 1929 in Chicago, and from 1927 to 1929 he served as the assistant medical director for the Victory Life Insurance Company.

First African-American Dean at Howard University School of Medicine

At this time, African American medical schools were challenged by recent advances in medicine and by funding difficulties. Howard University School of Medicine, along with Meharry Medical College, were among the only surviving such schools, and they were struggling to maintain accreditation. Although Howard had been open to train both African American and white students since 1868, the school had never had an African American dean. This ended when the president of Howard University selected Adams for the position, and Adams became dean in June 1929. In 1930, he was also appointed as a professor of medicine at Howard. Adams had a number of difficult tasks to complete when he arrived at Howard, and while working virtually alone, he made significant advancements.

Adams's first challenge was to reorganize the curriculum at Howard. He also did everything he could to bring excellent African American instructors from all over the country to the school. He secured funding to train African American physicians for teaching positions, and made a point of utilizing the Freedmen's Hospital in teaching. Another of Adams's policies involved the strengthening of Howard's medical students. Adams enforced these policies by raising entrance standards. He was subject to a great deal of criticism, however, as the size of entering classes began to decline. Through his efforts, Adams not only shaped Howard as a distinguished medical school, he encouraged African American students to make their own paths in medicine. For example **Charles R. Drew**, the first person to set up a blood bank, was considered in high esteem by Adams.

During the years he worked as dean at Howard, Adams also taught neurology and psychiatry at the Provident Hospital School of Nursing. Over the course of his career, Adams served as a member of the National Medical Association and a member of the Board of Directors of the Tuberculosis Association of the District of Columbia. He was a member of the Advisory Health Council of Washington, the Council on Social Agencies, and the Cook County Physicians Association in Illinois. He was also a fellow of the American Association for the Advancement of Sciences.

Recalling Adams in 1951, his colleague Dr. **W. Montague Cobb** described him as "a man of slight build, handsome, kindly face and shy, retiring manner." Besides taking delight in music, Adams enjoyed traveling from Washington, D.C., where he lived, to Fauquier County, where he grew up. According to Cobb, Adams "and his wife would. . . walk for hours through the woods over familiar ground so rich in memories. By some strange magic he seemed to gather strength there to come back and carry on." When Adams relaxed with friends, he demonstrated his humor and wit.

Adams died in Chicago on August 29, 1940, of pneumonia after an operation, without gaining the uncontested faith of his peers at Howard. Nevertheless, by the early to mid-1950s, recognition for his work at Howard emerged. Adams was featured in the January 1951 volume of the *Journal of the National Medical Association,* and his portrait graced the cover of a 1955 volume of the journal. In a tribute to Adams, the Dean of Howard University School of Medicine at the time, Joseph L. Johnson, wrote that Adams was a great man who cared about his patients. Johnson continued, "To know Numa Adams was to respect, to admire and to love him. He was of a brilliant mind. . ." In another tribute, the former Associate Medical Director of The Rockefeller Foundation, Dr. Robert A. Lambert, described Adams as a "man of wisdom, fine sensibility, clear judgment, patient determination, and courageous action."

SELECTED WRITINGS BY ADAMS:

Periodicals

Adams, Numa P.G. "Recent Developments in Medical Education at Howard University." *Howard University Bulletin.* (1935): 1-18.

FURTHER READING:

Books

Epps, Charles H. Jr., Davis G. Johnson, and Audrey L. Vaughan, eds. *African-American Medical Pioneers.* Rockville, MD: Betz Publishing Company, 1994.

Logan, Rayford W. *Dictionary of American Negro Biography.* Edited by Rayford W. Logan and Michael R. Winston. New York: W.W. Norton and Company, 1982.

Morais, Herbert M. *The History of the Negro in Medicine.* New York: Publishers Company, 1967.

Sammons, Vivian Ovelton. *Blacks in Science and Medicine.* New York: Hemisphere Publishing Co. 1990.

Smith, Jessie Carnie, ed. *Black Firsts.* Detroit: Gale Research, 1994.

Periodicals

The Crisis. (April 1924): 266.

George Edward Alcorn

Cobb, W. Montague, M.D., "Numa P.G. Adams, 1885-1940."*Journal of the National Medical Association.* (January 1951): 42-52.

Johnson, Joseph L., Dr. *Journal of the National Medical Association.* (January 1951): 53-54.

Journal of the National Medical Association. (November 1940): 257-58.

Lambert, Robert A. *Journal of the National Medical Association.* (January 1951): 52-53.

—*Sketch by R. Garcia-Johnson*

George Edward Alcorn
1940-
Physicist

George Edward Alcorn is responsible for a number of inventions now widely used in the semiconductor industry. He is perhaps best known for inventing an imaging x-ray spectrometer which uses the thermomigration of aluminum, an achievement which earned him the 1984 Inventor of the Year Award from the National Aeronautics and Space Administration (NASA) and the Goddard Space Flight Center (GSFC). Alcorn has worked in industry and government, as well as academics, and he is currently chief of the Office of Commercial Programs for the Goddard Space Flight Center.

Alcorn was born on March 22, 1940, to George and Arletta Dixon Alcorn. His father was an auto mechanic who sacrificed so Alcorn and his brother could get an education. Alcorn attended Occidental College in Pasadena, California, where he maintained an excellent academic record while earning eight letters in baseball and football. Alcorn graduated with a B.A. in physics in 1962, and in 1963 he completed a master's degree in nuclear physics from Howard University. During the summers of 1962 and 1963, Alcorn worked as a research engineer for the Space Division of North American Rockwell, computing trajectories and orbital mechanics for missiles. A NASA grant supported Alcorn's research on negative ion formation during the summers of 1965 and 1966. In 1967 he earned his doctorate from Howard University in atomic and molecular physics. After earning his Ph.D., Alcorn spent twelve years in industry. He was senior scientist at Philco-Ford, senior physicist at Perker-Elmer, and advisory engineer at IBM Corporation. In 1973, Alcorn was chosen to be IBM Visiting Professor in Electrical Engineering at Howard University, and he has held positions at that university ever since, rising to the rank of full professor. Alcorn is also a full professor in the department of electrical engineering at the University of the District of Columbia, where he has taught courses ranging from advanced engineering mathematics to microelectronics.

Alcorn left IBM, where he worked as a Second Plateau Inventor, to join NASA in 1978. While at NASA, Alcorn invented an imaging x-ray spectrometer using thermomigration of aluminum, for which he earned a patent in 1984, and two years later he devised an improved method of fabrication using laser drilling. His work on imaging x-ray spectrometers earned him the 1984 NASA/GSFC Inventor of the Year Award. During this period he also served as deputy project manager for advanced development, and in this position he was responsible for developing new technologies required for the space station *Freedom*. Alcorn served as manager for advanced programs at NASA/GSFC from 1990 to 1992, and his primary duties concerned the managing of technology programs and evaluating technologies which were required by GSFC. He also managed the GSFC Evolution Program, concerned with ensuring that over its 30-year mission the space station develops properly while incorporating new capabilities. Since 1992, Alcorn has served as chief of Goddard's Office of Commercial Programs supervising programs for technology transfer, small business innovation research, and the commercial use of space programs. He managed a shuttle flight experiment that involved Robot Operated Material Processing System, or ROMPs, in 1994. The experiment involved the manufacture of materials in the microgravity of space.

Alcorn holds over 25 patents. He is a recognized pioneer in the fabrication of plasma semiconductor devices,

and his patent "Process for Controlling the Slope of a Via Hole" was an important contribution to the process of plasma etching. This procedure is now used by many semiconductor manufacturing companies. Alcorn was one of the first scientists to present a computer-modeling solution of wet etched and plasma etched structures, and he has received several cash prizes for his inventions of plasma-processing techniques.

Alcorn has been extensively involved in community service. In 1984, he was awarded a NASA-EEO medal for his contributions in recruiting minority and women scientists and engineers and his assistance to minority businesses in establishing research programs. He is a founder of Saturday Academy, which is a weekend honors program designed to supplement and extend math-science training for inner-city students in grades six to eight. Alcorn also works with the Meyerhoff Foundation, whose goal is to encourage and support African American males interested in pursuing doctorates in science and engineering. Alcorn was honored by his alma mater Howard University in 1994 in its Heritage of Greatness awards ceremony. Alcorn was celebrated as a Black Achiever in the Science and Technology category. Alcorn married Marie DaVillier in 1969; they have one son, born in 1979. Alcorn's younger brother Charles is a research physicist at IBM.

SELECTED WRITINGS BY ALCORN:

Periodicals

IBM Technical Disclosure Bulletin, Aluminum-Copper-Silicon Subetch Process, Volume 19, 1976, p. 981.

IBM Technical Disclosure Bulletin, Stepped-Oxide CCD With Asymmetrical Oxide Geometry, Volume 24, 1981, pp. 1383–1387.

International Electron Devices Meeting, Proceedings, X-ray Spectrometer by Aluminum Thermomigration, 1982, pp. 312–314.

FURTHER READING:

Periodicals

Journal of the NTA, Space Station Freedom, fall, 1988, p. 22.

Other

Alcorn, George E., *Interview with Mark J. Kaiser,* conducted February 24, 1994.

—Sketch by Mark J. Kaiser

Archie Alphonso Alexander
1888-1958
Civil engineer

Archie Alphonso Alexander was an African American civil engineer who built tunnels, bridges, freeways, airfields, railroad trestles, viaducts, and power plants. Alexander maintained a successful engineering firm for over 35 years. He was also a Republican who was active in politics, and he was appointed Governor of the Virgin Islands in 1954 by President Dwight D. Eisenhower. Alexander was born in Ottumwa, Iowa, on May 14, 1888. His father was a janitor who later moved the family to a farm outside Des Moines. The oldest son of a large family, Alexander worked his way through high school and graduated in 1905. After working a few years, he enrolled in the College of Engineering at the University of Iowa in 1908. Although discouraged by officials from pursuing an academic degree because of his race, Alexander persevered and graduated in 1912 with a B.S. in civil engineering. He maintained an excellent scholastic record, and became such an effective tackle for the university football team that he was known as "Alexander the Great" during his years in college. In 1913, Alexander married Audria Linzey; they moved into a house which Alexander had designed and built himself. The couple would have one child, a son.

After graduating from college, Alexander worked for two years as a design engineer for the Marsh Engineering Company, a bridge-building firm. In 1914, while still only 26 years old, he formed his own firm, A. A. Alexander, Inc., with a fellow employee from the Marsh Company, George Higbee. The firm secured contracts to build concrete and steel bridges and sewer systems; they were quite successful by the spring of 1925, when Higbee died in an accident while supervising the construction of a bridge. In that same year, Alexander received an honorary civil engineering degree from his alma mater and was awarded the "Laurel Wreath," given to the member of Kappa Alpha Psi Fraternity who had the greatest accomplishment during that year. In 1928 Alexander was cited as the second most successful Negro in business, and the NAACP awarded him the Spingarn Medal, given annually for the "highest achievement of an American Negro."

In 1929 Alexander joined a fellow classmate from the University of Iowa named M. A. Repass to form the firm Alexander and Repass. The new company built a concrete tunnel, as well as a heating plant and a power house, for the University of Iowa. While much of their work was in Iowa, the firm also built the Tidal Basin Bridge and K Street Freeway in Washington, D.C. They were also responsible for a sewage-disposal plant in Grand Rapids, Michigan, a civilian airfield at Tuskegee, Alabama, a power plant in Columbus, Nebraska, and railroad bridges in Iowa and Missouri. Howard University bestowed an honorary doctorate in civil engineering on Alexander in 1946, and at the

centennial celebration of the University of Iowa in 1947, he was named one of its outstanding alumni and "one of the first hundred citizens of merit."

In April of 1954, President Eisenhower appointed Alexander the Governor of the Virgin Islands, but ill health forced him to resign the post in August of 1955. He died at his home in Des Moines in 1958. Ralph W. Bullock, writing in *In Spite of Handicaps,* said of Alexander: "When he was a lad he read that Abraham Lincoln said that if one will only prepare himself for his life's work, his opportunity will come some day, and . . . this has been the guiding principle of his life. Unquestionably, he . . . made good under it."

FURTHER READING:

Books

Blacks in Science and Medicine, Hemisphere Publishing, 1990, p. 14.

Bullock, Ralph W. *In Spite of Handicaps,* New York: 1927, pp. 79–84.

Negro Almanac, 5th ed. Gale, 1989.

Toppin, Edgar A. *Biographical History of Blacks.* David McKay, 1971, pp. 246–247.

Periodicals

Ebony, (September, 1949): 16.

New York Times, (February 14, 1954): 34.

Time, (April 19, 1954): 38.

—Sketch by Mark J. Kaiser

Benjamin Harold Alexander
1921-
Organic chemist

Though Benjamin Alexander's research career was cut short by a laboratory accident, he achieved much as both a chemist and as an administrator. Alexander co-holds four patents with the government for insecticide compounds related to his research. After his research days ended in 1967, Alexander began a second, related career as an administrator and lecturer, though he also continued to teach part time. He is perhaps best known as the controversial president of two universities, Chicago State and the University of the District of Columbia. Alexander is the author of over 45 research-related articles, and 150 for general audiences.

He was born on October 18, 1921, in Roberta, Georgia, one of six children born to Manoah Bush and Annie

Alexander. In 1924, the family moved to Cincinnati, Ohio, after his father lost all his money in failed cotton crops. Alexander's father found work in an iron foundry, but his failures weighed heavily upon him, and he began drinking. Alexander's parents divorced in 1927, and his mother worked as a hospital cleaning lady to support her family. She saved and sacrificed so each of her six children could go to college.

Benjamin Alexander went to public schools in Cincinnati. Because of his family's financial situation, he sold newspapers on street corners to help out. He graduated from Woodward High School at the age 16 and immediately entered the University of Cincinnati. One reason he was drawn to chemistry was that the department at the University would not tolerate racial prejudice, and there were other African American chemistry majors. He earned his B.A. in the subject 1943. For a year after graduation, 1944-45, Alexander was employed as a technician at the Cincinnati Chemical Works, where he worked in the manufacture of the chemical DDT.

Moves to Peoria, Serves in the Army

In 1945, Alexander went to Peoria, Illinois, to work at the United States Department of Agriculture's Agricultural Research Center as a chemist. He also did his own research on the side. His employment there was interrupted when he was drafted in 1946. He served in the Army in a laundry battalion in Japan as the Allies cleaned up the South Pacific after the end of World War II. Though this job was obviously beneath Alexander's skills and intellect, he used the time to study. He was eventually asked to be a science teacher for officer's children at their school. When he was discharged in 1947, Alexander had attained the rank of sergeant and earned 13 commendations and 12 citations. After his discharge, Alexander remained in the Army Reserves, attaining the rank of major by the time he retired in 1965.

When he returned to Peoria, Alexander went back to his job at the Agricultural Research Center and stayed until 1954. He also entered graduate school at local Bradley University and earned his M.S. in 1950. Upon his return from the service, Alexander also reunited with Mary Ellen Spurlock, a friend from the University of Cincinnati. They married in March 1948, and immediately had a son, Drew, together. Their marriage was strained, and they divorced in the early 1950s. Though Alexander had personal problems, he continued his work, and with one his professors, determined the true structure of a complex molecule.

Earns Ph.D. at Georgetown

In 1954, Alexander moved to Washington, D.C., where he wanted to earn his Ph.D. from Howard University in their newly created graduate chemistry program. He was not accepted. Scientists at Catholic Georgetown University, though, impressed with what they had heard about Alexander and his accomplishments, got the university to admit

him even though he was not Catholic and was black. He earned his Ph.D. in 1957. His dissertation was titled "The Phosphate Enzyme Activity of DDT Resistant and Normal House Flies, and Chlordane Resistant and Normal Cockroaches." In 1957, Alexander also reconciled with his wife, and they were married again in December of that year. In 1958, they had a daughter, Dawn Criket, together.

Again, while studying for his Ph. D., Alexander maintained his professional employment. He was employed as a research chemist at the United States Department of Agriculture in Beltsville, Maryland, from 1954 until 1962. There, his research continued to focus on insect control with chemicals. Alexander cultivated several compounds, which either repelled or attracted certain insects. His work in this area led to his four co-owned patents.

In 1962, he was hired by the Walter Reed Army Hospital to work as the chief research chemist in the immunology department. Alexander also was employed as an adjunct professor at the American University after his graduation, from 1958 until 1974. He took a similar post at the Graduate School of the United States Department of Agriculture, from 1960-68. An accident at Walter Reed, where Alexander and several colleagues were exposed to a chemical poison, forced him to quit doing laboratory research in 1967. Alexander had almost died from the exposure. Though he survived, he did lose most of his white blood cells and thus much of his immunity to disease.

Becomes a Science Administrator

Alexander turned then to the administration of science research and education. First, he received training at the National Institutes of Health in the Grants Associates Program. He began this phase of his career in a year-long stint (1967-68) as a health scientist administrator at the National Institute of Health. Alexander then worked for a year for the United States Public Health Service as a special assistant to the director for the disadvantaged at the National Center for Health Services Research and Development, Health Service & Mental Health Administration. Alexander worked another job for another year, 1969-70, as the administrator of new health career projects as well as deputy equal employment officer, before spending four years, 1970-74, as a program officer of the Health Care Organization and Resources Division of the U.S. Public Health Service.

Named President of Chicago State University

In 1974, Alexander's career took another unexpected turn. He was offered the presidency at Chicago State University, Chicago, Illinois. He stayed until 1982, cleaning up the troubled institution with hard line tactics. With his appointment, Alexander became involved several higher education organizations. He was a member of the committee on women in higher education of the American Council on Education, from 1975-77. Alexander was also a commissioner for the Northcentral commission of the Institute of

Higher Education from 1975 until 1978. Alexander was honored with a plaque naming him the Best College President in 1978.

Though his university presidency was demanding, Alexander remained involved in the world outside Chicago State. In 1977, for example, he became a consultant to the National Center for Health Services Research and the National Science Foundation. He held this post until 1984. He was also given an honorary LLD degree by Bradley University in 1979, and a year later he became a member of that university's board of trustees.

In 1982, Alexander took on the presidency of another troubled school, the University of the District of Columbia. Those who hired him expected the same results as he had gotten in Chicago State, but Alexander did not have the full support of the Trustees and other officials. He was forced out after a year. He took over as president and chief operating officer of Drew Dawn Enterprises, a research consulting firm, in 1983, when his daughter, who had founded the company, went to graduate school.

However, Alexander still remained active in both university and administrative circles. He began an on-going relationship as a distinguished visiting professor at the National Graduate University, Arlington, Virginia, in 1983. He also resumed his resident professorship at American University, which ended in 1994. In 1984, Alexander briefly served as interim deputy assistant secretary of the United States government Department of Education. He then held simultaneous positions in related academic bodies. In 1985-86, Alexander was the vice president of the Washington Academy of Sciences and the chairman of the Joint Board on Science and Engineering Education. (In 1997, Alexander became president elect of the Washington Academy of Sciences.) In 1985, he also became a member of the National Board Fund for Improvement of Postsecondary Education.

Throughout his life, Alexander has also been involved in his community, working with the YMCA, Boy Scouts, the NAACP, and CORE. He worked in the civil rights movement in Peoria and other cities. He became a member of the Board of Education in Washington, D.C. in 1966, and became involved with school administration and encouraging African American youths, especially in science. Since 1983, Alexander has been president of the YMCA Trustee Council. Of his work in this area, Alexander told *Ebony* magazine in March 1967, "Maybe it's old-fashioned to say it, but if we don't stoop down to help our brothers rise, we're going to rise less high ourselves."

SELECTED WRITINGS BY ALEXANDER:

Periodicals

(With Others) "Minority Biomedical Support: Program for Change," *Negro History Bulletin,* (August/September 1975): 442-447.

Other

"The Importance of Education in Today's America: Comprehending and Understanding the Written Word," *Vital Speeches of the Day,* (April 15, 1995): 403-07.
"Is the Time for People of Good Will to Act - Over?," *Vital Speeches of the Day,* (January 1, 1994): 174-79.
"The Letter C No Longer Stands for Courage in Chemist," *Vital Speeches of the Day,* (December 1, 1988): 155-57.

FURTHER READING:

Periodicals

"Controversial Ex-president of University Gets Top U.S. Student-assistant Post," *Chronicle of Higher Education,* (March 14, 1984): 23.
"Research Scientists Lends a Hand to Capital's Poor," *Ebony,* (March 1967): 124-26.

—*Sketch by A. Petrusso*

Leslie Luther Alexander
1917-
Radiologist

Since he began practicing medicine in the early 1950s, Leslie L. Alexander has gained wide respect for his contributions to radiology, a medical field in which specialists use radiant energy to treat malignant tumors. A physician, professor, administrator, and consultant, Alexander has done research on radiation therapy, nuclear medicine, radiobiology, and cancer. He has authored or coauthored more than 100 published articles.

Alexander was born on October 10, 1917, in Kingston, Jamaica. His family moved to the United States, and he became a naturalized citizen in 1927. Alexander graduated from New York City's George Washington High School in 1937. Before beginning his college education, he served in the U.S. Army as a first lieutenant during World War II and continued his service in the U.S. Army Reserve from 1946-52.

He earned his bachelor's degree in 1947 and his master's degree in 1948 from New York University. He then attended Howard University College of Medicine, where he received his medical degree in 1952. In a 1975 interview with *Black Enterprise* magazine, he commented on the advantages of attending a predominantly African-American medical school. He noted that as a student, he met a cross-section of the nation's black physicians and developed a sense of fellowship with them and other students that would be difficult to achieve at a predominantly white institution.

Alexander completed his residency training and worked at the Kings County Hospital Center in Brooklyn for 13 years. He began as an assistant attending radiologist in 1956 and later became assistant director of radiation therapy, acting chair of the department of radiology, and director of radiation therapy and nuclear medicine. From 1957-72, he worked as an assistant attending radiologist at St. Johns Episcopal Hospital in Brooklyn, where he received promotions to associate attending radiologist and attending radiologist. For several months in the mid-1960s, he was associate director of radiology and chief of the division of radiation therapy at the Jewish Hospital-Greenpoint Hospital Medical Center in Brooklyn. During this period, Alexander also performed research at New York University in 1948; at Columbia University in 1954; at Queens General Hospital Center, studying operative radium therapy in 1957 and radioactive isotopes in 1959; at the University of Minnesota's General Extension Division in 1960; and the U.S. Armed Forces Institute of Pathology in 1962.

Alexander was assistant director of radiotherapy at the State University Hospital in Brooklyn from 1966-69 and attending radiotherapist there from 1966-76. He was attending radiotherapist at Brooklyn's Veterans Hospital from 1962-65 and director of radiation therapy at Cornell Medical College's North Shore University Hospital from 1970-77. Alexander has held positions as attending radiologist at the Long Island Jewish Medical Center from 1977-88 and director of radiology at Queens Hospital Center Affiliation/Mount Sinai Hospital Center from 1977-88.

In addition to his medical and administrative duties, Alexander has been an active teacher. He told *Black Enterprise* in 1975 that recruiting minority physicians and college students through the Central Brooklyn Model Cities program along with training radiology residents have been among his most significant experiences. Alexander moved through the ranks from instructor to full professor at the State University of New York Department of Radiology in Brooklyn from 1956 to 1976 and served as a full professor at the SUNY School of Medicine at Stony Brook from 1978 to 1988. He also spent a short time as a visiting professor at the University of Lagos in Lagos, Nigeria, in 1970.

Alexander has won numerous awards and honors over the years, including the National Medical Association's Distinguished Service Award in 1974. He has been a member of the American College of Radiology's Board of Chancellors, the Association of University Radiologists, the American Society of Therapeutic Radiologists, the New York Academy of Medicine, and the American Geriatrics Society. Alexander has also been honored as a diplomate of the American Board of Radiology and a fellow of the New York Academy of Medicine, an independent, nonprofit organization created to enhance public health, particularly the needs of urban populations. He participated in the White House Conference on Food, Nutrition and Health, and he was chair of the Post Convention African Tour and Scientific Assembly.

The National Medical Association has been a central part of Alexander's career. Since 1960, he has served on the editorial board of the organization's *Journal,* which provides a monthly forum for original communications in all fields of medical research and practice. The journal's editors focus primarily on topics vital to African American physicians and those who serve a predominantly African American patient population. Alexander became assistant editor in 1970 and has also been a frequent contributor to the publication, writing on such topics as hospitals in West Africa, the position of minority radiologists in the United States, and radiation therapy as opposed to surgery. He has also served as president and board member of the National Medical Association Foundation.

In the 1975 interview with *Black Enterprise* magazine, Alexander noted that he never planned to retire, because "there's still too much to be done." True to his word, he continues to act as a consultant at the Long Island Jewish Medical Center and the Queens Hospital Center Affiliation/Mount Sinai Hospital Center, and did not step down from his position as a staff physician at Monteflore-Rikers Island Health Services until 1998. He is married and has four children.

SELECTED WRITINGS BY ALEXANDER:

Periodicals

"Position of Minority Radiologists in the United States." *National Medical Association Journal* (March 1974).

FURTHER READING:

Books

American Men & Women of Science 1992-93. Providence, NJ: R. R. Bowker, p. 76.
Sammons, Vivian Ovelton. *Blacks in Science and Medicine.* New York: Hemisphere Publishing, 1990.

—*Sketch by Rose M. Estioco*

Lloyd Ephraim Alexander
1902-
Embryologist

Lloyd Alexander has enjoyed two careers in his lifetime. He was an eminent scientist in the early part of this century doing extensive research in the developing descipline of embryology. Later, as an educator, he was able to share his research, knowledge, and techniques with hundreds of students at various universities.

Alexander, the youngest of 12 children, was born in a log cabin near the Appalachian mountain town of Catawba, Virginia, about 15 miles northwest of Roanoke. His family was poor, so Alexander was often required gather wild fruits for the dinner table. He then sold whatever was left over at the market in nearby Catawba. Alexander enjoyed working on the land because it gave him the chance to explore and discover the wonders of nature. Living in the country sparked his interest in the native plants and animals.

Both of Alexander's parents died when he was only 14, and he had to move to the home of one of his brothers in Landgraff, West Virginia. At Kimball High School, Alexander demonstrated early on that he was an exceptional student; his superiority was noticed by the principal of the school. The curriculum at Kimball was not able to challenge Alexander, so the school principal contacted friends and colleagues across the state to inquire about institutions that could offer Alexander the education he deserved. A short time later, Alexander enrolled at the Bluefield Institute, a college preparatory school for African Americans.

Alexander excelled in school despite working two jobs—one at Bluefield to earn his room, board, and tuition, and the other at various jobs in town. To no one's surprise, he had an affinity for biology, and he graduated with honors from Bluefield as well as having the honor of being the first member of his family to earn a high school diploma.

Career One—Embryological Research

Alexander's education was just getting started, though. He was accepted into the University of Michigan, but was unable to go immediately since he had very little money. He stayed in Bluefield and worked for three years, earning enough money to begin his college career in 1923. He received his bachelor's degree in 1927 and was invited to continue at Michigan for graduate studies on the strength of his undergraduate work. He earned his master's degree in just one year. After finishing college Alexander once again had no money, so he moved back to West Virginia and took a job teaching classes in high school science and biology. Again, his excellent work did not go unnoticed. After two years he accepted a position as an instructor at Fisk College in Nashville, Tennessee.

During the 1930s the Rockefeller Foundation established a goal to improve the state of biological research in the United States. The General Education Board, a division of the Foundation that extended financial support to African Americans, offered a fellowship to Alexander that paid for his doctoral program. Alexander began his doctoral work at the University of Chicago under the supervision of preeminent embryologist B. H. Willier. The subject of Willier's research was the development of chicken embryos. Alexander further refined Willier's research and focused much of his work on the formation of the embryonic eye. Since the eye of a chicken develops from early brain tissue, learning

about the eye's development would answer questions about the development of the brain. Alexander also experimented with what happens when tissue from other parts of the chicken embryo is introduced into eye tissue. The effect that the eye tissue has on the introduced tissue is called "induction." The research team moved to the University of Rochester, New York in 1933, and Alexander was awarded his doctorate in embryology 1936. His research lasted a lifetime, though, and Alexander was considered an expert on grafting and transplanting tissues in vertebrates.

Career Two—Education

All throughout Alexander's doctoral work, he was able to continue his teaching position at Fisk University. Because he was one their best and brightest instructors, Fisk's administrators allowed him to commute between Nashville, where the university was located, and Chicago or Rochester when necessary. During Alexander's 19-year tenure at Fisk he trained numerous educators, scientists, and medical doctors. He also served his country in World War II as an instructor at Meharry Medical College, training doctors to help alleviate the critical shortages of medical personnel serving in the war.

In 1949 Alexander accepted a position as a biology instructor at Kentucky State College, where one of his major projects was creating science education curricula. His program was eventually used across the United States and the world. When his instructional material was used in Egypt, King Farouk I donated a 900-specimen butterfly collection to the university in gratitude. Alexander incorporated this treasure in his classes to demonstrate the classification system used by biologists as well as certain theories of evolution. Alexander was chairman of the biology department at Kentucky State for 23 years until his retirement in 1972.

Alexander was married to Evelyn Baker in 1934 in Rochester, New York, shortly after his doctoral team moved from Chicago. They had two sons, but his wife passed away at a young age. He married his second wife in 1952 in Louisville, Kentucky, and together they had a son and a daughter.

Lloyd Alexander's undergraduate and graduate work at Michigan and Fisk Universities set the stage for his achievements as an embryologist, researcher, and educator. The biology department at Kentucky State College, where he still serves as a professor emeritus, holds an annual Lloyd E. Alexander Day in recognition of his achievements to science and the university. The students of the biology department use this event to showcase their current research projects.

FURTHER READING:

Books

Kessler, James, et. al. *Distinguished African American Scientists of the 20th Century.* Oryx Press, 1996.

—Sketch by Roger Jaffe

William E. Allen, Jr.
1903-1981
Physician

As a radiologist, researcher, professor, and philanthropist, William E. Allen, Jr. was a significant influence in the field of radiology during its development in the 1930s. He focused his skills on shaping radiology as a science and as a profession and on increasing access to education and scientific careers for other African Americans.

William Edward Allen, Jr. was born August 14, 1903, just eight years after the x ray was discovered. The son of Marian and William Allen, a Pensacola, Florida building contractor, he attended Howard University and earned his B.S. degree in 1927 and his M.D. in 1930. By the time he completed his residency at City Hospital No. 2 in St. Louis, he had organized one of the nation's first approved training schools for black x-ray technicians at St. Mary's Infirmary. In 1935, one year after the American Board of Radiology examinations were established, he became the first African American certified x-ray technician. By the late 1930s Allen had established one of the first approved residencies in radiology for minorities. He also became a founding member of the National Medical Association's Commission on X-Ray and Radium.

Several months before the United States entered World War II, Allen volunteered for active military service. However, since there was no place in the segregated military for a black radiologist, he accepted assignment as a battalion surgeon. When a military hospital staffed by black medical officers was established at Ft. Huachuca, Arizona, Allen became its chief of x-ray service. He provided elementary radiology training for medical officers headed for hospitals in most of the war's theaters. He also established the first and only black Women's Army Corps school for x-ray technologists. In 1945 he was elected to fellowship in the American College of Radiology.

Returning to Homer G. Phillips Hospital in St. Louis after the war, Allen immediately established yet another school for x-ray technologists, which eventually gained international recognition. For the first two years after the war, he served as consultant on radiology to the U.S. Secretary of War. In 1949 the National Medical Association (NMA) radiology section was born, and Allen served as its first chairman. Long active with the NMA, he was elected vice-president of the organization in the early 1960s.

As radiology developed from a chiefly diagnostic tool in its early years to having treatment applications for tumors and cancer, Allen's career followed the emerging fields of radiology and radiation oncology. His later research focused on nuclear medicine and radiation therapy in prostate tumors and carcinoma of the cervix. In addition to his research and writings, Allen taught for many years at St. Louis University Medical School and gained the rank of emeritus professor at the Washington University School of Medicine.

In addition to founding several training schools, he developed scholarships for students from Haiti, Nigeria, Liberia, and South Africa to study radiology. Through his efforts more than two dozen men and women became x-ray technologists; five became diagnostic radiologists. He also spearheaded efforts that brought West Africa its first cobalt treatment unit.

The American College of Radiology presented Allen with a gold medal in 1974. Homer G. Phillips Hospital, Howard University, the St. Louis chapter of the NAACP, the American Cancer Society, and the National Medical Association all presented him their highest awards for service. In 1978 the American Board of Radiologists inaugurated a series of annual lectures in his honor. On December 31, 1981, Allen succumbed to stomach cancer at the age of 78. He was survived by his wife Para Lee Batts Allen, a former head nurse at Homer G. Phillips Hospital.

SELECTED WRITINGS BY ALLEN:

Periodicals

"Malignancy of the Esophagus with Bronchial Fistula," *Radiology*, (March 1934): 366.
"Transverse Fracture of the Sacrum," *American Journal of Roentgenology*, Vol. 31 (1934): 676.
"Scout Film of the Abdomen in Appendicitis," *Journal of the National Medical Association*, Vol. 41 (1949): 119.

FURTHER READING:

Periodicals

Alexander, Leslie L. "Section on Radiology Celebrates Thirtieth Year," *Journal of the National Medical Association*, Vol. 72 (1980): 277.
Evens, Ronald G. "In Memoriam: William E. Allen, Jr., M.D.," *Radiology*, Vol. 143 (1982): 575.

Other

Pamphlet on History I, edited by John W. Coleman, National Medical Association Section on Radiology.

—Sketch by Penelope Lawbaugh

Harold Amos

Harold Amos
1919-
Microbiologist

Harold Amos, former chairman and professor emeritus of the microbiology department at the Harvard Medical School, has conducted extensive research in microbiology and bacteriology, primarily focused on hexose metabolism in mammalian cells. Amos is also involved with promoting the scholarship of underprivileged minority youth.

Harold Amos was born on September 7, 1919, in Pennsauken, New Jersey, and he grew up on a farm in that rural area. In 1941, he received his bachelor of science degree in biochemistry from Springfield College in Massachusetts. Drafted, he served in the Army for five years during World War II. After his discharge, he attended Harvard Medical School, earning his medical degree in 1947 and his doctorate in bacteriology and immunology in 1952.

Under the guidance of J. Howard Mueller, the chairman of the department of bacteriology and immunology of the Harvard Medical School, Harold Amos studied the effect of the treatment of purified herpes virus particles with phosphatase and protease enzymes. He aimed to identify a treatment that reduced the infectivity of the virus for the membrane of embryonated chick eggs. His dissertation was entitled, "Study of the Factors Contributing to the Loss of Infectivity of Herpes Simplex Virus." A Fulbright Scholarship enabled Amos to pursue research at the Pasteur Institute in Paris from 1951-52. From 1952-54, he was a research fellow at Harvard Medical School.

In 1957, Amos began his academic career as an associate professor of bacteriology at Harvard Medical School. He became a full professor in 1969 and then went on to become the chairman of the department of microbiology and molecular genetics. Since 1975, Amos has been a Maude and Lillian Presley Professor of Microbiology and Molecular Genetics, emeritus.

Research on Viruses and Metabolism

The focus of Amos's research at the Pasteur Institute was the metabolic mutants of *E. coli*, with much attention paid to amino acid metabolism. However, after several years, Amos began to pursue research concerning mammalian cell metabolism, particularly sugar metabolism. Amos's first study of sugar metabolism concerned the glucose metabolism of cancer cells in comparison to normal cells. Most cancer cells studied have a great demand for glucose and die rapidly when deprived of it. Initially, his research compared the transport systems of cancer and normal cells, but he did not find a significant difference between them. He then shifted his attention to the glucose transport system itself. Amos made various discoveries that reveal the rate of the transport of cancer cells and the relationship between glucose and its transport system. Amos found that when cells are deprived of glucose, the rate of transport may increase from five to 15 times as a function of sugar deprivation.

Amos's current research concentrates on the regulation of the glut-1 transporter, one of the members of the glucose transport family. The glut-1 transporter is found in all cells and is especially sensitive to the level of glucose and certain amino acids in the culture medium. His objective at the present is to identify the metabolite of glucose that is responsible for its repressive effect on glut-1 transporters.

Amos has shown great devotion to programs that encourage minority students to pursue careers in medicine and biomedical research. He has worked with the Macy, Jr. Foundation in New York since 1965 and has been a board member since 1975. He is also the program director of the National Program of Minority Faculty Development at the Robert Wood Johnson Foundation at Princeton University and is a committee member for the Funding of Young Investigators in the Biological and Biomedical Sciences. Amos won the National Academy of Science's highest honor, the Public Welfare Medal, in 1995 for his success in mentoring and providing funds for minority students pursuing biomedicine.

Along with teaching and lecturing, Harold Amos currently oversees the laboratory for medical students at Harvard. Amos never married and lives in Boston.

FURTHER READING:

Books

American Men and Women of Science, Volume 1. New Providence, New Jersey: R.R. Bowker, 1998.

Salzman, Jack, Smith, David Lionel, and West, Cornel, eds. *Encyclopedia of African American Culture and History, Volume 1.* New York: Simon and Schuster, 1996.

Sammons, Vivian Ovelton. *Blacks in Science and Medicine.* New York: Hemisphere Publishing Corp., 1990.

—Sketch by Alison Wellford

Caroline Still Anderson
1848-1919
Physician

Caroline Still Anderson rose to prominence in the late nineteenth century as a physician, educator, and social reformer. Originally a teacher of art and music, she returned to college to study medicine and built a practice in Philadelphia that flourished for more than 30 years.

She was born Caroline Virginia Still in Philadelphia on November 1, 1848. Her parents, William and Letitia Still, were important figures in the anti-slavery movement. William Still was famous as one of the "conductors" on the Underground Railroad; he helped escaped slaves travel from Philadelphia to New York.

William Still was also a successful businessman, and he was able to provide young Caroline with a first-rate education. After attending private schools, she entered Oberlin College in 1865 when she was not quite 16. When she graduated three years later, she was the youngest in her class as well as the only black student.

Caroline Still returned to Philadelphia, where she taught music, drawing, and elocution, or public speaking. In December 1869, she married Edward Wiley, whom she had met at Oberlin. The couple had two children.

In 1873, Wiley's health gave out and he died unexpectedly. His wife was suddenly a young widow with two children to raise alone. She continued to teach, but in 1875 she decided that she wanted to switch to a career in medicine. She began at Howard University's medical school

in 1875 and transferred to the Woman's Medical College of Pennsylvania the following year. She graduated in 1878, one of two black women out of a class of 17. She applied for an internship at New England Hospital for Women and Children in Boston. Initially turned down because of her race, she met with the board and impressed the members so much that they voted unanimously to accept her. After her internship was over, she returned to Philadelphia.

In 1880, she married Matthew Anderson, a minister who had helped found the Berean Presbyterian Church in Philadelphia. The couple had five children, two of whom died in infancy. Despite her busy home life, Caroline Anderson worked with her husband to help their community. She ran a dispensary out of the church, and with her husband helped found the Berean Manual Training and Industrial School in 1889. The school provided training in both industrial and liberal arts; Caroline Anderson taught hygiene, physiology, and public speaking, and also served as assistant principal. She also served on the board of the Home for Aged and Infirm Colored People of Philadelphia and was president of the Berean Women's Christian Temperance Union. In addition, she helped organize several Black Young Men's Christian Associations (YMCAs) within the city. With all this going on, she managed to maintain a private medical practice.

Anderson remained active until a stroke forced her retirement five years before her death in Philadelphia on June 1, 1919.

SELECTED WRITINGS BY ANDERSON:

Various letters and papers of Caroline Still Anderson are located in the following special collections: Charles L. Blockson Afro-American Collection, Temple University, Philadelphia, Pennsylvania Medical College of Pennsylvania, Philadelphia, Pennsylvania Oberlin College Archives, Oberlin, Ohio.

FURTHER READING:

Books

Hine, Darlene Clark, ed. *Black Women in America: An Historical Encyclopedia.* New York: Carlson Publishing, Inc., 1993

Still, William. *The Underground Railroad.* Philadelphia: Porter, 1883.

Smith, Jessie Carney, ed. *Notable Black American Women.* Detroit: Gale Research, 1995.

—Sketch by George A. Milite

Charles Edward Anderson
1919-1994
Meteorologist

Charles Edward Anderson was the first African American to receive a Ph.D. in meteorology, and he became the first African American professor to receive tenure at the University of Wisconsin. He was a nationally known expert on severe storms and tornadoes and held important positions in the government and academia.

Anderson was born in University City, Missouri (near St. Louis), on August 13, 1919. The name of his birthplace was prophetic: he would spend much of the rest of his life associated with one university or another as a student or professor. In 1937, he graduated first in his class from Sumner High School. Four years later, in 1941, he received his Bachelor of Science from Lincoln University in Jefferson City, Missouri, where, over 50 years later, he was laid to rest in his family burial plot. In 1943, he received a certification in meteorology (equivalent to a master's degree) from the University of Chicago. In 1943, he also married Marjorie Anderson, who was from Cary, North Carolina. They were to have two daughters, Cheryle and Linda.

During World War II, Anderson was commissioned an officer in the United States Army Air Forces, and served as a captain. He was the weather officer for the famous regiment of black air force pilots, the Tuskegee Airmen, based in Tuskegee, Alabama. In 1948, Anderson followed his certification in meteorology from the University of Chicago with a Master of Science in Chemistry from the Polytechnic Institute of Brooklyn. He then moved up the coast to Boston, Massachusetts, where he was the head of the Cloud Physics Branch of the Air Force's Research Center in Cambridge until 1961. In 1960, Anderson earned his Ph.D. in meteorology from the Massachusetts Institute of Technology. His doctoral dissertation, which was published immediately after he finished it (a considerable honor), was titled "A Study of the Pulsating Growth of Cumulus Clouds."

In 1961, Anderson left the Air Force Research Center for the Atmospheric Science Branch of the Douglas Aircraft Company in California. In 1965, he began work for the U.S. Department of Commerce as the Director of the Office of Federal Coordination in Meteorology in the Environmental Science Service Administration. Beginning in 1966 and continuing for over 20 years, Anderson held several important positions at the University of Wisconsin. He was a Professor of Space Science and Engineering, a Professor of Meteorology, Chairman of the Contemporary Trends Course, Chairman of the Afro-American Studies Department, Chairman of the Meteorology Department, and ultimately, in 1978, Associate Dean of the University.

In 1987, Dr. Anderson and his family moved to Raleigh, North Carolina, where he was a professor in the Department of Marine, Earth and Atmospheric Sciences at North Carolina State University. He retired in 1990 and died of cancer at the age of 75 in Durham, North Carolina, on October 21, 1994.

FURTHER READING:

Books

American Men and Women of Science. 13th ed. New York: Bowker, 1976.
Sammons, Vivian. *Blacks in Science and Medicine* New York: Hemisphere Publishing, 1990.

Periodicals

"Charles Anderson: Expert on Storms." *St. Louis Post Dispatch.* (October 27, 1994): 4B.

—Sketch by Patrick Moore

Gloria L. Anderson
1938-
Chemist

Gloria L. Anderson is a distinguished chemist, educator, and college administrator. Her scientific research has involved industrial, medical and military applications of fluorine–19 chemistry. As an educator, she has served as the Callaway professor of chemistry, chair of the chemistry department, and dean of academic affairs at Morris Brown College in Atlanta. Anderson, in addition, has been a board member and vice-chair of the Corporation for Public Broadcasting, for which she has lectured nationally on issues related to minorities and women in mass media and public television.

Anderson was born in Altheimer, Arkansas, on November 5, 1938, the daughter of Charley Long and Elsie Lee Foggie. She enrolled at the Arkansas Agricultural, Mechanical and Normal College (now the University of Arkansas at Pine Bluff), where she was awarded a Rockefeller Scholarship from 1956 to 1958. Anderson received her B.S. degree *summa cum laude* in 1958. She married Leonard Sinclair Anderson on June 4, 1960; they have one son, Gerald. In 1961, Anderson was awarded her M.S. degree from Atlanta University. For the next year, she worked as a chemistry instructor at South Carolina State College in Orangeburg. From 1962 to 1964, she held an instructorship at Morehouse

Gloria L. Anderson

College in Atlanta, then went on to take a position as a teaching and research assistant at the University of Chicago, where she received her doctorate in organic chemistry in 1968.

Researches Fluorine–19 Chemistry

Anderson's dissertation and aspects of her subsequent research have related to fluorine–19 chemistry. (The '19' following fluorine refers to a particular isotope of fluorine that, like other elements with odd numbered masses, has magnetic properties.) Fluorine–19 chemistry became an important field of research shortly before World War II when many commercial uses for fluorine compounds were discovered. Much of Anderson's research has involved nuclear magnetic resonance (NMR) spectroscopy, a method of investigating organic compounds by analyzing the nucleic responses of molecules subjected to radio-frequency radiation within a slowly changing magnetic field. NMR spectroscopy, which has been widely exploited for chemistry, biochemistry, biophysics, and solid-state physics research, enables extremely sophisticated analysis of the molecular structures and interactions of various materials. The small size, low reactivity, and high sensitivity of fluorine–19 make it particularly suited for NMR spectroscopy. Since the late 1960s, fluorine NMR spectroscopy has been applied to a range of biochemical problems, including the study of the human metabolism and the formulation of new pharmaceuticals.

Anderson joined the faculty of Morris Brown College in Atlanta in 1968 as associate professor and chair of the chemistry department. From 1973 to 1984, Anderson was the Fuller E. Callaway professor of chemistry at Morris Brown, and continued her service as the chemistry department chair. Anderson left the chemistry department to serve as dean of academic affairs at Morris Brown for the years 1984–89. In 1990, Anderson resumed her post as the Callaway professor of chemistry. In 1976, Anderson was recognized as an Outstanding Teacher at Morris Brown, and received a Scroll of Honor award from the National Association of Negro Business and Professional Women. In 1983, she received a Teacher of the Year award and was voted into the Faculty/Staff Hall of Fame at Morris Brown. In 1987, she received an Alumni All-Star Excellence Award in Education from the University of Arkansas at Pine Bluff.

In addition to her work at Morris Brown, Anderson has conducted research through a number of independent and government facilities. Beginning in 1971 she continued her investigations of fluorine–19 chemistry—first in association with the Atlanta University Center Research Committee, then under the National Institutes of Health, the National Science Foundation, and the Office of Naval Research. She also conducted research on amantadines (drugs used to prevent viral infection) under the Minority Biomedical Support Program of the National Institutes of Health. She held a faculty industrial research fellowship with the National Science Foundation in 1981, and with the Air Force Office of Scientific Research in 1984. In 1985, Anderson investigated the synthesis of potential antiviral drugs as a United Negro Fund Distinguished Scholar. In that same year, she conducted research on the synthesis of solid rocket propellants under the Air Force Office of Scientific Research. Since 1990, she has been affiliated with BioS-PECS of The Hague, Netherlands, as a research consultant.

In 1972, Anderson was appointed to a six-year term on the board of the Corporation for Public Broadcasting (CPB). At the CPB, Anderson chaired committees on Minority Training, Minorities and Women, and Human Resources Development; she was vice-chair of the CPB board from 1977–79. She is a member of the American Institute of Chemists, the American Chemical Society, the National Institute of Science, the National Science Teachers Association, the Association of Computers in Mathematics and Science Teaching, the Georgia Academy of Science, and the Atlanta University Science Research Institute, among other scientific and professional bodies. She has served as a proposal review panel member, contract reviewer, or field reader for the Department of Health, Education and Welfare's Office of Education, the National Science Foundation's Women in Science Program, the Nation Cancer Institute, the Department of Education, and the National Institute of Drug Abuse.

SELECTED WRITINGS BY ANDERSON:

Periodicals

"$_{19}$F Chemical Shifts for Bicyclic Fluorides," *Journal of the American Chemical Society,* Vol. 90 (1968): 212.

"$_{19}$F Chemical Shifts for Bicyclic and Aromatic Molecules," *Journal of the American Chemical Society,* Vol. 91 (1969): 6804.

"Transmission of Substituent Effects, Acid Dissociation Constants of 10-Substituted–9-Anthroic Acids," *Journal of the American Chemical Society,* Vol. 93 (1971): 6984.

"Synthesis of Triflate and Chloride Salts of Alkyl *N, N* -Bis (2, 2, 2-Tri-Fluoroethyl) Amines," *Synthetic Communications,* Vol. 17 (1987): 111–114.

"Novel Synthesis of 3-Fluoro–1-Aminoadamantane," *Synthetic Communications,* Vol. 18 (1988): 1967–1974.

"Novel Synthesis of Some 1-N-(3-Fluoroadamantyl) Ureas," *Synthetic Communications,* Vol. 19 (1989): 1955–1963.

FURTHER READING:

Periodicals

"Atlanta's Best and Brightest Scientists," *Atlanta Magazine,* (April 1983).

New York Times, (December 1, 1973): 39.

—Sketch by M. C. Nagel

Alexander Thomas Augusta
1825-1890
Physician

Alexander Thomas Augusta's career as a physician was punctuated with firsts. By appealing directly to President Abraham Lincoln, Augusta became the first black to be offered a commission with the U.S. Army's colored troops. The first black man to become the head of a hospital in the United States and the first black to be appointed to the faculty of a U.S. medical school, Augusta's leadership helped steer the fledgling Howard University medical department through the economic turmoil of 1873, ensuring the school's survival.

Born in Norfolk, Virginia, on March 8, 1825, Augusta, like all black Virginians, was barred by state law from learning to read. The Rev. Daniel Payne, later to become a bishop in the African Methodist Episcopal Church, defied the law and secretly taught young Augusta to read.

As a youth, Augusta was apprenticed to a Norfolk barber. After learning his trade, he worked his way to Baltimore; there, he cut hair and took private lessons, hoping to learn enough to enter medical school. Augusta then took his ambition to Philadelphia and began private studies with Dr. William Gibson. A faculty member of the University of Pennsylvania medical school, Gibson was impressed by Augusta's ability and determination; despite Gibson's support, Augusta was refused entrance in the University of Pennsylvania medical school because of his race.

In 1847, Augusta wed Mary O. Burgoin, a young woman from Baltimore. The couple set out for California and the gold boom in 1849, hoping to raise enough money to ease Augusta's entry into medical school. After a financially successful three-year stint, Augusta moved back east to pursue his medical school ambitions. Rejected by schools in Philadelphia and Chicago, he applied to and was accepted by Trinity Medical College of the University of Toronto, Canada, in 1850. Augusta graduated from medical school in 1856; he was promptly appointed head of a Toronto city hospital, then took charge of an industrial school while building a private practice. In Canada, Augusta's race seemed to pose few professional barriers; many of the patients in his private practice were white, and his academic and medical colleagues seemed to readily accept him for his medical and leadership skills.

Despite the opportunities Toronto made available, Augusta was, at heart, a patriotic American—and in 1863, he wrote a letter that earned him a place in the National Archives.

A Man of Letters and of Action

On January 1, 1863, the Congress passed the Emancipation Proclamation. On January 7, Augusta penned a letter to President Lincoln.

"Having seen that it is intended to garrison . . . forts with coloured troops, I beg leave to apply to you for an appointment as surgeon to some of the coloured regiments, or as physician to some of the depots of 'freedmen.' I was compelled to leave my native country and come to this [Canada] on account of prejudice against colour, for the purpose of obtaining knowledge of my profession; and having accomplished that object at one of the . . . educational institutions of the province, I am now prepared to practice it, and would like to be in a position where I can be of use to my race. If you will take this matter into favorable consideration, I can give satisfactory references as to character and qualification from some of the most distinguished members of the profession in this city [Toronto] where I have been in practice for about six years."

Lincoln's response to the letter was to issue a presidential commission to Augusta, naming him to the rank of major. Augusta was the first black physician to be granted a commission with the U.S. Army's colored divisions, and his service throughout the Civil War earned him the distinction of becoming first black to be promoted to breveted lieutenant-colonel, U.S. Volunteers.

In the military, Augusta faced the same intolerance that had barred him from medical schools in the United States. He was once confronted by an angry mob at a train station; his insignia was ripped from his uniform, and only the timely arrival of a group of Provost guards saved him from a beating or worse. Initially assigned to the 7th U.S. Colored Infantry at Camp Stanton, Maryland, Augusta was transferred to another post because two white officers complained that it was 'unnatural' and 'degrading' to serve under a black man of superior military rank. And although he was a physician, surgeon, and a major, Augusta had to fight for pay commensurate with his skills and rank. Initially, Augusta's military pay was set at $7 per month, and it took the intervention of Senator Henry Wilson of Massachusetts and the Secretary of War to convince the Army that Augusta's compensation should be adjusted.

Augusta served most of 1864 in Benedict, South Carolina, and in Baltimore as a military medical examiner on detached duty. Assigned to the Department of the South in 1865-66, he served as head of a Savannah hospital. Augusta was discharged from the military in October of 1866 with commendations for his meritorious service. He returned to Washington—where he had briefly served as head of the Freedmen's Hospital, the first black man to head a hospital in the United States—and established a private practice.

Shaping New Opportunities in Medical Education

When Howard University organized a department of medicine, Augusta was invited to join four other physicians to form the nucleus of medical school faculty. Augusta joined the university as a demonstrator in anatomy in 1869. It was another trail-blazing achievement for the doctor, who became the first black to hold a faculty position in a U.S. medical school. For the next nine years, he held various academic appointments at Howard while he continued to serve on the medical staff of the Freedmen's Hospital.

Despite his achievements, his military record, his academic standing, and his professional reputation, Augusta was denied membership in the Medical Society of Washington and American Medical Association. Disturbed by these rejections on behalf of the new generation of black physicians he was helping to educate, Augusta convinced some colleagues to join him in forming the National Medical Association, a professional medical organization built on a non-discriminatory membership policy.

Named to the chair of the anatomy department, Augusta's reputation helped the school attract qualified, dedicated faculty members. But none proved more dedicat-

ed than Augusta when the Panic of 1873 battered the country's economic health and threatened the financial stability of institutions across the nation, including Howard University. The university faculty voted to waive student tuition until times got better, but only two other faculty members joined Augusta in taking dramatic salary cuts to ease the university's financial straits.

Augusta remained at Howard until 1877, when the board of trustees asked him to step down from the chairmanship of the anatomy department and take over the chair of the pharmacology department. Augusta declined and returned to private practice. He remained in private practice in Washington until his death in 1890 at age 65. He died of pneumonia; his military service entitled him to burial in Arlington National Cemetery.

Augusta's original letter to President Lincoln, requesting a military appointment, is part of the National Archives.

SELECTED WRITINGS BY AUGUSTA:

Other

Gov. Doc. AE 1.102 H62.4, reproduction of Jan. 7, 1863 letter from A. T. Augusta to President Abraham Lincoln. *Researching Black History at the National Archives: Dr. Alexander T. Augusta* U.S. Depository, April 12, 1994.

FURTHER READING:

Books

Logan, Rayford W. and Michael R. Winston, eds. *Dictionary of American Negro Biography* New York: W. W. Norton & Company, 1982.

Low, W. Augustus, and Virgil A. Clift, eds. *Encyclopedia of Black America* New York: McGraw-Hill Book Company, 1980.

Rywell, Martin, ed. *Afro-American Encyclopedia, Vol. 1* North Miami, Florida: Educational Book Publishers, Inc., 1974.

Sammons, Vivian Ovelton. *Blacks in Science and Medicine* New York: Hemisphere Publishing Corporation, 1990.

Williams, Michael W., ed. *The African American Encyclopedia, Vol. 1* New York: Marshall Cavendish, 1993.

Periodicals

Cobb, W.M. "Alexander Thomas Augusta." *Journal* National Medical Association, vol. 44 (July 1952): 327-329.

—Sketch by A. Mullig

June Bacon-Bercey
1932-
Meteorologist

June Bacon-Bercey was one of the first black American women to rise to prominence in the field of meteorology. She has worked as a television news correspondent, held positions in the National Weather Service and National Oceanic and Atmospheric Agency (NOAA), and currently is an educator developing programs for young persons interested in the sciences.

June Bacon-Bercey was born on October 23, 1932, in Wichita, Kansas. In an interview with contributor Patrick Longe in May 1998, Bacon-Bercey indicated that early in her life she developed a drive to achieve success in the sciences. This resulted in her obtaining an undergraduate degree with honors in 1954 from the University of California at Los Angeles (UCLA) in mathematics and meteorology. Her master's degree in the same was earned at UCLA and awarded in 1955. Later in life, with her career flourishing in government, she obtained in 1979 a Masters in Public Administration to complement her work. In addition, she has done post-graduate work at New York University.

From 1956 to 1962, Bacon-Bercey worked as a meteorologist for the National Weather Service in Washington, D.C. It was here that she first prepared weather forecasting charts that were put into use worldwide. With this solid experience, she went to work later in 1962 for the Sperry Rand Corporation and stayed until 1974. It was then she became a consultant in high demand and soon was invited by National Broadcasting Company (NBC) television stations to impart her knowledge in their news broadcasts. In addition, she was both a news correspondent and morning hostess for these stations in Buffalo and New York City. In the years 1974-75, she was a professional lecturer in her field of expertise. Soon she was back at the National Weather Service, working as a meteorologist and broadcaster until 1979. Later that year, she joined the National Oceanic and Atmospheric Agency as a public affairs specialist and soon was appointed the chief of television services. She retained these duties until moving to California in 1982. There she began working as forecasting training officer for the state with the National Weather Service, a position she held until 1990.

Since 1990, Bacon-Bercey has been an educator, developing programs for young persons interested in the sciences. She has worked with private foundations, schools and universities, professional associations, and the NOAA. She contributed a weather lesson to the 1995 Harcourt Brace CD-ROM for elementary school students entitled *Science Anytime*. Her devotion to attracting young persons, particularly women and minority students, to the sciences is evident by her establishment of a scholarship to assist in educational expenses. The American Geophysical Union in Washington, D.C., administers the fund.

Bacon-Bercey is a member of, and held various posts in, the American Meteorological Society, Women in Science and Engineering, American Geophysical Union, American Association of Public Administrators, and the New York Academy of the Sciences.

She currently resides in Hillsborough, California with her husband George W. Brewer, a physician. They have two daughters.

SELECTED WRITINGS BY BACON-BERCEY:

Books

(Contributor) *Science Anytime (CD-ROM),* Harcourt Brace, 1995.

Periodicals

"Summary of AMS participation in the 1986 science and engineering affiliated fairs," *Bulleting of the American Meteorological Society,* (December 1986).

FURTHER READING:

Books

Who's Who of American Women, 14th ed. Marquis Who's Who, 1985.

—Sketch by Patrick J. Longe

Benjamin Banneker

Benjamin Banneker
1731-1806
Inventor, mathematician, and astronomer

It is difficult to place Benjamin Banneker's accomplishments into any single category. Over the course of his life he was an inventor, an astronomer, a mathematician, a surveyor, a clockmaker, and the publisher of an almanac. Nor was he concerned only with science. He wrote frequently and eloquently against slavery, both in his almanac and in private letters; among his correspondents was Thomas Jefferson. It was thanks to Jefferson, in fact, that Banneker became the first black American to receive a presidential appointment. By the time he died, he was known in the United States and overseas as an outstanding contributor to scientific knowledge.

Early Life

Benjamin Banneker was born on November 9, 1731, on a tobacco farm near Baltimore, Maryland. His maternal grandmother, Molly Walsh, had been a dairymaid in England; in 1698 she was sent to colonial Maryland as an indentured servant. Upon her release from servitude, she

secured a farm and purchased two slaves—one of whom, named Bannaky, she married. Their daughter, Mary, did the same; she purchased and married a slave named Robert. Under colonial law, children such as Benjamin, born to a free mother and a slave father, were themselves free.

Although the Bannaky farm prospered, there was no school in the region. Benjamin and his brothers and sisters received their early education from their grandmother Molly, who taught them to read the Bible. In 1743, a Quaker named Peter Heinrich came to the area and started a school for boys. Twelve-year-old Benjamin was the only black to attend; Heinrich changed the spelling of his last name to "Banneker" and the spelling stuck.

Young Banneker proved a quick learner, particularly in mathematics. It was not long before his understanding of math had surpassed even his teacher's; to amuse himself, he would make up complicated math problems and solve them. Banneker also learned the ways of the Quakers from Heinrich. Their belief in social justice became one of his core values.

The Celebrated Clock

When Banneker was 21, he met a man who owned a pocket watch. Banneker, who had never seen a pocket watch before, was fascinated, and its owner generously presented his watch to the young man as a gift. Banneker spent days taking the watch apart and putting it back together. He was so entranced with the mechanism that he decided to build a clock of his own. Borrowing a geometry book and a copy of Sir Isaac Newton's *Principia* from his old teacher Peter Heinrich, Banneker drew up plans for his clock. Based on both his calculations and his careful examination of the pocket watch, he meticulously carved a series of gears out of wood. By 1753 he had created a working clock that struck the hour—the first clock actually built in America. The clock kept accurate time for more than 40 years, and as its fame spread it became something of an early tourist attraction for American colonists. Banneker built a number of clocks over the years, and he also became an expert repairer of clocks, watches, and sundials.

Astronomer and Patriot

Banneker, who never married, continued to live on the family farm, building and studying whenever he had free time. In 1772 the Ellicott family bought land near Banneker's farm to build a mill. The father, Joseph Ellicott, wanted to plant wheat instead of tobacco, which he felt was eroding the soil's nutrients. Banneker (who by now was running his farm), continued to grow tobacco, but he helped Ellicott design the mill and became friends with the family. When Joseph Ellicott died a few years later, he left Banneker several books on astronomy, along with several scientific instruments including a telescope. Banneker built a "work cabin" on his farm, complete with a skylight, from which he studied the stars and made astronomical calculations. He soon earned a reputation for accuracy. In one famous example, he predicted that a solar eclipse would take place on April 14, 1789. Several other noted astronomers had calculated a different date, but Banneker found flaws in their predictions. On April 14, Banneker's calculations proved correct.

Eventually, Banneker's interest led to the publication of his Almanac. The first, called *Benjamin Banneker's Pennsylvania, Delaware, Maryland, and Virginia Almanack and Ephemeris,* was published in 1791. Banneker's almanac included information on tides, eclipses, sunrise and sunset times, weather, lunar phases, and common medicines. His Quaker influence came through in a section outlining his ideas for the creation of a "Secretary of Peace" and free schools for all children. The Almanac was published for several years and became as common in American homes as the Bible.

Banneker also included a number of articles condemning slavery. Perhaps especially because he was free, he felt a strong duty to speak out against the plight of blacks. Banneker had been a strong supporter of the American Revolution; during the war he switched from tobacco to wheat to help feed the soldiers. He was proud to be an American, and also proud of his heritage. When he published his first Almanac, he sent a copy to Thomas Jefferson, then George Washington's Secretary of State. Jefferson, himself a slave owner, had once written that blacks were intellectually and physically inferior to whites. Banneker sent a letter with his Almanac in which he noted Jefferson's own words, "... that all men are created equal," and asked Jefferson how he could still justify slavery. Jefferson replied to Banneker, beginning a long correspondence between the two men about the evils of slavery.

A Design for the Capital

Jefferson was so impressed with Banneker's intellect that he sent a copy of the Almanac to the Academy of Sciences in Paris. He made use of Banneker's skills closer to home as well. In 1790 plans were being made to move the U.S. capital from Philadelphia to its present location in Washington, D.C. President Washington engaged the French engineer Pierre L'Enfant to design the new city. Andrew Ellicott, one of Joseph's sons, was chosen to assist L'Enfant as a surveyor. At Ellicott's—and Jefferson's—request, Banneker was also appointed to the project.

L'Enfant was talented but high-strung and easily angered. Two years into the project, L'Enfant walked out and returned to France—taking his plans with him. Everyone was convinced that the project was doomed and that a new design would have to be created from scratch. Only Banneker was calm. He had examined the plans several times, and he told his colleagues he thought he could reconstruct them from memory. They were skeptical, but they had nothing to lose. It took Banneker a mere two days to do what he had promised. His ability to visualize the plans and reproduce them saved the group from having to

start completely from scratch. It is completely thanks to Banneker that L'Enfant's design was not abandoned.

In his later years, Banneker continued to publish his Almanac until sales fell off; even then, he still continued to make astronomical recordings. He also entertained many of the leading intellectuals of the day at his farm. He died there on October 25, 1806; his manuscripts and letters are on display at the Maryland Historical Society.

SELECTED WRITINGS BY BANNEKER:

Books

Benjamin Banneker's Pennsylvania, Delaware, Maryland and Virginia Almanack and Ephemeris for the Year of Our Lord 1792; Being Bissextile, or Leap-Year, and the Sixteenth Year of American Independence. Baltimore, Goddard and Angell, printers, 1797.

FURTHER READING:

Books

African-American Almanac. Gale Research, Inc., 1994.

Bedini, Silvio A. *The Life of Benjamin Banneker.* New York: Charles Scribner's Sons, 1972.

Biography Index: A Cumulative Index to Biographical Material in Books and Magazines. New York: H. W. Wilson, 1949 (ongoing).

Elliott, Clark A. *Biographical Dictionary of American Science: The Seventeenth Through the Nineteenth Centuries.* Westport, Connecticut: Greenwood Press, 1979.

Farragher, John Mack, ed. *Encyclopedia of Colonial and Revolutionary America.* New York: Facts on File, 1990.

Filler, Louis. *Dictionary of Social Reform.* New York: Philosophical Library, 1963.

Foner, Eric, and John A. Garraty, eds. *Reader's Companion to American History.* Boston, Houghton Mifflin Company, 1991.

Haber, Louis. *Black Pioneers of Science and Invention.* New York: Harcourt Brace Jovanovich, 1970.

Handy, William Christopher. *Unsung Americans Sung.* New York: Handy Brothers Music Co., Inc., 1944.

Hart, James D. *Oxford Companion to American Literature.* New York: Oxford University Press, 1983.

Woodson, Carter Goodwin. *Negro Makers of History.* Washington, D.C., The Associated Publishers, Inc., 1945.

Periodicals

Baker, Geoffrey S. "Benjamin Banneker." *Electronic Journal of the Astronomical Society of the Atlantic.* Vol. 6, No. 1 (August 1994).

Baker, Henry E. "Benjamin Banneker, the Negro Mathematician and Astronomer," *Journal of Negro History.* Vol. 3: 99-118.

—Sketch by George A. Milite

Robert Percy Barnes
1898-1990
Organic chemist

R obert Percy Barnes was an organic chemist with a distinguished career. He was one of the first African Americans to hold a faculty-related position at Amherst College, his alma mater. Barnes also served on the first National Science Board of the National Science Foundation beginning in 1950. Barnes published regularly throughout his career, including 40 papers in prestigious journals like the *Journal of Organic Chemistry*, but mostly in the *Journal of the American Chemical Society.*

Barnes was born on February 26, 1898, in Washington, D.C., to William and Mary Jane (nee Thomas) Barnes. After gradating from Dunbar High School in Washington, D.C., he earned his B.A. in 1921 from Amherst College, where he was a member of Phi Beta Kappa. Upon graduation, he worked as a research assistant in the chemistry department for a year, 1921-22. In that position, Barnes was the first black faculty member to be appointed at Amherst. (The college did not appoint a full-time African American professor until the 1960s.) In 1922, Barnes was also married for the first time to Ethel Hasbrock and began his teaching career.

After working at Amherst, Barnes returned to his home town of Washington, D.C., to teach at Howard University. While working his way through the professorial ranks at Howard, beginning as an instructor, Barnes attended graduate school at Harvard University. He also earned a prestigious fellowship for three years while attending Harvard. He was a General Education Board fellow from 1928 until 1931. Harvard granted him an M.A. in 1930 and his Ph.D. in chemistry in 1933. His dissertation was titled, *The Reactions and Keto-Enol Equilibria of an Alpha Diketone.* In 1933, Barnes married for the second time, to Florence Adams.

By 1945, Barnes was an associate professor, and he granted a full professorship at Howard that same year. Barnes was a generous teacher. He co-wrote many of his papers with graduate students he was mentoring, including future prominent scientists such as George W. Reed and Wendell M. Lucas. In 1950, President Truman appointed Barnes to the first National Science Board of the National Science Foundation. The Board was made up of 24

important science scholars, who met to produce a national policy for the advancement of science education and research. He held this board position until 1958. Barnes retired from Howard in 1967. He died on March 18, 1990, in Washington, D.C.

—Sketch by A. Petrusso

William Harry Barnes
1887-1945
Otolaryngologist, surgeon, and inventor

D r. William Harry Barnes was a distinguished ear, nose, and throat specialist who invented an instrument to facilitate reaching the pituitary gland surgically. He was Chief Otolaryngologist at Frederick Douglass Hospital in Philadelphia, and, as a diplomate of the American Board of Otolaryngology, he was the first black to become a board-certified specialist. Barnes was active in the National Medical Association, an organization of black doctors, dentists, and pharmacists, and served as its 37th president from 1935 to 1936.

Barnes was born on April 4, 1887, in Philadelphia, Pennsylvania, and spent nearly his entire life in that city. He grew up in a poor neighborhood, and his parents worked at menial jobs to support him and his two sisters. During high school he walked 10 miles (16 km) a day to school and work because he couldn't afford the trolley. His family and friends ridiculed his idea of becoming a doctor, but they were not aware of his fierce determination to rise out of poverty and to pursue a career as a professional.

After graduating from Philadelphia's Central High School in 1908, Barnes spent the summer preparing for the University of Pennsylvania Medical School scholarship exam. He won the scholarship, becoming the first black to do so. He received his M.D. in 1912 and interned at Douglass and Mercy Hospitals the following year, with a specialty in ear, nose, and throat. Douglass Hospital appointed him assistant otolaryngologist in 1913. In 1918 he served in the U.S. Public Health Service as an acting assistant surgeon.

In 1921, having completed seven years of clinical experience, Barnes returned to the University of Pennsylvania to do postgraduate work in ear, nose, and throat treatment and surgery. He desired further advanced training but couldn't find it in the United States, so he went to France in 1924 to study at the University of Paris and the University of Bordeaux. Later, in the United States, the renowned Dr. Chevalier Jackson of Philadelphia also served as Barnes's mentor, teaching him to use the bronchoscope, a device used for inspecting the bronchial tubes. The first black to master bronchoscopy, Barnes set up a department of bronchoscopy at Mercy Hospital. In 1931 he accepted a teaching position in bronchoscopy at Howard University Medical School in Washington, D.C.

Barnes was an innovator in his field. His invention of the hypophyscope, an instrument used to visualize the pituitary gland through the sphenoid sinus, made him famous. His accomplishments included other innovative operative techniques as well as a streamlined, efficient medical record system. Barnes was very active in the National Medical Association, for which he presented papers and gave demonstrations. One such demonstration showed the speedy and bloodless technique of his ten-minute tonsillectomy. He became the president of the association in 1935. Barnes was also one of the founders of the Society for the Promotion of Negro Specialists in Medicine. Among his other affiliations were the American Medical Association and the American Laryngological Association. Locally, he served as president of the Philadelphia Academy of Medicine and Allied Sciences for three years.

Barnes was married to Mattie E. Thomas in 1912. The couple had five sons: W. Harry Barnes, Jr., a mortician; Lloyd T. Barnes, an internist; Ralph W. Barnes, an industrial designer; Leroy T. Barnes, a radiologist; and Carl L. Barnes. In 1938 Barnes began to suffer from hypertension, and in 1943, he incurred a spinal injury with paraplegia. He later died of bronchial pneumonia on January 15, 1945, at the age of 58. His obituary in the March 1945 *Journal of the National Medical Association* paid tribute to him as a nationally recognized ear, nose, and throat specialist whose "ability as a diagnostician and surgeon was equalled by few, and surpassed by none."

SELECTED WRITINGS BY BARNES:

Periodicals

"A Simplified Method of Removing Naso-Pharyngeal Fibromas," *Eye, Ear, Nose, and Throat Monthly,* (November 1924).
"An Improved Hypophyscope," *Laryngos,* (1927): 379–380.

FURTHER READING:

Books

Dictionary of American Medical Biography. Greenwood Press, 1984, pp. 37–38.
Sammons, Vivian Ovelton. *Blacks in Science and Medicine.* Hemisphere Publishing, 1990, pp. 20–21.

Periodicals

Cobb, W. Montague, "William Harry Barnes, 1887–1945," *Journal of the National Medical Association,* (January 1955): 64–66.

Cobb, W. Montague, "In Memoriam, W. Harry Barnes, A Tribute," *Journal of the National Medical Association,* (March 1945): 72.
Venable, H. Phillip, "Pseudo-Tumor Cerebri," *Journal of the National Medical Association,* (November 1970): 435–436.

—*Sketch by Linda Lewin*

Andrew Jackson Beard
1849-1921
Inventor

Andrew Jackson Beard was a noted nineteenth-century inventor. He patented several important designs, including a new coupler to join railroad cars with much greater safety. His new coupler saved the lives of many railroad workers.

Beard was born a slave in Eastlake, Alabama, in 1849. While a teenager, he was a farmer in Birmingham, Alabama. He never learned to read and write well. In fact, one of his highly detailed and well-illustrated patent applications, which was prepared by his attorney based on a model Beard provided, listed his name as "Andrew J. X Beard." The "X" was his legal signature mark. Though illiterate, Beard was astute, inventive, and creative in developing tools to make agricultural and mechanical work more economical and safe. As a result of his experience with farming, Beard invented and then patented a plow in 1884. He sold the patent rights for $4,000, a sum that could support a family for many years in those days. In 1887, he sold another patent for a plow, this time for $5,200.

After these agricultural inventions, Beard turned to inventing devices for the flourishing railroad industry. In the later part of the nineteenth century, competition was intensifying in corporate America, and one way to beat the competition was to provide products and services more cheaply. In response, in 1892, Beard patented a rotary steam engine which cost less to operate than the other engines of the time.

Beard's most famous invention is the "Jenny coupler." It was the first automatic coupler that allowed train cars to be joined safely without human intervention. Before Beard's coupler, joining railroad cars was risky business. A railroad car would have a link with a hole in it extending from both ends of the car. When the hole in the link from one railroad car was lined up with the hole in the link of the next car, the trainman would insert a heavy metal pin through both of the holes in the links to join the cars. Unfortunately, however, one car was moving and perhaps lurching, so the trainman would have to insert the pin at the exact moment that he lined up the hole in one link with the hole in the other. If the trainman missed or the car lurched, he might lose a finger, an arm, a leg, or his life, depending on the situation. Beard himself lost a leg trying to couple two cars. Beard's coupling system consisted of horizontal jaws, one jaw on one car and the other on the next car. When the two jaws joined, they locked automatically to create the coupling.

Beard wanted to make sure his device would be regularly used, so he made sure that his coupling design was simple, that it had relatively few parts, and that the parts could be easily replaced when they wore out. He sold his patent in 1897 for $50,000 to a New York company. After 1897, Beard's activities are not well known. He died in 1921.

FURTHER READING:

Books

Encyclopedia of African-American Culture and History. Vol. 1. New York: Macmillan, 1996.

Burt, McKinley Jr. *Black Inventors of America.* Portland: National Book Company, 1989.

James, Portia P. *The Real McCoy: African-American Inventors and Innovation, 1619-1930.* Washington D.C.: Smithsonian Institution, 1989.

—Sketch by Patrick Moore

Ruth Winifred Howard Beckham
1900-
Psychologist

R uth Winifred Howard Beckham was the first black woman in the United States to receive a Ph.D. in psychology.

Beckham was born in Washington, D.C. on March 25, 1900. She was the eighth and youngest child of the Reverend and Mrs. William James Howard. Her mother was a school teacher before she married, and her father was pastor of the Zion Baptist Church in Washington. Because her siblings were all older (some were educated professionals), Beckham had no one to play with. However, she was surrounded in her youth with plenty of reading material, and so she started reading voraciously at an early age. She loved reading and libraries so much that her first thought of an occupation was to be a librarian. In 1916, she graduated from Dunbar High School, and then moved north to major in social work at Simmons College in Boston, Massachusetts, where she received her bachelor's degree in 1921.

After graduation, Beckham moved west to Cleveland, Ohio, where she was a social worker. In 1927 she received her master's degree from Simmons College. From 1929-1930, Beckham attended the Teacher's College and School of Social Work at Columbia University on a Laura Spelman Rockefeller Fellowship. In 1930, after receiving another Rockefeller fellowship, she moved west to Minneapolis, Minnesota, where she studied child psychology at the Child Development Institute at the University of Minnesota from 1930 to 1934. In 1934, the University of Minnesota awarded Beckham a Ph.D. in psychology and child development. Her doctoral dissertation was titled "A Study of the Development of Triplets." One important conclusion of Howard's research was that preschool and school-age triplets did not perform as well on tests of general ability as single children in their age group.

After receiving her doctorate, Beckham moved to Illinois, where she first had a clinical internship at the Illinois Institute for Juvenile Research. Later she established a private practice as a clinical psychologist. In 1934, she also married Dr. Albert Sidney Beckham, a distinguished psychologist in his own right. Her long subsequent career was a series of important positions as a teacher, consultant, clinical practitioner of psychology, and manager of psychological health care services.

Like other health care professionals, Howard held several positions concurrently. She was co-director (with her husband) of the Center for Psychological Services from 1940 to 1964. During the same period, she was the staff psychologist for the Provident Hospital School of Nursing in Chicago, and she was a psychological consultant at schools of nursing in Missouri and Florida. She also lectured, provided psychology clinics, and consulted for various organizations.

After her husband died in 1964, she continued to work in private practice and as a consultant. She worked as a psychologist for the McKinley Center for Retarded Children from 1964 to 1966. She was a staff psychologist for Worthington and Hurst Psychological Consultants from 1966 to 1968, and she was a psychologist for the Mental Health division of the Chicago Board of Health from 1968 to 1972.

SELECTED WRITINGS BY BECKHAM:

Periodicals

"Intellectual and personality traits of a group of triplets." *The Journal of Psychology.* Vol. 21 (January, 1946): 25-36.

FURTHER READING:

Books

Guthrie, Robert V. *Even the Rat Was White, 2nd Ed.* Boston: Allyn and Bacon, 1998.

O'Connell, Agnes N. and Nancy F. Russo. *Models of Achievement: Reflections of Eminent Women in Psychology.* New York: Columbia University Press, 1983.

American Men and Women of Science, Social and Behavioral Sciences, 13th edition. New York: R.R. Bowker, 1978.

—*Sketch by Patrick Moore*

Leonidas Harris Berry
1902-1995
Physician

As a leading physician and educator, Leonidas Harris Berry was an active force in the Chicago-area medical community for more than 40 years. The first African American internist at Cook County Hospital and the first black doctor at Michael Reese Hospital and Medical Center, Berry was an inspiration to minority medical students throughout his long career. In 1955 Berry invented the gastrobiopsyscope, a first-of-its-kind instrument for exploring the digestive tract, now part of the medical collection at the Smithsonian Institution. In 1993 a scholarship fund was established at Rush Medical College in Berry's name.

Berry was born on July 20, 1902, in Woodsdale, North Carolina, to Lewellyn and Beulah Anne Harris Berry. He received a B.S. degree from Wilberforce University in Ohio in 1924. At the University of Chicago, he earned a second B.S. in 1925 and an M.D. in 1930. The University of Illinois awarded him an M.S. in pathology in 1933. After an internship at Freedmen's Hospital in Washington, he served a residency in internal medicine and gastroenterology, then joined the medical staff at Cook County Hospital in Chicago. Following his residency, he joined the medical staff of Provident Hospital in 1935, founded the division of gastroenterology, and served 34 years as its chairperson. For eight of those years, 1966 to 1974, Berry also was chief of Cook County Hospital's gastrointestinal endoscopy service. He taught at the University of Illinois Medical School from 1950 to 1957, then at the Cook County Graduate School of Medicine until 1967. In 1955, he invented the direct-vision gastrobiopsyscope, the first instrument for viewing the inside of the digestive tract.

Known for his long involvement in medical and civic affairs from the local to the international level, Berry organized and coordinated clinics for medical counseling on narcotics for the Illinois Department of Health, helped found the Council on Medical Careers, served as chairperson of the health committee for the Chicago Commission on Human Relations, and organized Flying Black Medics in

Chicago and Cairo, Illinois. At the national level he served from 1966 to 1968 on the U.S. Department of Health, Education, and Welfare's first national advisory council on regional medical programs in heart disease, cancer, and stroke. Sponsored by the U.S. Department of State, he traveled to East Africa, West Africa, Japan, Korea, the Philippines, and France as a foreign cultural exchange lecturer in 1965, 1966, and 1970.

Berry also served as senior author and editor of the textbook *Gastrointestinal Panendoscopy,* published in 1974, and contributed various articles to medical publications and books. He conducted research on racial, sociological, and pathological aspects of tuberculosis, on gastroscopy techniques, gastrobiopsy instrumentation, therapy for chronic gastritis and peptic ulcer, gastric cancer, and narcotic rehabilitation. In 1977 he was the recipient of the Rudolph Schindler Award. Berry wrote a personal chronicle entitled *I Wouldn't Take Nothin' for My Journey: Two Centuries of an Afro-American Minister,* published in 1981.

In 1937 Berry married Ophelia Flannagan Harrison, with whom he had a daughter, Judith Berry Griffin. After the marriage ended, he wed Emma Ford Willis in 1959. For his energy, dedication, and achievement in the medical profession, Berry received two honorary doctorate degrees and many other awards and honors. Chief among these are the first Clinical Achievement Award from the American College of Gastroenterology; professional achievement and distinguished service awards from the Cook County Physicians Association; and the Marshall Bynum Service Award from the Chicago branch of the NAACP. The Leonidas Berry Society for Digestive Diseases was organized in his honor in 1983. In 1993 graduates and members of the staff of Rush Medical College established a fund in Berry's name to provide scholarships to promising minority students, and kicked off a fund-raising campaign on the occasion of his ninety-first birthday. Berry died on December 4, 1995, at his home in Chicago.

SELECTED WRITINGS BY BERRY:

Books

Gastrointestinal Panendoscopy. Springfield, IL: Charles C. Thomas, 1974.
I Wouldn't Take Nothin' for My Journey: Two Centuries of an Afro-American Minister. Johnson, 1981.

Periodicals

"The Continuing Task of Medicine in a Great Democratic Society." *Journal of the National Medical Association* 57 (1965): 412-15.
"How Important Is Endoscopic Premedication?" *Gastrointestinal Endoscopy* 51 (1969): 170-71.

FURTHER READING:

Periodicals

Carwell, Hattie. "Blacks in Science." *Exposition* (1977): 30.

———. "Rush Medical College Sets up Scholarship Fund for Minorities in Honor of Dr. Leonidas Berry." *Jet* (December 13 1993).

Saxon, Wolfgang. "Leonidas H. Berry is Dead at 93; Medical Expert Helped Blacks" (obituary). *New York Times*(December 12, 1995).

—*Sketch by Penelope Lawbaugh*

Albert Turner Bharucha-Reid
1927-1985
Mathematician

Albert Turner Bharucha-Reid made significant contributions to mathematics, statistics, and physics. Over the course of his career, he taught at universities throughout the United States and lectured in other countries around the world; some of his work was translated in Russian. He won prestigious grants as a principal or co-investigator, including two National Science Foundation grants. Bharucha-Reid was an aggressive researcher, advancing knowlege in much-studied fields and forging paths in new ones. He wrote numerous academic books and articles in the field of probability theory, and served as the editor of several journals. Bharucha-Reid's work as a mathematician and statistician was still being cited in the late 1990s, and had implications for biologists, economists, and engineers as well as mathematicians and physicists.

A. T. Bharucha-Reid was born Albert Turner Reid in Hampton, Virginia, on November 13, 1927 to William Thaddeus and Mae Elaine (Beamon) Reid. He studied biology and math at Iowa State University and earned a B.S. in 1949. He went on to study mathematics, mathematical biology, probability, and statistics and to work as a research assistant in mathematical biology at the University of Chicago from 1950 to 1953. During these years the young scholar published eight articles; most of these addressed topics in mathematical biology.

Reid began work as a research associate in mathematical statistics at Columbia University in 1953. He married Rodab Phiroze Bharucha on June 5, 1954, and the couple eventually had two sons, Kurush Feroze and Rustam William. Bharucha-Reid left Columbia University to work as an assistant research statistician at the University of California at Berkeley from 1955 to 1956. In 1956, he became an instructor of mathematics at the University of Oregon. He left the United States in 1958 to take up a fellowship at the Mathematical Institute at the Polish Academy of Sciences in Wroclaw, Poland. The following year, he returned to the University of Oregon as an assistant professor.

Increasingly, throughout the decade of the 1950s, Bharucha-Reid's published work demonstrated an interest in stochastic processes and Markov chains. His first book, *Elements of the Theory of Markov Processes and Their Application,* published in 1960, was devoted to this area of statistics. Stochastic processes and Marchov chains are concepts developed within the study of probability theory. A stochastic process is a sequence of values, each of which is random, but for which a probability can be calculated. A Markov chain is a type of stochastic process.

Moving up the ranks of academia with his work on stochastic processes, Bharucha-Reid was appointed associate professor of Mathematics at Wayne State University in Detroit, Michigan, in 1961. He held that post until 1965, when he was promoted to full professor there. During his time with Wayne State University, Bharucha-Reid served one year as a visiting professor at the Institute of Mathematical Sciences in Madras, India. Bharucha-Reid was a visiting professor at the Mathematics Research Center at the University of Wisconsin in Madison, from 1966 to 1967. He published *Probabilistic Methods in Applied Mathematics* in 1970. He also edited a three volume work, *Probabilistic Analysis and Related Topics,* that included articles from scholars around the world. Probabilistic analysis, as the preface to this work explained, "is that branch of the general theory of random functions (or stochastic processes) that is primarily concerned with the analytical properties of random functions." Excited by the theory of random equations and its potential applications, Bharucha-Reid wrote a survey of the research about them, published as *Random Integral Equations* in 1972.

During the early 1970s, Bharucha-Reid continued to work at Wayne State University. He spent the 1973-74 school year as a professor at the Georgia Institute of Technology. By 1976, he was named a Graduate Dean of Arts and Sciences and Associate Provost of Graduate Studies at Wayne State. By the late 1970s, Bharucha-Reid had earned two National Sciene Foundation grants (one with another investigator), and grants from the United States Air Force and the United States Army. He was also a member of several academic societies, including the American Association for the Advancement of Sciences, the American Mathematical Society, the Society for Industrial and Applied Mathematics, and the Academy of Sciences of New York and Iowa. Outside the United States, the Indian Mathematical Society, Indian Statistical Institute, and Polish Mathematical Society counted him among their members. Bharucha-Reid was also a member of the fraternity Sigma Xi. From 1977 to 1980, he served on the board of governors at the Cranbrook Institute of Science, near Detroit, Michigan, and from 1978 to 1982, he was a member of the Graduate Record Examination Board.

In 1981, Bharucha-Reid left Wayne State University for a post as a Professor of Mathematics at the Georgia Institute of Technology in Atlanta. He became a distinguished professor of Mathematics at Atlanta University in 1983, where he also held posts at the Center for Computational Sciences and Department of Mathematics and Computer Science. In 1984, he was granted an honorary science degree from Syracuse University. During the last few months of his life, reported **Ronald E. Mickens**, a colleague at Atlanta University in *Physics Today*, Bharucha-Reid "made direct contributions" to research in "computational and plasma physics." Bharucha-Reid also continued to write articles and edit *The Journal of Integral Equations* until his death on February 26, 1985. His book, *Random Polynomials*, written with M. Sambandham, was published posthumously in 1986.

SELECTED WRITINGS BY BHARUCHA-REID:

Books

Elements of the Theory of Markov Processes and Their Application. New York: McGraw Hill, 1960.
Probabilistic Methods in Applied Mathematics. New York: Academic Press, 1968.
Random Integral Equations. New York: Academic Press, 1972.
Probabilistic Analysis and Related Topics. New York: Academic Press, 1978.
(With M. Sambandham) *Random Polynomials.* New York: Academic Press, 1986.

Periodicals

"A Probability Model of Radiation Damage." *Nature* (1952): 369-370.
"On Stochastic Processes in Biology." *Biometrics* (1953): 275-289.
"Markov Branching Processes and Semi-Groups of Operators." *Journal of Mathematical Analysis and Application* (December 1965): 513-36.
(With D. Kannan) "Random Integral Equation Formulation of the Generalized Langevin Equation." *Journal of Statistical Physics* (1972).
(With W. Romisch) "Projective Schemes for Random Operator Equations." *Journal of Integral Equations.* (1985): 95-112.

FURTHER READING:

Books

American Men & Women of Science. 14th Edition. Ed. Jaques Cattell Press. New York: R.R. Bowker Company, 1979.
Black Mathematicians and Their Works. Eds. Virginia K. Newell, Joella H. Gipson, L. Waldo Rich, and Beauregard Stubblefield. Ardmore, PA: Dorrance & Company, 1980.
DeGroot, Morris H. *Probability and Statistics.* Second Edition. Reading: MA, Addison-Wesley, 1989.
Neter, John, William Wasserman, G.A. Whitmore. *Applied Statistics.* Third Edition. Boston: Allyn and Bacon, 1988.

Sammons, Vivian Ovelton. *Blacks in Science and Medicine.* New York: Hemisphere Publishing Company, 1990.
Who Was Who in America. Chicago: Marquis Who's Who, 1985.

Periodicals

Mickens, Ronald E. "Albert Turner Bharucha-Reid." *Physics Today.* (December 1985).

—Sketch by R. Garcia-Johnson

Alfred A. Bishop
1924-
Chemical and nuclear engineer

Alfred A. Bishop is a nuclear engineer whose career with Westinghouse Corporation focused on the development of safety devices for nuclear reactors. In addition to writings in the field of heat transfer and fluid mechanics, he holds a patent for a flow distributor for a nuclear reactor core.

Bishop was born in Philadelphia on May 10, 1924. After a stint in the U.S. Army from 1943 to 1946, during which he won three battle stars, Bishop entered the University of Pennsylvania, where he obtained his B.S. degree in 1950. In 1965, he earned his M.S. in chemical engineering at the University of Pittsburgh. In 1974, at the age of 50, he obtained his Ph.D. in mechanical engineering from Carnegie Mellon University. After working as a chemical engineer for the Naval Experimental Station in Philadelphia from 1950 to 1951, Bishop spent three years with the Fisher & Porter Company as an engineer and manager before taking an engineering position with the Westinghouse Corporation. An engineer with Westinghouse from 1956 to 1965, he served as manager of reactor safety, thermal and hydraulic design and development from 1965 to 1970. In 1970, Bishop became a consulting engineer with Westinghouse, and in 1974 became a partner in BB Nuclear Energy Consultants as well. He also taught at the University of Pittsburgh beginning in 1970, serving as the director of the university's nuclear engineering program from 1974 to 1980.

Bishop's contributions to nuclear engineering focus on the problem of heat control in a nuclear reactor core. The nuclear power industry depends on the heat generated by controlled nuclear chain reactions. By applying that heat to a suitable absorbing material (most often water, but sometimes gases or liquid metals like sodium), steam can be produced to run the turbines that generate electricity. The core of a nuclear reactor, where the fission reactions take place, must have the coolant material flowing through it to absorb the heat evenly. The engineering requirements of such a system are very high; it must be leak-tight, stable under conditions of high radioactivity, with special monitoring instrumentation and valves for redistributing the flow to avoid hot spots. Bishop was granted a patent for a flow distributor, a device to regulate water flow for cooling purposes, for a nuclear reactor core.

Bishop won a DuPont Research Award in 1971 and a National Science Foundation Award in 1975. He holds memberships in several professional societies, including the American Society of Chemical Engineers and the American Society of Mechanical Engineers, and served on the board of directors of the Pennsylvania Youth Centers and the United Fund. He now serves as a consultant in his field.

FURTHER READING:

Books

Blacks in Science and Medicine. Hemisphere Publishing, 1990.

Taylor, Julius H. *The Negro in Science.* Morgan State College Press, 1955.

—Sketch by Gail B. C. Marsella

Keith Lanier Black
1957-

Neurosurgeon

Keith Lanier Black is an internationally respected neurosurgeon, researcher, and teacher. He is best known for working with the most difficult brain tumors—many of which other neurosurgeons deem inoperable—and for his groundbreaking research. Black averages more than 200 brain tumor operations annually, has published more than 100 scientific articles, and presented his research findings at more than 200 national and international meetings.

A native of Tuskegee, Alabama, Black was born on September 13, 1957 to Lillian and Robert Black. The elder Black was principal of a segregated elementary school in Auburn, Alabama. He taught his children to cross racial boundaries during the governorship of ardent segregationalist George Wallace. Robert Black also encouraged the young Black's keen interest in science. "He was the ultimate educator," Keith Black said of his father in an article by Michael D. Lemonick in a fall 1997 issue of *Time* magazine.

"He instilled in us an attitude that there is nothing that you cannot do."

During his eighth-grade year, Black's family moved to Cleveland, Ohio. There, Black was drawn to the laboratories of Case Western Reserve University. When Black was a youngster, his father brought home a cow's heart from a local slaughterhouse for his son to dissect, and by the time Keith Black reached high-school age, he was performing organ transplants and heart-valve replacements on dogs. When he was 17, Black published his first scientific paper on the damage done to red blood cells in patients with heart-valve replacements, which earned him the Westinghouse Science Award.

At the University of Michigan in Ann Arbor, Black completed an accelerated college program in biomedical science and medicine, and earned his undergraduate and medical degrees in six years. Fascinated by the human brain, Black told Lemonick in the *Time* article that he initially wanted to understand consciousness. Later, however, he questioned whether scientists could comprehend the mystery, and he began to focus more on researching the physical brain.

Black completed his internship in general surgery and residency in neurological surgery at the University of Michigan Medical Center. During his residency, when viewing post-operative scans that showed damage to the brain as a result of surgery, Black decided to never touch the brain. "It's a concept I try to teach the residents," Black noted in *Time.* "The whole goal is to extract the tumor without disturbing the normal brain. It's as if the brain is asleep and you want to sneak in and remove the tumor and never wake the brain up."

Black has also been a pioneer in research related to techniques to open the blood-brain barrier, allowing chemotherapeutic drugs to be delivered directly into the cancerous tumor. He is well-known for discovering that bradykinin, a natural body peptide that forms locally in injured tissue, is effective in opening the blood-brain barrier. In 1996, Black and some of his patients, who were undergoing the first clinical trials of the cancer drug RMP-7, were profiled in a Public Broadcasting Service program, "The New Explorers." In addition, he has conducted progressive research to develop a vaccine to enhance the body's immune response to brain tumors.

Of the approximately 5,000 neurosurgeons in the United States, about 50 are considered brain-tumor specialists. Black is among those—performing well over 200 operations each year on patients referred to him from across the country, as well as from Europe, the Middle East, Asia, South America and Australia. Many of his patients have complex lesions and have exhausted other treatment options.

Black served on the University of California, Los Angeles, faculty from 1987 to 1997. He received the Ruth and Raymond Stotter Chair in the Department of Surgery in 1992, and was head of Neurosurgical Oncology and head of the Comprehensive Brain Tumor Program. He received a promotion to full professor in the UCLA Department of Surgery, Division of Neurosurgery in 1994.

In 1997, Black joined Cedars-Sinai Medical Center as director of the institution's new multi-million-dollar Neuro-surgical Institute. The institute provides a wide range of services for adult and pediatric patients, with programs that encompass brain tumors, vascular conditions, functional disorders and other complex conditions that require neuro-logical intervention. Black told the *Los Angeles Times* that the offer to direct the institute was difficult to resist: "The resources they are putting into this are really just an incredible opportunity to fulfill a dream. We are going to build a world-class center that does state-of-the-art re-search," he commented.

At the Cedars-Sinai Medical Center, Black also serves as director of the Division of Neurosurgery and director of the Cedars-Sinai Comprehensive Brain Tumor Program. He oversees a staff of 50 health care professionals.

In addition to his surgical, research and teaching responsibilities, Black serves on the editorial boards of the *Journal of Neuro-Oncology, Neurological Research, Perspectives in Neurological Surgery, Critical Reviews of Neurosurgery*, and the *Journal of Radiosurgery*. He serves on the National Institutes of Health's Board of Scientific Counselors for Neurological Disorders and Stroke as well. Black was a founding member of the North American Skull Base Society and is a member of many other professional associations, including the American Association of Neuro-logical Surgeons, the Neurological Society of America, and the Academy of Neurological Surgery.

Black continues to work toward his long-term goal of finding a true cure for brain cancer. An aggressive, but careful, surgeon, he also enjoys adventurous activities outside of the operating room and laboratory, such as mountain climbing, skydiving, and whitewater rafting. Black is married to Carol Bennett, a University of California Los Angeles (UCLA) urologist, and has two children.

SELECTED WRITINGS BY BLACK:

Periodicals

"Adult Giant Arteriovenous Malformation of the Vein of Galen," *Surgical Neurology*, (1984): 215-217.

FURTHER READING:

Periodicals

Lemonick, Michael D., *Time*, (Special Issue, Fall 1997): 46-53.
Jet (June 23, 1997): 24.

—*Sketch by Rose M. Estioco*

David Blackwell

David Blackwell
1919-
Mathematician

David Blackwell is a theoretical statistician noted for the rigor and clarity of his work. Blackwell's career has been dedicated to exploring and teaching topics in set theory and probability theory, and he has made important contributions to Bayesian statistical analysis (a method of incorporating observation into the estimate of probability), dynamic programming (the theory of multistage decision processes), game theory (the analysis of decision-making in situations of conflict or competition), and information theory (the application of probability to the storage and transmission of information). In 1979, Blackwell was awarded the von Neumann Prize by the Operations Research Society of America and the Institute of Management Science. In 1986, he received the R. A. Fisher Award from the Committee of Presidents of Statistical Societies, the most prestigious award in the field of statistics.

David Harold Blackwell was born in Centralia, Illinois, on April 24, 1919, to Grover Blackwell, a hostler for the Illinois Central Railroad, and Mabel (Johnson) Blackwell. Although two of the city's elementary schools were racially segregated, Blackwell attended one that was integrated.

Blackwell was intrigued with games like checkers, and wondered about such questions as whether the first player could always win. His interest in mathematical topics increased in high school. The mathematics club advisor would challenge members with problems from the *School Science and Mathematics* journal and submit their solutions; Blackwell was identified three times in the magazine as having solved a problem, and one of his solutions was published.

After graduating from high school at the age of 16, Blackwell entered the University of Illinois in 1935. Through a family friend, he was assured of a job teaching elementary school upon graduation. However, he enjoyed his mathematics courses so much that he never got around to taking the education courses that were required for teacher certification. After his freshman year at the University of Illinois, Blackwell became concerned because his father was borrowing money to send him to college, and supported himself with jobs such as washing dishes, waiting tables, and cleaning entomology lab equipment. Nonetheless, by taking summer courses and proficiency exams, Blackwell graduated in 1938, after only three years of enrollment.

Blackwell stayed at Illinois to earn a master's degree, shifting his aspirations to teaching at the high school or perhaps college level. As he noted in an interview with Donald J. Albers in *Mathematical People:* "During my first year of graduate work I knew that I could understand mathematics.... But whether I could do anything original I didn't know." Blackwell completed his master's degree in 1939, and received a fellowship from the university to work toward a doctorate. His dissertation, under American mathematician Joe Doob, was on Markov chains (in which the probability of each "state" in a sequence of events depends exclusively on what occurs in the preceding state; named after the Russian mathematician Andrei Markov). This research led to his first publications in 1942 and 1945. After receiving his Ph.D. in 1941, Blackwell was a Rosenwald Fellow for a year at the Institute for Advanced Study in Princeton. At the Institute, he became acquainted with the Hungarian mathematician John Neumann, whose work provided the basis for game theory. In 1942, Blackwell launched a job search by writing to each of the 105 black colleges in the country, simply assuming that his role would be teaching at a black institution. The Polish Jewish mathematician Jerzy Neyman did interview Blackwell for a position at the University of California at Berkeley, where Neyman chaired the mathematics department. Neyman's support for hiring Blackwell, however, would not prevail until over a decade had passed. Southern University in Baton Rouge, Louisiana was the first of three schools to offer Blackwell a position, and he taught there for the 1942–1943 academic year. The following year, he was an instructor at Clark College in Atlanta. In 1944, Blackwell joined the faculty of Howard University in Washington, D.C., the most prestigious black institution of higher learning in the country. In this same year, Blackwell

married Ann Madison; they have three sons and five daughters.

The focus of Blackwell's research shifted to statistics in 1945, when he heard the mathematician Abe Girshick lecture on sequential analysis (the analysis of an experiment that does not have a fixed number of trials, such that the analysis can respond to provisional outcomes). He was intrigued by the presentation, and later contacted Girshick with what he thought was a counterexample to a theorem presented in the lecture. That contact resulted in an enduring friendship and fruitful collaboration. Blackwell's first statistical paper, "On an Equation of Wald," appeared in 1946. A year later, Blackwell published what is perhaps his most significant contribution to modern statistics, "Conditional Expectation and Unbiased Sequential Estimation." In this paper, he helped establish what is now known as the Rao-Blackwell theorem, which relates to the sufficient statistic (whereby, in the study of the distribution of a population, a characteristic of the entire population can be determined if the distribution of a sample population is known). Blackwell was promoted to full professor at Howard in 1947, and served as head of the mathematics department until 1954.

Explores Problems in Game Theory

During the summers of 1948 to 1950, Blackwell developed an interest in game theory while working at the RAND Corporation headquarters in Santa Monica, California. In game theory, game-like situations are devised in which opposing "players" are assigned specific objectives (which can partially but not fully coincide) and capabilities. The decision-making options of these players are then statistically analyzed. Blackwell and a few colleagues, including Girshick, became interested in the theory of duels, a form of two-player zero-sum game. In zero-sum games, the players are assigned no common objectives, so the gain of one player involves an equivalent loss for the other. In the theory of duels, the initial condition concerns two players who advance toward each other, each holding a gun with one bullet. If one fires and misses, that player is required to continue walking toward the opponent. The problem is how a dueler should decide the optimal time to shoot. After developing the theory of that situation, Blackwell proposed and investigated the more challenging case where each gun was silent, such that a dueler doesn't know whether the opponent has fired unless that dueler has been hit.

The "conflict" situation in Blackwell's duelling game suggests the Cold War context within which game theory was developed. The RAND corporation, principally funded by the Air Force, was formed in the wake of World War II as a nonprofit consortium of scientists investigating problems with implications for military strategy and technology. Although Blackwell's own work remained at the theoretical level, his involvement with game theory began when an economist at RAND consulted him about determining funding recommendations for the Air Force in relation to the probability of war within a given period. The RAND corporation's fifteenth anniversary monograph describes game theory's utility for policy analysis in "the way it focuses attention on conflict with a live, dynamic, intelligent, and reacting opponent" and for tactical applications such the timing of missile fire, radar detection, and inspection for arms control.

Blackwell and Girshick subsequently coauthored *Theory of Games and Statistical Decisions,* first published in 1954. In the same year, Blackwell accepted a professorship in statistics at Berkeley, serving as chair of the department from 1956 to 1961. An important contribution of this period was applying game theory to topology (a branch of mathematics concerned with the properties of geometrical configurations that remain unaltered by certain forms of deformation) by finding a game theory proof for the Kuratowski Reduction Theorem (named after the Polish mathematician Kazimierz Kuratowski). During the 1973–1975 academic years, Blackwell directed the University of California Study Center for the United Kingdom and Ireland. In 1974, he gave the prestigious Rouse Ball Lecture at the University of Cambridge.

Blackwell was less interested in doing systematic research than in exploring problems that interested him personally. "I guess that's the way scholars *should* work," Blackwell commented in an interview with Morris H. Degroot in *A Century of Mathematics in America.* "Don't worry about the overall importance of the problem; work on it if it looks interesting. I think there's probably a sufficient correlation between interest and importance." Indeed, in addition to the military strategy context of game theory, Blackwell's work has found application in a variety of fields, including economics and accounting. Moreover, Blackwell's enthusiasm for mathematical knowledge was contagious, and he was a compelling and effective teacher. In his interview with Albers, Blackwell responded to a question about what made teaching fun: "Why do you want to share something beautiful with somebody else? It's because of the pleasure he will get, and in transmitting it you appreciate its beauty all over again."

Blackwell has been president of the Institute of Mathematical Statistics (1955) and the International Association for Statistics in the Physical Sciences, and is a member of the American Statistical Association, the National Academy of Sciences (the first black mathematician to be elected), and the American Academy of Arts and Sciences. He has also served on the Committee on National Statistics and the Mathematical Sciences Education Board. Blackwell, who retired from Berkeley in 1989, has been awarded honorary degrees by Howard, Harvard, and the National University of Lesotho, among other institutions.

SELECTED WRITINGS BY BLACKWELL:

Books

Theory of Games and Statistical Decisions. Wiley, 1954.

Basic Statistics. McGraw-Hill, 1970.

Periodicals

"On An Equation of Wald," *Annual of Mathematical Statistics* Vol. 17 (1946): 84–87.
"Conditional Expectation and Unbiased Sequential Estimation," *Annual of Mathematical Statistics,* Vol. 18 (1947): 105–110.
"Bayes and Minimax Solutions of Sequential Decision Problems," *Econometrica,* Vol. 17 (1949): 213–244.
"On Multi-Component Attrition Games," *Naval Research Logistics Quarterly,* Vol. 1 (1954): 210–216.
"An Analogue of the Minimax Theorem for Vector Payoffs," *Pacific Journal of Mathematics,* Vol. 6 (1956): 1–8.
"Infinite Games and Analytic Sets," *Proceedings of the National Academy of Science,* Vol. 58 (1967): 1836–1837.

FURTHER READING:

Books

A Century of Mathematics in America, Part III, American Mathematical Society, 1989, pp. 589–615 (reprinted from Statistical Science, February, 1986, pp. 40–53).
Mathematical People, Contemporary Books, 1985, pp. 18–32.
The Rand Corporation: The First Fifteen Years, Rand, 1963.

Other

Blackwell, David, *Interview with Loretta Hall,* conducted January 14, 1994.

—Sketch by Loretta Hall

Henry Blair
1804-1860
Inventor

Henry Blair is the first man to be identified as a black on a U.S. patent award.

Blair was born in Glenrose, Maryland, in 1804. Almost nothing is documented about his life. It is assumed he was a free man because slaves were prohibited by law from applying for patents. When Blair was born, there were about 60,000 "free people of color" in the United States. The U.S. Patent Act of 1790 did not exclude free blacks from obtaining patents, but data on an applicant's race was not usually recorded on a patent application or award.

Blair is the first black on record to be awarded a patent, which was granted in 1834 for his design for a corn seed planter. Blair's design, according to the drawings that accompanied his patent application, featured a seed hopper on a two-wheel cart. A v-shaped extension on the front of the cart was the mounting for a blade that dug a furrow; a harrow—a frame with heavy spikes—was added to the back of the cart. Because two long handles extend from the cart at the rear of the hopper, the device looks as if it were meant to be pushed, but it probably could have been hitched to a horse or mule. The user could drape the animal's reins over the handles and use the handles to guide the device in straight furrows.

As the planter was pushed or dragged, the front blade broke the earth. The hopper dropped seed evenly in the furrow and the harrow pushed soil over the newly planted seeds. Blair's invention combined three separate operations—plowing, seeding, and covering seed with soil—into one task.

In 1836, Blair was granted a second patent for a cotton seed planter based on the design for his corn planter.

Although Blair is the first black identified as an inventor by the Patent Office, research indicates that others preceded him, although race was not listed on their patent applications. Several sources list Thomas L. Jennings as the first black patent holder in the United States. A tailor who lived in New York, Jennings patented a method for dry cleaning clothes in 1821.

Henry R. Baker, the first black examiner in the U.S. Patent Office, compiled a list of early black inventors which he published in a pamphlet, *The Colored Inventor*, in 1913, the 50th anniversary of the Emancipation Proclamation. He acknowledges Blair's place as the first black man identified as an inventor on a patent, but describes inventors and inventions that predated Blair's patent awards. He notes such people as Benjamin Banneker of Maryland, who invented a sophisticated timepiece prior to his death in 1806; James Forten, who designed a device to manage ships' sails well before his death in 1842; and Robert Benjamin Lewis of Maine, credited with developing an oakum picker which Baker noted was "in use today (1913) in all the essential particulars in its original form by the shipbuilding interests of Maine, especially at Bath."

Despite the fact that Blake began compiling information on black inventors at a time when many innovators were still alive, he faced considerable difficulty in gathering information. Racism proved a stumbling block, as he wrote in his pamphlet, which was issued as a reprint in 1988:

"Sometimes it has been difficult to get this information by correspondence even from colored inventors themselves. Many of them refuse to acknowledge that their inventions are in any way identified with the colored race on the ground, presumably, that the publication of that fact might adversely affect the commercial value of their invention;

and in view of the prevailing sentiment in many sections of our country, it cannot be denied that much reason lies at the bottom of such conclusion. . . . One practicing attorney, writing from a small town in Tennessee, said that he not only has never heard of a colored man inventing anything, but that he and the other lawyers to whom he passed the inquiry in that locality were 'inclined to regard the whole subject as a joke.'"

At the end of his pamphlet, Baker wrote that he intended to compile a book to deal more fully with the contributions of black inventors to the advancement of science and technology. The book was never written; Baker himself faded into the kind of obscurity that has hidden the achievements of Blair and other black inventors.

FURTHER READING:

Books

Bergman, Peter M. *The Chronological History of the Negro in America.* New York: Harper & Row Publishers, Inc., 1969.

Garrett, Romeo B. *Famous First Facts About Negroes.* New York: Arno Press, 1972.

James, Portia P. *The Real McCoy* Washington, D.C.: Smithsonian Institution Press, 1989.

Rywell, Martin, ed. *Afro-American Encyclopedia, Vol. 2* North Miami, Florida: Educational Book Publishers, Inc., 1974.

Sammons, Vivian Ovelton. *Blacks in Science and Medicine.* New York: Hemisphere Publishing Corporation, 1990.

Other

Baker, Henry E. *The Colored Inventor (pamphlet)* Salem, New Hampshire: Ayer Company Publishers, Inc. 1988 (reprint).

—Sketch by A. Mullig

Guion S. Bluford
1942-
Engineer and astronaut

Guion S. Bluford, the first African American astronaut to fly in space, participated in four shuttle missions. An aerospace engineer and Air Force pilot, Bluford performed a variety of experiments in life sciences, materi-

Guion S. Bluford

Williams Air Force Base in Arizona, moving on to advanced training in the F–4C Phantom fighter-bomber a year later. In 1967, Bluford's 557th Tactical Fighter Squadron was sent to Vietnam, where he flew 144 combat missions. After his tour Bluford served as an instructor pilot, logging thirteen hundred hours as an instructor in the supersonic T–38 trainer at Sheppard Air Force Base in Texas. He also served as an executive support officer in the same unit until he applied and was accepted to the Air Force Institute of Technology (AFIT) at Wright-Patterson Air Force Base in Ohio. There he earned his master's degree in 1974 and went to work as a staff development engineer at the Air Force Flight Dynamics Laboratory. Serving in the aeromechanics division as deputy for advanced concepts, he later became chief of the aerodynamics and airframe branch. In 1978, Bluford received his doctorate from AFIT in aerospace engineering with a minor in laser physics. Bluford considered his dissertation, "A Numerical Solution of Supersonic and Hypersonic Viscous Flow Fields Around Thin Planar Delta Wings," to be his most important contribution to engineering.

Holding the rank of major, Bluford applied for mission specialist astronaut training at the Lyndon B. Johnson Space Center and was among the 35 astronaut candidates selected in January, 1978. Group 8, as NASA called Bluford and his classmates, included two other black men and the first women chosen for American space flight.

als research, and other disciplines during his shuttle flights. In recognition for his service as an astronaut, he was awarded the NASA Exceptional Service Medal, the 1991 Black Engineer of the Year Award, and 11 honorary doctorates.

Guion S. Bluford, Jr., was born in Philadelphia, Pennsylvania, on November 22, 1942, the oldest of three sons. His father, Guion S. Bluford, Sr., was a mechanical engineer and inventor and his mother, Lolita Harriet (Brice) Bluford, was a special education teacher. Devout Christian Scientists, Bluford's parents encouraged him to study, to be determined, and to have faith in himself as well as God. Bluford developed an early interest in aviation, earning a reputation as the best model airplane builder in his neighborhood. By the time he entered high school, he had already decided he wanted a military career and an engineering degree. Graduating in 1960, Bluford enrolled at Pennsylvania State University, where he concentrated on engineering studies and joined the Air Force Reserve Officer Training Corps. Bluford also volunteered for ROTC flight training, in large part because he felt having hands-on experience as a pilot would make him a better engineer.

Flying and Research Lead to Astronaut Program

Bluford graduated in 1964 with a bachelor's degree in aerospace engineering. That same year he married Linda Tull, an accountant, with whom he would have two sons, Guion Stewart III and James Trevor Bluford. Second Lieutenant Bluford then entered air force flight training at

Becomes First African American in Space

Publicity over the selection of Bluford and the other minority candidates was intense, and when he was selected to fly the eighth space shuttle mission in April, 1982, the attention increased even more dramatically. Aware of his place in history, Bluford did not dwell on it publicly and played down his role as the first black U.S. astronaut in space (while Bluford was to be the first African American, a black Cuban had flown earlier as a "guest cosmonaut" in a Soviet spacecraft). Bluford coped with the spotlight by focusing on what he saw as most important: doing a good job and accomplishing the work of the mission.

Bluford's first flight, on the shuttle *Challenger,* began on August 30, 1983, with a spectacular nighttime takeoff. On that mission Bluford ejected the main payload, a multipurpose satellite for India called INSAT–1B. He also operated the Continuous Flow Electrophoresis System, studying ways to isolate proteins from living cells in a weightless environment for medical research. The successful flight resulted in numerous honors for Bluford, including the Ebony Black Achievement Award and an NAACP Image Award. Accepting speaking engagements across the country, he encouraged young people to be dedicated and persevering in pursuit of their dreams.

Bluford flew for the second time in October 1985, as part of the largest crew ever to fly in space. He and seven other astronauts—again aboard the *Challenger* —spent a week in orbit. This was the twenty-second shuttle flight, designated STS 61-A. The crew's main task was to operate the German-built Spacelab module, which filled most of the cargo bay with pressurized workspace, in effect turning the shuttle into a short-duration space station. There were 76 experiments on the agenda, encompassing the fields of materials solidification, life science, fluid physics, medicine, and navigation. After that flight, Bluford became the Astronaut Office's specialist on all issues involving Spacelab missions and space shuttle pallet experiments.

Bluford returned to space on April 28, 1991. This time, he rode the orbiter *Discovery* on the first dedicated military shuttle mission. Bluford and his crewmates operated a variety of Strategic Defense Initiative experiments on ballistic missile tracking. They also studied the environment of orbital space and of the Earth below, and launched a classified experimental satellite. Bluford's fourth and final spaceflight, lasting from December 2 to December 9, 1992, was another military mission, which deployed a classified satellite payload and also performed a variety of experiments for the Defense Department and NASA. Subsequently, Bluford served as lead astronaut of the Space Station Operations Group, specializing in defining and presenting the astronauts' point of view on all aspects of space station design and operation.

Bluford left NASA and the Air Force in July, 1993, having logged 688 hours in space in addition to 5,200 hours in jet aircraft. He then became the vice president and general manager of Engineering Services Division of NYMA, Inc., in Greenbelt, Maryland. In this position, Bluford directs engineers, scientists, and technicians who provide engineering support to NASA's Lewis Research Center. Their research encompasses aircraft propulsion, aircraft structures, and space experiments.

FURTHER READING:

Books

Furniss, Tim. *Space Shuttle Log.* Jane's, 1986.
Hawthorne, Douglas B. *Men and Women of Space.* Univelt, 1992.

Periodicals

Ebony, (March, 1979): 54–62.
Leavy, Walter. "A Historic Step Into Outer Space," *Ebony,* (November, 1983): 162–70.

Other

Bluford, Guion S., Jr., *Interview with Matthew A. Bille conducted January 25,* 1994.
Bluford, Guion S., Jr., curriculum vitae, June, 1993.

—Sketch by Matthew A. Bille

Charles F. Bolden, Jr.

Charles F. Bolden, Jr.
1946-
Astronaut

Charles F. Bolden, Jr. was an astronaut on four shuttle missions. His devoted services to NASA and the military have made significant contributions to both organizations and their advances in science.

Charles F. Bolden, Jr. was born on August 19, 1946, in Columbia, South Carolina, to Charles F. Bolden, Sr. and Ethel M. Bolden. He graduated with a bachelor of science degree in electrical science from the United States Naval Academy in 1968. Bolden received his masters of science degree in systems management from the University of Southern California in 1977.

Following his graduation from the U.S. Naval Academy, Bolden worked as second lieutenant in the U.S. Marine Corps. In May 1970, after flight training in Florida, Mississippi, and Texas, he was commissioned as a naval aviator. He was then assigned to Nam Phong, Thailand from June 1972 through June 1973. In the A-6A Intruder, Bolden flew more than 100 sorties into North and South Vietnam, Laos, and Cambodia. In 1974, Bolden returned to the United States to spend five years as a Marine Corps selection and recruiting officer in Los Angeles, California and El Toro, California. He graduated from the United States Naval Test Pilot School at Patuxent River, Maryland in June 1979. Enlisted as an test pilot, Bolden flew test projects in the A-6E, EA-6B, and A-7C/E airplanes.

In 1980, Bolden applied his Marine Corps and aviating experience towards earning a position with NASA's Space Shuttle flight crews. Bolden was selected as an astronaut in 1981. A veteran of four space flights, Bolden has also accumulated numerous technical positions, some of which include: Astronaut Office Safety Officer, Technical Assistant to the Director of Flight Crew Operations, Special Assistant to the Director of the Johnson Space Center, Chief of the Safety Division at the Johnson Space Center, and Lead Astronaut for Vehicle Test and Checkout at the Kennedy Space Center.

Makes First Space Flight

On his first mission in space, Bolden piloted the Space Shuttle *Columbia*. *Columbia* was launched January 12, 1986 from the Kennedy Space Center, Florida. The shuttle orbited the earth six days and two hours, and completed its mission within 97 orbits of the earth. The mission entailed deploying the SATCOM KU satellite and performing a variety of astrophysical experiments and materials processing. Some of these tasks included infrared imaging, hand-held protein crystal growth, and the photography of Halley's comet. Bolden and the *Columbia* crew successfully completed their mission, although, due to camera battery trouble, Halley's comet could not be photographed. After the shuttle's voyage, Bolden and the *Columbia* crew safely landed at Edwards Air Force Base, California on January 18, 1982.

Bolden's second mission required him to pilot the Space Shuttle *Discovery*, which was launched on April 24, 1990 from the Kennedy Space Center, Florida. The Hubble Space Telescope was deployed into the Earth's orbit during Bolden's five-day mission. Because of the telescope's optimal location, far from the reaches of the Earth's blurring atmosphere, the Hubble Space Telescope has proven to be the most significant optical astronomical telescope in existence. After deploying the telescope, the *Discovery* astronauts made Earth observations with IMAX in cabin and cargo bay cameras. An optimal distance for Earth photography, the *Discovery* crew set the highest Shuttle altitude record at 329.5 miles (628 km). Completing a variety of gravitational experiments and a total of 75 orbits of the earth, the shuttle landed after its rewarding journey on April 29, 1990.

The March 24, 1992 launch of the Space Shuttle *Atlantis* sent Bolden on his third mission into space. He commanded *Atlantis's* seven man crew and its search for atmospheric and astrophysical data. Twelve experiments under the heading ATLAS-1 (Atmospheric Laboratory for Applications and Science) were conducted. Equipped with instruments from all over the world, the experiments examined atmospheric chemistry, solar radiation, space plasma physics, and ultraviolet astronomy. ATLAS-1 gath-

ered atmospheric chemical and physical property measurements that have advanced the knowledge of our atmosphere and climate. Also aboard *Atlantis* was a device that for the first time created an artificial beam of electrons used to stimulate a man-made auroral discharge. On April 2, 1992, *Atlantis* landed at the Kennedy Space Center, Florida.

Bolden led as Mission Commander on his final flight into space on February 3, 1994, in the space shuttle *Discovery*. Among the six-member crew was the Russian cosmonaut Sergei K. Krikalev, designating the *Discovery* mission as the first joint U.S. and Russian space shuttle mission. During the flight, the crew deployed and retrieved a free-flying disk created to generate semiconductor films for advanced electronics. Experiments were also carried out by the SPACEHAB Module involving materials processing, biotechnology and hardware, and technology development payloads. After a successful flight of nine days, *Discovery* landed on February 11, 1994.

Bolden has logged on more than 6,000 hours flying time and 680 hours in space. His contributions to NASA are abundant. His dedication to service has awarded him with the following decorations: the Legion of Merit, the Distinguished Flying Cross, the Defense Meritorious Service Medal, the Air Medal, the Strike/Flight Medal (8th award), the NASA Outstanding Leadership Medal, and three NASA Exceptional Service Medals. Bolden has also made significant contributions to his community. He often revisits his hometown, Columbia, to educate and inspire young people. As a mentor, he provides students with prerequisites for the space program, advice, and support.

In April 1992, Bolden was assigned to the Assistant Deputy Administrator at NASA. Bolden left NASA in 1994 and returned to active duty as Deputy Commandant of Midshipmen at the U.S. Naval Academy. Bolden currently holds the rank of Major General and is located at the naval station Miramar, in San Diego, California. Bolden is married to the former Alexis (Jackie) Walker of Columbia, South Carolina and has two children, Anthony and Kelly.

FURTHER READING:

Periodicals

"After the Cheating: Astronaut Charles Bolden Has a New and Daunting Mission—Helping Restore Integrity at the U.S. Naval Academy," *The Charlotte Observer,* (May 1, 1994).

"Astronaut Charles Bolden Inducted into S.C. Hall of Science and Technology," *A Matter of Facts,* (Spring 1994).

"Astronaut Says Segregated School Taught Him How to Deal with Adversity," *The News and Courier/ The Evening Post,* (October 9, 1993).

Hook, Debra Lynn. "Kennedy Space Center," *The State,* (February 4, 1994).

Hook, Debra Lynn. "Charles Bolden is Flying that Space Shuttle's Roar Ignites Columbia Kids' Dreams," *The State,* (February 1, 1994).

Livingston, Mike. "Astronaut to Pilot Discover after Helping to Steer NASA," *The State,* (February 1, 1994).

Patterson, Leslie. "Bolden Mission Successful," *The State,* (February 1, 1994).

Other

"Charles F. Bolden, Jr." *Strong Men & Women.* http://marsha.nflux.com:2222/s/strong/CharlesBolden.html (April 10, 1998).

Platoff, Annie. "Charles F. Bolden, Jr. (Colonel, U.S. Marine Corps): Former Astronaut." February 23, 1996. http://www.jsc.nasa.gov/pao/blackhistory/black-history.html (April 7, 1998).

—*Sketch by Alison Wellford*

Theodore Edward Bolden

Theodore Edward Bolden
1920-

Pathologist and dentist

For several decades, Theodore Edward Bolden has maintained his status as one of the nation's foremost pathologists, dentists, dental researchers, and educators. His research in histology, the microscopic study of tissue structure; periodontal disease, ailments affecting the gums; and salivary gland pathology has helped to further knowledge regarding the nature of disease as well as advance the field of dentistry.

Bolden was born in Middleburg, Virginia, on April 19, 1920, to Mary Elizabeth Jackson Bolden and Theodore Donald Bolden. He attended country and urban public schools in Virginia and New Jersey, and graduated from New Jersey's Montclair High School in 1937.

He earned a number of degrees during the 1940s and 1950s, while also serving in the U.S. Army as a private and sergeant from 1943 to 1944 and later as a first lieutenant from 1951 to 1952. He received an A.B. from Lincoln University in Pennsylvania in 1941 and a D.D.S. from Meharry Medical College in Tennessee in 1947. Bolden received a certificate for postgraduate training from New Jersey's Hudson County Dental Society in 1948 and completed his postgraduate training at the University of Illinois during 1949 to 1951.

As a John Hay Whitney Foundation opportunity fellow, Bolden obtained an M.S. in 1951, and as a U.S. Public Health Service fellow, he earned a Ph.D. in pathology in 1958 from the University of Illinois. For Bolden, education has been a lifelong pursuit. He continued to take courses up until the time he retired, including the Armed Forces Institute of Pathology's 20th Annual Course in Oral Pathology in 1973 and a postgraduate short course in oral pathology, oral diagnosis, and oral medicine at the Walter Reed Army Medical Center in 1989. He received an honorary L.L.D. degree from Lincoln University in 1981.

Bolden began his academic career as an instructor of operative dentistry, pedodontics, and periodontics at the Meharry Medical College's School of Dentistry in 1948. Founded in 1876, Meharry was the largest private, historically black institution exclusively dedicated to educating health care professionals and biomedical scientists. Leaving and returning over the years, he gradually advanced through the college's faculty ranks, often serving in multiple roles— beginning as a lecturer in 1956. At Meharry, Bolden was professor of dentistry and chairman of the department of oral pathology and oral medicine from 1962 to 1969, director of research from 1962 to 1973, and associate dean of the School of Dentistry from 1967 to 1974.

In addition, Bolden held faculty positions at several other colleges and universities throughout his career. He was an instructor of pathology and lecturer in postgraduate studies at the University of Illinois School of Dentistry from 1955 to 1957. At the Seton Hall University College of

Medicine in New Jersey, he was an associate professor of general and oral pathology from 1957 to 1960 and associate professor of oral diagnosis and pathology from 1960 to 1962.

Founded in 1970 as the College of Medicine and Dentistry of New Jersey and granted status as a free-standing university in 1981, the University of Medicine and Dentistry of New Jersey brings together all of New Jersey's public programs in medical and dental education. During the 1970s and '80s, Bolden taught and conducted research at the university and its various entities. He was dean of the Dental School from 1977 to 1978, acting chairman of general and oral pathology from 1979 to 1980, professor of general and oral pathology from 1977 to 1988, professor of oral pathology, biology, and diagnostic services from 1988 to 1990, and has been professor emeritus since 1991.

Despite his academic obligations, Bolden has been a prolific writer, coauthoring, publishing, contributing to, and editing more than 300 professional and scientific publications, including 10 books. In 1960, with John Manhold Jr., he wrote *Outline of Pathology*. In 1982, with E. Mobley and E. Chandler, Bolden wrote the fourth edition of the *Dental Hygiene Examination Review Book*.

Because of his expertise in oral pathology and dentistry, a number of companies and organizations have turned to Bolden as a consultant, including Colgate-Palmolive and the American Association of Dental Schools. He was a trustee and adviser to the American Fund for Dental Health from 1978 to 1986. Bolden has also served as a member, chairman, editor, or president on the advisory boards and committees of many prestigious organizations, such as the National Institutes of Health, the National Dental Association, the American Association for Cancer Education, the International Association of Dental Research, the Nashville section of the American Association of Dental Research, and the American Cancer Society.

Throughout his career, Bolden has received various honors and awards. He has been a fellow of the American Academy of Oral Pathology and the International College of Dentists and a diplomate of the American Board of Oral Medicine and the American Board of Oral Pathology. He received the National Dental Association Inc.'s Dentists of the Year Award and the Capital City Dental Society and Pan-Tennessee Dental Association Plaque in 1977, and the National Council of Negro Women's Service to the Community as Dean Plaque in 1978, among other awards. Bolden is a member of Sigma Xi, the Scientific Research Society with a membership of 90,000 scientists and engineers who have been elected to the society because of their research achievements or potential; Omicron Kappa Upsilon, the national dental honor society; and Kappa Sigma Pi.

Since retiring in 1990, Bolden has continued his involvement in various educational and community-related activities, including the National Alliance of Black School Educators, Children and Families of Iowa Educational Tutoring Services, the Irvington Neighborhood Improve-

ment Corp., and the Senior Youth Fellowship of St. Mark's United Methodist Church. He has continued to write, producing non-scientific publications, such as the 1997 *55 Years Ain't So Baaaaaaaad.* In 1998, he made his acting debut on stage as Professor Johnson in the "Family Album." He was married to Dr. Dorothy M. Forde, who is now deceased.

SELECTED WRITINGS BY BOLDEN:

Books

Dental Hygiene Examination Review Book. 4th edition, 1982.
Outline of Pathology. 1960.

FURTHER READING:

Books

Sammons, Vivian Ovelton. *Blacks in Science and Medicine.* Hemisphere Publishing, 1990, p. 31.
Who's Who in America 1997. 51st Edition, Volume I, Marquis Who's Who, p. 418.

—*Sketch by Rose M. Estioco*

Walter M. Booker
1907-1988
Biologist and pharmacologist

Walter M. Booker was a biologist, physiologist, and pharmacologist who served for 20 years as the chairman of the Department of Pharmacology of the College of Medicine at Howard University, Washington, D. C. As the author of over one hundred scientific papers, Booker studied liver damage in trauma, the effects of anesthesia, and gastrointestinal physiology. He was very active even after his retirement, focusing on such important issues as drug abuse and addiction.

Walter Monroe Booker was born in Little Rock, Arkansas on November 4, 1907. A 1928 graduate of Morehouse College in Atlanta, Georgia, where he obtained a B. A. degree, he received a master's degree from the University of Iowa in 1932, and a doctorate in physiology and chemistry from the University of Chicago in 1943. During those years, he also taught biology and chemistry at Leland College in Louisiana and at Prairie View College. After receiving his Ph.D., he accepted a teaching position at Howard University in 1943, and became an associate professor in 1948. He was appointed Chairman, Department of Pharmacology of the College of Medicine, Howard University in 1954. Booker remained in that position until 1973 when he retired as a full professor.

Booker had done a great deal of research on the heart's response to drugs, and participated in conferences on the subject in nearly a dozen nations. Besides running the pharmacology department at Howard University, Booker was a consultant to the Walter Reed Army Research Institute where he taught during the 1960s and 1970s. He was a consultant to the National Institute on Drug Abuse and the Department of Health, Education and Welfare. His specialization proved useful to the Washington Heart Association, and he was a representative of the American Society for Pharmacology and Experimental Therapeutics to the National Research Council.

Among the many groups to which he belonged were the American College of Clinical Pharmacology and the American Physiological Society. He was a fellow of the American College of Cardiology and a charter member of Sigma Xi, an honorary scientific society. As a senior Fulbright scholar, he studied at the Heymans Institute in Ghent, Belgium, during 1957 and 1958.

When he died of cardiac arrest on August 29, 1988, at Howard University Hospital, he was survived by a son, Walter Jr., a daughter, Marjorie Courm, and four grandchildren. His wife, the former Thomye Collins, died in 1986.

FURTHER READING:

Periodicals

Journal of Negro History, Vol. 35 (1950): 145.
Washington Post, (September 1, 1988): C6.

—*Sketch by Leonard C. Bruno*

Edward Alexander Bouchet
1852-1918
Physicist

Edward Alexander Bouchet, sometimes called the "patron saint of black scientists," was the first African American to earn a Ph.D. An intellectual giant who gained top academic honors, studied with some of the best-known American physicists of his day, and transformed education for African Americans wherever he taught, he was nevertheless unable to find employment as a scientist. Only five years before his death did he finally gain a collegiate appointment at Bishop College in Marshall, Texas. Bouchet was also known as an active, early supporter of the National

Association for the Advancement of Colored People (NAACP).

Bouchet was born on September 15, 1852, to William Francis Bouchet and Susan (Cooley) Bouchet. William Bouchet was a janitor at Yale University in New Haven, Connecticut, who first came there in the 1840s as valet to a Yale student named Robertson; Susan Bouchet did laundry for the students at Yale. Ironically, Robertson's and Bouchet's sons attended Yale together 30 years later. William was an active leader in the black New Haven community, serving as deacon at the Temple Street Church, and may have had big plans for his son from the beginning. The Robertson family also may have seen early promise in young Edward, as they may have contributed to the costs of his Yale education.

Bouchet's Education: the Best of the Best

Edward Bouchet began his education at the Artisan Street Colored School, one of a number of charity primary schools in the country operated by women reformers of the day. He attended New Haven High School from 1866 to 1868, transferring to the more prestigious Hopkins Grammar School from 1868 to 1870. That year, he enrolled at Yale.

As is often the case with minorities breaking new ground, Yale's first black student had to be the best of the best; Edward fit the bill, earning the first bachelor's degree awarded to an African American at Yale in 1874 with top honors. Although Edward was the first black American to earn entry into the prestigious Phi Beta Kappa society, and is sometimes referred to as the first black Phi Beta Kappa, he was not, because the Yale chapter of the society had become inactive and elected no members in the year he graduated. Bouchet was officially elected into the society in 1884.

Despite the relatively progressive philosophy at Yale, Bouchet may have begun to face prejudice even before he graduated. The sixth highest ranked student in his class, he was nevertheless one of only two who were not invited to join campus fraternities. This pattern—conspicuous achievement followed by disappointment—was to plague the rest of his career, showing that nineteenth century post-slavery America still had a long way to go in offering equal opportunity to its black citizens.

Bouchet's greatest educational achievement was to come in 1876, when he received a Ph.D. in physics from Yale—the first Ph.D. awarded to any African American. A relatively new degree in the United States, the doctorate had only been awarded by Yale for 10 years at the time. Bouchet's was only the sixth Ph.D. in physics awarded in the U.S.

In graduate school, Bouchet had the opportunity to study with two legendary nineteenth century American physicists, Josiah Willard Gibbs and Arthur Wright. He studied refractive indices, the numbers that can be used to calculate how much a light beam will bend when it passes from one medium to another—such as between water and air, or between air and the glass of a prism. Bouchet developed methods for measuring refractive indices.

Disappointment at Hiring Time

Had Bouchet been white, it seems likely that his career would have been made at that point. But a scientific career was to elude him. Instead, he joined the faculty of the Institute for Colored Youth in Philadelphia as a science teacher in 1876.

" . . . he had no library, no laboratory, no graduate students, and no colleagues of his caliber," lamented Curtis Patton, a professor of epidemiology and amateur historian at Yale to a Yale publication in 1995. Still, the Quaker-run Institute had a reputation for high standards, and Bouchet did have a sharp mind and a powerful motivation to offer his students the best education he could.

Bouchet taught at the Institute until 1902, when he resigned in protest over a decision to cease offering college preparatory work at the school. From there he went to Sumner High School in St. Louis, Missouri, to teach in their college preparatory program. In 1903 he moved again, to serve for a year as business manager at Provident Hospital in that city. From 1904 to 1905 he was U.S. Inspector of Customs for the Louisiana Purchase Exposition. But Bouchet could not stay away from education. In 1905 he was named director of academics at St. Paul's Normal and Industrial School in Lawrenceville, Virginia.

In 1908 he moved once again, to Lincoln High School in Galipolis, Ohio, to serve as principal. The school's campus was in disrepair, and Bouchet knew as well as anyone the huge obstacles facing his African American students. But once again he launched into the job whole-heartedly, sticking to his philosophy that black students could not afford to aim any lower than college.

"I had very good lessons today," one of his students wrote in her diary in 1912, offering perhaps a glimpse of Bouchet the teacher. "Mr. Bouchet did not scold very much."

In 1913, Bouchet finally realized a lifelong dream, gaining a position on the faculty of Bishop College in Marshall, Texas—another teaching appointment, but at least one at the college level. But he was sadly not to enjoy this position for long; in 1916 cardiovascular illness forced him to retire. He returned to New Haven that year, where he lived until his death in 1918. Bouchet never married.

SELECTED WRITINGS BY BOUCHET:

Books

Measuring Refractive Indicies. Yale University dissertation, 1876.

FURTHER READING:

Books

Osterweis, Rollin G. *Three Centuries of New Haven. 1638-1938,* Yale University Press, 1953.
Shumway, Floyd and Hegel, Richard. *New Haven: An Illustrated History,* Windsor Publications, 1987.

Periodicals

Lore, David. *Columbus Dispatch,* (January 31, 1995): section B.

Other

Kelly, Jill. "Yale's First Black Undergraduate, 120 Years Later," *Yale Daily News, 1995,* http://www.yale.edu/ydn/paper/2.1.96/2.1.96storyno.ED.html (April 9, 1998).
"Edward Alexander Bouchet: Physicist." February 13, 1998, http://www.lib.lsu.edu/lib/chem/display/bouchet.html (March 25, 1998).

—Sketch by Kenneth B. Chiacchia

Midian Othello Bousfield
1885-1948
Physician

During his 40 years as a physician and civic leader, Midian Othello Bousfield helped bring national attention to the health-care needs of African Americans. In his private practice, Bousfield took special interest in the spread of tuberculosis among residents of America's inner cities, and as a member of two White House subcommittees in 1940, he made recommendations regarding medical care for minorities. During World War II Bousfield established the first United States Army hospital staffed entirely by black medics, a significant step toward equality for African American military personnel. Throughout his career, he maintained a heavy involvement in civic and professional groups, becoming the first black member of the Chicago Board of Education and president of the National Medical Association. In part through his leadership as a physician and insurance company executive, Bousfield assisted numerous other African Americans in securing greater opportunities and a higher quality of life.

To Brazil and Back

Bousfield was born in Tipton, Missouri, on August 22, 1885, the son of William Hayman Bousfield, a barber, and Cornelia Gilbert Bousfield. In 1907 he obtained his A.B.

degree from the University of Kansas, and two years later earned his M.D. degree at Northwestern University School of Medicine. From 1909 to 1910, he served an internship at Freedman's Hospital in Washington, D.C., and in the latter year became one of the first four African American physicians appointed to the staff of General Hospital in Kansas City.

Believing that better opportunities awaited him outside the United States, Bousfield moved to Brazil in 1911. However, he discovered that the prospects for a black physician in South America were even less favorable than they were at home; therefore, he gave up his intention of practicing medicine in Brazil. However, he did not leave that country immediately. For a time he attempted to make a living as a prospector for precious metals. When this did not work out either, he returned to the United States.

Bousfield spent a year working for a railroad as a barber and porter. He did this in part to raise the funds he needed to open his medical practice, but also because he planned to marry. From 1912 to 1914, he served two years at Kansas City General Hospital as a visiting physician. Then on September 9, 1914, he married Maudelle Tanner Brown, and the couple settled in Chicago. They would have one child, a daughter they named after her mother, and would remain in Chicago for the rest of Bousfield's life.

Activities Outside the Doctor's Office

In 1914, Bousfield began his medical practice, serving as a school health officer and tuberculosis physician until 1916. At that time, tuberculosis or TB (sometimes called consumption), a lung disease characterized by coughing, fever, weakness, and other symptoms, was prevalent in the United States. This was particularly so in the nation's inner cities and poorer communities, where air pollution and unsanitary conditions greatly increased the incidence of TB.

Outside of his practice, Bousfield became involved with the Railway Men's Association, an early African American labor union. Although unions had already become a significant factor in American political life, many of them excluded blacks. Since African Americans were already prevented from numerous fields of work, and were thus relegated to positions such as railway worker or porter, black labor unions had the potential to be strong motivating forces in their community. During Bousfield's six years as the organization's secretary, from 1915 to 1920, the union's membership grew from 250 to 10,000.

Bousfield in 1919 joined with a group of black businessmen in incorporating Liberty Life Insurance Company, for which he became medical director. Over the next three decades, as Liberty Life became Supreme Liberty Life following a 1929 merger, Bousfield would hold a number of positions with the company, including the presidency, vice presidency, and membership on the board. He maintained the medical director position for most of the remaining years of his life.

During the 1920s, Bousfield continued his medical practice, but devoted a great deal of his professional attention to the insurance company. He served as medical director and first vice president from 1919 to 1925, and president from 1925 until the merger in 1929. From 1929 to 1933, he served as chairman of the executive committee for the newly created Supreme Liberty Life Insurance Company, and from 1933 to his death 15 years later he held the positions of vice president and medical director.

The White House Calls on Bousfield

In the 1930s and 1940s, Bousfield turned increasingly to public affairs. He acted as occasional consultant to the U.S. Children's Bureau and the Chicago Board of Health in the 1930s, and from 1934 to 1936 was president of the National Medical Association. He served as president of the Chicago Urban League from 1935 to 1939, and became a member of the executive committee of the National Urban League. From October 1939 to June 1942, Bousfield sat on the Chicago Board of Education as its first African American member. Ultimately he would hold positions on some 30 civic and governmental bodies.

Bousfield helped establish an infantile paralysis unit at the Tuskegee Institute in Alabama, and at Provident Hospital in Chicago. He would serve on the board of the latter institution for 25 years, and as technical director of Providence Medical Associates was instrumental in securing scholarships and educational opportunities for black medical students. He also acted in a support and advisory capacity for several African American medical colleges, as well as the National Association of Colored Graduate Nurses. In addition, he assisted a number of black physicians in becoming members of state boards of health.

In 1939 Bousfield received an appointment to the directorship of the Negro Health Program of the Julius Rosenwald Fund, a charitable foundation. The fund helped many African American medical students through college, and thus Bousfield assisted in the educations of numerous doctors, nurses, and public health officials.

Bousfield's tireless contributions to the community did not go unnoticed, even by President Franklin D. Roosevelt. In 1940, Bousfield was appointed to the planning committee for the White House Conference on Children in a Democracy. As a member of two subcommittees, on Children in Racial and Ethnic Minorities and Public Health and Medical Care, Bousfield made recommendations for improvements in health conditions among members of minority groups. In the South, as he noted in 1945, more than 20% of all blacks died without the care of a physician in their final period of illness.

Organizes First Black Army Medical Center

Bousfield joined the army as an officer in 1942, just after the United States entered World War II. At Fort Huachuca (pronounced "whah-CHOO-kuh"), Arizona, he organized Station Hospital Number One, the first United

States Army hospital staffed entirely by black personnel. Integration of the armed forces still lay several years in the future, but Bousfield's effort was a significant contribution toward equal facilities for black and white servicemen.

Later, Bousfield became the first African American colonel in the Army Medical Corps. During his time in the military, he continued to devote attention to tuberculosis, which remained a significant medical concern among African Americans in the 1940s. While in the military, from 1942 to 1943, Bousfield served as an executive committee member for the Children's Bureau Commission on Children in Wartime. In 1945, Bousfield left the army, and in 1946 was awarded its Legion of Merit.

Two years later, on February 16, 1948, Bousfield died of a heart attack in his Chicago home. He was survived by his wife Maudelle, a high school principal, and his daughter, who had become Mrs. Maudelle Evans. In the course of his life, Bousfield earned several awards, including a University of Kansas alumni citation for distinguished service in 1941. But perhaps the greatest symbol of his achievement was the large number of black medical personnel who had secured their training, and in some cases their positions, in part because of Bousfield's efforts.

SELECTED WRITINGS BY BOUSFIELD:

Periodicals

"Major Health Problems of the Negro," *National Conference of Social Work Proceedings,* June 1933.
"Reaching the Negro Community," *American Journal of Public Health,* March 1934, pp. 209-15.
"The Home and Health Education Program," *JNE,* July 1937.
"An Account of Physicians of Color in the United States," *Bulletin of History of Medicine,* January 1945, 61-84.
"A Control Program in a Metropolitan Area for Tuberculosis Among Negroes," *Journal of the National Medical Association* 38, (1946): 45.

FURTHER READING:

Books

Kaufman, Martin et al., eds. *Dictionary of American Medical Biography,* Volume I: A-L, Greenwood Press, 1984, pp. 83-84.
Logan, Rayford W. and Winston, Michael R. *Dictionary of American Negro Biography.* W.W. Norton, 1982, p. 51.
Sammons, Vivian Ovelton. *Blacks in Science and Medicine.* Hemisphere Publishing, 1990.

Periodicals

American Medical Association Journal, (April 17, 1948): 1059.

Murray, Peter Marshall. "Midian O. Bousfield, M.D., 1885-1948," *Journal of the National Medical Association* 40, (1948): 120.
New York Times, (February 17, 1948): 25.
Survey, (March 1948): 89.

—Sketch by Judson Knight

Otis Boykin
1920-1982
Electronics engineer and inventor

Otis Boykin was an inventor of some 26 electronic devices widely used today in computers and guided missiles. Perhaps most noteworthy of his inventions, though, was a regulating unit for the first heart pacemaker.

Otis Frank Boykin was born in Dallas, Texas, on August 29, 1920, to Walter Benjamin and Sarah Boykin. The young Boykin's academic career started in 1938 at Fisk University in Nashville, Tennessee. Boykin's first job after graduating in 1941 was with Majestic Radio & TV Corporation in Chicago. Although he had become a foreman, he left Majestic Radio in 1944 to take a position as a research engineer with P. J. Nilsen Research Labs of Oak Park, Illinois. He stayed at Nilsen Labs for five years before leaving to found his own company, Boykin-Fruth, Inc.; at the same time, he attended the Illinois Institute of Technology. In 1949 Boykin became chief chemist for ceramics and plastics at Radio Industries in Chicago; he remained there just two years, after which time he took a position as a senior research engineer at C. T. S. Corporation in Elkhorn, Indiana. Boykin left C. T. S. in 1964 to work as an electronics consultant for several American and European firms, three of them in Paris.

Many of the devices Boykin invented and patented became components in computers and guided missiles. He invented, for example, a type of resistor that became common in radios, computers, and television sets. He also invented a chemical air filter, a burglar-proof cash register, and a thick-film resistor for use in computers. Most notable of Boykin's inventions was probably the electronic device he built for regulating the pacemaker; first invented by Paul Zoll and perfected in 1960 by Wilson Greatbatch, the pacemaker is a device that uses electrical pulses to maintain the regular beating of the heart.

Boykin's inventiveness and his many patents won him the Cultural Science Achievement Award from the Old Pros Unlimited Club. Boykin's professional memberships included the American Association for the Advancement of the Sciences, the International Society for Hybrid Micro-electronics, and the Chicago Physics Club. Boykin died of heart failure in Chicago in 1982; he was 61.

FURTHER READING:

Books

Ploski, Harry A. and James Williams, eds. *The Negro Almanac: A Reference Work on the African American,* 5th ed. Gale, 1989, p. 1080.

Sammons, Vivian Ovelton. *Blacks in Science and Medicine.* Hemisphere, 1990, p. 34.

Van Sertima, Ivan, ed. *Blacks in Science: Ancient and Modern,* Transaction Books, 1984, p. 226.

Periodicals

Jet, (April 12, 1982): 13.

—Sketch by Karl Preuss

Robert Henry Bragg

Robert Henry Bragg
1919-
Physicist

Robert Henry Bragg used x-ray techniques to study the structure and electrical properties of carbon and other materials. He pursued this highly specialized work throughout his career. He worked in several industrial research centers and was a professor at the University of California at Berkeley. Later in his life he was a scientific advisor in Washington, and also did work in Nigeria.

Early Life

He was born in Jacksonville, Florida on August 11, 1919, the son of Robert Henry Bragg and the former Lilly Camille McFarland. His father worked as an organizer for a longshoremen's union in Mobile, Alabama. His mother worked as a seamstress, following a 1928 separation from Bragg's father. In 1933 the young Bragg was sent to Chicago to live with an uncle, William McFarland, who was a plumbing contractor.

"His idea was, you should be an engineer," Bragg said of his uncle to contributor T. A. Heppenheimer in a telephone interview on May 7, 1998. "He was very much into technical things." This advice suited Bragg, who recalls that "I was always good at technical things—math, and I could draw." He attended Tilden Technical High School, graduating in 1937, then enrolled at Woodrow Wilson

Junior College. With war approaching, he entered a program of the Army's Signal Corps that trained people to work in defense plants. This program introduced him to electronics and to the Illinois Institute of Technology (IIT), where he received his training.

He joined the Army in 1942 and became a second lieutenant. He served in combat zones in New Guinea and the Philippines, and twice received the Bronze Star as a military decoration. Then in 1946, after the war, he returned to IIT in Chicago. Initially he studied electronics, because, as he tells Heppenheimer, "I just loved the idea of radar and electrons and all that stuff." But he soon switched to physics, because he found that the courses in this field offered greater depth in the topics that interested him. He received a Bachelor of Science degree in physics from IIT in 1949.

Builds a Career Using X Rays

Bragg stayed on at IIT and pursued a Master of Science degree in physics. At the advice of his department chairman, he wrote a critical review of the existing state of knowledge of quantum-mechanical scattering. In physics, the science of quantum mechanics provides a fundamental description of subatomic particles and phenomena, including the behavior of atoms, electrons, and x rays. Scattering is an experimental technique wherein beams of electrons or x rays bounce off atoms that have a regular arrangement. Atoms in a regular arrangement form crystals, such as diamond or quartz. Bragg's work on scattering led him to the research laboratory of the Portland Cement Association in nearby Skokie, Illinois, which he joined following receipt of his degree in 1951.

His work at Portland Cement introduced him to the powerful methods of x-ray crystallography. He directed beams of x rays at samples of materials; the x rays scattered in specific directions and formed characteristic patterns of spots on photographic film. By studying these patterns, Bragg could learn which chemical compounds were present within his samples, and in what quantity. But as he tells Heppenheimer, "After I had been at Portland Cement for a couple of years, I realized I didn't know enough." He returned to IIT for a Ph.D. in physics. He received this degree in 1960, conducting further research and writing a dissertation in the field of x-ray crystallography.

The methods of x-ray crystallography allow physicists to do more than merely establish the presence of certain compounds. These methods have sufficient power to permit determination of how atoms are arranged within molecules. This makes it possible to describe the molecular structures of materials, and thus characterize them at deep levels of understanding. After finishing at IIT, Bragg pursued continued his research at the laboratory of Lockheed Aircraft Corp., in Palo Alto, California.

Working at this lab with a staff of graduate students from 1961 to 1969, he emphasized the study of carbon. Lockheed was a leader in building heat shields for spacecraft that re-enter the atmosphere. Carbon offers strong advantages as a material for such shields because it is lightweight, withstands high temperatures, and readily absorbs heat. On the space shuttle, carbon protects the hottest parts during re-entry. Bragg describes it as "the best material known, the best nature makes."

Proceeds to Berkeley—and to Washington

In the late 1960s, the University of California at Berkeley was actively recruiting black scientists as faculty members. Bragg joined this university in 1969, as a professor in the Department of Materials Science and Mineral Engineering. He also received a post as a senior scientist at the adjacent Lawrence Berkeley Laboratory, with these two positions constituting a joint appointment. He served as chairman of his university department from 1978 to 1981, then returned to his professorship, which allowed him to resume his research.

His research continued to focus on carbon. It is known that substances containing carbon, when heated strongly, turn to graphite, which has a well-ordered molecular structure. The heated substances might produce formless arrays of carbon atoms, but they don't. Bragg's work at Berkeley contributed to understanding how the atoms form these orderly arrays.

Though he retained his professorship at Berkeley until his retirement in 1987, he also held a number of advisory positions in Washington from 1980 on. He worked as a program director within the Department of Energy's Divi-

sion of Materials Science during 1981-82. As he recalls, "All the contracts that they had were my responsibility." He served on panels of the National Research Council, critically reviewing the quality of research programs in materials science at the Naval Research Laboratory and the National Institute of Standards and Technology. At the National Science Foundation, he joined a committee that advised the director of the Division of Materials Research, helping him pick topics that merited support. He also worked with the Fulbright fellowship program, and spent a year in Nigeria as a Fulbright Scholar in 1992-93.

Bragg married Violette Mattie McDonald on June 14, 1947. They have two children: Pamela and Robert Henry. His personal activities include a life membership in the National Association for the Advancement of Colored People (NAACP). Among his professional awards, he particularly treasures the status of Fellow of the National Society of Black Physicists, which he received in 1995.

SELECTED WRITINGS BY BRAGG:

Periodicals

(with D. Baker) "The Electrical Conductivity and Hall Effect of Glassy Carbon," *Journal of Non-Crystalline Solids,* Vol. 58 (1983): 57-69.
(with K. Kawamura) "Graphitization of Pitch Coke: Kinetics of Interlayer Spacing and Weight Changes," *Carbon,* Vol. 24 (1986): 301-309.

FURTHER READING:

Books

Ovelton, Vivian. *Blacks in Science and Medicine.* Sammons, NY: Hemisphere Publishing, 1990.
Who's Who among African Americans. Detroit: Gale Research, 1998.
Who's Who in Frontier Science and Technology. Chicago: Marquis Who's Who, 1984.

—Sketch by T. A. Heppenheimer

Fitzgerald B. Bramwell
1945-
Chemist

Fitzgerald B. Bramwell has made important contributions to the field of chemistry, but his commitment to science education at the high school and college levels has been a highlight of his career. He has actively developed opportunities for students to learn about science and conduct original research—a role he continues to play as vice president for research and graduate studies at the University of Kentucky.

Bramwell was born in Brooklyn, New York, on May 16, 1945, the son of a chemical engineer and a school principal. The importance of education was never in question in Bramwell's home, and he excelled in school. He attended the Phillips Academy in Andover, Massachusetts, graduating at 17. He then entered Columbia University, where he majored in chemistry.

After graduating in January 1966, after only three and one-half years, he was awarded a scholarship to study at Royal Dutch Shell's laboratories in the Netherlands. Upon his return, he enrolled at the University of Michigan at Ann Arbor, where he studied under Drs. Thomas Dunn and Julien Gendell. His research focused on the effects of light beams on carbon-based compounds; he received his master's degree in 1967 and his Ph.D. in 1970.

After graduation, Bramwell worked briefly in industrial research, accepting a position at the ESSO Research and Engineering Company in Linden, New Jersey. Although he enjoyed the research (he explored the electrical properties of petroleum-based products), he soon decided that an academic career would be more rewarding. He accepted a position with the City University of New York (CUNY) system in 1971, where he directed graduate students in chemical research. He also continued to conduct research on carbon-based compounds, helping develop superconductors and carbon-based fungicides. In 1990 he was named CUNY's dean of research and graduate studies.

During his years at CUNY, Bramwell developed and revised laboratory manuals to make them more comprehensive for students. He also became active in CHEMCOM, the pre-college program of the American Chemical Society. Bramwell's belief is that more students will choose the sciences as a profession if they receive the right encouragement early on. In 1995, Bramwell accepted a position as vice president for research and graduate studies at the University of Kentucky.

FURTHER READING:

Books

Kessler, James H., et al. *Distinguished African American Scientists of the Twentieth Century.* Phoenix: Oryx Press, 1996.

—Sketch by George A. Milite

Herman Branson
1914-1995
Physicist

Herman Branson was one of few African Americans to direct graduate research in physics. He collaborated with chemist Linus Pauling on defining the structure of proteins, which was a significant contribution to the fields of biochemistry and biology. As head of the physics department at Howard University and president of Central State University and Lincoln University, Branson has been devoted to the development of black scientists and other scholars.

Herman Russell Branson was born on August 14, 1914, in the small town of Pocahontas, Virginia, and he received his early education there. His family moved to Washington, D.C., and Branson graduated as valedictorian in 1932 from segregated Dunbar High School, which was famous for its outstanding faculty and curriculum. He attended the University of Pittsburgh for two years, then transferred to Virginia State College in Petersburg. He graduated *summa cum laude* in 1936, and received a fellowship to study physics in the graduate program at the University of Cincinnati. His dissertation included a practical section, on measuring x-ray intensity, and a theoretical section, on the quantization of mass. Branson was the first African American to obtain a Ph. D. in a physical science at the University of Cincinnati when he graduated in 1939. He left for New Orleans, Louisiana, to teach mathematics and physics at Dillard University for two years, then accepted an appointment as assistant professor of physics and chemistry at Howard University in Washington, D.C., in 1941. He was named professor in 1944, and served as head of the Physics Department from 1941 to 1968.

At Howard University, Branson was able to obtain research grants and develop an undergraduate major in physics as well as a graduate program, both of which were rare in black colleges. In the 1940s, physics courses at those colleges were for the most part service courses for premedical students and other science majors, but Branson was able to expand the department at Howard, and to offer an accredited physics major. Later, he added graduate courses and provided research opportunities at the University and at nearby government laboratories in Washington. Branson's own research at Howard was varied. He investigated biological reaction kinetics using isotopic labeling (isotopes are species of an element having identical atomic numbers, but varying masses), and he studied mass spectral fragmentation on an instrument he acquired for Howard. In the 1948-49 academic year, he received a National Research Council Senior Fellowship to travel to the California Institute of Technology, where he worked with Linus Pauling. His research led to one of Pauling and Robert B. Corey's first papers on the helical structure of proteins, which had a profound effect on the development of molecular biology and biochemistry, and to the understanding of diseases like sickle cell anemia, which are the result of aberrant protein structure.

Branson was always involved in the educational and economic improvement of African Americans, and he believed that the nation's demand for scientists would provide great opportunities for them. During World War II, he directed a program in physics in the Engineering, Science and Management War Training Program at Howard, to provide science education for civilians in the war effort. It was one of the few programs of its kind in physics at a black college. He was also involved in programs for increasing the number of African Americans enrolled in science courses in high school, and in the health professions. He served on many boards which gave scholarship aid and research grants, as well as in other civic and professional organizations.

In 1968, Branson accepted an offer from Central State University, in Wilberforce, Ohio, to serve as its president, and after two years, left to become president of Lincoln University, near Philadelphia, Pennsylvania. Lincoln University was the first college for black students in the United States, founded for the training of ministers. The appointment of Branson as president indicated that the University hoped to improve its science curriculum, and increase its prestige. Branson served as president until his retirement in 1985, at the age of 71. He returned to Howard at that time, and supervised a program which recruited bright high school students into science careers. Branson has received many awards and honors, including honorary degrees from institutions such as Brandeis University, Western Michigan University, Shaw College at Detroit, Virginia State University, Drexel University, University of Cincinnati, and Lincoln University. In 1939, Branson married Corolynne Gray of Cincinnati, Ohio, at the end of his graduate studies. They had one son, Herman Edward, and one daughter, Corolynne Gertrude, both physicians.

After his retirement, Branson lived in Silver Springs, Maryland. He died on June 7, 1995, at Washington Hospital Center.

SELECTED WRITINGS BY BRANSON:

Periodicals

"Structure of Proteins: Two Hydrogen-Bonded Helical Configurations of the Polypeptide Chain." *Proceedings of the National Academy of Sciences of the U. S.* 37 (1951): 205-11.

FURTHER READING:

Periodicals

Elliott, Michael J. "Herman Branson, 80, a Scientist who Headed Lincoln University" (obituary). *New York Times* (June 10, 1995): H10.

—*Sketch by Martin R. Feldman*

Randolph Wilson Bromery
1926-
Geologist and geophysicist

In his youth, Randolph W. Bromery worked hard to gain an education in mathematics, geology, and geophysics in the classroom and in the workplace. He was a pioneer in the airborne acquisition, reduction, and interpretation of geophysical information. Early in his career, he began to share his academic, practical, and administrative experience with others as an educator, and by the early 1990s, he earned a post as a college president. With over 150 professional articles, distinguished alumni awards from Howard University and the Johns Hopkins University, and several honorary doctorates and other awards to his credit, Bromery was named one of the nation's outstanding black scientists by the National Academy of Science in 1997.

Randolph Wilson Bromery was born January 18, 1926, Cumberland, Maryland, to Edith E. and Lawrence R. Bromery. It was in Cumberland that Bromery's education began. He attended a segregated high school, where African American boys were not allowed to take math courses. Instead, they were placed in industrial arts courses. Bromery recalled in an interview with contributor R. Garcia-Johnson on April 6, 1998, that his grandmother went to the school and "complained bitterly," but "to no avail. I was told that the superintendent of schools said that black men didn't need it [math] given what they were going to do in life." Bromery's grandmother arranged for him to learn math at night, from those who instructed his sister. (African American girls were allowed to take math in school). This arrangement eventually worked to Bromery's benefit: he learned math one-on-one, with the exclusive attention of his teachers. After high school, Bromery went to Tuskegee, where he wanted to become a navigator. Officials were concerned because, on paper, it looked as though he had no mathematics instruction. Bromery persuaded them to let him take a test, and he passed it. He became a member of U. S. Air Force Tuskegee Airmen, and flew in the United States (not overseas, as some sources relate) during World War II.

After the war, Bromery wanted to attend the University of Michigan, since he had family in Detroit, and had worked there for two summers. Once again, officials thought he had no math training. Again he proved with a test that he was capable; he took a correspondence course from Brigham Young University and entered the University of Michigan. He studied there until 1946, when he went to summer school at Howard to be near his mother, who was ill. Bromery's mother was, in fact, dying of multiple sclerosis (although the family was unaware of that at the time). Bromery's mother died the next spring, but Bromery stayed at Howard. There he worked with Professor **Elbert F. Cox**, the first African American to earn a Ph.D. in mathematics.

Bromery's Background Flies With the U.S. Geological Survey

Bromery's senior year, he married Cecile Trescott and prepared to graduate in the summer of 1948. However, he had a problem with the registrar; without receiving his degree, he left the university and began looking for work. He left application after application at the U.S. Naval Research Lab—which kept losing his application—and began to worry. "We had run out of money, the GI bill had stopped, and we had about 15 dollars," he told Garcia-Johnson. One day after a visit to the Naval Research lab, Bromery caught a trolley and saw an abandoned African American newspaper on a seat. He saw an advertisement for the U.S. Geological Survey, which was looking for physicists and mathematicians. Bromery transferred to another trolley and rode over the office. Officials there were excited about Bromery's background in math and physics and happy that he did not get air-sick. "Within two or three hours they put me on the payroll," he said.

Although he did not know much about geology, Bromery began work with the airborne geophysics group. For years, he worked to develop aeromagnetic maps of the East Coast, from New Hampshire to Pennsylvania. According to Bromery, aeromagnetic maps measure the variation in magnetic materials in rocks. Variations in the rocks allow scientists to discriminate different kinds of rocks, so they could map rocks from a plane. He explained, "We could analyze magnetic expressions . . . calculate how far below the aircraft was the body that caused them . . . and calculate the size and shape" of those bodies. Bromery also worked to find radioactive minerals in rocks. As the United States entered the nuclear era and needed a secure supply of uranium, Bromery flew over the Colorado plateau, searching for uranium deposits, mapping as he went. He also was a part of a team that worked for U.S. A.I.D., making geophysical maps of Liberia and Nigeria.

Bromery's thorough understanding of math was invaluable in his work; acquiring information about rocks and potential fields of valuable elements required analysis of magnetic expressions and interpretation of data. Yet he wanted to know more. In 1956, Bromery's degree from Howard University was finally awarded, and later, while still working for the U.S. Geological Survey, he began studies of geology at American University to earn undergraduate and masters degrees. In 1961, he began to lecture at Howard University. He told Garcia-Johnson that, during this time, he worked full time, took night school courses on Monday, Wednesday, and Friday, and began teaching at Howard on Tuesday and Thursday nights—"I made just enough money to pay tuition on Monday, Wednesday, and Friday." After earning an M.S. degree in 1962, he continued his graduate studies at Johns Hopkins University, where he was a Gillman Fellow.

Bromery Brings Hard-Won Knowledge to Academia

Bromery taught at Howard until 1965 and worked with the U.S. Geological Survey until 1967. During this time,

airborne geophysical acquisition, reduction, and interpretation as practiced by Bromery and others with the U.S. Geographic Survey was not yet widely taught in the United States. Bromery was asked to give lectures all over the country, and received calls from several colleges asking him to come as a faculty member to teach. Bromery decided to teach at the University of Massachusetts at Amherst. Bromery's Ph.D. from Johns Hopkins was conferred in 1968.

Bromery's career as an academic was off to a fast start. By 1969, he served as the head of the department of geology and geophysics at the University of Massachusetts. In 1971, the chancellor left, and Bromery was asked to serve as the acting chancellor. With faith in the management skills he acquired working for the U.S. Geological Survey, he accepted. He served as the senior vice-president and chancellor of the University from 1972 to 1980, when he returned to teaching and research as the Commonwealth professor of geophysics. During those years, he received several honorary doctorates.

Bromery kept busy with his academic work and some business ventures. In 1981, he served as the Weston Geophysical International Corporation president, and in 1983, he moved on to become the president of Geoscience Engineering Corporation. These were not Bromery's only activities in the business world. He worked as a consultant for Exxon and Kennecott Copper. He was a member of the board of directors for corporations including Exxon, NYNEX, and Singer, for banks including Chase Manhattan Bank and Chemical Bank, and for John Hancock Mutual Life Insurance.

In 1988, Bromery became the acting president of Westfield State College, and held that post until 1990. In 1989, he served as the president of the Geological Society of America. Next, he was called to Boston when the state and the governor and the board of Regents asked him to head up the board. Bromery did, but then retired from the University of Massachusetts in 1992. Six days after his retirement, he decided to serve as the acting president of Springfield College in Massachusetts. When the search committee for a new president organized, however, they decided that he should lead the institution. On October 30, 1993, Bromery was inaugurated as the president of Springfield College.

At Springfield College, Bromery provided leadership and sound administration. Bromery successfully dealt with the school's financial problems, and decided to retire during or after 1998. Yet retirement, for Bromery, does not mean "going fishing or sitting in a rocking chair." He told Garcia-Johnson, "I do want to write about some of my experience. As an African American, being 70 years old I've seen many changes." Life in the south in the early 1940s was difficult, and Bromery feels that young African Americans should know about it. Bromery and his wife, who have celebrated 50 years of marriage, live in Amherst, Massachusetts. They have five children: Keith, Carol, Dennis, David, and Christopher, as well as seven grandchildren.

FURTHER READING:

Books

American Men and Women of Science, 1998-99. 20th edition. Providence, NJ: R.R. Bowker, 1998.

Kessler, James H., J. S. Kidd, Renee A. Kidd, and Katherine A. Morin. *Distinguished African American Scientists of the 20th Century.* Phoenix, AZ: Oryx Press, 1996, pp. 22-27.

Phelps, Shirelle, ed. *Who's Who among African Americans.* 10th edition. Detroit: Gale Research, 1997.

—Sketch by R. Garcia-Johnson

Carolyn Branch Brooks
1946-
Microbiologist

Carolyn Branch Brooks has made numerous contributions to the fields of microbiology and molecular biology, but it is her work as a mentor to her students that most defines her as a person. She has spent most of her career at the University of Maryland Eastern Shore, where her research has concentrated on improving agricultural productivity through plant and microbial biotechnology.

Carolyn Branch was born on July 8, 1946, to Shirley Booker Branch and Charles Walker Branch. The family, including an older sister, lived with Carolyn's great grandparents in Richmond, Virginia. Her mother, an antique store worker, and father, a truck driver, worked long hours to provide for their daughters, and Carolyn showed her appreciation by doing her best at school.

In the 1950s her parents moved to a new neighborhood in Richmond. Carolyn continued to attend her old school, where she was surrounded by supportive teachers who recognized her potential. She took part in a special summer school for African American science students, where she was impressed by a guest speaker's description of his work as a medical microbiologist. Carolyn decided that she wanted to pursue a career in that field.

Her dreams became possible when she was offered scholarships at six different colleges. She chose to attend Tuskegee University in Alabama, where she majored in biology. There she met Henry Brooks, whom she married at the end of her second year. She graduated in 1968, remaining in the program through the birth of two sons, encouraged to continue with her career plans by her new husband and her professors. She earned her master's degree from Tuskegee in 1971, by which time she also had the first of two daughters.

Carolyn Brooks went on to receive a doctoral degree in 1977 from Ohio State University, where her dissertation research focused on the human immune system, and how macrophages in the blood destroy invading malaria parasites.

Following her graduation, Dr. Brooks worked at Kentucky State University, where she studied the nutritional needs of the elderly. She discovered a correlation between trace minerals found in hair and mineral intake in the subjects' diet, which enabled some medical problems caused by improper diet to be more easily diagnosed.

In 1981, Dr. Brooks took a position at the University of Maryland Eastern Shore (UMES), where she became Dean of the School of Agriculture and Natural Sciences and 1890 Research Director in 1994, and Executive Assistant to the President and Chief of Staff in 1997. Her research at UMES has primarily involved agricultural productivity, and includes studies of nitrogen-fixing soil bacteria and their relationship with plants in the legume family (peas and beans), as well as increasing plant resistance to insects and other predators through selective breeding and genetic engineering.

In 1984-85, she visited Togo and Senegal in West Africa, where she studied the microbes associated with an African groundnut. Her research helped to improve the food value of the plant by increasing the nitrogen-fixing ability of the microbe. In 1988, she helped local scientists in Cameroon, West Africa improve productivity of a number of food crops. In 1998, Dr. Brooks helped establish collaborative ties with research centers and universities in South Africa as a member of the U.S. A.I.D.-U.S.D.A. Team, and also represented UMES in linkage meetings with Egyptian universities.

Throughout her career at UMES, Dr. Brooks has also guided the research of her students. She has received numerous awards for her research, community service, and her abilities as a mentor. Simply by knowing, teaching, and helping her students, she says, her life has been enriched daily.

FURTHER READING:

Kessler, James H., J. S. Kidd, Renée A. Kidd, and Katherine A. Morin. "Carolyn Branch Brooks." In *Distinguished African American Scientists of the 20th Century.* Phoenix: The Oryx Press, 1996.

—Sketch by David E. Fontes

Arthur McKimmon Brown
1867-1939
Physician

Arthur McKimmon Brown was the first African American surgeon to secure a commission in the regular army of the United States, and he was the only African American surgeon to serve in Cuba during the Spanish-American War. Throughout his life and professional career, he received praise for his skill as a surgeon, businessman, civic leader, and humanitarian.

Brown was born on November 9, 1867, in Raleigh, North Carolina, to Winfield Scott and Jane M. Brown. Obtaining a good education for their son was very important to Brown's parents and to his grandmother, who was one of the first public school teachers in Raleigh. He began his education in the public school system, then entered Shaw University. Two years later in 1881 he returned to the public school.

In 1884 Brown received a scholarship to Lincoln University in Pennsylvania. An excellent student, he performed well in his studies and was a member of the glee club. Brown earned an A.B. in 1888. After graduation, he started his medical studies at the University of Michigan in Ann Arbor. The only African American in his class, Brown worked as a medical assistant and received his M.D. degree in 1891. He passed the difficult examination of the Medical Board of Alabama—with the highest score ever made in the history of the board at the time.

Brown began practicing medicine in Bessemer, Alabama. He spent some time as a surgeon in Chicago and Cleveland before beginning a successful practice in Birmingham, Alabama. He worked as a surgeon in the city's Provident and John C. Hall Hospital as well as at the Andrew Memorial Hospital in Tuskegee, Alabama. He also conducted a large drug business in Birmingham, called the People's Drug Store. During that period in his life, Brown served as chairman of the Alabama Prison Improvement Board and director of the Alabama Penny Saving Bank as well.

The Surgeon Goes Into Battle

When the United States Congress declared war on Spain in 1898, Brown was determined to serve in the U.S. Army. He organized and was captain of a company of soldiers. After waiting to be called into service with no response from the governor, the surgeon prepared to offer his services to the sick and wounded on the battlefield. Surgeon General M. Sternberg commissioned Brown as a first lieutenant and as a surgeon stationed at an immune regiment in Santiago, Cuba. There he would care for troops suffering with yellow fever, an infectious tropical disease caused by a virus spread through the bite of a certain

mosquito. When he arrived, however, the disease was no longer a significant threat within the regiment. He then received orders to join the Tenth Cavalry.

Along with several others who served in the all-black Ninth and Tenth Calvary regiments, Brown co-authored *Under Fire With the Tenth U.S. Cavalry.* The book captures the soldiers' experiences with war and racism while fighting during the Indian Wars as the nation spread westward and later during the Spanish-American War. Although he was a surgeon, Brown also faced danger on the battlefield. The enemy fired on doctors, as well as members of the hospital corps and American Red Cross. For nearly three months, Brown was the sole commander of the entire regiment.

Sergeant Horace W. Bivins, one of the authors of *Under Fire With the Tenth U.S. Cavalry,* wrote about the effect Brown had on the regiment upon his arrival: "He moved the hospital to where General Wheeler's headquarters were, put in bunks for all of the sick and members of the corps. It seemed as though he was just in time to save us. We received our meals from our respective organizations, but, indeed, it was so rough that the sick could not eat it. Under Surgeon Brown's supervision, our sick list soon began to decrease." Bivins also recalled how Brown's "skillful treatment" helped revive a soldier who was near death.

After the war ended, Brown returned with the regiment to the United States as an acting assistant surgeon. He served in Huntsville, Alabama, and Fort McIntosh, Texas. Brown received his discharge in 1899, but the director of pensions denied him a pension in 1930 for the services he provided during the war. The director of pensions indicated that Brown was appointed as a contract surgeon; therefore he was not considered a commissioned officer or an enlisted man, but a civilian employee.

In 1914, Brown served as president of the National Medical Association, an organization created to meet the needs of black physicians and those who serve a primarily black population. He was also a member of the Tri-State Medical, Dental and Pharmaceutical Association. Brown married Mamie Lou Coleman in 1895. Following her death in 1903, he married Mamie Nellie Adams in 1905. He had four children: Arthur, Herald, Walter, and Majorie. Brown died on December 4, 1939.

SELECTED WRITINGS BY BROWN:

Books

Under Fire with the Tenth U.S. Cavalry. Arno Press and The New York Times, 1969.

FURTHER READING:

Books

Logan, Rayford W.and Winston, Michael R. *Dictionary of American Negro Biography.* W. W. Norton & Company, 1982, p. 64.

Dorothy Lavinia Brown

Sammons, Vivian Ovelton *Blacks in Science and Medicine.* Taylor & Francis Publishers, p. 38.

—*Sketch by Rose M. Estioco*

Dorothy Lavinia Brown
1919-
Surgeon

Dorothy Lavinia Brown was the first black female surgeon in the South. She was also the first black woman admitted to the American College of Surgeons, the first black woman to serve in the Tennessee State Legislature, and the first single woman to adopt a child in Tennessee.

Brown was born on January 7, 1919, in Philadelphia, Pennsylvania, to Edna and Kevin Thomas Brown. Her mother took her to Troy, New York, within weeks of her birth, and Brown did not meet her father until she was an adult. Unable to care for her daughter, Brown's mother left her at Troy Orphanage when she was about five months old. Brown spent the next 12 years of her life there. She decided to become a doctor after having surgery to remove her tonsils when she was five years old.

When Brown was 13, her mother reclaimed her from the orphanage, hoping to prevent her daughter from being put in domestic service. Brown was not happy with her mother, who was a virtual stranger. She ran away at least five times, returning to Troy Orphanage each time. At the age of 15, Brown returned again to Troy and enrolled in Troy High School. With the help of the school's principal, Brown was placed with Samuel and Lola Redmon, who became her foster parents. With their support, she graduated near the top of her high school class. A local organization, the Women's Division of Christian Service of the Methodist Church, arranged a scholarship for her to attend Bennett College in Greensboro, North Carolina.

Brown's first year at Bennett was tough; college administrators initially told the Methodist Women's Division that she was not suitable for Bennett. But Brown held on to her scholarship and completed her bachelor's degree in 1941. While attending Bennett, Brown took as many science courses as possible, though school officials discouraged her from entering medical school. They thought she should set her sights on being a schoolteacher instead. After graduation, she worked as an inspector in the Rochester Army Ordinance Department, during World War II.

In 1944, Brown entered Meharry Medical College in Nashville, Tennessee. She graduated with her medical degree in 1948 and worked a year-long internship at Harlem Hospital in New York City. She decided she wanted to pursue surgery but was discouraged by her superiors at Harlem Hospital. Brown returned to Meharry Medical College and did her surgical residency at George W. Hubbard Hospital. In the course of her residency, Brown was the first woman to be chief resident in general surgery at Meharry. She completed her surgical residency in 1954 and in 1955 became an assistant professor of surgery. Eventually, Brown became a clinical professor of surgery at Meharry. Brown also maintained her own private practice. In 1956, Brown took advantage of recent changes in state laws to adopted an infant, Lola Denise; she was the first single mother to adopt in Tennessee. Three years later, in 1959, Brown became the first black female surgeon to become a fellow of the American College of Surgeons.

By 1960, Brown was the chief of surgery and educational director at Riverside Hospital in Nashville, a position she held until the hospital closed in 1983. Brown also was an attending surgeon at Nashville Memorial Hospital and Metro General Hospital, as well as student health services director at Meharry Medical College and Fisk University. In 1966, while maintaining her professional responsibilities, Brown was elected to the Tennessee State Legislature, the first black woman to achieve this position. Her two years in the legislature were controversial. She authored and sponsored an abortion rights bill which could, she believed, save many women's lives. Though Brown initially intended to only serve one term, she decided to run for the Tennessee State Senate. The furor over the abortion bill, and other controversies, led to Brown's defeat in 1968.

While juggling teaching and medicine with motherhood, Brown served as a trustee for several universities, including Philander Smith College, Bennett College, and Russell Sage College in Troy, New York. Russell Sage College honored her in 1972 with an honorary doctorate of science, one of several honorary doctorates Brown received over the course of her career. Brown also held important committee memberships. In 1976, she served on the Joint Committee on Opportunities for Women in Medicine, sponsored by the American Medical Association. Brown was also a sought-after public speaker, both nationally and internationally.

Throughout her career, Brown maintained memberships in numerous professional and civic organizations. In addition to being a fellow of the American College of Surgeons and of the American College of Medicine, Brown is a member of the Nashville Academy of Medicine, the R.F. Boyd Medical Society, and the National Medical Association. She is also a life member of the National Association for the Advancement of Colored People (NAACP). Brown has been recognized many times for her professional and civic work. These honors include the 1970 renaming of the Women's Building at Meharry Medical College to the Dorothy L. Brown Building.

FURTHER READING:

Books

Organ, Claude H. and Margaret M. Kosiba, eds. *A Century of Surgeons: The U.S.A. Experience, Volume II.* Norman, OK: Transcript Press, 1987, pp. 591-93.
Sammons, Vivian Ovelton. *Blacks in Science and Medicine.* New York: Hemisphere Publishing, 1990.

Periodicals

"Bachelor Mother." *Ebony* (September 1958): 92-96.
"Meharry Gets Woman Chief of Surgery." *Afro-American* (July 25, 1953).

—*Sketch by A. Petrusso*

Russell Wilfred Brown

Russell Wilfred Brown
1905-1986
Microbiologist

Russell Wilfred Brown's work as a microbiologist was critical both in the development of experimental techniques and in scientific results. In addition to his work as a researcher, he was also an important figure in education at the Tuskegee Institute, where he served in top administrative posts for several years.

Brown was born in Gray, Louisiana on January 17, 1905. He attended Howard University, graduating with a bachelor of science degree in 1926. He began his graduate work at the University of Chicago, and in 1930 took a position as an instructor in biology at Rust College in Mississippi. He remained there for a year and moved on to Iowa State University, where he received his master's degree in 1932. (That year, he also married Mildred McConnell.) Brown took a position as assistant professor of bacteriology at Langston University in Oklahoma and later returned to Iowa State to complete his doctoral work. While there, he had the opportunity to work with such noted scientists as Harland G. Wood and C. J. Werkman. Brown was awarded his Ph.D. in 1936.

Upon receiving his doctorate, Brown accepted a post as instructor at the Tuskegee Institute. In 1943 he returned to Iowa State as a research assistant, but he came back to Tuskegee in 1943 as a professor of bacteriology. In 1944 he was named head of the Carver Research Foundation at Tuskegee.

Brown gave up this post in 1951 when he was asked to lead a research group creating a special strain of cells that would be used for experimentation in the development of a polio vaccine. Part of the work Brown and his team conducted involved culturing enough of the cells to make experimentation possible. Among other things, this meant determining the exact effect temperature had on the cultures, which were extremely sensitive to any temperature change (even during shipment from one research center to another). Between 1953 and 1955 the Tuskegee team had manufactured and shipped 600,000 cultures to laboratories around the country that were conducting polio research.

Dr. **James H. M. Henderson** of Tuskegee was brought on board by Brown to work on this project. In an April 1998 interview with contributor George Milite, Henderson remembered Brown as "an outstanding researcher and a meticulous scientist." Brown's attention to detail, he added, is "a quality that is critically important, particularly in a field such as microbiology where environments must be strictly controlled."

Brown remained on the board of the Carver Foundation, a post he held until 1970. He also remained at Tuskegee. During the 1956-57 academic year he was a postdoctoral fellow at Yale. In 1962, Brown became vice president and dean at Tuskegee. He retired from Tuskegee in 1970 and spent a year as Distinguished Professor of Microbiology at the University of Reno School of Medicine in Nevada. In 1971 he was awarded an honorary doctorate by Tuskegee. Brown died on July 29, 1986.

SELECTED WRITINGS BY BROWN:

Periodicals

Brown, Russell W. and James H. M. Henderson. "The Mass Production of HeLa Cells at Tuskegee Institute", 1953-55. *Journal of the History of Medicine and Allied Sciences,* vol 38, no. 4: 415-431.

FURTHER READING:

Books

Taylor, Julius, ed. *The Negro in Science.* Morgan State University Press, 1955.
Sammons, Vivian O. *Blacks in Science and Medicine.* Hemisphere Publishing, 1990.
Who's Who Among Black Americans, second edition. Who's Who Among Black Americans Press, 1977.

—*Sketch by George A. Milite*

Marjorie Lee Browne

Marjorie Lee Browne
1914-1979
Mathematician

In 1949 Marjorie Lee Browne, along with **Evelyn Boyd Granville**, was one of the first African American women to receive a Ph.D. degree. By training a topologist (specializing in a branch of mathematics that deals with certain geometric aspects of spaces and shapes), Browne made her greatest contributions in the areas of teaching and university administration. She also provided a leadership role in seeking funding for better educational opportunities; her goals included the strengthening of mathematical preparation for science and mathematics teachers in secondary schools and the increased presence of females and minorities in the mathematical sciences.

Browne was born in Memphis, Tennessee, the second child of Lawrence Johnson Lee, a transportation mail clerk; her stepmother, Lottie Taylor Lee, was a school teacher. As a young woman growing up in Memphis and New Orleans, she was an expert tennis player, a singer, an avid reader—a trait she inherited from her father—and a gifted mathematics student. Browne graduated from LeMoyne High School in Memphis in 1931. In 1935 she received a B.S. degree *cum laude* in mathematics from Howard University, then earned a M.S. in mathematics in 1939 and a Ph.D. in 1949 from the University of Michigan. She wrote her doctoral dissertation on one-parameter subgroups in certain topological and matrix groups, and her dissertation served as the basis for one of her major publications on the classical groups in 1955.

Browne began her teaching career in 1935 at Gilbert Academy in New Orleans, Louisiana, where she taught physics and mathematics for a year. From 1942 to 1945, she served as an instructor at Wiley College in Marshall, Texas. In 1949, Browne was appointed to the faculty in the department of mathematics at North Carolina Central University (NCCU), where she rose to the rank of professor and became the first chair of the department from 1951 to 1970. She served as a principal investigator, coordinator of the mathematics section, and lecturer for the Summer Institute for Secondary School Science and Mathematics Teachers, a program funded by the first National Science Foundation grant awarded to NCCU in 1957. Browne continued this role until 1970.

Browne was acutely aware of the obstacles which women and minorities faced in pursuing scientific careers. Shortly after receiving her doctorate in 1949 she sought, unsuccessfully, to obtain an instructorship at several major research institutions. After receiving many polite letters of rejection, she decided to remain in the South and resolved that her greatest contributions would be directing programs designed to strengthen the mathematical preparation of secondary school mathematics teachers and to increase the presence of minorities and females in mathematical science careers.

Thus, Browne spent her summers teaching secondary school teachers, and her objective was to insure that the teachers whom she taught would be able to understand and teach their students the so-called "modern math" or "new math." Browne's teaching standards were exacting and her methods were thorough; her demands for excellence and concise, clear ideas contributed greatly to the academic growth and development of her students, and many of her students have made significant contributions in a number of professions. Nine of them have earned doctorates in the mathematical sciences or related disciplines. Browne was also a steady, outspoken critic of racism and the discriminatory practices prevalent among funding agencies relative to minorities and predominantly minority universities and colleges. She was an ardent advocate for the integration of the previously segregated meetings of the national mathematics organizations of which she was a member.

Honored For Her Work

For her work in mathematics education, Browne was awarded the first W. W. Rankin Memorial Award from the North Carolina Council of Teachers of Mathematics in 1974. During her acceptance speech, she described herself as "a pre-*Sputnik* mathematician." She was referring to the purist nature of her advanced mathematical preparation and the practice of many American industries and businesses,

prior to the launching of the first Russian satellite in 1957, to allow scientists and mathematicians to pursue research projects that had no immediate real world or job-related applications. The launching of *Sputnik* had a tremendous impact on mathematics education in the United States. America was viewed as having fallen behind the Russians in space explorations, and as a result there was a shift in emphasis from pure abstract mathematical and scientific research to investigations that were of an applied nature. Browne, however, remained a mathematical purist, and like many great mathematical philosophers of the nineteenth century, she viewed mathematics as an intellectual quest, free from the limitations of the physical universe.

Browne was a member of the Woman's Research Society, American Mathematical Society, Mathematical Association of America, and the International Congress of Mathematicians as well as the author of several articles in professional and scholarly journals. In 1960, she received a $60,000 grant from IBM to establish one of the first electronic digital computer centers at a predominantly minority university, and in 1969, she received the first of seven Shell Foundation Scholarship Grants, awarded to mathematics students for outstanding academic achievements. The director of the first Undergraduate Research Participation Program at NCCU during 1964 and 1965—which was sponsored by the National Science Foundation—Browne was also one of the first African American females to serve on the advisory panel to the National Science Foundation Undergraduate Scientific Equipment Program in 1966, 1967, and 1973. In addition, she served as a Faculty Consultant in Mathematics for the Ford Foundation from 1968 to 1969 at their New York office. Browne was awarded numerous fellowships, including one from the Ford Foundation at Cambridge University in England from 1952 to 1953.

Browne died of an apparent heart attack at her home in Durham, North Carolina, in 1979. At the time of her death, she was preparing a monograph on the development of the real number system from a postulational approach. Browne was a generous humanitarian who believed that no good student should go without an education simply because he or she lacked the financial resources to pay for it. Thus, it was not uncommon for her to assume the financial responsibilities for many able students whose families were unable to provide tuition, books, board, or transportation for them. To continue the philanthropic legacy which she began, four of her former students established the Marjorie Lee Browne Trust Fund at North Carolina Central University in 1979. This fund supports two major activities in the mathematics and computer science department: the Marjorie Lee Browne Memorial Scholarship—which is awarded annually to the student who best exemplifies those traits which Browne sought to instill in young people—and the annual Marjorie Lee Browne Distinguished Alumni Lecture Series.

SELECTED WRITINGS BY BROWNE:

Periodicals

"A Note on the Classical Groups," *American Mathematical Monthly,* (August 1955).

FURTHER READING:

Periodicals

"$57,500 Granted for High School Teachers Summer Institute at NCC," *Durham Sun,* (December 21, 1956).

Other

Personal information supplied to William T. Fletcher by the department of mathematics and computer science of North Carolina Central University, 1994.

—*Sketch by William T. Fletcher*

Charles Wesley Buggs
1906-1991
Bacteriologist

Charles Wesley Buggs was primarily concerned with the resistance of different bacteria to antibiotics—substances that can kill or prevent their growth. Buggs did research on several kinds of antibiotics, including streptomycin, penicillin, and sulfa. He devised an ingenious method for treating traumas such as burns and wounds from under the skin. Buggs taught at several universities including Howard University and Wayne University (later known as Wayne State University). At Wayne, he was the first black person to hold a full-time position on the faculty.

Buggs was born on August 6, 1906, in Brunswick, Georgia, to John Wesley and Leonora Vane (Clark) Buggs. His father was a doctor. Buggs graduated from Brunswick's St. Athanasius High School in 1924 and then entered Morehouse College. Majoring in zoology, Buggs earned his bachelor's degree from Morehouse in 1928. While still a student at Morehouse, Buggs married Marguerite Lee Bennett, with whom he would have one daughter, Margaret L. Buggs. After working as an instructor for a year at Dover State College in Delaware, Buggs began his graduate studies at the University of Chicago. However, lack of funds forced him to leave school and work as a teacher again, this time at a high school in Key West, Florida. With the support of his wife, Buggs was able to continue his graduate work at the University of Minnesota, earning his master of science

degree in 1931. He continued at Minnesota with the funding from a Shevlin fellowship and the Julius Rosenwald Fund, earning his doctorate in 1934. His dissertation was entitled "Cataphoretic Phenomena." After graduation, he worked from 1934-35 as a chemistry professor at Bishop College.

In 1935, Buggs joined Dillard University, located in New Orleans, Louisiana. From 1935-43, Buggs was a biology professor as well as the chairman of the natural sciences division there. He spent 1943 in Woods Hole, Massachusetts, as a Rosenwald fellow. He then accepted a position at the College of Medicine at Wayne University in Detroit, Michigan, where he remained until 1949. Buggs worked through the ranks, from instructor to associate professor; he was also associated with the Office of Science Research and Development at Wayne. He returned to Dillard in his former positions as professor and division chair in 1949. That year, Buggs published *Premedical Education for Negroes,* a study partially funded by the federal government. In the book, Buggs outlined the lack of sufficient support on every level for African Americans trying to get an education to prepare themselves for medical school.

In 1956, Buggs moved his family to Washington, D.C., when he took a position at Howard University. Buggs was professor of microbiology there from 1956-71. He was also head of the department from 1958-70. Beginning in 1969, Buggs held a simultaneous position as project director for the faculty of allied health science in the **Charles R. Drew** Postgraduate Medical School at the University of California, Los Angeles. From 1969-76, Buggs was also a visiting professor at the University of Southern California. In 1971, Buggs moved to California, and by 1972, he was dean of Drew Postgraduate Medical School. This position lasted for only one year, and in 1973 he became a microbiology professor at California State University, Long Beach. He retired from this professorship in 1983.

Buggs was a member of several professional organizations, including the American Association for the Advancement of Science, the American Association of Pathologists and Bacteriologists, the National Institute of Science, and the Society of Experimental Biology and Medicine. Buggs died on September 13, 1991.

SELECTED WRITINGS BY BUGGS:

Books

Premedical Education for Negroes: Interpretations and Recommendations Based Upon a Survey in Fifteen Selected Negro Colleges. Washington, D.C., 1949.

Periodicals

"Antibiotic Agents and Some General Principles of Antibiotic Therapy." *Journal of the National Medical Association* (1947): 45-47.

FURTHER READING:

Books

American Men & Women of Science. New Providence, NJ: R.R. Bowker, 1992.

Sammons, Vivian Ovelton. *Blacks in Science and Medicine.* New York: Hemisphere Publishing, 1990.

—Sketch by A. Petrusso

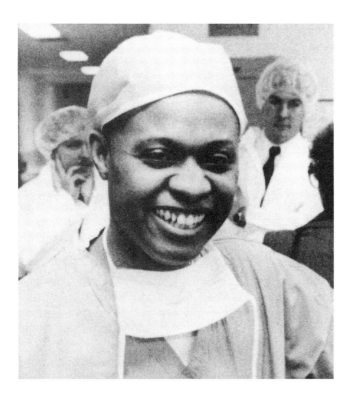

Clive O. Callender

Clive O. Callender
1936-
Surgeon

Clive O. Callender has been at the forefront of promoting organ donor programs in the United States and abroad. As the transplant director at Howard University Hospital in Washington, D.C., and as professor of the hospital's department of surgery, Callender is a leading transplant surgeon and spokesperson for health issues pertaining to the African American community.

Clive Orville Callender was born on November 16, 1936, to Joseph Callender and Ida Burke in New York City. He was inspired at an early age to become a missionary doctor after hearing a sermon in his church. Callender graduated from Hunter College in New York in 1959 with degrees in chemistry and physiology and then attended Meharry Medical College in Nashville, Tennessee. In 1963 he graduated first in his class and won the Charles Nelson Gold Medal. He married Fern Irene Marshal in May of 1968, and they eventually had three children: Joseph, Ealena, and Arianne.

During his internship at the University of Cincinnati, Callender became interested in surgery and obtained further training in the specialty as chief resident at Howard University and Freedmen's Hospital. He became an instructor at the university in 1969; the following year he became a medical officer at D.C. General Hospital. Shortly thereafter, his invitation to work as a surgeon at Port Harcourt General Hospital in Nigeria (during the Biafran Civil War) fulfilled his dream of being a missionary doctor.

Upon returning to the United States, Callender became interested in transplant surgery and was granted a two-year National Institutes of Health fellowship and a one-year fellowship at the University of Minnesota to become a transplant specialist. Following this, he formed a transplant center at Howard University. Ten years later, in 1983, Callender established another transplant center in the Virgin Islands, which was named in his honor.

Callender became concerned when he detected a resistance among African Americans toward donating organs. His inquiry into the issue uncovered that many felt that needy minorities were less likely to receive an organ transplant than white patients. Some objected to transplants because the procedure violated their religious beliefs about not disturbing the body after death. Others were afraid they would be declared dead prematurely if they had promised an organ.

Callender has travelled throughout the United States, Europe, and the Caribbean on his mission to dispel these misconceptions about organ and tissue transplants. Together with organ donors, recipients, and those waiting for transplants, he has given workshops aimed at increasing the number of minority donors. In addition, he testified before the U.S. Senate in 1983, in a successful attempt to increase government funding for community education on the issue. Callender's efforts have begun to pay off—a 1990 Gallup poll found that 24 percent of African Americans surveyed said they had signed organ donor cards, up from seven percent in 1985.

Callender sees organ transplant awareness as a crucial issue for African Americans because they represent 30 percent of all dialysis patients and because they often fare poorly after the procedure. To prevent a backlash, Callender told *New York Times* writer Paul Delaney that "blacks themselves have to do more," and become more involved in health care issues.

In 1989 Callender was elected to the Hunter College Alumni Hall of Fame. As of 1994, he was the only African American member of the Task Force on Organ Procurement and Transplantation. Since 1979, he has also been the president of the National Capitol Area branch of the National Kidney Foundation.

SELECTED WRITINGS BY CALLENDER:

Periodicals

"Organ Donation in Blacks: Once a Dilemma, Now a National Commitment," *Black Health,* Vol. 1 (1988): 22–25.
"Special Report: Organ Donation and Blacks, A Critical Frontier," *New England Journal of Medicine,* (August 8, 1991).

FURTHER READING:

Books

Burgess, Marjorie. "Clive O. Callender," in *Contemporary Black Biography,* Gale, 1993.

Periodicals

Delaney, Paul. "Fighting Myths in a Bid to Get Blacks to Consider Transplants," *New York Times,* (November 6, 1991).

—Sketch by Linda Lewin

Nathaniel Oglesby Calloway
1907-1979
Physician and organic chemist

Nathaniel O. Calloway—often called "N. O."—was a talented physician and social activist whose work was surrounded by controversy. The son of a former slave, Calloway rose to a position of respect as a physician and as a leader in the African American community. His role in reorganizing the Chicago chapter of the Urban League in the late 1950s helped transform it from an embarrassment for the national organization to one of its most successful chapters. His later life teachings on genetics and race at University of Wisconsin, Madison, helped debunk racist notions of white superiority.

However, Calloway was not always well-respected by those around him. His controversial attempts to prevent the Chicago Urban League from adopting the activism of the early 1960s led to bad publicity for the organization and his eventual ouster. As a private physician in Madison, he became embroiled in a prescription drug scandal that resulted in charges from the Wisconsin State Medical Examining Board.

Chemist, physician

Calloway was born on October 10, 1907, in Tuskegee, Alabama. He received both a B.S. in 1930 and a Ph.D. in chemistry in 1933 from Iowa State University. In the latter year, he became head of the chemistry department at the Tuskegee Institute. He was named assistant professor at Fisk University in 1936. As a medical student at the University of Illinois, Chicago, he became an instructor in pharmacology at the University of Chicago in 1940. In 1943, when he received his M.D. from Illinois, he became a lieutenant in the U.S. Army Medical Corps.

Calloway's best-known work as a chemist concentrated on the use of metal halide catalysts to improve reaction yields in the production of ketones, a basic workhorse molecule in industrial organic chemistry. In particular, these studies identified ways of avoiding unwanted side reactions, as well as finding alternative conditions and catalysts for optimizing these reactions.

As a physician, Calloway rapidly rose to positions of authority. After a lecturer position at the University of Illinois Medical School that began in 1945, in 1947 he was promoted to assistant professor and senior physician at Illinois, as well as being named assistant chief of medicine at Percy Jones Army Hospital. The Army made him a major in 1950. In 1958 he left the university to begin a group medical practice in Chicago; in 1963 he moved again, to become chief of the medical staff at the Tomah, Wisconsin, Veterans Administration Hospital. Finally, in 1966, he moved to Madison, Wisconsin, where he opened a private practice that he kept until shortly before his death in 1979.

In the 1960s, Calloway became interested in the process of aging, particularly the physical effects of aging on biological cells and tissues, called senescence. Today his work in this field—largely theoretical—is difficult to place in context, because so much more information about the processes involved is known than was available to him at the time. His assertion that *systems, energy systems,* and *not things* senesce [his emphasis]" is not entirely correct. Today we know that an organism's DNA (deoxyribonucleic acid) and proteins can indeed collect physical damage and become less efficient with age. On the other hand, this accumulation of damage results from the increasing inefficiency of cellular repair mechanisms—so in that sense, the system rather than its components is at fault, as he postulated. Similarly, his observation that organisms tend to die when they reach a certain low point in the ability to produce heat may yet prove significant—or may just be a general indication of the body's inability to carry out housekeeping functions.

Chicago and the Urban League years

Undoubtedly Calloway is best known for his presidency of the Chicago Urban League and his involvement in the Urban League's national board of directors in the late 1950s and early 1960s. When Calloway was appointed president in 1955, the Chicago chapter was in a shambles. Confidence in the organization among members of the black community and fundraising were down drastically. In addition, the chapter was torn in a debate between moderates, who wanted the organization to work in a low-key manner with the white establishment (as stipulated by the organization's bylaws) and progressives, who wanted to see the organization take a more confrontational pose.

While Calloway was known as a "conservative" or "moderate" member, he claimed at the time that there was little opposition to his appointment because "our friends all thought we could improve [the chapter] and our enemies thought . . . Nothing could be any worse . . . " Given the brief to clean house by the Chicago Urban League board of directors, Calloway and white advertising executive Hugo B. Law essentially dissolved the organization, allowing them to reform it as they wished without the resistance of non-like-minded members and employees. To design and run programs based on the policies Calloway and the board formulated, he hired an Urban League executive director from Portland, Oregon, named Edwin C. Berry, to serve as the Chicago director in 1955. Berry was known for helping to transform Portland from one of the worst cities in the country in terms of race relations to one of the best.

There is little doubt that Calloway accomplished everything he set out to do. Where earlier, many Chicago business leaders avoided working with the Urban League because of its perception as a "radical" organization, under his leadership many of them joined the chapter's advisory board and began contributing financially to the organization. Within a few years, the chapter's budget grew and stabilized, allowing Berry to begin a number of educational and aid projects in the Chicago inner city. One big coup was gaining powerful Mayor Richard Daley's consent to become honorary chairman. Soon the Chicago chapter was the pride of the national Urban League. In 1959, the National Urban League gave Calloway and Law its highest honor, the Two Friends Award.

However, Calloway's commitment to working "within the system," coupled with his sometimes explosive way of confronting political enemies, proved his downfall. Berry, while an effective director, was from the beginning more progressive than Calloway and the initial Chicago board. Soon he was testing the limits of the board's willingness to let him interpret its policies. Initially, Calloway supported Berry and his sometimes controversial quotes in the press, saying, "those who would like to see the Chicago Urban League become docile . . . should realize that such an Urban League would be worthless . . . " But eventually

Calloway pushed to limit Berry's power, even as Berry pushed to expand it. In 1960 the Chicago board, which had grown more progressive in the previous five years, voted Calloway out of office as president—although he remained a member of the board until 1961, when he resigned in protest over the direction that the chapter was going.

The debate over school bussing was the flashpoint that completed Calloway's fall from power. When a Chicago newspaper photographed Berry at a demonstration against school segregation in 1962 (Berry claimed to be there as an observer only), Calloway began a series of letter-writing campaigns criticizing Berry, sending this and other embarrassing photos of Berry to influential businessmen and civic leaders. These letters, coming from a prominent physician and member of the National Urban League board, embarrassed both the Chicago and national organizations. The situation worsened from there, with the board supporting Berry and the national organization trying to stay out of the fight. In 1962, Calloway resigned from the National Urban League board. Although he joined the board of the Madison Urban League and served as the president of the Madison chapter of the National Association for the Advancement of Colored People (NAACP) when he moved there in 1966, he never again attained the national prominence that he enjoyed in Chicago.

Madison: Persuasive Lectures and More Controversy

In 1970, Calloway became a lecturer at the prestigious University of Wisconsin, Madison, campus. He taught a class on genetics, race, and racial stereotypes there until 1978. Never forgetting his origins as the son of a former slave, Calloway attacked the underpinnings of the arguments for genetic differences between the races, pointing out alternate explanations having to do with the history of black Americans as slaves and then as a segregated underclass. "Often what are called racial differences are social and economic differences," he argued. Although these issues are still being debated today, Calloway's arguments have not weakened with time.

But the Madison years ended in controversy for Calloway. In 1975, the State Medical Examining Board prohibited him briefly from prescribing methaqualone, pending an investigation into the large number of prescriptions for college students that he was writing for this depressant, often known by the brand name Quaalude. In 1978, the Madison Press Connection printed a story alleging that Calloway had prescribed three quarters of the entire city of Madison's prescriptions for methaqualone in 1976—a staggering 60,000 prescriptions.

Calloway didn't deny the number of prescriptions he wrote for methaqualone, but he did argue that they were medically necessary, and challenged accusers to identify patients of his who were abusing the drug. He also said that his accusers were motivated by racial bias.

Late in 1978 the medical board acted again, charging him with endangering his patients by writing excessive numbers of prescriptions for this drug. But their investigation into his prescription practices was never completed; in 1979 Calloway, who had fought a long battle with cancer, retired from his medical practice. He died soon afterward, survived by his wife, Mary Ann, sons David and Aubrey, and daughters Constance, Candace, Kathlyn, Sharon, and Roslyn.

SELECTED WRITINGS BY CALLOWAY:

Periodicals

(With Louis D. Green) "Reactions in the presence of metallic halides. I. Beta-unsaturated ketone formation as a side reaction in Friedel-Crafts Acylations," *Journal of the American Chemical Society*, (May, 1937).

"Reactions in the presence of metallic halides. II. The behavior of fluorides and the reactivity of the halogens," *Journal of the American Chemical Society*, (August 1937).

"The nature of senescence," *Journal of the American Geriatrics Society*, Vol. 14, (1966).

"Heat production and senescence," *Journal of the American Geriatrics Society*, Vol. 22, (1974).

FURTHER READING:

Books

Strickland, Arvarh E. *History of the Chicago Urban League*. University of Illinois Press, 1966.

Periodicals

Detering, Susan. "Black genetic differences disputed," *Wisconsin State Journal*, (May 6, 1973).

"Blacks, whites differ in learning, not inheritance," *The Capital Times* (Madison), (May 9, 1973).

Mayer, Dean. "Doc Calloway returns from bout with cancer," *Daily Cardinal* (Madison), (January 26, 1978).

Makward, Edris. "Rebut to Calloway story (letter)" *Daily Cardinal* (Madison), (February 3, 1978).

Dorgan, Michael. "Doctor is main 'downer' source," *Madison Press Connection*, (March 1, 1978).

"Noted physician, activist Dr. N. O. Calloway, 72, dies," *Jet*, (December 27, 1979).

—Sketch by Kenneth B. Chiacchia

Herman George Canady
1901-1970
Psychologist

Herman George Canady was the first race psychologist in America, and he was a leader in demonstrating experimentally that performance on intelligence quotient (I.Q.) tests was significantly influenced by the social situation of the test, for example, who the tester was. Canady also led the way in showing that a student's gender influenced how she or he performed on I.Q. tests.

Canady was born on October 9, 1901, in Okmulgee, Oklahoma. His mother was Anna Carter Canady, and his father, a Methodist minister, was Howard T. Canady. His family was poor, and he moved frequently around the rural Midwest as a child, but his parents had high expectations for their children. After his father died in 1914, the Canady family moved to Sedalia, Missouri. There Canady attended the high school department of George R. Smith College with his sister, Estella. His mother worked at the college as a cook.

After graduating from high school in 1923, Canady entered Northwestern University on a scholarship to study for the ministry. He paid his way through school as a railroad worker, short order cook, waiter, caretaker, and handyman. He also worked part-time for his room and board as a chauffeur for one of his professors. Besides working and studying, he began swimming at the university swimming pool in 1924. Unfortunately, the president of the university threatened expulsion, so he had to swim elsewhere. After a while, Canady became interested in the behavioral sciences and changed his mind about his major. He received his bachelor's degree in sociology in 1927, and his master's degree in clinical psychology in 1928, both from Northwestern. Later in 1928, he began to teach at West Virginia State College in the town of Institute, West Virginia. There, on August 16, 1934, he married his wife, the former Julia Witten, who also worked for the college. They were to have two children, Joyce and Herman, Jr. Herman Jr. later became a circuit judge.

In 1939, Canady returned to Northwestern to earn his Ph.D. He paid his way with a scholarship, the General Education Board Fellowship, which he held from 1939-1941. For his dissertation, he studied factors that influenced the scores of black students on intelligence tests. He suspected that students' social and environmental situations had a greater influence on I.Q. scores than their races. His doctoral dissertation was titled, "Test Standing and Social Setting: A Comparative Study of the Intelligence-Test Scores of Negroes Living Under Varied Environmental Conditions." When he received his Ph.D. in psychology on May 17, 1941, from Northwestern University, Canady was only the tenth black American to get a Ph.D. in psychology.

He returned to West Virginia State College as a full professor.

Challenging Assumptions about I.Q. Tests

In the words of James L. Spencer, Canady "was the first true race psychologist in the United States." Some of Canady's research focused on finding out why black students did poorly on intelligence tests. For centuries, many people had believed that blacks were less intelligent than whites because they had inferior genes. Canady did not agree. He thought that one factor influencing the outcomes of I.Q. tests might be stress. If there was racial hostility in a culture, and if the races of the tester and the students were different, then Canady thought that the stress from the hostile social environment might influence test performance. But Canady needed a rigorous way to prove that people performed poorly on intelligence tests because of the social environment. In 1936, Canady published a well-known article titled, "The Effect of 'Rapport' on the IQ: A New Approach to the Problem of Racial Psychology." The article, which was based on his master's thesis written eight years earlier, showed that the social situation of the I.Q. test had an impact on a person's test performance. If the person testing black students was black, then the students performed better than if the tester was white. Canady found a similar result for white students: if the person testing white students was white, then the students performed better than if the tester was black. Canady's research showed that the social environment was also a factor in performance on I.Q. tests.

In 1938, Canady showed how another factor—gender—influenced I.Q. test scores. In a study of 1,306 students, Canady discovered that female students did better than males on verbal portions of I.Q. tests, while males outperformed females on the math portions of I.Q. tests. It took a while for Canady's results to get around, but his work helped to show other researchers that simple experiments could be developed to demonstrate that other influences besides genes affected student performance on intelligence tests. Canady's work is a landmark in the struggle to create fair testing environments for all people, regardless of race or gender.

Nobody Chews Gum in His Classes

Canady's long experience in the school of hard knocks taught him that a college education was not just about reading books and taking tests. Developing personal character was more important. His students had to be disciplined, neat, and well prepared. Canady insisted that his students come to class on time, and he locked out latecomers. He also criticized students who chewed gum, and he lectured women students who he felt wore too much makeup. Cheaters were expelled from his classes and were forbidden to take any other classes from him. Canady also had high academic standards. He was notorious for long, difficult

tests, and he gave out few As. Only 5% of his 380 students in 1937 earned As.

Though Canady could be tough in the classroom, he was also humorous and entertaining, and many of his students thought well of him and appreciated his standards and his personality. He would tell students that his middle initial "G" did not stand for "George" but for "God." If a student exclaimed, "Oh God!" while taking one of his demanding tests, Canady would say "Yes?" to ease the tension. On the first day of class, Canady would sometimes enter the darkened room from the back, turn on the lights, and say, "Let there be light!" to set the tone for the class.

In addition to publishing and teaching, Canady was active in founding several professional organizations and participating in many others. He served his college in a variety of capacities, gave many presentations locally and at universities around the United States, served as a board member for numerous organizations, and consulted with a variety of groups. He retired from West Virginia State College in 1968, and he died on December 1, 1970.

SELECTED WRITINGS BY CANADY:

Periodicals

"The Effect of 'Rapport' on the IQ: A New Approach to the Problem of Racial Psychology." *Journal of Negro Education.* Vol. 5 (1936): 209-219.

FURTHER READING:

Books

Guthrie, Robert V. *Even the Rat Was White, 2nd Ed.* Boston: Allyn and Bacon, 1998.
Spencer, James L. *Recollections and Reflections: A History of the West Virginia State College Psychology Department, 1892-1992.* Institute: West Virginia State College, 1993.

Periodicals

Watson, Peter. "IQ: The Racial Gap." *Psychology Today* (September 1972): 48-50, 97-99.

—Sketch by Patrick Moore

Thomas C. Cannon, Jr.

Thomas C. Cannon, Jr.
1943-
Communications engineer

The fiber optic cables that today we take for granted could not function properly without a thorough understanding of their structure. Thomas C. Cannon, Jr. has provided much of the research that makes fiber optic technology possible. He helped design, plan, and install the first commercial fiber optic system in the United States.

He was born in Houston, Texas on January 8, 1943, to Thomas C. Cannon, Sr. and Lillian Bland Cannon. As a boy, young Thomas was interested in building model airplanes—which presaged his future career. He attended Purdue University in Indiana, receiving his bachelor's degree in aeronautical engineering in 1964. He stayed on at Purdue for his master's, which he received in 1966; and for his Ph.D., which he was awarded in 1970. (He was named a Stanford Sloan Fellow in 1987 and received a master's in management science in 1988.)

After leaving Purdue, Cannon joined the Federal Systems Division of Bell Labs (formerly part of AT&T, now part of Lucent Technologies) in Whippany, New Jersey. He helped design a cable system that would help detect submarine activity. One of his tasks was to ensure that the cables, which were being made with the synthetic material Kevlar instead of steel, would be able to withstand the same stresses as those made with steel. His study of cable design principles for this project was good preparation for his next assignment at Bell Labs' Atlanta facilities in 1974.

Bell researchers were experimenting with fiber optics. A key problem they faced was determining how much stress would be placed on the fibers (which were made of glass) during cable manufacture and installation. Without this information, the cables would function poorly or break outright. Cannon developed the mathematical equations necessary to predict the effects of physical force on the fibers. These equations allowed manufacturers to design cables that could be manufactured and installed without creating harmful stresses on the fibers. Another problem that Cannon helped solve was figuring out how to connect the hair-thin fibers without losing light energy at their junction. Cannon and his co-inventors came up with a solution, the ST Connector, which is the most widely manufactured optical connector in the world.

The first practical application of this was the experimental fiber optic lightwave system that was installed under the streets of Chicago in 1976. Cannon supervised the group that designed the cable terminators and optical connectors, and he actually went down manholes and did some of the splicing himself. On a different level, Cannon and his group also developed the Tactical Fiber Optic Cable (TOFC), which was the first optical connector certified by the military. The TOFC was used in Operation Desert Storm during the Gulf War to transmit firing signals to Patriot missiles.

Between 1989 and 1992, Cannon was on special assignment at Sandia National Laboratories. At Sandia, Cannon helped devise ways to improve the reliability and safety of nuclear devices by helping develop more effective means of arming nuclear devices. He also helped create a program that identified and evaluated methods for making hazardous sites more environmentally safe.

More recently, Cannon has led the development of new communication products and identifying potential markets for them. He has also been active in mentoring programs, particularly for young minority professionals, both at Bell Labs and at several universities including Purdue, the University of Michigan, and the Massachusetts Institute of Technology (MIT). He is the author of *Survival Routines for Professionals: Moving Toward Corporate Success* (1988).

Outside of work, Cannon coaches community youth basketball and baseball teams; he was selected as a torch bearer for the 1984 Olympics. Cannon married the former Joyce Elaine Stott in 1967; the couple has four sons.

SELECTED WRITINGS BY CANNON:

Books

Cannon, Thomas C. *Survival Routines for Professionals: Moving Toward Corporate Success.* Prentice-Hall, 1988.

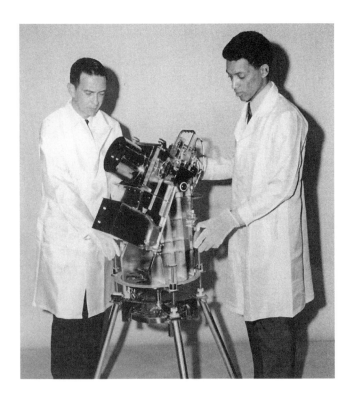

George R. Carruthers (right)

FURTHER READING:

Books

Van Sertima, Ivan, ed. *Blacks in Science, Ancient and Modern.* Journal of African Civilizations, Ltd., 1984.

—*Sketch by George A. Milite*

George R. Carruthers
1939-

Astrophysicist

George R. Carruthers is best known for his invention of a camera and spectrograph—imaging devices — which use ultraviolet light to capture images of both Earth and space from the surface of the moon. A team of engineers built a model according to his design for use during the *Apollo 16* mission in 1972, and the resulting photographs provided startling new evidence about ways to control pollution in the Earth's atmosphere and about the presence of hydrogen in deep space.

Carruthers was born on October 1, 1939, in Cincinnati, Ohio. At an early age he developed an interest in physics, which his father, a civil engineer, encouraged. Carruthers was also an avid science fiction reader and enjoyed constructing model rockets. He grew up on the South Side of Chicago, graduated from Englewood High School in 1957, and entered the College of Engineering at the University of Illinois. He earned a B.S. in physics in 1961 and a M.S. in 1962; in 1964 he earned his Ph.D. in aeronautical and astronautical engineering, with a thesis written on atomic nitrogen recombination. In 1964 he was awarded a National Science Foundation fellowship in rocket astronomy at the Naval Research Laboratory in Washington, D.C.

In 1966, Carruthers became a research assistant at the Navy's E. O. Hulburt Center for Space Research, and here he began the work that would occupy him for much of the next several decades: the development of imaging devices to elucidate the make up of deep space. In particular, he concentrated on ultraviolet imaging mechanisms and spectroscopy—the use of the color spectrum of substances to detect their constituent parts. In 1969, he patented an image converter for detecting electromagnetic radiation. He then invented the Far Ultraviolet Camera/Spectrograph, a device which would examine both the Earth's atmosphere and deep space from a location that would avoid the distortions created by Earth.

Carruthers's imaging device was designed in effect to use the moon as a deep-space observatory. It took several years for the idea to become reality, but by 1972 Carruthers's camera/spectrograph was constructed—a gold-plated instrument mounted on a tripod. Commander John W. Young carried the device aboard the *Apollo 16* mission and placed it on the surface of the moon. Over 200 pictures of the Earth's atmosphere and geocorona, as well as of the Milky Way and deep space, were taken from this lunar observatory. Much was learned about the Earth's atmosphere, including possible new ways to control air pollution. Most startling of all was the detection of hydrogen in deep space. This was evidence that plants are not the only source of Earth's oxygen, and the discovery also led to new thinking on the origins of stars. Carruthers' camera was also used on *Skylab 4,* when it observed Comet Kohoutek in 1974.

A private man, Carruthers devotes his life to his research and is characteristically low-key about his own contributions. Married in 1973, he has continued his work at the Naval Research Laboratory, developing a telescope to be used in space, as well as other photometric devices. A member of the American Astronomical Society and several other professional organizations, Carruthers won the Arthur S. Fleming Award in 1971, the Exceptional Achievement Scientific Award from NASA in 1972, the Warner Prize, and the National Civil Service League Exceptional Achievement Award.

SELECTED WRITINGS BY CARRUTHERS:

Periodicals

"Far-Ultraviolet Photography of Orion: Interstellar Dust," *Science,* (October 30, 1970): 527–531.

"*Apollo 16* Far-Ultraviolet Camera/Spectrograph: Earth Observations," *Science,* (September 1, 1972): 788–791.

"Sounding Rockets in Space Astronomy," *Sky and Telescope,* (October 1972): 218–221.

"Astronomy with the Space Shuttle," *Sky and Telescope,* (September 1974): 152–156.

"Far-Ultraviolet Rocket Survey of Orion," *Sky and Telescope,* (April 1977): 270–275.

"The Hydrogen Coma of Comet P-Halley Observed in Lyman Alpha Using Sounding Rockets," *Astronomy and Astrophysics,* (May 1992): 555–565.

FURTHER READING:

Books

Blacks in Science: Ancient and Modern. Transaction Books, 1984, pp. 258–262.

Carwell, Hattie. *Blacks in Science: Astrophysicist to Zoologist.* Exposition Press, 1977, pp. 13–14.

Sammons, Vivian Ovelton. *Blacks in Science and Medicine.* Hemisphere Publishing Corporation, 1990, p. 49.

Periodicals

"Earth's Eye on the Moon," *Ebony,* (October 1973): 61–63.

"Star Radiation Investigator," *Ebony,* (October 1970): 6.

—*Sketch by J. Sydney Jones*

George Washington Carver

George Washington Carver
1865-1943
Agricultural chemist

George Washington Carver, born in slavery and orphaned in infancy, rose to national and international fame as an agricultural scientist. Carver grew up and was educated in the northern states and later became a faculty member at the all-black Tuskegee Institute in Alabama, working in the forefront of the infant discipline of "scientific agriculture." Carver devised and promoted scores of uses for peanuts and sweet potatoes, and he had a significant effect on the diversification of southern agricultural practices. His testimony in 1921 before the House Ways and Means Committee achieved a tariff to protect the U.S. peanut industry and was the beginning of his identity as the peanut wizard. He also worked with hybrid cotton, conducted experiments in crop rotation and restoration of soil fertility, and developed useful products from Alabama red clay. Carver was a widely talented man who became an almost mythical American folk hero. He was deeply religious, explaining his wide-ranging interests as attempts to understand the work of the "Great Creator."

Carver was born near the end of the Civil War in Newton County, Missouri. His birth date is uncertain, although historian Linda O. McMurry suggests that he was likely born in the spring of 1865. His mother, Mary, was owned by Moses and Susan Carver, who were successful farmowners in the state. His father is believed to be a slave on a nearby plantation, and he was killed in an accident soon after Carver was born. His mother disappeared following a kidnapping by bushwhackers, and Carver and his brother were brought up by Moses and Susan. Carver was a frail and sickly child, and because of his weak health, he helped with the lighter tasks on the farm. He quickly mastered various household tasks, including cooking, laundering, canning, crocheting, needlework, as well as learning the alphabet and music. He also spent considerable time indulging his deep curiosity about nature, building a pond for his frog collection and keeping a little plant nursery in the woods. His talent with plants made him the neighborhood "plant doctor." At the nearby Locust Grove Church,

Carver heard a variety of Methodist, Baptist, Campbellite, and Presbyterian circuit preachers, and acquired a nondenominational faith.

Pursues an Education

In 1877 Carver left home for the county seat of Neosho, to attend a school for blacks. This was the beginning of a long journey through three states in pursuit of basic education. In these years he supported himself with odd jobs working for, and living with, various families along the way. In Neosho, he lived with a black couple, Andrew and Mariah Watkins, and helped with chores. He learned herbalism from Mariah, and he quickly recognized that his knowledge outstripped that of his teacher. In the late 1870s he hitched a ride to Fort Scott, Kansas, and moved in with the family of a blacksmith. Shortly thereafter he moved to Olathe, Kansas, where he made his home with another black couple, Ben and Lucy Seymour. He entered school, helped Lucy with her laundry business, and taught a class at the Methodist church. In the summer of 1880 he followed the Seymours to Minneapolis, where he established a laundry business and spent four years attending school. In 1884 he moved to Kansas City, acquired a typewriter, and took a job as a clerk at the Union Depot. His thirst for education continued, and he was accepted, by mail, into a small college in Highland, Kansas, only to be told when he arrived there that the college did not accept blacks. He stayed in Highland for a while, then moved to Ness County as a homesteader. On the frontier, Carver built a sod house, farmed, took his first art lessons, played accordion for local dances, and joined the literary society.

Around 1890 he sold his homestead and moved to Winterset, Iowa, where his talents and industry impressed a white couple, Dr. and Mrs. John Milholland. They persuaded him to enter Simpson College, a small Methodist College in Indianola. Carver quickly made friends on campus. He had intended to pursue art, but his art teacher, Etta Budd, encouraged him to consider a career in botany and suggested he enroll at the agricultural college at Ames, where her own father was a faculty member. The idea appealed to Carver; agriculture would allow him to be of service, and in 1891 he left for Ames and the Iowa State College of Agriculture and Mechanic Arts.

At Iowa, Carver was a popular student and active in a variety of campus affairs. During this time his painting entitled *Yucca and Cactus* was exhibited in Cedar Rapids and selected as an Iowa representative for the World's Columbian Exposition in Chicago in 1893. For his wide-ranging abilities, Carver was affectionately called "doctor" by the other students. His academic record was excellent, and his skills in raising, cross-fertilizing, and grafting plants were recognized by his professors. His bachelor's degree thesis, "Plants as Modified by Man," described the positive aspects of hybridization. He stayed on at Iowa for graduate work and was appointed an assistant in botany. Freed at last from odd jobs, Carver could now devote himself to greenhouse studies and teaching.

The Tuskegee Years

Carver received his master's degree from Iowa in 1896 and accepted a position at Tuskegee Institute, Alabama, at the invitation of its president, Booker T. Washington. He was to spend 47 years at Tuskegee, living most of that time in Rockefeller Hall, a dormitory occupied by students. The early years were difficult for Carver as he had numerous responsibilities at the institute. Besides heading the agriculture department, Carver was also director of the newly established Agricultural Experiment Station. Additionally, he managed the school's two farms, taught classes, and served on committees and councils. Despite all this, in 1910, unhappy with the number of agriculture graduates, Washington removed Carver from his charge of the Agriculture Department. Carver submitted his resignation, following which, Washington made him director of a new research department and "consulting chemist."

Experimental work was more to Carver's liking. From the beginning Carver had worked on a number of projects to help improve the lot of poor southern farmers. He analyzed water, feed, and soil. He experimented with paints that could be made with clay. He worked with organic fertilizers. He demonstrated uses for cheap and locally available materials, such as swamp muck. He searched for new, cheap foodstuffs to supplement the farmers' diets. In addition to human food items, he developed stock feeds, cosmetics, dyes, stains, medicines and ink from peanuts and sweet potatoes. In his agricultural bulletins, he offered elementary information to uneducated farmers.

In 1916 Carver received two prestigious invitations: to serve on the advisory board of the National Agricultural Society and to become a fellow of the Royal Society for the Arts in London. In 1919, under Tuskegee president Robert Russa Moton, he received his first salary increase in 20 years. He had become increasingly popular as a lecturer and his testimony before the House Ways and Means Committee in 1921 thrust him into the national limelight. In 1923 he was awarded the Spingarn Medal from the NAACP (National Association for the Advancement of Colored People) for his contributions to agricultural chemistry and for his lectures to religious, educational, and farming audiences that had "increased inter-racial knowledge and respect." Other honors included an honorary doctorate from Simpson College in 1928.

Becomes a Spokesman for "Chemurgy"

In the mid–1930s, the word *chemurgy* was coined to mean putting chemistry to work in industry for the farmer. Carver became a spokesman for chemurgy, just as he had been for the peanut industry and the "New South." In 1937 Carver met the industrialist Henry Ford at a chemurgy conference Ford had sponsored. A long friendship developed between the two men and when, in 1940, Carver established a foundation to continue and preserve his work, the Carver Museum in Tuskegee was dedicated by Ford.

The museum contained 71 of Carver's pictures as well as handicrafts, case studies, and results of his research.

Carver received numerous awards and honors for his contributions to the field of scientific agriculture. Noteworthy among these were the Roosevelt Medal, which he received in 1939, an honorary doctorate from the University of Rochester, and the first award for "outstanding service to the welfare of the South" from the Catholic Conference of the South. In 1942 Ford erected a Carver memorial cabin in Greenfield Village, Michigan, and established a nutritional laboratory in Carver's honor in Dearborn, Michigan. Carver also received an honorary doctorate from Selma University, a fellowship from the Thomas A. Edison Institute, and was a member of Kappa Delta Pi, an honorary education society.

Carver's health had begun to fail in the 1930s. When he died on January 5, 1943, Tuskegee Institute was flooded with letters of sympathy from many people. Carver was buried in the Tuskegee Institute cemetery near the grave of Booker T. Washington. On January 9, 1943, President Franklin D. Roosevelt paid tribute to Carver in an address before Congress, and on July 14, 1943, Roosevelt signed legislation making Carver's Missouri birthplace a national monument.

FURTHER READING:

Books

Elliott, Lawrence. *George Washington Carver: The Man Who Overcame.* Prentice Hall, 1966.

Graham, Shirley, and George D. Lipscomb. *Dr. George Washington Carver: Scientist.* Julian Messner, 1944.

Holt, Rackham. *George Washington Carver: An American Biography.* Doubleday, 1943.

Kremer, Gary R., ed. *George Washington Carver: In His Own Words.* University of Missouri Press, 1987.

McMurry, Linda O. *George Washington Carver: Scientist and Symbol.* Oxford University Press, 1981.

Periodicals

McMurry, Linda O. "Dr. Carver Is Dead: Negro Scientist," *New York Times,* (January 6, 1943): 25.

Mackintosh, Barry. "George Washington Carver: The Making of a Myth," *Journal of Southern History,* (November, 1976): 507–28.

—Sketch by Jill Carpenter

Vivian Murray Chambers
1903-1984
Entomologist

The potential dangers of pesticides, such as DDT, to the environment were initially viewed as minimal compared with their effectiveness against destructive insects. Vivian Murray Chambers was one of the first individuals to question the true ecological costs of using pesticides indiscriminately. His research showed how pesticide residue could run off into nearby lakes and rivers; later research determined that this runoff could cause possibly irreversible damage.

Chambers was also a noted educator with a long and distinguished career at Alabama A & M University in Huntsville. He was the founder and first dean of Alabama A & M's School of Arts and Sciences.

Early Life

Vivian Murray Chambers was born in Salisbury, North Carolina, on June 4, 1903, the third child of Will and Fannie Campbell Chambers. Will Chambers died when Vivian was an infant, and Fannie, a seamstress, supported herself and her three young children. She instilled in her children a strong sense of values, particularly the importance of hard work. Young Vivian was eight years old when he started his first job—lighting fires for neighbors' coal furnaces.

Fannie Chambers also placed a high value on education, and her children worked hard in school. After she married the Rev. W. H. Howard, the family moved to a larger house in Salisbury, close to the campus of Livingstone College. By now young Chambers had shown a definite interest in science, and living near the college gave him the opportunity to meet professors and other students. "All during the time Vivian was growing up he had good role models," his widow, Mary McCray Chambers, said in an April 1998 interview with contributor George Milite.

Beginnings of a Career

Chambers chose Shaw University in Raleigh for his undergraduate work. He excelled both as a student and as a football player. He graduated in 1928 with B.S. and returned briefly to North Carolina, where he taught high school and coached football. He then went to New York, where he attended Columbia University (from which he received a B.A. in 1931). During the Great Depression, Chambers held a position under the Works Progress Administration (WPA) as a researcher at the American Museum of Natural History. Initially, the museum had turned down his application, claiming he had no laboratory experience. But Chambers had gotten extensive lab experience while at Shaw, and he made it clear that he was qualified for the job being offered.

Through no small degree of perseverance, he succeeded in getting the museum post.

It was at the American Museum of Natural History that Chambers developed his interest in entomology. Until them, his primary interest had been medicine. But he was fascinated by the insects he studied, and he decided to pursue an entomological career.

He was accepted at Cornell, but found it nearly impossible to get into the entomology department. The department chair simply did not want to let him in. Chambers found out the reason: an earlier black student in the program had done poorly, and the chair had decided not to admit any more blacks. Once again, however, Chambers persevered, and he got his master's from Cornell in 1935. Afterwards, he taught science at the Lincoln Normal School in Alabama. In 1937 he began his long association with Alabama A & M University, teaching in the biology department. One of his students was Mary McCray, who became his wife in 1941.

Chambers returned to Cornell to earn his Ph.D. While there, he boarded at the home of Cornell president Edmund E. Day, who took a liking to him and introduced him to a number of influential people. Chambers' thesis was in "economic entomology"—the cost factors involved in pest control, for example.

Research Yields Important Findings

Chambers chose as his dissertation topic the environmental effects of the pesticide DDT. His research focused on DDT sprayings similar to those done at government installations in Alabama, along the Tennessee River (a tributary of the Mississippi). His research confirmed that the spray residue could run off into nearby bodies of water and have an adverse impact on the ecological balance. Up until then, farmers and others who used potent pesticides gave little thought to their overall impact on the environment. However, while pest control was important in the short term, it was essential that the long-range effects of the pesticides would not do more harm than good.

Upon successful completion of his Ph.D. in 1945, Chambers returned to Alabama A & M as a professor of biology. He was the first black to earn a Ph.D. from Cornell's entomology program, and the first Alabama A & M faculty member besides the university president to hold a doctorate. A year later his daughter, Vivian Marie, was born. (Not surprisingly, she shared her parents' interest in science and today is a physician.)

Chambers earned a reputation as a first-rate scientist and as an educator during his years at Alabama A & M. Thanks to his experience at the American Museum of Natural History, he was an expert in preparing entomological specimens—a skill he taught many students. In later years, he worked to establish the university's arts and sciences division. The School of Arts and Sciences was officially opened in 1970, and Chambers served as its first dean.

Upon his retirement in 1973, Chambers continued to remain active within the university community (his home, where Mary Chambers still lives, is across the street from the school). He also took more time to indulge in photography, which had been a longtime avocation. Vivian Chambers died on February 23, 1984, in Huntsville. The Chambers Science Building on the Alabama A&M campus is named in his honor.

SELECTED WRITINGS BY CHAMBERS:

The papers of Vivian Murray Chambers are primarily held by his wife, Mary McCray Chambers, who can be contacted through Alabama A & M University.

FURTHER READING:

Books

Sammons, Vivian O. *Blacks in Science and Education.* Washington, D.C.: Hemisphere Publications, 1989.
Taylor, Julius, ed. *The Negro in Science.* Baltimore: Morgan State College Press, 1955.

—Sketch by George A. Milite

Emmett W. Chappelle
1925-
Biochemist

With at least 13 patents to his credit, Emmett W. Chappelle has made significant findings in several fields within biology and chemistry. Perhaps his most important contribution was the discovery that a readily available combination of chemicals can make living organisms emit light, a quality called bioluminescence. He developed this idea originally to test for life on Mars. Chappelle's other interests include iron metabolism in mammalian body systems, methods for the quantitative analysis of proteins and amino acids (the building blocks of proteins), the utilization of carbon monoxide in green plants, interstellar molecules, and the analysis of large tracts of land using the spectrum emitted by its plant life.

Chappelle was born on October 24, 1925, in Phoenix, Arizona. He grew up in poverty, beginning his education in a one-room school. Chappelle attended a segregated high school in Phoenix, graduating first in his small class in 1942. Upon graduation, Chappelle was drafted into the

Emmett W. Chappelle

United States Army and fought in Europe during World War II. He returned to Phoenix in 1946 and entered Phoenix College's two-year program in electrical engineering. Chappelle graduated with his associate of arts degree in 1947. Soon after, he married Rosemary Phillips, his childhood sweetheart; they eventually had four children together. Using funding from the GI Bill, Chappelle entered the University of California, Berkeley in the fall of 1947, intending to continue his engineering studies.

While at Berkeley, Chappelle found his interests shifting from engineering to biology. He eventually changed his major, earning his bachelor's degree in biology in 1950. After graduation, Chappelle spent two years in Nashville, Tennessee, at Meharry Medical College, where he was an instructor in biochemistry for nursing students. While at Meharry, Chappelle also did research of his own, including two studies using radioactive iron. He studied how red blood cells work, focusing on how they recycle iron. Chappelle measured levels of the radioactive iron in various organs and fluids to chart that process. Similarly, Chappelle studied anaphylactic shock, an extreme and sometimes fatal allergic reaction. By using radioactive iron and measuring its levels in various parts of the body, he determined that the body releases a chemical during anaphylactic shock and that this chemical causes the lungs' air tubes to contract and restricts the ability to breathe. Chappelle's work drew the attention of graduate schools, and he moved his family to Seattle, where he attended the University of Washington.

While a graduate student, Chappelle continued to do original research. He studied the amino acids that, when linked, can form proteins. He found that when certain enzymes (biochemical catalysts) are introduced, an amino acid can regenerate into a different amino acid all together. Chappelle was awarded his master's degree in 1954 and accepted an offer to do his doctoral work at Stanford University. At Stanford, he also worked as a research associate in the chemistry department, from 1955-58. He continued to research amino acids, discovering glycine, a key enzyme for amino acid production in both plants and animals. Chappelle also showed that glycine is exactly the same in both plants and animals and could be interchanged.

At Stanford, Chappelle made another important discovery, that of a chemical that can predictably split protein molecule chains by clipping the amino acids found at the ends of the chain. The clipped acids can be converted to another molecule type called aldehydes and used in other studies. Though Chappelle did not receive a degree, he decided to leave Stanford in 1958 and join the private sector. He was hired by the Research Institute of Advanced Studies, a part of the Martin Marrietta Corporation, which designs both aircraft and spacecraft. While at the Research Institute in Baltimore, Maryland, Martin worked on using plants to ensure a safe air supply for astronauts. He determined that even one-celled plants can absorb enough carbon monoxide to make the air safe on a spacecraft. In 1963, Chappelle left the Research Institute to work for Hazelton Laboratories in Falls Church, Virginia.

From 1963-66, Chappelle worked as a biochemist at Hazelton Laboratories, which had a number of research contracts with National Aeronautics and Space Administration (NASA), including one to develop a method to determine if there was life on Mars. Chappelle helped design instruments for *Viking,* the spacecraft that would land on Mars, including an instrument that would collect soil samples. Chappelle came up with a way to test the soil for life by using three chemicals, one found in all living creatures and the other two extracted from fireflies. When mixed with soil containing any life, the chemical combination emits light. Chappelle's test was not used when *Viking* was launched in 1975, but he used the basic idea in other areas of his research, including counting cells.

In 1966, Chappelle took a position at NASA's Goddard Space Flight Center, where he continued to use the light-emission idea. He applied the concept to a method for detecting drinking-water bacteria. He also used it to establish which parts of a farmer's field are growing the fastest. The faster crops grow, the more light they emit. Each plant also has a slightly different color, so a picture taken from space can show crop productivity. Chappelle also discovered that applying lasers can make cells produce more light, allowing for more accurate measurements. Other light sources can also be used. One such study of his concerned red spruce trees, and he made a correlation between acid rain damage and chlorophyll's fluorescence spectrum.

In addition to his numerous research studies, Chappelle worked from 1973-74 as a consultant for the Applied

Magnetics Corporation. From 1975-77, Chappelle held a fellowship sponsored by NASA at Johns Hopkins University. During this period, he was unsuccessful in developing a test for the early signs of cancer. After the fellowship ended, Chappelle returned to his work with plants and light, helping the U.S. Department of Agriculture develop tests to improve food production by determining when crops need fertilizer and water. Chappelle is a member of the American Chemical Society, the New York Academy of Science, and the American Society of Photobiology.

FURTHER READING:

Books

Kessler, J.H., et al. *Distinguished African American Scientists of the 20th Century.* Phoenix, AZ: Oryx Press, 1996.
Sammons, Vivian Ovelton. *Blacks in Science and Medicine.* New York: Hemisphere Publishing, 1990.

Periodicals

Ebony. (November 1961): 7.
"Fireflies' Light Gains New Uses in Medical and Technical Research." *The New York Times* (August 25, 1975): 25.

—*Sketch by A. Petrusso*

Kenneth Bancroft Clark
1914-
Psychologist

Many psychologists have made history within their profession; few, however, have had an impact on the laws of a nation. Such was the case with Kenneth Bancroft Clark, whose work the Supreme Court cited in its historic *Brown v. Board of Education* ruling. In the 1954 case, which overturned racial segregation in public schools, the Court referred to a 1950 paper by Clark, and described him as a "modern authority" on the psychological effects of segregation. His recognition by the highest court in the land made Clark an instant celebrity, and on the heels of this success, he set out to develop a prototype community action program for young people in Harlem in 1962. However, political workings brought an early end to his vision. Disillusioned by this experience, Clark penned the most well-known of his many books, *Dark Ghetto: Dilemmas of*

Kenneth Bancroft Clark

Social Power (1965), which would become an important text for sociologists studying inner-city life in America.

A World of Opportunities in Harlem

Clark was born on July 24, 1914, in the Panama Canal Zone. His father, Arthur Bancroft Clark, had come from the West Indies and worked as a cargo superintendent for the United Fruit Company, a major employer in Central America at that time. Clark's mother, Miriam Hanson Clark, was from Jamaica, and she and his father disagreed over their children's upbringing. Miriam wanted to move the family to the United States, where Kenneth and his younger sister Beulah would have greater educational and career opportunities than they would in Panama. But the father refused to go with them. He had a good position at United Fruit, and under the harsh racism and segregation that prevailed even in the northern United States at that time, he did not believe he could obtain a similar job in America. Therefore Miriam and her two children boarded a boat for New York harbor, leaving the children's father behind.

In New York City, Miriam got a job as a seamstress in the New York garment district, and the family settled in Harlem. At that time Harlem was a mixed community, and besides other black families, the Clarks found themselves living alongside Irish and Jewish neighbors. This experience undoubtedly had an effect on Clark's later commitment to integrated education. In school, he told the *New Yorker* magazine in 1982, all students were expected to excel, regardless of skin color: "When I went to the board in Mr.

Ruprecht's algebra class," he recalled, " . . . I had to do those equations, and if I wasn't able to do them he wanted to find out why. He didn't expect any less of me because I was black."

In spite of this positive educational environment, the rest of the world was filled with people who had low expectations for black students. Hence when Clark finished junior high and had to choose a high school, counselors urged him to enroll in a vocational school. In spite of his strong academic record, he was black, and therefore he could only hope to gain employment in a limited range of jobs, all of which involved working with one's hands. That, at least, was the logic, and to many people it would have made sense—but not to Miriam Clark. When her son told her what the school counselor had suggested, she went to the counselor's office and informed him that she had not struggled to bring her family from Panama so that her son could become a factory worker.

She enrolled Kenneth in George Washington High School, an academic school where he performed well in all subjects. He was particularly interested in economics, and had begun to consider becoming an economist. But when he earned an award for his outstanding performance in the class, the teacher refused to give it to him. This example of racial discrimination, Clark's first clear-cut experience with it, would have enormous impact on his life. Because of it, he decided not to study economics, and it may have led to his lifelong interest in the psychology of racism.

Meetings with Remarkable Men—And a Woman

Clark had not yet decided to become a psychologist; in fact, when he entered Washington, D.C.'s Howard University in 1931, he planned to study medicine. But in his sophomore year, he took a psychology course taught by Professor Frances Sumner. Sumner's method of psychological study, Clark recalled in his 1982 *New Yorker* interview, offered "the promise of . . . systematic understanding of the complexities of human behavior and human interaction"— including insight into "the seemingly intractable nature of racism." Intrigued, Clark switched his major to psychology. Another professor at Howard who had an influence on Clark was Ralph Bunche. Bunche, who would later gain fame as a diplomat and winner of the Nobel Peace Prize in 1950, taught Clark in several political science courses.

After graduating in 1935, Clark went on to obtain his M.S. in psychology the next year, then accepted a teaching position at Howard. But Sumner, recognizing his great potential, encouraged him to obtain his doctorate at Columbia University. Therefore Clark returned to New York City and enrolled in the doctoral program at Columbia. On April 14, 1938, he married Mamie Phipps, a psychology student from Arkansas whom he had met at Howard. The couple would eventually have two children, Kate Miriam and Hilton. Clark, the first black doctoral candidate in Columbia's psychology program, earned his Ph.D. degree in 1940.

For a short period of time, Clark taught at Hampton Institute in Virginia, an old and highly conservative black college. But Clark had strong differences of opinion with the administration at Hampton, and resigned after one semester. From 1941 to 1942, Clark worked for the federal government's Office of War Information, studying morale conditions of America's black population as the country entered World War II. In 1942, he accepted a position as an instructor at City College of New York (CCNY), and in 1949 became an assistant professor.

Clark and his mentor Bunche had worked together on research for renowned Swedish economist Gunnar Myrdal, another future Nobel laureate. Myrdal's study of conditions among African Americans in the United States would be published in 1944 as *An American Dilemma: The Negro Problem and Modern Democracy*. But his work with Bunche and Myrdal would not prove to be the most significant collaboration of Clark's career; his most important partner was closer to home, in the person of his wife Mamie.

The Rising Young Social Scientist

In 1946, the Clarks established the Northside Testing and Consultation Center in Harlem. In time this would become the Northside Center for Child Development, and the name change reflected a shift of emphasis. In the course of their research and therapy for troubled black youngsters, the Clarks had discovered evidence that racism helped to create a pervasive negative self-image. For instance, when given a choice between a brown doll and a white one and told "Give me the doll that looks bad," black children would usually choose the brown doll; told to point out "the doll that is a nice color," they would select the white one.

The Clarks had been conducting such studies for some time. Between 1939 and 1950, they published five articles on the effect that segregated schooling had on kindergartners in Washington, D.C. For the Midcentury White House Conference on Children and Youth in 1950, Clark wrote another article that summed up his and Mamie's research, as well as the work of other social scientists who had studied the psychological effects of segregation.

Up to that time, the law of the land regarding segregated schooling had been governed by the Supreme Court's decision in *Plessy v. Ferguson* (1896). In that case, the Court held that the establishment of separate schools for blacks and whites—as long as the schools were of equal quality—did not violate the concept of equal protection under the law guaranteed by the Fourteenth Amendment to the Constitution. In practice, of course, schools for blacks were certainly separate, but rarely equal. Furthermore, Clark's research had shown that even if they *were* equal in quality, the very fact of enforced separation created an inherent inequity.

When the National Association for the Advancement of Colored People (NAACP) began to challenge institutionalized segregation in the nation's courts, the organization turned to Clark. In three of the four cases that led to the Supreme Court's review of the segregation issue, Clark testified as an expert witness. When the case went before the Supreme Court, the NAACP presented a special paper, prepared by Clark and others, called "The Effects of Segregation and the Consequences of Desegregation: A Social Science Statement." It was the first time in American legal history that a brief prepared by a social scientist, illustrating the human consequences of a law in terms of its social and psychological impact, had been presented before the Supreme Court.

In its ruling on *Brown v. Board of Education,* the historic 1954 case which struck down institutionalized segregation, the Court cited Clark's work as valuable evidence. More important, it reiterated the theme he had presented as the evidence mounted from his studies: "Separate educational facilities are inherently unequal."

Highs and Lows, Disappointment and Hope

On the heels of the May 17, 1954, Supreme Court decision, Clark became a celebrity in the community of social scientists. He was feted and honored at universities around the country, bestowed with honorary degrees and described in glowing terms by his colleagues. A generation later, three young graduate students writing in the *Journal of Applied Behavioral Science* would sum up the extent of his reputation: "We approached our telephone interview with Dr. Kenneth Clark with awe. After all, his contribution to U.S. history had enabled our own education to occur in an integrated society."

For the next decade, Clark went from triumph to triumph. In 1960, CCNY made him a full professor, and he thus became the first African American awarded a permanent position at any of New York's city colleges. The next year, the NAACP gave him its Spingarn Award for his contributions to race relations. With the support of the federal government, Clark in June 1962 established Harlem Youth Opportunities Unlimited, or HARYOU. With HARYOU, he planned to reorganize the schools of Harlem by integrating classes, enforcing higher standards on teachers, and involving members of the community—especially parents—in the education of its young people. It was to be the prototype for the sort of community-action programs which come into increasing prominence in the 1980s and 1990s.

HARYOU outlined these principles in a 620-page report, which took two years to prepare; unfortunately, as Clark would later say in his *New Yorker* profile, "As it turned out, all we did at HARYOU was to produce a document." Clark's dream for the organization would never become a reality, and his opposition came not from white racists but from a black politician. The federal government in May 1964 allocated $110 million for the program, and arranged a merger of HARYOU with Associated Community Teams (ACT), a group in which Democratic Congressman Adam Clayton Powell had a hand. Clark and Powell disagreed over who should lead the program, and when

Clark accused Powell of trying to take it over for political purposes, Powell claimed that Clark was profiting financially from the program. In disgust, Clark resigned from the organization on July 31, 1964.

As a result of his disappointing experience, Clark wrote *Dark Ghetto,* which would become the most well-known of his more than 16 books. In 1967 he formed the Metropolitan Applied Research Center, or MARC, with a group of other social scientists. Three years later, in 1970, MARC attempted to resurrect a program similar to that of HARYOU, this time in Washington, D.C. Yet again, however, power politics defeated Clark's dream. Teachers' unions rejected Clark's attempts to hold educators to higher standards, and the city school board chairman disagreed with Clark's central idea that black children should be expected to do as well in school as their white counterparts. To add to his misfortunes, in the late 1960s, Clark was subjected to scorn by black militants who rejected his integrationist approach.

Just as the decade leading up to the HARYOU debacle had been characterized by triumphs, the decade that followed had proven to be one of disappointments. In 1975, Clark retired from teaching and with his wife and children founded Clark, Phipps, Clark & Harris, Inc., a consulting firm that assisted corporations such as AT&T in setting up affirmative action programs. Clark continued with this work after he lost his most important partner, Mamie, when she died in 1983.

Meanwhile, the idealist who had dreamed of fully integrated schools watched with disappointment as society became more segregated. This time the segregation was not a matter of law, but of choice, and the growing gap between the performance of black students and those in the mainstream only threatened to increase the division. But Clark managed to retain his hope that society could make a change. The key, as he wrote in *Newsweek* in 1993, was to teach genuine respect for humankind: "We have not yet made education a process whereby students are taught to respect the inalienable dignity of other human beings. . . . [But] by encouraging and rewarding empathetic behavior in all of our children. . . . [w]e will be helping them to understand the commonality of being human. We will be *educating* them."

SELECTED WRITINGS BY CLARK:

Books

Prejudice and Your Child. Beacon Press, 1955.
Dark Ghetto: Dilemmas of Social Power. Foreword by Gunnar Myrdal, Harper, 1965.
(With Jeannette Hopkins) *A Relevant War Against Poverty: A Study of Community Action Programs and Observable Change.* Harper, 1969.
The Pathos of Power. Harper, 1974.

Periodicals

(With Mamie Clark) "The Development of Consciousness of Self and the Emergence of Racial Identification in Negro Preschool Children," *Journal of Social Psychology* 10 (1939).

"Desegregation: An Appraisal of the Evidence," *Journal of Social Issues* 9, no. 4 (1953).

"The Pathos of Power: A Psychological Perspective," *American Psychologist* 26 (1971).

"The Social Sciences and the Courts," *Social Policy* 17, no. 1 (1986).

"Unfinished Business: The Toll of Psychic Violence," *Newsweek,* (January 11, 1993).

FURTHER READING:

Books

Bigelow, Barbara Carlisle, ed. *Contemporary Black Biography,* Volume 5. Detroit: Gale, 1994, pp. 51-55.

Contemporary Authors, Volume 36. Detroit: Gale, 1978.

Keppel, Ben. *The Work of Democracy: Ralph Bunche, Kenneth B. Clark, Lorraine Hansberry, and the Cultural Politics of Race.* Harvard University Press, 1995.

Markowitz, Gerald and Rosner, David. *Children, Race, and Power: Kenneth and Mamie Clark's Northside Center.* University Press of Virginia, 1996.

McGuire, William and Wheeler, Leslie. *American Social Leaders.* ABC-Clio, 1993, pp. 99-100.

Sammons, Vivian Ovelton. *Blacks in Science and Medicine.* Hemisphere Publishing, 1990.

Young, Margaret. *Black American Leaders.* Watts, 1969, pp. 28-30.

Periodicals

Guthrie, Robert V. *Even the Rat Was White,* Harper's (1976): 150-1

Hentoff, N. "Profiles," *New Yorker,* (August 23, 1982): 37-40.

Latting, Jean Kantambu et al., "Dr. Kenneth Bancroft Clark: A Biography," *Journal of Applied Behavioral Sciences,* (September 1991): 263-64.

"Light in the Ghetto," *Newsweek,* (May 31, 1965): 78.

"10 Forces Behind U.S. Education," *Scholastic Update,* (February 3, 1984): 9.

Willie, C.V., "Five Black Scholars," *Change,* (September 1983): 27.

—Sketch by Judson Knight

Jewel Plummer Cobb

Jewel Plummer Cobb
1924-
Cell biologist

Jewel Plummer Cobb is known for her contributions to the field of cell biology and for promoting minority involvement in the sciences. She has focused much of her research on melanin, a brown or black skin pigment, and the factors that affect the causes and growth of normal and cancerous pigment cells. Her research into the effects of drugs on cancer cells was important to future work in the field of chemotherapy. As an educator, Cobb initiated a number of programs to encourage ethnic minorities and women in the sciences.

Born in Chicago on January 17, 1924, Cobb was the only child of Frank V. Plummer, a doctor and graduate of Cornell University, and Carriebel (Cole) Plummer, who taught dance in public schools and participated in the Works Projects Administration (WPA) efforts. Cobb's family had a history in the sciences: not only was her father a doctor, but her paternal grandfather was a pharmacist who had graduated from Howard University in 1898.

As an upper-middle-class African American, Cobb was exposed to a variety of African American professionals through her parents, all accomplished in their fields. She also socialized with well-off peers during her summers at a northern Michigan resort. Although the schools in Chicago were largely segregated, Cobb received a solid public school education, bolstered by her exposure to her father's library at home. Her interest in biology was sparked in her sophomore year by her first look through the lens of a microscope.

A member of her high school's honor society, Cobb attended the University of Michigan after graduation. She was drawn there partly by the knowledge that some of her summer friends would be there and by the university's nationally known football team. The segregation she had experienced in public schools continued in college, however: all the African American students had to live in one house. After three semesters at Michigan, Cobb transferred to Alabama's Talladega College, and in 1944 she graduated with a bachelor of arts degree in biology. She then accepted a teaching fellowship at New York University, which had at first turned her down. Her poise and credentials finally tipped the scales in her favor. She maintained her fellowship for five years and undertook graduate studies in cell physiology.

Pursues Career as Cell Biologist

By 1950 Cobb had completed her master's degree and doctorate. Because she enjoyed research and a theoretical approach to biology, Cobb decided to become a cell biologist. As a cell biologist, her focus was the action and interaction of living cells. She was particularly interested in tissue culture, in which cells are grown outside of the body and studied under microscopes. Among her most important work was her study with Dorothy Walker Jones of how new cancer-fighting drugs affected human cancer cells.

As a researcher, Cobb has held a series of positions at various colleges and research facilities throughout the United States. She was a fellow at the National Cancer Institute for two years after receiving her doctorate, and from 1952 to 1954 she was the director of the Tissue Culture Laboratory at the University of Illinois. At the end of this period Cobb married, and in 1957 she and her husband had a son, Roy Jonathan Cobb. After leaving Illinois, Cobb worked at several universities, including New York University and Hunter College in New York, and in 1960 she was appointed professor of biology at Sarah Lawrence College. There Cobb taught and continued her research into skin pigment. She was particularly interested in melanoma, or skin cancer, and melanin's ability to protect skin from damage caused by ultraviolet light.

Establishes Programs for Minority Students

In 1969, two years after she and her husband divorced, Cobb was appointed dean of Connecticut College and professor of zoology. In addition to teaching and continuing her research, she established a privately funded premedical graduate program and a pre-dental program for minority students. Numerous other colleges used these programs as models for their own, but after she left in 1976, the programs at Connecticut were discontinued. From 1976 to 1981 Cobb served as dean and professor of biological sciences at Douglass College. Although she had to give up her research in order to fulfill her administrative and teaching obligations, she continued to press for the advancement of minorities and women in the sciences.

Cobb wrote about the difficulties women face in scientific fields in a 1979 paper, "Filters for Women in Science," published in the book *Expanding the Role of Women in the Sciences,* which was edited by Anne M. Briscoe and Sheila M. Pfafflin. In this piece, Cobb argued that various pressures, particularly in the educational system, act as filters that prevent many women from choosing science careers. The socialization of girls has tended to discourage them from pursuing math and the sciences from a very early age, and even those women who got past such obstacles have struggled to get university tenure and the same jobs (at equal pay) as men.

In 1981 Cobb was named president at California State University (CSU) in Fullerton. She was extremely active in initiating improvements for the campus, notably in obtaining state funding for a new engineering and computer science building and a new science building. In addition, she built an apartment complex for students (later named in her honor), ending the university's years as a commuter campus, and established the president's opportunity program for ethnic students. Her work also extended to the community, for which she founded a privately funded gerontology center.

Cobb became a trustee professor at California State College in Los Angeles in 1990, and in 1991 she was made principal investigator for Southern California Science and Engineering ACCESS Center and Network. A trustee of several colleges, with numerous honorary degrees, Cobb worked with a consortium of six colleges to raise private funds to replace diminishing government grants and fellowships for minorities in science and engineering. The group worked to motivate minorities in the sciences, to bring more of them into the field. Over the years, Cobb had become increasingly aware of the disparity between the number of black men in sports and those in the lab, for instance. As part of her group's effort, faculty members tutored students on an individual basis in order to solidify their math skills, which Cobb felt were a crucial foundation for a career in the sciences. President emeritus of CSU since 1990, Cobb continues to use her skill as an educator, administrator, and scientist to promote the educational needs and careers of minorities in the sciences.

SELECTED WRITINGS BY COBB:

Periodicals

"Studies on Human Melanoma Cells in Tissue Cultures. I. Growth Characteristics and Cytology," *Cancer Research,* Vol. 20, (1960): 858–67.

"Cytologic Studies on Human Melanoma Cells in Tissue Culture after Exposure to Five Chemotherapeutic Agents," *Cancer Chemotherapy Reports,* Vol. 51, (1968): 543–52.

"I Am Woman, Black, Educated," *Hartford Courant Sunday Supplement,* (February 4, 1973).

"Filters for Women in Science," *Expanding the Role of Women in the Sciences,* ed. by Anne M. Briscoe and Sheila M. Pfafflin, New York Academy of Sciences, 1979, pp. 236–48.

"The Role of Women Presidents/Chancellors in Intercollegiate Athletics," *Women at the Helm,* ed. by J. A. Sturnick, J. E. Milley, and C. A. Tisinger, AASCU Press, 1991, pp. 42–50.

FURTHER READING:

Books

Hine, Darlene Clark, ed. *Black Women in America: An Historical Encyclopedia.* Carlson Publishing Inc., 1993, pp. 257–58.

Notable Black American Women. Gale, 1992, pp. 195–98.

—*Sketch by Geeta Kothari*

William Montague Cobb

William Montague Cobb
1904-1990
Anatomist

As an educator, scientist, and civic activist, William Montague Cobb devoted his career to the advancement of African Americans. He taught anatomy to medical and dental students at Howard University over the course of more than 40 years, and he fought for the integration of hospitals and medical societies to provide opportunities for his students when they graduated. He is also considered an important historian of African Americans in medicine, and he often used his scientific knowledge to argue against racist characterizations. Active in many professional societies and civil rights organizations, Cobb was recognized both as a scholar and an aggressive proponent of justice. He is quoted in *New Directions* as saying, "I'm a seasoned fighter and the battle never bothered me."

Cobb was a lifelong resident of Washington, D.C., except for a few years spent in college and graduate school. He was born there October 12, 1904, the son of William Elmer and Alexzine Montague Cobb. His father was a printer who had moved to Washington from Selma, Alabama, in 1899 to work for the Government Printing Office; he later opened his own printing shop. Cobb attended segregated Patterson Elementary School and Dunbar High School in Washington. Dunbar was famous for the high quality of its teaching staff and curriculum, and its many notable alumni. He graduated from Dunbar in 1921 and enrolled in Amherst College in Massachusetts. At Amherst, Cobb distinguished himself in scholarship and athletics. He won the Blodgett Scholarship as the outstanding biology student in his class, which allowed him to study embryology the summer after graduation at the Marine Biological Laboratory at Woods Hole, Massachusetts. He was also a successful athlete, winning the intramural cross-country championships three times and boxing championships twice.

Cobb's career in medical science began in 1925, after he graduated from Amherst and enrolled in the College of Medicine at Howard University in Washington. When he was a senior, he was invited to teach a course in embryology, as a result of his summer at Woods Hole, and it was because of this experience that he decided that he would prefer to teach medical science than to practice medicine. After graduation in 1929, he completed his internship at Freedmen's Hospital (now Howard University Hospital), and left to study anatomy and physical anthropology at Western Reserve (now Case Western) University in Cleveland. His dissertation advisor at Western Reserve was Thomas Wingate Todd, who had collected a large number of human and mammalian skeletons for the university's Hamann Museum of Comparative Anthropology and Anatomy, which inspired Cobb's own collections later at Howard University. Cobb's investigations of skeletons of different races convinced him of the erroneous and worthless arguments of white supremacists who contended that African Americans were mentally inferior, supposedly based on anatomical studies. He published his observations and conclusions in a number of professional journals and in popular magazines. He later analyzed x-ray photographs of Olympic champions of 1936 to show that there were no fundamental differences in bone structure between black and white runners.

Cobb received his Ph.D. in 1932 and returned to Howard as an assistant professor of anatomy in the medical school; he was promoted to associate professor in 1934 and professor in 1942. In 1947 he was appointed head of the anatomy department, a position which he held for 22 years. As an educator, Cobb was innovative and inspiring. His unique personality made his anatomy classes memorable. He interjected quotations from the Bible, William Shakespeare, and classic literature into his lectures. He imitated the movements of the embryo in the womb and occasionally played his violin during dissections in the anatomy laboratory in order to help the students relax. He assembled a varied collection of more than 600 human skeletons, used slides and motion pictures which he produced himself in his courses, and developed a graphic method of teaching anatomy through student drawings. Although 6000 students received anatomy instruction from Cobb, in 1969 many complained that his course was outdated and did not cover the material on licensing examinations. A struggle ensued, with the students demanding that Cobb relinquish the chair, and the university administration eventually removed Cobb from his post. However, he was immediately appointed the university's first Distinguished Professor, a position in which he remained until retiring in 1973.

Cobb served in a variety of scientific, medical, and civic organizations, and made distinguished contributions to all of them. He was president of the Anthropological Society of Washington and the American Association of Physical Anthropologists, and was council member, vice-president, and chair of Anthropology of the American Association for the Advancement of Science (AAAS). Cobb vigorously opposed the AAAS convention site of Atlanta in 1955, because of the segregated facilities in that city. He refused to attend the meeting when it was held there, and his pressure led to the adoption in 1956 of an antisegregation policy for future meetings. Cobb was able to obtain the same kind of policy for the American Association of Anatomists in 1958.

Cobb was prominent in several medical associations, particularly those whose members were African American. As president of the Medico-Chirurgical Society of the District of Columbia, he successfully fought for the admission of black physicians to the present D.C. General Hospital in 1948, and to the Medical Society of the District of Columbia in 1952. He served the National Medical Association as editor of its journal from 1949 to 1977 and as its president in 1964. He is credited with changing the

Journal of the National Medical Association from a modest house organ to an influential medical periodical. He published numerous editorials and articles in this journal, many about the history of medicine, especially biographies of black physicians. He is quoted in *Modern Medicine* as saying, "Negro physicians . . . have contributed to the health care of the American populace under handicaps which no other segment of the population has had to suffer." When he was president of the National Medical Association, he testified in Congress in support of Medicare, the only representative of a medical association who actually endorsed the proposed legislation. He was a guest of President Lyndon B. Johnson's the signing of the bill.

For many years, Cobb was active in the National Association for the Advancement of Colored People (NAACP). In 1946, on behalf of the NAACP, he wrote "Medical Care and the Plight of the Negro" and "Progress and Portents for the Negro in Medicine" in support of government financed health care. He served on the board of directors for many years, and was national president from 1976 to 1982. The latter position gave Cobb the opportunity to speak on contemporary issues to a wide audience.

In 1929, Cobb married Hilda B. Smith, who taught in the Washington schools for over 40 years. They had two daughters and four grandchildren. Cobb had a wide circle of friends in the medical community and at Howard University, with whom he spent many pleasant hours. He enjoyed playing the violin and reading. When he was 77 years old, he made his debut as an actor at the Kennedy Center, playing the role of W. E. B. Du Bois in a production directed by his daughter. Near the end of his active and rewarding life, Cobb was quoted in *New Directions* as saying, "When I go down, I hope I'll go down still pushing for something in the forward direction." He died in Washington on November 20, 1990, at the age of 86.

SELECTED WRITINGS BY COBB:

Periodicals

"Physical Anthropology of the American Negro," *American Journal of Physical Anthropology,* Vol. 29 (1942): 113–223.
"The Skeleton," *Problems of Ageing,* edited by A. I. Lansing, Williams & Wilkins, 1952, pp. 791–856.

FURTHER READING:

Periodicals

Lawlah, John W. "The President-Elect," *Journal of the National Medical Association,* Vol. 55 (November, 1963): 551–554.
Scarupa, Harriet Jackson. "W. Montague Cobb," *New Directions,* (April, 1988): 6–17.

Price Mashaw Cobbs

Scarupa, Harriet Jackson. "W. Montague Cobb," *Modern Medicine,* (December 28, 1970): 16–25.

—*Sketch by Martin R. Feldman*

Price Mashaw Cobbs
1928-
Psychiatrist

Price Mashaw Cobbs is best known for his work in ethnotherapy, a group therapy that is sensitive to ethnic differences and seeks to help individuals resolve racially based identity issues. With another black psychiatrist, William H. Grier, Cobbs published *Black Rage* in 1968. The title of this book gives a name to the repressed frustration and anger often felt by African Americans, and it explores the effects of these emotions—effects which include increased health problems. Since the late 1960s, Cobbs has been engaged in working with corporations, government agencies, and nonprofit groups as a consultant on issues of diversity in the workplace.

Cobbs was born in Los Angeles, California, on November 2, 1928, the son of Peter Price and Rose (Mashaw) Cobbs. Cobbs's father was also a doctor. After graduating from high school in Los Angeles, Cobbs attended the University of California, Los Angeles for two years, until he was drafted during the Korean War. From 1951-53, he served in the U.S. Army, attaining the rank of corporal.

After his discharge, Cobbs completed his undergraduate degree at the University of California at Berkeley, where he was awarded his bachelor's degree in 1954. He then entered Meharry Medical College in Nashville, Tennessee. While a student there, Cobbs married Evadne Priester on May 30, 1957. They would have two children together, Price Priester and Marion Renata, before his wife died in 1973. Cobbs earned his medical degree from Meharry in 1958. He spent the next year as an intern at the San Francisco General Hospital. He began his psychiatric residency at Mendocino State Hospital, in Talmadge, in 1959. When his residency ended in 1961, Cobbs opened a private practice in San Francisco.

While maintaining his practice, Cobbs held several related positions. In 1961, Cobbs conducted psychiatric research at the Langley Porter Neuropsychiatric Institute. From 1963-64, Cobbs was a consultant to the State of California Department of Corrections. He became an assistant clinical professor at the University of California, San Francisco in 1966. Cobbs also became a board certified psychiatrist that year.

It was at this university that Cobbs met William H. Grier. In his private practice, Cobbs told *Black Enterprise* magazine, he had begun to see "that black people, whether they were middle class, unemployed, or young professionals trying to get started, were angry." With Grier, he coauthored *Black Rage,* which was published in 1968. *Black Rage* explores racial anger for many African Americans and examines how it affects them and their health. The book ends by celebrating the merits of diversity and its future promise. Cobbs and Grier published their study as a clinical handbook for other psychiatric professionals, but its accessibility insured it was read well beyond these circles. They coauthored a second book, published in 1971. Entitled *The Jesus Bag*, this work explores the complicated role and effect of religion on the lives of African Americans.

The University of California, San Francisco gave Cobbs a grant to study ways to lessen racism on college campuses. In addition to his private practice, this experience helped him develop ethnotherapy, an idea which he had been working on for most of his career as a psychiatrist. Ethnotherapy employed group therapy techniques to question and hopefully transform attitudes and suppositions related to differences of race, ethnicity, and values.

In 1967, Cobbs founded Pacific Management Systems, a consulting firm that specializes in executive development and diversity management. Through this San Francisco-based company, Cobbs began his career as a consultant to businesses and organizations of all kinds. He began with the

San Francisco area, but his work spread throughout the United States and the world. Using ethnotherapy as a basis, Cobbs helped people of all races to understand the dynamics of racism, as well as its effects. He promoted the value of understanding differences between people as a means to making work environments more effective. His seminars encouraged managers of multi-racial workplaces to use diversity as a way to benefit the company. Cobbs also worked with minority managers and other professionals who were trying to overcome the challenges of working in traditionally white organizations. Cobbs eventually took the title of chief executive officer of Pacific Management Systems. He also formed his own company, Cobbs, Inc.

In 1985, Cobbs married again, to Frederica Maxwell. In the late 1980s and early 1990s, Cobbs received two significant awards. *Black Enterprise* magazine named him Outstanding Psychiatrist in 1988. The Association of Humanistic Psychology gave him a Pathfinder Award in 1993. Cobbs is a fellow of the American Psychiatric Association, and a member of the International Association of Social Scientists, the National Medical Association, the Institute of Medicine, the National Academy of Sciences, and the International Association of Social Psychiatrists. Cobbs is also a charter member of the National Urban League as well as a life member of the National Association for the Advancement of Colored People (NAACP). Cobbs also served on the advisory board for *Black Scholar* and on the board of directors for Foundation for National Progress, and he held a chairmanship at Renaissance Books.

SELECTED WRITINGS BY COBBS:

Books

(with William H. Grier) *Black Rage.* New York: Basic Books, Inc., 1968, reprinted 1980.
(with William H. Grier) *The Jesus Bag.* New York: McGraw Hill, 1971.

Periodicals

"Journeys to Black Identity: Selma and Watts." *Negro Digest* (July 1967).

FURTHER READING:

Books

Sammons, Vivian Ovelton. *Blacks in Science and Medicine.* New York: Hemisphere Publishing, 1990.

Periodicals

"Prescribing Strong Medicine for the Mind." *Black Enterprise.* (October 1988): 86.

—*Sketch by A. Petrusso*

Johnetta Betsch Cole

Johnnetta Betsch Cole
1936-
Anthropologist

Johnnetta Betsch Cole was the first African American woman to become president of Spelman College, the liberal arts school for black women in Atlanta, Georgia. Cole's writing has helped to correct the tendency of earlier academic feminism to focus exclusively on white, middle-class women.

Cole was born on October 19, 1936, in Jacksonville, Florida. Her mother, Mary Frances Lewis Betsch, was a college administrator and insurance company executive. Her father, John Betsch Jr., was also an insurance company executive. In 1952, she entered Fisk University at the age of 15, and after one year, transferred to Oberlin College in Ohio with the intention of studying medicine. After taking a fascinating course on racial and cultural minorities, she changed her major to anthropology. She graduated from Oberlin with a degree in anthropology in 1957.

Cole then enrolled at Northwestern University and earned a master's degree in anthropology in 1959. At Northwestern she met Robert Cole, the son of an Iowa dairy farmer and a graduate student in economics. They were married in 1960 and later had three sons: David (born in 1962), Aaron (born in 1966), and Ethan Che (born in 1970). When Cole and her husband returned to Jacksonville so that he could meet her parents, the insurance company owned by her family was threatened by white extremists because Cole had married a white man. Shortly after her marriage, she and her husband left for Liberia for two years so that they could collect data for their respective doctoral dissertations.

Cole and her husband moved to Washington state in 1962 so that he could take up a teaching job. She taught part-time and finished her dissertation, titled "Traditional and Wage Earning Labor in Liberia." Northwestern awarded Cole a Ph.D. in anthropology in 1967, after which she became a full-time assistant professor of anthropology at Washington State University and helped to found a program in black studies. In 1970, Cole and her husband left for Massachusetts, where she had been offered a tenured professorship at the University of Massachusetts at Amherst. There, Cole later was promoted to full professor and became provost of undergraduate education from 1981-1983. She and her husband were divorced in 1982. In 1983, she began to teach at Hunter College of the City University of New York. Until she left Hunter in 1987 to become president of Spelman College, she was a full professor of anthropology, and she directed the Latin American and Caribbean studies program.

Expanding Rights for All Women

Cole's writing recognized that early feminist studies tended to focus on white, middle-class women and generalize from their experience to all other women. A social problem that especially concerned white, middle-class women, such as their lack of voting rights, would be characterized as a women's rights problem in general, and a goal would be set and pursued until it was achieved. Thus women gained the right to vote in the United States in 1920. But after such a triumph, women's activism would decline considerably, leaving many other problems relating to women unsolved, such as unfair wages, sexual harassment, racism, spousal abuse, disproportional child-care responsibilities, sexual discrimination in job promotion, and limited access to birth control, to name a few. These other problems, however, would not necessarily be the concerns of white, middle-class women and would not be addressed with the vigor that the voting rights issue received. Though voting rights were good for women in general, they were not as important to other groups of women, for example, to poor, black, unwed, teenage mothers, who faced different sets of problems.

Cole set out in her publications to raise the public's consciousness about the problems of women who were not white and middle-class. These other problems concerned work, families, sexuality and reproduction, religion, and politics. Cole's approach to solving this problem was very even-handed, as the title of her most important book shows: *All American Women: Lines that Divide, Ties that Bind.* She recognized that ignoring the common ground between all women would promote divisiveness, which women did not need. Yet she also recognized that ignoring differences between women would promote race, class, age, and sexual discrimination, among other problems. An even-handed respect for the commonalities and differences between people permeates her work.

"Sistah Prez" Runs Spelman College

In 1987, Cole succeeded Donald Stewart as president of Spelman College. Spelman was founded in 1880 by abolitionists from New England who wanted freed slave women to learn Christian virtues and get a good education. For many years after its founding, Spelman's presidents had been white women, a situation which finally changed in the 1950s, when an African American, Albert Manley, became president. Cole was the first black woman president of the first black women's college in America. In an interview early in her term, she referred to herself as "sister president," and she soon became known affectionately to everyone around the campus as "Sistah Prez."

Among many other activities, presidents of private colleges must spend a lot of time raising money, and Cole was a smashing success, raising $114 million by the end of one funding drive. Comedian and television star Bill Cosby and his wife Camille donated $20 million to Spelman at Cole's presidential inauguration in 1987, and Cole's charisma, sincerity, creativity, and enthusiasm have made her one of the most effective fund raisers in the history of higher education in America. While president of Spelman, she taught one course per term in addition to her other academic responsibilities, and she kept a busy pace creating new programs and opportunities for her students, serving on boards of directors of corporations, giving interviews, publishing, and collecting scores of awards and honorary degrees from a variety of organizations and academic institutions. In December 1988, Cole took time from her busy schedule to marry Arthur Robinson Jr., a public health care administrator.

In June 1997, after ten years in office, Cole resigned her presidency of Spelman College. After some time off to rest, she became a full professor at Emory University in Atlanta. In spite of her success, Cole remains pragmatic and modest. Late in 1997, as she prepared for her new job teaching at Emory, she wrote in *Dream the Boldest Dreams*, "To the African proverb 'She who learns must teach,' let us add: 'She who teaches must continue to learn.'"

SELECTED WRITINGS BY COLE:

Books

All-American Women: Lines that Divide, Ties That Bind. New York: Free Press, 1986.
Conversations: Straight Talk with America's Sister President. New York: Doubleday, 1993.

Dream the Boldest Dreams: And Other Lessons of Life. Atlanta: Longstreet Press, 1997.

FURTHER READING:

Books

Bateson, Catherine. *Composing a Life.* New York: Atlantic Monthly Press, 1989.

Bigelow, Barbara Carlisle, ed. *Contemporary Black Biography.* Volume 5. Detroit: Gale Research, 1993.

Smith, Jessie Carney, ed. *Notable Black American Women.* Detroit: Gale Research, 1991.

—Sketch by Patrick Moore

Rebecca J. Cole
1846-1922
Physician

Rebecca J. Cole was the second black woman in the United States to obtain a medical degree. She received her degree just after the Civil War—a period when neither blacks nor women were readily accepted as doctors. But Cole persevered, and her more than 50-year career was dedicated to helping poor women and children.

Not much is known about Cole's early life. She was born in Philadelphia on March 16, 1846, the second of five children. She attended the Institute for Colored Youth (now Cheyney University), graduating in 1863. She taught for a year and then entered the Female Medical College of Pennsylvania (now part of Allegheny University of the Health Sciences). She graduated in 1867. In addition to being the second black woman physician in the U.S., she was the first black woman to graduate from the Female Medical College.

After graduating, Cole went to New York, where she became a resident physician at the New York Infirmary for Women and Children. This hospital had been founded a decade earlier by Elizabeth Blackwell, the first white woman to obtain a medical degree in the United States. Cole had a strong interest in assisting poor women and children, and Blackwell assigned her to the post of "sanitary visitor." In this capacity, Cole would visit poor families and provide advice and instruction on proper hygiene, prenatal and infant care, and maintaining good general health. This was no easy task; New York's population was rapidly growing, and there was no shortage of impoverished families living in slum conditions. Cole carried out this demanding work for several years.

Cole eventually left New York and briefly practiced medicine in Columbia, South Carolina. She next went to Washington, D.C., where she served as a superintendent of the Government House for Children and Old Women. Eventually, she returned to Philadelphia, where she operated a private practice. In 1873, she and another doctor, Charlotte Abby, created a "Woman's Directory," which provided medical and legal services to poor women and children. She continued to provide services to the poor, as well as running her private practice, until her death in Philadelphia on August 14, 1922.

FURTHER READING:

Books

Abram, Ruth J., ed. *Send Us a Lady Physician: Women Doctors in America, 1835-1920.* New York: W.W. Norton, 1986.

Hine, Darlene Clark, ed. *Black Women in America: An Historic Encyclopedia.* New York: Carlson Publishing, Inc., 1993.

Keene, John A. *The Negro in Medicine.* Tuskegee, Alabama: Tuskegee Institute, 1912.

Kerr, Laura. *Doctor Elizabeth.* New York: Thomas Nelson, 1946.

Marais, Herbert Montfort. *History of the Negro in Medicine.* New York: NY Publishers Company, 1967.

Smith, Jessie Carney, ed. *Notable Black American Women.* Detroit: Gale Research, Inc., 1995.

Sterling, Dorothy, ed. *We Are Your Sisters: Black Women in the Nineteenth Century.* New York: W. W. Norton, 1984.

—Sketch by George A. Milite

John William Coleman
1929-
Molecular physicist

John William Coleman's best known contribution to science was his instrumental role in developing the American electron microscope at RCA. He also holds a patent on electron optics research. For his effort, he was honored with RCA's David Sarnoff Award. Some of Coleman's primary areas of research interest include electron optical design, differential microspectrophotometry, electron diffraction, and light optical systems.

Coleman was born in New York City on December 30, 1929, to John William and Melissa Teresa (nee Preston) Coleman. He attended Howard University and was awarded his B.S. in 1950. After graduation, Coleman was given several awards that allowed him to study abroad for a year. He won the Lucy E. Moten Award, the Göttingen Award, and a Fulbright fellowship. Before entering graduate school, Coleman worked as a physicist for the National Bureau of Standards from 1951 until 1953.

Coleman then began his graduate work. While a graduate student at the University of Illinois, Urbana, he was a National Science foundation Award for the 1955-56 school year. He earned his M.S. in 1957, and before going on to earn his Ph.D., Coleman worked as an physics instructor at his alma mater, Howard University, from 1957-58. In 1958, he became an engineer at RCA. While at RCA, Coleman earned his Ph.D. in biophysics at the University of Pennsylvania in 1963. His dissertation was titled "The Diffraction of Electrons in Ultramicroscopic Biological Particles of Ordered Structure."

Before graduation, Coleman was already helping in the development of the American electron microscope. An electron microscope uses a beam of electrons instead of light to magnify objects too small for conventional microscopes. Coleman was awarded the David Sarnoff Award from RCA the same year he completed his graduate studies, 1962-63. Coleman also married that year. He wed Diane Mea Vaitses in June 1962, and they had two daughters, Melissa Paula and Crystal McCleod.

Coleman left RCA in 1969 to become the director of engineering at Forglo Corporation, in Sunbury, Pennsylvania. In 1972, Coleman was hired as a physicist associated with the Massachusetts Institute of Technology, in their Developmental Electrons Optics Laboratory. Throughout his career, Coleman has contributed articles to relevant journals. He is also associated with several relevant profession societies: the Electron Microscopy Society, the Physical Society, the Biophysical Society, and the Society of Cell Biology.

—Sketch by A. Petrusso

James Pierpont Comer
1934-
Psychiatrist

James P. Comer is a psychiatrist who founded the Comer School Development Program (CSDP), a visionary approach to improving troubled schools. The program is based on Comer's belief in the importance of providing children with experiences that promote their social, emotional, cognitive, and moral development. He believes that

James Pierpont Comer

the development of these qualities is more important than genetics in determining a child's performance in school and in life. Comer established his first CSDP schools in New Haven, Connecticut, in 1968. The program's success there and around the country prompted the Rockefeller Foundation to spend $15 million over five years to support Comer's efforts. By 1998, about 600 schools in the United States had adopted CSDP.

The tenets of CSDP reflect Comer's own upbringing by parents who emphasized education and instilled in him the drive to succeed, despite obstacles. Comer was born in East Chicago, Indiana, on September 25, 1934, into a working-class family. His father, Hugh Comer, was a steelworker and a janitor. His mother, Maggie, was a domestic worker who had little formal schooling. His parents gave him the middle name Pierpont, to help him remember the achievements of the financier J. Pierpont Morgan. The second oldest of five children, Comer and his siblings made frequent trips to the library, museums, and any other place that their parents thought might stimulate their intellect and build their self-esteem.

Comer was a top student at East Chicago's Washington High School, sang in the chorus, and served as student-body president in his senior year. However, he faced a traumatic personal challenge when he left the nurturing atmosphere of his family to attend Indiana University. "All of a sudden I was a black, poor kid," he explained to the *Washington Post.* "I had to deal with racial antagonisms. My confidence was shot. I was petrified."

He earned a bachelor's degree from Indiana University in 1956. Because of his experience there, he decided to transfer to a predominantly black university. He chose Howard University in Washington, D.C., where he received his medical degree in 1960. In 1964, he received a master's degree in public health from the University of Michigan. Between 1964-67, Comer trained in psychiatry at the Yale University School of Medicine and its Child Study Center. In addition, he received a year of residency training at the Hillcrest Children's Center in Washington, D.C. Comer complemented his ongoing training in medicine with service in the U.S. Public Health Service from 1961-68, during which time he attained the rank of lieutenant colonel.

Founds the Comer School Development Program

Comer returned to Yale in 1968. That year, he established his school development program, forming a collaboration between two public elementary schools in New Haven. The philosophy of the program was, and is, that even failing inner-city schools can achieve on a high level if society sustains them with "an interlocking network of services." This strategy of "services integration" requires medical clinics, mental health centers, libraries, and child-care centers to work together for the benefit of children. The crucial element of the model, however, is ensuring that parents understand how important they are in their children's lives. Of children, Comer said to the *Washington Post*: "They develop well by making an emotional attachment to the meaningful adults in their environment. Adults become meaningful by helping children manage their environment." In other words, parents must learn to reinforce the attitudes and behaviors that good schools value.

The *Washington Post* reported in 1997 that there were CSDP models operating in 650 schools in 28 states, about a third of which Comer considered were very successful and another third somewhat successful. Despite his zealous pursuit of nurturing school environments, he wrote in his 1997 book, *Waiting for a Miracle—Why Schools Can't Solve Our Problems—and How We Can,* that schools cannot be expected to solve society's problems. Rather, that challenge rests with children, families, and communities.

From 1996-97, Comer supervised the development of the Kidpreneurs Program sponsored by *Black Enterprise* magazine. The two-year program taught children aged 3-17 the rudiments of entrepreneurship, emphasizing concepts such as cash flow, business plans, marketing, and customer service. Comer also injected his own deeply felt belief in the importance of parental involvement by including an interactive session for parents. The aim of parental involvement was to make the entrepreneurial spirit an integral part of the childrens' home lives.

Comer served as a consultant to the Children's Television Workshop, which produces "Sesame Street" and "Electric Company." In 1989 he was a consultant to the Pre-Education Summit, along with President George Bush and Secretary of Education Lauro F. Cavazos. He has also been a member of the National Commission on Teaching and America's Future since 1994. Comer has also contributed to numerous books and magazines, including *Parents, Ebony,* and *Redbook*. In addition, he has served on the editorial boards of the *American Journal of Orthopsychiatry* (1970-76); *Youth and Adolescence* (1971-87); and the *Journal of Negro Education* (1978-83).

The wide recognition accorded to Comer has included 37 honorary degrees, the 1996 Heinz Award for the Human Condition for his work on behalf of disadvantaged children; and the 1996 Healthtrac Foundation award. Among Comer's other honors are the Charles A. Dana Award for Pioneering Achievement in Education (1991); the James Bryant Conant Award given by the Education Commission of the States (1991); the Harold W. McGraw, Jr. Prize in Education given by McGraw-Hill, Inc. (1990); the Special Presidential Commendation of the American Psychiatric Association (1990); the Rockefeller Public Service Award (1980); and the John and Mary Markel Foundation Scholar Award in Academic Medicine, a five-year award ending in 1979.

Comer married Shirley Ann Arnold in 1959; they have two children, Brian Jay and Dawn Renee.

SELECTED WRITINGS BY COMER:

Books

Beyond Black and White. Quadrangle Press, 1972.
Maggie's American Dream: The Life and Times of a Black Family. Plume, 1988.
Rallying the Whole Village: The Comer Process for Reforming Education. Teachers College Press, 1996.
Waiting for a Miracle—Why Schools Can't Solve our Problems—And How We Can. E.P. Dutton, 1997.

FURTHER READING:

Periodicals

The Boston Globe (Dec. 21, 1997): E5.
The Washington Post (Oct. 24, 1997): A27.
Black Enterprise (January 1998): 91.
Black Enterprise (December 1997): 113.

Other

The Heinz Awards www.awards.heinz.org/comer.html
James P. Comer, M.D. http://info.med.yale.edu/comer/comer.html

—*Sketch by Marc Kusinitz*

Lloyd M. Cooke

Lloyd M. Cooke
1916-
Industrial chemist

Lloyd M. Cooke spent 30 years working in chemical, technical, and market research in cellulose and carbohydrate chemistry for companies. Although he worked in industry throughout his career, he developed a respected reputation in the scientific community and was instrumental in preparing a publication on chemistry and the environment that was widely adopted as a university textbook. He is a member of a number of scientific boards and societies, and has received many awards and honors, including the Proctor Prize in Science from the Science Research Association in 1970. Cooke transferred to the area of urban affairs (a community relations position) for Union Carbide in 1970, a position which made him responsible for areas such as equal opportunity employment and education.

Lloyd Miller Cooke was born in La Salle, Illinois, on June 7, 1916, the son of William Wilson and Anna (Miller) Cooke. His father, an engineer and architect for the U.S. government, advised him against his first choice for a career, aeronautical engineering, because he said a black wouldn't be able to find work in the field. Hoping for more opportunity, Cooke elected to major in chemistry instead.

Although he graduated first in his class in 1937 with a bachelor of science from the University of Wisconsin, he could not get a job. Cooke went on to McGill University in Canada and received his doctorate in organic chemistry in 1941.

Cellulose Research Leads to Employment

Cooke's studies in the chemistry of cellulose (a polysaccharide found in plant cell walls and used in the manufacture of goods such as rayon, paper, and cellophane) led to a job as researcher and section leader in starch chemistry at the Corn Products Refining Company in Argo, Illinois. In 1946, Cooke moved to the Visking Corporation in Chicago to do research in carbohydrate chemistry. Cooke advanced steadily within the films and packaging division of Visking, whose products included hot dog casings. He was manager of the cellulose and casing research department from 1950 to 1954, then assistant manager of a technical division from 1954 to 1957. Cooke's areas of chemical research, on which he has published in professional journals, include the structure of lignin (a polymer related to cellulose), starch modification and derivatives, cellulose derivatives, the chemistry of viscose (a solution of cellulose treated with caustic alkali and carbon disulfide, used in the manufacture of rayon and films), and carbohydrate and polymer chemistry.

When Visking was taken over by Union Carbide, a leading chemical company, in 1957, Cooke volunteered for challenging assignments. "I decided I was happiest when I was on a problem with a time limit where, come a date, I had to make a decision," he told the *New York Times.* At Union Carbide in Chicago, Cooke served as assistant director of research from 1957 to 1965, manager of market research from 1965 to 1967, and manager of planning from 1967 to 1970. It was as manager of planning that he was responsible for the preparation of the book *Cleaning our Environment—The Chemical Basis for Action,* which was published by the American Chemical Society in 1969. Although the book was written for the lay person, especially for politicians and environmental leaders, it was also adopted as a college text by 20 universities, and sold more than 50,000 copies.

Shifts Focus to Urban Affairs

In 1970, Cooke accepted a new challenge as director of urban affairs for Union Carbide in New York, where he became responsible for issues of equal employment and education access for minorities. Cooke explained his shift in direction to the *New York Times:* "I had decided to make a career change anyway before this offer came. . . . My real interest was in problem solving and I'd had fun getting involved in the environmental problem." In this new position, which Cooke held until 1978, he fostered an innovative partnership between Union Carbide and the New York City public school system and focused on secondary science and mathematics education. Between 1978 and his retirement, Cooke served as a senior consultant to Union Carbide.

Cooke was awarded both the Proctor Prize in Science and the Honor Scroll Award of the Chicago Chapter of the American Institute of Chemists in 1970. He is a member of the National Academy of Sciences, the American Institute of Chemists, the American Chemical Society, and the American Marketing Association, among other scientific and professional organizations. Cooke served as a member of the National Science Board from 1970 to 1982, a trustee for the Carver Research Foundation of the Tuskegee Institute from 1971 to 1978, president of the National Action Council on Minorities in Engineering from 1981 1983, and as a senior advisor to the chancellor of the New York public schools from 1984 to 1987. In 1957, Cooke married Vera E. Schlegel, a biochemist he met at Visking. He acknowledged in the *New York Times* in 1971, "Every single thing I've written she's approved." Cooke and his wife have two children, Barbara and William.

SELECTED WRITINGS BY COOKE:

Books

Cleaning Our Environment: The Chemical Basis for Action, American Chemical Society, 1969.

FURTHER READING:

Books

Scientists in the Black Perspective. Lincoln Foundation, 1974, pp. 142–143.

Periodicals

New York Times, (April 25, 1971): section III, p. 7.

—*Sketch by M. C. Nagel*

Edward Sawyer Cooper
1926-
Cardiologist

Cardiologist Edward Sawyer Cooper has done extensive research into strokes and stroke prevention, especially among African Americans. He has published numerous articles on this subject, as well as on heart disease and the incidence of high blood pressure in poor. Cooper

Edward Sawyer Cooper

was the first African American to head the American Heart Association, serving as president in 1992-93. He was also the first black tenured professor of medicine at the University of Pennsylvania School of Medicine, the oldest medical school in the United States. Cooper has used his position to encourage minorities to pursue careers in the medical profession.

Cooper was born on December 11, 1926, in Columbia, South Carolina, to Henry Howard Cooper, Sr., and Ada (Sawyer) Cooper. Cooper's father was a dentist, and both of his brothers pursued careers in dentistry. After graduating first in his class from Columbia's Booker T. Washington High School, Cooper entered Lincoln University in Pennsylvania. He graduated with a bachelor's degree in 1946. Then he entered Meharry Medical College in Nashville. Cooper earned his medical degree in 1949, again graduating first in his class. Meharry honored Cooper with the Hartley Gold Medal that year. With his degree in hand, Cooper returned to Pennsylvania.

In 1949, Cooper began his year-long internship at Philadelphia General Hospital. While working there, he had a patient who suffered a debilitating series of strokes. This woman was still young—less than 40 years old—but the strokes robbed her of speech and use of one side of her body. This experience inspired Cooper to become a cardiologist, a doctor who specializes in heart disease, high blood pressure, and strokes. After completing his internship, Cooper worked a residency in cardiology at Philadelphia General Hospital until he joined the United States Air Force in 1954.

From 1954-56, Cooper was the chief of the Air Force's regional hospital in the Philippines, reaching the rank of captain. Cooper then returned to accept a year-long National Heart Institute fellowship in cardiology, again at Philadelphia General Hospital. He also opened his own private practice. He became certified by the American Board of Internal Medicine in 1957. In 1958, Cooper became a staff member at Philadelphia General Hospital as well as a faculty member at the University of Pennsylvania School of Medicine. A year later, in 1960, he was named a master of the American College of Physicians.

Cooper directed Philadelphia General's Stroke Research Center, which opened in 1968 with a federal grant of $1,000,000. He retained this position until the center was closed in 1974 when federal funding was cut. In 1969, Cooper moved his private practice to the hospital at the University of Pennsylvania, where he was also a staff member; that year, he became president of the medical staff at Philadelphia General, an office he held until 1971. Throughout the 1970s, Cooper held other professional positions and won several awards. From 1970-84, Cooper was a member of the council of the College of Physicians of Philadelphia, and he returned to this post in 1994. In 1971, Meharry Medical College honored Cooper with the Distinguished Alumni Award. He became chief of medical service at Philadelphia General in 1972, a position he held until 1976. Cooper won the **Charles Drew** Award for Distinguished Contributions to Medical Education in 1979.

President of the American Heart Association

Cooper was associated with the American Heart Association for over 25 years before being elected to his year-term as president in 1992. Cooper had been a board member, the chairman, and the director of the American Heart Association's Stroke Council. He also chaired the Credentials and Nominating Committee as well as the Writing Committee. The latter produced an important scientific paper, "Cardiovascular Disease and Stroke in African-Americans and Other Racial Minorities." In 1986, Cooper was given the association's Award of Merit.

When Cooper became the American Heart Association's first black president, he used his position to advocate for health education and a national health care system. He argued that prevention and early treatment are less costly and better for the patient. One of his main goals was increasing the number of people receiving treatment for high blood pressure. When he took office, only half of people suffering from high blood pressure were receiving treatment. "Access to health care is something that Americans want," he told *Ebony*, "It's a political process . . . [R]educing disability and deaths from cardiovascular diseases and strokes are a part of our mission."

Throughout his career, Cooper has been active in other professional and civic organizations, using his position to promote better treatment and prevention of strokes, as well as to encourage minorities to become medical professionals. Cooper is a fellow of the American College of Physicians,

and he belongs to the American Medical Association, the National Medical Association, the Association of University Professors, and the Alpha Omega Alpha. Cooper chaired the talent recruitment council for the National Medical Association, an organization of African American doctors. Cooper was also a founding member and one-time chairman of the executive committee of American Health Education for African Development (AHEAD) and the American Foundation for Negro Affairs (AFNA). He has served on numerous editorial boards, including a consulting editorship for *Stroke,* and he has won numerous awards.

Cooper married Dr. Jean Marie Wilder, and with her had four children: Edward Sawyer Cooper, Jr., who died at a young age; Lisa Cooper Huggins, a pediatrician; Jan Cooper Jones, an endocrinologist; and Charles Wilder Cooper, a psychologist. He is currently professor emeritus of medicine at the University of Pennsylvania School of Medicine.

FURTHER READING:

Periodicals

"Edward S. Cooper, M.D.: American Heart Association President. *Ebony* 47, no. 12 (October 1992): 25-27."

"Seeking an Rx For Stroke Prevention." *Black Enterprise* (October 1988): 68.

Books

Hawkins, Walter L. *African American Biographies, Volume 2.* Jefferson, NC: McFarland and Co., 1994.

Sammons, Vivian Ovelton. *Blacks in Science and Medicine.* New York: Hemisphere Publishing, 1990.

—*Sketch by A. Petrusso*

Paul Bertau Cornely
1906-
Physician

In 1934 Paul Bertau Cornely became the first African American to earn a Ph.D. in public health, and in 1969 the American Public Health Association elected him its first black president. During the 1940s and 1950s, he studied the treatment black patients received at hospitals in the southern and northern United States. To the surprise of many who assumed the conditions would be better in the North, Cornely's research found that African Americans received substandard medical treatment on either side of the Mason-

Paul Bertau Cornely

Dixon Line. During the 1950s Cornely, along with two other leaders in the medical and civil rights community, spearheaded an effort to integrate health-care facilities in the United States. Their work would culminate in the 1964 Supreme Court case *Simkins v. Moses H. Cone Memorial Hospital,* which integrated health care as the more famous *Brown v. Board of Education* (1954) integrated schooling. Cornely taught at Howard University for some 40 years, and directed the Freedmen's Hospital in Washington, D.C., for more than a decade.

Becomes First African American to Earn Ph.D. in Anatomy

Paul Bertau Cornely was born in Born in Poin-à-Pitre, Guadeloupe, in the French West Indies, on March 9, 1906. The son of Eleodore and Adrienne (Mellon) Cornely, he was raised and educated in Puerto Rico, and in 1920 migrated to the mainland United States. In 1924 he began his studies at the College of the City of Detroit, but soon afterward switched to the University of Michigan. After earning his B.A. at Michigan in 1928, Cornely continued his studies there, and in 1931 received his M.D. degree. Three years later, in 1934, Cornely earned his Ph.D. degree as well, making him one of those rare individuals who possess a double doctorate. Of greater historical significance was the fact that his degree made him the first African American to earn a Ph.D. in anatomy.

Cornely's area of specialty was public health, and his dissertation—which was later published—carried the title *A*

Survey of Post-Graduate Medical Education in the United States and an Inquiry into the Educational Needs of the General Practitioner. In 1934 Cornely became an assistant professor in the Medical College of Howard University, where he would remain until his retirement nearly 40 years later. He moved up to the position of associate professor in 1935, and worked as Director of Health Service from 1937 to 1947. In 1937, Cornely experienced another milestone when he became a United States citizen. He served as head of the university's Department of Bacteriology, Preventive Medicine, and Public Health in 1943, and held that position until 1947.

Cornely became a full professor in 1947, and would continue to teach at Howard for another quarter-century, until 1973. In the meantime, he stayed active in his profession. From 1947 to 1958, he was medical director of Freedmen's Hospital in Washington, D.C., which at one time had been the only health-care facility in the area that would treat black patients. In 1955, he became director of Howard's Department of Community Health Service, a position he held until 1970.

Helps to Integrate Hospitals

In addition to his job at Howard, Cornely was consulting for the National Urban League, conducting studies of the health-care services available to blacks in the southern and northern United States. Facilities in the South, Cornely discovered by observing two cities, were abominable; but services in the North, as his studies of three cities showed, where not much better. On both sides of the Mason-Dixon Line, there was a much lower ratio of hospital beds for black patients, and even the provision of beds served as no guarantee that patients would be admitted.

One of the many unfortunate cases Cornely observed involved the death of a black college administrator and national Young Women's Christian Association (YWCA) executive, who had the misfortune to get into a car crash near Dalton, Georgia. Because Dalton's hospital had a "no Negroes" policy, an ambulance had to be called from 66 miles (105 km) away, and the woman died before she could receive proper treatment. In another instance, a white man was forced out of Atlanta's Grady Hospital in the middle of a pouring rain because someone saw his son-in-law, who happened to be a black man, and said "What! Have we put a nigger in the white ward?" The son-in-law was Walter White, executive director of the National Association for the Advancement of Colored People (NAACP).

Between World War II and the passage of Medicare in the 1960s, the largest federal grant program for public health was the Hospital Survey and Construction Act of 1946, known as "Hill-Burton" for the two Senators who wrote it. The Act provided for so-called "separate but equal" medical facilities for black patients, which tended to be all too separate, but not particularly equal. Cornely—along with **Louis Tompkins Wright**, a Harlem surgeon and chairman of the NAACP board of directors, and Howard

University anatomist **William Montague Cobb**—set out to challenge segregation in hospitals.

In the 1950s Cornely, Wright, and Cobb brought together forces from the NAACP, National Medical Association, National Urban League, and American Public Health Association to deal with what they called "perhaps the greatest of all discriminatory evils, differential treatment with respect to hospital facilities." The NAACP, its leadership inspired by the efforts of the three, from 1957 to 1963 sponsored the Imhotep Conference, at which doctors, leaders of professional organization, and members of the media came together to discuss the issue of racial integration in hospitals.

These discussions would ultimately yield tangible results when a black dentist from North Carolina, George Simkins, brought a legal challenge to the "separate but equal" policies of a medical facility that received Hill-Burton funds. Helped by NAACP legal counsel, Simkins took his case to the Supreme Court, whose March 2, 1964, decision in *Simkins v. Moses H. Cone Memorial Hospital* forced the integration of hospitals. *Simkins* was to health care what *Brown v. Board of Education* had been to schooling ten years before, and though Cornely did not take part in the actual case, his efforts had been instrumental in paving the way for it.

Establishes Facilities in Africa

During the 1950s, Cornely served as chief negotiator for the United States in helping to establish educational facilities for two newly independent or soon-to-be independent African countries. As Africa saw the end of European colonialism, it was a time of great optimism, and many Americans believed that conditions for Africans could be greatly improved by the infusion of Western aid. Cornely helped set up a nursing school in Sierra Leone, near the far western tip of Africa; and a medical school in Ghana, on the southern coast of the African "hump" that juts out into the Atlantic Ocean. As was typical of subsequent African history, Sierra Leone succumbed to a series of coups and dictatorships; but the later history of Ghana offered more hope. An ancient civilization whose charismatic leader Kwame Nkrumah was a figure of world renown during the time Cornely worked with the Ghanaians, Ghana would devolve into poverty and unrest—partly through Nkrumah's mismanagement—but would undergo a recovery in the 1980s under the leadership of Jerry Rawlings. As a consultant to the U.S. Agency for International Development (AID), Cornely was heavily involved in the affairs of emerging African nations for a period of time.

In 1969, Cornely became the first black president of the American Public Health Association, and in 1972 he received that body's Sedgwick Memorial Medal. From 1970 to 1972, he served on the President Richard M. Nixon's Committee on Population Growth and the American Future. The University of Michigan gave him an honorary degree in 1968, as did the University of the Pacific in 1973. In the latter year, Cornely retired from Howard to become an

emeritus professor, and in 1992 the university awarded him an honorary degree. After his retirement, he served as a staff member of Health Services Evaluations Systems, Inc. from 1973 to 1981.

Throughout his years in academia, Cornely continued to write extensively, contributing to journals and popular magazines, and publishing some 100 articles. An example of his work was "The Health Status of the Negro Today and in the Future" for the *American Journal of Public Health* (April 1968), in which he discussed the major health-care problems facing black Americans. As Cornely wrote, the situation was urgent and needed to be addressed soon; at the conclusion of the article, he offered possible solutions. Cornely has also published several books on public health and medical education.

Cornely married Mae Stewart of Macon, Georgia in 1934, and they had one child, Paul B. Cornely, Jr. The Cornelys live in Silver Springs, Maryland, and in religion are Catholics. Among Cornely's many professional and civic memberships are, or have been, the American Public Health Association (of which, as noted above, he served as president from 1969 to 1970), the American College of Preventive Medicine (fellow), the American College of Health Care Executives (honorary fellow), and the Community Group Health Foundation (president, 1968-74).

SELECTED WRITINGS BY CORNELY:

Books

Postgraduate Medical Education and the Needs of the General Practitioner. Edwards Brothers, 1934.
Report on the Field Services of the Specialist in Health. National Urban League, 1945.
(With Stanley K. Bigman) *Cultural Considerations in Changing Health Attitudes.* Howard University, 1961.
Public Health Imperatives for the Great Society (John Sundwell Memorial Lecture). University of Michigan, 1966.

Periodicals

"The Economics of Medical Practice and the Negro Physician," *National Medical Association Journal,* (March 1951.)
"The Health Status of the Negro Today and in the Future," *American Journal of Public Health,* (April 1968): 647-54.

FURTHER READING:

Books

American Men & Women of Science, 19th edition. R. R. Bowker, 1992-93.

Biographical Dictionary of the American Public Health Association. R. R. Bowker, 1979.

Sammons, Vivian Ovelton, *Blacks in Science and Medicine.* Hemisphere Publishing, 1990.

Periodicals

"The Earliest Ph.D. Awards to Blacks in the Natural Sciences," *Journal of Blacks in Higher Education,* (March 31, 1997).

Reynolds, P. Preston, "Hospitals and Civil Rights, 1945-1963: The Case of *Simkins v. Moses H. Cone Memorial Hospital,*" *Annals of Internal Medicine,* (June 1, 1997): 898-906.

—Sketch by Judson Knight

Elbert Frank Cox
1895-1969
Mathematician

Elbert Frank Cox was the first African American to earn a Ph.D. in pure mathematics. Cox entered the teaching profession as a high school instructor and eventually rose to become the head of Howard University's mathematics department. In addition to his contributions to abstract mathematics, he made his mark as an educator by helping to craft Howard's grading system in 1947 and guiding scores of successful masters degree candidates in mathematics.

Cox was born in Evansville, Indiana, on December 5, 1895. He was the oldest of three boys born to Johnson D. Cox, an elementary school principal, and his wife, Eugenia D. Cox. Close knit and highly religious, the Cox family had a respect for learning that reflected Johnson's educational occupation. When young Elbert demonstrated unusual ability in high school mathematics and physics, he was directed toward Indiana University. While at Indiana, he was elected to undergraduate offices and joined the Kappa Alpha Psi fraternity. After graduation in 1917, Cox entered the U.S. Army as a private during World War I and was promoted to staff sergeant in six months. Upon discharge, he became an instructor of math at a high school in Henderson, Kentucky.

In 1920 or 1921 (sources vary) Cox joined the faculty of Shaw University in Raleigh, North Carolina, and left there two years later to attend Cornell University with a full scholarship. In the summer of 1925, when Cox graduated from Cornell with his Ph.D., he became the first black to earn such a degree in pure mathematics. This abstract and highly difficult field is largely concerned with mathematical theory rather than with practice or application. The title of Cox's dissertation demonstrates this point very well: "The

Polynomial Solutions of Difference Equations of $(X-1)$ $6F(X) = $ Phi (x)."

In the fall of 1925, Cox became the head of the mathematics and physics department at West Virginia State College and remained there until 1929 when he joined the faculty of Howard University in Washington, D.C. Cox became chair of the university's department of mathematics in 1947 and held that position until 1961 when a university rule mandated that all department heads resign at the age of 65. He remained as a full professor in the department until his retirement in 1966.

During his career Cox specialized in difference equations, interpolation theory, and differential equations. Among his professional accolades were memberships in such educational societies as Beta Kappa Chi, Pi Mu Epsilon, and Sigma Pi Sigma, and he was also active in the American Mathematical Society, the American Physical Society, and the American Physics Institute. He married Beulah P. Kaufman, an elementary school teacher, on September 14, 1927. They had three sons, James, Eugene, and Elbert. Cox died at Cafritz Memorial Hospital on November 28, 1969, after a brief illness.

FURTHER READING:

Periodicals

"Cox, James D.," *The Washington Post,* (December 2, 1969): C6.

Other

Written biographical information provided to Leonard C. Bruno.

—Sketch by Leonard C. Bruno

Thomas J. Craft, Sr.
1924-
Biologist

Thomas J. Craft, Sr., made significant contributions to the sciences, both as a researcher and as an administrator. Early in his career he did important studies in skin grafts and the mechanism by which the body rejected them. Later, he turned his focus to academic administration, advising educators in the United States and abroad on establishing effective scientific education and training programs.

Thomas Craft was born on December 27, 1924, in Monticello, Kentucky. His father, Thomas M. Craft, owned a farm, and his mother, Wonnie Alta Travis Craft, was a teacher. Education was important to both the Craft and Travis families. Thomas's grandfather, Jacob Travis, had owned a general store in nearby Albany. To protest Albany's practice of cutting off public education for black students after only the second grade, Travis managed to convince most of the blacks in the town to move to Monticello. (Education for blacks in Monticello continued to the sixth grade.) He also relocated his general store to Monticello.

Young Thomas was the younger of two children; the family farm did well enough during the Great Depression that the Crafts were also able to raise a foster boy and girl. Craft was a quick learner; his older sister read to him, and he was reading on his own before he was five years old. He also developed an interest in science as a student. He spent his last year of high school in Wilberforce, Ohio and after graduating, enrolled in Wilberforce University.

The United States entered the Second World War shortly after Craft began his college studies. He was drafted in 1943 and served in the U.S. Marines. He became a drill instructor and was assigned to an active combat unit in the Pacific theater in the spring of 1945. Fortunately, the war ended before he actually saw active combat. Instead, his unit occupied Japan until 1946.

Upon his return from duty, he went back to Wilberforce under the GI Bill. In 1947, Wilberforce split into two schools, a private school and Central State University, from which Craft took his bachelor's degree in 1948. He married Joan Hunter, a fellow biology student, that year, and the couple moved to Milwaukee. Uncertain of what sort of career he wanted—he was thinking about becoming a researcher or a high school teacher—he thought a break from academia might provide him with an answer. He briefly took first a factory job and then a job with the Post Office. It did not take long for him to enroll in graduate school, at Kent State in Ohio. He obtained his master's degree in developmental biology in 1950, the same year his son, Thomas Jr., was born.

It was during this time that Craft developed his interest in human organs. In particular, he was intrigued by the mechanics of skin grafts and the reasons why the body rejects them. Craft's research, conducted with amphibians, showed a correlation between the production of stress-induced hormones and the rejection rate of grafts. The more stress, the less successful the graft.

After receiving his master's degree, Craft returned to Central State University as a biology instructor. He realized that career advancement would only come with an advanced degree, and in 1955 he began working part-time on a doctorate in zoology at Ohio State University in Columbus. He received his Ph.D. in 1963.

Craft continued to teach at Central State for an additional 20 years, although his interests were beginning to shift. After completing a program on the history and philosophy of science (sponsored by the National Science Foundation) at American University in Washington, D.C. in 1966, he began to devote more of his attention to education instead of research. He was still an active researcher; his work with transplants and grafts led to his appointment to advisory boards by the National Institutes of Health and the Ohio state government. He also conducted research on the protective qualities of melanin, the substance responsible for skin pigmentation.

But he also involved himself more with developing education programs at the high school and early college levels. In particular, he was interested in making the sciences attractive to students, especially minority students, who were often steered away from scientific careers. He became a volunteer district director for the Ohio Junior Academy of Science. He also offered his administrative services to the government of India; he spent a total of six months there between 1967 and 1968, advising on how to train college-level science instructors.

Appointed a full professor at Central State in 1980, Craft took a position at the same time as director of Florida Memorial College's Energy Program. He continued on at central State for another two years and then went to Florida Memorial full time. He chaired the school's Division of Natural Sciences and Mathematics, and in 1984 he was named academic dean.

Craft retired in 1987 and moved back to Ohio, where he continued to use his skills as an educator and administrator as a volunteer for several organizations.

FURTHER READING:

Books

Kessler, James H., et al. *Distinguished African American Scientists of the Twentieth Century.* Phoenix: Oryx Press, 1996.

—Sketch by George A. Milite

Michael Croslin
1933-
Inventor

Michael Croslin is best known for inventing a highly reliable computerized blood pressure and pulse monitor which eliminated problems caused by earlier manual systems. Croslin's monitor determines blood pressure based on blood motion, rather than having a medical professional use the less reliable method of listening for the sound of the patient's pulse.

Michael Croslin was born in 1933 in Frederiksted, St. Croix, in the U.S. Virgin Islands. His parents abandoned him when he was a baby. The Britto family took him in, named him Miguel, and raised him through childhood. In 1945, when he was 12 years old, Croslin ran away to the continental United States. For a time he lived in Georgia, picked up whatever work he could, and briefly attended a school run by Jesuit priests. Then he moved to Wisconsin and was adopted by the Croslin family, who gave him his name. An exceptionally bright student, he graduated early from high school at 14. He soon entered the University of Wisconsin and graduated with a Bachelor of Science degree only three years later. That was the first of five degrees he was to earn from major American universities.

Croslin joined the Air Force in 1950 and did tours of duty in Korea and Vietnam. After his discharge from the service, he studied Mechanical Engineering at New York University in New York City, where he received a second B.S. degree. A few years later, in 1963, he received a master's degree, this time in Electrical Engineering, and in 1968, he earned a Ph.D. in Biomedical Engineering. Both of these degrees were from NYU. His fifth degree was a Master's in Business Administration from Columbia University, which he earned while he was getting his doctorate from NYU.

Croslin's computerized blood pressure and pulse measuring device, marketed as the Medtek 410, provided significant advances over the old technique. Before Croslin's device, a nurse measured a patient's blood pressure by listening to the sound of the patient's pulse through a stethoscope while simultaneously watching the moving needle in a pressure gauge. The measurement taken using this old method could be distorted by the nurse's hearing or vision limitations, by the nurse's judgment of where the moving needle registered when the nurse heard the patient's pulse, or by distracting noises or high humidity in the environment. Croslin's device neutralized all the environmental problems and any potential physical limits of the nurse or doctor. His device, which can easily be held in one hand, also displayed the results of the measurement on a digital screen.

Croslin founded the Medtek Corporation in Princeton, New Jersey, in 1978 to produce his invention. A later, improved version of Croslin's invention, the Medtek 420, is accepted for use in medical air evacuation helicopters because it automatically calibrates for barometic pressures and because the surrounding noise does not affect measurements.

FURTHER READING:

Other

"Cardiac Medtek BPI 420 Blood Pressure/Pulse Monitor." Brooks Air Force Base. http://www.alcft.

brooks.af.mil/HTMLPOOL/SG160.htm. (April 14, 1998).

—Sketch by Patrick Moore

David Nelson Crosthwait, Jr.
1892-1976
Engineer

David Nelson Crosthwait Jr. was a mechanical engineer who specialized in heating, ventilation, and air conditioning (HVAC). During his long career with the C. A. Dunham Company, his research led to innovations in the field, and he received over 30 U.S. patents for HVAC apparatus. Crosthwait was also a National Technological Association (NTA) Medalist in 1936 and the first African American honored by the American Society of Heating, Refrigeration, and Air Conditioning Engineers (ASHRAE). Among his many accomplishments is the design for the heating system of New York's Radio City Music Hall.

Crosthwait was born in Nashville, Tennessee, on May 27, 1892 (some sources lists 1890, 1891, or 1898), to Dr. David Nelson and Minnie (Harris) Crosthwait. He attended elementary and high school in Kansas City, Missouri, and studied mechanical engineering at Purdue University. In 1913, after receiving his bachelor of science degree, he began his long association with the C. A. Dunham Company. At Dunham, Crosthwait progressed from engineer to engineering checker in 1915 to research engineer in 1919. During this time he continued his education, earning his M.S. degree from Purdue in 1920 while also contributing to technical magazines, including *Power* and *Industrial Management*. In 1925 Crosthwait was named director of research, and five years later he was promoted to technical advisor. As research director Crosthwait was responsible for heat transfer research, steam transport research, and application of the resistance thermometer principle to thermostats.

On May 3, 1930, Crosthwait married E. Madolyne Towels in Chicago, Illinois. They had one child, David Nelson III, who died before the age of six. Madolyne died in August of 1939, and two years later Crosthwait married Blanche Ford.

From 1930 until he retired in 1969, Crosthwait remained a technical consultant and advisor at C. A. Dunham, which later became Dunham-Bush. He continued to conduct research on heating systems, including devising and applying techniques for reducing noise caused by steam and non-condensible gases in heating systems. Additionally, he was responsible for product and process development applications and the policies regarding these developments. Crosthwait continued contributing to the HVAC field as an author, rewriting chapters of the *American Society of Heating and Ventilation Engineers Guide* for the 1939, 1959, and 1967 editions. He also wrote articles for *Heating and Ventilation* magazine.

Crosthwait was active in technical societies, including ASHRAE, the American Chemical Society, the National Society of Professional Engineers, and the American Association for the Advancement of Science. Crosthwait was involved in community affairs as well, serving on the North West Comprehensive Health Planning Executive Committee, and as president of the Michigan City Redevelopment Commission in his home town of Michigan City, Indiana. He was also active in the Masons, having held the positions of Grand Junior Warden and Grand Senior Warden.

In addition to receiving the NTA medal, Crosthwait became the first African American to be honored for excellence in engineering when he was made a fellow of ASHRAE in 1971. In the spring of 1975 Crosthwait was honored by Purdue University with an honorary doctorate in technology. He enjoyed studying history, reading biographies, and listening to classical music. Crosthwait died on February 25, 1976, after a brief hospital stay.

SELECTED WRITINGS BY CROSTHWAIT:

Books

American Society of Heating and Ventilation Engineers Guide, 1939.
American Society of Heating, Refrigeration and Air Conditioning Engineers Guide, 1959.

Periodicals

"Making Up the Labor Shortage," *Industrial Management,* (May, 1918): 412–413.
"Heating System Vacuum," *Power,* (October 21, 1919): 614–616.

FURTHER READING:

Periodicals

"Retired Michigan City Inventor David Crosthwait Jr. Dies," *Michigan City News Dispatch,* (February 25, 1976): 1.

—*Sketch by George A. Ferrance*

Rebecca Lee Crumpler
1833-??
Physician

R ebecca Lee Crumpler was the first black woman to receive a medical degree in the United States. She spent her lifetime working to improve the health of the black community, and described her lifelong sense of vocation in the following words: "I early conceived a liking for and sought every opportunity to relieve the suffering of others."

Rebecca Lee was born in Richmond, Virginia, in 1833. She was raised in Pennsylvania by an aunt who spent much of her time attending to the health needs of the local black population. This woman became her first inspiration and prompted her to work as a nurse. Crumpler spent eight years, from 1852-60, helping others in this capacity in Massachusetts. Her work gained the attention of her supervisors, who encouraged her to pursue a career as a doctor. With recommendations from her employers, Crumpler was accepted into the New England Female Medical College in Boston, Massachusetts. Upon graduation from the school in March 1864, she was awarded a Doctress of Medicine degree. This was 15 years after the first white woman received a medical degree.

Immediately after completing school, Crumpler embarked on her medical career. She set up practice in Boston, gaining experience as a general practitioner serving many families. After the end of the Civil War, she recognized the need for health care services among former slaves in the South. This prompted her to relocate her medical practice to Richmond, Virginia. Her excellent reputation and hard work soon resulted in her serving many patients. After many years of working with the black community in Richmond, Crumpler decided to move back to where in career began in Boston.

In Boston, Crumpler began to organize her research and experience with the goal of publishing her insights. In 1883, her desire to educate others in general medical principles resulted in the publication of her *A Book of Medicinal Discourses in Two Parts.* In the book, based on her personal journals, she focused on instructions for women on how to provide medical care for themselves and their children.

Crumpler spent a lifetime caring for the welfare of others. The first black woman to receive a medical degree, she is also an inspiration for generously providing essential medical services in the local black communities she served.

SELECTED WRITINGS BY CRUMPLER:

Books

A Book of Medical Discourses in Two Parts. Boston: Cushman, Keating & Company, 1883.

FURTHER READING:

Books

Hine, Darlene Clark. *Black Women in America.* Brook-lyn, NY: Carlson Publishing, 1993.

Sammons, Vivian. *Blacks in Science and Medicine.* New York: Hemisphere Publishing, 1990.

—Sketch by Patrick J. Longe

Ulysses Grant Dailey
1885-1961
Surgeon

In an era when African Americans still faced discrimination in the practice of medicine, Ulysses Grant Dailey rose to become an internationally respected practioner in the field of surgery. Dailey was more than just a surgeon, however. As a teacher, he trained physicians who went on to positions of great responsibility in the medical community. As an editor, he helped shape a forward-looking editorial policy for the *Journal of the National Medical Association.* As an administrator, he founded a hospital in Chicago that offered training opportunities to physicians and treatment opportunities to patients regardless of race. Finally, as an ambassador of American medicine, he helped study and improve health care systems in many different countries.

Dailey was born in Donaldsonville, Louisiana, on August 3, 1885. His father, S. Toney Hanna Dailey, was a bartender; his mother, Missouri (Johnson) Dailey, was a teacher and a dressmaker. Dailey was a bright child, learning fluent French from his mother and aspiring to play classical piano music. In one of the most formative experiences of Dailey's childhood, Missouri took him and his brother Henry to the 1893 World Columbian Exposition in Chicago. There the young Grant, as he was called, met villagers from Dahomey, Africa, as well as the legendary black statesman Frederick Douglass. This taste of national politics and international culture was to bear rich fruit later in Dailey's life.

Dailey attended high school in Fort Worth, Texas. His education took an unexpected turn when Ernest L. Stephens, a local physician, encouraged him to study medicine. Dailey went on to earn a bachelor's degree from Dillard University in 1902; he chose to apply to Northwestern University Medical School. At the time, the choice of such a prestigious medical school was an audacious one for a young black man; in addition, he was the youngest student in the school that year. Dailey did not disappoint the medical school's admissions committee. Peter T. Burns, director of the Anatomical Laboratory, was sufficiently impressed with his performance to invite Dailey to work as his assistant in the summer of 1903. Dailey received his M.D. in 1906, graduating fifth in a class of 123.

A Promising Young Surgeon

Dailey experienced prejudice early in his career. In 1906, Mercy Hospital of Chicago refused to allow him to serve a two-week obstetrics rotation in the hospital's charity ward. Allen B. Kanavel, a professor at Northwestern, decided against offering him a position as an assistant because of his race. But these events only seemed to increase Dailey's determination to succeed.

If some faculty at Northwestern slowed Dailey's progress, others proved his allies. From 1906-08, he served as assistant demonstrator of anatomy at the medical school, a prestigious position for such a young physician. From 1907-08 he also served in a civil service position as an ambulance surgeon for the city of Chicago.

The year 1908 was a watershed year for Dailey's career. The pioneering black surgeon **Daniel Hale Williams** hired Dailey as his assistant at Provident Hospital in Chicago, giving the young surgeon invaluable experience assisting in the operating room and preparing lectures and papers. That year Dailey also joined the National Medical Association, a society of African American physicians which he was later to serve in many capacities. In 1909, Provident Hospital also offered Dailey a position as instructor in anatomy and physiology for its nursing school, a position he filled until 1917. From 1920-25, Dailey served as instructor of surgical nursing at Provident Hospital.

Most importantly, though, Dailey began writing a series of journal articles on surgery, which earned him recognition throughout the medical community. In 1910, he was promoted to associate surgeon at Provident Hospital. He left briefly in 1912 to pursue postgraduate study in Paris and Berlin and returned to Provident Hospital in that same year as an attending surgeon. In 1915, his growing status in the medical community led to his election as president of the National Medical Association.

Hospital Founder and Teacher

Dailey served as an attending surgeon at Provident Hospital until 1926, when he grew tired of what he saw as racial and political barriers at that institution. Dailey was determined to found a hospital that he could run according to his own judgment, and in that year he purchased two houses in Chicago which he converted into the Dailey Hospital and Sanitarium.

Dailey closed his hospital in 1932, partly because of the Great Depression. Although Dailey Hospital only existed for six years, it had amassed an impressive record for the safety of the surgical procedures performed there, as well as the number of them. Dailey decided to return to Provident Hospital as director of surgical residency and, later, senior attending surgeon and senior attending surgeon emeritus. In these roles, he trained a number of African

American surgeons who would later rise to leadership positions in the medical community. Despite travels around the world, he retained a position at Provident Hospital until his death in 1961.

In his later years, Dailey received more recognition from his surgical peers. In 1942, he completed the American Board of Surgery examination and became board certified. In 1945, the American College of Surgeons ended a longstanding moratorium on allowing black members and inducted Dailey and three other senior black surgeons as fellows of the college. In that same year, Dailey became a founding member of International College of Surgeons. In 1949, the National Medical Association awarded him with its Distinguished Service Medal. In 1952, he was elected to the International College of Surgeons' board of trustees. And in 1956, Northwestern University's Alumni Association awarded him the Golden Reunion Certificate for being the most distinguished member of the medical school class of 1906.

Dailey also played a large role in shaping the careers of younger African American physicians by serving in various positions at the *Journal of the National Medical Association*. He served on the journal's editorial board from 1910-43, helping to select papers for publication in the journal. He continued contributing articles on medicine as well as political and educational topics relevant to the black medical community. From 1948 to 1949, he served as the journal's editor-in-chief, and from then until nearly his death he served as a consulting editor.

An Ambassador of American Medicine

Although Dailey's career as a surgeon and medical educator was impressive, he may well have made an even more enduring contribution in his second career, as an ambassador for American medicine. In 1942, the Caribbean nation of Haiti invited him to come and study the impoverished country's struggling health care system. A lifelong admirer of Frederick Douglass—who had served as Haiti's American Consul—and a fluent French speaker, Dailey jumped at the chance. In Haiti, Dailey practiced medicine, taught, and offered recommendations to his Haitian colleagues.

The taste of diplomacy and foreign travel was not be enough for Dailey. In 1946, he became the first African American surgeon to speak on an international medical panel, in Lima, Peru. (Dailey eventually learned Spanish and German as well as French.) In 1951, the U.S. State Department made him a delegate on a four-and-a-half-month mission to Pakistan. As in Haiti, Dailey lectured, performed surgery, and gave surgical clinics in Pakistan's three largest medical centers. He also developed warm relationships with Pakistani colleagues that would last the rest of his life.

Dailey made a number of other international trips, including one to Bordeaux, France, in 1952, where his lecture on surgery in French made such an impression that

he was named a corresponding member of the Society of Surgeons of the University of Bordeaux. In 1953, he made another State Department trip, a whirlwind tour of Paris, Athens, Israel, Pakistan, India, and Ceylon. In Pakistan, Dailey and colleagues there founded the Pakistan Section of the International College of Surgeons. Yet another trip in 1953 took him to Africa, where he toured a school for midwife training in Nairobi, held consultations in Uganda, and visited and consulted with world-renowned physician and humanitarian Albert Schweitzer in what was then called the Belgian Congo. In 1954, he traveled to Haiti once again; later that same year he was presented by the Haitian government with the post of Honorary Consul of Haiti in Chicago. And in 1955, the International College of Surgeons sent him to Japan, the Phillipines, China, India, Pakistan, and Turkey. Also in 1955, his medical alma mater, Northwestern University, awarded him with an honorary doctorate in law as a "successful ambassador of democracy."

Dailey retired in 1956, moving to Haiti in 1957 with his wife of 40 years, Eleanor (Curtis) Dailey. But in less than two years, his health deteriorated. He received his last honor—a testimonial dinner from Provident Hospital colleagues—in Chicago in 1960, only a year before his death in 1961 of heart failure. Dailey was survived by Eleanor and their adopted children, Grant and Eleanor, twins born in 1919.

SELECTED WRITINGS BY DAILEY:

Periodicals

"Total Congenital Absence of the Veriform Appendix in Man." *Surgery, Gynecology and Obstetrics* (July/December 1910): 413-416.

"Vasovesiclities Acute Appendix." *New York Medical Journal* (June 1924).

"The Future of the Negro in Medicine." *Journal of the National Medical Association* (July/Spetember 1929).

"Proposals with Reference to the Idea of a Negro College of Surgeons." *Journal of the National Medical Association* (March 1942).

FURTHER READING:

Books

Organ, Claude H. Jr. and Kosiba, Margaret M. (eds.) *A Century of Black Surgeons*. Norman, OK: Transcript Press, 1987.

Logan, Rayford W. and Winston, Michael R. *Dictionary of American Negro Bography*. New York: W. W. Norton & Company Inc., 1982.

—Sketch by Kenneth B. Chiacchia

Marie M. Daly
1921-
Biochemist

Marie M. Daly was the first African American woman to earn a Ph.D. in chemistry. Throughout her career, her research interests focused on areas of health, particularly the effects on the heart and arteries of such factors as aging, cigarette smoking, hypertension, and cholesterol. In addition to research, she taught for 15 years at Yeshiva University's Albert Einstein College of Medicine.

Marie Maynard Daly was born in Corona, Queens, a neighborhood of New York City, on April 16, 1921. Her parents, Ivan C. Daly and Helen (Page) Daly, both valued learning and education and steadily encouraged her. Her father had wanted to become a chemist and had attended Cornell University, but was unable to complete his education for financial reasons and became a postal clerk. Daly attended the local public schools in Queens and graduated from Hunter College High School in Manhattan. She credits her interest in science to both her father's scientific background and to influential books such as Paul DeKruif's *The Microbe Hunters.*

Daly enrolled in Queens College as a chemistry major, graduating with a B.S. degree in 1942. The following year she received her M.S. from New York University and then went to Columbia University where she entered the doctoral program in biochemistry. In 1948 she made history at that university, becoming the first African American woman to earn a Ph.D. in chemistry.

Daly began teaching during her college days as a tutor at Queens College. She began her professional career a year before receiving her doctorate, when she accepted a position at Howard University in Washington, D.C., as an instructor in physical sciences. In 1951 she returned to New York first as a visiting investigator and then as an assistant in general physiology at the Rockefeller Institute. By 1955 she had become an associate in biochemistry at the Columbia University Research Service at the Goldwater Memorial Hospital. She taught there until 1971 when she left Columbia as an assistant professor of biochemistry to become associate professor of biochemistry and medicine at the Albert Einstein College of Medicine at Yeshiva University in New York.

Daly conducted most of her research in areas related to the biochemical aspects of human metabolism (how the body processes the energy it takes in) and the role of the kidneys in that process. She also focused on hypertension (high blood pressure) and atherosclerosis (accumulation of lipids or fats in the arteries). Her later work focused on the study of aortic (heart) smooth muscle cells in culture.

During her career, she held several positions concurrently with her teaching obligations, such as investigator for the American Heart Association from 1958 to 1963 and career scientist for the Health Research Council of New York from 1962 to 1972. She was also a fellow of the Council on Arteriosclerosis and the American Association for the Advancement of Science, a member of the American Chemical Society, a member of the board of governors of the New York Academy of Science from 1974 to 1976, and a member of the Harvey Society, the American Society of Biological Chemists, the National Association for the Advancement of Colored People, the National Association of Negro Business and Professional Women, and Phi Beta Kappa and Sigma Xi. In 1988 Daly contributed to a scholarship fund set up at Queens College to aid African American students interested in the sciences. Daly, who married Vincent Clark in 1961, retired from teaching in 1986.

SELECTED WRITINGS BY DALY:

Books

"Hypertension: A Precursor of Arteriosclerosis." In *Hypertension: Mechanisms and Management,* edited by Gaddo Onesti, Kwan Eun Kim, and John H. Moyer, Grune & Stratton (New York), 1973.

FURTHER READING:

Books

Grinstein, Louise S., Rose K. Rose, and Miriam H. Rafailovich, eds. *Women in Chemistry and Physics.* Greenwood Press, 1993, pp. 145–149.

Periodicals

Prestwidge, K. J. "Scientifically Speaking . . . !" *New York Voice,* (February 4, 1984).

—Sketch by Leonard C. Bruno

Walter T. Daniels
1908-1991
Structural engineer

Walter T. Daniels was the first African American to earn a Ph.D. in engineering. During his long career as an educator and administrator at Howard University, he realized his professional goal of developing a renowned engineering program for black students.

Walter Thomas Daniels (some sources cite the surname as "Daniel") was born in Fort Ring Gold, Texas, on

April 26, 1908, and was raised in Arizona. Daniels enrolled in Prairie View A&M College in 1925, intent on pursuing a career in engineering. The following year he was accepted into the engineering program at the University of Arizona. Due to the racial barriers then enforced at the university, Daniels was not permitted to associate with his classmates and was therefore prevented from taking laboratory classes, which required interaction with a lab partner. Furthermore, he was made to sit physically apart from the other students in the classroom. Despite these obstacles, he graduated with a bachelor of science degree in 1929.

Daniels returned to Prairie View College and taught there for two years. During that time, his goal of creating professional engineering opportunities for African Americans was crystallized. Energized by this ambition, Daniels first sought advanced education for himself and entered the civil engineering graduate program at Iowa State University. He received a master of science degree in 1932, and, following several years of teaching at North Carolina A&T College, he returned to Iowa State to take a Ph.D. in civil engineering in 1941. In doing so, Daniels became the first African American to earn a doctoral degree in the field. After graduating he taught for one year at Southern University. Upon receiving his professional license in 1943, he also became the first African American engineer to be licensed in the state of Louisiana.

Daniels became a member of the civil engineering faculty at Howard University in Washington, D.C., in 1943. He eventually became chair of the civil engineering department and was dean of the School of Engineering for a short time. During his years as professor of structural engineering he was able to realize his dream, developing a curriculum that comprised an outstanding engineering program for African American students. Although he resigned his position as department chair in 1971, he continued to teach at Howard until 1976 when he retired due to health problems

Daniels made significant contributions not only in engineering education, but also in the real world of the practicing engineer. He designed structures that were constructed in Washington, D.C., Baltimore, Maryland, and West Africa. On the Howard campus, he designed the L. K. Downing Engineering Building and helped develop the University Physical Plant, including designing its water loop system. Daniels also served as a curriculum consultant in science and mathematics to the District of Columbia public school system. He was a member of the American Society of Civil Engineers, the American Concrete Institute, the American Society for Engineering Education, the Pre-stressed Concrete Institute, Tau Beta Pi, and Sigma Xi. He was married and had two children.

FURTHER READING:

Periodicals

"Walter Daniels: A Special Tribute to an Engineering Giant," *The Black Collegian,* (January/February 1979): 136, 138.

—*Sketch by Leonard C. Bruno*

Stephen Smith Davis

Stephen Smith Davis
1910-1977
Engineer and educator

Stephen Smith Davis brought graduate programs to the engineering curricula of Howard University. Howard has long stood at the top of the nation's black colleges and universities, but as recently as 1967, its engineering departments offered only bachelor's degrees. Davis emphasized the hiring of new faculty members with advanced degrees, and introduced programs leading to the master's degree in 1968 and later, the Ph.D. As a result of Davis's work, Howard's engineering school rose to stand on a par with those of other major universities. Davis's field was mechanical engineering, and he held a patent for his design of supersonic wind tunnel nozzles.

Davis was born in Philadelphia on October 24, 1910, the son of Stephen Davis and the former Rosa Elizabeth Norris. His father worked for the city gas company, and according to family lore this influenced young Davis's choice of engineering as a career. Following the death of his father, his mother moved to Boston, where Davis went to high school at the Lowell Institute, which was affiliated with the Massachusetts Institute of Technology.

Davis graduated from Lowell in 1933 and then went to Howard University in Washington, D.C., where he received a Bachelor of Science degree in mechanical engineering in 1936. He then found work at Howard's power plant as a boiler operator. His son Stephen told contributor T. A. Heppenheimer in a telephone interview on May 7, 1998, that his father's job had been simply to maintain the boilers that heated the campus. Still, the work had fringe benefits, for in the course of his duties, he met the woman he would marry. In the words of his son Stephen, "She was sitting on a bench, and one day he popped up through one of the manholes. That's apparently when he first met her."

He quickly made his way from boiler rooms to classrooms, as in 1938 he joined the faculty of Howard as an instructor in engineering. In that year he also became a registered professional engineer, specializing in heating, ventilation, and air conditioning. Then in 1941 the nation entered World War II. This led him into a career in defense research that paralleled his career at Howard.

Guided Missiles and Wind Tunnels

Davis worked at the National Bureau of Standards as a mechanical engineer during the war years of 1943-45. Here he contributed to early work on the development of guided missiles. Such missiles were to strike targets under remote control, carrying out military tasks that presented danger to piloted bombers and fighters. Davis's particular project was the Bat, a naval missile that was carried by an airplane. The Bat had a television camera that allowed controllers to see where it was flying, along with radio equipment with which an operator could control its course. Launched from the air, it enabled carrier aircraft to conduct attacks while remaining out of range of antiaircraft fire. It entered service late in the war, and was used with some success.

Following the war, Davis enrolled at Harvard University, receiving a Master of Science degree in mechanical engineering after only a single year of study. At Howard, this qualified him for promotion to associate professor, which gave him a permanent position on the faculty. But he continued to work in defense research. From 1953 to 1963 he served as a consultant and aeronautical engineer at the Naval Ordnance Laboratory, a leading research center. Here he made a useful contribution to the design of wind tunnels, for which he was awarded a patent.

Wind tunnels are used extensively in designing new aircraft and in developing their engines. Investigators place an engine or a model of the aircraft within a chamber, and blow air through the chamber at high speed. This allows them to study the engine's performance in a laboratory, and to observe the characteristics of the airplane design without having to build and fly a full-size version.

It is often useful to conduct tests at several different speeds of airflow. When the airflow is subsonic—less than the speed of sound—this can usually be done simply by changing the power that drives the flow. But when the airflow is supersonic—faster than sound—the procedure

could be cumbersome. Engineers achieve a supersonic airflow by having the flow expand through a nozzle, which resembles a rocket engine. In Davis's day, changing the speed meant changing the nozzle, which called for physically removing this major component and replacing it with another one. Davis addressed this problem by inventing a flexible nozzle for use in high-speed wind tunnels. By changing the shape of this nozzle, investigators could vary the airspeed at will, without removing the entire component. This invention was part of Davis's broader involvement with wind tunnels. He also studied temperature-resistant materials for use in airflows of particularly high speed. He worked on the development of air compressors as well, and co-authored a report on this topic that was published by the Office of Naval Research.

Leads Howard University Toward Doctoral Program

Meanwhile, he continued to teach at Howard University, where he became a professor of mechanical engineering in 1956. Among some 100 black colleges and universities within the United States, Howard stood out. Its location in Washington, D.C. placed it within a major city, whereas many similar institutions were located in towns of the rural Deep South. In addition, it received funds from the federal government. Its alumni included the diplomat Ralph Bunche, who won the Nobel Peace Prize in 1950.

Yet despite Howard's prominence, its School of Engineering and Architecture, where Davis was a member of the faculty, offered a restricted range of technical programs and awarded only bachelor's degrees. Students could earn the bachelor's simply by taking courses. And while the coursework at Howard was more demanding than that of a high school or community college, a bachelor's degree represents no more than a step toward the Ph.D.

It takes more than coursework to earn a Ph.D.; it takes original research. Typically, a graduate student works with one or more professors, often solving a problem posed by them, with the solution representing a new contribution to knowledge within some field. The student writes a dissertation, a book-length presentation of the problem and its solution, and the dissertation is reviewed by faculty in that area of study. The award of the Ph.D. then certifies that the student is ready to pursue a career in research, contributing to the progress of this field.

The right to award Ph.D. degrees is so important that it defines the very name of an institution. A "university" is qualified to grant this degree in at least some fields; a "college" can not. Howard was indeed a university, but it awarded the Ph.D. only within a restricted range of subjects, and these did not include engineering.

Davis set out to change this. He started by broadening his own background, attending Cornell University in 1958 and the University of Michigan in 1959, taking courses in nuclear engineering. This suited his background in naval research, as the Navy's Hyman Rickover had built the first nuclear-powered submarines and was preparing to build nuclear aircraft carriers. At the time there was also strong interest in generating electricity using nuclear power plants.

Responding to these developments, Davis succeeded in building a nuclear reactor at Howard. It was of a commercial design, and was incapable of sustaining a true nuclear reaction; it merely increased the rate of radioactive decay of its uranium fuel. Nevertheless, his son Stephen notes that "this was the only active nuclear reactor in the Washington area." Davis also built a subsonic wind tunnel with a testing chamber that was four feet square (0.36 sq m), making it large enough to accommodate aeronautical models of some size.

He became chairman of the Department of Mechanical Engineering in 1962, and quickly began recruiting holders of the Ph.D. as new faculty members. He pursued this effort with new vigor after he became dean of the School of Engineering and Architecture in 1964. By 1970, his last year as dean, he had increased the number of faculty members with Ph.D.s from two to 40. His colleague Lucius Walker, who succeeded him as dean, assessed his contribution in a telephone interview with contributor T. A. Heppenheimer on May 12, 1998: Davis directed "the transition from a faculty that was degreed at the master's level to one that was degreed at the Ph.D. level."

Davis also broadened the range of programs, introducing the first undergraduate curriculum in chemical engineering at any black university or college. He introduced new graduate programs in nuclear engineering, architecture, and city planning. Howard began offering master's degrees in civil, mechanical, and electrical engineering in 1968. Davis's newly-hired faculty members, with their doctorate degrees, expanded these graduate programs to offer the Ph.D. The first such program was initiated in 1974. Meanwhile, Davis remained on the faculty, stepping down as dean in 1970 but continuing to teach until his death in 1977.

Makes Washington Attractive to Tourists

In addition to his professional work, Davis was active in civic affairs. His son Stephen notes that "there are a lot of commissions around here, that political friends of anyone in power can get appointed to." Davis knew the political leader Walter Washington. When Washington became mayor, he appointed Davis vice chairman of the District of Columbia Redevelopment Land Agency. Davis served from 1967 to 1975 and authorized a redevelopment of part of the city waterfront, adding upscale hotels and restaurants to the area, along with a marina.

He was married on June 25, 1938, to Aileen Priscilla Harris, the woman he met while emerging from his manhole. They had one child, Stephen Harris, who currently practices as an attorney. Davis's professional distinctions included a certificate of appreciation in 1945, signed by James Conant, president of Harvard University, and by Vannevar Bush, head of the wartime Office of Scientific Research and Development. (*Newsweek* later described

Bush as "the most powerful scientist in the world" during World War II.)

Davis enjoyed tennis and photography, and was an enthusiastic sailor. He also became one of the first black members of Washington's exclusive Cosmos Club. He died in that city on January 15, 1977, of heart failure.

FURTHER READING:

Books

The National Cyclopedia of American Biography. Clifton, NJ: James T. White and Co., 1980.

—*Sketch by T. A. Heppenheimer*

Ellen Irene Diggs
1906-
Anthropologist

E llen Irene Diggs was one of the first black women anthropologists. Holder of a doctoral degree, she was a longtime assistant to W.E.B. Dubois and a faculty member of Morgan State College for more than 30 years before her retirement in 1976. She has spent her life studying race relations and cultural differences among blacks in the United States and Latin America.

Irene Diggs was born on April 13, 1906, in Monmouth, Illinois, a small college town surrounded by farms. Growing up quite aware of the inequality black persons were subject to, she focused on education as a means of advancement. Her first year at Monmouth College was funded by a scholarship provided to the high school student with the highest grade point average. She then transferred to the University of Minnesota for its more extensive curriculum. There she majored in sociology, graduating in 1928. Immediately, she proceeded to Atlanta University to pursue a graduate degree in sociology. In 1933, she received the school's first master's degree. While taking W.E.B. Dubois's classes, she so impressed her professor that he asked her to become his research assistant. Their professional relationship lasted 11 years, during which time she contributed to five of his books. Together they founded the journal *Phylon: A Review of Race and Culture.*

In the early 1940s, Diggs traveled to Cuba for language study as a Roosevelt Fellow of the Institute of International Education. She continued her studies at the University of Havana with the renowned professor of ethnography, Fernando Ortiz. In 1945, she earned her doctorate from this university. After World War II, she continued her research in Uruguay and Argentina as a visiting scholar under the auspices of the U.S. State Department. While in South America she developed an interest in the fine art of the peoples she was studying and went on to become a recognized authority on this subject, providing articles to many publications. In 1947, she joined the faculty of Morgan State College, where she remained a prominent member of the sociology and anthropology department until her retirement in 1976.

Diggs's work focuses on cultural continuity and cultural change. She studied the transformation of African culture not only in Latin America but also in the United States, and she examined how race relations varied in these different geographic locations. Due to teaching duties, her writings have consisted mostly of articles for numerous publications, including contributions to several histories of the African experience.

Diggs is a fellow of the American Anthropological Association, the American Association for the Advancement of Science, the American Association of Applied Anthropology, and the American Association of Physical Anthropologists. She is a member of the American Sociological Association, New York Academy of Sciences, International African Institute, and the American Association of University Women.

The Association of Black Anthropologists presented her with their Distinguished Scholar award in 1978. A dedicated community activist, she is also involved with many community organizations near her home in Baltimore.

SELECTED WRITINGS BY DIGGS:

Books

(Contributor) *Black Chronology from 4000 B.C. to the Abolition of the Slave Trade.* Boston: G.K. Hall, 1983.
(Co-editor) *The Encyclopedia of the Negro.* New York: HW Wilson Company,1945.

Periodicals

"Zumbi and the Republic of Os Palmares." *Phylon*14 (First Quarter 1953): 62-70.
"Color in Spanish America." *Journal of Negro History* 38 (October 1953): 403-27.
"Legacy." *Freedomways* 5 (Winter 1965): 18-19.
"Cuba before and after Castro." *The New American* (July 15, 1976).
"The Biological and Cultural Impact of Blacks on the United States." *Phylon* 41 (Summer 1980):152-166.

FURTHER READING:

Books

Notable Black American Women. Detroit: Gale Research, 1992.

Who's Who Among Black Americans. Detroit: Gale Research,1994.

Periodicals

Bolles, A. Lynn. "Irene Diggs: A Biographical Sketch." *Outreach* 5 (1983): 1-2.

—*Sketch by Patrick J. Longe*

Linneaus C. Dorman
1935-
Organic chemist

As a boy, one of Linneaus Dorman's favorite pastimes was playing with a friend's chemistry set. His early interest pointed him toward a career at the Dow Chemical Company, where his research led to important breakthroughs in medicine and environmental protection.

Linneaus C. Dorman was born in Orangeburg, South Carolina, on June 28, 1935. Both his parents were teachers, and they encouraged their son to take his studies seriously. In truth, they did not have to do much in the way of encouragement; young Linneaus was an eager and curious student who showed an early interest in science.

He attended the "laboratory school" of South Carolina State College; this was where college students in the teaching program got their first experience, under the direction of experienced teachers. This experience provided Dorman with a solid educational program at a time when many black children in the South could expect little more than perfunctory schooling.

Dorman's early interest in chemistry was spurred on by his high school teachers, and in 1952 he entered Bradley University in Peoria, Illinois. He majored in chemistry and excelled in his studies, but he was also able to devote time to activities at the nearby Ward Chapel AME Church. He sang in the church's junior choir, and he made a number of friends. One of them, a librarian named Phae Hubble, would become his wife in 1957.

He graduated in 1956 and was accepted into the graduate program at Indiana University (he was the second black student from Bradley to be accepted there). To help finance his studies—and later to help support his wife and small child—he worked summers as a chemist for the U.S. Department of Agriculture's Northern Regional Research Laboratory, and as a teaching assistant at Indiana. He also received a research fellowship from the Dow Chemical Company. In 1960, shortly before his graduation, he was co-winner of the American Oil Chemist Society's Bond Award for a research paper he presented.

Immediately after receiving his Ph.D. in 1961, Dorman was offered a position at Dow's research center in Midland, Michigan. For more than 30 years, until his retirement in 1997, he was involved in a variety of chemical research projects. He worked with proteins and their building blocks, the peptides; his research helped develop compounds that kept blood from clotting and relieved asthma. Later, he found ways to mix agricultural chemicals (such as insect repellants) with other compounds that would lessen the harmful impact on the environment. He was awarded a patent for an artificial bone material that could serve as a replacement for irreparably damaged natural bone.

He was named Dow's Inventor of the Year in 1983 and received an honorary degree from Saginaw Valley State University in 1988. He also received awards from the American Chemical Society and Bradley University. Over the years, he has also involved himself in community activities, working with students to build an interest in science.

FURTHER READING:

Books

Kessler, James H. et al. *Distinguished African American Scientists of the Twentieth Century.* Phoenix: Oryx Press, 1996.

—*Sketch by George A. Milite*

Charles R. Drew

Charles R. Drew
1904-1950
Surgeon and blood researcher

Charles R. Drew was a renowned surgeon, teacher, and researcher. He was responsible for founding two of the world's largest blood banks. Because of his research into the storage and shipment of blood plasma—blood without cells—he is credited with saving the lives of hundreds of Britains during World War II. He was director of the first American Red Cross effort to collect and bank blood on a large scale. In 1942, a year after he was made a diplomat of surgery by the American Board of Surgery at Johns Hopkins University, he became the first African American surgeon to serve as an examiner on the board.

Charles Richard Drew was the eldest of five children. He was born on June 3, 1904, in Washington, D.C., to Richard T. Drew, a carpet layer, and Nora (Burrell) Drew, a school teacher and graduate of Miner Teachers College. As

a student, Drew excelled in academics and sports, winning four swimming medals by the age of eight. In 1922 he graduated from Paul Laurence Dunbar High School, where he received the James E. Walker Memorial Medal in his junior and senior years for his athletic performance in several sports, including football, basketball, baseball, and track.

Drew attended Amherst College in Western Massachusetts on an athletic scholarship. He would be one of 16 black students to graduate from Amherst during the years 1920 to 1929. He served as captain of the track team; he was enormously popular and was awarded several honors, including the Thomas W. Ashley Memorial Trophy for being the football team's most valuable player.

Although Drew was a gifted athlete, he worked hard in school to keep high grades. By the time he graduated in 1926, he had decided to apply to medical school. However, his funds were severely limited. Before he could go to medical school, he had to work for a couple of years. He accepted a job at Morgan State College in Baltimore, Maryland, as a professor of chemistry and biology, as well as director of the college's sports program. During the next two years, he paid off his undergraduate loans and put some money aside for medical school.

In 1928 he was finally able to apply to medical school. However, African Americans who wished to become doctors at that time did not have many opportunities. There were two colleges open to them. Drew applied to Howard University and was rejected because he did not have enough credits in English. Harvard University accepted him for the following year, but he did not want to wait so he applied to and was immediately accepted to McGill University in Montreal, Canada.

Embarks on Research in Blood

At McGill, Drew continued to excel in sports and academics. In 1930 he won the annual prize in neuroanatomy and was elected to Alpha Phi Omega, the school's honorary medical society. During this time, under the influence of Dr. John Beattie, a visiting professor from England, Drew began his research in blood transfusions. The four different types of blood—A, B, AB, and O—had recently been discovered. Subsequently, doctors knew what type of blood they were giving to patients and were avoiding the negative effects of mixing incompatible blood types. However, because whole blood was highly perishable, the problem of having the appropriate blood type readily available still existed. In 1930 when Drew and Beattie began their research, blood could only be stored for seven days before it began to spoil.

In 1933 Drew graduated from McGill with his Medical Degree and Master of Surgery degree. He interned at the Royal Victoria Hospital and finished his residency at Montreal General. During this time, he continued researching with Beattie. Because of his father's death in 1934, Drew decided to return to Washington, D.C., to take care of his family. In 1935 he accepted a position to teach pathology at Howard University Medical School. The next year he obtained a one-year residency at Freedmen's Hospital in Washington, D.C.

Develops Process to Preserve Plasma

In 1938, having accepted a two-year Rockefeller Fellowship, Drew continued his work in blood at Columbia University-Presbyterian Hospital in New York. Under the auspices of the Department of Surgery, he worked with Dr. John Scudder and Dr. E. H. L. Corwin on the problem of blood storage. Drew began to study the use of plasma as a substitute for whole blood. Because red blood cells contain the substance that determines blood type, their absence in plasma means that a match between donor and recipient is not necessary, which makes it ideal for emergencies. In 1939, while supervising a blood bank at Columbia Medical Center, Drew developed a method to process and preserve blood plasma so that it could be stored and shipped to great distances. (Dehydrated plasma could be reconstituted by adding water just before the transfusion.)

Drew graduated from Columbia University in 1940, with a Doctor of Science degree; he was the first African American to receive this degree. In his dissertation, "Banked Blood: A Study in Blood Preservation," Drew showed that liquid plasma lasted longer than whole blood. He was asked to be the medical supervisor on the "Blood for Britain" campaign, launched by the Blood Transfusion Betterment Association. At the height of World War II,

Nazi warplanes were bombing British cities regularly and there was a desperate shortage of blood to treat the wounded. In order to meet the huge demand for plasma, Drew initiated the use of "bloodmobiles"—trucks equipped with refrigerators. The Red Cross has continued to use them during blood drives. In 1941 after the success of "Blood for Britain," Drew became director of the American Red Cross Blood Bank in New York. He was asked to organize a massive blood drive for the U.S. Army and Navy, consisting of 100,000 donors. However, when the military issued a directive to the Red Cross that blood be typed according to the race of the donor, and that African American donors be refused, Drew was incensed. He denounced the policy as unscientific, stating that there was no evidence to support the claim that blood type differed according to race. His statements were later confirmed by other scientists, and the government eventually allowed African American volunteers to donate blood, although it was still segregated. Ironically, in 1977 the American Red Cross headquarters in Washington, D.C., was renamed the Charles R. Drew Blood Center.

Drew was asked to resign from the project. He returned to Washington, D.C., and resumed teaching. In 1941 he was made professor of surgery at Howard University, where he had been rejected 13 years earlier, and chief surgeon at Freedmen's Hospital. In 1943 he became the first black surgeon to serve as an examiner on the American Board of Surgery. He was an inspiration and role model to his students and received numerous honorary degrees and awards during this period of his life, including the National Association for the Advancement of Colored People (NAACP) Spingarn Medal in 1944. He wrote numerous articles on blood for various scientific journals, and in 1946 was elected Fellow to the International College of Surgeons.

In 1939 Drew married (Minnie) Lenore Robbins, and they had four children. Drew continued teaching in Washington, D.C.; during the summer of 1949, as a consultant to the Surgeon General, he travelled with a team of four physicians, assessing hospital facilities throughout Occupied Europe. On March 31, 1950, after performing several operations, Drew allowed his colleagues and some of his students to talk him into attending a medical meeting being held at Tuskegee Institute as part of its Founder's Day celebrations. When Drew dozed off while driving near Burlington, North Carolina, his car overturned, and he was killed.

Despite his untimely death at the age of 45, Drew left behind a legacy of life-saving techniques. Additionally, many of his students rose to prominence in the medical field. In 1976 Drew's portrait was unveiled at the Clinical Center of the National Institutes of Health, making him the first African American to join its gallery of scientists. Four years later, his life was honored with a postage stamp, issued as part of the U.S. Postal Service's "Great Americans" series.

FURTHER READING:

Books

Haber, Louis. *Black Pioneers of Science and Invention.* Harcourt, 1970, pp. 151–167.
Hardwick, Richard. *Charles Richard Drew: Pioneer in Blood Research.* Scribners, 1967.
Lichello, Robert. *Pioneer in Blood Plasma: Dr. Charles Richard Drew.* Simon & Schuster, 1968.
Sammons, Vivian Ovelton. *Blacks in Science and Medicine.* Hemisphere Publishing, 1990, pp. 78–79.
Wynes, Charles. *Charles Richard Drew: The Man and the Myth.* University of Illinois Press, 1988.

Periodicals

Bims, Hamilton. "Charles Drew's 'Other' Medical Revolution," *Ebony,* (February 1974): 88–96.
Journal of the National Medical Association, (March 1971): 156–57; (July 1950): 239–45.

—Sketch by Geeta Kothari

Joseph C. Dunbar, Jr.
1944-
Physiologist

With over 100 publications to his credit, Joseph C. Dunbar, Jr., is a recognized authority on diabetes, including the roles of insulin and the pancreas in the disease. The primary focus of his research is how insulin levels affect the nervous system and increase the likelihood of cardiovascular problems such as heart attacks and strokes.

Dunbar was born on August 27, 1944, in Vicksburg, Mississippi. The son of the Joseph C. Dunbar, Sr., and Henrienne M. (Watkins) Dunbar, he grew up in the town of Port Gibson, where his father was an agricultural extension agent and his mother was a schoolteacher. Dunbar and his two sisters all chose careers related to biology. Like his parents and elder sister before him, Dunbar attended Alcorn College in Lorman, Mississippi, where he earned his bachelor of science degree in 1963.

When he graduated from Alcorn, Dunbar worked for one year as a biology teacher and band director at a high school in Bassville, Mississippi, while he applied to graduate schools and saved money to pay his fees. In 1964, Dunbar began his graduate work at Texas Southern University in Houston. He focused in part on gland functions, and this would be key to his later work on diabetes. He was awarded his master's degree in 1966. After graduation,

Texas Southern University asked him to join their faculty, and Dunbar taught there for one year. During this year, he met Agnes Estorge, whom he married on July 1, 1967. They would eventually have two daughters together, Andrea and Erica.

In 1967, Dunbar relocated to Detroit, Michigan, where he entered Wayne State University's doctoral program. While a graduate student, Dunbar worked as a research assistant, conducting studies related to diabetes. Diabetes is a disease wherein a gland in the pancreas does not produce enough insulin, a hormone that regulates blood sugar in the body. Dunbar's research concerned chemical alternatives to insulin, and new methods of testing these alternatives. He earned his doctoral degree in 1970 and began postgraduate work at Detroit's Sinai Hospital. Dunbar continued to work on research related to diabetes. He studied glands, including the reaction of the pancreas to insulin injections, the relationship of body weight to pancreatic function, and how certain glands work and their reaction to certain medicines.

Dunbar remained affiliated with Sinai Hospital until 1978. In 1972, Dunbar was also hired as assistant professor in the physiology department at Wayne State University's school of medicine. His research subjects included the possibilities and implications of pancreas transplants, the relationship of the pancreas and pancreatic functions on other organs, and the effect of hormones other than insulin on sugar storage and their use in the human body. He is currently trying to determine how diabetes increases the incidence of heart attacks and strokes in people suffering from the disease. His research is concerned specifically with the effect of diabetes on the central nervous system and insulin's role in regulating it.

Dunbar was awarded a Minority Achievement Award in 1989. Three years later, in 1992, Dunbar was given the Charles Gershenson Distinguished Faculty Fellowship. By 1998, Dunbar was the chairman of the physiology department at Wayne State University.

SELECTED WRITINGS BY DUNBAR:

Periodicals

(with Y. Hu) "Regional Vascular and Cardiac Response to Systemic Neuropeptide-Y in Normal and Diabetic Rats." *Peptides* 18 (1997): 809-15.
(with Z. Duanmu and K. Lapanowski) "Insulin-like Growth Factor-1 Decreases Sympathetic Nerve Activity. The Effect is Modulated by Glycemic Status." *Proceedings of the Society of Experimental Biological Medicine* 216 (1997): 93-97.

—Sketch by A. Petrusso

Katherine Mary Dunham

Katherine Mary Dunham
1909-

Anthropologist and dance choreographer

Katherine Mary Dunham has spent a lifetime contributing to the areas of dance and anthropology. As one of the founders of the anthropological dance movement, Dunham combined aspects of traditional ballet with jazz rhythms, Caribbean dance, and African ritual to create a new dance form known today as the Dunham technique. She has toured over 57 countries, mounted dozens of Broadway revues, formed dance companies, choreographed numerous films, and taught inner-city black youth the virtues of African heritage.

Katherine Dunham was born in Glen Ellyn, Illinois on June 22, 1909, to Albert Dunham and Fanny June (Taylor) Dunham. As a child of a mixed-race marriage, her diverse ancestral heritage includes African, Madagascan, French-Canadian, and American Indian blood. Her mother died when Katherine was four, and she moved to the poverty-stricken south side of Chicago with her brother, Albert Jr., and their aunt Lulu while her father worked as a traveling salesman. In Chicago, she was exposed to chorus and theater, which taught her the joys of music and dance.

Studies in Anthropology and Dance

A short time thereafter, Albert Dunham married former schoolteacher Annette Poindexter, and Katherine moved with them to Joliet, Illinois. After graduating from high school, she attended Joliet Township Junior College and then attended the University of Chicago. She studied anthropology while beginning to teach dance, a skill she had learned from years of classes. In 1931, as a means of supporting herself through school, Katherine Dunham helped form Ballets Negre, a troupe which made its debut at the Beaux Arts Ball in Chicago. The group closed shortly thereafter due to a lack of funds, and Dunham formed the Negro Dance Group, later known as the Katherine Dunham Dance Company. In 1934, she performed with the Negro Dance Group at Chicago World's Fair. After performing in *La Guiablesse,* a ballet based on West Indian legend, Dunham decided to pursue research about the cultural and anthropological origins of dance.

Before Dunham earned her bachelor's degree in anthropology from the University of Chicago in 1936, she won a Rosenwald Foundation travel fellowship to research West Indian and African dance. She studied with the head of Northwestern University's African studies program for three months and then left for her field study in Haiti, Martinique, Jamaica, and Trinidad. In her travels, she encountered ancient dance customs and religious voodoo rituals. Living and dancing with Haitians, she developed an African-based theory of movement that she incorporated into her choreography. Dunham wrote three books about her experiences in the Caribbean: *Katherine Dunham's Journey to Accompong* (1946), *The Dances of Haiti,* (1947), and *Island Possessed* (1969). After returning from the Caribbean, Dunham continued her research in dance and anthropology; she received a master of science degree from the University of Chicago and a doctoral degree from Northwestern University.

Success in Dance and Politics

Dunham launched her professional career as a choreographer in 1938, and the year 1939 marked the beginning of her success. She wrote, choreographed, and directed *L'Ag'Ya,* based on a Martinican fighting dance, which won great acclaim. Dunham and her company performed African-American dance routines with Duke Ellington and his orchestra. Her company was hired for numerous successful shows and films. By the late 1940s, the Katherine Dunham Dance Company was making their first overseas tour.

The dance troupe toured Europe, Australia, and the Far East in the 1950s. During this time, she composed an autobiography of the first 18 years of her life, *A Touch of Innocence,* which was published in 1959. In 1963, Dunham choreographed a highly praised production of *Aida,* performed by the New York Metropolitan Opera. In 1965, she dissolved her dance company. She left the United States for Senegal, where she served as the technical cultural advisor to President Leopold Sedar Senghor and helped train the

Senegalese National Ballet for the First World Festival of Negro Arts in Dakar. Contemplating retirement as a performer, Dunham returned to the United States in 1967 and accepted an invitation from Southern Illinois University to work as an artist in residence. She created the Performing Arts Training Center and Dynamic Museum in East St. Louis in order to reach black inner-city youth through African culture and living arts.

Throughout her career, Dunham collected many awards, some of which include the Professional Achievement Award from the University of Chicago Alumni Association, the Dance Magazine Award, the Distinguished Service Award from Southern Illinois University, the St. Louis Argus Award, the National Center of Afro-American Artists Award, the Black Merit Academy Award, the Albert Schweitzer Music Award, the Kennedy Center Honors Award, and an induction into the Black Filmmakers Hall of Fame. After Dunham retired, she founded the Children's Workshop and the Dunham Technique Seminar and Institute for Interculture Communication. She is also the founder of the Foundation for the Development and Preservation of Cultural Arts and the Dunham Fund for Research and Development of Cultural Arts. In the early 1990s, Dunham made headlines around the world as an activist for her support of Haitian refugees.

In 1939, Dunham married John Pratt, a white American of Canadian birth. He was the chief stage and costume designer for her shows throughout her career. In 1952 Dunham and Pratt adopted their daughter, Marie Christine, a five-year-old French Martinique girl. After a long and happy marriage, Pratt died in 1986. Today, Dunham divides her time between St. Louis and Haiti.

SELECTED WRITINGS BY DUNHAM:

Books

Katherine Dunham's Journey to Accompong. 1946.
The Dances of Haiti. 1947.
A Touch of Innocence. Chicago: University of Chicago Press, 1959.
Island Possessed. New York: Doubleday, 1969.

FURTHER READING

Books

Aschenbrenner, Joyce. *Katherine Dunham.* Congress on Research in Dance, 1981.
Beckford, Ruth. *Katherine Dunham, a Biography.* New York: M. Dekker, 1979.
Bigelow, Barbara Carlisle, ed. *Contemporary Black Biography,* vol. 4. Detroit: Gale Research, 1993.
Dannett, Sylvia G. L. *Profiles of Negro Womanhood,* vol. 2. Yonkers, New York: Educational Heritage, 1966.

Harnan, Terry. *African Rhythm—American Dance.* New York: Knoft, 1974.
Haskins, James. *Katherine Dunham.* New York: Coward, McCann and Geoghegen, 1982.
Mangione, Jerre. *The Dream and the Deal: The Federal Writers' Project, 1935-1943* Boston: Little, Brown and Co., 1972.
Smith, Jessie Carney, ed. *Notable Black American Women.* Detroit: Gale Research, 1992.

Other

"Katherine Dunham." *The American Dance Festival.* http://www.americandancefestival.org/dunham.html (April 1998).
"Katherine Dunham." *The Kennedy Center Honors,* http://kennedy-center.org/1983/dunham.html (April 1998).

—*Sketch by Alison Wellford*

James Durham (Derham)
1762-18??
Physician

James Durham, born a slave, became the first black physician to practice in the United States. His success in treating such life-threatening diseases as yellow fever and diphtheria earned him the respect of many prominent doctors, notably Benjamin Rush of Philadelphia. Durham became well-known as an expert on diseases of the throat, and he was also noted for his theories on the connection between disease and climate.

Early Life

Durham, or Derham (he was known by both but he spelled his name Durham) was born in Philadelphia on May 1, 1762. Philadelphia at this time was an important base for the Quakers, a religious sect that opposed slavery and later became active in the abolitionist movement. Although there were slaveowners in Philadelphia, they were often more lenient than those in more agricultural areas, particularly in the South.

The family that initially owned Durham taught him to read and write and gave him some schooling in Scripture. While still a child, Durham was sold to Dr. John Kearsley, Jr., a highly regarded physician. Kearsley gave young Durham his first experience with medicine, allowing him to compound simple medicines and perform rudimentary medical duties. Kearsley died in 1772, and Durham became the property of Gregory West, an apothecary. At the war's end he became the property of yet another physician, Robert

Dove, who had emigrated from Scotland to New Orleans in the 1770s.

In New Orleans, Dove gave Durham additional medical training and allowed him to assist in numerous medical procedures. Durham was allowed to make money as a medical assistant and apothecary, and on April 2, 1783, he purchased his freedom from Dove for 500 pesos. Durham opened a medical practice and soon became well acquainted with the diseases common to the New Orleans region. He also learned to speak French (in which he became fluent) and some Spanish.

Makes His Mark

Other blacks before Durham had earned reputations in medicine in colonial America. One slave had found effective treatment for certain skin diseases; another one had been able to cure scurvy. But Durham was the first black to serve as a bona fide physician. The respect he earned from other doctors during his lifetime serves as proof of his knowledge and abilities.

Durham returned to Philadelphia for a visit in 1788. While there, he met Dr. Rush, who was one of the nation's most respected physicians. By now Durham was himself quite well-regarded in New Orleans, drawing a salary of around $3,000 per year from his practice. Rush was quite favorably impressed with Durham and said as much in a letter he wrote to the Philadelphia Abolition Society. Rush wrote, "I have conversed with him upon the most acute and epidemic diseases of the country where he lives and was pleased to find him perfectly acquainted with the modern simple mode of practice in those diseases. I expected to have suggested some new medicines to him; but he suggested many more to me."

Rush encouraged Durham to remain in Philadelphia and open a practice there. Durham did extend his visit and eventually stayed for nearly a year. He made the acquaintance of Philadelphia's leading physicians during his time there. After his return to New Orleans, he continued to correspond with Rush for more than a decade.

Shortly after his return to New Orleans, Durham sent Rush a paper describing his treatment for diphtheria, known more commonly at the time as "putrid sore throat." Rush was so impressed with Durham's success that he read the paper during a presentation before the College of Physicians of Philadelphia. Later, Durham described his methods for treating yellow fever, which he was able to test during two particularly crippling epidemics in 1796 and 1798. Durham lost only 17 patients out of 114 whom he had treated. Diseases such as yellow fever were common in semitropical climates like that of New Orleans, and Durham became an expert on how diseases and climate related to one another.

Despite his success, his lack of a formal medical degree eventually meant the end of his practice in New Orleans. In August 1801 (when Durham was only 39), New Orleans' city council decreed that all medical practitioners must have degrees and licences. They did made special provisions for Durham to continue treating throat diseases, but what ultimately became of his practice remains a mystery. He did write to Rush in 1802 asking for information on cowpox, from which he believed New Orleans might be suffering an epidemic. In an 1800 letter he had also mentioned to Rush that he might wish to leave New Orleans and settle elsewhere, possibly Philadelphia. His name does not appear in the 1805 edition of the New Orleans City Directory, which would indicate that he left some time between 1802 and 1805. But if he left any sort of paper trail, it has not yet been discovered.

FURTHER READING:

Books

Hayden, Robert and Jacqueline Harris. *Nine Black American Doctors.* Addison-Wesley, 1976.

Logan, Rayford W. andMichael R. Winston, eds. *Dictionary of American negro Biography.* W. W. Norton, 1982.

Woodson, Carter G. and Charles H. Wesley. *Negro Makers of History.* The Associated Publishers, 1928.

—Sketch by George A. Milite

Annie J. Easley
1933-
Computer scientist

Annie Easley was a key member of the National Aeronautics and Space Administration team (NASA) that developed computer software for the *Centaur,* a high-energy rocket used to launch space vehicles and communication satellites.

Easley was born in Birmingham, Alabama. She attended Xavier University in New Orleans and worked as a substitute teacher in Jefferson County, Alabama, before moving to Ohio. In 1955, Easley joined the staff of NASA's Lewis Research Center in Cleveland. At that time, the United States was on the verge of the space age, and a tense competition with the former Soviet Union had just begun. The Soviet Union dedicated much of its resources—including many of its most capable scientists—to the race for space. But support in the United States for the fledgling space program was not as strong; Americans were dismayed by military action in Korea and reluctant to continue in the role of international guardian of democracy. They were also disturbed by the allegations of Communism that had been part of the much-publicized McCarthy hearings. Most people focused their efforts on striving to succeed in the post-World War II economy and were uninterested in visionary quests.

The mood changed abruptly in 1957, when the Soviet Union launched *Sputnik,* the first satellite to be placed in orbit around the Earth. American pride was pricked (and American fears of a possible Soviet military advantage were awakened) by the feat. In that year, the Air Force studied a proposal for a high-energy space booster with a new propulsion system that mixed liquid hydrogen and oxygen. Dubbed the *Centaur,* the booster's development was authorized by the United States government in 1958.

Easley was assigned to the Flight Software Section at the Lewis Research Center. The space race pushed forward the development of computer hardware and software because complex, miniaturized systems were required to monitor and run space vehicles. Easley developed and helped implement computer programs used to determine solar wind and solve numerous energy monitoring and conversion problems. Easley also worked on projects related to energy while at Lewis. She studied the life use of storage batteries that powered electric utility vehicles and the efficiency of energy conversion systems. While at the Lewis

Research Center, Easley attended Cleveland State University and completed a bachelor of science degree in mathematics in 1977.

Easley's work with NASA's *Centaur* developed the technological foundations for today's shuttle launches, as well as for the launches of communication, weather, and military satellites. Easley retired in 1991, but her work contributed to the 1997 flight to Saturn of the *Cassini*—launched on its way by the *Centaur.*

SELECTED WRITINGS BY EASLEY:

Other

"Effect of Turbulent Mixing on Average Fuel Temperatures in a Gas-Core Nuclear Rocket Engine." *NASA-TN-D-4882* (November 1968).
"Performance and Operational Economics Estimates for a Coal Gasification Combined-Cycle Cogeneration Powerplant." *NASA Technical Memo 82729* (March 1982).

FURTHER READING:

Books

Sammons, Vivian O. *Blacks in Science and Medicine.* New York: Hemisphere Publishing Company, 1990.

Other

Brown, Mitchell C. *Faces of Science: African Americans in the Sciences* http://www.lib.lsu.edu/lib/chem/display/easley.html
NASA *Centaur: America's Workhorse in Space* http://www.lerc.nasa.gov/WWW/PAO/html/centaur.htm

—Sketch by A. Mullig

Cecile Hoover Edwards
1926-
Nutritional researcher

Cecile Hoover Edwards, a nutritional researcher and educator, devoted her career to improving the nutrition and well-being of disadvantaged people. In recognition of her achievements, she was cited by the National Council of Negro Women for outstanding contributions to science and by the Illinois House of Representatives for "determined devotion to the cause of eliminating poverty through the creation of a quality environment."

Edwards was born in East St. Louis, Illinois, on October 26, 1926. Her mother, Annie Jordan, was a former schoolteacher and her father, Ernest Hoover, was an insurance manager. Edwards enrolled at Tuskegee Institute, the college made famous by Booker T. Washington and **George Washington Carver**, at age 15, and entered a home economics program with minors in nutrition and chemistry. "I knew from the first day that I had no interest in dietetics," Edwards told contributor Laura Newman in an interview. "My real interest was in improving nutrition through research." Edwards was awarded a bachelor of science degree with honors from Tuskegee in 1946. With a fellowship from Swift and Co. she conducted chemical analyses of an animal source of protein. In 1947, she earned a master's degree in chemistry from Tuskegee. Edwards received a Ph.D. in nutrition from Iowa State University in 1950. Edwards's doctoral dissertation was a study of methionine, an essential amino acid that she said has "not only the good things needed to synthesize protein, but also has sulfur, which can be given to other compounds and be easily released." Edwards wrote at least 20 papers on methionine.

Appointed Head of Tuskegee's Food and Nutrition Department

After completing her doctorate, Edwards returned to Tuskegee as a faculty member and a research associate of the Carver Foundation, remaining there for six years. "Staying in nutrition at Tuskegee seemed like an opportunity," said Edwards. "I felt obligated to pay back the opportunity Tuskegee had given me." In 1952 she became head of Tuskegee's department of foods and nutrition. Edwards's nutritional research later expanded to studies of the amino acid composition of food, the utilization of protein from vegetarian diets, and the planning of well-balanced and nutritious diets, especially for low-income and disadvantaged populations in the United States and developing countries.

Develops Human Ecology Curriculum at Howard University

Designing a new curriculum for the School of Human Ecology at Howard University, Washington, D.C., in the 1970s was a high point of Edwards's career. Just before she came to Howard, in 1969, Arthur Jensen had argued in his paper, "How Much Can We Boost IQ," that blacks were inherently inferior, and that providing education, nutrition, and other resources could not bring them equality. Disproving the Jensen hypothesis became a major goal for Edwards. Howard's School of Human Ecology conducted research and evaluated work in providing resources for low-income people so that they could help themselves. It taught

parenting, childcare, nutrition, budgeting, job skills, and other skills useful in overcoming obstacles. In 1974, Edwards was appointed Dean of the School of Human Ecology, a position she held until 1987.

In 1985 Edwards became director of a five-year project sponsored by the National Institute of Child Health and Human Development to study the nutritional, medical, psychological, socioeconomic, and lifestyle factors which influence pregnancy outcomes in low-income women. In 1994 she served as editor of the *Journal of Nutrition* May supplement on "African American Women and Their Pregnancies." A humanitarian and prolific writer who published numerous scientific papers, Edwards helped to establish a family resource development program in her birthplace, East St. Louis, Illinois.

SELECTED WRITINGS BY EDWARDS:

Books

Current Knowledge of the Relationships of Selected Nutrients, Alcohol, Tobacco, and Drug Use, and Other Factors to Pregnancy Outcomes. School of Human Ecology, Howard University, 1988.
Human Ecology: Interactions of Man with His Environments. Kendall-Hunt, 1991.

Periodicals

"Utilization of Methionine by the Adult Rat, Distribution of the alpha-carbon of DL-methionine–2-C$_{14}$in Tissues, Tissue Fractions, Expired Carbon Dioxide, Blood and Excreta," *Journal of Nutrition,* Vol. 72, (1960): 185.
"Utilization of Wheat by Adult Man: Vitamins and Minerals," *American Journal of Clinical Nutrition,* Vol. 24, (1971): 547.
"Low Income Black Families: Strategies for Survival in the 1980s," *Journal of Negro Education,* Vol. 51, (1982): 85–89.
"Quality of Life: Black Families," *Human Ecology Monograph,* School of Human Ecology, Howard University, 1991.

FURTHER READING:

Periodicals

Edwards, Cecile Hoover, *Interview with Laura Newman,* conducted March 12, 1994.

—Sketch by Laura Newman

M. Joycelyn Elders

M(innie) Joycelyn Elders
1933-
Physician, former U.S. Surgeon General

Joycelyn Elders's controversial ideas about health care education have won her stalwart admirers and fierce critics. But neither her supporters nor her foes probably know that this pediatric endocrinologist, medical professor, and former U.S. Surgeon General did not visit a doctor until she was 15 years old. Where Elders grew in rural Arkansas, medical care was only for emergencies. By the time she became "the nation's doctor," Elders had become quite practiced in fighting stereotypes and defending unpopular causes—something she has never shied away from doing.

Early Life

Minnie Joycelyn Jones was born on August 13, 1933, in Schaal, Arkansas. She was the oldest of eight children. Her parents, Haller and Curtis Jones, eked out a living as sharecroppers, supplementing their meager cotton income by trapping raccoons. Minnie Jones grew up in a loving but destitute environment. Her home had no electricity or running water. She and her brothers and sisters worked in the cotton fields with their parents.

However, Minnie was also a studious child—so studious that at age 15 she received a scholarship from the United Methodist Church to go to Philander Smith College in Little Rock, Arkansas. It was as a college student that the young woman first saw a doctor. It was also then that she became interested in medicine. She met **Edith Irby Jones**, the first black woman to attend the University of Arkansas Medical School, and Jones inspired Elders to strive for a medical degree.

Elders worked her way through college and graduated with a B.A. in three years. She was just 19 at the time. She joined the U.S. Army, attaining the rank of first lieutenant. She trained to become a physical therapist while in the Army, and upon her discharge she went to the University of Arkansas Medical School, assisted by the G.I. Bill. She received her M.D. in 1960, the only woman graduate in her class. That same year she married Oliver Elders, a high school teacher and basketball coach. The couple had two sons.

Elders's internship was spent in Minneapolis at the University of Minnesota Hospital, and she served as a resident at the University of Arkansas Medical Center in Little Rock. In 1963 she was named chief pediatric resident, and a year later she was named a pediatric research fellow. Over the next several years her career continued to build momentum. She enrolled in the master's program in biochemistry at the University of Arkansas, from which she graduated in 1967. Soon after her graduation she was named an assistant professor of pediatrics. In 1971 she became an associate professor, and in 1976 she was made a full professor. In 1978 she was board certified as a pediatric endocrinologist.

Impresses Governor Clinton

A tragedy during the 1970s led to a meeting that would prove important in Elders's career. Her brother was murdered in Arkansas in a much publicized case. Among those who attended the funeral was the governor of Arkansas—Bill Clinton. The two got to know each other, and Clinton saw in Elders a pragmatic and dedicated physician.

Clinton was so impressed, in fact, that in 1987 he selected Elders to serve as the chief public health director for the state of Arkansas. In this capacity, she oversaw a staff of 2,600 employees across the state. In five years, Elders made significant strides in improving health care for Arkansans. She initiated a childhood immunization program that nearly doubled the number of immunized toddlers. The number of early childhood screenings rose from 4,000 to 45,000. Elders expanded the state's prenatal care program, which cut down the infant mortality rate. She made it easier for poor women to get mammograms, and she increased home-care options for the chronically or terminally ill.

Elders also tackled such difficult issues as teenage pregnancy and AIDS (acquired immune deficiency syndrome). Under her tenure, HIV (human immunodefiency virus, which causes AIDS) testing and counseling services were serving nearly twice as many people. She also worked to cut down the state's teenage pregnancy rate, which was then the second highest in the United States. Her advocacy of sex education and contraception rankled many political and religious conservatives, but she refused to cave in. A portent of the outspokenness that was to cut short her career as Surgeon General revealed itself at a 1987 press conference; asked whether she would distribute condoms to students, she replied, "Well, I'm not going to put them on their lunch trays, but yes."

When Clinton became President in 1993, he nominated Elders to replace Antonia Novello as U.S. Surgeon General. If confirmed, Elders would be second woman, and the first black, to serve in that office. Not surprisingly, her nomination faced enormous opposition, especially from conservative members of Congress who saw her views on contraception and abortion rights as too liberal. After an often bitter fight, Elders was finally confirmed to the position by the Senate in September 1993.

An Opponent of Ignorance

Elders proved to be as outspoken as ever in her new role, which she saw as a "bully pulpit." She called for higher taxes on both tobacco and alcohol, citing the harm both substances could do. She also supported a physician's right to use marijuana medicinally, and even suggested that perhaps the legalization of marijuana and other drugs should be explored. In an interview co-sponsored by the American Civil Liberties Union and America Online in June 1995, Elders elaborated on her views: "Our present policy of locking [marijuana offenders] up and throwing away the key without treatment, without consideration of the nature of the offense, is not doing anything but promoting the prison industry and costing this country billions of dollars."

Increasingly, high officials in the government—even allies of the President—questioned whether Elders's candor was helpful to her or to her causes. But Elders continued to speak out, convinced that the only way to deal with important issues was to confront them. Eventually, the pressure became too much for the Clinton administration, and Elders resigned in December 1994. She returned to the University of Arkansas. In 1995 she was named to the national board of the American Civil Liberties Union, and she published her autobiography in 1996. Today she continues to speak out frequently on controversial issues; her belief in the importance of combating ignorance with education remains unshaken.

SELECTED WRITINGS BY ELDERS:

Books

Elders, M. Joycelyn, with David Chanoff. *Joycelyn Elders, M.D. From Sharecropper's Daughter to Surgeon General of the United States of America.* New York: Morrow, 1996.

FURTHER READING:

Books

Jones, Chester R. *Dancing With the Bear and Other Facts of Life: The Story of M. Joycelyn Elders.* Pine Bluff, Arkansas: Delta Press, 1995.

Periodicals

Popkin, James. "A Case of Too Much Candor." *U.S. News and World Report,* December 19, 1994, p. 31.
Rosellini, Lynn. "Joycelyn Elders is Master of Her Own Domain." *U.S. News and World Report,* November 3, 1997, p. 65.
"What I Would Say," *Time,* (December 9, 1996): 30.

—Sketch by George A. Milite

Irvin Wesley Elliott, Jr.
1925-
Organic chemist

Irvin Wesley Elliott, Jr. is known for his development of simple procedures that can be used to synthesize complex molecules with specific three-dimensional structures. He has used these procedures to prepare a series of related alkaloid compounds. He has also helped to educate the next generation of chemists, with over 35 of his former students or laboratory assistants going on to receive doctoral degrees.

Born in Newton, Kansas, on October 21, 1925, Wesley was the middle child and only son of Irwin and Leota (Jordan) Elliott. His father worked for the Santa Fe Railroad, which ran through the town. Two incidents in Newton's childhood led him toward chemistry. First, his older sister complained that her high school chemistry textbook was difficult to understand. Elliott, a freshman at the time, spent the Christmas holiday reading the entire text—it fascinated him. The second incident occurred the next year in his speech class, where he had to present a talk on what field he wanted to enter. Though his parents were encouraging him to study law, the information on lawyers had been taken by another student. He found information on pharmaceutical chemistry available and chose this field as the subject of his talk instead.

Soon money he earned over the summers was being used to purchase glassware and basic chemicals for experiments. He bought an elementary organic chemistry textbook and the laboratory manual that went with it. Elliott set up a

Irvin Wesley Elliott, Jr.

laboratory in his basement, where he not only amazed his friends but had an accidental explosion or two as well. Right after high school he entered the University of Kansas to begin his studies. He was expecting to be drafted, as World War II was in progress, but his nearsightedness prevented him from joining the armed forces.

Fighting Segregation and Launching His Career

His college years were greatly influenced by the segregationist practices that pervaded the south. Joining the university track team, Elliott entered and won many intramural events but was prevented from competing in intercollegiate competitions because of the athletic conference's policies. He and the other members of his track team, most of whom were white, campaigned to integrate the athletic conference. Though this did eventually happen, it occurred too late for Elliott to compete.

Housing at the University of Kansas was also segregated, and the school provided no dormitories for black students. As a sophomore, some of his white friends convinced the other students to let him move into a student-owned house with them. This was the start of interracial housing at the school, and this precedent eventually convinced university administrators to open the dormitories to black students. For his work on improving relations between races, he was awarded a William A. White-Hillel Foundation grant.

In chemistry, Elliott found a mentor in Calvin Van der Werf, one of his professors. Wesley completed an under-

graduate project with Van der Werf involving stereoisomers—two compounds that have exactly the same formula and bonds but are mirror images of each other, like right and left hands. Van der Werf convinced Elliott to attend graduate school at the University of Kansas, once he had completed his bachelor of science degree. There Elliott chose William E. McEwen as his research advisor, who introduced him to methods for synthesizing heterocyclic compounds. These compounds contain rings that are composed of carbon plus another element such as oxygen or nitrogen. To pay for school, Elliott worked at the Eastman Kodak Company over the summer of 1948, where he became interested in x-ray diffraction, a method for determining the three-dimensional structure of molecules.

After earning his master's degree, Elliott took a job as a chemistry instructor at Southern University in Baton Rouge, Louisiana. The university had no laboratory facilities, so he set up his own laboratory in his office, using a small grant from the Carnegie Foundation. He was trying to complete some of the synthesis work he had begun at the University of Kansas. After one of his experiments exploded and destroyed his office, the Southern University refused to renew his contract. One good thing did come out of his time in Louisiana, however: he met his future wife there, Joan Louise Curl.

Unable to find a full-time position, Elliott returned to the University of Kansas and began work on his doctoral degree under McEwen. At the same time, he was working at the Kansas Geological Survey Laboratory to support himself. His former professor, Van der Werf, received a grant to synthesize lubricating oil compounds and hired Elliott to carry out the work. This work became part of his graduate project and allowed him to complete his doctorate in 1952.

His marriage to Joan took place as soon as he graduated, and Elliott moved to Florida A&M College in Tallahassee, where his wife had a position teaching German. He was soon made chairman of the chemistry and physics department and was given responsibility for selecting laboratory equipment for a new science building. He selected advanced equipment such as he had learned about at Eastman Kodak. At the same time, he remained involved in social problems, participating in a bus boycott which ended segregated buses in Tallahassee.

Increasing Recognition in Organic Chemistry

In 1957 Dr. Elliott was awarded a National Science Foundation Faculty Fellowship, which allowed him to spend a year at Harvard University working with Peter Yates. Here he continued investigating the structure of pure organic compounds. Receiving a grant from the Petroleum Research Fund, he moved to Fisk University in Nashville, Tennessee, where he inherited samples of natural compounds collected by **Percy Julian**.

Through this collection, he became interested in the synthesis of natural products, particularly alkaloids, such as morphine and other polycyclic compounds. While continuing his research at Fisk, Elliott served as a visiting professor at both Howard University in 1964 and Wellesley College in 1984. He also spent time at the University of Copenhagen in Denmark in 1974, where he studied methods that used electricity to carry out particular steps in a chemical synthesis procedure. He applied these methods when he returned to Fisk and developed new procedures for synthesizing certain alkaloids. One compound his group synthesized and patented may be active against the virus that causes AIDS (acquired immune deficiency syndrome).

Elliott served as chairman of the chemistry department at Fisk from 1960 until his retirement in 1995. In 1996, he was elected professor emeritus and honored by the National Organization of Black Chemists and Chemical Engineers as their teacher of the year. He and his late wife have two children, Derek and Karen.

SELECTED WRITINGS BY ELLIOTT:

Periodicals

"Nature of the Organic Base in Reissert Compounds." *Journal of the American Chemical Society* 77 (1955): 4408.
"New Synthetic Approaches to Isoquinoline Alkaloids. (+/-)-Laudanosine." *Journal of Heterocyclic Chemistry* 7, (1970): 1229.
"Synthesis of an Isopavine Alkaloid. (+/-)O-Methylthalisopavine." *Journal of Organic Chemistry* 44 (1979): 1162.

FURTHER READING

Books

Distinguished African American Scientists of the 20th Century. Phoenix, Arizona: Oryx Press, 1996, p. 80-4.

—*Sketch by Jerome Ferrance*

Effie O'Neal Ellis
1913-1994
Physician

A specialist in maternal, prenatal, postnatal, and preventative health care, Effie O'Neal Ellis was the first black woman administrator in the American Medical Association. She dedicated her career to treating and

Effie O'Neal Ellis

advising new and expectant mothers. An equally important contribution to public health was her determination to encourage health maintenance throughout life at all socioeconomic levels.

Ellis was born in Hawkinsville, Georgia, on June 15, 1913. Her parents were Joshua P. O'Neal, a home builder, and Althea (Hamilton) O'Neal. Ellis excelled in academics. She received her bachelor's degree in biology and chemistry from Spelman University in 1933. She then earned a master's degree in biology from Atlanta University in 1935, the same year she married Arthur W. Ellis. She planned to continue her research in parasitology, and in recognition of O'Neal's capable research, Atlanta University awarded her a grant to investigate parasites and disease in Puerto Rico.

Her experience in Puerto Rico changed the direction of her career. Struck by the limited access that poor people had to medical care, she resolved to become a medical practitioner. She entered the Illinois College of Medicine, graduating fifth in her class of 160 on June 16, 1950. After an internship at the University of Illinois Hospital and a residency in pediatrics at Massachusetts General Hospital, Ellis served a postdoctoral fellowship in pediatric cardiology at Johns Hopkins University (1952-53). On March 23, 1953, she married James Solomon, who was also a physician. They had one daughter, Elaine.

From 1953-61, Ellis served as pediatrician and director of medical education at Baltimore's Provident Hospital. In 1961, she became director of maternal and child health for the Ohio State Department of Health, where she remained until 1965. From 1965-67, Ellis served on the Ohio Commission for Mental Health and Mental Retardation Planning; during this period, she became the first regional commissioner for social and rehabilitation service in the Department of Health, Education and Welfare.

Ellis resolved to increase the scope of family-planning education, particularly among the poor. Apart from contraception, she encouraged the development of adequate nutritional and sanitary conditions to meet the growth and development needs of children, beginning in the prenatal stage. She chaired a panel at the White House Conference on Food and Nutrition in 1969.

In 1970, Ellis became the first black woman administrator of the American Medical Association. It was in this capacity that she influenced the formation of the first national congress on the quality of life. As special assistant for health services, she traveled the United States extensively, speaking to promote public awareness of family health, sanitation, and prenatal care. Ellis also developed parenting programs and procedures for the March of Dimes.

Ellis was a member of the National Association for Maternal and Child Health, the American Public Health Association, the American Public Welfare Association, and the American Association on Mental Deficiency. She was also a member of Alpha Omega Alpha and the Delta Sigma Theta sorority. In 1970, she received the American Academy of Achievement's Golden Plate Award and the Trailblazer Award from the American Medical Association. Ellis was inducted into the Chicago Hall of Fame in 1989.

Ellis died of cancer at age 81 on July 5, 1994, at Northwestern Memorial Hospital in Chicago. In an obituary, *Jet* magazine quoted Ellis' definition of the quality of life as "good health, good interpersonal relationships, appropriate values, the opportunity to learn what you want to learn and to work at what you wish to work at."

FURTHER READING:

Books

American Men & Women of Science, 20th Edition. New Providence, NJ: R.R. Bowker, 1998.
Smith, Jessie Carney, ed. *Notable Black American Women.* Detroit: Gale Research, 1992.

Periodicals

Jet 86 (July 24, 1994): 54.

—*Sketch by Virginia H. Canton*

Philip Emeagwali

Philip Emeagwali
1956-
Computer scientist

Much has been made of the rise of Bill Gates, who dropped out of Harvard to create what would eventually become Microsoft. Philip Emeagwali dropped out of school in Nigeria at the age of 14 and went on to become a renowned computer scientist and mathematician, whose computational skills are being translated into such practical uses as the recovery of additional oil reserves in OPEC nations.

Philip Emeagwali, the oldest of nine children, was born in 1956 in the town of Akure, Nigeria. The family was poor; his father James was a nurse and his mother Agatha was a homemaker. Philip showed an early talent for mathematics. By the time he got to high school, his mathematical skills were so evident that his classmates gave him the nickname "Calculus."

Unfortunately, the family could not afford to send Philip to school after he turned 14, so he was forced to drop out. This did not keep him from studying, however. Making use of his local public library, he taught himself advanced math, physics, and chemistry. He passed a high school equivalency exam at 17.

Soon afterward, Emeagwali was awarded a scholarship to Oregon State University, where he majored, not surprisingly, in mathematics. He received his bachelor's degree from Oregon State; he later received two master's degrees from George Washington University in Washington, D.C. (in ocean/marine engineering and civil/environmental engineering), and a master's from the University of Maryland in applied mathematics. He earned his Ph.D. in scientific computing from the University of Michigan.

Emeagwali's most important contribution to computer science is his work with supercomputers. He proved that supercomputer research could be conducted by remotely programming a supercomputer using the National Science Foundation Network (NSFNET). What Emeagwali proved was that users could hook into many smaller computers instead of one supercomputer to access information or solve complex computational problems. In 1989, he used the Internet to access more than 65,000 computers in order to perform a complex calculation—which he did at three times the anticipated speed of a supercomputer. He discovered that this was possible by using the earlier calculations of a German scientist, Paul Fillunger. Fillunger had been unable to prove his calculations correct, but Emeagwali re-examined them and was able to solve key equations to do prove Fillunger's calculations.

Emeagwali used these equations to help map petroleum reservoirs in simulation. By using complex calculations, he showed how oil engineers could more accurately track oil flow underground and get the maximum amount of oil out of any reserve. Experts expect that the new technology could eventually increase oil revenues by billions of dollars.

Emeagwali has received several awards for his discoveries, including the Gordon Bell Prize and the National Society of Black Engineers' 1996 "Pioneer of the Year" award. He is married to Dale Brown Emeagwali, herself a noted microbiologist; the couple have a young son. Emeagwali's hobbies include exploring the Internet, but he also plays tennis, swims, and runs.

FURTHER READING:

Periodicals

"African-American Computer Wizard Wins 'Pioneer of the Year' Award." *Michigan Citizen,* (June 8, 1996): B4.

Connors, Cathy, "Nigerian Scientist Leads Computer Field with Discoveries, Inventions." *Amsterdam News,* (April 13, 1996).

"Practical Math: Emeagwali Puts Math to Work in Real World." *Detroit Free Press,* (May 29, 1990).

Romanseko, James, "Computer Scientist Wants PC to Top TV." *Saint Paul Pioneer Press,* (January 27, 1996).

Williams, Brandt, "Real Genius." *Insight News,* (May 11, 1996).

—Sketch by George A. Milite

Herman Eure
1947-
Parasitologist

Herman Eure has spent his entire professional career at Wake Forest University, in Winston-Salem, North Carolina. The primary focus of his research has been the interactions of parasites and aquatic vertebrates, including frogs, toads, turtles, and fish. He is also taken a prominent role in the recruitment of minorities into advanced scientific training and scientific occupations.

Herman Eure was born on January 7, 1947, in Corapeake, North Carolina. He was the seventh of 10 children born to Sarah Goodman Eure and Grover T. Eure. Herman, along with his three younger brothers, enjoyed exploring the large forest behind their home, part of North Carolina's and Virginia's Great Dismal Swamp. Observing the wide variety of wildlife there helped to spark Herman's interest in the biological sciences.

Eure went to T.S. Cooper School in Sunbury, North Carolina, and then Central High School in Gatesville. He excelled at his studies, was active in student government, and was captain of the track team, basketball team, and football team. He graduated at the top of his class and was offered a track scholarship by Maryland State College (now the University of Maryland Eastern Shore).

In college as in high school, Eure realized high academic achievement and continued his involvement in student government, as well as maintaining his participation in sports. He graduated in 1969 and won a Ford Foundation Fellowship to finance his graduate studies, which he conducted at Wake Forest University.

Eure's graduate research concerned the parasites that attack freshwater fish, in particular an intestinal worm that infects largemouth bass. He wanted to determine if bass that lived in waters unnaturally heated by industrial use were more prone to infection. What he discovered was that such fish were in fact healthier, grew faster, and were more productive.

Eure joined the faculty of Wake Forest as soon as he completed his graduate studies, continuing his research on the parasites of fish and other aquatic animals. He also spent a semester in England at the University of Exeter, where he studied the parasites of trout.

In addition to his research activities, Eure has been active in administrative functions, including the recruitment of minorities into the sciences, working with traditionally minority-oriented educational institutions to ensure they are aware of opportunities provided by new federal programs, and providing advice to the administrators of national standardized tests to help bring these tests into balance from a cultural standpoint.

Eure also participates in the Society for the Social Study of Science and the Graylyn Group, an organization dedicated to placing minority women in science, mathematics, and engineering careers. In 1991, he was promoted to full professor at Wake Forest, where he continues his teaching and research, and also serves as a mentor for minority students who have been awarded scholarships that Eure himself helped create.

FURTHER READING:

Kessler, James H., J. S. Kidd, Renée A. Kidd, and Katherine A. Morin. "Herman Eure." In *Distinguished African American Scientists of the 20th Century*. Phoenix: The Oryx Press, 1996.

—Sketch by David E. Fontes

Matilda Arabella Evans
1872-1935
Physician

Matilda Arabella Evans was the first licensed African American female medical doctor in South Carolina. She founded several hospitals and clinics, including the first free clinic in the state, where she treated both black and white patients. One of her hospitals, Taylor Lane, was the first black hospital in Columbia, South Carolina, and also served as a training school for nurses. Evans was especially concerned with the welfare of children, and she developed a program for providing medical examinations to students in public schools. Additionally, Evans founded the Negro Health Association of South Carolina.

Evans was born on May 13, 1872, in Aiken County, South Carolina, to Anderson and Harriet (Corely) Evans. As a child, Evans attended the Schofield Normal and Industrial School located in Aiken. The Schofield School was founded in 1868 by Martha Schofield, a Quaker from Philadelphia, under the patronage of the Pennsylvania Freedmen's Relief Association. The school was established to educate young African American children, and attracted students from every part of South Carolina.

Martha Schofield became Evans's mentor, and she encouraged her to attend Oberlin College. In 1887, Evans enrolled in the college's preparatory department, and within three months she was awarded a scholarship for her tuition. To pay her living expenses, Evans worked as a waitress in Oberlin's dining hall during the school year, and during the summer she canned fruit. She left Oberlin in 1891, three months before her graduation, to pursue her goal of becoming a doctor, perhaps a medical missionary.

Evans worked for several years as a teacher, first at the Haines Institute in Augusta, Georgia, and then at the Schofield School. In 1893, again with Martha Schofield's encouragement, Evans enrolled in the Women's Medical College of Pennsylvania. Evans was given a scholarship by a wealthy Philadelphia philanthropist, Alfred Jones. The only African American in her class, she graduated with her medical degree in 1897 and returned home to South Carolina.

Evans settled in Columbia, South Carolina, where she opened a private medical and surgical practice which attracted patients of both races. It was immediately successful, and soon Evans had so many patients that she began to use her own home as a hospital. In 1901, Evans rented a building and founded the Taylor Lane Hospital and Training School for Nurses. This was the first black hospital in Columbia, a city whose population was half African American. Evans eventually had to give up her own practice to manage and work at Taylor Lane. When this hospital burned down, Evans founded St. Luke's Hospital in its place. In both hospitals, Evans played a critical role in the education of nurses and the clinical training of black doctors and surgeons.

In addition to practicing medicine, managing a hospital, and teaching, Evans also worked to improve public health. After researching and observing public health clinics in several major cities, including Durham, North Carolina, Philadelphia, and New York City, she founded the Columbia Clinic Association. The association provided basic health maintenance education and medical services, including vaccinations, to the poor free of charge. Evans recruited doctors and other medical practitioners of both races—including specialists—to work in the association's clinics. Along similar lines, Evans founded the Negro Health Association of South Carolina to provide statewide education about basic health and sanitation.

One of Evans's primary concerns as a doctor and a humanitarian was the welfare of children. She founded a clinic dedicated to treating infants and teaching their parents proper health care. Under the auspices of South Carolina public schools, she took it upon herself to examine the health of black schoolchildren. When she found disturbing results—many were afflicted with ringworm, tooth decay, scabies, and other treatable illnesses—officials began a program to examine and treat students routinely. Evans also took a more personal role in children's well-being. She opened up a pond for swimming on her own property for poor boys, though she did not know how to swim. She taught herself to swim and then taught many others. Though Evans never married, she adopted eight children, and took in others. Her eight adopted children were John B. Evans, Mattie O. Evans, Jessie Trottie Evans, Myrtle Evans Lee, Edward Evans Robinson, Gresham Evans, and Sydney Trottie Evans.

Evans received numerous accolades. Active in professional societies, Evans served as president of the Palmetto State Medical Society and as vice-president of the National

Medical Society. Beginning in 1930, she also served as a trustee of Haines College, formerly known as the Haines Institute, where Evans once taught. The National Council for Defense gave her a commission, and she was an appointed member of the Volunteer Medical Service Corps during World War I. Evans also honored those who helped her. In 1916, she published a biography of her mentor, entitled *Martha Schofield: Pioneer Negro Educator.* That same year, Evans also contributed to several issues of the *Negro Health Journal.* Evans died on November 17, 1935, in her home in Columbia, after a short illness.

SELECTED WRITINGS BY EVANS:

Books

Martha Schofield: Pioneer Negro Educator, Columbia, South Carolina: DuPre Printing Company, 1916.

FURTHER READING

Books

Hine, Darlene Clark, ed. *Black Women in America: An Historical Encyclopedia.* New York: Carlson Publishing, 1993. Lerner, Gerder, ed. *Black Women in White America.* New York: Pantheon, 1972.

—Sketch by A. Petrusso

Slayton A. Evans, Jr.
1943-
Organic chemist

Slayton A. Evans, Jr. is an internationally known researcher in organophosphorus chemistry. He has collaborated with colleagues in France, Germany, and India and assisted in organizing international conferences on phosphorus chemistry. He has been the Kenan Professor of Chemistry at the University of North Carolina at Chapel Hill since 1992.

Evans was born in Chicago, Illinois, on May 17, 1943, the oldest of three children of Slayton A. Evans Sr. and Corine M. (Thompson) Evans. While he was young, the family moved to Meridian, Mississippi, where Evans attended parochial school. Evans showed an early fascination with science, collecting and researching plants and insects. After the launch of *Sputnik* by the Russians, he designed and tested his own rockets, preparing some of the chemicals that he needed by himself.

After high school, Evans attended Tougaloo College in Tougaloo, Mississippi, where he was awarded both an academic and an athletic scholarship. During the summer between his junior and senior years he worked at Abbott Laboratories in Chicago, where he began to apply what he learned in his chemistry classes. Receiving his bachelor's degree in 1965, he returned to Abbott Laboratories for a second summer. He began a postgraduate program at the Illinois Institute of Technology in September 1965 and continued working part-time at Abbott Laboratories. In 1966, on the advice of a teacher, he transferred to Case Western Reserve University in Cleveland, Ohio, where he accepted a research assistantship. His research at Case Western included work on controlling schistosomiasis, a disease caused by a parasite common to southeast Asia. This research was important to the war effort in Vietnam. In 1970 he received his doctoral degree from Case Western.

Following postdoctoral work at the University of Texas, Evans accepted a second postdoctoral position at the University of Notre Dame under Ernest Eliel. Here, Evans began working with stereoisomers; these compounds have the same composition and bonds but the bonds are arranged differently in space. Because stereoisomers are very hard to separate but can have very different biological properties, it is important to synthesize only one arrangement of the isomer.

After two years at Notre Dame, Evans joined the faculty of Dartmouth College. Because of limited resources for carrying out his research, he accepted a faculty position at the University of North Carolina in 1974. In 1983-84, he received a Ford Foundation Fellowship and a Fulbright-Hays Fellowship, which allowed him to travel to France as a visiting professor at the Universite Paul Sabatier. His work at the University of North Carolina has been honored with the Tanner Teaching Award for Excellence in Undergraduate Teaching in 1994, and the Howard University Outstanding Achievement Award in 1996.

Evans's research on stereoisomers has led to the development of several organophosphate compounds that allow scientists to generate selectively single isomeric forms of new compounds. He has also developed applications of nuclear magnetic resonance, where certain elements can be detected in a magnetic field, for organophosphate and organosulfur compounds. He has written more than 95 papers related to his work and has presented seminars on his work throughout Europe and the United States.

In July 1967, Evans married Tommie A. Johnson. They had two children, Amy Rebecca and Slayton Alvin III, before she passed away.

SELECTED WRITINGS BY EVANS:

Periodicals

(with I. Lefebvre) "Studies toward the Asymmetric Synthesis of Alpha-Amino Phosphonic Acids via the Addition of Phosphites to Enantiopure Sulfinimines." *Journal of Organic Chemistry*, vol. 62 (1997): 7532.

(with T. Powers) "Lanthanide Induced Oxygen-17 NMR Shifts of Diastereotopic Oxygen Atoms in 1-Thiadecalin-1,1-dioxide and Related Compounds," *Tetrahedron Lett.*, vol. 31 (1990): 5835.

(with J. Kelly) "Oxygen-17 NMR Spectral Studies of Selected Aromatic Sulfones," *Magnetic Resonance Chemistry*, vol. 25 (1987): 305.

FURTHER READING:

Books

Distinguished African American Scientists of the 20th Century. Phoenix, Arizona: Oryx Press, 1996, p. 87-91.

—Sketch by Jerome Ferrance

Dorothy Boulding Ferebee
1897-1983
Physician

Born into privilege but mindful of the needs of those less fortunate, Dorothy Boulding Ferebee was a leader in the fight to bring health care to the disadvantaged. In addition to her 40-year career as a physician and educator at Howard University, she led several health projects for the poor, founded the Southeast Neighborhood House in Washington, D.C., and chaired the D.C. Commission on the Status of Women.

Dorothy Celeste Boulding was born in 1897 (some sources list 1893 or 1898) in Norfolk, Virginia to Benjamin Richard and Florence Ruffin Boulding. When she was still a child, the family moved to Boston, and young Dorothy grew up in the affluent neighborhood of Beacon Hill. The Ruffins were one of the most prominent black families in Boston. Dorothy's great-uncle, George L. Ruffin, had been the first black to graduate from Harvard Law School and the first black judge in Massachusetts.

Early Interest in Helping Others

Ferebee told interviewers late in her life that she wanted to be a doctor from her earliest days. As a child, she would nurse sick birds and other animals. She did well in her studies and went to Simmons College in Boston. Upon graduating from Simmons she went on to Tufts University Medical School. Out of 137 students in her class, only five were women, and she was the only black. She recalled in one interview that women were the last to get assignments, and that she was usually the last among the five women to get assignments. Yet she graduated first in her class in 1924.

Her applications for internships (which required a photograph) were all rejected, but she finally got a civil service position at the Howard University Hospital in Washington, D.C. (Then known as Freedmen's Hospital). She completed her internship and became an instructor in obstetrics, but her desire to help others took her beyond teaching.

Expands Services for the Poor

In the late 1920s she became involved in an incident that led to her founding what is now known as the Southeast Neighborhood House in Washington. A nine-year-old black boy, left alone to babysit his three-year-old brother while his mother worked as a domestic servant across town, stole a bottle of milk from a neighbor's porch. The boy was arrested. Ferebee went to the police precinct, paid for the milk, and retrieved the boy. She realized, as she noted in a 1978 interview with The Washington Post, that "we needed a place for black children of working mothers." No such place existed, and what facilities did exist for poor children were not open to blacks.

Ferebee approached the Friendship House, an all-white settlement house, and asked for donations to create such a place. At first the Friendship House board balked at her request, but she persisted and eventually they agreed to help, as did the city's Community Chest. The result, orientally known as the Southeast Settlement House, opened on G Street in 1929.

Ferebee did not limit her work with the underprivileged to Washington. During the Great Depression of the 1930s, she spent seven summers in rural Mississippi, where she directed a health project, sponsored by the black sorority Alpha Kappa Alpha, that included educating the poor in proper nutrition and providing treatment for children and the elderly. Largely thanks to her efforts, the Mound Bayou Hospital was founded to help meet the medical needs of these rural poor.

Back in Washington, Ferebee continued to work at Freedmen's. She had also set up a private practice in a poor neighborhood. Often, she would drive her patients to Freedman's because ambulances would not come into her neighborhood. In 1941 she was named medical director of Howard University's student health service, a position she held for 27 years.

She married Claude Thurston Ferebee, also a physician, in 1928, and the couple had a twin son and daughter, Claude, Jr. and Mary. Unfortunately, the marriage did not survive, and Ferebee's daughter Mary died at the age of 18. Despite these personal blows, Ferebee never cut back on her commitment to helping others.

Nationally and Internationally Active

Later in her career, Ferebee built on her reputation as an advocate for the rights of the underprivileged. In 1949 she succeeded Mary McLeod Bethune as president of the National Council of Negro Women, a position she held until 1953. In the 1960s she served as a medical consultant to the U.S. Department of Health and the Peace Corps. President John F. Kennedy appointed her to the U.S. Food for Peace Council, and President Lyndon B. Johnson named her as a representative to the World Health Organization. She retired from Howard University in 1968 but remained active. She served as chair of the D.C. Commission on the Status of Women, and she traveled widely throughout Europe, Africa, and South America. In 1975 she found The Women's Institute in Washington, D.C.

In her later years, poor health slowed her down somewhat, but she managed to stay involved in the causes that were important to her. She maintained her private medical practice for many years, always putting the needs of the poor at the top of her agenda. Dorothy Boulding Ferebee died of congestive heart failure in Washington on September 14, 1980.

FURTHER READING:

Books

Hine, Darlene Clark, ed. *Black Women in America: An Historical Encyclopedia* Brooklyn: Carlson Publishing, 1993.

Periodicals

Ebony, (February 1948): 22.
Roy, J. H. "Portrait of Dr. Dorothy Boulding Ferebee." *Negro History Bulletin,* (April 1962): 160.
Trescott, Jacqueline. "A Voice for the Disadvantaged: Dorothy Ferebee Has Spent Her Life Speaking Up for the Community." *Washington Post,* (May 5, 1978): B1.

—*Sketch by George A. Milite*

Angella Dorothea Ferguson
1925-
Pediatrician

Angella Ferguson is both a pediatrician and a well-respected researcher in the area of sickle-cell anemia. She began studying the disease, an illness that mainly strikes people of African descent, while in medical school. Ferguson drew up guidelines to identify it and established procedures for treatment. She also did research work in the area of growth and development in infants and children, especially African Americans. In the 1960s, Ferguson became involved in health and hospital administration. She oversaw the construction of the Howard Medical Center before her retirement in 1990.

Ferguson was born on February 15, 1925, in Washington, D.C. She was one of eight children born to George Alonzo and Mary (Burton) Ferguson. Ferguson's father worked several jobs; he was a schoolteacher, an architect,

and a lieutenant colonel in the Army Reserves, but Ferguson and her family lived in poverty. Ferguson attended Washington's Cordoza High School, and while a sophomore, she became interested in chemistry and mathematics. Ferguson decided to attend college to study science, and upon her high school graduation in 1951, she enrolled in Howard University.

While attending Howard, Ferguson became more interested in biology. Her experiences with other biology students influenced her decision to become a doctor. Ferguson earned her bachelor of science degree from Howard in 1945 and then entered the medical school at Howard that same year. While a medical student, Ferguson took a class in pediatrics with Roland Scott, who became her mentor. Ferguson graduated with her medical degree in 1949. After graduation, Ferguson did a year-long internship in general medicine at Freedmen's Hospital, the teaching hospital attached to Howard. As part of her rotation, she worked in pediatrics, and this experience helped her decide on a specialty. She was admitted to a two-year residency program in pediatrics at Freedmen's Hospital. She later did postgraduate training at Bethesda Naval Hospital in radioisotopes and their clinical uses; she also held a fellowship at Cornell University Hospital in hematology. In 1951, she married Charles M. Cabanis, who was also a doctor. Together they would have two daughters, Carla Victoria and Caryn Leota.

Begins Sickle Cell Research

When her residency was completed and her board examinations were passed, Ferguson opened her own private pediatric practice. The developmental questions that came up in the course of treating infants and children intrigued her. Most of the available information about child development focused on those of European, not African, descent. With the help of Scott, Ferguson studied the developmental physiology of African American children as a research associate at Howard's medical school. While conducting this research, Ferguson noticed the large number of black children suffering from sickle-cell anemia. This is a usually nonfatal though potentially serious condition; in sickle-cell anemia, red blood cells are sickle shaped rather than donut shaped as healthy red blood cells are, and this creates painful blockages in small blood vessels.

Throughout the 1950s and early 1960s, Ferguson continued to study sickle-cell anemia. In 1953, she became an instructor in the pediatric department of Howard University's school of medicine and an assistant pediatrician at Freedmen's. By 1959, she was promoted to assistant professor in the medical school. In her sickle-cell research, she first devised guidelines for identifying the illness in children under 12 years of age, since symptoms were difficult to distinguish from other childhood maladies. She promoted the use of a blood test in infants to check for the condition, something that had not been done before her time. After accomplishing this goal, she turned to treatment methods. For small active children, about five years of age,

Ferguson recommended drinking at least one extra glass of water with some baking soda dissolved in it each day to relieve any extreme symptoms. Drinking water adds more volume to the blood, increasing its flow. When a patient suffering from sickle-cell anemia underwent surgery, symptoms of the disease would increase because of the strain from the operation. Ferguson recommended that doctors give such patients extra oxygen as they emerge from the anesthetized state to reduce the symptoms.

As a result of this research, Ferguson was awarded two certificates of merit from the American Medical Association. In 1963, she became an associate professor at Howard and an associate pediatrician at Freedmen's. She was also hired as member of the attending staff at D.C. General Hospital that year.

In 1965, Freedmen's Hospital was being torn down so that a new hospital could be built in its place. Ferguson was initially involved in the development of the children's wing but became director of programs and facilities for the entire hospital in 1970. That year, she was promoted to director of the University Office of Health Affairs at Howard Medical School. In addition to facility development, she oversaw student health services, research, and instruction in the medical school's advanced degree programs. Ferguson continued to supervise the planning and construction of the new hospital building. She also dealt with the United States Congress and their budgetary restrictions, eventually persuading them to increase funding. When the hospital, named the Howard University Medical Center, was completed in 1975, Ferguson became the associate vice-president of health affairs. She continued to be involved in new building development, including projects such as Howard College of Medicine's Seeley G. Mudd Building, the Animal Research Center, and the renovation of the College of Allied Health and Sciences and the College of Nursing.

Throughout her career, Ferguson was active in professional societies including the Society for Pediatric Research, the Society for Nuclear Medicine, and the National Medical Association. She also served on the board of directors for the Association for Sickle-Cell Anemia Research. Ferguson retired in 1990.

FURTHER READING:

Books

Hayden, Robert C. *Eleven African-American Doctors.* Frederick: 1992.
Kessler, J.H., et al. *Distinguished African American Scientists of the 20th Century.* Phoenix, AZ: Oryx Press, 1996.
Sammons, Vivian Ovelton. *Blacks in Science and Medicine.* New York: Hemisphere Publishing, 1990.

Periodicals

Ebony. (August 1960): 44.

Lloyd N. Ferguson

Ebony. (May 1964): 70.

—*Sketch by A. Petrusso*

Lloyd N. Ferguson
1918-
Chemist

After a long and distinguished career as a chemist and educator at the California State University, Los Angeles, Lloyd N. Ferguson achieved emeritus status in 1986. In addition to teaching, Ferguson conducted important research on the relationship between the chemistry of organic compounds and properties such as odor and taste, alicycles (organic compounds with unusual molecular structures), and cancer chemotherapy during his years at California State. Despite all these accomplishments, Ferguson considers his efforts to encourage minority youth to pursue careers in science as one of his more significant contributions through the years. An active educator and writer, Ferguson has published six textbooks and numerous pedagogical articles, and he is the recipient of several awards, including the Distinguished Teaching award of the Manufacturing Chemists Association in 1974, the American Chemical Society award in chemical education in 1978, and the Outstanding Teaching award from the National Organization of Black Chemists in 1979.

Lloyd Noel Ferguson was born in Oakland, California, on February 9, 1918, the son of Noel Swithin and Gwendolyn Louise (Johnson) Ferguson. He studied chemistry at the University of California at Berkeley, receiving his Bachelor of Science degree, with honors, in 1940 and his doctorate in 1943. Additionally, at intervals between 1941 and 1944, Ferguson worked on National Defense research projects, and he was assistant professor at the Agricultural and Technical College at Greensboro, North Carolina, during 1944–45. He married Charlotte Olivia Welch on January 2, 1944; they have two sons and a daughter.

Studies the Chemistry of Aroma and Taste

In 1945, two years after receiving his doctorate, Ferguson joined the faculty of Howard University in Washington, D.C., becoming a full professor in 1955 and chairing the chemistry department from 1958 to 1965. Ferguson's research during this period included studies of the chemical properties of aromatic molecules; in particular, he investigated halogenation, the complex mechanisms by which aromatic molecules combine with a halogen. Ferguson also studied the molecular components and biochemical processes of taste—research that is valuable, as Ferguson argued in his 1958 article titled "The Physicochemical Aspects of the Sense of Taste," in gaining a fuller understanding "about the ways chemicals stimulate biological activity." Exploring one aspect of such research, Ferguson investigated whether a chemical compound's structural configuration has an effect on its taste by measuring the absorption of sweet and nonsweet compounds by various surfaces. Ferguson wrote three of his textbooks as a professor at Howard University: *Electron Structures of Organic Molecules, Textbook of Organic Chemistry,* and *The Modern Structural Theory of Organic Chemistry.* In 1953, Ferguson was awarded a Guggenheim fellowship, which took him to the Carlsberg Laboratory in Copenhagen, Denmark. Between 1961 and 1962 he was a National Science Foundation fellow at the Swiss Federal Institute of Technology in Zurich, Switzerland.

Studies Alicycles and Chemotherapy

In 1965 Ferguson joined the faculty at California State University in Los Angeles as professor of chemistry; he then chaired the chemistry department from 1968–71. During this period, Ferguson's areas of research included the chemistry of alicycles. In his 1969 article "Alicyclic Chemistry: The Playground for Organic Chemists," Ferguson describes alicycles as providing "ideal systems for measuring electrical and magnetic interaction between nonbonded atoms and for studying the [structural] and mechanistic aspects of organic reactions," and as supplying

"models for elucidating the chemistry of natural products such as steroids, alkalids, vitamins, carbohydrates, [and] antibiotics."

In 1970, Ferguson received an honorary doctorate of science degree from Howard University. He published three additional textbooks during the following decade: *Organic Chemistry: A Science and an Art, Highlights of Alicyclic Chemistry,* Volumes 1 and 2, and *Organic Molecular Structure.* Along with his national teaching and educational awards, Ferguson received Outstanding Professor awards from California State University in 1974 and 1981. Ferguson's interest in cancer chemotherapy is reflected by his service on the chemotherapy advisory committee of the National Cancer Institute from 1972–75 and by articles such as "Cancer: How Can Chemists Help?" In 1973 Ferguson was appointed to the United States national committee to the International Union of Pure and Applied Chemistry (IUPAC) for three years. He also served on the National Sea Grant Review Panel from 1978–81 and was affiliated with the National Institute of Environmental Health Sciences from 1979–83. In 1986, Ferguson retired as emeritus professor of chemistry at California State University.

Ferguson is a member of the American Chemical Society, the National Cancer Institute, the American Association for the Advancement of Science, and the Royal Chemical Society, among other professional and scientific bodies. Ferguson accepted a post as visiting professor at the University of Nairobi in Kenya during 1971–72. In 1976, he was awarded the Distinguished American Medallion from the American Foundation for Negro Affairs. In 1984–85, Ferguson taught at Bennett College in Greensboro, North Carolina, as a United Negro College Fund scholar-at-large. He has helped establish both the National Organization of Black Chemists and Engineers (1989) and the American Chemical Society's SEED (Support of the Educationally and Economically Disadvantaged) program.

SELECTED WRITINGS BY FERGUSON:

Books

Electron Structures of Organic Molecules. Prentice-Hall, 1952.
The Modern Structural Theory of Organic Chemistry. Prentice-Hall, 1963.
Organic Chemistry: A Science and an Art. Willard Grant, 1972.
Highlights of Alicyclic Chemistry. 2 volumes, Franklin, 1973–77.
Organic Molecular Structure. Willard Grant, 1974.

Periodicals

"Absorption Spectra of Some Linear Conjugated Systems," *Journal of the American Chemical Society,* (September 1944): 1467–75.

"Aromatic Compound and Complex Formation," *Journal of the American Chemical Society,* (February 20, 1954): 1167–69.

"The Physicochemical Aspects of the Sense of Taste," *Journal of Chemical Education,* (September 1958): 437–44.

"Alicyclic Chemistry: The Playground for Organic Chemists," *Journal of Chemical Education,* (July 1969): 404–12.

"Cancer: How Can Chemists Help?" *Journal of Chemical Education,* (November 1975): 689–94.

"Bio-Organic Mechanisms II: Chemoreception," *Journal of Chemical Education,* (June 1981): 456–61.

—Sketch by M. C. Nagel

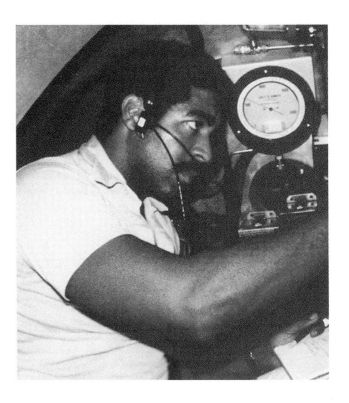

Evan B. Forde

Evan B. Forde
1952-
Oceanographer

Evan Forde's work at the National Oceanic and Atmospheric Administration (NOAA) has included research and experimentation, but he has also been active in the organization's equal opportunity program. He is a frequent speaker at Miami area schools, and for three years he wrote a science column for *Ebony Jr.* magazine.

Forde's interest in the ocean perhaps stems from his having grown up in coastal Florida. He was born in Miami in 1952 and attended local schools. In 1970 he went to Columbia University, where he majored in geology (with an oceanographic specialty) and received a bachelor's degree in 1974.

Forde had his first experience with NOAA (a branch of the U.S. Department of Commerce) while a student at Columbia; in the summer of 1973 he worked at NOAA as a scientific technician. Upon his graduation, he won a NOAA Fellowship for graduate studies. He became a full-time NOAA employee and returned to Columbia for his master's degree. He studied at Columbia's Lamont-Doherty Earth Observatory and received his master's in marine geology in 1976. He became a part of NOAA's Ocean Chemistry Division in 1982.

Forde's work involves examining how changes in the environment affect the ocean. His research showed, for example, how sediment caused by oil drilling off the Atlantic Coast could have a negative ecological impact, and resulted in the Department of the Interior's decision to sharply curtail offshore drilling rights. He has also examined how the environmental process of global warming has affected the content of carbon dioxide in the ocean. He has won several government awards for his work.

Forde was the first black oceanographer to participate in submersible dives aboard research ships (known as research submersibles). Throughout his career, he has been actively involved in creating more opportunities in science for minorities. As manager of NOAA's Community Outreach Program, he has given many speeches to students in the Miami area in which he encourages young minority students to explore science as a career. From 1980 to 1983 he wrote the "Science Corner" column, which outlined various experiments, for *Ebony Jr.* He serves on the Equal Employment Opportunity Committee of NOAA's Atlantic Oceanographic and Meteorological Labs (AOML), and serves as the committee's Webmaster. He is actively involved in school and church in his home of North Miami.

Forde and his wife, Priscilla (whom he married in 1983), have two sons.

SELECTED WRITINGS BY FORDE:

Periodicals

"Science Corner," *Ebony Jr.,* (1980-83).

Other

"Evan B. Forde, NOAA/AOML/OCD" (Web page), http://www.aoml.gov/ocd/people/forde/forde.html

—Sketch by George A. Milite

Joseph S. Francisco
1955-
Atmospheric and physical chemist

A noted atmospheric and physical chemist, Joseph Francisco's interest in the subject was sparked by an after-school job in the local pharmacy when he was just a teenager. This early introduction spawned a career in research, first in the private sector and later at Wayne State and Purdue Universities.

Francisco was born in New Orleans on March 26, 1955, but was raised by his grandparents, Merlin and Sarah Walker, in Beaumont, Texas. Strong believers in the work ethic, the Walkers put young Joseph to work as part-time bookkeeper for their real estate business when he was in his teens. His part-time job in the pharmacy allowed him to learn something practical about how chemical compounds are put together.

Francisco excelled in science in school, and entered the Texas state science fair. He sought the help of professors in nearby Lamar University, and with their encouragement he designed a project that won him third place in the state competition. They also encouraged him to continue his pursuit of science, and in 1973 he entered the University of Texas at Austin.

Almost immediately, Francisco showed himself to be an outstanding chemistry student. He was recruited by his professors to work on an x-ray crystallography project, and in the summer of 1975, he was invited to a student research program at the Argonne National Laboratories outside Chicago.

Francisco was accepted to MIT's graduate program, but his grandfather's death caused financial hardship for the family. Francisco postponed his education and took a job with the Monsanto Chemical Company. The job paid well, but it was not particularly challenging. As soon as Francisco had saved up some money, he reapplied to MIT and began his studies there in 1978.

Francisco joined a research team that was studying the effects of lasers on chemical reactions. He was sent to Australia, where he worked with researchers at Sydney and Adelaide Universities. Armed with new data on laser energy, Francisco brought many new perspectives to his team when he returned to MIT. He received his Ph.D. in 1983 and went to England to do postdoctoral work. He returned to MIT in 1985 and was offered a position at Wayne State in Detroit a year later.

While at Wayne State, Francisco conducted important research on the effects of chemical reactions that destroyed ozone, a gas which helps protect the earth from the harmful rays of the sun. His research confirmed that gases from aerosol and air-conditioning units created reactions that destroyed ozone. For his valuable contribution he was given several awards, including an Alfred P. Sloan Research Fellowship in 1990. In 1994, Francisco moved on to Purdue University.

Francisco has been actively involved in creating more opportunities for minority students who want to enter the sciences. At Wayne State he established the first student chapter of the National Organization for the Professional Advancement of Black Chemists and Chemical Engineers. He has worked to encourage black graduate students to mentor undergraduates, and speaks frequently to students about confronting obstacles to find opportunities. The American Baptist Church, U.S.A. awarded Francisco their Outstanding Teacher Award in 1992.

FURTHER READING:

Books

Kessler, James H., et al. *Distinguished African American Scientists of the Twentieth Century.* Phoenix: Oryx Press, 1996.

—*Sketch by George A. Milite*

Renty Benjamin Franklin
1945-
Physiologist

R enty Benjamin Franklin is an expert in the functioning of the human prostate gland. Formerly on the faculty of the Howard University College of Medicine, today he is a Professor of Physiology at the University of Maryland Dental School, where he continues his research. In addition to his academic activities, he devotes considerable time to the recruitment of minorities to scientific professions.

Renty Benjamin Franklin was born September 2, 1945, in Birmingham, Alabama, to George and Pinkie (Smith) Franklin. A former schoolteacher, his mother helped out in the family store and instructed her children. This tutoring resulted in Renty skipping grades in elementary school and entering high school two years ahead of schedule. He became one of the school's star pupils. Already attracted to a career in the sciences, he became fixed on this ambition after attending a summer session of the Tuskegee Institute, where he was exposed to other academic high achievers. At the age of 16, he entered Morehouse College. There he majored in biology, intending to become a physician. With the encouragement of his professors, he began to focus instead on a career in scientific research. In 1966, he was awarded his undergraduate degree.

In the graduate program at Atlanta University, Franklin was selected for a research teaching assistant position that provided tuition and some money for living expenses. In 1967, he received his master of science degree. Although wishing to pursue his education, for financial reasons he took work as an instructor at St. Augustine's College in Raleigh, North Carolina. By 1969 he was able to resume his graduate studies, this time at Howard University, where he was again awarded a research teaching assistant position. It was for his dissertation there that he first focused on studying the body's glands. In 1972, he received his doctoral degree from Howard University.

Upon graduation, Franklin joined the faculty of Howard University Medical School, teaching courses in physiology. In 1974, he received a fellowship from the Porter Foundation and conducted his research at Harvard University. Soon thereafter, he moved to the Dental School of the University of Maryland, in Baltimore. It was here that he completed his major research on glands, particularly the prostate gland. In 1986, he was named a full professor at the school.

Franklin is a member of the American Physiology Society, the New York Academy of Sciences, and the Endocrinal Society. In 1994, he was honored with the Howard Hughes-Morehouse Distinguished Scientist Award. As part of his efforts to recruit young persons to the sciences, he advises the National Science Foundation in this regard. He still regularly contributes articles and abstracts to scientific journals. He is married to Therese C. Langston and they have two children, LaTania and Omari.

FURTHER READING:

Books

Phelps, Shirelle, ed. *Who's Who Among Black Americans.* Gale Research, 1994, p. 499.
Kessler, James H., et. al. *Distinguished African American Scientists of the 20th Century.* Phoenix, Arizona: Oryx Press, 1996, p. 106.

—Sketch by Patrick J. Longe

A. Oveta Fuller
1955-

Microbiologist

A. Oveta Fuller is a research scientist who primarily studies viruses and how they attach to the cells they infect. Her research has two main objectives: to better understand the interaction between viruses and cells in order

to gain insight into the control of viral diseases; and to explore the possibility of using certain viruses as a means of facilitating genetic engineering.

Oveta Fuller was born on August 31, 1955, in Mebane, North Carolina. She grew up on the family farm operated by her father, Herbert R. Fuller. Her mother, Deborah Woods Fuller, worked as a junior high school teacher to help supplement the family's income.

While her parents were working, young Oveta spent a great deal of time with her paternal grandmother, Lillie Willis Fuller Graves, who lived on the farm. Oveta had an early experience with the powers of medicine when her grandmother was bitten by a water moccasin. Oveta was worried when her grandmother was rushed to the hospital, but relieved when she returned safely, having been treated with a medicine known as antivenin.

Fuller moved further along the path to becoming a scientist in high school, where she had inspiring biology teachers, and was able to attend the North Carolina Governor's School, a highly regarded summer school, following her junior year. The program focused on mathematics, but also involved a range of topics from music to literature.

Following high school, Fuller was awarded a full four-year scholarship to the University of North Carolina (UNC) at Chapel Hill, where she majored in biology. She did not follow a strict premedical curriculum and greatly enjoyed classes in English literature, composition, and journalism. She also worked for one of the college newspapers.

Following her junior year, Fuller took a summer job at a local health clinic, where she discovered the job she most enjoyed was working in the laboratory. She began to consider a career as a research scientist. Nevertheless, she still had a strong interest in writing, and after graduating, she worked for a summer with a large publishing company in Louisiana, where she marketed children's reference books. Her scientific inquisitiveness soon took hold, however, and she decided to return to UNC for graduate studies in biology.

Fuller's doctoral research at UNC involved the biological actions of plant toxins, but she became increasingly interested in the study of viruses and cell surface chemistry. Following her graduation in 1983, she joined the research team of Professor Patricia G. Spear at the University of Chicago, where she studied the behavior of the herpes virus.

Fuller spent nearly five years at the University of Chicago, during which time she helped to identify certain molecules found in cell walls which appear to bring about at least a partial immunity to the herpes virus. In 1987, Fuller received a fellowship from the Ford Foundation, which enabled her to soon become a independent research scientist.

She joined the faculty of the medical school at the University of Michigan in 1987, where she has continued to pursue her research interests. She also teaches in the medical, dental, and graduate schools, and is a mentor to several graduate students and part-time undergraduates who are a part of her research team. Her team continues to report new information on the interactions between viruses and the cells they infect.

FURTHER READING:

Kessler, James H., J. S. Kidd, Renée A. Kidd, and Katherine A. Morin. "A. Oveta Fuller" In *Distinguished African American Scientists of the 20th Century*. Phoenix: The Oryx Press, 1996.

—*Sketch by David E. Fontes*

Solomon Carter Fuller
1872-1953
Neurologist and psychiatrist

The first prominent black psychiatrist in American history, Solomon Carter Fuller made significant contributions to scientific knowledge of the degenerative brain condition known as Alzheimer's disease. Fuller postulated that the disease was not caused by arteriosclerosis, or hardening of the arteries. His theory would later be confirmed by other researchers. He was also ahead of his time in his views of the linkage between organic causes and psychological effects, an idea which would come into increasing acceptance within the medical community during the course of the twentieth century. One of the first African American physicians to serve on the faculty of a medical school that was not exclusively black, in his case the Boston University School of Medicine, Fuller enjoyed a 54-year career as an instructor and professor emeritus.

Coming to America

Born on August 11, 1872, in Monrovia, Liberia, Fuller was the son of Solomon Fuller, a coffee planter and government official whose father had been a slave in Virginia. John Lewis Fuller had bought himself out of slavery and moved his family to Liberia, an African nation established in 1847 as a haven for freed American slaves.

Fuller's mother, Anna Ursula James, the daughter of a physician-missionary couple, established a local school to teach her son and other children. There Fuller was educated to the age of 10, when he enrolled in the College Preparatory School of Monrovia. Fuller completed his education at the preparatory school when he was 16, and a year later, in 1889, he sailed to the United States.

He enrolled in Livingstone College, in Salisbury, North Carolina, from which he graduated in 1893. After completing his undergraduate education, Fuller began his medical studies at Long Island College Hospital in Brooklyn, New York, but soon transferred to the Boston University School of Medicine (BUSM), from which he received his M.D. degree in 1897.

Meeting Freud—and Other Pivotal Encounters

Following his graduation, Fuller began his internship at the Westborough State Hospital pathology lab in Massachusetts. In 1899, Westborough State appointed him to a position as a pathologist, and he would remain at Westborough State until 1922. Also in 1899, Fuller became a pathology instructor at his alma mater, BUSM. During the next 34 years, he would also teach neurology and psychology, and would progress from instructor to lecturer, associate professor, and ultimately emeritus professor of neurology.

His interest in neurology and psychology—the realms in which Fuller would establish his name—emerged only after he attended a lecture by S. Weir Mitchell, a neurologist. Speaking at a meeting of the American Medico-Psychological Association, Mitchell lambasted hospitals in the United States for their failure to conduct serious studies of mental illness, particularly its pathology and psychology. Inspired by Mitchell's call to action, Fuller began his own study of mental patients. In 1900 he enrolled in New York's Carnegie Laboratory, where he studied under several leading psychiatrists.

Four years later, in 1904, Fuller took his psychological studies much further—all the way across the Atlantic Ocean, to the University of Munich in Germany. At the university's psychiatric clinic, he studied under professors Emil Kraepelin and Alois Alzheimer, the discoverer of the disease that bears his name. During his stay in Germany, in 1905, Fuller had an opportunity to spend an afternoon with Paul Ehrlich, who in 1908 would win the Nobel Prize for his research in immunology. Later Fuller would credit this encounter as one of the most important in his life.

Upon his return to Westborough General and his teaching work at BUSM, Fuller pursued his study of Alzheimer's disease and other neurological phenomena. The year 1909 would prove to be a significant one for him. In that year, he ceased to be a pathology instructor and began teaching neurology at BUSM, commencing a course of work that would continue for the remainder of his career. Also in 1909, he had an opportunity to meet Sigmund Freud when the famous Austrian psychiatrist visited the United States. Fuller was photographed along with Freud and a number of other distinguished members of the psychiatric community during Freud's visit to Clark College in Worcester, Massachusetts. But his encounter with Freud would not be the most significant in Fuller's life during that pivotal year: 1909 also marked his marriage to Meta Vaux Warrick. A sculptor, she had studied under Auguste Rodin, the renowned French sculptor. The couple would have three children, Solomon, Thomas, and Perry.

Alzheimer's, Syphilis, and the Link Between Body and Mind

In 1913, Fuller became editor of the *Westborough State Hospital Papers,* a journal with a focus on mental diseases. In it he published several articles, but his writings on pathology, psychiatry, and neurology also appeared in numerous other publications. During this time, Fuller's interest in Alzheimer's disease continued, and he made perhaps his most significant contribution to the field of medical knowledge.

Alzheimer's is a degenerative disease of the brain cells that results in memory loss and impaired thinking, usually in patients over 65 years of age. By the latter part of the twentieth century, scientists still had not reached full agreement as to its cause, though researchers postulated a variety of theories, including the possibility that genetic factors were at the root of the disease. At the time of Fuller's work, however, the prevailing belief was that arteriosclerosis, commonly known as hardening of the arteries, caused Alzheimer's. Fuller disagreed, and put forth this opinion in the course of diagnosing the ninth documented case of Alzheimer's. But he was not able to support his ideas with research work. That proof would have to wait until 1953, the year he died, when other medical researchers would confirm the lack of any linkage between arteriosclerosis and Alzheimer's.

From 1919 to 1921, Fuller taught neuropathology at BUSM, returning to the teaching of neurology in the latter year. His research continued, and he explored the chemical causes of mental disorders such as schizophrenia and manic-depressive psychosis, or bipolar disorder. Here again Fuller was forward-thinking in his attempt to find a link between a physical cause and a psychological effect.

Fuller also assisted in the development of the neuropsychiatric unit of the Tuskegee, Alabama Veterans Administration Hospital. At the latter facility, which treated black soldiers, he personally trained a number of doctors who eventually took over the leadership of the unit. Later, during World War II, a number of servicemen would arrive at the hospital showing signs of what appeared to be mental illness. But thanks in part to data Fuller had gathered from his neuropathological research, doctors at the Tuskegee hospital would be able to diagnose the actual cause of the apparent dementia as syphilis, a venereal disease.

A Memorable Life

During the last three decades of his life, Fuller served variously on the neuropathology staffs of Westborough State, Massachusetts Memorial, Framingham Union, and Marlboro General Hospitals in Massachusetts, as well as Allentown State Hospital in Pennsylvania. Although in 1937 Fuller retired from his regular teaching responsibilities to become a professor emeritus, he practiced psychiatry even in his last years. On January 16, 1953, Fuller died at the age of 80.

His legacy was manyfold. Fuller, the grandson of slaves, had become the first black psychiatrist of note, if not *the* first black psychiatrist. He had contributed to physicians' knowledge of Alzheimer's, as well as to the understanding of the link between physical causes and psychological states. On a social level, he was one of the first African American instructors in the United States to teach at a medical school other than Howard or Meharry, both institutions with all or mostly black student bodies.

In May 1971, the Black Psychiatrists of America presented Fuller's portrait to the American Psychiatric Association in Washington, D.C. The next year, the Black Psychiatrists, in conjunction with the American Psychiatric Association, established the Solomon Carter Fuller Institute. In October 1973 BUSM, then commemorating its centennial, held a day-long conference in honor of Fuller's contributions; also during that time, the BUSM library was presented with a bust of Fuller. Finally, the university renamed its mental health unit the Dr. Solomon Carter Fuller Mental Health Center.

SELECTED WRITINGS BY FULLER:

Periodicals

"Four Cases of Pernicious Anemia Among Insane Subjects," *New England Medical Gazette,* 1901.
"A Statistical Study of 109 Cases of Dementia Praecox," *Journal of the American Institute of Homeopathy* 1 (1909): 322-37.
"Alzheimer's Disease (Senilium Praecox): The Report of a Case and Review of Published Cases," *Journal of Nervous and Mental Disorders* 39 (1912): 440, 536.
(With H.I. Klopp), "Further Observations on Alzheimer's Disease," *American Journal of Insanity* 69 (1912-13): 17-29.

FURTHER READING:

Books

Gifford, George E., Jr., ed. *Psychoanalysis, Psychotherapy, and the New England Medical Scene, 1844-1944,* Science History Publications/USA, 1978, pp. 181-195.
Hayden, Robert C. and Harris, Jacqueline. *Nine Black American Doctors,* Addison-Wesley, 1976, pp. 16-29.
Kaufman, Martin et al., eds. *Dictionary of American Medical Biography,* Volume I: A-L, Greenwood Press, 1984, p. 268.
Logan, Rayford W. and Winston, Michael R. *Dictionary of American Negro Biography,* W.W. Norton, 1982, pp. 247-248.
Sammons, Vivian Ovelton. *Blacks in Science and Medicine,* Hemisphere Publishing, 1990.

Periodicals

American Medical Association Journal, (March 28, 1953): 1122.

Cobb, W. Montague. "Solomon Carter Fuller, 1872-1953," *National Medical Association Journal,* (September 1954): 370-372.

McNamara, Owen J., "Solomon Carter Fuller," *Centerscope,* (Winter 1976): 26-30.

National Medical Association Journal, (January 1972): 93.

—Sketch by Judson Knight

Charles Herbert Garvin
1890-1968
Physician and surgeon

Charles Herbert Garvin was the first black doctor to receive a commission in the Army and the first black staff physician in the Genito-Urinary Department of Lakeland Hospital of Western Reserve University, Cleveland, Ohio.

Born in Jacksonville, Florida, on October 27, 1890, Garvin was the son of Edward and Theresa Decorse Garvin. He began his studies at Atlanta University and completed his undergraduate degree at Howard University in 1911. He entered Howard University Medical School, where he won the Edwin Hiram Reade Prize in Physical Examination and the Perry Prize in Obstetrics.

Garvin graduated from medical school in 1915 and served a one-year internship at Freedmen's Hospital in Washington, D.C. In 1916, he served as assistant visiting surgeon on the hospital staff, then moved to Cleveland, Ohio, to launch a private practice in general medicine and his specialty, genitourinary surgery.

Garvin's medical career was interrupted by World War I. In 1917, he became the first black to be commissioned as a First Lieutenant in the Army. He rose to captain in the Medical Corps, 367th Infantry, and he served as the commanding officer of the 368th Ambulance Company in the 92nd Division in France for 11 months.

After completing his tour of duty, Garvin returned to Cleveland and his practice. In 1920, he received an appointment as a staff physician and faculty member of the Genito-Urinary Department of Lakeland Hospital, Western Reserve University Medical School.

Garvin married Rosalind West in 1920. The couple had a son, Charles West Garvin on June 29, 1921. Some sources state a second son, Harry C. Garvin, was born and became a physician who worked in his father's practice.

Evolving as a Community Leader

Garvin's academic and professional success was acknowledged by his peers. He was a member of the Cleveland Academy of Medicine, the American Venereal Disease Society, the American Medical Association, the National Medical Association, and Alpha Phi Alpha.

However, Garvin had to fight for acceptance within the Cleveland community. In 1927, he built a home in an exclusive city neighborhood. After moving into his house, he was dogged by threats of violence that escalated. Garvin's home was bombed, not once, but twice. Garvin, though, refused to be intimidated. He would not move and yield to terrorists. He became a symbol of courage and was among the first to demand and ultimately win the right for a black person to live in the neighborhood of his or her choice.

The ugly episode fueled Garvin's determination to improve his community for all residents. Before the attack on his home, Garvin had championed—in philosophic and practical terms—black entrepreneurship. He was one of the founders of the Dunbar Life Insurance Company and the Quincy Savings and Loan Company, which he served as board chairman for several years. He also served as treasurer of the Cleveland Peoples Finance Corporation and as an advisory director of the Empire Savings and Loan Company. His business acumen earned political recognition, and Garvin was a member of the committee which welcomed the Republican National Convention to Cleveland in 1923.

Garvin now expanded his professional and political activities and embraced organizations that addressed social concerns. He became a trustee of Karamu House, a settlement house established to ease racial tensions by helping all people tap their potential. A life member of the National Association for the Advancement of Colored People (NAACP), he served on the board of the NAACP's local chapter and on the board of the Cleveland Urban League.

In 1938, the Cleveland Board of Education asked him to serve as a trustee for the Cleveland Public Library, which he served as president in 1940 and 1941 and as secretary until his retirement in 1963. Garvin also served as a trustee of the Mt. Zion Congregational Church and as a trustee for Howard University from 1932 to 1964.

Combining Activism with Professional Achievement

While making time for numerous community obligations, Garvin never neglected his busy practice and professional responsibilities. In addition to scholarly works published in the Journal of the National Medical Association, Garvin wrote articles for more general publications. The pieces covered not only health-related topics, but subjects such as the social and professional progress of black physicians and the experiences of black soldiers in World War I.

A fellow of the International College of Surgeons, Garvin was also a member of the Ohio State Medical Association and served as president of the Cleveland Medical Association. He also was a member of the editorial board of the Journal of the National Medical Association and the John Andrew Clinical Society.

After a 43-year career with Western Reserve University and its medical facilities, Garvin retired from academia as an associate professor of urology and from private practice in 1963. In that year, he was named the fourth recipient of the William Alonzo Warfield Award by the Association of Former Interns and Residents of Freedmen's Hospital, Howard University. Garvin died in 1968 at the age of 78.

SELECTED WRITINGS BY GARVIN:

Periodicals

"Immunity to Disease Among Dark Skinned Peoples," *Opportunity* (1926).

FURTHER READING:

Books

Boris, Joseph J., ed. *Who's Who in Colored America* New York: Who's Who in Colored America Corporation, 1927.
Logan, Rayford W. and Michael R. Winston, ed. *Dictionary of American Negro Biography* New York: Norton & Company, 1982.
Low, W. Augustus, ed. *Encyclopedia of Black America* New York: McGraw-Hill Book Company, 1980.
Sammons, Vivian Ovelton. *Blacks in Science and Medicine* New York: Hemisphere Publishing Corporation, 1990.

Periodicals

Profile *Jet* (Oct. 30, 1969).

—*Sketch by A. Mullig*

Joseph Gouverneur Gathings
1898-1965
Dermatologist

Joseph Gouverneur Gathings was a well-respected dermatologist who won several awards over the course of his career in both Houston, Texas, and Washington, D.C. Gathings was also instrumental in the development of the

National Medical Association, a primarily African American organization of medical professionals, as well the organization's *Journal of the National Medical Association.*

Gathings was born on July 11, 1898, in Richmond, Texas, the son of the Reverend Joseph and Clara (Hill) Gathings. After earning his bachelor's degree at Howard University in 1924, Gathings enrolled at Meharry Medical College in Nashville, Tennessee. This was also the year he married Elizabeth Parr, with whom he would have one child. In 1925, he transferred back to Howard Medical College; he received his medical degree from this institution in 1928. When Gathings graduated, he was given the Marshall Ross Prize in gynecology. Gathings spent the next year as a rotating intern at Freedmen's Hospital in Washington, D.C., again receiving a citation for outstanding work, before returning to Texas. From 1929-41, he had a private practice in Houston.

In 1941, Gathings accepted a Julius Rosenwald Fellowship in Dermatology and Syphilology, and he moved his family to New York while he spent two years at the New York Skin and Cancer Hospital. By 1944, Gathings returned to Houston, where he reopened his private practice. He also worked as a clinical assistant in dermatology at Baylor University Medical Center, as a clinician for the city health department, and as head physician at several venereal-disease clinics, including at least one that was interracial. Gathings only stayed in Texas for two years. In 1946, he moved his family and his private practice back to Washington, D.C., where he became a member of the clinical faculty of Howard Medical College's dermatology and syphilology department.

Throughout his career, Gathings was active in the National Medical Association, serving on several committees. He was a member of the board of directors from 1941-49, serving as that board's chair from 1947-49. In 1949, Gathings was elected to the first vice-presidency, and in 1951, he was elected the National Medical Association's fifty-first president. Gathings was also a diplomate of American Board of Dermatology and Syphilology and a fellow of the American Academy of Dermatology and Syphilogy. He belonged to the Medico-Chirurgical Society of the District of Columbia and several other professional organizations, including the National Medical Committee of the National Association for the Advancement of Colored People (NAACP).

Gathings died on June 28, 1965, in Washington, D.C.

SELECTED WRITINGS BY GATHINGS:

Periodicals

"Physician Heal Thyself." *Journal of the National Medical Association* 44 (September 1952): 333-58.
"Speech to the AMA from NMA." *Journal of the National Medical Association* 44 (July 1952): 313-14.

FURTHER READING:

Periodicals

Cobb, W. Montague. "Joseph Gouverneur Gathings, M.D., 1989-1965." *Journal of the National Medical Association* 57 (September 1965): 427-28.

—*Sketch by A. Petrusso*

Roscoe Conkling Giles
1890-1970
Surgeon

Roscoe Conkling Giles was the first black graduate of Cornell Medical School, the first black diplomate of the American Board of Surgery, and the first black attending surgeon at Cook County Hospital in Chicago. He was also one of the first four black members of the American Medical Association. Giles had a distinguished career both as doctor and a leader in professional and civic societies. He worked to reform the treatment of black doctors within the profession. For example, while serving as committee chair of the National Medical Association, Giles was instrumental in getting the abbreviation "col." (for colored) removed from the names of black members included in the directory of the American Medical Association. Giles also pushed for reforms in the armed forces, trying to get them to hire black doctors and admit black officers to medical facilities.

Giles was born in Albany, New York, on May 6, 1890. He was the son of Francis Fenard and Laura (Caldwell) Giles. Giles's father was both a minister and an attorney in New York City. Giles grew up in Brooklyn, graduating from the Boy's High School in 1907. While a high school student, Giles was a gifted orator, winning the B. B. Christ medal in the subject as well as a scholarship to Cornell University in Ithaca, New York. At Cornell, Giles majored in literature and was a member of the crew team. However, his father had influenced Giles since childhood to pursue a medical career, and Giles entered medical school after earning his bachelor's degree from Cornell in 1911. He received his medical degree from Cornell in 1915, the first black to do so.

Giles then returned to New York City and passed the entrance examinations to the Harlem and Bellevue Hospitals. In 1915, supported by the National Association for the Advancement of Colored People (NAACP) and the Sons of North Carolina of Brooklyn, Giles helped open admission to Bellevue and other city hospitals to black interns. Giles himself, however, chose to go to Chicago. In 1915, he began a two-year internship at Provident Hospital there. In 1917, his admission exams for a junior physician position at the

Chicago Municipal Tuberculosis Sanitarium outscored the other 250 applicants, but because of his color, he was not allowed to work there. Giles became an associate surgeon with Provident Hospital in 1917, and he also worked as a supervisor in the Chicago Health Department for eight months of that year.

On January 9, 1917, Giles married Frances Reeder, a registered nurse. They eventually had three sons together: Roscoe C. Giles I (who died as a child), Oscar DePriest Giles, and Roscoe C. Giles II. In 1917, Giles also was an attending surgeon for Southside hospital, and he began a private practice that would last until his death in 1970. In 1925, Giles served as president of the Cook County Physicians Association. By 1926, Giles was a full attending surgeon at Provident, a position he also held until 1970. Giles also became a member of the executive board of the National Medical Association in 1926. He left this position in 1935.

Publishes Surgical Research and Fights Discrimination

In 1930-31, Giles traveled to Vienna, Austria, to study surgery for a year at several institutions there on a Rockefeller fellowship. While in Vienna, he was elected to membership in the American Medical Association of Vienna's executive committee. After returning from Europe, Giles continued to do postgraduate work at the University of Chicago, in anatomy and other subjects. In 1933, he held a General Education Board and Rosenweld Foundation Fellowship at the University of Chicago to study bone pathology. This experience resulted in the publication of several papers.

Giles was elected the president of the National Medical Association for a year term in 1936. Giles held many such positions throughout his career. He was also elected president of the John A. Andrews Clinical Society, Tuskegee, Alabama, and the Alpha Phi Alpha fraternity. Additionally, Giles was a fellow of the American Medical Society, a trustee and founder of the Metropolitan Community Center Church of Christ in Chicago, and a member of the NAACP and the Urban League. He also belonged to the Chicago Medical Society.

In 1938, Giles passed a competitive examination to become a diplomate of the American Board of Surgery. He was the first black doctor to achieve this honor. While still president of the National Medical Association, Giles formed the Goodwill Committee to remove the "colored" designation from the American Medical Association directory. When Giles's term as president was up, he chaired this committee beginning in 1938. The designation ceased to be included, beginning in the 1940 edition. The Goodwill Committee continued as Special Liaison Committee, to oversee matters that were of mutual concern to both the National Medical Association and the American Medical Association.

During World War II, Giles worked in the Army Medical Corps. He was chief of surgical services in hospitals at Fort Huachuca, Arizona, from 1942-45. He eventually attained the rank of lieutenant colonel. In 1945, Giles returned to Chicago and served in the Medical Reserve Corps. A year later, through the Surgeon General, Giles was appointed surgical consultant to the Secretary of War. Giles fought for black rights within the armed forces. He battled for the appointment of black doctors on local Selective Service System boards and the opening of military hospitals to black officers. He also sought to have black personnel admitted to all parts of the navy.

In 1945, Giles became a fellow of the American College of Surgeons, and the following year he became a founder and a charter fellow of the International College of Surgeons. Giles was also given an assistant professorship of surgery at the Chicago Medical School at Northwestern University in 1946, another position he held until 1970. In 1947, Giles became an honorary attending surgeon at Cook County Hospital. This was an empty symbol, however; he was not actually allowed to practice medicine there. In 1949, Giles became attending physician in surgery at Westside Veterans Hospital. By the late 1940s and early 1950s, Giles became more involved in medical education and residency training at Northwestern. In 1947, he became the alternate attending physician in Northwestern's department of surgery, a position he held until 1952. A year later, in 1953, he became the associate attending physician there. That year, Giles also became a full attending surgeon at Cook County Hospital, the first black doctor to be given such a position.

While teaching and working, Giles continued to publish. In 1953, he published an article on gall bladder surgery, "A Ten-Year Survey of Gall Bladder Surgery at Provident Hospital" in the *Journal of the National Medical Association*. His research proved that this disease is not as uncommon among African Americans as was previously thought.

For his continuing work in the community and his profession, Giles was named one of Chicago's 100 outstanding citizens on December 12, 1957. Giles died on February 19, 1970, in Chicago's Veterans Hospital. In 1985, Cornell honored its alumnus by establishing the Roscoe C. Giles Award for outstanding contributions in minority education and the Roscoe Giles Award for minority students.

SELECTED WRITINGS BY GILES:

Periodicals

"A Report of Three Hundred and Forty-two Consecutive Cases of Appendicitis." *Journal of the National Medical Association* 37 (November 1945): 177-80.

"A Ten-Year Survey of Gall Bladder Surgery at Provident Hospital." *Journal of the National Medical Association* 45 (January 1953): 46-50.

FURTHER READING:

Periodicals

"The Special Liaison Committee." *Journal of the National Medical Association* 32 (1940): 260-61.

Books

Organ, Claude H. and Margaret Kosiba, eds. *A Century of Black Surgeons: The U.S.A. Experience, Volume I.* Norman, OK: Transcript Press, 1987, pp. 297-309.

—Sketch by A. Petrusso

Isaac Thomas Gillam, IV
1932-
Aerospace engineer and NASA administrator

Isaac Thomas Gillam IV was manager for the Delta program, which developed launch vehicles to send weather and communications satellites into orbit. Gillam was also director of shuttle operations during the flight tests of the space shuttle *Enterprise*. In 1978, he became director of National Aeronautics and Space Administration's (NASA) Dryden Flight Research Center at Edwards Air Force Base in California, where testing of the shuttle was conducted. Later, he worked at NASA headquarters in Washington on the early development of the space station, before entering private industry.

Gillam was born in Little Rock, Arkansas, on February 23, 1932, the son of Isaac Thomas and Ethel McNeal (Reynolds) Gillam. As a boy, Gillam lived with his grandparents and attended school in Little Rock, where his grandfather was a high school principal. During summers he stayed with his parents, who were both working in Washington, D.C. His father worked for the United States Post Office and his mother worked for the State Department. After graduation from Dunbar High School in 1948, Gillam attended Howard University, where his father and grandfather had also studied. At Howard, he joined the Air Force ROTC; a newsreel about the Tuskegee airmen had first made him interested in becoming a pilot. He earned a bachelor's degree in mathematics in 1952.

After graduation, Gillam trained as an Air Force pilot, earning his wings in 1953. He married Norma Jean Hughes, a former teacher, on December 21, 1956. Gillam taught as an ROTC instructor at Tennessee State University from 1957-61. He also studied mathematics and physics while he was there. From 1961-63 he was commander of a missile crew for the Strategic Air Command. He later told *Ebony* that 24-hour shifts in the missile silos stretched to 30 hours with briefings and debriefings; instead of sleeping on his days off, he had to put in time flying to maintain his certification as a pilot. By 1963, these conditions convinced him to leave the Air Force, where he had reached the rank of captain.

In 1963, Gillam joined NASA as a resources management specialist. He was appointed assistant manager for the Delta program in 1966, and in 1968 he became manager of the program. From 1971-76, Gillam held the position of program manager for small launch vehicles and international projects, as NASA sent satellites into orbit not only for the United States government but also for governments in Asia and Western Europe. Gillam's division also launched satellites for companies such as Comsat, RCA, and Western Union, beginning a new era in modern communications. From 1976-77, Gillam was director of shuttle operations at the Dryden Flight Research Center, where critical tests of the space shuttle were being conducted. In these tests, the shuttle was carried into the air by a modified Boeing 747 and released to glide to the desert landing strip. Gillam served as the director of Dryden from 1978-81.

Gillam moved to NASA's Washington headquarters in 1981 as a special assistant. He worked at the White House, in the Office of Science and Technology Policy, helping to develop a national space policy. He became an assistant associate administrator at NASA in 1982; in this position, he helped manage the space shuttle program and the beginnings of the space station program. From 1984-87 Gillam was assistant administrator in charge of commercial programs, the first to hold the post. As part of this position, he presented papers at meetings of aerospace organizations in Europe and Asia.

In 1987, Gillam left NASA to join Orbiting Astronomical Oberservatory Corporation, which provides information services and other technological support for NASA as well as other government agencies and private corporations. He became vice president for mission and computing support in 1988 and senior vice president of the aerospace systems group in 1989. In 1998, Gillam went to work for Allied Signal Technical Services in Pasadena as program manager for a communications network, commissioned by NASA, that enables control centers to communicate with distant spacecraft.

In 1976, Gillam received NASA's highest award, the Distinguished Service Medal, for his work on the Delta program. He received the Exceptional Service Medal from NASA twice, once in 1981 and again in 1982. He also was named a distinguished Howard University alumnus in 1981, and in 1986 he was presented with the Presidential Meritorious Excellence Award. He is a fellow of the American Astronautical Society and an associate fellow of the American Institute of Aeronautics and Astronautics.

Gillam and his wife have four children: Michael, Teri Forte, Traci Evens and Kelli.

SELECTED WRITING BY GILLAM:

Periodicals

"Business in Orbit: The Commercial Use of Space." *Journal of International Affairs* 39 (Summer 1985):115-20.

FURTHER READING:

Books

Hallion, Richard P. *On the Frontier: Flight Research at Dryden, 1946-1981.* Washington: National Aeronautics and Space Administration, 1984.
Macknight, Nigel. *Shuttle.* Nottingham, England: Macknight International, 1985.
Ploski, Harry A. and Williams, James, eds. *The Negro Almanac: A Reference Work on the African American.* Detroit: Gale, 1989.
Sammons, Vivian Ovelton. *Blacks in Science and Medicine.* New York: Hemisphere, 1990.

Periodicals

"Space Shuttle Research Chief." *Ebony* (April 1977): 124-9.

—*Sketch by Sally M. Moite*

Cornelia Denson Gillyard
1941-
Organic chemist

Cornelia Denson Gillyard is known for her work on identifying and eliminating compounds that harm the environment. She has also worked hard to increase the number of African American women going into science and engineering careers.

Cornelia Denson was born on February 1, 1941, in the town of Talladega, Alabama, the oldest of three children. Her father, Frank Denson, worked in the steel industry; her mother worked part-time as a nurse, in addition to volunteering in church and community organizations. An avid student, Denson found her high school science courses fascinating, and she devoted her free time to studying advanced concepts with her chemistry teacher. After graduating as valedictorian of her class, she chose to continue her education at Talladega College, both because of its excellent reputation and because it was close enough to allow her to live at home and save money.

When she started college, Denson planned to major in biology. Within a year, a chemistry teacher had convinced her to switch her major to chemistry. Her work in chemistry, however, integrated her interest in biology. Her senior project used chemistry to determine the nutritional value of nuts. Following graduation, she thought about attending medical school but realized she would need money to continue her education. Finding employment in the nuclear medicine laboratory of Ohio State University Hospital, she learned to work with the radioactive tracers used in modern medicine. In 1964, she transferred to Children's Hospital in Columbus, Ohio, and this job gave her the opportunity to help set up and run a new isotope laboratory.

Denson loved the experimental research carried out in this new laboratory, and her enthusiasm led her back to graduate school. She attended Clark Atlanta University, graduating with her master's degree in organic chemistry in 1973. Her thesis project was a study to determine the chemistry and function of vitamin B_{12}. She returned to Columbus, working now at the Battelle Memorial Institute on developing compounds that would turn sunlight into electricity. She stayed only for a year; in 1974, she married and moved back to Atlanta.

Within three years she was back in school, entering a specially designed chemical education program at Clark Atlanta University. While working on her doctoral dissertation, she began teaching at Spelman College, a private women's college in Atlanta. She taught organic chemistry as well as chemistry courses for nonscience majors. After receiving her doctorate in 1980, Gillyard joined the faculty at Spelman, where she is now an associate professor.

At Spelman, Gilllyard joined a team of researchers investigating arsenic contamination of waterways. The goal of the project was to find microorganisms that could convert the toxic chemicals into benign compounds. Gillyard focused on determining the amounts of arsenic compounds that are destroyed by each microorganism. Her current research involves the identification and destruction of toxic contaminants in the environment.

In addition to teaching and research, Gillyard is involved with programs designed to encourage African American women to choose careers in science. Sponsored by the National Aeronautics and Space Administration and the National Science Foundation, these programs offer scholarships to black women at Spelman who are majoring in science or engineering.

SELECTED WRITINGS BY GILLYARD:

Periodicals

(with J. Grainger, et al.) "Isomer Identification of Chlorinated Dibenzo-p-dioxins by Orthogonal Spectroscopic and Chromatographic Techniques." *Chemosphere* 32 (1996): 13.

(with J. Grainger, et al.) "Isomer Identification of Non-laterally Tetrachlorinated Dibenzo-p-dioxin isomer groups by Gas Chromatography/Fourier Transform Infrared Spectroscopy." *Organohalogen Compd.* 19 (1994): 143.

FURTHER READING:

Books

Distinguished African American Scientists of the 20th Century Phoenix, Arizona: Oryx Press, 1996, p. 116.

—*Sketch by Jerome Ferrance*

Mack Gipson, Jr.
1931-1995
Structural geologist

Mack Gipson, Jr., was the first African American to receive a doctoral degree in geology from the University of Chicago. As chair of the geological science department at Virginia State University, he trained many earth scientists. Some of these students taught this subject in high school; others went on to receive advanced degrees in geology, a field that had previously been closed to African American scientists.

Mack Gipson, Jr., was born on September 15, 1931, in Trenton, South Carolina, to Artie (Mathis) Gipson and Mack Gipson, Sr. His family worked as sharecroppers. Gipson's grandmother raised him and his sister Margaree, while other family members did the farming. Growing up in the country, Gipson became very interested in rocks and how they were formed. He studied geology in junior high school and then convinced his whole family to move to Augusta, Georgia, where he could complete high school. During that period, rural areas of the South rarely offered blacks a high school education.

With his family's help, Gipson attended Paine College in Atlanta, while working part-time at menial jobs. He first studied English literature but then changed his major to science, with minors in mathematics and education. He received his bachelor's degree from Paine College in 1953. He then spent a year teaching high school mathematics in Madison and then Augusta, Georgia, before being drafted in June 1954. He served as a radio technician in the Army from 1954-56. A friend in Gipson's unit convinced him to pursue graduate studies in geology so that he could work outside rather than being confined to a laboratory or classroom. On completing military service, Gipson married

Alma D. Gadison, who had studied with him at Paine College.

During the 1950s and 1960s, the University of Georgia would not accept blacks but paid promising students to pursue their studies at another university that offered the same courses. Gipson attended the University of Chicago on one of these grants. His wife, who had become a psychiatric nurse, helped support them. Gipson worked part-time as a substitute teacher in the Chicago public school system. He also worked as a geologist for the Walter H. Flood Company in Chicago, and he served as a research assistant in the department of geophysical sciences at the University of Chicago. Gipson received his master's degree in 1961. For his doctoral dissertation, he studied the deeply buried rock layers near the coal fields of central Illinois. Analysis of these rocks required professors of chemistry and physics as well as geology to oversee Gipson's work. His dissertation was entitled *A Study of the Relations of Depth, Porosity, and Clay Mineral Orientation in Pennsylvanian Shales.* He received his doctoral degree in 1963.

After graduating, Gipson continued to work as geologist with the Walter H. Flood Company, conducting core samples. In core sampling, machines drive a metal sleeve into the ground to collect various layers of soil. Gipson conducted core sampling to select suitable ground for the runways at Chicago's O'Hare International Airport. During this period, he also participated in a study of ocean sediment for the University of Chicago. This research examined samples of clay and rock taken from the bottom of the sea to determine how oceans evolved over millions of years.

In 1964, Gipson accepted a position at Virginia State University. He would remain there until 1975, becoming professor and chair of the geological sciences department. While there, Gipson was asked by the National Aeronautics and Space Administration to explain pyramid-shaped formations on Mars. He and fellow researchers discovered that sandstorms, which occurred frequently on Mars, had gradually smoothed the sides of extinct volcanoes.

In 1973-74, Gipson took a sabatical to conduct oil exploration for Exxon Company. He then joined the company as a research associate in June 1975. Seismic stratigraphy was the method of oil exploration that he employed. This process makes use of artificially induced waves, simulating an earthquake, to study the lowest layers of rocks. He explored possible oil fields in Alaska, Florida, Mexico, Czechoslovakia, and Pakistan. In 1982, he joined ERCO Petroleum, where he worked on improving the production levels of oil and gas wells. After a six months with Aminoil, Inc., Gipson joined Phillips Petroleum Company as a senior project specialist in 1985. Gipson returned to academia in 1986. In that year, he accepted a position as professor of geology at the University of South Carolina, in Columbia. He taught general geology and did his best to open up careers such as oil exploration to minority students.

Gipson received many awards during his career, including the Elmer Thomas Fellowship in Geology (1961-63) and the Outstanding Scientist Award from the National Consortium for Black Professional Development (1976). His memberships included the Geological Society of America and the National Association of Geology Teachers. Gipson died of cancer in Columbia, South Carolina on March 10, 1995. He was survived by his wife Alma and their four children: Jacquelyn, Deborah, Mack, and Byron.

SELECTED WRITINGS BY GIPSON:

Periodicals

(with Ablordeppey, V.K.) "Pyramidal Structures on Mars." *Icarus* (June 1974).

FURTHER READING:

Books

Kessler, James H., et al. *Distinguished African American Scientists of the 20th Century.* Phoenix, AZ: Oryx Press, 1966, pp. 120-123.

Sammons, Vivian Ovelton. *Blacks in Science and Medicine.* New York: Hemisphere Publishing Corporation, 1990, pp. 101-102.

Periodicals

Ebony (May 1976): 7.

—Sketch by Robert J. Teitler

Meredith Charles Gourdine
1929-
Engineer and inventor

Meredith Charles Gourdine is a pioneer in electrogasdynamics (EGD) technology, an energy conversion process with many practical applications. The holder of over 70 patents, Gourdine is the president and CEO of Energy Innovations, a Houston-based firm devoted to overseeing and improving the many technological innovations for which Gourdine is responsible. The practical applications of his research and development in energy conversion systems have affected the daily lives of people throughout the world.

One of four children, Gourdine was born in Newark, New Jersey, on September 26, 1929. Although his father had won a scholarship to Temple University, he decided not

Meredith Charles Gourdine

to go and worked instead at various maintenance jobs. Gourdine's mother was a teletype operator who was also interested in mathematics. In 1936 the family moved to Harlem, where Gourdine was inspired by a math teacher at his elementary school. Gourdine went on to attend the highly competitive Brooklyn Tech High School, where he combined schoolwork with swimming and track and excelled as a quarter-mile runner. He also worked long hours for a radio and telegraph company, which provided him with funds to finance his first semester of college at Cornell University. Entering Cornell in 1948, Gourdine soon distinguished himself as a student and was awarded with a scholarship.

At Cornell, Gourdine became interested in physics as a more practical application of mathematics, a discipline which he felt was too abstract. However, as a freshman, he was not allowed to take classes in engineering physics—considered the most demanding and selective course at the university—because his high school grades were not good enough. Gourdine worked hard during his first term to score high grades in chemistry, engineering, physics, and calculus and was later allowed to transfer from electrical engineering to engineering physics.

Gourdine balanced his studies at Cornell with a developing career as a star athlete. In 1952 he earned a place on the United States Olympic Track team and won a silver medal in the broad jump competition at Helsinki, Sweden, missing the gold by four centimeters. Graduating in 1953 with a bachelor's degree in engineering physics, Gourdine

married June Cave, whom he met during his sophomore year (they would have four children together and later divorce). He then joined the Navy for two years as an ex-NROTC student, but found the work undemanding. Turning his attention back to math and physics, he applied for fellowships at Princeton and Cornell universities, as well as the California Institute of Technology.

Discovers Formula for Electrogasdynamics

Gourdine decided to go to CalTech on a Guggenheim Fellowship. During his graduate school years, he also received the Ramo-Woolridge Fellowship and developed the formula for electrogasdynamics (EGD) while working at Jet Propulsion Labs. Electrogasdynamics involves the interaction between an electrical field and charged particles suspended in gas, an event which produces high voltage electricity. The phenomenon of EGD had been known since the eighteenth century, but its uses were limited until Gourdine figured out how to employ the principle to produce enough electricity for practical applications in the modern world. Although Gourdine was put off by Jet Propulsion Lab's lack of interest in his research, he was not yet ready to take on the responsibility of his own company.

By 1960 Gourdine had earned his Ph.D. in engineering science, an interdisciplinary field based on a comprehensive understanding of all branches of physics. From 1960 to 1962 Gourdine was laboratory director of Plasmadyne Corporation, where he continued his research into magnetohydrodynamics (MHD), another conversion method that generates power through the interaction between magnetic fields and gases. However, again, he had no corporate support and moved on. After two more years, serving as chief scientist of Curtiss-Wright Corporation's Aero Division, Gourdine struck out on his own.

As the president and chairman of the board for Gourdine Systems, based in Livingston, New Jersey, Gourdine worked on patenting practical applications of EGD, MHD, and plasma physics (the study of electrically-charged, extremely hot gases). From 1964 to 1973, Gourdine invented or co-invented close to 70 patents. Knowing his own limitations, both personal and financial, Gourdine decided not to manufacture or sell his inventions. Instead, he licensed the patents to other companies.

One of Gourdine's inventions was the Electradyne Spray Gun, which used electrogasdynamics to atomize and electrify any kind of paint, allowing for the easy spray-painting of irregularly shaped objects, such as bicycles. He also invented Incineraid, a device to reduce air pollution emitted by apartment building incinerators. In 1970, Gourdine Systems became a publicly owned company and decided to do its own manufacturing and selling of products, although it soon fell prey to bad timing and poor business strategies. For example, Gourdine Systems spent more money marketing the spray gun than it made, and when incinerators were outlawed in New York City, Incineraid became unsalable.

Establishes New Company to Develop and License Technology

Despite these setbacks, Gourdine held fast to his goal to invent and license practical applications for the highly specialized technologies of EGD, MHD, and other direct energy conversion methods such as thermovoltaics (which involves the conversion of chemical and thermal energy into electricity). In 1974, Gourdine founded a new company, Energy Innovations, based in Houston, Texas.

In 1986 Gourdine lost his eyesight due to diabetic retinopathy. He first developed diabetes during his time in the Navy, with his eyesight gradually deteriorating over the years. This disability, however, did not prevent him from running Energy Innovations. Although Gourdine cannot read Braille (the diabetes has reduced sensation in his fingertips), he continues to produce new applications for his technologies and license them to other companies with the help of his son and second wife, Carolina. Known for his vigor and positive attitude, Gourdine practices yoga and meditation, swims, and enjoys spectator sports.

Gourdine's career as a researcher and inventor spans over thirty years and continues to grow. His many honors include election to the National Academy of Engineering and a citation for service as a member of the United States Army Science Board. He is a member of the Black Inventors Hall of Fame and in 1987 was honored for outstanding contributions as a scientist by North Carolina State University. Some of Gourdine's energy-saving and cost-efficient applications include a battery for electric cars, a system for clearing fog at airports, a method of extracting oil from oil shale, a procedure for repairing potholes by recovering rubber from old car tires and combining it with asphalt, and the means for producing better refrigerators and air conditioners.

SELECTED WRITINGS BY GOURDINE:

Periodicals

"Nuclear Power in Space," *Discovery,* (1963).
"Electrogasdynamic Power Generation," *AIAA Journal,* (August 1964): 1423–1427.
"EGD and Precipitation," *Industrial & Engineering Chemistry,* (December 1967): 26–29.

FURTHER READING:

Books

Van Sertima, Ivan, ed. *Blacks in Science: Ancient and Modern.* 1983, Transaction Books, pp. 226–227.

Periodicals

Ebony, (August 1972): 125.
Field, Alan M. "Father of Invention," *Houston Metropolitan,* (February 1991): 43–45, 53–54.

Evelyn Boyd Granville

Pierce, Ponchitta. "Science Pacemaker," *Ebony,* (April 1967): 53–58.

—Sketch by Geeta Kothari

Evelyn Boyd Granville
1924-
Mathematician

Evelyn Boyd Granville earned her doctorate from Yale University in 1949; in that year she and **Marjorie Lee Browne** (at the University of Michigan) became the first African American women to receive doctoral degrees in mathematics; it would be more than a dozen years before another black woman would earn a Ph.D. in the field. Granville's career has included stints as an educator and involvement with the American space program during its formative years.

Granville was born in Washington, D.C., on May 1, 1924. Her father, William Boyd, worked as a custodian in their apartment building; he did not stay with the family, however, and Granville was raised by her mother, Julia

Walker Boyd, and her mother's twin sister, Louise Walker, both of whom worked as examiners for the U.S. Bureau of Engraving and Printing. Granville and her sister Doris, who was a year and a half older, often spent portions of their summers at the farm of a family friend in Linden, Virginia.

Achievement Encouraged throughout Academic Career

The public schools of Washington, D.C., were racially segregated when Granville attended them. However, Dunbar High School (from which she graduated as valedictorian) maintained high academic standards. Several of its faculty held degrees from top colleges, and they encouraged the students to pursue ambitious goals. Granville's mathematics teachers included Ulysses Basset, a Yale graduate, and Mary Cromwell, a University of Pennsylvania graduate; Cromwell's sister, who held a doctorate from Yale, taught in Dunbar's English department.

With the encouragement of her family and teachers, Granville entered Smith College with a small partial scholarship from Phi Delta Kappa, a national sorority for black women. After her freshman year, she lived in a cooperative house at Smith, sharing chores rather than paying more expensive dormitory rates. During the summers, she returned to Washington to work at the National Bureau of Standards.

Granville majored in mathematics and physics, but was also fascinated by astronomy after taking a class from Marjorie Williams. She considered becoming an astronomer, but chose not to commit herself to living in the isolation of a major observatory, which was necessary for astronomers of that time. Though she had entered college intending to become a teacher, she began to consider industrial work in physics or mathematics. She graduated *summa cum laude* in 1945 and was elected to Phi Beta Kappa.

With help from a Smith College fellowship, Granville began graduate studies at Yale University, for which she also received financial assistance. She earned an M.A. in mathematics and physics in one year, and began working toward a doctorate at Yale. For the next two years she received a Julius Rosenwald Fellowship, which was awarded to help promising black Americans develop their research potential. The following year she received an Atomic Energy Commission Predoctoral Fellowship. Granville's doctoral work concentrated on functional analysis, and her dissertation was titled *On Laguerre Series in the Complex Domain*. Her advisor, Einar Hille, was a former president of the American Mathematical Society. Upon receiving her Ph.D. in mathematics in 1949, Granville was elected to the scientific honorary society Sigma Xi.

Granville then undertook a year of postdoctoral research at New York University's Institute of Mathematics and Science. Apparently because of housing discrimination, she was unable to find an apartment in New York, so she moved in with a friend of her mother. Despite attending segregated schools, Granville had not encountered discrimination based on race or gender in her professional preparation. Years later she would learn that her 1950 application for a teaching position at a college in New York City was turned down for such a reason. A female adjunct faculty member eventually told biographer Patricia Kenschaft that the application was rejected because of Granville's race; however, a male mathematician reported that despite the faculty's support of the application, the dean rejected it because Granville was a woman.

In 1950, Granville accepted the position of associate professor at Fisk University, a noted black college in Nashville, Tennessee. She was a popular teacher, and at least two of her female students credited her with inspiring them to earn doctorates in mathematics in later years.

Begins Affiliation with Space Program

After two years of teaching, Granville went to work for the Diamond Ordnance Fuze Laboratories as an applied mathematician, a position she held for four years. From 1956 to 1960, she worked for IBM on the Project Vanguard and Project Mercury space programs, analyzing orbits and developing computer procedures. Her job included making "real-time" calculations during satellite launchings. "That was exciting, as I look back, to be a part of the space programs—a very small part—at the very beginning of U.S. involvement," Granville told contributor Loretta Hall in a 1994 interview.

On a summer vacation to southern California, Granville met the Reverend Gamaliel Mansfield Collins, a minister in the community church. They were married in 1960, and made their home in Los Angeles. They had no children, although Collins's three children occasionally lived with them. In 1967, the marriage ended in divorce.

Upon moving to Los Angeles, Granville had taken a job at the Computation and Data Reduction Center of the U.S. Space Technology Laboratories, studying rocket trajectories and methods of orbit computation. In 1962, she became a research specialist at the North American Aviation Space and Information Systems Division, working on celestial mechanics, trajectory and orbit computation, numerical analysis, and digital computer techniques for the Apollo program. The following year she returned to IBM as a senior mathematician.

Return to Teaching Marked by Involvement with Children

Because of restructuring at IBM, numerous employees were transferred out of the Los Angeles area in 1967; Granville wanted to stay, however, so she applied for a teaching position at California State University in Los Angeles. She happily reentered the teaching profession, which she found enjoyable and rewarding. She was disappointed in the mathematics preparedness of her students, however, and she began working to improve mathematics education at all levels. She taught an elementary school supplemental mathematics program in 1968 and 1969 through the State of California Miller Mathematics Improvement Program. The following year she directed a mathematics enrichment program that provided after-school classes for kindergarten through fifth grade students, and she taught grades two through five herself. She was an educator at a National Science Foundation Institute for Secondary Teachers of Mathematics summer program at the University of Southern California in 1972. Along with colleague Jason Frand, Granville wrote *Theory and Application of Mathematics for Teachers* in 1975; a second edition was published in 1978, and the textbook was used at over 50 colleges.

In 1970, Granville married Edward V. Granville, a real estate broker. After her 1984 retirement from California State University in Los Angeles, they moved to a 16-acre (6.4 ha) farm in Texas, where they sold eggs produced by their 800 chickens.

From 1985 to 1988, Granville taught mathematics and computer science at Texas College in Tyler. In 1990, she accepted an appointment to the Sam A. Lindsey Chair at the University of Texas at Tyler, and in subsequent years continued teaching there as a visiting professor. Smith College awarded Granville an honorary doctorate in 1989, making her the first black woman mathematician to receive such an honor from an American institution.

Throughout her career Granville shared her energy with a variety of professional and service organizations and boards. Many of them, including the National Council of Teachers of Mathematics and the American Association of University Women, focused on education and mathematics. Others, such as the U.S. Civil Service Panel of Examiners of the Department of Commerce and the Psychology Examining Committee of the Board of Medical Examiners of the State of California, reflected broader civic interests.

When asked to summarize her major accomplishments, Granville told Hall, "First of all, showing that women can do mathematics." Then she added, "Being an African American woman, letting people know that we have brains too."

SELECTED WRITINGS BY GRANVILLE:

Books

Theory and Application of Mathematics for Teachers. Wadsworth Publishing, 1975.

Other

On Laguerre Series in the Complex Domain. (dissertation), Yale University, 1949.

FURTHER READING:

Books

Grinstein, Louise S., and Paul J. Campbell, eds. *Women of Mathematics.* Greenwood Press, 1987, pp. 57–61.

Hine, Darlene Clark, ed. *Black Women in America,* Vol. 1, Carlson, 1993, pp. 498–499.

Women, Numbers and Dreams. U.S. Department of Education, 1982, pp. 99–106.

Periodicals

Kenschaft, Patricia C. "Black Women in Mathematics in the United States," *The American Mathematical Monthly,* (October 1981): 592–604.

Other

Granville, Evelyn Boyd, *Interview with Loretta Hall conducted January 11,* 1994.

—Sketch by Loretta Hall

Artis P. Graves
1907-1977
Zoologist and embryologist

Artis P. Graves made a name for himself as a researcher and administrator, but he was equally well known as a teacher. Throughout a busy career spanning nearly half a century, he always made time to teach because he believed in the importance of sharing his knowledge with others.

Born in Hiawatha, West Virginia on September 23, 1907, Artis Paris Graves was the son of a coal miner. The elder Graves was killed in a coal mining accident when Artis was a small child, and the family remained in Hiawatha until Mrs. Graves remarried. The family then moved to Tennessee.

Graves became interested in science and entered Bluefield State College in West Virginia as a chemistry major. (He was also an All-American fullback for three years.) He soon realized that he was more interested in the biological sciences and switched majors. He received his bachelor of science degree in 1931 and became an instructor in biology at Morristown College, a two-year college in Tennessee. He remained there until 1935 when he took a position at Shorter College, a two-year institution outside Little Rock. After a year at Shorter, he joined the faculty of Morris Brown College in Atlanta as an instructor in biology, and as coach of the Wolverines football team, which he led to two National Negro Championships.

He decided to pursue graduate studies at around this time, and chose the University of Iowa, where he worked with the researcher Emil Witschi. Graves received his master's degree in 1938 and returned to Morris Brown. In

1940 he returned to Iowa for his doctoral work. His dissertation, on the development of the golden hamster (*Cricetus auratus Waterhouse*), earned him his doctorate in zoology in 1943. It was so highly regarded that it was accepted for publication in the *American Journal of Anatomy*.

Graves returned to Morris Brown as chair of the biology department, and remained there until the spring of 1950. In the summer of 1950 he taught at Texas Southern University in Houston, and in the fall he accepted the chairmanship of the biology department of North Carolina A & T University in Greensboro. When Graves arrived at North Carolina A & T, the biology department "was housed in a small one-story building," his widow, Anne Graves Kornegay, said in an interview with contributor George Milite in May 1998. "It's thanks to him that the biology department today is as large as it is." Graves was responsible for the construction of the new biology building, Barnes Hall (which was partially funded with grants from the National Science Foundation). Over the course of his quarter century as department chair, he increased the biology staff from four to 14, and the number of biology majors from 75 to more than 300.

He continued to remain active as a teacher—both for students and for other teachers. Between 1959 and 1963 he was involved in a series of National Science Foundation-sponsored training programs for high school biology teachers who would come to North Carolina A & T for advanced training. In addition, he chaired the school's athletic committee and was one of the founders of the Mid-Eastern Athletic Conference (MEAC).

Graves married the former Anne Collins in 1940; the couple had three daughters. In his spare time, Graves was an avid hunter and fisherman. He taught himself taxidermy; several of his birds are on display at North Carolina A & T.

Illness forced Graves's retirement in June 1977; he died two months later on August 17. In 1978 his family established the Artis P. Graves Memorial Scholarship for Biology, which is awarded to a biology major at North Carolina A & T each year.

FURTHER READING:

Books

Sammons, Vivian O. *Blacks in Science and Medicine.* Hemisphere Publishing, 1990.

—Sketch by George A. Milite

Ida Gray
1867-1953
Dentist

Ida Gray was the first African American woman to earn the doctor of dental surgery degree in the United States. She earned her degree from the University of Michigan, Ann Arbor. Gray was also the first African American woman to practice dentistry in Chicago.

Ida Gray was born on March 4, 1867, in Clarksville, Tennessee. Her mother's name was Jennie Gray John; her father's name is not known. Her family moved to Cincinnati, Ohio, and Gray attended Gaines High School, graduating in 1887. While attending high school, Gray worked in the office of the only dentist in Cincinnati then, Dr. Jonathan Taft. Unlike many of his colleagues, Taft believed that women should become dentists. Indeed Taft helped the first female dentist in the world, Lucy Hobbs, begin her career. Gray was inspired by Hobbs's accomplishment, and Taft helped her gain admission to his alma mater, the University of Michigan Dental School, in Ann Arbor.

Gray enrolled in the University of Michigan Dental School in October 1887. She earned her doctor of dental surgery degree from the University of Michigan in 1890. Upon graduation, she practiced for several years in her hometown of Cincinnati. In 1895, she married James S. Nelson. A veteran of the Spanish-American War, Nelson had served as the Eighth Regiment's quartermaster in Chicago. Gray moved to this city with her new husband. While Nelson worked as a lawyer and an accountant, Gray set up another successful dental practice. She was again the first black female dentist in Chicago; she would spend the rest of her life and career there. She was also involved in a number of women's organizations in Chicago.

While working as a dentist, Gray influenced another woman to enter the profession. Olive M. Henderson, a patient of hers, became the second African American woman dentist in Chicago in 1912. Nelson died in 1926, and three years later Gray married William A. Rollins. She took his name and practiced as Ida N. Rollins. William Rollins died in 1938. Gray died in 1953; she had had no children with either husband.

FURTHER READING:

Books

Driskell, Claude Evans. *History of Chicago Black Dental Professionals, 1850-1983.* Chicago: C.E. Driskell, 1983-84, pp. 22-23.

Periodicals

Kelsey, Charles. "Ida Gray: Class of 1890." *University of Michigan School of Dentistry Alumni Bulletin.* (1977-78): 50-52.

—Sketch by A. Petrusso

Harry James Green, Jr.
1911-
Chemical engineer

Harry James Green, Jr. pursued a highly successful professional career in engineering despite obstacles posed both by racism and by the Depression. He was born in St. Louis, Missouri on December 7, 1911, the son of Harry James Green, Sr. and the former Olivia Jones. His father was a clerk in the U.S. Post Office; his mother was a housewife.

Although the young Green grew up within the segregated school system of St. Louis, he nevertheless found opportunity. "In high school I took the scientific course," he told contributor T. A. Heppenheimer in a telephone interview conducted on May 7, 1998. "Most of the young men took manual training; they were more or less encouraged to do so, but I didn't want that." His courses included college algebra; he also made good use of the city's public library. He even built a steam engine while in high school, and used it to drive a boat.

Pursues a Career Amid Difficulties

Green graduated from high school in 1928 and entered Ohio State University. He chose chemical engineering as his major, picking this field with a shrewd eye to his prospects within a segregated nation. He knew that this field was expanding rapidly, amid strong growth of both the petroleum industry and the production of industrial chemicals. He nevertheless anticipated that even with a degree in this subject, racial prejudice might prevent him from working as a chemical engineer. But he was aware that America's black colleges offered positions to teachers of chemistry, and he expected that he might win such a position if he could not work as an engineer.

He graduated from Ohio State in 1932, with the degree of Bachelor of Chemical Engineering. Then, as he tells Heppenheimer, he "couldn't get a job in industry." This involved more than racism, for the nation was in the depths of the Depression; graduates with even the best qualifications had to take whatever they could get. Unable to find a job in engineering, Green nevertheless won a position as an instructor in chemistry at North Carolina Agricultural and Technical College, which was one of the black institutions on which he had expected to rely. It served as his base during the subsequent ten years. In 1937 he received a fellowship from the General Education Board and entered a graduate program at the Massachusetts Institute of Technology, emerging in 1938 with a Master of Science degree. This qualified him for promotion to assistant professor at North Carolina A & T. In 1941 he returned to Ohio State to study, with support from a Julius Rosenwald fellowship. He received a Ph.D. in chemical engineering two years later.

Green's dissertation dealt with the chemical process of dialysis, which separates substances in solution by arranging for them to diffuse through a membrane. During subsequent decades, this process gained great importance in medicine, for it made possible the construction of artificial kidneys that could remove waste products from the blood. Green did not contribute to this medical work, but complied with terms of his doctoral program by returning for a final year at North Carolina A & T. Here he received another promotion, to full professor. Then in 1944, with industry booming during World War II, he left this college to pursue, at last, a career in chemical engineering.

Wins Success in Industrial Management

Green joined the firm of Stromberg-Carlson, a builder of radios, in Rochester, New York. He remained with this company through the next quarter century, as it merged with the firm of General Dynamics and became that corporation's Electronics Division. Green worked in research on materials. He particularly recalls contributing to improvements in telephone transmitters. We speak into a transmitter whenever we talk on the phone; it uses carbon granules and converts the vibrations of speech into an electrical signal. Green worked with anthracite coal as a source for the carbon, as it was both readily available and offered high purity.

He came in at the level of Senior Engineer; in 1959 he was promoted to Supervisor of Manufacturing Research and Development within the Production Engineering Department. In 1967, following the merger with General Dynamics, he became a Principal Engineer in microelectronics. Then in 1970, the Electronics Division moved from Rochester to San Diego, California. Green stayed in Rochester and joined the Xerox Corporation as a staff scientist within that firm's research department. He remained at Xerox until he retired, in 1976.

Research in materials engineering was an ongoing activity for him during his career in industry. At Stromberg-Carlson he directed work on metals, with emphasis on magnetic materials used in electronics. He joined the American Society of Metals, and was a member of a group that edited a handbook on metallurgy. He also served as chairman of a group that wrote a review of the use of copper alloys. He went on to conduct studies of the electrical properties of plastics, and of the packaging of microelectronic circuits.

In 1939 he married Ruth Williams. They had two children: Richard, and Harry James Green III. He and his wife continue to live in Rochester, where he has remained active by teaching at the Rochester Institute of Technology.

In his youth, he faced severe difficulties due to race prejudice, while the Depression made things worse. He nevertheless won his way to academic achievement and to a highly successful professional career. Today, amid prosperity and with opportunities for black people having expanded greatly, he urges others to take heart from his accomplishments. As he told Heppenheimer, "You have to move into whatever the situation is, regardless of the barriers."

FURTHER READING:

Books

American Men and Women of Science. New Providence, NJ: R.R. Bowker, 1982.

Low, W. Augustus, and Clift, Virgil A. *Encyclopedia of Black America*New york: Norton, 1982.

Sammons, Vivian. *Blacks in Science and Medicine.* Sammons, NY: Hemisphere Publishing, 1990.

—*Sketch by T. A. Heppenheimer*

Frederick Drew Gregory

Frederick Drew Gregory
1941-
Astronaut

In 1985, Frederick Drew Gregory became only the second black astronaut in space, the first having been Colonel **Guion "Guy" Bluford** in 1983. Gregory, who flew the space shuttle *Challenger,* was also the first black space shuttle pilot. In his later work as a safety administrator for the National Aeronautics and Space Administration (NASA), he redesigned the shuttle cockpit and assisted in the development of revolutionary landing technology.

Fighter Pilot, Test Pilot

Frederick Drew Gregory was born on January 7, 1941, in Washington, D.C., the son of Francis and Nora (Drew) Gregory. Through his mother, he was nephew to the renowned African-American blood plasma specialist **Charles Drew**. He attended Anacostia High School, and later entered the United States Air Force Academy.

Graduating from the Academy in 1964 with a B.S. degree, Gregory entered the Air Force pilot-training program. He earned certification as a pilot and, in 1965, as a helicopter pilot. In 1968, he received training as a fighter pilot, and began flying F-4 Phantoms. He attended the United States Naval Test Pilot School, and following his graduation in 1971, received an assignment as a research and engineering test pilot.

This continued until 1974, when NASA asked Gregory to come to work as a test pilot for them. He continued in this role for several years, during which time he earned his M.S.A. in information systems from George Washington University in 1977. In 1978, NASA selected him as an astronaut candidate.

Second Black Astronaut in Space

Gregory began his astronaut training in the summer of 1978, and completed a one-year training and evaluation cycle in August of the following year. In 1983, Bluford became the first black man in space, but Gregory's opportunity was not far behind. On April 29, 1985, NASA launched mission STS 51-B of the space shuttle *Challenger* from the Kennedy Space Center in Florida. Gregory served as pilot on the flight, which returned to earth a week later, on May 6; thus he was not only the second black astronaut in space, but the first black pilot of a space shuttle.

Gregory flew several other missions with the space shuttle in the late 1980s and early 1990s. He also became NASA's associate administrator of its Office of Safety and Mission Assurance at the Lyndon B. Johnson Space Center in Houston, Texas. In his capacity as a safety administrator, Gregory redesigned the space shuttle cockpit and worked with a team that developed an innovative landing system that utilized microwave instrumentation. The Bendix Aircraft Company has adapted this technology, which it predicts will be used after the year 2000 to facilitate landing of planes without pilots. Gregory's expertise has also been called upon in studies of NASA safety and the viability of continuing joint American and Russian missions through the combined NASA and *Mir* programs.

Gregory has received numerous honors and awards in his career. NASA has awarded him its Outstanding Leadership Award, Distinguished Service Medal, three Space Medals, and two NASA Space Flight Medals. The Air Force awarded him its Defense Superior Service Medal, two Distinguished Flying Crosses, the Meritorious Service Medal, the Air Force Commendation Medal, the Defense Meritorious Service Medal, 16 air medals, and the Air Force Association Ira Eaker Fellowship. In addition, he has earned the Distinguished National Scientist Award from the National Society of Black Engineers (1979), the Top 20 Minority Engineers Award (1990), the George Washington University Distinguished Alumni Award, and an honorary degree from the University of the District of Columbia. Among the professional, academic, and civic organizations to which he belongs are the American Helicopter Society, the Association of Space Explorers, the National Technical Association, Omega Psi Phi, Sigma Pi Phi, the Society of Experimental Test Pilots, the Tuskegee Airmen, the United States Air Force Academy Association of Graduates, and the Young Astronaut Council of the National Capital Area Boy Scouts (board of directors).

Gregory married Barbara Ann Archer on June 3, 1964, and they have two children, Frederick D. Gregory, Jr., and Heather Lynn Gregory Skeens. His son followed in his father's career path, becoming an officer in the Air Force working at the Johnson Space Center. Among Gregory's avocational interests are water and snow skiing. The Gregorys live in Washington, D.C.

FURTHER READING:

Books

Mabunda, L. Mpho, ed. *The African American Almanac.* Gale, 1997.

Sammons, Vivian Ovelton. *Blacks in Science and Medicine.* Hemisphere Publishing, 1990.

Who's Who Among African Americans, eleventh edition. Gale, 1998.

Periodicals

Broad, William J., "Has NASA Forgotten the Lesson of *Challenger?*" *Star-Tribune,* (February 15, 1998): 21-A.

Major, Michael, "Black Engineer of the Year Awards," *U.S. Black Engineer,* (December 31, 1990).

Vaughn, Leroy, "Black Inventors," *Los Angeles Sentinel,* (February 15, 1995).

Wheeler, Larry, "NASA Expected to Get Serious Grilling Over *Mir* Before House Panel," Gannett News Service, (September 15, 1997).

—*Sketch by Judson Knight*

Margaret Elizabeth Grigsby
1923-
Physician

Margaret Elizabeth Grigsby began her medical career in the 1940s—at a time when few women, especially black women, aspired to such ambitions. In addition to her work as a physician, her career includes research in internal medicine, service as an advisor to the United States government, and many years as an educator at Howard University.

Margaret Elizabeth Grigsby was born in Prairie View, Texas, on January 16, 1923. She earned her bachelor's degree in her hometown, graduating in 1943 from Prairie View State College. She received her medical degree in 1948 from the University of Michigan in Ann Arbor, Michigan. In 1963, she obtained an additional advanced degree from the University of London in England.

Shortly after graduating from the University of Michigan, Grigsby moved to St. Louis, Missouri, where she joined the staff of Homer G. Phillips Hospital. During 1950, Grigsby moved to Washington, D.C. to practice medicine at the Freedmen's Hospital. From 1951-52, she completed a Rockefeller Foundation Research Fellowship at the Harvard Medical School. While remaining an attending physician at Freedmen's Hospital, Grigsby found additional challenges in 1952 at Howard University, also in Washington. Her first position was as a course instructor in the medical school. Before long, she was promoted to associate professor. Beginning in 1958, she expanded her duties by treating patients at D.C. General Hospital as an attending physician. In 1966, Grigsby was named a professor of medicine in the College of Medicine.

Grigsby's medical research included work in internal medicine, tropical medicine, infectious diseases, antibiotics, and the electrophoresis of proteins. In 1966, she began her service to various United States government health agencies. In that year she traveled to Ibadan, Nigeria, as a medical epidemiologist for the United States Public Health Service. From 1970-71, she served as a consultant to the United States Agency for International Development and as a member of the Anti-Infective Agents advisory committee of the United States Food and Drug Administration.

In 1956, Grigsby was named a China Medical Board Fellow of the School of Tropical Medicine at the University of Puerto Rico. The American College of Physicians named her a fellow in 1962. Grigsby is also a member of the American Medical Association and the National Medical Association. Now retired from Howard University, Grigsby continues to reside in the Washington, D.C. area.

FURTHER READING

Sammons, Vivian. *Blacks in Science and Medicine.* New York: Hemishpere Publishing, 1990, p. 107.

—*Sketch by Patrick J. Longe*

Lucille Constance Gunning

Lucille Constance Gunning
1922-
Pediatrician

Lucille Constance Gunning has made important advances in rehabilitating children with disabilities. Her work has included studies in the care of handicapped children and the establishment of vitally needed extended-care facilities for children with chronic health problems.

The elder of two children, Gunning was born on February 21, 1922, in New York City. Her parents, who were from Jamaica, were Susan and Roland Gunning. Because of poor health, Gunning was sent back to Jamaica shortly after her first birthday to live with her paternal grandmother. One formative event in her decision to become a doctor occurred at the age of five, when she visited an aunt, who was a midwife. Her aunt was helping with a delivery; the birth went badly, and a doctor was called in to help. He came too late, though and the baby died. Gunning remembered years later their faith in the doctor—everyone in the house believed, unquestioningly, that the baby would have lived if the doctor had been there. She too would become a baby doctor.

Gunning graduated from high school in Jamaica; she wanted to go to college in England but World War II prevented this. She returned to the United States and entered New York University. She received her bachelor's degree in 1945 and promptly went to medical school at the Women's Medical College of Pennsylvania. She received her medical degree in 1949. In 1950, she served her internship at the Harlem Hospital Center in New York City. After a residency in infectious diseases in Detroit, she returned to Harlem Hospital Center, where she was chief resident in pediatrics from 1951-52. She then became the chief pediatric resident at the Woman's Medical College of Pennsylvania Hospital from 1952-53. In 1953, she married Carlton E. Blackwood, a fellow Jamaican and a chemist.

After 1953, Gunning focused her interests on the longterm illnesses of children, especially on rehabilitating children with disabilities. In 1964, she began work at the Montefiore Hospital, and by 1966 she had established a division of pediatric rehabilitation there and become its head. In 1971, she moved to the Harlem Hospital Center, where she became the chief of pediatric rehabilitation. At Harlem Hospital Center, Gunning created a developmental center for children with Down's syndrome. She was careful to involve the parents of the children in the activities of the center, because she recognized that they were the most important caregivers in the children's lives and that they also needed support. In addition, Gunning observed that the parents were some of her best sources for information about what treatments worked for children.

Gunning became one of the founding members of the **Susan Smith McKinney-Steward** Medical Society of New York City—a group of black women physicians who mentor minority female medical school students. In 1981, she moved to Dayton, Ohio, where for two years she was director of physical medicine and rehabilitation in the Children's Medical Center. While in Dayton, she served as an associate clinical professor of rehabilitative medicine at the medical school of Wright State University. Beginning in 1983, she worked for the state of New York as the deputy director of medical services for the office of Mental Retardation and Developmental Disabilities.

In 1983, Gunning received the Physicians Recognition Award from the American Medical Association; in 1985, she received the Charles Drew Pre-Medical Society of Columbia University Honorary Award. In the early 1990s, Gunning took a position supervising health physicians for school districts in Manhattan. She also has a private consulting practice. Her husband, Carlton E. Blackwood, died in 1974. They have four children, Elaine, Alexander, Lydia, and Ann.

SELECTED WRITINGS BY GUNNING:

Periodicals

"Management of the Handicapped Child in Central Harlem." *Bulletin of the New York Academy of Medicine,* 50, no. 1 (January 1974): 45-9.

FURTHER READING:

Books

Smith, Jessie Carney, ed. *Notable Black American Women.* Detroit: Gale Research, 1991.

—Sketch by Patrick Moore

John Langston Gwaltney
1928-
Anthropologist

John Langston Gwaltney has distinguished himself as an anthropologist, writer, and educator. He has contributed to the ethnographic understanding of African American culture and researched the role of blindness in the Chinantec Indian culture.

John Gwaltney was born in Orange, New Jersey, on September 25, 1928, to Mabel Harper Gwaltney and John Stanley Gwaltney. At two months of age, it was determined that John Gwaltney was blind. His large extended family surrounded and supported him throughout his childhood. His father, a merchant seaman, was frequently absent from the household, making the presence of his other family members even more important. Mabel Gwaltney made several attempts to find a cure for her son's blindness. Neither medical science nor religious healers corrected his vision. Once John was old enough to attend school, Mabel Gwaltney wrote a letter to Eleanor Roosevelt about the First Lady's efforts to establish special education for handicapped children. Eleanor Roosevelt responded and helped John Gwaltney enroll in a school for the blind. As an avid and independent student, he excelled in his studies.

Gwaltney entered Upsala College in East Orange, New Jersey, in order to remain in close proximity to his family, as his mother had grown ill from diabetes. He studied political science and sociology, inspired by his father's travels and his childhood memories of Margaret Mead's radio speeches. Gwaltney received his bachelor of arts degree in 1952, a short time after his mother passed away.

Gwaltney attended the New School of Social Research, completing the master's program there in 1957. He studied the conflicts of the colonization of Africa, paying particular attention to the Mau Mau uprising, a bloody war fought for Kenya's independence. After earning his master's degree, he briefly taught at the Henry George School of Social Science in New York City in order to finance his graduate studies. In 1959, he enrolled in Columbia University's graduate school of anthropology. He began working on his doctoral dissertation with Margaret Mead, who supervised his field study of the Chinantec Indians near Oaxaca, Mexico.

Partially supported by a fellowship grant from the National Institutes of Health, Gwaltney conducted ethnographic research in the remote Chinantec village with special reference to an endemic disease, borne by flies, that resulted in blindness. One out of every 20 villagers suffered from this condition, which was known as Roble's disease or river blindness. Gwaltney spent more than a year with the Indians collecting data for his dissertation. In 1967, his study won the prestigious Columbia University Ansley Dissertation Award. In 1970, is thesis was published as a book entitled, *The Thrice Shy: Cultural Accommodations to Blindness and Other Disasters in a Mexican Community.*

Gwaltney received his doctoral degree in 1967 and accepted a position at the State University of New York at Cortland. During his associate professorship, he studied the Shinnecock and Poospatuck Indians of Canada and embarked on his first study of African American culture. He transferred to Syracuse University in 1971, where he taught anthropology courses and started to accumulate a series of African American oral narratives. Gwaltney compiled these narratives together to create his book, *Drylongso,* African American slang meaning "ordinary" or "nothing unusual." *Drylongso,* published in 1981, documents the ideas, values, and attitudes of the ordinary African American. Gwaltney did not impose his interpretations onto the narratives. His ethnographic research allows each individual's voice to stand alone and function as its own interpretation of culture—a technique known as "native anthropology." For this publication he won the first Association of Black Anthropologists Publication Award.

Gwaltney has accepted numerous positions within anthropological organizations. He is a fellow of the American Anthropological Society, the American Ethnological Society, and the Society for Applied Anthropology. He also contributes to a program in African studies funded by the National Science Foundation. In 1987, Gwaltney won the Robert F. Kennedy Book Award for *The Dissenters* (1986), a collection of interviews with revolutionaries from "all walks of life." In this book, Gwaltney explores the social and anthropological necessity of dissent and rebellion.

In 1991, Gwaltney retired from Syracuse University to devote more time to his family, his writing, and other pursuits. He currently lives in Oregon with his wife Judith Gwaltney, where he spends time with his two children, Karen and Peter, and works as a writer and an artist. Gwaltney carves wood into works of art that represent his African American heritage; his carving of an African ceremonial staff was exhibited at Syracuse University in 1983.

SELECTED WRITINGS BY GWALTNEY:

Books

The Dissenters. New York: Random House, 1986.

Drylongso: A Self-Portrait of Black America. New
   York: The New Press, 1993.
*The Thrice Shy: Cultural Accommodations to Blindness
   and Other Disasters in a Mexican Community.*
   New York: Columbia University Press, 1970.

FURTHER READING

Books

Chandler, Sue P., and Shockley, Ann Allen. *Living
   Black American Authors: A Biographical Directory.*
   New York: R. R. Bowker Co., 1973.

Kessler, James H., et. al. *Distinguished African American Scientists of the 20th Century.* Phoenix, Arizona: Oryx Press, 1996.
Sammons, Vivian Ovelton, ed. *Blacks in Science and
   Medicine.* New York: Hemisphere Publishing Corporation, 1990.
Page, James A. *Selected Black American Authors: An
   Illustrated Bio-Bibliography.* New York: G.K. Hall,
   1977.

                                    —Sketch by Alison Wellford

Lloyd Augustus Hall
1894-1971
Chemist

Chemist Lloyd Augustus Hall is best known for his work in the field of food technology, where he developed processes to cure and preserve meat, prevent rancidity in fats, and sterilize spices. In 1939, he cofounded the Institute of Food Technologists, establishing a new branch of industrial chemistry.

Hall was born in Elgin, Illinois, on June 20, 1894. His father, Augustus Hall, was a Baptist minister and son of the first pastor of the Quinn Chapel A.M.E. Church, the first African American church in Chicago. Hall's mother, Isabel, was a high-school graduate whose mother had fled to Illinois via the Underground Railroad at the age of 16.

Hall became interested in chemistry while attending the East Side High School in Aurora, Illinois, where he was active in extracurricular activities such as debate, track, football, and baseball. He was one of five African Americans attending the school during his four years there. By the time he graduated among the top ten in his class, he'd been offered scholarships to four Illinois universities.

Hall chose to attend Northwestern University, working his way through school while he studied chemistry. During this time, he met Carroll L. Griffith, a fellow chemistry student, who would later play a part in his career. Hall graduated in 1916 with a bachelor of science degree in chemistry and continued his studies in graduate classes at the University of Chicago.

During World War I, Hall served as a lieutenant in the Ordnance Department, inspecting explosives at a plant in Wisconsin. However, he was subjected to such prejudice and discriminatory behavior that he asked to be transferred. The discrimination was also apparent in the civilian world: at one point, he was hired over the telephone by the Western Electric Company. When he arrived for work, he was told there was none.

In 1916, however, he was able to find a position in the Chicago Department of Health Laboratories. Within a year, he was made senior chemist. For the next six years, he worked at several industrial laboratories. In 1921, he was made chief chemist at Boyer Chemical Laboratory in Chicago. By then, he'd become interested in the developing field of food chemistry, and in 1922, he became president and chemical director of the Chemical Products Corporation, a consulting laboratory in Chicago.

In 1924, one of Hall's clients, Griffith Laboratories (his old lab partner at Northwestern had been Carroll L. Griffith) offered him a space where he could work for them while continuing his consulting practice. By 1925, Hall had become chief chemist and director of research at Griffith; in 1929, he gave up his consulting practice and devoted himself full-time to Griffith until 1959.

Develops "Flash-Drying" Method

When Hall started at Griffith, current meat curing and preservation methods were highly unsatisfactory. It was known that sodium chloride preserved meat, while chemicals containing nitrogen—nitrates and nitrites—were used for curing. However, not much was known about how these chemicals worked, and food could not be preserved for an extended period of time.

In experiments, Hall discovered that nitrite and nitrate penetrated the meat more quickly than the sodium chloride, causing it to disintegrate before it had a chance to be preserved. The problem was to get the salt to penetrate the meat first, thereby preserving it before it was cured. Hall solved this through "flash-drying"—a quick method of evaporating a solution of all three salts, so that crystals of sodium chloride enclosing the nitrite and nitrate were formed. Thus, when the crystals dissolved, the sodium chloride would penetrate the meat first.

Discovers How to Sterilize Spices

Hall's next accomplishment was in the area of spices. Although meat could now be preserved and cured effectively, the natural spices that were used to enhance and preserve it often contained contaminants. Spices such as allspice, cloves, cinnamon, and paprika as well as dried vegetable products like onion powder contained yeasts, molds, and bacteria. Hall's task was to find a way to sterilize the spices and dried vegetables without destroying their original flavor and appearance. Heating the foods above 240° F (115° C) would sterilize them, but it would also destroy their taste and color. Hall discovered that ethylene oxide, a gas used to kill insects, would also kill the germs in the spices. He used a vacuum chamber to remove the moisture from the spices so that the gas could permeate and sterilize them when introduced into the chamber. The times and temperatures varied according to the type of bacteria, mold, or yeast to be destroyed.

The ability to sterilize spices had a major impact on the meat industry. The process also became popular in the hospital supplies industry and was used to sterilize bandages, dressings, and sutures. In fact, a number of industries in the United States benefited enormously from Hall's invention.

Researches Effects of Antioxidants on Fats

In his work at Griffith, Hall also discovered the use of antioxidants in preventing rancidity in foods containing fats and oils. Rancidity is caused by oxidation when constituents in the fats react with oxygen. By experimenting with various antioxidants, Hall found that certain chemicals in crude vegetable oil worked as antioxidants. Using some of these combined with salt, he produced an antioxidant salt mixture that protected foods containing fats and oils from spoiling.

During his 35 years at Griffith, Hall worked in several areas of food chemistry, including seasoning, spice extracts, and enzymes. In 1951, Hall and an associate developed a way to reduce the time for curing bacon from between six and 15 days to a few hours. The quality of the bacon was also improved, both in appearance and stability. He was also very interested in vitamins and the development of yeast foods. By 1959, Hall held over 105 patents in the United States and abroad and had published numerous papers on food technology. Hall served on various committees during his time at Griffith. During World War II, he was a member of the Committee on Food Research of the Scientific Advisory Board of the War Department's Quartermaster Corps; in that position he advised the military on the preservation of food supplies from 1943 to 1948. In 1944, he joined the Illinois State Food Commission of the State Department of Agriculture, serving until 1949.

As a further sign of the establishment of food chemistry as a field of science, the Institute of Food Technologists was founded in 1939. Hall was a charter member; he edited its magazine, *The Vitalizer,* and served on its executive board for four years. In 1954, Hall became chairman of the Chicago chapter of the American Institute of Chemists. The following year, he was elected a member of its national board of directors, becoming the first African American man to hold that position in the Institute's 32-year history.

Upon his retirement from Griffith in 1959, Hall continued to serve as a consultant to various state and federal organizations. He also continued to work, and in 1961, he spent six months in Indonesia, advising the Food and Agricultural Organization of the United Nations. From 1962 to 1964, he was a member of the American Food for Peace Council, an appointment made by President John F. Kennedy. After retiring, Hall and his wife, Myrrhene, moved to California to benefit her health. Hall lived in Altadena, where he remained active in community affairs, until his death on January 2, 1971.

FURTHER READING:

Books

Carwell, Hattie. *Blacks in Science: Astrophysicist to Zoologist.* Exposition Press, 1977, pp. 27–28.

Haber, Louis. *Black Pioneers of Science and Invention.* Harcourt, 1970, pp. 102–111.

Miles, Wyndham D., ed. *American Chemists and Chemical Engineers.* American Chemical Society, 1976, pp. 193–194.

Sammons, Vivian Ovelton. *Blacks in Science and Medicine.* Hemisphere Publishing, 1990, pp. 109–110.

Periodicals

Drew, Charles Richard. "Negro Scholars in Scientific Research," *Journal of Negro History,* Vol. 35, 1950, pp. 135–189.

—Sketch by Geeta Kothari

Benjamin Franklin Hammond
1934-
Dentist and microbiologist

Benjamin Franklin Hammond is a distinguished dental professor who does research in the area of microbiology, especially on the physical and molecular biology of oral lactic acid bacteria. Hammond has served as the chair of the department of microbiology in the School of Dentistry at the University of Pennsylvania, as well as the associate dean for academic affairs.

Hammond was born on February 23, 1934, in Austin, Texas. He received his undergraduate education at the University of Kansas, where he earned his B.A. in 1954. Hammond attended dental school at Meharry Medical College, receiving his D.D.S. in 1958. Hammond went on to the doctoral program at the University of Pennsylvania, the institution with which he would remain affiliated throughout his career. Hammond won a four-year fellowship from the United States Public Health Service (USPHS). In 1959, while still a graduate student, Hammond earned the Hatton Award from the International Association for Dental Research. He was granted his doctorate in microbiology in 1962, with a dissertation entitled *Studies on Capsule Formation in Lactobacillus Casei.*

Hammond began teaching as a graduate student at the University of Pennsylvania. He was an assistant instructor from 1958-62. From 1962-70, Hammond was first an assistant professor and then an associate professor. In 1970, he was made a full professor in the microbiology department at the School of Dentistry. In 1972, Hammond became the chair of the microbiology department. Twelve years later, in 1984, he was named the University of Pennsylvania's associate dean for academic affairs. While affiliated with the University of Pennsylvania, he has held other positions. He was a lecturer for a research seminar at Meharry Medical College in 1965; he has served as a consultant for the Council of Dental Education, the USPHS, the National Science Foundation, and the American Fund for Dental Education. Hammond also is a member of the National Institutes of Health.

A member of the American Society for Microbiology and the International Association for Dental Research, Hammond has earned many honors throughout his career. In 1966, he won the USPHS Career Development Award. Three years later, he was selected for the Lindback Award for Distinguished Teaching at the University of Pennsylvania. In 1976, the city of Paris, France, gave him the Medaille D'Argent. Hammond has had outside interests as well. In 1981, he served as president of the Lecture University of Pennsylvania. He is also a committee member for the Philadelphia College of Art at the Museum of Art of Philadelphia.

—Sketch by A. Petrusso

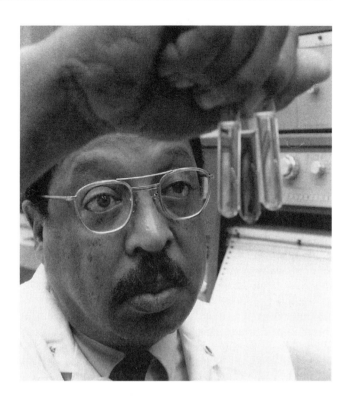

Don Navarro Harris

Don Navarro Harris
1929-
Biochemist

Don Navarro Harris was born on June 17, 1929, in New York City to Virginia natives John Henry Harris, an electrician, and Margaret Vivian Berkley-Harris, a seamstress and housewife, who had moved to New York during the mid-twenties. As a young boy, Don attended integrated public schools in the city and early on decided on a career in science. He went on to study chemistry at Lincoln University, a small college in rural Pennsylvania, where the student body was almost entirely African American. To help pay his way through school, Harris worked part-time at the student infirmary, and thus gained experience relevant to his field. Upon his graduation in 1951, he returned to New York and worked for a couple of years at government agencies and medical laboratories.

In 1953, just after the Korean War, Harris was drafted into the army and sent to serve as a medical technician, first at Fort Sam Houston in Texas and then to an army hospital in France. While in Texas he met and married Regina

Brooks on July 29, 1954, and when he returned from France in 1955 the couple moved to New York. At first, Harris took up a position with the city's Public Health Service but soon moved to a basic research laboratory at Columbia University in search of more challenging work. There he was a part of a team that was just beginning to understand the influence of cholesterol on the arteries and heart. In 1958 he decided to return to school and enrolled in the graduate program in biochemistry at Rutgers University in New Brunswick. Within one year he was able to complete his master's and went straight on to his Ph.D., graduating in 1963.

Harris's graduate work was concerned with ribonucleic acid (RNA) molecules, an essential part of all cells. He investigated the basic problem of how RNA controlled the building of specific amino acid units that make up different proteins in the body. In his first job, at the Research center of the Colgate-Palmolive Company at Piscataway, N. J., Harris turned his attention to applied problems and supervised students in a study of dental caries and plaque. He switched back to Rutgers and basic science one year later, and in 1965 switched yet again to applied science, this time as a member of the research staff at Bristol-Meyers Squibb Research Institute near Princeton, N.J. He has remained associated with the company ever since.

Harris wore many different hats at Bristol-Meyers. First he was a supervisor in a laboratory that focused on developing methods to analyze how complex molecules such as proteins and hormones are built. Over the years, he attempted to answers such diverse questions as how sex hormones influenced protein synthesis; how enzymes affected physiological processes such as blood clotting and blood pressure; what role cholesterol played in heart attacks, and also how compounds called eicosanoids were processed in the blood stream. During this time he rose in the company to a position of research leader, which entails making strategic decisions and integrating different research projects directed towards the development of different products. His work produced a total of over 60 scientific articles. Harris is also the co-holder on five U.S. patents for various medical compounds developed as a result of his work.

In 1993 Harris left full-time work at his company to become a Human Resources consultant, advising the department on the recruitment and training of young scientists and coordinating their activities. He also took up an adjunct appointment in the pharmacology department of the Temple University School of Medicine. He maintains an avid interest in community affairs and has made valuable contributions to advancing the careers of minorities both within his own company and at a broader level. After 40 years of married life, Harris's wife Regina, who had worked as a teacher's aide, passed away. The couple had three children, two sons and daughter, all whom enjoy professional careers.

—*Sketch by Neeraja Sankaran*

James Andrew Harris

James Andrew Harris
1932-
Chemist

J ames Andrew Harris was a leader within a group of investigators at Lawrence Berkeley Laboratory in California. During 1969 and 1970, this group discovered two new chemical elements: element 104, rutherfordium, and element 105, now called dubnium. These were the first new elements found since the early 1960s. In addition, the Berkeley researchers refuted a claim to the discovery of element 104 that Soviet scientists had presented in 1964. Harris's careful work made it possible for other laboratories to reproduce the Berkeley results, thus confirming their discovery.

Harris was born in Waco, Texas on March 26, 1932, the son of Frank Harris and the former Martha Green. His father was a farmer who died when his son was a young child. His mother worked as a cook in a junior high school cafeteria. Then at age 12, the young Harris went to live with an aunt, Matilda Robinson, in Oakland, California. Here he received his introduction to science.

Harris held a strong interest in music, performing with his high school's marching band, jazz band, and concert band. But as he told contributor T. A. Heppenheimer in a telephone interview on May 15, 1998, he also remembers his high school chemistry teacher. At that teacher's urging, Harris took the course. "I enjoyed it so much, I decided when I got to college to major in music and chemistry. But I only ended up getting a degree in chemistry. I went on the road to play music during my first year in college. I decided that wasn't the thing I wanted to do."

He attended Huston-Tillotson College in Austin, Texas, a black institution, and received a Bachelor of Science degree in chemistry in 1953. He then joined the U.S. Army and served for two years as a sergeant. Returning to the civilian world in 1955, he set out to find work. "I could write a book on my job-hunting experiences," he told the magazine *Ebony* in 1973. Doubtful secretaries refused to believe he was applying for a job as a chemist and not a janitor. "At one point, I was even given a job test simple enough for elementary kids—basic addition and subtraction. I told the secretary I didn't need a job that badly."

But during 1955 he found a job as a chemist at Tracerlab, Inc., in Richmond, California, close to Oakland where he had grown up. Here his work brought him into a realm where sophisticated chemical analyses could shape national defense policy. He was actively involved in detecting secret Soviet tests of nuclear weapons.

Uncovering Moscow's Nuclear Secrets

Tests of atomic and hydrogen bombs that took place above ground produced fallout, or radioactive debris, that dispersed into the atmosphere and rode with the winds. Aircraft with special equipment could recover samples of the fallout. Studies of this material then could disclose that a secret test had taken place. Such studies could also indicate the design of the weapon and the power of the explosion.

Tracerlab had pioneered in this work, and had detected evidence in September 1949 that showed the Soviet Union possessed the atomic bomb. In response, Truman ordered the stepping up of America's nuclear weapons program, and okayed the development of the hydrogen bomb, a weapon significantly more powerful than the atomic bomb. In August 1953, Soviet scientists detonated a new weapon, and a top Soviet official boasted that his country now had the hydrogen bomb. American scientists studied the fallout, and concluded that the 1953 bomb was not a hydrogen bomb, though the Soviet Union seemed well on its way to making one. This was the background to the work Harris did at Tracerlab, though he came along too late to take part in these events. He nevertheless worked there for five years, meanwhile taking night courses in chemistry and physics through the University of California and through San Francisco State College. Then in 1960 he joined the Nuclear Chemistry Division of Lawrence Berkeley Laboratory. Initially he contributed to the development of detectors that used the element germanium, and which saw use in neutron activation analysis, a sensitive method for detecting trace amounts of chemical elements. By the decade's end he was ready to take a leading role in pursuing the lab's specialty: the creation and detection of new elements.

Discovers Elements 104 and 105

Ninety-two chemical elements exist in nature and are ennumerated in the periodic table in order of molecular weight, with uranium as the heaviest. Uranium is used in nuclear reactors, and as early as 1940 the chemist Glenn Seaborg, working at the University of California at Berkeley, used uranium to create element 94, plutonium. Plutonium could be made within such reactors and became the prime material for crafting nuclear weapons. Because plutonium was both artificial and of enormous importance to national defense, the study of additional artificial elements became a major topic for research following World War II. By the early 1960s, chemists and physicists extended the roster to element 103, lawrencium.

No one ever found other elements that were as world-shaking as plutonium, but this research nevertheless was of high interest. Chemists had developed means to predict the chemical properties of new elements; the newly-created ones served to test and to confirm their methods. In addition, physicists sought fundamental understanding concerning the nature of atoms, and worked to test their theories by creating the atoms of new elements.

In 1964, a group of Soviet scientists conducted experiments and obtained what they believed to be a new element, number 104. They named it kurchatovium, after Igor Kurchatov, who had directed that nation's atomic bomb program. Scientists at Berkeley were eager to test the Soviet claim with their own experiments, but element 104 was not producible with their existing equipment. They needed new equipment, which took shape as the HILAC, or Heavy Ion Linear Accelerator. It could bombard a target with a beam of carbon or nitrogen atoms, producing not only element 104 but heavier elements as well.

Harris led a group that prepared a target of californium, element 98. He received the world's entire supply of this rare substance, totaling no more than two millionths of an ounce. He then refined it using more than 22 separation techniques, as he worked to remove all traces of impurity. The purified californium took the form of "a very thin, small dot," as he describes it to Heppenheimer. The target was said to be the best that this laboratory had ever produced.

Why was such extreme purity necessary? Harris feared that atoms of lead, contaminating the californium, would readily combine with the bombarding carbon or nitrogen. These combinations then could give experimental results that would look like newly-created elements of a novel type, such as number 104—and yet would amount merely to new versions of known elements.

The Berkeley researchers launched their experiments in mid-1968, seeking to produce element 104. They created it literally atom by atom, with these atoms being radioactive. To detect this product, the investigators used techniques from both physics and chemistry, and again Harris played a leading role. This element was predicted to have specific chemical properties, and Harris relied on this prediction as he extracted the newly-formed atoms from the parent californium. Another test came from physics, as these atoms emitted alpha particles, which amount to atoms of helium, element 2. Following these emissions, the atoms showed a pattern of radioactive decay that was known to signal the presence of nobelium, element 102. Then, since 102 plus 2 equals 104, Harris and his colleagues concluded that they had the newest element.

The question remained whether their findings matched those of the Soviets. "Nobody could ever duplicate their work," Harris told Heppenheimer. By contrast, "Los Alamos and Livermore were able to reproduce our work." These were two of America's premier nuclear laboratories; by duplicating the findings of the Berkeley group, they confirmed that these scientists had indeed found element 104. Then, during 1970, the Berkeley researchers went on to produce element 105. And because the Soviet work had failed to stand up, those investigators lost the right to give element 104 its name. The name "kurchatovium" fell into disuse, as Albert Ghiorso, a colleague of Harris, proposed the name rutherfordium, after the nuclear physicist Lord Rutherford who had discovered how atoms are put together.

Nevertheless, the Soviets would receive a consolation prize. Ghiorso went on to propose the name "hahnium" for element 105, after Otto Hahn, a German chemist who first split uranium atoms and thereby launched the atomic age. But other scientists eventually decided to call the new element "dubnium," after Dubna, site of the principal Soviet laboratory for the study of artificial elements.

Worked While Young, Retired Early

Harris retired in 1988, while still in his mid-50s. "I had always wanted to retire young," he told Heppenheimer. Certainly he had started working while young, for he recalls that when he was only five years old, "I had a little red wagon. I used to go get ice and sell it to the neighbors." At age nine he was setting pins in a bowling alley.

In 1957 he married Helen Harris, whose last name was the same as his. They had five children: Cedric, Keith, Hilda, Kimberly, and James. His honors include an honorary Doctor of Science degree from Huston-Tillotson, his alma mater, in 1973, as well as a key to the city of Oakland, California in 1988. In 1997 he was inducted into the Hall of Fame for Black Colleges and Universities.

These honors have not turned his head, for he remains active in such organizations as the PTA in Pinole, California, where he resides. Moreover, he has never received an earned degree beyond the bachelor's. As he told *Ebony* in 1973, "I've been too busy working to even think about a Ph.D."

FURTHER READING:

Books

Carwell, Hattie. *Blacks in Science: Astrophysicist to Zoologist.* Hicksville, N.Y.: Exposition Press, 1977.

Periodicals

Holcomb, Robert W. "Element 105 Synthesized and Named Hahnium by Berkeley Researchers." *Science*, (May 15, 1970): 810.
Holcomb, Robert W. "Heavy Elements: A Feud over 104 and a Future for 114." *Science*, (December 5, 1969): 1254-1255.
Slater, Jack. "Putting Soul into Science." *Ebony*, (May 1973): 144-150.
Stone, Richard. "Transuranic Names Finally Final." *Science*, (September 12, 1997): 1601.
York, Herbert F. "The Debate over the Hydrogen Bomb." *Scientific American*, (October 1975): 106-113.

—Sketch by T. A. Heppenheimer

Mary Styles Harris
1949-
Geneticist

As a researcher, Mary Styles Harris has studied the relation between genetics and diseases such as sickle cell anemia. As an educator and administrator, she has been a stalwart advocate for public health education. For nearly a quarter century she has worked closely with scientists and government officials to make health information accessible to the people who need it most.

Mary Styles was born in Nashville, Tennessee, on June 26, 1949, and raised in Miami, Florida. Her father was a doctor, and Mary showed an early interest in science. Dr. Styles died when Mary was nine years old, but she continued her avid pursuit of science. She excelled in science in high school, and she volunteered after school at a local medical laboratory, where she learned firsthand about research techniques.

Styles entered Lincoln University in Lincoln, Pennsylvania, in 1967. Her interest in science was still strong, and she followed what was ostensibly a pre-med program. But she decided that research was her true passion. Upon graduating from Lincoln University in 1971, she was awarded a Ford Foundation Doctoral Fellowship to study molecular genetics.

While in college she had met Sidney Harris, whom she married shortly after her graduation. (The couple later had a daughter.) They both went on to Cornell University; he to study engineering, and she to continue her genetics studies. Her faculty advisor at Cornell had worked closely with the geneticist Barbara McClintock, who later won the Nobel Prize in Biology.

After graduating from Cornell in 1975, Mary Styles Harris was awarded a postdoctoral fellowship by the National Cancer Institute. She spent the next two years studying virus structures at the New Jersey University of Medicine and Dentistry. She continued to conduct research for two years. In 1977 she was offered the executive directorship of the Sickle Cell Foundation of Georgia. This position was administrative rather than research-based, but it afforded her the opportunity to educate the public about the disease. Using her knowledge and her research skills, she succeeded so well that the National Science Foundation awarded her a Science Residency Award.

Harris used this award as a springboard from which to further publicize sickle cell and other genetically based diseases. Working with broadcasters, she created a series of television documentaries that explained health and science issues to the general public. Later, she became State Director of Genetics for the Georgia Department of Human Resources; she also served as an assistant professor at Morehouse College and later at Atlanta University.

After several years of teaching and administrative work, Harris founded her own company, Harris and Associates, which provided consulting to companies whose products were based on genetic research. Harris relocated her company to the West Coast when her husband accepted a position at Claremont College in California. In addition to her consulting work, she has been active in producing audio-visual materials focusing on public health topics, such as breast cancer, that are particularly prevalent among minorities.

FURTHER READING:

Books

Kessler, James, et al. *Distinguished African American Scientists of the Twentieth Century.* Oryx Press, 1996.

Sammons, Vivian O. *Blacks in Science and Education.* Hemisphere Publishing, 1990.

Who's Who Among Black Americans, 1985. Who's Who Among Black Americans Publishing Company, 1985.

Periodicals

"Doctor Gets Grant to Simplify Medicine." *Jet,* vol. 57 (23), (February 21, 1980): 27.

—Sketch by George A. Milite

Wesley L. Harris

Wesley L. Harris
1941-
Aerospace engineer

As an engineer and an administrator for the National Aeronautics and Space Administration (NASA), Wesley L. Harris has participated in or directed a broad range of research initiatives that advanced aircraft, helicopter, and spaceflight technology. As an educator, he has increased opportunities for minority students and strengthened engineering education programs at three major universities.

Born in Richmond, Virginia, on October 29, 1941, Wesley Leroy Harris was one of three children of tobacco factory workers William and Rosa Minor Harris. Rosa Harris encouraged her children to educate themselves and learn all they could. For young Wes, that meant pursuing his fascination with airplanes. He not only read about them but built models of all types. When his elementary school held a writing contest on students' career ambitions, fourth-grader Harris won with his essay on his dream of becoming a test pilot.

Harris attended Armstrong High School in Richmond, where he found math and physics the most rewarding subjects. He also played football for a demanding coach, an experience he credited with teaching him that hard work and never giving up were the keys to success in any endeavor. Harris's imagination was sparked when the Soviet Union orbited *Sputnik I,* the first artificial satellite, in 1957, and his interest in aviation and space guided his life even more strongly from then on.

In 1960 Harris graduated from high school and went on to attend the University of Virginia. At the time only certain programs were open to black students, and Harris was not allowed to pursue his original idea of majoring in physics; he enrolled instead in aerospace engineering. He also married in that year. Despite the strain of having a family and being one of only a handful of African Americans at the school, Harris's determination made him a success. As a senior, he won an award from the American Institute of Aeronautics and Astronautics (AIAA) for his research on the turbulent flow of air over wing surfaces. Another honor was being chosen to introduce Dr. Martin Luther King, Jr., when the civil rights leader made a speech at the campus. In 1964 he received his bachelor's degree with honors.

On the advice of his professors, Harris moved on to Princeton University with the goal of earning a doctorate in engineering and becoming a professor himself. He earned a master's in aerospace engineering in 1966 and a Ph.D. in 1968 before returning to the University of Virginia as the school's first black engineering professor. He also became the first African American faculty member to receive tenure there. In addition to teaching, Harris performed research on aerodynamic noise analysis, hypersonic airflow, and short-takeoff-and-landing airplane technology. Harris eventually moved on to teach at two other universities. First came a year of teaching physics at Southern University in Louisiana. Then he moved to the Massachusetts Institute of Technology (MIT), where he stayed from 1972 to 1979. There he taught aeronautics, astronautics, and ocean engineering. He also started MIT's Office of Minority Education, charged with encouraging minority students in their studies. Harris's efforts won him MIT's 1979 Irwin Sizer Award, given for the most significant improvement to education at the school.

In 1979 Harris took his first position with the National Aeronautics and Space Administration. At NASA's Washington headquarters he served as manager of computational methods in the Office of Aeronautics and Space Technology. He also served as a program manager in the Fluid and Thermal Physics Office. There he performed groundbreaking research in using computers to model airflow, a field known as computational fluid dynamics. He returned to MIT in 1980 and taught until 1985, when he accepted the position of dean of the school of engineering at the University of Connecticut.

Harris's achievements in five years at Connecticut were many. He established an institute for environmental research and began partnerships between the school and area aerospace companies, such as United Technologies and Pratt & Whitney. He greatly boosted the recruiting and enrollment of minority students. Harris, whose earlier marriage had ended in divorce, married again in 1985. He had a total of seven children.

Among the areas Harris investigated during his academic career were shock wave patterns in gas mixtures, new techniques for analyzing aerodynamic noise, and hypersonic airflow. His study of the broadband noises created by helicopter rotors was of special interest to the U.S. Defense Department. Defense engineers used his discoveries to design quieter military helicopters, and Harris considered these studies and the several papers he produced on the subject to be his most significant achievement as an engineer.

In 1990 Harris was appointed vice president of the University of Tennessee Space Institute, where he steered the school through a reputation-threatening plagiarism scandal. He also reshaped its research program, focusing on space propulsion, energy conversion, laser applications, environmental studies, and applied mathematics. In the course of Harris's career in academia, he published more than one hundred technical papers.

In 1992 Harris was named a fellow of the AIAA for his research and education achievements, and he was also appointed the Herbert S. and Jane Gregory Distinguished Lecturer at the college of engineering of the University of Florida. That same year, Harris returned to NASA. He was drawn by new NASA administrator Daniel Goldin's call for NASA to put a new emphasis on aeronautics and lead a new age of American aviation progress.

Joins NASA in New Post

As NASA's first associate administrator for aeronautics, Harris supervised the Langley, Lewis, and Ames Research Centers and the Ames-Dryden Flight Research Facility and oversaw the agency's $1.6 billion aeronautics research budget. Programs under his direction included efforts to design an advanced supersonic transport, the runway-to-orbit national aerospace plane, and work on new supercomputers to improve modeling of aerodynamic forces and design better aircraft. Engineers employed under Harris also pursued work on improving the structure, engines, and instrumentation of airliners, testing new sensors to detect dangerous wind shear, and modernizing air traffic control.

While at NASA, Harris also served on the U.S. Army Science Board. This continued his long tradition of participating in advisory groups, including the National Research Council's Commission on Engineering and Technical Systems, the Board on Engineering Education, the Air Force Studies Board, the Committee on Aeronautical Technologies, and the National Science Foundation's Engineering Advisory Committee. In the August 11, 1994, issue of *Black Issues in Higher Education* Harris urges women and minorities to engage in scientific and technical endeavors so that the scientific community will be more of a reflection of the cultural diversity of the country.

FURTHER READING:

Other

Anderson, Priscilla, NASA Aeronautics Public Affairs office, *Interview with Matthew A. Bille,* February 18, 1994.

"Dr. Wesley L. Harris," (biographical data sheet), NASA Public Affairs Office, December, 1993.

"The First 'A': NASA," *Aeronautics Research,* (booklet), NASA Public Affairs Office, undated.

"Wes Harris: In Love with the Sky," (biographical sketch), NASA Public Affairs Office, undated.

—Sketch by Matthew A. Bille

Faye Venetia Harrison
1951-
Anthropologist

Faye Venetia Harrison is a political anthropologist whose main work has concerned social inequality and its related political economy. She has done extensive research in Jamaica, but also has written about Americans such as Alice Walker and W.E.B. DuBois. Harrison is also interested in dance and theater, which she has used as outlets for her anthropological and ethnographic work.

Harrison was born November 25, 1951, in Norfolk, Virginia, to James and Odelia Blount (nee Harper) Harrison. She earned her A.B. degree from Brown University in 1974. While a graduate student at Stanford, she did research in 1974-75 in Brixton, London, England, where she researched adolescents from the West Indies and the issues they face as they grow to maturity in Great Britain. Harrison went on to earn her M.A. 1977. In 1978, Harrison began doing research in Kingston, Jamaica. Harrison also married in this period. She wed William Louis Conwill on May 17, 1980. They have three children, Giles, L. Mondlane, and Justin. She was awarded her Ph.D. in 1982, with a dissertation entitled "Semiproletarianization and the Structure of Socioeconomic and Political Relations in a Jamaica Slum."

Harrison began her teaching career at the University of Louisville, where she worked as an associate professor from 1983-89. While in Louisville, Harrison was active in several local organizations. She served as organizer for the Kentucky Rainbow Coalition from 1988-89. It was at the first convention for this organization that Harrison performed a dramatic experiment, a soliloquy titled "I Am Somebody!," one of several pieces she has performed on other occasions throughout the late 1980s-90s. While in Louisville, Harrison was also associated with two women's group, Black Women Organized for Power (1984-86) and Alliance Against Women's Oppression (1988-89). Harrison also served as editor of a book, *Black Folks in Cities Here and There* (1988).

In 1989, Harrison became an associate professor at the University of Tennessee, Knoxville. Soon after, Harrison became editorially associated with several professional journals, *Woman and Aging* (1990) and *Urban Anthropology* (1992), and edited a book, *Decolonizing Anthropology* (1991).

Harrison has received numerous accolades in her short career. She was a Ford Foundation fellow from 1987-88 and received a certificate of merit from Phi Beta Kappa in 1993. A member of the Association of Black Anthropologists, she served as its president from 1989-91. Harrison is also a member of the International Union of Anthropologists and Ethnology Sciences, where she served as co-chair of the Commission on Women from 1993-98. Harrison is associ-ated with numerous other professional associations and editorial boards.

SELECTED WRITINGS BY HARRISON:

Books

Behar, Ruth, and Deborah Gordan, ed., "Writing Against the Grain: Cultural Politics of Difference in Alice Walker's Work," in *Women Writing Culture.* University of California Press, 1995, pp. 233-45.

Periodicals

"Crime, Class, and Politics," *TransAfrica Forum,* (1987): 29-38.
"The Du Boisian Legacy in Anthropology," *Critique of Anthropology,* (1992): 239-60.
"Racial and Gender Inequalities in Health and Health Care," *Medical Anthropology Quarterly,* (1994): 90-95.

FURTHER READING:

Other

The Faye Harrison Home Page: funnelweb.utcc.utk.edu/~innes/fharris.htm

—Sketch by A. Petrusso

Robert Walker Harrison, III
1941-
Endocrinologist

A fully licensed medical doctor and internist, Robert Walker Harrison, III chose a career as a research scientist who studies hormonal glands and diseases that affect them. His later research includes the hormonal aspects of infectious diseases.

Harrison was born on October 13, 1941, in Natchez, Mississippi, the son of Robert and Charlotte Harrison. His mother was a schoolteacher and his father was a dentist. Harrison grew up in Yazoo City, Mississippi, and he attended a college preparatory high school at the teacher training center of Tougaloo College, which is near Jackson. Harrison continued his education at Tougaloo as an undergraduate, majoring in chemistry; he received his bachelor's degree in 1961. His focus changed over the last years of college, and he decided that he wanted to become a doctor. His father had studied dentistry at Northwestern University; Harrison attended medical school there, earning his medical degree in 1966.

After graduating from medical school, Harrison did his internship and residency at Chicago Wesley Memorial Hospital, from 1966-68. From 1968-70, Harrison served in the United States Navy as a medical officer for a destroyer squadron. He remained a member of the Naval Reserves until 1980. After leaving the Navy in 1970, he started another residency, this time at Hartford Hospital in Hartford, Connecticut. When his residency was completed, he passed his boards and became a certified internal medicine practitioner.

Instead of going into practice, Harrison became a research scientist, focusing on hormonal glandular disease. In 1972, Harrison was hired by the medical school at Vanderbilt University, in Tennessee. He moved through the ranks quickly, from instructor, 1972-74, to assistant professor, 1974-81, and associate professor, 1981-85. In 1973, Harrison became the codirector of the Steroid Receptor Core Laboratory in the Center for Population Research and Reproductive Biology at Vanderbilt University. His work concentrated on glucocorticoids, which are hormones produced by the adrenal glands' outer covering. In 1977, Harrison was given a research associateship with the Howard Hughes Medical Institute. This relationship gave Harrison access to funding for his projects. A year later, he began an association with the physiology department at Vanderbilt's medical school. Harrison also took a sabbatical in 1980 to further his glucocorticoid research.

In 1985, Harrison moved to the medical sciences division at the University of Arkansas. Though he remained a research scientist, directing the university's clinical endocrine laboratory, Harrison was also hired as the associate dean for special projects in the medical sciences divison. As associate dean, Harrison worked to diversify both the faculty and the student body. Harrison also diversified his research to infectious diseases, like AIDS (acquired immune defiency syndrome), and their hormonal aspects. In 1993, Harrison moved to the University of Rochester as chief of the endocrinology and metabolism division of their school of medicine. Harrison's research focused on a better comprehension of hormonal functions through the study of individual biochemical molecules.

A member of the Endocrine Society, Harrison is married to Gayle Johnson, and has two sons with her, Robert and Seth.

FURTHER READING:

Books

Kessler, James H., et al. *Distinguished African American Scientists of the 20th Century.* Phoenix, AZ: Oryx Press, 1996.

—*Sketch by A. Petrusso*

W. Lincoln Hawkins
1911-1992
Chemical engineer

A longtime employee of Bell Laboratories, W. Lincoln Hawkins was a chemical engineer whose work helped make universal telephone service possible. Until the late 1940s telephone cables were insulated with a lead coating, which was very expensive; this coating was also too heavy for use in the multi-cable conduits which would be required if most homes were to have telephones. It was clear to many that plastics could be a cheaper and lighter insulating alternative, but every plastic then in existence broke down rapidly when exposed to the elements. Hawkins, working at Bell Laboratories, helped to solve the problem by co-inventing a plastic coating that withstood heat and cold and had a life span of many decades.

Hawkins was always a tinkerer. Born Walter Lincoln Hawkins on March 21, 1911, in Washington D.C., he was the son of William Langston Hawkins, a lawyer for the Census Bureau, and Maude Johnson Hawkins, a science teacher. As a child, he was fascinated with how things worked, and he made spring-driven model boats to sail on Washington's Reflecting Pool. He also constructed a simple radio to listen to baseball games. "I always loved building things," he told Kim E. Pearson in a 1983 interview for *The Crisis.* "When I was about eleven years old, a friend and I tried to build a perpetual motion machine. We didn't know anything about thermodynamics—we had no idea that it couldn't be done." Hawkins's parents hoped their son would pursue a career in medicine, but it was engineering that captured his imagination. He attended Dunbar High School in Washington, a segregated public school renowned for its science and engineering programs—the faculty consisted primarily of African Americans with doctoral degrees who could not get a job elsewhere because of their race. One of his teachers had a new car every year, and when Hawkins learned it was partial compensation for the man's patent on a component of the car's self-starter, he realized that tinkering could actually earn a person a living.

After graduation from Dunbar High School, Hawkins and one other African American student attended the well-known engineering school in Troy, New York, Rensselaer Polytechnic Institute. They were the only black students in the school. The next year they were followed by two more African American students from Dunbar. While nearly two out of three students dropped out of Rensselaer, Hawkins and the three other black students completed their studies in four years. But the Depression awaited Hawkins upon graduation in 1932, so he continued his studies, and by 1934 he had earned a master's degree in chemistry at Howard University in Washington. Following this, he taught for a time in a trade school and then was convinced by a counselor at Howard University to apply for a fellowship in chemistry at McGill University in Canada. He won the fellowship and completed his Ph.D. in chemistry at McGill in 1938. That same year he won a National Research Council Fellowship in alkaloid chemistry, and he accepted a position at Columbia University, where he would remain until 1942. During his time at Columbia he met Lilyan Varina Bobo, whom he married on August 19, 1939. They would have two sons.

Becomes First African American at Bell Laboratories

In 1942 Hawkins joined Bell Laboratories in Murray Hills, New Jersey, the first African American scientist to be hired there. Hawkins would stay at Bell for the next 34 years, researching and inventing new materials and products for the preservation and recycling of plastics; he completed his career as assistant director of the Chemical Research Laboratory. "I had a ball," Hawkins told Pearson, describing his years of service at the research lab. "There's a world of excitement there that's like nowhere else." Of the 18 domestic and 129 foreign patents Hawkins himself held, by far the most important was that to replace the lead insulation of telephone cables with a new weather-resistant plastic coating. Working together with Vincent Lanza in the late 1940s, he developed additives to create a new polymer that could resist both thermal degradation and the effects of oxidation and last up to 70 years in the elements. "Hawkins's work is arguably one of the major achievements which made universal telephone service economical," a colleague at Bell Laboratories told John Burgess of the *Washington Post*.

But engineering was only part of Hawkins's long and distinguished career. Retiring at age 65, he remained a consultant to Bell on the education and employment of minorities. He also became research director for the Plastics Institute of America in Hoboken, New Jersey, from 1976 to 1983, and he worked privately as a materials consultant. In addition, he often spoke to minority youth about the importance of education. In 1981, he became the first chairman of the American Chemical Society's Project SEED, a campaign to promote science careers to minority students around the country. Hawkins worked for many years with the National Action Council for Minorities in Engineering (NACME), a committee set up by several major companies to get minorities into the field. He was also a member and chair of the board of trustees of Montclair State College in New Jersey. This second career in counseling was as successful as his first in engineering, and the kids listened to him as if he were a member of their own family. Robert Stephens of Montclair State College told Burgess of the *Washington Post* that the students said to themselves: "This guy is my uncle, this guy is my grandfather, but this guy is also somebody important."

Hawkins was widely honored for his pioneering work in polymers, winning the Honor Scroll of the American Institute of Chemistry in 1970, the **Percy Julian** Award from the National Organization of Black Chemists and Chemical Engineers in 1977, and the International Medal of

the Society of Plastics Engineering in 1984. But by far his most important honor was the 1992 National Medal of Technology, awarded to him not only for his work in chemical engineering, but also for his labors in attempting to bring minorities into the sciences.

Hawkins remained vital and active through his eighth decade. He and his wife traveled around the world and then moved to San Marcos, California, to be near one of their sons. On August 20, 1992, Hawkins died of heart failure at the age of 81. Shortly after his death, an undergraduate research fellowship was established in his name by the National Action Council for Minorities in Engineering.

SELECTED WRITINGS BY HAWKINS:

Books

Polymer Degradation and Stabilization. Springer Verlag, 1984.

FURTHER READING:

Books

Sammons, Vivian Ovelton. *Blacks in Science and Medicine,* Hemisphere Publishing Corporation, 1990, pp. 114–115.

Periodicals

Burgess, John. "High Honors for a Telephone Pioneer," *Washington Post,* (June 24, 1992): F1-F2.
"Honoring a Pioneering Leader in Science," *About . . . Time,* (March 1993): 9.
Lambert, Bruce. "W. Lincoln Hawkins, 81, a Chemist and Inventor," *New York Times,* (August 23, 1992): L46.
Pearson, Kim E. "Pioneering Black Bell Labs Engineer Still at Work at 71," *The Crisis,* (April 1983): 192–193.
"W. Lincoln Hawkins Honored by President Bush," *American Chemical Society Chemunity News,* (September 1992): 3.

—Sketch by J. Sydney Jones

John Kermit Haynes
1943-
Biologist

John Kermit Haynes is one of this country's foremost African American scientists in biological studies. He has been an educator for 34 years in his chosen field and is currently Chairman of the Biology Department at Morehouse College in Atlanta, Georgia. A widely published scholar, he also has been awarded numerous significant research grants throughout his career. His research interests are sickle cell membranes and the mechanism by which cells regulate their volume.

John Kermit Haynes was born October 30, 1943, in Monroe, Louisiana, to parents John Kermit Haynes Sr. and Grace Quanita Ross Haynes. In high school he developed an interest in the health sciences. It was with the ambition of becoming a physician that he enrolled in Morehouse College. With a major of biology he was soon exposed to research scholars and began to view the field as full of opportunity for scientific discovery. In 1964 he earned his Bachelor of Science degree from Morehouse. In 1970 he was awarded a Ph.D. in developmental biology from Brown University in Providence, Rhode Island. From 1971-73 he completed post-doctoral work at Brown University and the renowned Massachusetts Institute of Technology (MIT) in Cambridge, Massachusetts.

Soon after completing his studies, Haynes was teaching aspiring medical students as Assistant Professor in the Division of Genetics and Molecular Medicine at Meharry Medical College in Nashville, Tennessee, where he taught until 1978. Since 1979 he has been a faculty member at Morehouse College, where he has been named David E. Packard Professor in Science and Chair of Department of Biology. During his tenure at Morehouse, he has served as Director of the Office of Health Professions, Director of the collegewide Honors Program, and as Director of the College's Self-Study Program. Haynes is also an adjunct professor of Physiology at Brown University and Clark Atlanta University.

In 1980 Haynes was named one of the Outstanding Young Men of America. Throughout his distinguished career, he has been advisor to many academic projects and professional organizations. The highlights of activities during the past decade include member of the review panel of Minority Science Improvement Program of Washington, DC, in 1990. In 1991 he was a panelist for Research-Based Curriculum (also in Washington, D.C.) and for the Advisory Committee to the Director, National Institutes of Health. From 1991 to the present, he has been a member of the Minorities Affairs Committee of the American Society for Cell Biology and currently serves as its Chair. Since 1991 he has been a member of the Internal Advisory Committee to the Sickle Cell Comprehensive Center Grant at the Emory University School of Medicine. From 1994 to 1996, he was a member of the Committee on Undergraduate Science Education of the National Research Council.

In 1998, he was principal investigator on grants from the Howard Hughes Medical Institute, the National Science Foundation, the Centers for Disease Control, the National Institutes of Health, and co-investigator on a $6.9 million dollar grant to Morehouse College from the U.S. Department of Defense. Since 1970 he has published his research and continues to regularly present his findings in academic publications.

Married to the former Carolyn Ann Price in 1969, they reside in the Atlanta metropolitan area.

SELECTED WRITINGS BY HAYNES:

Periodicals

"A Simple Screening Procedure for Hemoglobin S," *New England Journal of Medicine,* 288:49 (1973).
"Structural and Functional Studies of the Isohemoglobins from Fundulus Heteroclitis," *Biological Bulletin,* 151:413 (1976).
"In Vitro Studies of Some New Anti-Sickling Agents," *The Physiologist,* (August 1978).
"Finding A Cure For Sickle Cell," *Atlanta Tribune,* (April 1989).
"Volume Regulatory Amino Acid Transport in Erythrocytes of the Little Skate Raja Erinacea," *American Journal of Physiology,* 34:R173-R179 (1993).
"Volume Activated Taurine Efflux from Squalus Acanthias Rectal Gland Cells," *The Bulletin, Mount Desert Island Biological Laboratory,* 35:79-82 (1996).

—Sketch by Patrick J. Longe

James H. M. Henderson
1917-
Plant physiologist and botanist

While James H. M. Henderson has had a prestigious teaching career, primarily at the Tuskegee Institute, he has also done significant research into plant physiology. He is primarily interested in tissue cultures, specifically those related to plant growth, such as auxins. (Auxins are a plant hormones that promote longitudinal plant growth.) Henderson has studied both normal and abnormal plant tissue physiology, and compared their growth mechanisms to animal growth hormones. His work has potential human applications in such areas as the regulation of the growth of cancer cells. Henderson has also spent a lifetime as a community activist, working in voter registration drives in the 1960s and with the Boy Scouts.

Born James Henry Meriwether Henderson in Falls Church, Virginia, on August 10, 1917, Henderson was the son of Edwin Bancroft and Mary (nee Meriwether) Henderson. Henderson's father was a forerunner of African Americans in sports and sports education. In Washington, D.C., Edwin Bancroft Henderson was the first African American professional teacher of physical education. Henderson later wrote a biography of his father entitled *Molder of Men: Portrait of a Grand Old Man: Edwin Bancroft Henderson*, with his wife Betty.

The scientist also had more famous relatives. Henderson's maternal grandfather, James Henry Meriwether, for whom he was named, was a descendant of Meriwether Lewis, of Lewis and Clark Expedition fame. Henderson is also a grand-nephew to Booker T. Washington, the man who founded the Tuskegee Institute, where Henderson spent the majority of his career.

As an undergraduate at Howard University, Henderson was a four-year honor student majoring in biology and chemistry. He earned his B.S. degree in 1939. He did his graduate work at the University of Wisconsin, where he studied chemistry, biochemistry, and plant physiology. Henderson earned his masters degree, an M.Ph., in 1940, then his Ph.D. in plant physiology in 1943. For his thesis, Henderson studied the tomato plant and how it regulates the nutrients and water absorbed through its roots. His dissertation was entitled "The Effect of Respiratory Intermediates and Inhibitors on the Growth and Respiration of Tomato Roots."

During his final years of graduate school, 1942-43, Henderson worked as a junior chemist in the Badger Ordnance Works, a U.S. civil service position he held as part of the effort in support of World War II. The research there focused on developing substances that could be used as propellants for rockets, such as gun powder. Upon graduation, Henderson worked at the Toxicity Laboratory of the University of Chicago for two years, 1943-45. His post as a research assistant at the National Defense Research Committee was again part of the war effort, but the research was more relevant to Henderson's primary interests. He explored the poisons that plants naturally make to stave off predators.

In 1945, Henderson moved to Tuskegee, Alabama, which remained his personal and professional base for the rest of his life. His primary professional association has been with the Tuskegee Institute, where he has made the sweet potato the focus of his research. Henderson began as an assistant professor and research associate in plant physiology at the Carver Research Foundation, Tuskegee Institute. He held this post until 1950.

In 1948, Henderson married Betty A. Francis, a native of Washington, D.C., and together they eventually had four children, Edith Ellen, Dena, James F., and Edwin B. II. From 1948-50, Henderson took a leave of absence from Tuskegee to work as a research fellow at the California Institute of Technology. There he continued his plant growth research and used his methodology on plants like sunflowers.

When he returned to the Institute, Henderson continued to move through the ranks at the Carver Foundation, serving as research associate and professor of biology from 1950-68, and the head of the department from 1957-68. While gaining professional prominence in Tuskegee, Henderson continued to garner related experiences in other parts

of the United States and abroad. For example, from 1961-62, Henderson was a senior faculty fellow, under the auspices of the National Science Foundation, at the National Center for Science Research in Le Phytotron-Gil-sur-Yvette, France. There he continued his ongoing research, studying the effect of certain chemicals on plant growth.

Henderson became the director of the Carver Research Foundation in 1968, a post held until 1975. He was also appointed chairman of the Science Division at Tuskegee in 1968. Several more appointments came Henderson's way in the 1970s. In 1973, Henderson was named the director of the Minority Biomedical Research Program. This program helps in the development of high school students committed to getting a college education. Henderson was named a senior research professor at the Carver Research Institute in 1975. That same year, Henderson was awarded his second Alumni Award from Howard University. (He received his first in 1964.) A year later, in 1976, the Tuskegee Institute honored him with an Eminent Faculty Award. He was recognized with this award again in 1980.

Throughout the 1980s and 1990s, Henderson continued to receive accolades for both his professional and public work. In 1982, UNCF honored him with an Distinguished Scholars Award. He received two honors in 1984: one from the SS-ASPP, and the Lamplighter Award from Beta Kappa Chi. An active member of the American Society of Plant Physiologists, for which he served as chairman of the Southern Sector in 1970, Henderson received two awards, a distinguished scholars award, and, in 1997, the Charles Reid Barnes Life Member Award.

Henderson earned other honors for his many contributions to the community. For his many years of work with the Boy Scouts—he has invested much time and energy in organizing programs in Alabama—the organization awarded him a Silver Beaver Award in 1961. He was a long-time member of the board of trustees for Stillman College, Tuscaloosa, Alabama. Henderson was also member of the Macon County, Alabama, school board, serving as vice-chairman from 1968-74. He was also active in his Presbyterian Church. However, much of his community activity involves the promotion of science. Henderson devised a program at the Tuskegee Institute in which gifted high school students could come for the summer and become exposed to scientific research.

SELECTED WRITINGS BY HENDERSON:

Books

(With Betty F. Henderson) *Molder of Men, Portrait of a Grand Old Man: Edwin Bancroft Henderson.* Vantage Press (New York), 1985.

Periodicals

(With Russell Brown) "The Mass Production and Distribution of Hela cells at Tuskegee Institute," *Jour-*

nal of the History of Medicine and Allied Sciences,
(October 1983): 415.

—*Sketch by A. Petrusso*

Walter Lester Henry, Jr.
1915-
Physician and endocrinologist

Walter Lester Henry had a long and distinguished career at Howard University as a physician, educator, and researcher. In particular, he conducted important research into the function of insulin and the causes of diabetes.

Henry (known as Lester) was born in Philadelphia on November 19, 1915 to Walter Lester Henry, Sr. and Vera Robinson Henry. He was educated in Philadelphia and received his bachelor of arts degree from Temple University in 1936. From there, he went on to Howard University Medical School, where he graduated first in his class in 1941. He married the former Ada Palmer.

Henry served in the United States Marine Corps during the Second World War, attaining the rank of major and winning the U.S. Army Bronze Star. Upon his return, he went into practice, joining the faculty of Howard's medical school in 1953 as an assistant professor. He later became associate professor, and in 1962 was named chair of the department of medicine (a position he held until 1973. He was named a full professor in 1963 and was named the John B. Johnson Professor of medicine in 1973—a post he held until his retirement in 1988.

A Career of Diabetes Research

It was in the field of diabetes research that Henry made his greatest contribution to medicine. According to *Ebony* magazine, he was considered the "dean" of the nation's roughly two dozen black physicians specializing in diabetes. As an endocrinologist, he examined the role of insulin in the body and explored the many causes of diabetes to determine which might be preventable.

Henry was particularly interested in the onset of diabetes among blacks, who have a proportionally higher percentage of sufferers. What he tried to do was find out whether there was a natural predisposition for blacks to become afflicted with diabetes. His research showed that the high proportion of blacks who developed the disease was related more to diet and exercise than other causes. Blacks (and those of any race) whose diets are high in rich foods full of sugar, starch, and carbohydrates, gain weight—a key

trigger for diabetes. As they gain weight, they become less active. The combination of obesity and sweet or fatty foods is almost a formula for diabetes. "There is no doubt," Henry said in a 1979 interview with *Ebony*, "that when people become obese they become insulin-resistant and they are, in a sense, digging their graves with their teeth."

Some people do have a genetic predisposition to diabetes. But as Henry pointed out, the high rate of diabetes among black Americans stands in stark contrast to the relatively low rate among Africans. The reason? African native diets were low in the foods that trigger diabetes. In his book, *The Black Health Library Guide to Diabetes*, Henry notes that the Bantu of Tanzania have traditionally had one of the world's lowest rates of diabetes—around one percent. "But when rural Africans such as the Bantu move to the city, their lifestyle often changes radically," he continues. "They give up their traditional diet . . . and learn to enjoy western favorites—refined white bread, meats, sweets, alcohol." Interestingly, he adds, slaves in eighteenth- and nineteenth-century America, whose diets were far from rich, had very little diabetes.

Henry worked to help educate people about the causes of diabetes—but also how to minimize or even prevent the disease. He also conducted research to find ways for the body to use insulin more efficiently—since diabetes is often caused by the inability to use the otherwise adequate amount of insulin being secreted. This research was important in identifying possible ways to treat severe diabetes without subjecting the sufferer to daily injections of insulin.

In addition to his research and practice, Henry was active in a number of professional organizations, including the American Board of Internal Medicine, the American College of Physicians, the National Association for the Advancement of Colored People (NAACP), and the Howard University Board of Trustees. In 1974 he became the first black Regent of the American College of Physicians. He was also the first black to receive the College's Master Award in 1987, and was named a College laureate in 1993. Even after retirement, Henry has continued to be active in providing information about diabetes and its treatment and prevention.

SELECTED WRITINGS BY HENRY:

Books

Henry, W. Lester, with Kirk A. Johnson. *The Black Health Library Guide to Diabetes*. Henry Holt & Co., 1993.

FURTHER READING:

Books

Phelps, Shirelle, ed. *Who's Who Among Black Americans 1996/97*. Gale Research, Inc., 1997.

Sammons, Vivian O. *Blacks in Science and medicine.* Hemisphere Publishing, 1990.

Periodicals

Howell, Ron. "Diabetes: Black Women Are Its No. 1 Victim." *Ebony,* (March 1979): 65-71.

—*Sketch by George A. Milite*

Warren Elliott Henry
1909-

Physicist

Warren Elliott Henry was among the most highly regarded African American physicists in the field of missile research in the post-World War II era. A specialist in cryogenics, electronics, and magnetism, he worked at the U.S. Naval Research Laboratory for 12 years before moving to the Lockheed Missiles and Space Company in 1960 and then to Howard University in 1969. During his career, he produced over 100 publications and collaborated with more than 20 Nobel Prize laureates. Much of the work he did 40 years ago has become important to the new interest in the connection between magnetism and superconductivity.

Henry was born in Evergreen, Alabama, on February 18, 1909. His parents, Nelson Henry and Mattye (McDaniel) Henry, were public school teachers, and were extremely supportive of their seven children, the oldest of whom was Warren. His parents took education very seriously and would allow their children to stay up past their normal bedtime only if they were reading or studying. When Henry was in the eleventh grade, his school was forced to close in February of the school year. His parents immediately borrowed railroad fare for him to attend another school in Greenville, Alabama. Henry later worked his way through college and received his B.S. from the Tuskegee Institute in 1931. That year he was appointed principal at the Escambia County Training School in Atmore, Alabama. He remained in this position until 1934 when he took a position as instructor of physics at both Spelman and Morehouse Colleges in Atlanta, Georgia. In 1936, Henry returned to school and earned his M.S. degree from Atlanta University the following year. After returning to Tuskegee as an instructor in chemistry in 1936, he reentered graduate school at the University of Chicago and received his Ph.D. in physics in 1941. In 1943, he left Tuskegee as an instructor in chemistry, physics, and radio and became a staff member at the radiation laboratories of the Massachusetts Institute of Technology in Cambridge. He remained there until 1946 when he returned to teaching at the University of Chicago. A year later he was named the acting head of the physics department at Morehouse College.

In 1948 Henry left teaching and accepted a position as a supervisory physicist at the Naval Research Laboratory (NRL) in Washington, D.C. He then entered the private sector in 1960 when he joined the Lockheed Missiles and Space Company as a senior staff scientist and engineer. Before he returned to teaching in 1968 at Howard University in Washington, D.C., Henry had established an impressive record in research specializing in magnetism, cryogenics (the science of refrigeration at very low temperatures), and solid state physics. The results of his work at both NRL and Lockheed have been used in space technology, oceanography projects, and cryogenic and electronic programs. At Howard, Henry was a professor of physics until his retirement in 1977; he also served as department chairman for one year. Henry was named professor emeritus in 1980 and since then has served Howard as Student Research Coordinator in the MARC Honors Undergraduate Research Training Program. In April 1997 he received a lifetime achievement and excellence award from Howard.

Henry has lectured in his field in France, Germany, Japan, and the former Soviet Union. He is also the designer of the Henry Elevator Lift, a device that allows for the precise mechanical placement of materials for study. A fellow of the American Physical Society, he has always been intensely interested in minorities in the sciences and served as chairman of that society's committee on minorities in physics. He is also a fellow of the American Association for the Advancement of Science and a member of the American Association of Physics Teachers, the Federation of American Scientists, the Scientific Research Society of America, the American Chemical Society, the Institute of Radio Engineers, Sigma Xi, and the Washington Philosophical Society. A winner of the Carver Award, he was also named a Presidential Associate of Tuskegee Institute. In 1997 he was honored by the Ernest Orlando Lawrence Berkeley National Laboratory for his contributions to the study of magnetism and superconductivity. He is married to Jeanne Sally (Pearlson) and has one daughter, Eva Ruth.

FURTHER READING:

Books

Maclin, A. P., T. L. Gill, and W. W. Zachary, ed. "Magnetic Phenomena: The Warren E. Henry Symposium on Magnetism." In *Lecture Notes in Physics,* Springer-Verlag, 1989.

Sammons, Vivian O. *Blacks in Science and Medicine.* Hemisphere Publishing Co., 1990, p. 117.

—*Sketch by Leonard C. Bruno*

Henry A. Hill

Henry A. Hill
1915-1979
Chemist

Henry A. Hill was an expert on polymers, with a particular interest in resins, rubber, and plastics. Conscious of the limited opportunities for African Americans in the sciences in the 1940s and 1950s, Hill turned adversity to advantage and held a number of management positions in the chemical industry before starting his own company, Riverside Research Laboratory. Hill was frequently sought out by his colleagues for a range of consulting and advisory positions. He was responsible for developing guidelines for employers in the chemical industry, and was appointed by President Lyndon Johnson to the National Commission on Product Safety. In 1977 Hill served as president of the American Chemical Society.

Henry Aaron Hill was born May 30, 1915, in the small river town of St. Joseph, Missouri. His undergraduate education was completed at Johnson C. Smith University, a liberal arts school in North Carolina. Hill received a B.S. in chemistry in 1936. He then spent a year in graduate school at the University of Chicago, but went on to earn a Ph.D. in organic chemistry from the Massachusetts Institute of Technology (MIT) in 1942. At MIT Hill came briefly but

memorably under the influence of James Flack Norris, who impressed Hill by being more interested in Hill's abilities as a chemist than in his heritage. Hill was later instrumental in establishing the American Chemical Society's Norris award.

Following his formal schooling, Hill held jobs involving several different research concerns, beginning as head of chemistry research at Atlantic Research Associates in Massachusetts from 1942 to 1943. In 1943 he was made a research director. In 1945 Hill was promoted to vice president in charge of research at what was now the National Atlantic Research Company. While moving quickly up the ranks, Hill spent his research time developing water-based paints, rubber adhesives, and synthetic rubber, among other projects. It was also there that Hill began to conceive of operating his own research laboratory.

Hill then spent six years, from 1946 to 1952, as group leader at the Dewey & Almy Chemical Company, working on polymer research. (Polymers are large molecules consisting of similar or identical small molecules or monomers linked together. Examples of naturally occurring polymers are proteins and silk; polymers synthesized in the laboratory include plastics and synthetic fibers.) Hill's experience led him to the collaborative development of National Polychemicals Inc., in Wilmington, Massachusetts, where he spent the next nine years beginning in 1952, the first four as assistant manager, and the last five as a vice president. This corporation was a manufacturer of chemical intermediaries used for polymers, and grew to have annual sales in 1971 of over 10 million dollars. The company's success was largely credited to Hill's personal research contributions.

In 1961 Hill realized his ambition of operating his own research facility, establishing Riverside Research Laboratory. The mission of the corporation would be to provide research and development, as well as consulting, in the area of organic chemistry. Hill had a particular interest in resin, rubber, and plastics. By 1964 the company had moved to more spacious accommodations, where it would remain for the remainder of Hill's life. Hill eventually became known as an authority in polymer chemistry on fabric flammability.

Hill was active in the professional aspects of his field. In 1968 he served as chair of the committee on professional relations of the American Chemical Society. This committee produced widely used personnel guidelines for employers of chemists and chemical engineers. In 1968 Hill was appointed by President Lyndon Johnson to the National Commission on Product Safety, a position that galvanized Hill's interest in product liability and product safety. Hill was a fellow of both the American Association for the Advancement of Science and the American Institute of Chemists. He was a member of the American Chemical Society for 38 years, served on its board of directors from 1971 to 1978, and was elected president in 1977. He was chair of the compliance committee of the National Motor Vehicle Safety Advisory Council, and a member of the Information Council on Fabric Flammability. He was married in 1943, and had one child.

Whatever obstacles Hill may have faced in his career owing to racial discrimination, his talent and persistence served him well in a highly competitive industry. In 1971 he was quoted in *Chemistry* as saying, "My successes have hinged upon a scratch below the surface, a little extra persistence." Hill died of a heart attack on March 17, 1979.

FURTHER READING:

Books

Young, Herman, and Barbara Young. *Scientists in the Black Perspective.* Lincoln Foundation, 1979.

Periodicals

Young, Herman, and Barbara Young. "Henry Hill Dead of Heart Attack at 63," *Chemical and Engineering News,* (March 26, 1979): 6–7.

Massie, Samuel P. "Henry A. Hill: The Second Mile," *Chemistry,* (January 1971): 11.

—Sketch by Kimberlyn McGrail

Mary Elliot Hill
1907-1969
Chemist

Analytical chemist Mary Elliot Hill worked and taught at a number of universities in Kentucky, Tennessee, and Virginia during the decades from the 1930s to the 1960s. Little is known about this extraordinary woman, one of the few black female chemists—or indeed, scientists of any kind—who flourished during those years. Her research work concerned properties of light in the ultraviolet spectrum and the synthesis of molecules for creating plastics.

Years of Teaching and Research

Mary Elliot Hill was born Mary Elliot in South Mills, North Carolina, on January 5, 1907. She earned her B.S. degree from Virginia State College in Petersburg, Virginia, in 1929, when she was 22 years old. She went on to teach at the Virginia State College Laboratory School from 1930 to 1932; then at Hampton Institute in Hampton, Virginia, from 1932 to 1936. In 1938, she returned to Virginia State College. Perhaps it was during this brief hiatus from teaching that she married Carl McClellan Hill; certainly during this time she continued her education, and in 1941 earned her M.S. degree from the University of Pennsylvania.

Hill's work at Virginia State College continued until 1942, and in the latter year she moved to Bennett College, in Greensboro, North Carolina. She served there for one school year, and in 1944 became assistant professor of chemistry at Tennessee A & I State University in Nashville. In 1951 she became acting head of the chemistry department, and held that position until 1962. The latter year marked the beginning of her last appointment, to Kentucky State College in Frankfort.

Research in Light and Synthesis of Molecules

Hill must have been a brilliant woman to have succeeded in environments where there were few female scientists, to say nothing of black female scientists. As for her areas of research, a person lacking a scientific education would not at first glance even understand the meaning of her two specialty areas, ultraviolet spectrophotometry and synthesis of ketenes.

A photometer is an instrument for measuring the intensity of varying degrees of light, and a spectrophotometer measures this intensity in various parts of the spectrum that contain invisible light. Among the invisible forms is ultraviolet light, which exists beyond the violet end of the spectrum and has rays shorter than those for visible light, but longer than x rays. Hence ultraviolet spectrophotometry concerns measurement and experiments regarding the intensity of ultraviolet light.

Ketene synthesis is even more complex, involving as it does radicals, acetyls, and acetic acid. Acetic acid is the chief acid found in vinegar; a radical is a group of bonded atoms that react as an entity; and a radical of acetic acid is called an acetyl. Acetyls are used in creating, or synthesizing, plastics. Hill worked specifically with ketene, a poisonous gas with a strong odor which is used as an acetylating agent. In her specialty, she worked with monomeric ketenes, a monomeric compound being one that can undergo polymerization—that is, a chemical reaction in which two or more molecules combine to form larger ones with repeating structural units. Polymerization, too, is an activity key to the creation of plastics.

Hill was a member of the American Chemical Society, the Tennessee Academy of Science, Beta Kappa Chi, and the National Institute of Science. She died in 1969.

FURTHER READING:

Books

Sammons, Vivian Ovelton. *Blacks in Science and Medicine.* Hemisphere Publishing, 1990.

Spradling, Mary Mace, ed. *In Black and White.* Gale, 1980.

Who's Who of American Women, 4th edition, 1966-67. Marquis Who's Who, 1965.

—Sketch by Judson Knight

Walter Andrew Hill
1946-
Agronomist

Walter Andrew Hill is a renowned soil scientist and plant physiologist who has foregone what could have been a lucrative career in private industry to be an educator and researcher. His well-known research on the sweet potato and other crops includes groundbreaking work for the National Aeronautics and Space Administration (NASA). A full professor at Tuskegee University, he is involved with numerous professional organizations and has received extensive recognition for contributions to his field.

Walter Andrew Hill was born on August 9, 1946, in New Brunswick, New Jersey. As a young child, his parents moved to North Little Rock, Arkansas. His mother, a schoolteacher, and his father, a minister, placed great value on education—not only for their own children but also for the children of other families. At that time, there were no high schools for blacks in rural areas of Arkansas; the Hills organized a network of families that housed these children while they attended high school in North Little Rock. The opportunities his parents provided for young black people inspired Walter. Their example, combined with his interest in the work of **George Washington Carver**, led him to pursue a career as a scientist and educator.

Hill's performance in high school earned him a scholarship to Lake Forest College in Lake Forest, Illinois, where he received a bachelor's degree in 1968. He then began teaching high school chemistry, while attending graduate school at the University of Chicago. In 1970, he was awarded a master of science degree. To fulfill his goal of helping farm families, he chose to study soil science. This required an additional master's degree, which he earned from the University of Arizona in 1973. His teachers in Arizona recognized his ability and encouraged him to continue his studies in the College of Agriculture, at the University of Illinois. In 1978, he earned a doctoral degree in soil science from the school.

That same year, Hill joined the faculty of Tuskegee University, teaching soil science. He frequently encouraged his students to join him in research projects, and his pupils have won numerous awards for their research projects. Hill was named a Danforth Associate in 1980 for his teaching; in 1990, the American Society of Agronomy presented him with the Outstanding Education Award for his teaching efforts.

Hill's research has focused on the sweet potato plant. In 1983, he was awarded the Plucknett Award of the International Society of Tropical Root Crops for his work on the plant. Soon afterward, NASA provided him the funds to research whether the sweet potato plant could be part of a sustained life-support system in space. NASA was particularly interested in the ability of the sweet potato plant to transform waste material into food, oxygen, and purified water. Prior to Hill's studies, no root crop had successfully been grown in a water tank. He was successful in solving the numerous problems associated with this project and was awarded a U.S. patent for his procedure.

Hill is a member of the Soil Science Society of America, the American Society of Agronomists, the International Society of Soil Science, the American Chemical Society, the American Society of Horticultural Science, the Crop Science Society of America, and the American Society of Gravitational and Space Biology. Today he is a full professor, dean, and research director of the School of Agriculture and Home Economics at Tuskegee University. Hill married Jill Harris in 1984, and they have three children: Shaka, Asia and Osei.

FURTHER READING:

Books

Sammons, Vivian. *Blacks in Science and Medicine* New York: Hemisphere Publishing, 1990, p.120.
Kessler, James H. *Distinguished African American Scientists of the 20th Century.* Phoenix, Arizona: Oryx Press, 1996, p.168.
American Men & Women of Science. New Providence, New Jersey: R.R. Bowker, 1989, p. 848.

—*Sketch by Patrick J. Longe*

William Augustus Hinton
1883-1959
Medical researcher

William Augustus Hinton was the first black professor at Harvard Medical School, where he taught preventative medicine and hygiene, as well as bacteriology and immunology. He earned an international reputation as a medical researcher with his work on the detection and treatment of syphilis and other sexually transmitted diseases. He was integral in developing two common diagnostic procedures for syphilis, the Hinton test and the Davies-Hinton test.

Hinton was born on December 15, 1883, in Chicago, Illinois. His parents were Augustus Hinton and Maria Clark, both former slaves. Hinton grew up in Kansas and became the youngest student to ever graduate from Kansas City High School. After high school, he studied at the University of Kansas, completing the three-year premed program in

William Augustus Hinton

two years. Hinton did some additional undergraduate work at Harvard University and received his B.S. there in 1905.

After graduation, Hinton spent some time working in a law office, but, as he reported in *Twenty-fifth Anniversary Report—Harvard Class of 1905,* he "discovered that legal appetite can't always be cultivated." Instead of pursuing work in law, Hinton turned to education, teaching science at Waldo University in Tennessee from 1905 to 1906 and at State School in Langston, Oklahoma, from 1906 to 1909. It was during this time—in Langston—that Hinton met and married Ada Hawes, a teacher, in 1909. They subsequently had two daughters, Ann and Jane.

In 1909, Hinton entered Harvard Medical School. Though offered a scholarship reserved for African American students, Hinton instead chose to compete for a scholarship offered to all students. He won the Wigglesworth scholarship two years in a row. By skipping the second year of school and finishing the Harvard medical program in only three years, Hinton received his M.D. in 1912.

After graduating, Hinton's first job was as a serologist at the Wassermann Laboratory of the Harvard Medical School. By 1915, he was named the director of the lab, which at the time had become the official lab for the Massachusetts State Department of Public Health. In 1916, Hinton also became chief of the laboratory department at the Boston Dispensary. One of his accomplishments there was developing a program to train women as lab technicians, a profession that at the time was not generally open to women.

From the start of his career until his retirement, his attention was directed toward "syphilis and the laboratory tests used in connection with its diagnosis and treatment," Hinton reported in *Fiftieth Anniversary Report—Harvard Class of 1905.* In 1927, Hinton developed a test—subsequently known as the Hinton test—to diagnose syphilis. Because it was easier, less expensive, and more accurate than previously used tests, the Hinton test was adopted as standard procedure for diagnosing syphilis. Later, with Dr. J. A. V. Davies, Hinton developed another diagnostic test for syphilis, know as the Davies-Hinton test.

Hinton began teaching at Harvard Medical School in 1923, as assistant lecturer in preventive medicine and hygiene. He continued teaching for 27 years. Hinton wrote one book during his career—*Syphilis and Its Treatment,* published in 1936. At the time, the book was considered controversial. In *Fiftieth Anniversary Report—Harvard Class of 1905,* Hinton wrote that the book contained "specific ways in which laboratory tests for syphilis should be used correctly." Though the book had "little support" at first, by 1955 Hinton noted that "except where new and superior drugs have replaced those then in use, most of it has been recognized." The *Harvard Medical Alumni Bulletin* of July 1959, in fact, described the book as "widely acclaimed." In an interview with the *Boston Daily Globe* in 1952, Hinton told reporter Frances Burns that he considered the book his most important contribution because it summed up both his research and the experience he gained through patients in clinics who had syphilis. "I had learned that race was not the determining factor but that it was, rather, the socioeconomic condition of the patient," he told Burns. "It is a disease of the underprivileged."

In addition to his work as a researcher, Hinton was a special consultant to the U.S. Public Health Service and, beginning in 1936, chief of the labs of the Boston Floating Hospital. He also taught at both Tufts University and Simmons College. In 1940, Hinton lost a leg in a car accident. This disability, however, did not keep him from teaching. In fact, in 1949, Harvard appointed Hinton clinical professor of bacteriology and immunology. He was the school's first black professor. Hinton retired one year later, in 1950. According to the *Boston Daily Globe,* however, he continued to teach without a salary. Hinton retired from the Massachusetts Department of Public Health Wassermann Laboratory in 1953.

At home, Hinton's hobbies were gardening and making furniture. He died at the age of 75 on August 8, 1959, in Canton, Massachusetts.

SELECTED WRITINGS BY HINTON:

Books

Syphilis and Its Treatment. Macmillan, 1936.

FURTHER READING:

Books

Fiftieth Anniversary Report—Harvard Class of 1905, Harvard University Printing Office, 1955, pp. 247–248.

Twenty-fifth Anniversary Report—Harvard Class of 1905, Harvard University Printing Office, 1930, p. 304.

Periodicals

Boston Daily Globe, (September 15, 1952).
Boston Herald, (June 30, 1949).
Boston Sunday Globe, (August 9, 1959).
Boston Transcript, (January 25, 1916).
Harvard Medical Alumni Bulletin, (July 1959).

—*Sketch by Devera Pine*

Freeman Alphonsa Hrabowski, III
1950-

Mathematics educator

Freeman A. Hrabowski, III's achievements in educating young African Americans have drawn national attention, and his contributions to this cause have enriched the lives of countless people. Hrabowski was born in Birmingham, Alabama on August 13, 1950, and even as a young child, his ambition was to follow in the footsteps of his parents, educators Maggie and Freeman, Jr. He skipped two grades in elementary school, and as a result, he entered high school at the age of 12. When he first started high school, he participated in a civil rights demonstration. He was arrested and spent a week in a Birmingham jail with Dr. Martin Luther King Jr. Although jail is no place for a 12-year-old, Hrabowski received a dramatic life lesson in the consequences of standing up for your beliefs.

Hrabowski graduated from high school at the tender age of 15, but his young age was not a detriment to his continuing education. He entered the Hampton Institute in Hampton, Virginia, which had a fine reputation and offered excellent educational opportunities to African American scholars. His teaching abilities were spotted immediately, and he soon became a tutor for hearing-impaired students at the college.

While at the Hampton Institute, Hrabowski took advantage of an offer to study in Cairo, Egypt for a year. He furthered his education in the scientific disciplines of mathematics and physics, but he also availed himself of classes in Arab culture as well as the sights and attractions of the Middle East.

His scientific background served him well, and upon graduation with high honors from Hampton, he entered the University of Illinois in Champaign to begin work on his master's degree. He completed the requirements in just one year, then continued to work for his doctorate degree. At this time, his educational focus shifted from pure mathematics to math education, and he applied his talent to teaching African Americans. Since he also had a background in statistics, his doctoral thesis investigated the difference in the performance of African American math students from universities that were historically black versus those at schools that were mainly white.

Hrabowski's flair for education was rewarded when he was offered the position of assistant dean for student services at the University of Illinois. While in this position, he took a leadership role in the Upward Bound and the Educational Opportunities programs, both of which reached out to the low-income and minority community. This leadership furthered his career and helped others to achieve greatness in education and in their personal and professional lives. In the final year of his dissertaion Hrabowski was also appointed as an assistant professor of statistics at Illinois. He earned his doctorate in 1975 in higher education administration and statistics.

After the University of Illinois, Hrabowski accepted positions as an associate professor of statistics and research, and later as the Associate Dean of Graduate Studies at Alabama A&M University. His tenure lasted only a year as he later accepted a position at Coppin State College in Baltimore as a professor of mathematics and Dean of the College of Arts and Sciences. In 1981 he became the Vice-President for Academic Affairs.

Hrabowski was lured away from Coppin State by the University of Maryland, Baltimore County in 1987, when he became the Vice Provost. Later, in 1990, he served as the Executive Vice-President, then in 1993 he became President of the university.

Of the many programs on which he has worked during his time at the University of Maryland, one his finest achievements was his collaboration with local Baltimore philanthropists Robert and Jane Meyerhoff. Together they formed the Meyerhoff scholarship program, which attempts to mitigate the shortage of African American young people in the science and engineering disciplines. The program now helps support over 150 students, giving them the opportunity to work side by side during the summer months with notable scientists in universities throughout the country.

Not only does Hrabowski fill his schedule with his duties as President of the University of Maryland, Baltimore, he is also a co-author of two books on science education for African Americans, he has received research grants, and he serves on the board of numerous companies and organizations including the American Council on

Education, Mercantile Safe Deposit and Trust Company, and Baltimore Gas and Electric Company. He also serves as a consultant to many educational programs including the Educational Testing Service and the Maryland State Department of Education. Hrabowski also shares his expertise by giving numerous lectures each year.

Hrabowski lives near Baltimore, Maryland and is married to Jacqueline Coleman. They have one son, Eric.

SELECTED WRITINGS BY HRABOWSKI:

Books

(With Geoffrey Greif and Kenneth Maton) *Beating the Odds*, Oxford University Press, 1998.

Periodicals

(With Kenneth Maton) "Enhancing the Success of African-American Students in the Sciences: Freshman Year Outcomes," *School Science and Mathematics*, Volume 95, (January 1995).

"Language and Literature: Inferences for the Twenty-First Century," *Maryland English Journal*, Vol. 24, Nos. 1 and 2, (1989-90).

"Graduate School Success of Black Students from Black and White Colleges," with E.G. Anderson, *Journal of Higher Education*, Vol. 57, No. 3, (1977).

"The Joy of Being Recognized: Success in Public Schools," *Baltimore Evening Sun*, (April 18, 1986).

FURTHER READING:

Books

Phelps, Shirelle. *Who's Who Among African Americans, 1998-99,* Gale Research, 1998, p. 729.

Kessler, James H., et.al. *Distinguished African American Scientists of the 20th Century,* Oryx Press, 1996, pp. 174-177.

—*Sketch by Roger Jaffe*

Philip G. Hubbard
1921-
Electrical engineer

Philip G. Hubbard is a well-respected researcher in fluid dynamics (the study of the motion of matter in gas, liquid, plastic, or plasma state) who pioneered methods of measuring and analyzing turbulence in fluid flow. He was born Philip Gamaliel Hubbard in Macon, Missouri, on March 4, 1921, to Philip Alexander Hubbard, a semi-skilled craftsman and Rosa Belle Guy, a teacher. Both parents were believed to be direct descendants of freed slaves. Tragically, just 18 days after the birth of young Hubbard his 51-year-old father succumbed to pneumonia. While his mother continued teaching, the job of caring for the baby fell to his grandparents, Molly and Richard Wallace.

In 1925 Rosa Belle, her three sons from a previous marriage, and young Hubbard moved to Iowa so the four boys could enroll in unsegregated schools. In an interview with contributor Roger Jaffe, Hubbard noted he was usually the only non-white student and was accepted on an equal basis in school; outside of school things were very different and the races were highly unequal.

Hubbard Begins Association with the University of Iowa

Philip Hubbard entered the University of Iowa in 1940, graduated in 1943 with a degree in chemical engineering and married Wynonna Marie Griffin. Hubbard and his wife had five children, four boys and one girl. After serving two years in the army he received another bachelor's degree in electrical engineering in 1946; he was offered a full-time position at the university as a research engineer and later as the head of the instrumentation division. He received his master's degree in mechanics and hydraulics in 1949; his Ph.D. was awarded in 1954 in the same field.

The Hot Wire Anemometer

Hubbard's electrical engineering degree gave him the necessary background to investigate fluid measurement instrumentation and would later prove invaluable in his research of fluid flow. At the time there was a need to measure turbulence in a fluid flow. In a water distribution system for a city, for example, many miles of pipes are required. If certain types of pipeline cause less turbulence and fewer interruptions of the smooth fluid flow than others, those pipes are better suited for the job since they are more efficient. Industry needed a way to measure this kind of turbulence.

Hubbard developed the hot wire anemometer, a device that has a length of very thin wire that is heated with an electric current and placed in fluid. Measuring the rate at which heat is dissipated from the wire leads to the measurement of fluid turbulence. The wire is only 50 microns in diameter—about one-seventh the thickness of a human hair. The small wire allows the device to respond very quickly so fluid turbulence can be measured as it happens.

The instrument became so popular with industry that while in the university environment, Hubbard could not make enough to satisfy the demand. He formed the Hubbard Instrument Company in 1951 to manufacture and market hot wire anemometers and related measuring devices while retaining his position at the University of Iowa.

Hubbard's Focus on Education

Hubbard joined the teaching faculty of the University as an assistant professor of mechanics and hydraulics in 1954, became an associate professor in 1956, and then a professor in 1959. This made Hubbard the first African American tenured professor at the University of Iowa. In 1966 Hubbard was appointed the dean of academic affairs, a position he held until his retirement. During his tenure as dean, he also held the positions of vice provost, vice president of student services, and the director of the "Opportunity at Iowa" program. Even after his retirement in 1991, Hubbard remains active in the university community. He sits on numerous boards for various academic and educational organizations and has three awards in his name given to deserving students at the university each year.

SELECTED WRITINGS BY HUBBARD:

Books

Rouse, Hunter, ed. *Advanced Mechanics of Fluids*. John Wiley, 1959.
"Whence Come Megatrends?" *Megatrends in Hydraulic Engineering,* Colorado State University Press, 1986.

Periodicals

"The Hot-Film Anemometer: A New Device for Fluid Mechanics Research," *Journal of Applied Sciences,* (September 1956).

Other

Hubbard, Philip G., letter and personal information provided to Roger Jaffe, January, 1994.
Interview with Roger Jaffe, conducted January 20, 1994.

—*Sketch by Roger Jaffe*

Benjamin Franklin Hubert
1884-1958
Agriculturist

Benjamin Franklin Hubert shaped agricultural education and introduced scientific farming principles in Georgia. His work influenced both the academic and economic evolution of agriculture.

Hubert was born in Hancock County, Georgia, in 1884 to Zacharias and Camilla Hubert, owners of a thriving farm. Hubert earned a bachelor of arts degree from Morehouse College in 1909; he then attended Massachusetts Agricultur-

al College in Amherst and earned a bachelor of science degree in agriculture in 1912. He attended both the University of Wisconsin and the University of Minnesota, but it is unclear if he completed the requirements for a master of science degree in agriculture.

Hubert served as the chief of the Agricultural Department at Tuskegee Institute, then joined South Carolina State College, Orangeburg, as a professor of rural social sciences. In 1918, he was named director of agriculture and agricultural extension and professor of agriculture.

Hubert's most significant appointment came in 1926, when he was selected as the third president of Georgia State Industrial College, a post he was to hold for 21 years. Georgia State (known today as Savannah State College) was established in 1891 under a federal program and was the first state-supported institution of higher education for blacks in Georgia.

Georgia State was in deplorable condition when Hubert arrived. He launched a vigorous renovation program. He recruited faculty from prestigious institutions and lobbied tirelessly for laboratories, additional teaching facilities, and student resources. He reorganized the academic programs and instituted a bachelor of science degree in agriculture.

In 1935, Georgia State launched a serious agricultural research program, and the college's faculty and students conducted research on such topics as developing a cotton plant that could withstand the onslaught of boll weevils (agricultural pests capable of destroying large fields of cotton) and the value of phosphates as a fertilizer.

Hubert feared the impact of urban migration on farming and the quality of life. In 1928, he organized the Association for the Advancement of Negro Country Life and purchased 466 acres from his parents' estate, the farm on which he was born, to establish the Log Cabin Center. There, he worked with destitute tenant farmers, teaching modern agricultural techniques and sound business practices. The center also became a resource for rural educators.

Social, economic, and political changes after World War II drastically altered the shape of higher education in the United States, and Hubert decided his talents could be better used in a different capacity. He resigned as president of Georgia State Industrial College in 1947 and focused his energies on the Log Cabin Center. But those efforts to rebuild the center met with failure. Hubert died in 1958; today, only a few ruins mark the location of the Log Cabin. Center.

FURTHER READING:

Books

Boris, Joseph J., ed. *Who's Who in Colored America,* vol. 1. New York: Who's Who in Colored America Corp., 1927.

Hall, Clyde W. *One Hundred Years of Educating at Savannah State College* East Peoria, Illinois: Versa Press Inc. 1991.

Sammons, Vivian Ovelton. *Blacks in Science and Medicine* New York: Hemisphere Publishing Co., 1990.

Other

Elmore, Charles, historian, Savannah State College, telephone interview, April 22, 1998.

Schultz, Mark Roman. *A More Satisfying Life on the Farm: Benjamin F. Hubert and the Log Cabin Community* Unpublished master's thesis, University of Georgia, 1989.

Sewell, Lela, archivist, South Carolina State University, Orangeburg, South Carolina. Telephone interview, April 21, 1998.

—Sketch by A. Mullig

Roy Davage Hudson

Roy Davage Hudson
1930-
Neuropharmacologist

Roy Davage Hudson has contributed to science in several ways. As a pharmacology researcher, his discoveries shed light on how drugs impact neuronal control of movement. He has been a teacher and administrator at several universities, and was President of Hampton University. He worked in the pharmaceutical industry helping couple industrial and academic research. His career demonstrates that those willing to take advantage of life's smaller opportunities will often be presented with larger opportunities.

Roy Davage Hudson was born on June 30, 1930, in Chattanooga, Tennessee. His father, James Roy Hudson, worked for the Southern Railroad as a mail handler on the Tennessean. His mother, Everence Love Hudson (nee Wilkerson), was a country school teacher, and strongly influenced Hudson's love of learning. In a telephone interview with contributor Dónal O'Mathúna, conducted April 27, 1998, Hudson recalled his mother's motto: "Not to equal, but to excel."

Interest in science began for Hudson as a young boy on his grandfather's farm. He was curious about how organisms worked, and would collect and dissect them. He loved to take his toys apart, and would methodically lay out the pieces so he could put them together again correctly. His schools often lacked the best equipment, but they had concerned teachers who noted Hudson's aptitude and encouraged him towards science.

Hudson joined the Air Force in 1948 and served until 1952. He repaired structural damage to aircraft while stationed in Alaska during the Korean Conflict, and later worked on engine maintenance. What he learned during this time would later help him repair and modify research equipment. These experiences taught him important lessons. As he says, "Use your time wisely. Take advantage of every opportunity that comes your way because you never know when it might become of primary use to you."

After leaving the military, Hudson attended Livingstone College in Salisbury, North Carolina. He graduated with a B.S. in biology in 1955, where he was also a co-captain and all-conference guard on the football team. He was later named one of all-time top 22 football players at Livingstone, whose team played in the first football game between two black colleges in 1892. Hudson went to graduate school at the University of Michigan as a Danforth Fellow. He obtained an M.S. in zoology in 1957, but made the switch to pharmacology by taking advantage of what might have seemed like a trivial opportunity.

Switches Focus to Pharmacology

While in the zoology doctoral program, a friend told Hudson of a summer job in the pharmacology department. Hudson got the job, and worked diligently as a technician. He developed ways to handle research animals where he could do procedures quicker on his own than it usually took two technicians working together. A faculty member took a keen interest in Hudson, who went on to publish a paper with him while Hudson was still a technician. He soon switched his doctoral studies from zoology to pharmacology and obtained his Ph.D. in 1962. He started teaching pharmacology in the University of Michigan's Medical School in 1961, and remained on the faculty until 1966. He then moved to Brown University in Providence, Rhode Island, where he was both associate professor of neuroscience (1966-1970) and associate dean of the graduate school (1966-1969).

Hudson's research has made a significant contribution to our understanding of how certain drugs alter the transmission of nerve signals influencing muscle function. Some diseases and accidents lead to muscle stiffness and even paralysis by affecting these neurons. Hudson showed how some chemical agents can also influence these neurons. He was the first to show how certain drugs can distinguish between two specific neurons, called alpha and gamma motor neurons. He also studied the effects of nicotine from cigarette smoke on the brains of animals. This research has led to about 25 publications and to his work being cited in important sources, like Goodman and Gilman's *The Pharmacological Basis of Therapeutics* and the Merck Index.

While Hudson is a committed scientist, he also has a deep love of the arts. (He is still involved with his local Civic Black Theatre.) This influenced his reshaping of Brown University's medical school curriculum. Instead of concentrating humanities courses early in the program, he moved many to later years. These ideas are only now being implemented in other medical schools. Hudson's administrative duties expanded in 1970 when he became president of Hampton University in Hampton, Virginia, an historically black institution. However, he continued to teach pharmacology as a visiting professor at the University of Virginia, believing creative involvement with students to be an important aspect of administrative responsibilities. He has also published about 25 articles on administrative issues.

Moves from Academia to Industry

Another significant change occurred in Hudson's career in 1976 when he returned to Michigan to work for the pharmaceutical research division of Warner-Lambert/Parke-Davis. He was vice-president for Research, Planning and Coordination until 1979. This position involved evaluating research and development projects, doing cost-benefit analyses on proposed projects, and directing approved research projects. In 1981 he became director of Central Nervous System Research for Upjohn Company. He moved to Europe in 1987 to direct Upjohn's European Discovery Capabilities project. This unique initiative allowed the pharmaceutical industry to fund new drug research at universities. Having experience in both academia and industry enabled Hudson to make these initiatives as helpful as possible to both parties.

Hudson returned to the United States in 1990 as vice-president for worldwide corporate affairs and public relations. This was a difficult time for Upjohn as significant controversy surrounded a couple of their products. Again, Hudson's various experiences gave him the research background to understand and explain to others the scientific aspects of the controversy. Hudson retired from Upjohn in 1992, but has twice come out of retirement, most recently to serve as interim president of his alma mater, Livingstone College (1995-1996).

Hudson has received numerous awards during his distinguished and diverse career, including the Upjohn Prize (1987) and honorary degrees from Brown University (M.A. in 1968), Lehigh University (LLD in 1974), and Princeton University (LLD in 1975). Beneath the variety in Hudson's career is the constant drive of a man doing his best no matter what the situation. As he said, "Pray as if everything depended on God and work as if everything depends on you." His career demonstrates that if something is worth doing, it should always be done well.

Hudson married Constance Taylor in 1956, and they have two children, David and Hollye, and two grandchildren. Now retired, he and Constance live in Kalamazoo, Michigan.

SELECTED WRITINGS BY HUDSON:

Periodicals

"Effects of Chlorpromazine on Spinal Cord Reflex Mechanisms," *International Journal of Neuropharmacology,* Vol. 5, (January 1966): 43-58.

(With M. K. Wolpert) "Central Muscle Relaxant Effects of Diazepam," *Neuropharmacology,* Vol. 9, (September 1970): 481-8.

"Central Nervous System Responses to Cigarette Smoke Inhalation in the Cat," *Archives Internationales de Pharmacodynamie et de Therapie,* Vol. 237, (February 1979): 191-212.

FURTHER READING:

Books

American Men & Women of Science 1998-99. New Providence, NJ: R. R. Bowker. 20th Edition. Vol. 3, pp. 1050-1.

Sammons, Vivian Ovelton. *Blacks in Science and Medicine.* Taylor and Francis, 1990, p. 125.

Periodicals

Ebony, July 1978, p. 7.
Ebony, December 1987, p. 7.

—Sketch by Dónal P. O'Mathúna

I

Elmer Samuel Imes

Elmer Samuel Imes
1883-1941
Physicist

Elmer Samuel Imes was the second African American to receive a Ph.D. in physics. (The first was **Edward Bouchet**, who graduated from Yale in 1876.) He became internationally known for his research on the infra-red spectra and became head of the department of physics at Fisk University. An inspiring teacher knowledgeable in many fields, Imes also taught for many years in schools run by the American Missionary Association.

Imes was born in Memphis, Tennessee, on October 12, 1883. His parents, Benjamin A. and Elizabeth W. Imes, were missionaries, and his father was a graduate of Oberlin College and Theological Seminary. The elder Imes was among the pioneers in educational and church work in the southern field of the American Missionary Association. There were also two other sons in the family, Albert L. and William L. Imes. Before the younger Imes began his graduate studies in physics he, too, taught for several years in the American Missionary schools, mainly in Albany, Georgia, at the Albany Normal School. Imes received his B.A. in 1903 and his M.A. in 1910 from Fisk University in Nashville, Tennessee. He was later accepted in the doctoral physics program at the University of Michigan, where he was a fellow from 1916 to 1918. When he received his Ph.D. in physics from that university in 1918 with a dissertation entitled "Measurements on the Near Infra-red Absorption of Some Diatomic Cases," he had the distinction of being only the second African American to receive a Ph.D. in physics.

Imes worked in New York City as a research and consulting engineer and physicist both before and after earning his Ph.D., and in 1922 he took a position as a research physicist at the Federal Engineer's Development Corporation. In 1924 he moved to the Burrows Magnetic Equipment Corporation, and in 1927 he took a position as research engineer with E. A. Everett Railway Signal Supplies. Imes remained in the private sector until 1930, when he returned to teaching as professor and head of the department of physics at Fisk University. He was to remain in that position until his death in 1941, creating a well run and highly successful department.

A member of the Physical Society and the Society of Testing Materials, Imes was known for his appreciation of literature and music. A former student, W. F. G. Swann, remembered him as a considerate and sensitive man who brought "to any discussion an atmosphere of philosophic soundness and levelheaded practicalness." Imes died on September 11, 1941, at Memorial Hospital in New York.

FURTHER READING:

Books

Sammons, Vivian. *Blacks in Science and Medicine.* Hemisphere Publishing, 1990, p. 127.

Periodicals

New York Times, (September 12, 1941): 22.
Swann, W. F. G. "Elmer Samuel Imes," *Science,* (December 26, 1941): 600–601.

—Sketch by Leonard C. Bruno

Frederick Douglas Inge
1896-19??
Plant physiologist

F rederick Douglas Inge was a plant physiologist who did research in seed germination and seedling development. He also had an academic teaching career. Inge had a long association with Hampton Institute (later known as Hampton University), in Hampton, Virginia, where he served as chairman of both the biology and natural sciences department.

Inge was born in Charlottesville, Virginia, on May 30, 1896, to George P. and Kate V. (nee Ferguson) Inge. Inge served with the United States Army, attaining the rank of Sergeant during his 1917-19 tenure. When his stint in the army ended, he went to college and received all his higher education in the Midwest. He graduated from the University of Minnesota in 1924, with a B.S. (Some sources say a Ph.C, a degree in pharmacy.) Even before graduation, Inge was working as a professional scientist. He was a professor of pharmacy at the Meharry Medical College from 1923 until 1925. He also was employed as a pharmacist from 1924 until 1929. In 1929, Inge returned to teaching at the university level. He worked as an instructor in biology at Southern University, Baton Rouge, Louisiana, from 1929 until 1936. (Some sources say he was assistant professor or chairman of the biology department.)

Inge began his graduate work in Iowa that same year. He received his M.S. from Iowa State College in 1937 and his Ph.D. in plant physiology in 1940. His dissertation was titled "Growth Correlation in Maize Seedlings." While doing graduate work, Inge was also employed as a professor. Inge was a biology professor at Florida A & M University from 1938-40, then science department chair at Bennett College, Greensboro, North Carolina, from 1944-45. In 1945, Inge became associated with the Hampton Institute (later Hampton University), where he would spend the rest of his career. He was chair of the biology department there from 1945 until 1954, then chair of the department of natural sciences from 1954 until 1962. In 1970, Coleman was appointed to an emeritus professorship in biology.

Inge maintained membership in several key academic societies. They included the American Botanical Society, the American Institute of Biological Sciences, the American Society of Plant Physiology, American Association for the Advancement of Science, and the New York Academy of Science. He was also a member of the Botanical Society, the Torrey Botanical Club, and Sigma Xi.

SELECTED WRITINGS BY INGE:

Periodicals

"Growth Correlation in Maize Seedlings," *Iowa State Journal of Science,* (1941).

"Growth of the First Internode of the Epicoltyl in Maize Seedlings," *American Journal of Botany,* (1937).

"The Role of Education in a Changing Society," *Quarterly Journal, Florida A & M College,* (1939).

—*Sketch by A. Petrusso*

J

Jacquelyne Johnson Jackson
1932-
Sociologist

Jacquelyne Johnson Jackson has been a leading educator and researcher into those issues affecting elderly minority populations. As a Professor Emeritus from Duke University, Jackson has been a prominent voice in public policy debates over programs directed to elderly minority populations for over 30 years.

Jacquelyne Johnson was born on February 24, 1932, in Winston-Salem, North Carolina, to James A. and Beulah C. Johnson. Raised in Tuskegee, Alabama, she has retained lifelong connections to her hometown. She adopted her husband Murphy's name of Jackson when married. They have one child, Viola Elizabeth. Early in her educational career, an elderly couple who were friends of her parents were forced to sell their home to provide medical care for themselves (there was no Medicare/Medicaid at the time). Their resulting loss of home and life savings propelled Jackson to a career addressing issues of elderly minority populations. In addition, this couple was forced into public housing, creating Jackson's awareness of the law governing public services and in civil rights issues.

Jackson earned a B.S. in Sociology from the University of Wisconsin in 1953. In 1955 she received her M.S. in Sociology, also from the University of Wisconsin. At the Columbus campus of Ohio State University, she received her Doctorate in Sociology in 1960. Post-doctoral work began soon after in 1961 at the University of Colorado-Boulder. Her academic career includes additional post-doctoral work at Duke University from 1966-68 and at the University of North Carolina-Chapel Hill in the years 1977-78.

From 1959 to 1962, Jackson served as an Assistant Professor and Associate Professor at Southern University-Baton Rouge. Later in 1962 she left for Jackson State College, where she served as a Professor until 1964. Her passion for teaching took her next to Howard University, one of the nation's leading universities with a largely black enrollment. She stayed until 1966, when she left to join Duke University as Instructor and Associate Professor of Medical Sociology. Since 1969 she has been Visiting Professor at St. Augustine's College. In addition to teaching at the primarily black Jackson State College, she was also Professor at Howard University from 1978-1985.

At Duke University, Jackson was Associate Professor of Medical Sociology in the Department of Psychiatry. In a telephone interview with contributor Patrick Longe on April 14, 1998, she judged her most important work to be in the field of ethno-gerontology, which she stresses is not to be confused with efforts of social workers. Her research and writings have focused on the older African American population in the United States. Jackson's analyses measured the intra-variations within this population rather than comparing the variations against other ethnic groups. Examples of these intra-variations include sex, age, and ethnicity (within the black community). In addition, sociological impacts are also important. To illustrate, Jackson recalled that how during the 1960s research did not account for social discrimination against blacks. Some of her work during that era compared populations based on segregation influences.

A contributor of articles to more than 80 scholarly journals, Jackson has also published two books, *These Rights They Seek*, in 1962, and *Minorities and Aging*, in 1980. Recent topics which she has addressed in scholarly journals include the bell curve, race-based affirmative action, the Anita Hill/Clarence Thomas controversy, and ebonics.

Some of Jackson's more notable achievements include being named as John Hay Whitney Fellow 1957-59, National Institutes of Health Fellow 1966-1968 and 1977-1978, and National Science Foundation Fellow, beginning in 1959. Other professional activities include serving as President of the Association of Social and Behavorial Scientists and Chair of the Caucus of Black Sociologists. Jackson is also the recipient of numerous awards from the American Psychiatric Association, American Society of Black Sociologists, and Ohio State University.

Jackson has been a member of the Board of Directors of the Carver Research Foundation of Tuskegee University and currently serves as a Director of the National Council on Black Aging. She is also a member of the American Sociological Association, Southern Sociological Society, Gerontological Society of America, and the National Council on Family Relations. Jackson is a life member of the Tuskegee, Alabama, Civic Association, which she joined in 1959.

In her interview with Longe, Jackson summed up the challenge of her work as "keep[ing] pace with changes and identify[ing] characteristics and causes and address[ing] public policy to modify programs." In looking back, she sees tremendous improvements since the beginning of her academic career. Asked shortly after her retirement what achievement she was particularly proud of, she mentioned that beginning in 1978 she began a dialogue in public policy circles to explore options to our social security system focusing on differential age limits and educating recipients to better attain financial well-being. Her belief is that most Americans are unaware of the financial basis of the Social Security System and how benefits are distributed. In closing, she noted how this was one of the foremost topics on national agenda in 1998. Soon after her retirement, Jackson moved from Durham, North Carolina to Kansas.

SELECTED WRITINGS BY JACKSON:

Books

These Rights They Seek. Public Affairs Press, 1962.
Minorities and Aging. Wadsworth Publishing Co., 1980.

Periodicals

"Aging Black Women and Public Policies," *The Black Scholar,* (May/June 1988).
"Them Against Us: Anita Hill v. Clarence Thomas," *The Black Scholar,* (Winter 1991/Spring 1992).
"Race-based Affirmitave Action: mend it or end it?" *The Black Scholar,* (Summer 1995.)
"The Bell Curve: what's all the fuss about?" *The Black Scholar,* (Winter 1995).
"The Bell Curve (Book Review) intelligence and class structure in American Life," *The Black Scholar,* (Winter 1995).

—*Sketch by Patrick J. Longe*

Shirley Ann Jackson
1946-
Physicist

S hirley Ann Jackson is a theoretical physicist who has spent her career researching and teaching about particle physics—the branch of physics which uses theories and mathematics to predict the existence of subatomic particles and the forces that bind them together. She was the first African American woman to receive a Ph.D. from the Massachusetts Institute of Technology (MIT), and she spent many years conducting research at AT & T Bell Laboratories. She has been a professor of physics at Rutgers University since 1991 and was appointed chair of the Nuclear Regulatory Commission in 1995.

Jackson was born on August 5, 1946, in Washington, D.C. Her parents, Beatrice and George Jackson, strongly

Shirley Ann Jackson

valued education and encouraged her in school. Her father spurred on her interest in science by helping her with projects for her science classes. At Roosevelt High School, Jackson attended accelerated programs in both math and science, and she graduated in 1964 as valedictorian. Jackson began classes at MIT that same year, one of fewer than 20 African American students and the only one studying theoretical physics. While a student she volunteered at Boston City Hospital and tutored students at the Roxbury YMCA. She earned her bachelors degree in 1968, writing her thesis on solid-state physics, a subject then in the forefront of theoretical physics.

Although accepted at Brown, Harvard, and the University of Chicago, Jackson decided to stay at MIT for her doctoral work, because she wanted to encourage more African American students to attend the institution. She worked on elementary particle theory for her Ph.D., which she completed in 1973. James Young, the first African American tenured full professor in MIT's physics department, directed her research. Jackson's thesis, "The Study of a Multiperipheral Model with Continued Cross-Channel Unitarity," was subsequently published in the *Annals of Physics* in 1975.

Jackson's area of interest in physics is the study of the subatomic particles found within atoms, the tiny units of which all matter is made. Subatomic particles, which are usually very unstable and short-lived, can be studied in several ways. One method is using a particle accelerator, a device in which nuclei are accelerated to high speeds and then collided with a target to separate them into subatomic particles. Another way of studying them is by detecting their movements using certain kinds of nonconducting solids. When some solids are exposed to high-energy particles, the crystal lattice structure of the atoms is distorted, and this phenomenon leaves marks or tracks that can be seen with an electron microscope. Photographs of the tracks are then enhanced, and by examining these photographs physicists like Jackson can make predictions about what kinds of particles have caused the marks.

As a postdoctoral student of subatomic particles during the 1970s, Jackson studied and conducted research at a number of prestigious physics laboratories in both the United States and Europe. Her first position was as research associate at the Fermi National Accelerator Laboratory in Batavia, Illinois (known as Fermilab) where she studied hadrons—medium to large subatomic particles which include baryons and mesons. In 1974 she became visiting scientist at the accelerator lab at the European Center for Nuclear Research (CERN) in Switzerland. There she explored theories of strongly interacting elementary particles. In 1976 and 1977, she both lectured in physics at the Stanford Linear Accelerator Center and became a visiting scientist at the Aspen Center for Physics.

Jackson joined the Theoretical Physics Research Department at AT & T Bell Laboratories in 1976. The research projects at this facility are designed to examine the properties of various materials in an effort to discover useful applications. In 1978, Jackson became part of the Scattering and Low Energy Physics Research Department, then in 1988 she moved to the Solid State and Quantum Physics Research Department. At Bell Labs, Jackson explored theories of charge density waves and the reactions of neutrinos, one type of subatomic particle. In her research, Jackson has made contributions to the knowledge of such areas as charged density waves in layered compounds, polaronic aspects of electrons in the surface of liquid helium films, and optical and electronic properties of semiconductor strained-layer superlattices. On these topics and others she has prepared or collaborated on over 100 scientific articles.

In 1991 she became a professor of physics at Rutgers University. In 1995, while still a professor, Jackson was appointed chair of the Nuclear Regulatory Commission (NRC). Ten months after her appointment, George Galatis, an engineer for Northeast Utilities' nuclear division, which operates five nuclear power plants in New England, blew the whistle on the utility that was cutting costs by ignoring NRC regulations. In the past the NRC had been criticized for failing to enforce its safety rules, but Jackson took immediate action and ordered three plants in Waterford, Connecticut closed because of safety violations. Under Jackson's direction, the commission has become more aggressive about inspections and even forced top NRC officials (ones who had looked the other way when whistleblowers spoke up) to resign or retire. Jackson has not relaxed her policies. Since the Northeast Utilities scandal broke she has ordered several more shutdowns of nuclear

power plants and has stepped up inspections of all nuclear power facilities that it oversees. Jackson reorganized the commission to enable inspectors to detect problems early and allow managers to order changes more quickly.

Jackson has received many scholarships, including the Martin Marietta Aircraft Company Scholarship and Fellowship, the Prince Hall Masons Scholarship, the National Science Foundation Traineeship, and a Ford Foundation Advanced Study Fellowship. She has been elected to the American Physical Society and selected a CIBA-GEIGY Exceptional Black Scientist. In 1985, Governor Thomas Kean appointed her to the New Jersey Commission on Science and Technology. Then in the early 1990s, Governor James Florio awarded her the Thomas Alva Edison Science Award for her contributions to physics and for the promotion of science. Jackson is an active voice in numerous committees of the National Academy of Sciences, the American Association for the Advancement of Science, and the National Science Foundation, where her aim has been to actively promote women in science.

In addition to duties as a professor and government official, Jackson is on the board of trustees at Rutgers and MIT. She is also involved in civic organizations that promote community resources and developing enterprises. She is married to Morris A. Washington, a physicist with Lucent Technologies. They have one son, Alan.

SELECTED WRITINGS BY JACKSON:

Books

"Structurally Induced States from Strain and Confinement," *Semiconductors and Semimetals,* Academic Press, 1990.

Periodicals

"Amplitude Modulation of Discommensurations in Charge Density Wave Structures," *Bulletin of the American Physical Society,* Vol. 22, (1977): 280.
"The Polaronic State of Two Dimensional Electrons on the Surface of Liquid Helium," *Surface Science,* Vol. 142, (1984): 125.
"Frequency Dependent Response of an Electron on a Liquid Helium Film," *Physical Review,* Vol. B31, (1985): 7098.

FURTHER READING:

Books

Carwell, Hattie. *Blacks in Science: Astrophysicist to Zoologist.* Exposition Press, 1977, p. 60.
Notable Black American Women. Gale, 1992, pp. 565–566.

Blacks in Science and Medicine. Hemisphere, 1990, p. 130.

—*Sketch by Barbara A. Branca*

William M. Jackson
1936-
Physical chemist

William Jackson had a number of obstacles to overcome on his path to success. At the age of nine he contracted polio; at 13 his parents divorced. As a graduate student in chemistry he failed his first set of comprehensive chemistry exams. Yet his determination, his love of science, and his talent propelled him into a career as an important researcher in the field of physical chemistry.

Jackson was born in Birmingham, Alabama on September 24, 1936. His father was a teacher who also owned a taxicab company; his mother worked for the U.S. Government and later became a program director at Birmingham's only black radio station. Young Jackson was a good student from an early age, but his bout with polio caused him to miss a year of school.

After his parents divorced, Jackson moved with his mother to Mobile, where he did so well in school that he graduated two years early—and won a Ford Foundation Scholarship. He went to Morehouse College and initially planned to major in mathematics. But when he took a chemistry course with the prominent educator **Henry McBay**, he realized that chemistry was his true passion. Dr. McBay was a tough teacher, but Jackson worked hard and proved his scientific abilities and commitment.

Upon graduating from Morehouse in 1956, Jackson was accepted at several top graduate schools, but he lacked sufficient funds and the schools had already allotted out their fellowship money. He moved to Washington D.C. (where a cousin was living) in the hopes of finding a short-term job. Almost as a whim, he visited Catholic University, home of a highly regarded chemistry department. The department chair looked at Jackson's undergraduate work and was so impressed that he invited him to join Catholic's graduate program—the following week! Fortunately for Jackson, Catholic also still had some fellowship money available.

Jackson did well in his first year, and took a summer position at the U.S. Army's Harry Diamond Laboratory. While there, he studied how chemical compounds were affected by electric currents. After his return to Catholic, Jackson took the required comprehensive exams. He achieved high scores in mathematics and physics—but failed the chemistry exam. He first chose to switch his

major to physics, but by the end of the first semester he and his wife were expecting a child—so money was a concern. A professor suggested he take a job at the National Bureau of Standards, which turned out to be a serendipitous move. Jackson's supervisor steered him toward research that could lead to a dissertation topic, and also encouraged him to re-take the chemistry exam. Jackson examined the chemical effects of burning gasoline to find ways to make it more efficient. He re-took the chemistry comps and passed, and his research earned him his doctorate from Catholic University in 1961.

Jackson worked first at Martin-Marietta, the aerospace firm. But after two years he went back to the National Bureau of Standards to do post-doctoral research; he explored how light beams affect certain chemical compounds. In 1964 he joined the National Aeronautics and Space Administration's (NASA) Goddard Space Flight Center, where he continued his research on light's effects on different molecular structures. He took a leave of absence from NASA in 1969 to do some teaching and research at the University of Pittsburgh. He returned to NASA in 1970, but four years later joined Howard University's chemistry department. He remained there until 1985, when he moved to the University of California at Davis. His later research examined lasers and how they affected molecules.

Jackson has also been active in minority recruitment programs. He serves as director of a $1 million fund at Davis geared at increasing minority participation in science programs.

FURTHER READING:

Books

Kessler, James H., et al. *Distinguished African American Scientists of the Twentieth Century.* Phoenix: Oryx Press, 1996.

—*Sketch by George A. Milite*

Robert S. Jason
1901-1984
Physician and pathologist

Robert S. Jason was the first African American to earn a Ph.D. in pathology. Already a physician, Jason served as head of the department of pathology at Howard University and later as dean of its college of medicine. During his last years at Howard, he was coordinator for design and planning of its new University Hospital. In recognition of his many contributions to the university, the department of pathology at Howard's College of Medicine established in 1967 the Robert S. Jason Award in Pathology.

Robert Stewart Jason was born in Santurce, Puerto Rico on November 29, 1901. He was the son of Reverend Howard Talbot Jason, a Presbyterian missionary who was originally from Maryland, and his missionary wife, Lena B. (Wright) Jason. After attending local schools in Corozal, Puerto Rico and graduating from the Polytechnic Institute of San German, Puerto Rico, Jason entered Lincoln University in Pennsylvania and received his B.A. degree in 1924. He then attended the Howard University College of Medicine in Washington, D.C., and was awarded his M.D. degree in 1928. From the local schools of Puerto Rico through college and medical school, Jason was regularly ranked first in his class. In 1929 he completed his internship at Freedman's Hospital in Washington, D.C., and chose to continue his studies at the University of Chicago, where he was awarded his Ph.D. in pathology in 1932.

During that time, Jason joined the medical faculty at Howard's College of Medicine as an assistant professor of pathology. In 1934 he became associate professor and acting head of the department of pathology, and, by 1937, he was the department head and a full professor as well. He then served as vice dean of the college of medicine from 1946 to 1953, and as dean from 1955 to 1965. In that year he took on a new position as coordinator for the design and planning stages of a new facility to replace Howard's old Freedman's Hospital. He retired as professor emeritus in 1970 and lived in San Diego, California, before moving to New York City in 1979. As a pathologist, he was concerned with the structural and functional changes in cells, tissues, and organs caused by disease, and he focused specifically during his research career on the pathology of syphilis and tuberculosis. As department head and dean, he ran an extremely efficient operation, and these same skills were used to plan and organize Howard's new hospital.

Besides research, teaching, and administration, Jason held many professional appointments. He was a consultant in pathology to the National Institutes of Health from 1955 to 1970, consultant to the Veterans Administration Hospital from 1960 to 1970, member of the International Committee on Health of the Agency for International Development, and member of the National Advisory Council on Education for the Health Professions from 1964 to 1968. Jason also received several honors and awards during his long career. Besides two honorary doctorates and several awards from Howard University, he received the Professional Achievement Award given by the University of Chicago Alumni Association in 1970 and the Distinguished Service Award of the National Medical Association in 1969. Jason considered the most significant honor he received to be Howard University's College of Medicine naming an award after him in 1967. According to the *Journal of the National Medical Association,* "it is presented to a graduating student chosen on the basis of distinguished scholastic achievements, demonstrated interest in fundamental aspects of disease, integrity, self-discipline, and compassion, attributes common to the recipient and Dr. Robert S. Jason."

Jason was a volunteer with the American Cancer Society as well as a member of the American Medical Association, the American Association of Pathologists and Bacteriologists, and the International Academy of Pathologists. He was also a fellow of the College of American Pathologists and belonged to Alpha Omega Alpha (a national medical honor society), Alpha Phi Alpha Fraternity, and the Alpha Pi Boule of Sigma Pi Phi Fraternity.

Jason died of Alzheimer's disease at his home in New York City on April 6, 1984. He was survived by his wife, the former Elizabeth Gaddis, a daughter, Mrs. Jean Elizabeth Wright, a son, Robert S. Jason, Jr. M.D., and one brother and four sisters.

SELECTED WRITINGS BY JASON:

Periodicals

"Howard University and the College of Medicine," *New Physician,* Vol. 8, (1959): 61–70.

"Opportunities, Obligations and Challenges We Cannot Refuse," *Journal of the National Medical Association,* Vol. 61, (1969): 417–21.

FURTHER READING:

Books

Sammons, Vivian O. *Blacks in Science and Medicine.* Hemisphere Publishing, 1990, p. 131.

Periodicals

"Dr. Robert Stewart Jason Awarded Distinguished Service Medal for 1969," *Journal of the National Medical Association,* Vol. 62, (January 1970): 60–61.

"Jason and Harden to New Posts at Howard," *Journal of the National Medical Association,* Vol. 58, (March 1966): 131–32.

Obituary, *Washington Post,* (Saturday, April 14, 1984): B4.

"Robert Stewart Jason, S.R., M.D., Ph.D., D.Sc.: 1901–1984," (Obituary) *Journal of the National Medical Association,* Vol. 76, (September 1984): 934–35.

—*Sketch by Leonard C. Bruno*

James Monroe Jay

James Monroe Jay
1927-
Microbiologist

Microbiologist James Monroe Jay wrote the text *Modern Food Biology* in 1970. A classic relied on by Food Science educators worldwide, by 1996 it had gone into a 5th edition and appeared in Spanish, Hindi, Malaysian, and Chinese, and remains the preferred textbook used by instructors at the college level. *Modern Food Biology* is also widely referenced in the United Kingdom, South Africa, Saudi Arabia, and Israel. Professor Emeritus at Wayne State University and Adjunct Professor at University of Nevada, Las Vegas, Jay is recognized internationally as an authority in the study of meat spoilage.

Jay was born September 12, 1927, in Ben Hill County, Georgia, to John B. Jay, Sr., a minister in the Christian Methodist Episcopal Church, and Lizzie (Wells) Jay, a homemaker. A self-described "naive country boy," Jay knew early that he wanted to study science. According to Jay, his father had hoped for him to become a minister, while his mother encouraged him to pursue dentistry, one day to assume her brother's practice. Still, both supported their son's decision to study natural science.

Jay completed high school in 1945 and served as a sergeant in the United States Army, 1946-47. In 1950, he received his A.B. in Natural Sciences/Mathematics *cum laude* from Paine College in Augusta, Georgia, and enrolled in graduate courses at Western Reserve University in Cleveland, Ohio, with the intention earning a doctorate in chemistry. It was at Western Reserve University, Jay said, that he changed his educational plans, when he took a course in bacteriology and, "fell into it." Encouraged by an associate, he pursued his studies at Ohio State University, Columbus, Ohio in 1952, receiving a Ph.D. in bacteriology/biochemistry in 1956, followed by a postdoctoral fellowship in the Department of Agricultural Biochemistry, 1956-1957.

Jay joined the faculty of Southern University in Baton Rouge, Louisiana as an assistant professor in 1957; in 1961, he moved to Wayne State University in Detroit, Michigan. At Wayne State, Jay rose from assistant to associate professor, and finally to a full professorship in the Department of Biology. He remained there until 1994, the year he was named Professor Emeritus. In 1994, Jay also became adjunct professor in the Department of Biological Sciences at the University of Nevada, Las Vegas.

Notes Ethnic Trend

While at Ohio State University, Jay became intrigued by the relatively low number of blacks pursuing doctorates in mathematical, engineering and, particularly, natural, science. That interest remained with him and evolved into a 12-year study, beginning in 1958, during his tenure at Southern University. There, Jay and his colleagues were frequently called upon to provide, for staff recruitment purposes, the names of black doctorate holders. (According to Louisiana state law at that time, white persons were prohibited from the faculty at Southern University and denied enrollment in its student body.) Jay's compilation of names, along with the scholars' regional origins and educational background, became the subject of an informational text published in 1971, when Jay was at Wayne State University in Detroit.

Titled, *Negroes in Science: Natural Science Doctorates 1876-1969*, the study separated the data into demographic tables arranged and summarized by Jay. These lists include: geographical origins of black doctorate holders, institutions conferring the natural science degrees, and specific area of study. In the preface, Jay states, "It is the author's estimate that approximately 650 American Negroes obtained doctorate degrees in the natural sciences between 1876 and 1969 . . . Depending upon how one views the matter, this number is either extremely low or high. It is low when one considers that over 84,000 natural science doctorates were awarded by American universities between 1920 and 1962. On the other hand, it is a high number when one considers the adversities which the American Negro has had to endure over the years, especially in the area of higher education."

Jay maintains his interest in the numbers of blacks receiving doctorates in the sciences, and has continued to update his studies in the 1980s and 1990s, providing related historical background and encouragement to black Americans with published work and speaking engagements. Jay wrote, *An update on black Americans in the sciences; a bad situation getting worse*, (1988, Trans. National Institute of Science 32: 47), and contributed to the "African-American scientists and inventors" segment of *The African-American Experience*, a 1995 CD-ROM.

Jay's prolific research in the area of meat microbiology earned him an appointment to the United States Department of Agriculture National Advisory Committee for Microbiological Criteria for Foods, where he served from 1987-94. During that period, Jay chaired a subcommittee on consumer education, and was instrumental in developing a pioneering concept incorporated into guidelines used by regulatory agencies for food inspection programs.

Jay's fascination with bacterial growth, development, and interaction has provided material for his authorship or contribution to numerous text and reference books, beginning in the 1950s and continuing through the 1990s. Jay has also served as a reviewer and/or editorial board member of several publications, including *Journal of Food Quality, Journal of Bacteriology, Journal of Food Science, Journal of Food Protection,* and *Journal of Food Microbiology.*

Success in his chosen field has earned Jay recognition from his colleagues and various community organizations. He has received, among other accolades: Distinguished Alumni Award (Paine College, 1969); Probus Award, Probus Club of Metropolitan Detroit, for outstanding achievement in the sciences at Wayne State University, 1969; Founder's Award (Detroit Inter-Alumni Council of the United Negro College Fund, 1986); Michigan Science Trailblazer Award, Detroit, Michigan (1987); **Percy Julian** Award, National Organization for the Advancement of Black Chemists and chemical engineers, Indianapolis, Indiana; Sigma Xi Faculty Research Award for outstanding research (Wayne State University, 1988).

Jay has contributed his expertise to a wide range of panels and subcommittees for the National Science Foundation, the National Institutes of Health, and others, regarding awards for faculty professional development, Women in Science awards, and fellowship and pre-doctoral reviews. He has accepted international invitations to participate in meetings related to food microbiology, including journeys to Rome, Italy (1995), the 42nd International Conference on Meat Science and Technology in Norway (1997), and the World Congress on Food Hygiene in the Netherlands (1997). In 1996, he became a Fellow of the Institute of Food Technologists.

Jay is a member of: Sigma Xi; American Society for Microbiology (Fellow, 1997); American Academy of Arts and Sciences, Institute of Food Technologists, (Fellow, 1996); International Association for Milk, Food and Environmental Sanitation; Society for Industrial Microbiology; and Nevada Public Health Association. Past memberships include: Society for Applied Bacteriology, (1971-94); AAUP, 1962-1986; Corp of United States Public Health

Services (1957-80); American Chemical Society (1965-81); New York Academy of Sciences, 1960-77; American Meat Science Association, 1968-80; Michigan Academy of Arts and Sciences, 1963-78; Beta Beta Beta Biology Honor Society (1958-80); American Public Health Association (1962-82, Fellow, 1966).

Challenges Ethnic Labeling in Achievement

In an April 20, 1998, interview with contributor Virginia Canton, Jay said of his accomplishments, "I am a human being, an American, a male, a father, a scientist. Somewhere in there, I became an ethnic entity. It's human to want to understand what one loves, and I love science—watching and learning about bacteria. As a scientist, I refuse to wear my ethnic heart on my sleeve." In that line, Jay stated that his textbook, *Modern Food Biology*, "is a book that stands on its own."

Jay's post retirement research continues at his home laboratory in Henderson, Nevada. His primary area of study is *Escherichia coli*, the bacterium responsible in 1993 for the devastating outbreak which caused widespread illness and death in Seattle, Washington.

Jay married the former Patsy Phelps on June 6, 1959. They have three children: Mark E., Alicia D., and Byron R.

SELECTED WRITINGS BY JAY:

Books

Modern Food Biology. New York, Canada, 1970: Van Nostrand Reinhold Company.
NEGROES IN SCIENCE: Natural Science Doctorates, 1876-1969. Detroit, 1971, Balamp Publishing.

Periodicals

"Mechanism and detection of microbial spoilage in meats at low temperatures," *Journal of Agricultural Food Chemistry,* 24, (1972): 1113-1116.
"Rapid estimation of microbial numbers in ground beef by use of the Limulus test," *Journal of Food Protection,* 44, (1981): 275-278.
"Microorganisms in fresh ground meats: the relative safety of products with low versus high numbers," *Meat Science,* 43 (S), (1996): 59-66.
"Do background microorganisms play a role in the safety of fresh foods?" *Trends in Food Science Technology* 8, (1997): 421-424.
"Mycology of meat and fish," in *Food and Beverage Mycology,* 1st. ed., Avi Publishers, L.R. Beuchat, ed. Westport, CT, 1978, 129-144, 1978.
"Antibiotics as food preservatives," in *Food Microbiology,* A.H. Rose, ed. Academic Press, NY, 1983, 117-143.

"Analysis of food products for microorganisms or their products . . . nonculture methods," in *Food Analysis: Principles and Techniques,* J.R. Whitaker and D.W. Gruenwedel, eds., Marcel Dekker: NY, 1985, 81-126.

"Microbial quality control standards for processed foods," in *Advances in Food Industries Development in the Arab World,* I.Y. Hamdan, A. El-Nawawy, M. Mameesh, eds., Kuwait Institute for Scientific Research: Kuwait City, 1987, 273-289.

"Indicator organisms in foods," in *Handbook of Foodborne Diseases,* vol. 1, Y.H. Hui, ed., Marcel Dekker, NY, 1994, Chapter 15, 537-546.

FURTHER READING:

Books

Low, W. Augustus, ed., Clift, Virgil A., assoc. ed. *Encyclopedia of Black America.* McGraw-Hill, 1981, xi.

Goff, Neal, et al, R.R. Bowker Database Publishing Group. *American Men & Women of Science 1998-99,* 20th Ed., Vol. 4, J-L, R. R. Bowker, (c1998), p. 63.

Who's Who Among African Americans 1998-99, 10th Edition, Detroit: Gale Research, 1997, p. 777.

Cook, Robert, et. al, ed., *Leaders in American Science* 8th Edition—1968-69. Who's Who in American Education, Inc., 1968.

—*Sketch by Virginia Haskins Canton*

Ambrose Jearld, Jr.
1944-
Marine biologist

When Ambrose Jearld Jr. was a young boy, his ambition was to become a farmer like his uncles with whom he lived in rural North Carolina. Little did he imagine then the guise in which this dream would come true. Because instead of the farmland there is an ocean, and shad, cod, and flounder rather than cotton and tobacco are the primary cash crops. As the chief of research planning and evaluation at the U.S. Department of Commerce's Northeast Fisheries Science Center in Woods Hole, Massachusetts, Jearld is responsible for ensuring the quality and steady supply of various Atlantic fish all across the country.

Jearld was born in Annapolis, Maryland on March 6, 1944. At the time, his father Ambrose Sr., a Naval officer, was away at war and his mother, Katherine Marie Smith, was trying to raise his elder sisters by herself. Soon after his

birth Jearld was sent to North Carolina to live with his grandmother and uncles, where he stayed until he was 10. He then moved back to Annapolis to live with his family. After graduating from high school in 1961 he entered the Maryland State College (later the University of Maryland, Eastern Shore) in Princess Anne where, to help pay his way through school, he took up a job as an assistant in the biology department. He graduated in 1964 with a degree in biology, in addition to a senior biology achievement award. He then worked for a few years in Philadelphia for a chemical company and then enrolled for graduate work in biology at the Oklahoma State University in Stillwater, an institution which, despite its inland location, had an extensive fisheries research program. As a graduate student Jearld joined this program and for his dissertation worked on monitoring various aspects of fish behavior for an ongoing census. His work was interrupted in 1969 when he was drafted to serve in the Vietnam War, but the Army noted his scientific background and stationed him at a research laboratory in Edgewood, Maryland. While stationed there Jearld was able to use his free time to finish his masters degree (received in 1971), and in addition take psychobiology courses in the nearby Johns Hopkins University.

Upon completing military service, Jearld moved back to Oklahoma to work on a Ph.D., which he completed in 1975. He then moved to take up a faculty positions at Lincoln University in Oxford, Pennsylvania (1975-77) and married Anna C. Martin, now an Associate Professor of Social Work at Bridgewater State College in Massachusetts. Summers during these years were spent doing field research in different locations, including San Francisco and New Jersey. After spending one year at Howard University, Jearld accepted a summer appointment at the Northeast Fisheries Center and decided to take up a permanent position there.

His varied career armed Jearld with a broad knowledge base about the behavior of different types of fish under varying environmental stresses and allowed him to assess the growth of the area of fisheries research, both of which stood him in good stead as the new chief of the fishery biology investigation unit at the Woods Hole lab. In his own words during an interview with contributor Neeraja Sankaran, "A particularly interesting feature has been the evolution of marine fisheries biology from a traditional emphasis on assessment of stocks and their dynamics to a more holistic view, perhaps characterized best as fisheries oceanography, aimed at ecosystem understanding, conservation and fisheries resource management." Over the course of his career he was promoted to positions of increasing responsibility and became the regional coordinator of all the fisheries research areas in the Northeast. In recent years he has also been involved in many international issues. Since 1983 he has also held an adjunct appointment at his alma mater in Maryland.

SELECTED WRITINGS BY JEARLD:

Other

Expanding Opportunities in Ocean Sciences: Strengthening the links between HBMSCU undergraduates and oceanic graduate studies Proceedings of a Conference: 11-12 September 1995, Hampton university, Virginia. *Northeast Fisheries Science Center Reference Document* (Available from: National Marine Fisheries Service, 166 Water Street, Woods Hole, MA 02543-1026).

FURTHER READING:

Other

"Speaking of People. Blacks and the Future: Where Will We Be in the Year 2000?" *Ebony Magazine* Special Issue, Vol. XL, No. l0, p. 6.

—*Sketch by Neeraja Sankaran*

Mae C. Jemison

Mae C. Jemison
1956-

Physician and astronaut

Mae C. Jemison had received two undergraduate degrees and a medical degree, had served two years as a Peace Corps medical officer in West Africa, and was selected to join the National Aeronautics and Space Administration's astronaut training program, all before her thirtieth birthday. Her eight-day space flight aboard the space shuttle *Endeavour* in 1992 established Jemison as the United States' first female African American space traveler.

Mae Carol Jemison was born on October 17, 1956, in Decatur, Alabama, the youngest child of Charlie Jemison, a roofer and carpenter, and Dorothy (Green) Jemison, an elementary school teacher. Her sister, Ada Jemison Bullock, became a child psychiatrist, and her brother, Charles Jemison, is a real estate broker. The family moved to Chicago, Illinois, when Jemison was three to take advantage of better educational opportunities there, and it is that city that she calls her hometown. Throughout her early school years, her parents were supportive and encouraging of her talents and abilities, and Jemison spent considerable time in her school library reading about all aspects of science, especially astronomy. During her time at Morgan Park High School, she became convinced she wanted to pursue a career in biomedical engineering, and when she graduated in 1973 as a consistent honor student, she entered Stanford University on a National Achievement Scholarship.

At Stanford, Jemison pursued a dual major and in 1977 received a B.S. in chemical engineering and a B.A. in African and Afro-American Studies. As she had been in high school, Jemison was very involved in extracurricular activities including dance and theater productions, and served as head of the Black Student Union. Upon graduation, she entered Cornell University Medical College to work toward a medical degree. During her years there, she found time to expand her horizons by visiting and studying in Cuba and Kenya and working at a Cambodian refugee camp in Thailand. When she obtained her M.D. in 1981, she interned at Los Angeles County/University of Southern California Medical Center and later worked as a general practitioner. For the next two and a half years, she was the area Peace Corps medical officer for Sierra Leone and Liberia where she also taught and did medical research. Following her return to the U.S. in 1985, she made a career change and decided to follow a dream she had nurtured for a long time. In October of that year she applied for admission to NASA's astronaut training program. The *Challenger* disaster of January 1986 delayed the selection process, but when she reapplied a year later, Jemison was one of the 15 candidates chosen from a field of about 2,000.

Joins Eight-Day *Endeavour* Mission

When Jemison was chosen on June 4, 1987, she became the first African American woman ever admitted into the astronaut training program. After more than a year of training, she became an astronaut with the title of science-mission specialist, a job which would make her responsible for conducting crew-related scientific experiments on the space shuttle. On September 12, 1992, Jemison finally flew into space with six other astronauts aboard the *Endeavour* on mission STS–47. During her eight days in space, she conducted experiments on weightlessness and motion sickness on the crew and herself. Altogether, she spent slightly over 190 hours in space before returning to Earth on September 20. Following her historic flight, Jemison noted that society should recognize how much both women and members of other minority groups can contribute if given the opportunity.

In recognition of her accomplishments, Jemison received several honorary doctorates, the 1988 *Essence* Science and Technology Award, the *Ebony* Black Achievement Award in 1992, and a Montgomery Fellowship from Dartmouth College in 1993, and was named Gamma Sigma Gamma Woman of the Year in 1990. Also in 1992, an science and technology public school in Detroit, Michigan—the Mae C. Jemison Academy—was named after her. Jemison is a member of the American Medical Association, the American Chemical Society, the American Association for the Advancement of Science, and served on the Board of Directors of the World Sickle Cell Foundation from 1990 to 1992. She is also an advisory committee member of the American Express Geography Competition and an honorary board member of the Center for the Prevention of Childhood Malnutrition. After leaving the astronaut corps in March 1993, she accepted a teaching fellowship at Dartmouth and also established the Jemison Group, a company that seeks to research, develop, and market advanced technologies. The former astronaut also conducted the first annual International Space Camp in 1994.

FURTHER READING:

Books

Hawthorne, Douglas B. *Men and Women of Space.* Univelt, 1992, pp. 357–359.

Smith, Jessie Carney, ed. *Notable Black American Women.* Gale, 1992, pp. 571–573.

—Sketch by Leonard C. Bruno

Halle Tanner Dillon Johnson
1864-1901
Physician

Halle Tanner Dillon Johnson was recruited by Booker T. Washington as a resident physician for the Tuskegee Institute in Alabama and was the first woman to earn a medical doctor's license in the state.

Johnson was born in Pittsburgh, Pennsylvania, on October 17, 1864, the first of nine children born to Benjamin T. and Sara Elizabeth Miller Tanner. The Tanners were well educated and advocates of the arts, education, and intellectual achievement. Benjamin Tanner, a graduate of Avery College, was a minister of note who rose to a bishopric in the African Methodist Church. Prior to her marriage, Sara Tanner was a teacher. Halle was not the only child in the family to shine in their respectful fields of endeavor; Henry Ossawa Tanner became a celebrated painter, recognized primarily for his landscapes, and Carlton Tanner was ordained and became a well-known church leader.

In addition to his ministry, Benjamin Tanner served as the first editor of the Christian Recorder, and Halle served as a staff member for the publication. At the age of 22, she married Charles E. Dillon; their only child, Sadie, was born in 1887, the year after their marriage. Charles Dillon died shortly after, although the exact date and circumstances of his death are not known. Halle Dillon returned to the Tanner home in Philadelphia with her daughter.

At the age of 24, the young widow decided to enroll in the Woman's Medical College of Pennsylvania. The only black student in a class of 36 women, she graduated with honors from the three-year course in May 1891.

At the same time, Booker T. Washington was searching for a black resident physician for the Tuskegee Institute. The dean of the Woman's Medical College recommended Dillon. Washington offered room and board and a salary of $600 per year for duties that included teaching two daily classes, managing the health department, and preparing medications. The physician would be permitted to develop a private practice for additional income.

Intrigued by the challenge, Dillon agreed to sit for the Alabama licensing exam. Her decision attracted public attention at a time when women were generally discouraged from pursuing medical careers. She was the first black woman to sit for Alabama's medical boards, and this drew notice from the newspapers, sparking public debates.

Dillon underwent a 10-day trial in which she was tested on a different subject each day. She felt her performance was more critically evaluated than that of other applicants, and she was quoted in the Atlanta University Bulletin as saying "The critical medical pen has been perhaps too rigorously applied." Dillon passed with a respectable score, though, and she became the first woman of any race to be licensed to practice medicine in Alabama.

Dillon served as resident physician at Tuskegee from 1891 to 1894. During her relatively short tenure, she not only provided direct patient care, but established the Lafayette Dispensary to serve the health care needs of the campus and community. She also founded a nurses' training school at the institute.

At Tuskegee, she met a mathematics instructor, the Rev. John Quincy Johnson. They married in 1894; in 1895, Johnson accepted the presidency of Allen University, a private college for blacks in Columbia, South Carolina. Johnson, who held a doctorate of divinity from Morris Brown College in Atlanta, Georgia, later completed postgraduate work at Princeton Theological Seminary. The couple moved to Nashville, Tennessee in 1900 when Rev. Johnson was named pastor of Saint Paul AME Church. The new Mrs. Johnson apparently gave up medical practice when she left Tuskegee. In Nashville records, her occupation was listed as homemaker.

In their seven years of marriage, the couple welcomed sons John Quincy Jr., Benjamin T., and Henry Tanner. Johnson did not live to see her sons grow up; she died of complications from childbirth, worsened by dysentery, on April 26, 1901, at the age of 37.

FURTHER READING:

Books

Hine, Darlene Clark, ed. *Black Women in America: An Historical Encyclopedia, Vol. 1.* Brooklyn, NY: Carlson Publishing, 1993.

Rywell, Martin, ed. *Afro-American Encyclopedia, Vol. 5.* North Miama, Florida: Educational Book Publishers, 1974.

Sammons, Vivian Ovelton. *Blacks in Science and Medicine* New York: Hemisphere Publishing, 1990.

Smith, Jessie Carney, ed. *Notable Black American Women* Detroit: Gale Research, 1992.

Periodicals

Atlanta Univeristy. *Bulletin,* (1891).

Other

Johnson, Halle Tanner Dillon. *Collected Papers* University of Pennsylvania Archives.

—Sketch by A. Mullig

John B. Johnson, Jr.
1908-1972

Physician and cardiologist

John B. Johnson, Jr. was one of the first African American physicians to assume a leadership position as department chairman of the Howard University Medical College. A pioneer in the diagnostic use of angiocardiography and cardiac catheterization, he also was one of two African American physicians appointed to Georgetown University Hospital's staff in 1954 as part of a successful effort to offer District of Columbia physicians equal opportunity.

John Beauregard Johnson, Jr., was born in Bessemer, Alabama, on April 29, 1908. He was the eldest of three sons of John B., Sr., a postman, and his wife Leona Duff Johnson. After completing high school at Tuskegee Institute, Alabama, he attended Oberlin College in Ohio, and earned a letter in track as well as his B.A. degree in 1931. From there, he went directly to medical school at Western Reserve University in Cleveland and earned his M.D. there in 1935. After serving his internship at Cleveland City Hospital, he went to Howard University in 1936 as a laboratory assistant in physiology and spent his entire career in that institution. The following year he joined the Department of Medicine as an assistant and became an instructor in 1938.

When Johnson first joined Howard, its Dean, **Numa P. G. Adams**, was beginning to search for well-trained young physicians to staff the medical school's full-time clinical faculty. Adams selected Johnson as a promising potential candidate for leadership in the medical school, and sent him to the University of Rochester in 1939 for two years of postgraduate study in internal medicine. Johnson was given a General Education Board Fellowship. Upon returning to Howard, Johnson became director of Clinical Laboratories in 1941 and was made acting chair of the Department of Medicine from 1944 to 1949. During those years, Johnson spent one year at the Columbia University Division of Bellevue Hospital in New York under another General Education Board fellowship. In 1954, Johnson and another African American physician, Dr. R. Frank Jones, were appointed to the staff of Georgetown University Hospital. This marked a major breakthrough in the long campaign to secure parity of opportunity for minority physicians in the District of Columbia. At Howard, Johnson ended his career as the director of its Division of Cardiology.

As a cardiologist, or specialist in the treatment of heart disease, Johnson was an early proponent of angiocardiography, which is a diagnostic procedure that x rays the heart and its vessels after an intravenous injection of dye has been administered. The resulting picture shows blockages and abnormalities in the circulatory system. He also pioneered the technique of cardiac catheterization, in which a catheter—a thin, flexible tube—is inserted into the heart itself through a major vein in the arm. Johnson employed this technique to obtain samples of blood in the heart, to discover its abnormalities, and to determine the pressure of the heart itself. In addition, the physician studied hypertension—high blood pressure—and its disproportionate effects on African Americans. Johnson excelled in his field and published 64 papers during his career. One of these was awarded a citation from the journal *Angiology Research* for the Outstanding Publication of 1966.

As an educator, Johnson was described as an excellent teacher with infectious energy and enthusiasm whose lectures were both dramatic and exciting, as well as an individual who drove himself hard. He served on the board of directors of the American Heart Association from 1958 to 1961, and was awarded the Distinguished Service Medal of the National Medical Association. Twice he received the Susan B. and Theodore Cummings Humanitarian Award of the American College of Cardiology, in 1964 and 1965. After his retirement, the Howard University College of Medicine voted unanimously to name a chair after him. Its incumbent has the title of John Beauregard Johnson Professor of Medicine. When Johnson died in Freedman's Hospital on December 16, 1972, after a cerebral hemorrhage, he was survived by his third wife, Audrey Ingram Johnson, a stepdaughter, Adrienne, and a daughter from his second marriage, Linda.

SELECTED WRITINGS BY JOHNSON:

Periodicals

"Observations of the Effect of Pyrogens in the Treatment of Patients with Hypertension," *Journal of the American Medical Association,* Vol. 43, (1951): 300.
"Arteriovenous Fistula and Multiple Saccular Arterial Aneurysms of a Finger, Following Childhood Human Bite," *Angiology Research,* 16, no. 89, (1965).
"Hearts Too Good to Die—Problems in Acute Myocardial Infarction," *Journal of the National Medical Association,* 59, no. 1, (1967).

FURTHER READING:

Books

Dictionary of American Medical Biography, Vol. I, 1984, p. 397.

Periodicals

Cobb, W. Montague. "John Beauregard Johnson, M.D., D.Sc., F.A.C.P., 1908–1972," *Journal of the National Medical Association,* (March 1973): 166–170.
"Dr. J. B. Johnson, Medical Professor Howard U., Dies," *Jet,* (January 4, 1973): 17.
"Wide-Awake Patients Given Heart Surgery," *Evening Star,* (Washington, D.C.), (April 17, 1959).

—*Sketch by Leonard C. Bruno*

Joseph Lealand Johnson
1895-1991
Physiologist and physician

Joseph Lealand Johnson was the second African American to earn both a Ph.D. and an M.D. degree. Although his parents had been born into slavery in North Carolina, Johnson was able to secure an education and eventually became dean of the Howard University Medical School and chairman of its Department of Physiology. It was through his efforts that this department became a fully modernized place of research.

Johnson was born in Philadelphia, Pennsylvania, on January 14, 1895. His parents had moved there from North Carolina and eventually had 14 children. Johnson was the youngest of the 10 that survived infancy. His father was a laborer who died when Johnson was two, and his mother supported the family as a midwife. Although the 10-year-old Johnson was so interested in the law that he would regularly cut school to attend trials at City Hall, he took the advice of his high school principal and applied for a scholarship in agronomy at Pennsylvania State University. "I knew I first had to get to college if I wanted to study law," Johnson recalled later in an interview with Allen B. Weisse in *Conversations in Medicine,* "and this was the first step."

Upon admission, Johnson found himself to be the only black on the entire campus. His education was interrupted by World War I, and when Johnson discovered there were no officer training camps available to him as there were for his white classmates, he wrote directly to the Secretary of War. The Secretary responded that a special camp was being formed at Fort Des Moines, Iowa. Johnson joined up, was commissioned second lieutenant, and was assigned to the 350th Field Artillery at Fort Dix, New Jersey. After being honorably discharged in January, 1919, he returned to Penn State and received his B.S. degree in June of that year.

That autumn, Johnson began teaching at the Kansas Vocational and Industrial Institute in Topeka, Kansas, where he also was an assistant coach of the men's basketball team as well as coach of the women's basketball team. The next year he moved to Kansas City to teach general science and zoology at Lincoln High School. It was while attending a summer education course at the University of Chicago that Johnson first became interested in medicine as a way of helping the people of his poor Kansas City neighborhood called West Bottoms. "I got the feeling that those people were not getting the medical care that they should have because they couldn't afford it," Johnson explained to Weisse. "The idea struck me that I would go away and prepare myself thoroughly in medicine, and then come back to Kansas City and serve the people in the West Bottoms." With the help of the Lincoln High School principal who secured the backing of a wealthy friend, Johnson was able to resign from teaching and to dedicate himself to medical school.

By 1931, Johnson had earned his combined M. D. and Ph.D. degree in medicine and physiology at the University of Chicago. He was offered a physiology professorship at Howard University in Washington, D.C., by Dr. Numa P. G. Adams who had just become the first black dean of its medical school. Johnson accepted the offer, and it was under his guidance and direction that Howard's physiology department was completely revamped, renovated, and redirected into a modern facility where meaningful research could take place. When Dr. Adams died suddenly in 1940, Johnson became acting dean of Howard's medical school. In 1947 he became dean and remained in that position until 1955 when he returned to full-time teaching and research in physiology. He retired in 1971.

Johnson was a member of the board of directors of the National Medical Association and a member of the Medico Chirurgical Society of the District of Columbia. He also held memberships in the AAAS, NAACP, AMA, Foundation for Tropical Medicine, International College of Surgeons, Walter Reed Society, American Physiology Society, and was a fellow of the New York Academy of Sciences. He was a member of the honorary medical society, Alpha Omega Alpha, and Alpha Phi Alpha fraternity. He also served as the 1960–61 Imhotep Conference Chairman. Johnson died of cancer in Silver Spring, Maryland, in 1991.

FURTHER READING:

Books

Weisse, Allen B., ed. *Conversations in Medicine,* New York University Press, 1984, pp. 231–254.

Periodicals

Jet, (January 14, 1991): 18.

—*Sketch by Leonard C. Bruno*

Edith Mae Irby Jones
1927-
Physician and health administrator

Edith Irby Jones is an accomplished internist who was the first black student to attend racially mixed university classes in the South and the first to receive her medical degree from the University of Arkansas School of Medicine. Despite the discriminatory racial policies of the university and the South in general, Jones finished in the upper half of her class. From 1959-62, Jones was the first African American to participate in Baylor Affiliated Hospital's (Houston) internal medicine resident program. In 1975, she was appointed as the first woman to chair the National Medical Association's Council on Scientific Assembly; from 1984-86, she served as that organization's first woman president. Some credit a speech by Jones as being instrumental in former Surgeon General **Jocelyn Elders'** decision to study medicine.

Edith was born to Robert and Mattie (Buice) Irby, on December 23, 1927, in Conway, Arkansas. Her father died when she was eight years old, and her mother, employed as a cook, moved the family to Hot Springs. Edith's interest in health care was influenced in part by the loss of two siblings to typhoid fever. Observing the people who arrived in Hot Springs seeking medical benefit from its mineral waters furthered her desire to help. She came to believe that the best path to a healthy adulthood began with a healthy childhood, and she initially planned to study pediatrics.

Jones graduated from Langston High School in 1944. She received her bachelor of science degree from Knoxville College in Knoxville, Tennessee. Aided by the financial support of Langston High School alumni and Little Rock's black newspaper, the *State Press,* Jones attended the University of Arkansas School of Medicine. She received her medical degree in 1952. Jones opened a general practice in Hot Springs in 1953, which she operated until 1959, when she entered the residency program at Baylor Affiliated Hospital in Houston. In 1962, Jones established a private practice in Houston's Third Ward district. After pursuing studies at West Virginia College of Medicine (1965) and Cook County Graduate School (1966), Jones served as chief of cardiology at St. Elizabeth's Hospital in Houston and then associate chief of medicine at Riverside General Hospital.

In 1960, Jones married James B. Jones, whom she says was "both mentor and protector" until his death in 1989. The couple established a real estate business which purchased and renovated homes and then rented them to low-income families at rates substantially below market levels. Their efforts continue to be maintained by family members, and Jones is actively involved with Habitat for Humanity. In a telephone interview with contributor Virginia Canton, Jones expressed her commitment to working with people at the poverty level: "I had poor housing, and I resolved that if I ever got any money, I'd do my part" to help others in similar circumstances. Jones has not only fulfilled that pledge, but expanded on it, through memberships and financial contributions to numerous housing and educational programs in the United States as well as to the annual African-American Summit. In 1986, she started a clinic in Haiti, and in 198, she initiated an emergency-care program in Vera Cruz, Mexico.

A personal highlight, Jones says, was attending the forty-fifth reunion of the class of 1952 at the University of Arkansas School of Medicine. "In the beginning, it was predicted that I would not even finish the first year, and not only was I welcomed, but I was selected as the alumni liaison for the class, because I know everyone." As a student, she recalled, "any isolation I experienced came from how others felt about themselves. Once they got to know me, they were inclusive." Jones has received numerous university, state, and city awards and citations, most notably from the city of Houston and the state of Texas. In 1986, Houston honored her with Edith Irby Jones Day. In 1988, Jones was selected as the American Society of Medicine Internist of the Year. In 1998, the ambulatory center at the former Southeast Memorial Hospital was named in her honor.

Jones continues her private practice in Houston, where she resides. She is a member of the clinical faculty at Baylor College of Medicine. She has three children, Gary, Myra, and Keith, and seven grandchildren. Jones says her enthusiasm for life and helping others remains high, and she maintains that individual involvement—from financial gifts to a simple handshake and kind word—are essential to keeping that spirit alive. In her words, "People are hungry for being motivated and need anything positive to move them forward."

FURTHER READING:

Books

Smith, Jessie Carney, ed. *Notable Black American Women, Book II*. Detroit: Gale Research, 1996.

—*Sketch by Virginia H. Canton*

Eleanor Green Dawley Jones
1929-
Mathematician

In 1966 Eleanor Green Dawley Jones was one of the first black women to receive a doctorate in mathematics from a university in the United States. Jones, who says that she "cannot recall a time when I did not expect to become a teacher," has taught mathematics at Norfolk State University in Virginia for much of her career. She has served as a board member and officer of mathematics organizations and on committees shaping the undergraduate mathematics curriculum. She has also been active in encouraging minorities and women to pursue careers in mathematics and the sciences.

Jones was born in Norfolk, Virginia on August 12, 1929. She was the second of six children of George Herbert Green, a letter carrier, and Lillian (Vaughn) Green, who had been a domestic worker before her marriage. Both her parents had high academic expectations of their children, and all six would earn at least a bachelor's degree.

In 1945, Jones graduated as valedictorian of Booker T. Washington High School, a segregated public school in Norfolk. Mathematics was her favorite subject. She entered Howard University with a one-year scholarship from the university and a four-year scholarship from the Pepsi-Cola Corporation. As a mathematics major, she took classes from **Elbert Cox**, the first black to receive a doctorate in pure mathematics in the United States, and other black mathematicians with doctorates, including **David Blackwell**. Jones minored in education and physics. Upon graduating *cum laude* from Howard in 1949, Jones received a fellowship to study for a master's degree in mathematics, which she completed in 1950.

In 1950, Jones began teaching at Washington High School in Norfolk. In addition to teaching, she helped compile a curriculum guide for the secondary mathematics program. In 1951 she married Edward Armistead Dawley, Jr. a lawyer. She left teaching in 1953 due to the birth of their son, Edward Armistead III. Their second son, Herbert Green, was born the next year. Jones returned to teaching mathematics as an instructor at Hampton Institute near Norfolk in 1955. In 1957, formerly all-white schools were ordered to admit black students, and the public schools in Norfolk were closed. Battles over school segregation left black students in Norfolk without a school to attend; Jones tutored some of these students at the First Baptist Church in Norfolk. She was also vice chairman of CORE in Virginia from 1958-60.

To obtain a tenured position at Hampton Institute, Jones needed a doctoral degree. At that time, Virginia did not admit blacks to doctoral studies in the state but gave tuition and travel grants for studies elsewhere. In 1962, following a divorce, Jones went to Syracuse University in New York with her sons. She had a stipend from Hampton Institute and worked as a grader to support her family. The next year she received a National Science Foundation faculty fellowship, and from then on she worked as a teaching assistant at Syracuse until she received her doctorate in 1966. Her thesis on algebra, written under James D. Reid, was titled "Abelian Groups and Their Endomorphism Rings and the Quasi-Endomorphisms of Torsion Free Abelian Groups." An abstract of Jones's dissertation appeared in the *American Mathematical Monthly* in May 1967.

Jones returned to Hampton as an associate professor for the 1966-67 academic year. In June 1967, she married Everette Benjamin Jones, a pharmacist. They had one son, Everette Benjamin Jones, Jr. This second marriage was ended in divorce after 15 years. In 1967, Jones joined the mathematics department at Norfolk State University, as associate professor of mathematics. She has taught at Norfolk for more than 30 years. She usually teaches calculus, abstract algebra, linear algebra, and contemporary mathematics for nonscience majors. Jones has continued her education in mathematics by doing summer postgraduate courses at New York University in 1957, at University of Southern California in 1959 and 1960, and at University of Oregon in abstract algebra in 1971.

Jones has been Virginia representative for the National Association of Mathematicians since 1973. She served as vice president of that organization from 1975-79, on their nominating committee in 1984, as a member of their board of directors from 1988-94, and as chair of the legislation and nominating committee from 1990-94. She received the National Association of Mathematicians' Distinguished Service Award in 1994. Jones was on the board of governors of the Mathematical Association of America from 1983-86, and she has served on committees on mathematics remediation and teaching undergraduate mathematics. She has also contributed papers to this association. She was a board member of the Association for Women in Mathematics from 1989-94, and since 1990 she has served on a committee of the American Mathematical Society on opportunities in mathematics for underrepresented minorities. Jones was elected to the science honor society Sigma Xi at Syracuse in 1965 and became a full member in 1985.

Jones has been a speaker and consultant on the college mathematics curriculum and for events designed to interest and encourage women and minorities to follow careers in mathematics and science. She has also written about her experiences as a black woman mathematician. In 1981, Jones was a reviewer for course-improvement proposals for the National Science Foundation (NSF). In 1991, she was an evaluator for NSF minority fellowships for graduate research. She was a reader for the college board advanced placement test in calculus from 1989-94.

SELECTED WRITINGS BY JONES:

Books

"A Note on Abelian P-Groups and Their Endomorphism Rings." *Black Mathematicians and Their Works.* Newell, V.K., et. al., eds. Ardmore, Pennsylvania: Dorrance, 1980.
"A Minority Woman's Viewpoint." *Winning Women into Mathematics.* Patricia C. Kenschaft, ed. Mathematical Association of America, 1991.

Periodicals

(Co-author) "Black Women Mathematicians." *Association for Women in Mathematics Newsletter* (September 1978).
(Co-author) "Report of the Committee on Improving Remediation Efforts in Colleges." *American Mathematical Monthly.* (March 1981): 230-3.

FURTHER READING

Books

American Men and Women of Science, 1995-96, 19th Edition. New Providence, NJ: Bowker, 1994.

Percy Lavon Julian

Sammons, Vivian Ovelton. *Blacks in Science and Medicine.* New York: Hemisphere, 1990.

Periodicals

Kenschaft, Patricia C. "Black Women in Mathematics in the United States." *American Mathematical Monthly* (October 1981): 592-604.

—*Sketch by Sally M. Moite*

Percy Lavon Julian
1899-1975
Organic chemist

Percy Lavon Julian is best known for discovering how to synthesize physostigmine, a chemical used to treat the eye disease glaucoma. He also developed an economical method for producing sterols, making it possible for many people with arthritis to afford cortisone. An African American who eventually grew frustrated with the discrimination he faced in academia, Julian turned to industry and worked at the Glidden Company in Chicago, Illinois, before starting his own business.

Julian was born in Montgomery, Alabama, on April 11, 1899, to James and Elizabeth Adams Julian. His father was a railway clerk and his mother a schoolteacher. His paternal grandfather was a former slave who had two fingers cut off his right hand for learning to write. Julian was one of six children, all of whom went to universities and graduated with higher degrees. Julian attended public school until the eighth grade, but, because there was only one public high school in Alabama that accepted African American students, he attended a private school called the State Normal School. He graduated at the top of his class in 1916 and was admitted to DePauw University in Greencastle, Indiana. His high school education had not been satisfactory, however, and for two years he had to take remedial classes in addition to a regular course load. He lived in the attic of a fraternity house during this time and earned money by waiting on tables downstairs. He also played in a jazz band and tended furnaces. Despite his heavy workload, Julian graduated in 1920 with a degree in chemistry; he was class valedictorian and a member of Phi Beta Kappa.

When Julian had decided to major in chemistry, his father had tried to persuade him to become a physician instead, feeling that Julian would not find many career opportunities in chemistry beyond teaching because of his ethnicity. His father's concerns proved well-founded. Although Julian wanted to go to graduate school, the head of his department was told that an African American would not find work in the field; Julian was denied fellowships by the same people who had been his role models.

Julian taught chemistry at Fisk University in Nashville, Tennessee, for the next two years. In 1922, he received the Austin Fellowship in chemistry at Harvard University, which enabled him to earn his master's degree in chemistry by 1923. However, afraid that white students from the American South would object to an African American teacher, Harvard did not offer Julian a teaching assistantship, despite his high grades. Julian took various research assistantships in order to continue to work toward his doctorate. He stayed at Harvard until 1926, studying biophysics and organic chemistry.

From 1926 to 1927, Julian taught at West Virginia State College, and in 1928 he went to Howard University in Washington, D.C., as associate professor and head of the Department of Chemistry. By this time, Julian had begun to follow the research that was being done at the University of Vienna by Ernst Spath, who had developed methods for synthesizing nicotine and ephedrine. In 1929, Julian received a fellowship from the General Education Board and went to Vienna to study with Spath. While there, he became interested in the soya bean, which was then being used in Germany to manufacture certain drugs, including physostigmine and sex hormones. In 1931, he received his Ph.D. from the University of Vienna. When he returned to Howard, he resumed his teaching and was promoted to full professor.

Succeeds in Synthesizing Physostigmine

Working with two colleagues from Vienna who had come back to Howard with him, Julian began to investigate the structure and synthesis of physostigmine, which was used to treat glaucoma, an eye disease that eventually leads to blindness by slowly damaging the retina. In 1932, just as he and his colleagues began to see some results, a disagreement with the Howard administration forced Julian to leave. A former professor arranged for Julian to return to DePauw as a research fellow and teacher of organic chemistry. There he was able to identify the chemicals that lead to the formation of physostigmine. In 1934, he presented his findings to the American Chemical Society, challenging the work of Robert Robinson, the head of the chemistry department at Oxford University. By February, 1935, Julian had accomplished the first synthesis of physostigmine, proving his method and research correct.

Despite his successes, Julian continued to face discrimination; he was denied two positions, one at DePauw and one at the University of Minnesota, on the basis of his race. He decided to seek employment at an industrial laboratory and accepted a position as director of research and chief chemist at the Glidden Company in Chicago, becoming the first African American in United States history to direct a major industrial laboratory.

In 1936, a milk protein called casein was being used to coat paper. Because this was expensive, Julian's first task at Glidden was to extract the soya bean protein, which was cheaper but equally effective, for use in textiles, paints, and paper coating. The results of his work proved profitable for Glidden, and in one year the company went from a deficit of $35,000 to a profit of $135,000. Julian's experiments with soya protein also yielded a new product, "Aero Foam," which was used to extinguish oil and gas fires.

Develops Methods for Manufacturing Sex Hormones and Cortisone

One of Julian's most important achievements was the synthesis of sex hormones from sterols extracted from soya beans. Progesterone was used to prevent miscarriages, while testosterone was used to treat older men for diminishing sex drive. Both hormones were also important in the treatment of cancer. Traditionally, these hormones were made using cholesterol from the brains and spinal cords of cattle. German scientists had developed a process to extract sterols from the soya bean and convert them into hormones, but it was slow and very expensive. From watching how plaster of Paris puffed up into a porous, foamy mass after the addition of quicklime, Julian developed a method to convert the soya bean oil into a porous foam from which sterols could be easily extracted. He was able to synthesize progesterone and testosterone from the sterols, increasing the supply of these chemicals and reducing their cost.

Cortisone had recently been found to be effective in treating rheumatoid arthritis, but its method of production made it extremely expensive and beyond the reach of most patients: it took the bile of 14,600 oxen to produce enough cortisone to treat one patient for one year. Julian perfected an economical method for synthesizing cortexolone from soya beans. The difference between cortisone and cortexolone, which Julian called Substance S, was one oxygen atom; he devised a method to add this missing atom to cortexolone and the resulting synthetic cortisone was just as effective in the treatment of arthritis as the organic form.

In 1954, Julian left Glidden to open his own plant and company, Julian Laboratories Inc., in Chicago, and the Laboratorios Julian de Mexico in Mexico City, Mexico. He had found that using wild yams was more effective than soya beans in the production of Substance S, and within a few years Julian Laboratories had become of one of the world's leaders in the production of drugs using wild yams. In 1961, Julian sold his Oak Park plant to Smith, Kline, & French. He stayed on as president until 1964, when he founded the Julian Research Institute and Julian Associates Inc. in Franklin Park, Illinois.

In 1947, Julian received the National Association for the Advancement of Colored People's Spingarn Medal; in 1949, he was presented with the Distinguished Service Award from the Phi Beta Kappa Association for his work with Substance S and synthetic cortisone. In 1990, Julian was elected to the National Inventors Hall of Fame, along with agricultural chemist **George Washington Carver**. They were the first African Americans to be so honored since the institution was created in 1973.

Julian married Anna Johnson, who had a Ph.D. in sociology, on December 24, 1935. They had two children, a girl and a boy. Julian continued to investigate synthetic drugs and the chemistry of various substances until his death in 1975.

Ernest Everett Just

Periodicals

Cobb, W. Montague. "Percy Lavon Julian," *Journal of the National Medical Association,* (March 1971): 143–147.

—Sketch by Geeta Kothari

SELECTED WRITINGS BY JULIAN:

Periodicals

"Studies in the Indole Series. V. The Complete Synthesis of Physostigmine (Eserine)," *Journal of American Chemistry Society,* 57, (1935): 755.
"Process for the Recovering of Sterols," *Chemistry Abstracts,* 36, (1942): 3692.
"Procedure for the Preparation of Progesterone," *Chemistry Abstracts,* 42, (1948): 1710.

FURTHER READING:

Books

Current Biography. H. W. Wilson, 1947, pp. 29–31.
Haber, Louis. *Black Pioneers of Science and Invention.* Harcourt, 1970, pp. 86–101.
Toppin, Edgar Allen. *A Biographical History of Blacks in America since 1528.* McKay, 1971, pp. 341–343.

Ernest Everett Just
1883-1941
Zoologist and marine biologist

Ernest Everett Just was a zoologist who did groundbreaking work on the embryology of marine invertebrates. He conducted research on fertilization, as well as the development of eggs without fertilization—a process known as parthenogenesis—but his most important achievement was probably his discovery of the role the protoplasm plays in the development of a cell. As an African American, Just conducted his research despite widespread discrimination, and he spent most of his career at Howard University when that institution was still little more than a college, with few graduate students and fewer facilities. In addition to his international reputation as a zoologist, Just was a dedicated teacher whose scientific successes inspired many younger men and women. In *Black Pioneers of Science and Invention,* Louis Haber calls him "Howard's vindication before the scientific world."

Just was born on August 14, 1883, in Charleston, South Carolina, to Charles and Mary Cooper Just. His father was a dock builder who died when Just was still a young boy, and his mother was a schoolteacher who supervised his education. After sending him to the Colored Normal, Industrial, Agricultural and Mechanical College in South Carolina, she enrolled him at a northern preparatory school called Kimball Union Academy, in Meriden, New Hampshire. Just did extremely well there, completing the four-year course in three years, while serving as editor of the school newspaper and president of the debating society.

He then entered Dartmouth College, which was only a few miles away from Kimball. Here, he found himself the only black in a freshman class of 288 students. Although he performed exceptionally well in Greek during his first year, he majored in biology the next year, and by the time he graduated with an B.A. degree in 1907, he had taken all the courses the college offered in that subject. He had even supplied studies and drawings on frog embryo formation for a zoology textbook being written by the head of the biology department, William Patten. In recognition of his superior performance as an undergraduate, he was elected to Phi Beta Kappa; he also received special honors in zoology and history, and he was the only student in his class to graduate *magna cum laude.* Upon graduation, he gained a teaching appointment at Howard University in Washington, D.C., first in the English department, and then as professor of zoology and physiology in its medical school.

Makes Start at Woods Hole Laboratory

Although he was now teaching Just had no higher degrees, and he began his graduate training in 1909 at the Marine Biological Laboratory (MBL) in Woods Hole, Massachusetts. This world-famous research institution gives scientists an opportunity to pursue their investigations during the summer months without the interruptions of teaching or other duties. Just's teaching load at Howard was very heavy, and for the next 20 years he would do most of his research here. He found Woods Hole an ideal place to study marine organisms, and he was often called upon for advice by other scientific investigators. In 1911, he became a research assistant to the director of the MBL, Frank Rattray Lillie, who was also head of the zoology department at the University of Chicago. Their research focused on the fertilization process in the sandworm *Nereis;* in 1912, Just published his first paper, describing the results of research which showed that when the fertilized egg of the *Nereis* undergoes its first cleavage division, the polar bodies determine the plane of development of the embryo, together with the point of entrance of the spermatozoon.

Just's research on fertilization won him the first Spingarn Medal awarded by the National Association for the Advancement of Colored People. Designed to honor men and women of African descent, it was presented to him in 1915 by the governor of New York State, Charles S. Whitman. In a letter quoted in the *Journal of the National Medical Association,* Just called the award "a new day in my life." The recognition encouraged him in his effort to pursue his research despite the obstacles presented to him by an effectively segregated society: "I have suddenly become a real human being, alive and anxious to work. I have a feeling that *anything* in the way of sacrifice is worthwhile; somebody appreciates my striving and learning." At the time of this award, Just had not yet yearned his doctorate. Lillie had arranged for him to enter the doctoral program at the University of Chicago, but his teaching duties delayed completion of his dissertation and the awarding of his Ph.D. until 1916.

Just spent 20 summers at Woods Hole, and as Lillie recalled in an obituary in *Science:* "He became more widely acquainted with embryological resources of the marine fauna than probably any other person." Lillie praised Just for "the very fine methods he had developed for work in this field," and it was these skills that enabled him to advance the study of parthenogenesis. This was a subject which had been pioneered by Jacques Loeb, who discovered that sea urchin eggs and frog eggs could be induced to develop without being fertilized by sperm; development could begin after pricking the eggs with a needle or subjecting them to certain kinds of salt-water solutions. Just conducted numerous experiments on invertebrate eggs, subjecting them to outside influences, such as various concentrations of seawater and butyric acid. On the basis of the results of his experiments, he came to question aspects of Loeb's procedures, as well as his theory explaining parthenogenesis.

As Just returned to Woods Hole year after year, he became established as a member of the Corporation of the Marine Biological Laboratory. He also served as an associate editor of the laboratory's *Biological Bulletin.* In addition, he became associate editor of the *Journal of Morphology, Physiological Zoology,* and the German journal, *Protoplasma.* In recognition of his professional qualifications, he was elected to membership in such scientific societies as the American Society of Naturalists, the American Ecological Society, the American Association for the Advancement of Science, and the American Society of Zoologists, of which he became vice president. In 1920, the philanthropist Julius Rosenwald supported Just's research work with an individual financial grant that was to continue for a number of years, culminating in an overall grant to Howard University in 1928 of 80,000 dollars. This enlarged Just's work in the zoology department and allowed him to travel to European centers of research.

Contributes to Knowledge of Cell Function

In 1939, Just published *The Biology of the Cell Surface,* which was the result of research he had done at

Woods Hole in the 1920s and in Europe during the 1930s. Before Just completed his research on cell biology, it was widely believed that all the activities of the cell were controlled by the nucleus. Just established the important role played by the living substance that lay outside the nucleus in a cell, known as the protoplasm. He also emphasized the importance of the ectoplasm—the rigid, outer layer of the protoplasm. Drawing on two decades of observing the activity of the ectoplasm in the egg cells of marine animals undergoing the process of fertilization, he was able to demonstrate the important influence the ectoplasm exerts even before the nucleus of the sperm fuses with the nucleus of the egg. Just concluded that the combined influence the ectoplasm and the nucleus have on the protoplasm contributes to the actions of the gene in determining heredity. He further claimed that the factors influencing heredity are already present in the protoplasm and are then extracted from it by the genes.

Just was frequently consulted on selections to the National Academy of Sciences but he himself was never elected to this society, and during his career he became increasingly bitter about racial discrimination in the United States. The fellowships and research grants he won never lasted long enough to give him a sense of security, and despite his success in the laboratory he was never granted an appointment at a major research institution. Lillie wrote of him in *Science:* "An element of tragedy ran through all Just's scientific career due to the limitations imposed by being a Negro in America, to which he could make no lasting psychological adjustment despite earnest efforts on his part. . . . He felt this as a social stigma, and hence unjust to a scientist of his recognized standing." In 1929, Just left for Europe, and he returned there often for most of the rest of his life, in what Lillie described as "self-imposed exile." First invited by M. Hartmann to study at the Kaiser Wilhelm Institute for Biology in Berlin, Just also studied at the Sorbonne in Paris and the Stazione Zoologica in Naples. He died in the United States from cancer on October 27, 1941, at the age of 58. He was survived by his wife, Ethel Highwarden Just, and three children.

SELECTED WRITINGS BY JUST:

Books

The Biology of the Cell Surface. Blakiston's Sons & Co., 1939.
Basic Methods for Experiments on Eggs of Marine Animals. Blakiston's Sons & Co., 1940.

Periodicals

"The Relations of the First Cleavage Plane to the Entrance Point of the Sperm," *Biological Bulletin,* 22, (1912): 239–252.
"Fertilization-Reaction in Eggs of *Asterias rubens,*," *Anatomical Record,* 78, (1940): 132.

FURTHER READING:

Books

Haber, Louis. *Black Pioneers of Science and Invention.* Harcourt, 1970, pp. 113–121.
Manning, Kenneth R. *Black Apollo of Science, The Life of Ernest Everett Just.* Oxford University Press, 1983.

Periodicals

Cobb, W. Montague. "Ernest Everett Just, 1883–1941," *Journal of the National Medical Association,* 49, (1957): 349–351.
Lillie, Frank R. "Ernest Everett Just," *Science,* 95, (February 2, 1942): 10–11.

—Sketch by Maurice Bleifeld

James King, Jr.

1933-

Physical chemist

James King, Jr., is a physical chemist who made key contributions to a number of different fields, including nuclear energy, solar power, and anesthesia. He also managed research projects at the Jet Propulsion Laboratory at the California Institute of Technology and in the Office of Manned Space Flight of the National Aeronautics and Space Administration (NASA).

James King, Jr., was born on April 23, 1933, in Columbus, Georgia. King began first grade when he was only four and was offered further opportunities to skip grades during elementary school. He graduated from his segregated high school in January 1949 when he was only 15 years old. At age 16, King enrolled in Morehouse College in Atlanta, Georgia, with a full scholarship. He concentrated in chemistry, intending to study medicine, and graduated in 1953.

King entered the graduate program at the California Institute of Technology, supported by a General Education Board Scholarship from the Rockefeller Foundation and the Danforth Foundation Fellowship. He was the first graduate from Morehouse to attend the California Institute of Technology, and because of his achievements there, the university established a scholarship for Morehouse graduates. His early studies focused on the chemistry of iron, particularly its atomic relationship with oxygen and its various types of rust. He later studied the complex reactions between iron and organic molecules. In 1958, King received his doctorate degree in chemistry and physics.

King began working as a research engineer of electrochemistry with Atomics International—a division of North American Aviation, Inc. During this time, he developed a method to measure the temperature inside atomic reactors. In the 1960s, during a Middle Eastern oil crisis, King began to engineer solar-powered cars. He then accepted a post with the Jet Propulsion Laboratory, managed by Cal Tech, to conduct research on the physical chemistry of atomic hydrogen.

At the Jet Propulsion Laboratory, the object of most of his research was the chemistry of natural and artificial gases. After studying atomic hydrogen and its relationship with other gases, King explored the theories surrounding anesthetic gases, describing the process by which these gases enter the human body. He also studied the electrical effects caused by the bombardment of subatomic particles on unreactive gases. He proved that unreactive gases, such as helium or xenon, can influence chemical reactions even if they do not join with the newly formed molecules.

In 1969, King accepted an appointment as manager of the physics department at the Jet Propulsion Laboratory. In 1974, he joined NASA's Office of Manned Space Flight in Washington, D.C. There, he directed the space shuttle environmental effects program, which was designed to determine whether gases generated by the space shuttle would harm the atmosphere during either the shuttle's launch or its orbit of the earth. After two years with NASA, he returned to the Jet Propulsion Laboratory in California to manage several research programs. In the fall of 1984, King took a two-year leave of absence to return to Morehouse, where he assisted the college officials in building a new teaching and research program in atmospheric science. In 1988, he became senior technical manager for the Space Science and Applications Program at the Jet Propulsion Laboratory; in 1993, he was promoted to the director of science and engineering.

King currently works on reducing atmospheric pollution. He is a member of the Scientific Committee of the Los Angeles Air Pollution Control District and has been a major contributor towards the reduction of Los Angeles's air pollution. In 1993, King was also presented by the National Technical Association with the Technologist of the Year Award.

FURTHER READING:

Books

Kessler, James H., et al. *Distinguished African American Scientists of the 20th Century.* Phoenix, Arizona: Oryx Press, 1996.

Sammons, Vivian Ovelton. *Blacks in Science and Medicine.* New York: Hemisphere Publishing Corp., 1990.

American Men and Women of Science, 16th ed. Volume IV. New Providence, New Jersey: R.R. Bowker Company, 1986.

—Sketch by Alison Wellford

John Quill Taylor King
1925-
Mathematician

John Quill Taylor King was born on September 25, 1921, in Memphis Tennessee to John Quill Taylor, a physician and Alice Woodson Taylor, a public school teacher. His father died while he was still very young, and when he was 10 his mother got married again, to Charles B. King, a director of a funeral home in Memphis. John took up his stepfather's name and the family soon moved to Austin, Texas, where the couple co-founded another funeral home. King returned to Tennessee in 1937 to attend college and in 1941 graduated with a BA. in mathematics. With a view to helping his mother run the family business, he then entered mortuary school and in 1942 was licensed as a funeral director and embalmer. That year he also got married, to Marcet Alice Hines of Chicago, whom he had met while they were both students at Fisk.

King was drafted as a private in the Army in 1943 and served in World War II as a Captain in the Pacific Theater of Operations. When he returned in 1946 he fully intended to work with his mother, and even enrolled himself in a second bachelor's program in business administration at the Samuel Huston College in Austin. But while there, the president of the University "cajoled me into teaching math to veterans returning from the war," King related in an interview with contributor Neeraja Sankaran. He fell in love with the teaching profession and there was no turning back. In 1949 he and his wife, who taught music, took a year off from Huston and went to DePaul University in Chicago to obtain Master's degrees in their respective fields. When the University of Texas at Austin opened up to non-whites in 1950, King registered as a doctoral student and received his Ph.D. in the area of mathematical statistics in 1957.

After teaching at the college for several years—Huston merged with Tillotson College in 1952—King turned to administration, becoming Dean in 1960, president in 1965 and finally in 1987 the Chancellor of the college. Meanwhile, he stayed with the Army as a member of the Reserve, only retiring from active duty in 1983 by which time he had been promoted to rank of Major General. In 1985 King was promoted to the rank of Lieutenant General in the Texas State Guard. He retired from Huston-Tillotson in 1988 but continued to remain active as the Chair of a research branch of the college.

King's numerous awards and honors recognize not only his academic achievements but also his success and dedication to other spheres of his career—military and entrepreneurial. He is a successful writer, having co-authored several mathematical text books as well as biographical books—the latter in collaboration with his wife Marcet, who passed away in 1995. The couple had four children,

and, at last count, nine grandchildren and three great-grand children.

SELECTED WRITINGS BY KING:

Books

(with Marcet H. King) *Stories of Twenty Three Famous Negro Americans,* Steck-Vaughn Publishing Company, 1967.
(with Marcet H. King) *Famous Black Americans,* Steck-Vaughn Publishing Company, 1975.
(with Marcet H. King) *Mary McLeod Bethune: A Woman of Vision,* Commission on Archives and History of the United Methodist Church.

—Sketch by Neeraja Sankaran

Flemmie Pansy Kittrell
1904-1980
Nutritionist and educator

Flemmie Pansy Kittrell was an internationally known nutritionist whose emphasis on child development and family welfare drew much-needed attention to the importance of the early home environment. During her more than 40 years as an educator, she traveled abroad extensively, helping to improve home-life conditions in many developing nations. She was a founder of Howard University's school of human ecology and the recipient of several major awards which acknowledged her unique accomplishments. As the first African American woman to earn a Ph.D. in nutrition, she strove constantly to focus attention on the important role that women could play in the world and to push for their higher education.

Kittrell was born in Henderson, North Carolina, on Christmas Day, 1904. She was the youngest daughter of Alice (Mills) and James Lee Kittrell, both of whom were descended from African American and Cherokee forebears. Learning was of central importance to Kittrell's parents, and her father often read stories and poetry to her and her eight brothers and sisters. Her parents knew the importance of encouragement and the children frequently received praise for their perseverance and achievements.

After graduating from high school in North Carolina, Kittrell attended Hampton Institute in Virginia, receiving her Bachelor of Science degree in 1928. With the encouragement of her professors she enrolled at Cornell University, although there were not many black women during that era who became graduate students. In 1930 Kittrell received her M.A. from Cornell and in 1938, from the same institution, she accepted her Ph.D. in nutrition with honors.

Kittrell was offered her first job teaching home economics in 1928 by Bennett College in Greensboro, North Carolina, and it was to Bennett she returned after obtaining her Ph.D. She then became dean of women and the head of the home economics department at Hampton Institute in 1940, where she remained until 1944. In that year Kittrell accepted the personal offer of Howard University president Mordecai Johnson to preside over the home economics department at Howard University in Washington, D.C. At Howard, Kittrell developed a curriculum that broadened the common perception of home economics so that it included such fields as child development research.

In 1947 Kittrell embarked upon a lifetime of international activism, carrying out a nutrition al survey of Liberia sponsored by the United States government. Her findings concerning "hidden hunger," a type of malnutrition which occurred in 90% of the African nation's population, led to important changes in Liberian agricultural and fishing industries. Kittrell then received a 1950 Fulbright award which led to her work with Baroda University in India, where she developed an educational plan for nutritional research. In 1953, Kittrell went back to India as a teacher of home economics classes and nutritional seminars. Then, in 1957, Kittrell headed a team which traveled to Japan and Hawaii to research activities in those countries related to the science of home economics. Between 1957 and 1961, Kittrell was the leader of three more tours, to West Africa, Central Africa, and Guinea.

During this period Kittrell remained at Howard University. In 1963, her 15-year struggle to obtain a building for the school of human ecology resulted in the dedication of a new facility. This innovative building attracted national attention as it provided a working example for the nation's Head Start program, which was just getting off the ground. Retiring from Howard University in 1972, Kittrell was named Emeritus Professor of Nutrition.

Kittrell's achievements were regularly recognized by awards and honors. For instance, she was chosen by Hampton University as its outstanding alumna for 1955. In 1961 she received the Scroll of Honor by the National Council of Negro Women in recognition of her special services. Cornell University gave her an achievement award in 1968 and the University of North Carolina at Greensboro conferred on her an honorary degree in 1974. Also, a scholarship fund was founded in honor of Kittrell's career by the American Home Economics Association.

Kittrell continued to work despite her retirement from teaching in 1972. From 1974 to 1976 she was a Cornell Visiting Senior Fellow, and she served as a Moton Center Senior Research Fellow in 1977 and a Fulbright lecturer in India in 1978. Kittrell died unexpectedly of cardiac arrest on October 3, 1980, in Washington, D.C. During her life she had credited much of her success not only to her education, but also to the strength, love, and family unity she enjoyed in her parents' home, where learning was a very important aspect of family life.

FURTHER READING:

Books

Sammons, Vivian O. *Blacks in Science and Medicine.* Hemisphere Publishing, 1990, pp. 143–144.
Smith, Jesse Carney, ed. *Notable Black American Women.* Gale, 1992, pp. 636–638.

—Sketch by Leonard C. Bruno

William Jacob Knox, Jr.
1904-1995
Chemist

William Jacob Knox, Jr. made significant contributions as a chemist in two different areas. During World War II he participated in the Manhattan Project, which built the first atomic bombs. He became a group leader, addressing difficult problems involving uranium. Later, in a postwar career at Eastman Kodak, he worked with chemicals known as surfactants, which are important in the manufacture of photographic film. "He became the company's expert on surfactants," his colleague Walter Cooper told contributor T. A. Heppenheimer in a telephone interview on May 14, 1998. During a quarter century at Kodak, he received 21 patents in this area.

Knox was born in New Bedford, Massachusetts on January 5, 1904. His father worked in that town's post office. Knox had two brothers, Everett and Lawrence, both of whom earned Ph.D. degrees from Harvard. Everett received his in history and later became an ambassador; Lawrence obtained his in organic chemistry.

William Knox attended Harvard as well, receiving a Bachelor of Science in chemistry in 1925. He then interspersed work on advanced degrees with academic appointments within the nation's black colleges. He taught chemistry at Johnson C. Smith University from 1925 to 1928, then went to the Massachusetts Institute of Technology as a student, and received his Master of Science degree in 1929. He became a professor at Atlanta University in 1933, then received his Ph.D. from MIT in 1935, in physical chemistry. This qualified him for department chairmanships, which he held at the Agricultural and Industrial College of North Carolina and at Talladega College. Then in 1943, with World War II raging, he received an invitation to come to Columbia University and to help develop the atomic bomb.

Prepares Uranium for Nuclear Weapons

Uranium comes from mines, like copper or iron, and exists in two varieties, or isotopes: U235 and U238. The numbers refer to their weights, in appropriate units. U235 is the type that can produce a bomb, but it represents only 0.7% of natural uranium. The remaining 99.3% is U238, which is chemically identical but cannot sustain a nuclear chain reaction. In crafting the first atomic weapons, one of the most important problems was to separate the two isotopes, and to obtain U235 in substantial quantities.

This was exceedingly difficult to do. Both uranium isotopes have exactly the same chemical properties; hence no method based on chemistry would work. The minute difference in weight was the only important difference between them, and offered the only basis for a useful separation method. The method ultimately used by the Manhattan Project to separate U235 was known as gaseous diffusion. Gaseous diffusion relied on a highly corrosive substance, uranium hexafluoride. Studying corrosion became Knox's specialty. Knox began at Columbia as a research associate and eventually became leader for corrosive studies. He reported to the chemist Willard Libby, who won a Nobel Prize in 1960 for his founding work on carbon 14 dating techniques. "Libby made him head of that department," recalls his colleague Cooper. Then at war's end, Libby personally recommended Knox to the head of Kodak Research Laboratories.

Helps America Take Snapshots

In 1945 he joined the research staff of Eastman Kodak in Rochester, New York, where he remained until his retirement in 1970. He dealt extensively with surfactants, also known as wetting agents. These help to assure good quality in commercial photo film, which must be manufactured rapidly and on a large scale.

Photo film uses emulsions consisting of gelatin mixed with silver halide, a light-sensitive chemical. The manufacturing process places thin layers of emulsion on a base of plastic or heavy paper, or on a separate emulsion layer. The film requires anti-static and anti-abrasion layers as well, while color film uses three types of emulsion, in the colors yellow, magenta or deep purple-red, and cyan, a blue-green. "Photographic film is a very complicated system," John Wright, a longtime associate of Knox, told contributor T. A. Heppenheimer in a telephone interview on May 14, 1998.

Surfactants help emulsions to wet or cling to the underlying surface, promoting good bonding. Proper selection of surfactants produces thin emulsion layers that spread evenly and are free of defects. "Some surfactants may react or interact with the gelatin," Wright cautions. "So you get into all sorts of studies. That was the main program we were on."

In addition to his professional work, Knox was active for many years in upholding the rights of black people. From 1955 to 1959 he was a member of the New York State Advisory Council to the State Commission Against Dis-

crimination. He also served on the Federal Commission on Human Rights at that time, later joining the Rochester Housing Authority. He was president of the Legal Aid Society after 1974, and received the Annual Civic Award of the Rochester Chamber of Commerce in 1978.

Knox married Edna Jordan in 1932; they had one child, their daughter Sandra. He reached and passed age 90 before succumbing to prostate cancer. He died in July 1995.

FURTHER READING:

Books

Sammons, Vivian. *Blacks in Science and Medicine.* Sammons, NY: Hemisphere Publishing, 1990.
Who's Who among Black Americans. Lake Forest, IL: Educational Communications, 1985.

—*Sketch by T. A. Heppenheimer*

Wade M. Kornegay
1934-
Engineering physicist

Wade Kornegay's fascinating history is a prime example of the achievements one can realize with a positive attitude and strong motivation. Kornegay was born January 9, 1934, in Mount Olive, North Carolina to Gilbert and Estelle Williams Kornegay. Young Wade was the sixth in a family of nine—a family that was orphaned in 1940. After their parents died the children went to live with their maternal grandmother in a small country town in North Carolina.

Life was not easy; Kornegay and his brothers and sisters went to segregated schools, however, his pursuit of knowledge knew no bounds. With his teachers' help, Kornegay understood the important link between education and success, realizing that in order to be successful, he would need to get a college education. Kornegay went to Carver High School, and although his teachers were very supportive of his educational progress, the resources of the school were limited and his high school education suffered. He made do with the resources he had, and he did the best work he could to prepare himself to be a scientist.

Kornegay won a two-year scholarship at North Carolina Central University in Durham, and that, combined with his earnings from a summer job at a school for the mentally retarded, paid for some of his college education. He quickly found other jobs at the university to support himself the rest of the way through school.

Kornegay focused much of his attention on his core subjects of chemistry and math, but he knew that a well-rounded education would later be an asset, so he also took art, German, and music. In 1956 Kornegay graduated *summa cum laude* with a degree in chemistry. His foresight in taking a broad range of classes paid off when he was awarded a Fulbright fellowship at Bonn University and spent a year in West Germany.

After his stay in Germany, Kornegay received the Danforth Graduate Fellowship at the University of California, Berkeley. It was there that Kornegay investigated the chemical reactions that cause inert gases like xenon and krypton to form new compounds. Under normal circumstances inert gases do not combine with other elements, but when these gases are heated to extreme temperatures, chemical reactions happen. This research earned him his doctorate degree in 1961.

As Kornegay said in an April 1998 interview with contributor Roger Jaffe, his career path strayed somewhat from his formal university training. His work studying chemical reactions at Berkeley led to an appointment at the Lincoln Laboratory at the Massachusetts Institute of Technology, and his research in chemical compounds and reactions steered him into the investigation of radar design, specifically, identifying objects in the sky by their radar signatures. The radar signature of an object—the characteristics of the radio wave that bounces off the object in the sky—is partly determined by the chemical makeup of the object. Since the early 1960s, the beginning of the Soviet cold war, particular emphasis was given to identifying and tracking missles and other weapons of destruction. A method of identifying those objects while they were in the sky would obviously be a country's important weapon of defense. His work also focused on defensive maneuvers once missles were detected in the air.

Unfortunately, because of the sensitive nature of his work with radar and enemy weapons detection, Kornegay's findings have been kept classified by the United States Government and have remained unpublished in the general scientific literature. He was the leader of the Radar Signature Studies group at MIT from 1971 through 1986, and he served as an associate division leader from 1983 through 1993. Kornegay currently is the head of the Radar Measurements group.

Kornegay has also given back to the African American community during his career. For three years in the 1960s he was an official on the Task Force on Youth Motivation, a group set up by then vice-president Hubert Humphrey. He was also a leader in a group called the Pre-Engineering Program for Minority Students, which urged Massachusetts' minority students to pursue education in engineering. He won the Black Achiever Award from the Boston YMCA in 1979, MIT's Martin Luther King, Jr. Achievement Award in 1980, and the Scientist of the Year award from the National Society of Black Engineers in 1990.

Kornegay married Bettie Joyce Hunter, his childhood sweetheart in North Carolina, after returning from his fellowship in Germany. They have three children, Melvin, Cynthia, and Laura.

FURTHER READING:

Books

Kessler, James H., et.al. *Distinguished African American Scientists of the 20th Century,* Oryx Press, 1996, pp. 212-215.

Phelps, Shirelle. *Who's Who Among African Americans, 1998-99,* Gale Research, 1998, p. 880.

—Sketch by Roger Jaffe

Samuel L. Kountz
1930-1981
Transplant surgeon

Born in a small, poverty-stricken, all-black town in Arkansas, Samuel L. Kountz struggled to study medicine and eventually became one of the most renowned kidney transplant surgeons in the world. During his career he developed techniques not only to preserve donated organs, but also to overcome tissue rejection, thus making kidney transplants more feasible.

Born Samuel Lee Kountz Jr. on October 20, 1930, in Lexa, Arkansas, he was the son of a Baptist minister and grandson of a woman born a slave. Lexa was so poor that it had no doctor to serve its population of under 100, and Kountz's father doubled as nurse to the sick. At an early age Samuel Kountz, with his grandmother's encouragement, determined to become a doctor. But educational opportunities were extremely limited in Lexa, and Kountz did not pass the entrance examination to Arkansas A & M College. He was so determined to attend, however, that he appealed to the college president and was given a chance, working his way through school as a waiter and graduating third in his class in 1952. He then won a scholarship to the University of Arkansas Medical School in Little Rock and was the first African American to be enrolled at that institution. In 1956 he earned an M.S. in biochemistry and, upon attaining his M.D. in 1958, Kountz interned at San Francisco General Hospital for two years, completing his extensive surgical residency at Stanford University School of Medicine in 1965.

Focuses on Renal Transplants

It was while interning in San Francisco that Kountz assisted on the first West Coast transplant of a kidney.

Kidney transplant had come a long way by 1959, but the procedure still had some distance to go before it gained a degree of success. The first animal kidney transplant took place in 1902 in Austria; the first human transplant was performed by a Soviet surgeon in 1936. But only by 1959 had medicine begun to overcome the most difficult part of such an operation: rejection of the implanted organ by the immune system of the host body. Successful transplants between identical and fraternal twins had started in 1954, but it was only with the development of immunosuppressants such as azathioprine that transplants between non-siblings became a possibility. While interning at Stanford, Kountz began to study this rejection process and discovered that large amounts of the steroid methylprednisolone administered after the transplant operation helped to reverse the rejection of the new organ. He also teamed up with Folker O. Belzer to devise a technique for keeping organs healthy and functioning for up to sixty hours after they were cut out of donors. Additionally, he was responsible for setting up a system of organ donor cards through the National Kidney Foundation.

Most of all, however, Kountz was a master at surgery itself, transplanting more than a thousand kidneys over the course of his professional career. The American College of Cardiology honored him for his work in 1964 with an Outstanding Investigator Award, and his alma mater, the University of Arkansas, also paid him tribute in 1973 with an honorary doctor of law degree. Kountz was an associate professor of surgery at Stanford University from 1965 to 1967 and then transferred to the University of California at San Francisco, where he built one of the largest kidney transplant training and research centers in the nation. In 1972 he became full professor of surgery and department chair at the State University of New York, Downstate Medical Center in Brooklyn, as well as chief of surgery at Kings County Hospital Center. It became one of his goals after moving to New York to improve medical care in the African American community. On a teaching trip to South Africa in 1977, Kountz contracted an undiagnosed disease which caused brain damage and incapacitated him, ending his brilliant career. Married to Grace Yvonne Akin and the father of three children, Kountz died in Great Neck, New York, on December 23, 1981. He left behind a body of work including nearly 200 articles and papers on kidney transplants and related topics, as well as scores of students he had trained and patients to whom he had given new life.

SELECTED WRITINGS BY KOUNTZ:

Periodicals

"The Effect of Bioscience and Technological Momentum on the Surgical Treatment of Chronic Illness," *Surgery,* (June 1975): 735–740.

"Acute Effects of Stress on Renal Function in Healthy Donors. Preliminary Report," *New York State Journal of Medicine,* (October 1975): 2138–2139.

"Vascular Complications in Human Renal Transplantation," *Surgery,* (January 1976): 77–81.

"A New Vascular Access for Hemodialysis: The Arterial Jump Graft," *Surgery,* (April 1976): 476–479.

"Renal Transplantation in Children," *Urologia Internationalis,* 32, (1977): 277–283.

"Effects of Intravenous Bolus Dosages of Methylprednisolone and Local Radiation on Renal Allograft Rejection and Patient Mortality," *Surgery, Gynecology and Obstetrics,* (January 1977): 63–66.

"Organ Preservation and Tissue Banking," *Transplantation Proceedings,* (March 1977): 1255–1256.

"Immunosuppression with Melengestrol," *Transplantation Proceedings,* (June 1977): 447–453.

"The Impact of 1,000 Renal Transplants at One Center," *Annals of Surgery,* (October 1977): 424–435.

FURTHER READING:

Books

Robinson, Donald. *The Miracle Finders.* David McKay, 1976, pp. 77–80.

Periodicals

"Dr. Samuel Kountz," *San Francisco Chronicle,* (December 25, 1981): 42.

Journal of the National Medical Association, (December 1981 supplemen): 1229.

Organ, Claude H. "The Black Surgeon in the Twentieth Century: A Tribute to Samuel L. Kountz, M.D.," *Journal of the National Medical Association,* (September 1978): 683–684.

—Sketch by J. Sydney Jones

George M. Langford

George M. Langford
1944-
Cell biologist

G eorge Malcolm Langford was born on August 26, 1944, in Halif, North Carolina, to Maynard Langford and Lillie Grant Langford. His parents were both farmers, and Langford was raised in what he described later as a "sheltered but nurturing" rural community. As an undergraduate he attended the nearby Fayetteville State University, an historically black college from where he graduated in 1966 with a B.S. in biology. When he left North Carolina to pursue graduate studies at the Illinois Institute of Technology, it was his first time living away from home. He obtained both his M.S. (1969) and his Ph.D. (1971) in cell biology from this institute. Also in Chicago, Langford met Sylvia Tyler (now a Dean at Dartmouth College), whom he married in 1968. The couple have two sons and a daughter.

After spending the early part of his career moving through several universities, Langford returned to his home state in 1979 to take up an appointment at the University of North Carolina at Chapel Hill. After several years he moved to Dartmouth College in 1991, where he currently holds the position of **E.E. Just** Professor of Natural Sciences and professor of biology, in addition to an adjunct appointment at the medical school.

Throughout his career, Langford's primary area of research has been the study of the movements of the components of living cells, or intracellular motility. He has specificly studied the movement of subcellular organelles. He was first drawn to the subject by Jean Dan, a famous embryologist who spent a sabbatical year at Chicago while Langford was in graduate school. In 1992, Langford and his colleagues were the first to demonstrate that special filaments long known to be responsible for the movement of muscle cells were also responsible for the movement of particles within nerve cells.

As he explained in the 1996 television program, *Breakthrough: The changing face of science in America,* his Eureka moment came when peering through the microscope late one evening he observed, "bundles of proteins moving along like trucks on invisible highways." Tied to this finding was the discovery that the process was fueled by a protein similar to myosin, which is the motor protein in muscles. These findings have very important implications for scientists trying to understand the general traffic-control mechanisms in cells. Once this is understood, scientists can take steps to ensure the proper health of cells and, consequently, the organisms they belong to.

His scientific achievements have earned Langford numerous awards and honors in the course of his career. In 1988-89, he was the Program Director for the Cell Biology Program at the National Science Foundation. Since the early years of his career he has also maintained a summer laboratory at the Marine Biological Laboratory in Woods Hole and for a time served as Chair of the Science Council for this prestigious institution. In addition to his contributions to cell biology, Langford has also been a vital player in promoting minority students in the sciences. In fact, one of the reasons he was lured away from home to New Hampshire was the opportunity to work with minorities. He is responsible for establishing the E.E. Just program at Dartmouth, which provides internships to minority students in the sciences. From 1985-90 he served as the chair in the Minorities Affairs Committee of the American Society for Cell Biologists, whose main mission is to plan programs to increase minority participation in the society's activities.

SELECTED WRITINGS BY LANGFORD:

Periodicals

(With S.A. Kuznetsov and D.G. Weiss) "Actin-dependent organelle movement in squid axoplasm," *Nature* v356, (1992): 725-27.

FURTHER READING:

Periodicals

Kaufman, Wallace. "On becoming a scientist: two profiles," *Carolina Alumi Review,* General Alumni Association, The University of North Carolina,Chapel Hill, (Spring 1990): 34-39.

Raeburn, Paul, "Can dogfinch cure diabetes?" *National Wildlife* (December-January 1988): 34-39.

—*Sketch by Neeraja Sankaran*

Lewis H. Latimer

Lewis H. Latimer
1848-1928
Inventor, draftsperson, and engineer

Despite his lack of any formal education, Lewis H. Latimer, the son of an escaped slave, became a member of Thomas Alva Edison's research team and made several outstanding contributions to the development and commercialization of the electric light. Latimer was a self-taught draftsman who began as an office boy and rose to become chief draftsman for both the General Electric and Westinghouse companies.

Lewis Howard Latimer was born in Chelsea, Massachusetts, on September 4, 1848. His father, George A. Latimer, had been a slave in Virginia and had escaped to Boston; some years after he gained his freedom there, his former owner, James B. Gray, came to Boston to reclaim him. Latimer's case was taken up by abolitionists such as William Lloyd Garrison and Frederick Douglass, who raised the necessary $400 to purchase Latimer's freedom. The Latimer case was the first of several famous Boston fugitive cases, after which Massachusetts passed a personal liberty law forbidding state officers from participating in the tracking down of fugitive slaves. George Latimer deserted the family when Lewis was 10 years old, forcing the boy to leave school and take a job to help support his mother, Rebecca (Smith) Latimer, and her other four children.

Becomes A Self-Taught Draftsman

By 1864, Latimer had turned 16 and the Civil War had begun. He enlisted in the Union navy and served as a "landsman" on the gunboat *U.S.S. Massasoit.* Eventually, he became a lieutenant in the 4th Battalion of the Massachusetts Volunteer Militia. After receiving an honorable discharge in 1865, Latimer returned to Boston and accepted a job as an office boy in the patent firm of Crosby and Gould. It was there that Latimer first became interested in the craft of mechanical drawing, and he soon began to teach himself the art. Patent applications required that very detailed and accurate drawings be submitted, and Latimer was so fascinated by this craft that he saved his money to buy second-hand drafting tools and learned how to use them from library textbooks. After studying every night after work, Latimer felt he was ready to ask his employers for permission to make the drawings for a invention; once they saw how skilled he was, they promoted him to the position of junior draftsman.

In 10 years' time, Latimer had been promoted to chief draftsman for Crosby and Gould. In this position he was responsible for perfecting the final drawings that decided the success or failure of patent applications. One of the firm's clients was Alexander Graham Bell, and it fell to Latimer to execute the drawings for Bell's historic invention, the telephone; in 1876, Bell received his patent. Three years later, Latimer left Crosby and Gould to join the United States Electric Lighting Company. This new firm was the brainchild of American inventor and entrepreneur Hiram S.

Maxim, and was to be one of the first to enter the new and rapidly expanding field of electric lighting. Thomas Edison had just invented the first electric incandescent lamp, and Maxim was determined to improve upon Edison's invention and take the lead (which he did with Latimer's help). By 1882, Latimer had invented an improved carbon filament that lasted longer at high temperatures; in addition, he devised a cheaper method of making the filaments. The new light was called the "Maxim lamp" and was to be used in railroad stations throughout the United States, Canada, and other countries.

Begins Long Career At General Electric

While Maxim was attempting to seize world leadership in electricity away from Edison, Latimer left him in 1882 and joined the Olmstead Electric Light and Power Company of New York where he could continue his experimentation on improved filaments. Staying there for only two years, Latimer then joined one of Edison's companies, the Excelsior Electric Company, in 1884. There Latimer worked as a draftsman and engineer and was able to continue his pioneering electrical research. Upon joining Edison, Latimer no longer switched companies; when Excelsior was later incorporated into the Edison General Electric Company—which became known simply as GE— Latimer became one of its key members.

The electric light industry by the end of the 1880s was in a state of chaos and contention as the federal courts were asked to resolve scores of suits involving patent rights for incandescent lighting. One of the most significant legal contests involved Edison and the combined rival forces of Westinghouse and Thompson-Houston. The legal issue centered on Edison's 1880 invention of the carbon filament lamp, the challenger being the United States Electric Lighting Company, a Westinghouse subsidiary and Latimer's old employer. Latimer's value to Edison became immediately clear, since it was he who had received some of the patents that were now being used to challenge Edison. Latimer found himself in the unique position of being able to help his present employer discredit the originality of his own early designs. To accomplish this, Latimer was promoted to the company's legal department and began what would prove a career as an expert witness. His testimony aided Edison in eventually overcoming all challenges, and Latimer would continue as an expert witness in many of the other related trials that ensued. He remained with General Electric until 1912, when his expertise as a witness was no longer needed.

As a man of many talents, Latimer did not simply retire when he left General Electric at age 64. He worked as an independent electrical and mechanical engineer for another 16 years and taught mechanical drawing to immigrants at the Henry Street Settlement in New York City. Latimer also loved to write and in 1925 his friends and family published his *Poems of Love and Life*. Writing was nothing new to Latimer, however, since in 1890 he had written a groundbreaking book on electric lighting, *Incan-*

descent Electric Lighting: A Practical Description of the Edison System. Latimer's curiosity and probing mind led him to art and music as well, but his primary interest remained invention. This impulse was exhibited as early as 1874 when he received a patent for an improved railroad car water closet (toilet) while working for Crosby and Gould. Later Latimer also obtained patents for such varied devices as an apparatus for cooling and disinfecting, a rack for hats, coats, and umbrellas that locked, and a new device for supporting books.

When Latimer died in Flushing, New York, on December 11, 1928, he left behind his wife, Mary Wilson (Lewis) Latimer (whom he married on December 10, 1873), and two children, Louise Rebecca and Emma Jeanette. He had been a member of such diverse organizations as the New York Electrical Society, the Grand Army of the Republic, and the Negro Society for Historical Research. Most significantly, Latimer was the only African American member of the famous team of inventors called the "Edison Pioneers." On May 10, 1968, the Lewis H. Latimer public school in New York City was named for him, dedicated to honor the memory of a man who had worked in the background but whose inventiveness and perseverance made him a key figure in the history of electric lighting.

SELECTED WRITINGS BY LATIMER:

Books

Incandescent Electric Lighting: A Guide for Lighting Engineers, Van Nostrand, 1890.

FURTHER READING:

Books

Bigelow, Barbara Carlisle, editor, *Contemporary Black Biography,* Volume 4, Gale, 1993, pp. 148–150.

Hayden, Robert C., *Eight Black American Inventors,* Addison-Wesley, 1972, pp. 78–92.

Klein, Aaron E., *The Hidden Contributors: Black Scientists and Inventors in America,* Doubleday, 1971, pp. 97–108.

Logan, Rayford W., and Michael R. Winston, editors, *Dictionary of American Negro Biography,* Norton, 1982, pp. 385–386.

—Sketch by Leonard C. Bruno

Theodore K. Lawless

Theodore K. Lawless
1892-1971
Dermatologist

Theodore K. Lawless was a pioneer in developing treatments for the early stages of syphilis and established dermatological treatment programs for arsenic-damaged skin. In the course of his long career, he built a private practice in the heart of Chicago's African American community that became one of the most prestigious skin clinics of its day. Honored worldwide for his work, Lawless amassed wealth through his business ventures and furthered the causes of health and African American education with monetary donations.

Theodore Kenneth Lawless was born on December 6, 1892, in Thibodaux, Louisiana, the son of Alfred Lawless, a minister, and Harriet (Dunn) Lawless. In 1914 he received his A.B. degree from Talladega College in Alabama. After attending the University of Kansas from 1914 to 1916, he began studying medicine at the Northwestern University School of Medicine, from which he received his M.D. in 1919. It was during this time that he focused on a career in dermatology, becoming a fellow in dermatology and syphilology at Massachusetts General Hospital from 1920 to

1921 while also studying at both Columbia University and Harvard University. During the early 1920s, Lawless studied abroad at some of the most prestigious centers of dermatology in Europe.

Upon returning to America, Lawless began his private practice in Chicago, developing the largest dermatology clinic in the city. He also accepted a teaching post at Northwestern in 1924 and set up the University's first clinical laboratory. Throughout the 1920s and 1930s, Lawless not only kept up his practice but also taught and conducted dermatological research. He investigated and developed a diagnosis for sporotrichosis, a fungal disease that produces subcutaneous and lymphoid ulcerated lesions, and did important work in syphilis research. Lawless pioneered the use of electrically-induced fever as a therapy for the early stages of syphilis, a disease that was incurable before the advent of penicillin. He also researched leaks that occurred during injections of arsenical drugs, which were another method of treating syphilis at the time. If some of the arsenical preparation leaked out during injection, as frequently happened, tissues surrounding the vein where the injection was being made would be damaged. Lawless developed a treatment for such accidental leaks.

In 1941, Lawless resigned from his position at Northwestern University after having been assigned no students to teach, apparently in an incident inspired by racism. He concentrated on his private practice and became extremely successful both in his practice and in various investment businesses into which he entered. Lawless donated a research laboratory to Chicago's Provident Hospital and money to African American colleges in the American South. He was also active in international affairs, helping to establish a dermatology clinic at the Beilinson Hospital Center in Israel, which was named after him. During World War II, he served with the U.S. Chemical Warfare Board, as well on an advisory committee on venereal disease.

Lawless, who never married, continued to research in his later years. He was also a respected and tireless instructor whose dermatology lectures at Cook County Hospital were eagerly attended by medical students. Lawless was honored by many organizations for his research and philanthropy. Among other awards, he received the Harmon Award in 1929 for outstanding medical work and the National Association for the Advancement of Colored People's Spingarn Medal in 1954. He was also a fellow of the American Medical Association, associate examiner in dermatology for the National Board of Medical Examiners, president of the board of trustees of Dillard University, and Diplomate of the American Board of Dermatology. Lawless died in on May 1, 1971, in Chicago.

SELECTED WRITINGS BY LAWLESS:

Periodicals

"The Diagnosis of Sporotrichosis," *Archives of Dermatology and Syphilology,* 22, (1930): 381–388.

"Treatment of Accidental Perivascular Injections of Arsphenamine or Neoarsphenamine," *Journal of Laboratory and Clinical Medicine,* 16, (1931): 1910.

"The Treatment of Early Syphilis with Electropyrexia," *Journal of the American Medical Association,* 107, (1936): 194–199.

FURTHER READING:

Periodicals

Cobb, W. Montague. "Theodore Kenneth Lawless," *Journal of the National Medical Association,* 62, No. 4, (1970): 310–312.

—*Sketch by J. Sydney Jones*

Margaret Cornelia Morgan Lawrence
1914-
Psychiatrist

Margaret Cornelia Morgan Lawrence has had a distinguished career as a pediatric psychiatrist in the New York area. She is primarily known for her theories about the value of the ego strength in children.

Lawrence was born in New York City on August 19, 1914. Her mother, Mary Elizabeth (Smith) Morgan, worked as a teacher, and her father, Sandy Alonzo Morgan, was an Episcopal minister. Lawrence's father moved his family from one Episcopal church to another during her early childhood, but by the time she was seven, her parents had settled in Vicksburg, Mississippi. Lawrence grew up in a racially segregated neighborhood there, feeling loved and even privileged.

Lawrence had decided to be a doctor by her early teens, and at the age of 14 she went to live with her maternal aunts in New York City so she could get a good high school education. When she graduated, she was accepted to three distinguished colleges: Cornell, Smith, and Hunter. She entered Cornell in 1932 on a scholarship. Because she was not allowed to stay in the Cornell dormitories, she earned her board as a housekeeper. She received her bachelor's degree in 1936. Later that year, she entered Columbia University's medical school, one of 10 women (and the only black) in a class of 104. She would be the only black medical student at Columbia throughout her four years of study. In June of 1938, she married Charles Radford Lawrence II, whom she had met in Vicksburg in 1933. Margaret Lawrence received her medical degree from Columbia in 1940.

After medical school, Lawrence began to focus on pediatric psychiatry. From 1940-42, she was a pediatric intern at Harlem Hospital beginning. In 1943, she earned a master of science degree from the Columbia School of Public Health. There, she worked with Benjamin Spock, who was a powerful influence in her professional development. Lawrence taught at Meharry Medical College from 1943-47, where she rose to the rank of associate professor of pediatrics. She studied psychiatry from 1948-50 at the New York Psychiatric Institute, and she studied psychoanalysis at the Columbia Psychoanalytic Clinic. She had a fellowship in child psychiatry and a pediatric consultation from 1949-51 with the Council of Child Development Centers. In 1951, she and her family moved to Rockland County, 30 miles (48 km) northwest of New York City. There she had a private practice in pediatric psychiatry. Beginning in 1963, Lawrence was a child psychiatrist at the Harlem Hospital, where she was head of the Developmental Psychiatry Clinic. She was also an associate clinical professor of psychiatry at the College of Physicians and Surgeons of Columbia University. She retired from both positions in 1984.

Lawrence's most important contributions were her ideas about the ego strength of children and how to treat childhood psychological problems. As her daughter Sara Lawrence Lightfoot described her mother's treatment of childhood mental trauma, Lawrence had the patient "confront the deep wound, experience the knifelike pain, move through the zombielike period of 'depersonalization,' speak about the event, act it out, cry over it, stomp on it, and finally emerge from it usually with a scar."

After she retired, Lawrence continued her private practice in Rockland County, New York. Her husband died in 1988. Their three children are Charles Lawrence, Sarah Lawrence Lightfoot, and Paula Lawrence Wehmiller.

SELECTED WRITINGS BY LAWRENCE:

Books

The Mental Health Team in the Schools. New York: Behavioral Publications, 1971.
Young Inner City Families: Development of Ego Strength Under Stress. New York: Behavioral Publications, 1975.

FURTHER READING:

Books

Lightfoot, Sara Lawrence. *Balm In Gilead: Journey of a Healer.* Reading, Massachusetts: Addison Wesley, 1988.
Smith, Jessie Carney. *Notable Black American Women.* Detroit: Gale Research, 1991.
Salzman, Jack, David L. Smith, and Cornel West, eds. *Encyclopedia of African-American Culture and His-*

Robert Henry Lawrence, Jr.

tory. New York: Simon & Schuster Macmillan, 1996.

—*Sketch by Patrick Moore*

Robert Henry Lawrence, Jr.
1935-1967
Astronaut

Robert Henry Lawrence, Jr. was the first African American test pilot to be selected for astronaut training in the Air Force's Manned Orbiting Laboratory program. A distinguished Air Force officer and a senior test pilot, he logged more than 2,500 hours of flying time, over 2,000 of which was in jets. By the time of his death, he had attained the rank of major. If Lawrence had not been killed during a training flight in 1967, he probably would have been the first African American astronaut in space.

Lawrence was born on October 2, 1935, in Chicago, Illinois, to Robert Henry and Gwendolyn Lawrence. His parents divorced when Lawrence and his sister were still in preschool. His mother soon married again, to Charles

Duncan. Both Duncan and his father played important roles in Lawrence's upbringing. Lawrence did not grow up in affluence. His mother and stepfather both worked. His mother was a civil servant, and his stepfather worked as a Veterans Administration underwriter and in periodicals' circulation. His father was a disabled veteran.

A self-motivated, determined child, Lawrence grew up in the Christian Scientist church. He had numerous interests, including chess and piano, but he was particularly fascinated by model airplanes and chemistry sets—both of which foretold his future. After attending Haines Elementary School, Lawrence entered Chicago's Englewood High School, then a distinguished and predominantly African American school. There, Lawrence was deeply engaged by biology and chemistry; he also participated in track. He graduated from Englewood in the top 10 percent of his class.

Lawrence received his undergraduate education at Bradley University, where he waited tables and worked other part-time jobs around campus to help pay for his schooling. Though undistinguished academically until his senior year, Lawrence was awarded his bachelor's degree in chemistry in 1956. One of the most important experiences Lawrence had at Bradley was with the Air Force Reserve Officers Training Corps (ROTC). While in the ROTC, Lawrence attained the second-highest cadet rank on campus, lieutenant colonel; at one point, he was the cadet commander.

After graduation, Lawrence joined the Air Force and was given the rank of second lieutenant. Determined to become a pilot, he attended pilot instructional school at Craig Air Force Base in Alabama, before being stationed at the United States Air Force base in Furstenfeldbruck, West Germany. In Germany, Lawrence served as both a pilot-trainee instructor and a fighter pilot for the Military Assistance Advisory Group. On July 1, 1958, he married Barbara H. Cress, whom he had met while attending Bradley. They had one child together, a son named Tracey, in 1960.

In 1961, Lawrence and his family returned to the United States, and Lawrence enrolled in graduate school. He attended a joint program in the physical sciences at Ohio State University and the Air Force Institute of Technology, located at Wright-Patterson Air Force Base. Lawrence worked hard at Ohio State, earning a grade point average of about 3.5. In 1965, Lawrence was awarded his doctoral degree in physical chemistry. His dissertation was entitled *The Mechanism of the Tritium Beta-Ray Induced Exchange Reactions of Deuterium with Methane and Ethane in the Gas Phase*. Lawrence dedicated his thesis ". . . to those American Negros who have spent their lives in the performance of menial tasks struggling to overcome both natural and man-made problems of survival. To such men and women scientific investigation would seem a grand abstraction. However, it has been their endeavors which have supplied both the wherewithall and motivation that initiated and helped sustain this effort."

After earning his doctorate, Lawrence was assigned to Kirtland Air Force Base in New Mexico. There, he worked at the Air Force Weapons Laboratory as a research scientist for a short time. In 1967, Lawrence graduated from a one-year program at the Aerospace Research Pilot School at Edwards Air Force Base in California. On June 30 of that year, Lawrence was selected for the Manned Orbiting Laboratory program sponsored by the Air Force, and he began his training as an astronaut at Edwards Air Force Base. Lawrence was one of four men in the third group of Manned Orbiting Laboratory program.

The training lasted six months, but Lawrence was killed during instruction on December 8, 1967. He was on a proficiency-training flight in a modified F-104 Starfighter when the accident occurred. The plane, which could travel at twice the speed of sound, crashed on the runway while Lawrence was trying to make a complicated landing that simulated a spaceship. Lawrence was killed instantly. His instructor survived, though with severe injuries. Lawrence was the ninth fatality in the United States astronaut program. Had he lived, Lawrence would probably have traveled to space in a *Gemini* B spacecraft launched by a Titan 3M missile.

Before his death, Lawrence had been honored by the Air Force with a Commendation medal and an Outstanding Unit Award. Upon his death, Lawrence's family set up a memorial scholarship fund in his honor. The Robert H. Lawrence, Jr., Memorial Scholarship fund benefits black chemistry students at Bradley University.

FURTHER READING:

Books

Atkinson, Joseph D., Jr., and Jay M. Shafritz. *The Real Stuff: A History of NASA's Astronaut Recruitment Program.* New York: Praeger Scientific, 1985, pp. 105, 136.

Periodicals

Lorens, David. "Ode to an Astronaut." *Ebony* (February 1968): 90-92, 94.

Powers, Blake. "Space Personality: Robert Lawrence." *Space World* (December 1983): 21.

—*Sketch by A. Petrusso*

James Raymond Lawson

James Raymond Lawson
1915-1996
Physicist

James Raymond Lawson established himself as an experimental physicist, building up a research laboratory in spectroscopy at Fisk University. He went on to become president of that institution. His term was marred by the activities of student protesters, who burned down a campus building and contributed to Fisk's increasingly serious financial difficulties. Beset by ill health, he left Fisk and joined the National Aeronautics and Space Administration (NASA) in Washington. Here, in more peaceful surroundings, Lawson continued to serve his academic community.

He was born in Louisville, Kentucky on January 15, 1915, the son of Daniel Lamont Lawson and the former Daisy Harris. His father was a teacher and a graduate of Fisk in Nashville, Tennessee, where he had been one of the Jubilee Singers, a well-known choral group. The young Lawson went to Fisk as well, where he received a Bachelor of Arts degree in physics in 1935. He then went to the University of Michigan for graduate work.

Builds a Reputation and a Laboratory

At Fisk, Lawson had come up under the tutelage of the physicist **Elmer Imes**, who had received his Ph.D. at Michigan some two decades earlier. Now, in the mid-1930s, Lawson's professors included Samuel Goudsmit, who had made key discoveries concerning the nature of the electron, and who went on to become editor of the *Physical Review*, the nation's leading physics journal. Lawson received his master's from Michigan in 1936 and received a Julius Rosenwald fellowship that enabled him to pursue the Ph.D.

He did his doctoral research under Harrison M. Randall, the department chairman. His topic was far-infrared spectroscopy, a field in which Randall was a pioneer. This was part of the broad science of spectroscopy, which draws on the fact that atoms and molecules can be made to absorb and emit light at characteristic and sharply defined wavelengths. Chemists have used this to discover new elements, and to show that industrial activities have brought changes to the very atmosphere we breathe. Astronomers have used spectroscopy to learn what stars are made of, to determine stars' ages, and to trace the expansion of the universe itself.

Scientists working in spectroscopy initially dealt with visible wavelengths, which are well-suited for studying atoms. Randall and Lawson wanted to study molecules such as methyl alcohol, but these did not emit visible light. Instead they emitted at much longer wavelengths known as the far infrared, and study of these wavelengths demanded new instruments and innovative techniques. Lawson mastered these new requirements, and received his Ph.D. in physics in 1939.

He then launched his career within the nation's black colleges, working as an assistant professor at Southern University during 1939-40 and as an associate professor at Langston University from 1940 to 1942. In that latter year, Lawson's mentor at Fisk, Elmer Imes, died. Lawson accepted an invitation to return to his alma mater and chair the physics department.

Fisk University has long held high distinction within the black community. Its alumni include W. E. B. DuBois, a founder of the National Association for the Advancement of Colored People (NAACP). But in 1942 Fisk had only about three hundred students, and lacked graduate programs in physics. Lawson saw an opportunity to build a physics program centered on infrared spectroscopy. He learned that a group of his colleagues at the University of Michigan were to build two research-grade infrared spectrophotometers, instruments that could not only observe infrared emissions but could measure their intensity. He arranged for them to build a third, and persuaded the president of Fisk to authorize its purchase.

Such instruments were rare. Lawson used his as bait to lure additional researchers to Fisk, where they could work with it. He won research grants and recruited five graduating seniors to stay on to use this equipment while pursuing Master of Arts degrees. In this fashion, Lawson founded a research center, the Fisk Infrared Research Laboratory. In 1950 he and his colleagues broadened the scope of their work by founding the Fisk Infrared Spectroscopy Institute. It sponsored a summer program that introduced other scientists to infrared spectroscopy.

Meanwhile, he was overreaching himself, for in 1949 he accepted the chairmanship of the physics department at Tennessee Agricultural and Industrial State University. He did this without consulting the president of Fisk, who fired him immediately from his professorship at that university. Lawson built up a new infrared research lab at Tennessee A & I, but remained close to the activities at Fisk. Then in 1957 he returned to Fisk to chair the physics department once again, and to work there full time.

A decade later, he became acting vice president of Fisk, serving for 18 months during 1966 and 1967. He took over the presidency during that latter year. Then, very quickly, his university entered a time of turmoil.

Faces Student Riots and Hard Times

The late 1960s were a time of upheaval. The historian William Manchester, in his book *The Glory and the Dream*, writes that during 1968 "there were 221 major demonstrations, involving nearly 39,000 students, on 101 American campuses. Buildings were dynamited, college presidents and deans were roughed up, obscenities were painted on walls." At Columbia, students took officials hostage and seized campus buildings; they were evicted using police force. That summer, at the Democratic National Convention in Chicago, student radicals outraged the nation and sparked what was later called a police riot. At Cornell, a year later, student radicals were armed with rifles.

At Fisk, students took over the library and seized another campus building. One issue was the appropriateness of white financial support of the black institution. The president of the Student Government Association sent some two hundred letters to individuals and organizations that had provided Fisk with aid, cursing them and advising them to keep their money. Then in May 1970, arsonists burned the university's Livingstone Hall.

Philanthropists rarely appreciate people who bite the hand that feeds them. Fisk relied on their good will, and while Lawson tried to encourage their continued support, the destruction of Livingstone was more than anyone cared to accept. Incoming flows of cash dried up, and Lawson found himself compelled to spend money from the principal of the university's modest endowment in order to pay debts.

Some new funds continued to arrive, particularly from Washington, as Fisk received grants from the Department of Housing and Urban Development and from the Office of Education. The Ford Foundation also came in with a grant, in 1972. Nevertheless, in a report on higher education, the Carnegie Commission in New York cited Fisk as "a famous and venerable southeastern institution headed for financial difficulty unless fresh resources could be developed immediately." By 1975, the university was cutting salaries by

20% and chopping its operating budget by one-fourth. The value of the endowment had shrunk by half, to $4 million.

By 1975, Lawson had lost the confidence of his university. He also entered a time of ill health, as he developed serious complications following gall bladder surgery. Thus beset, he stepped down as president in July of that year. His departure did not rescue Fisk, as financial problems persisted through the presidency of his successor, Walter Leonard. Not until the term of Leonard's successor, Henry Ponder, was Fisk restored to financial health.

Lawson at first planned to take a year's leave of absence from Fisk, then go back to teaching there. But he changed his mind, and instead took a position in Washington as Director of University Affairs within the equal-opportunity office of the National Aeronautics and Space Administration. Here he worked to steer contracts to black colleges. Nevertheless, his health continued to deteriorate. "His wife told me that during his last 20 years, he was in the hospital at least 20 times," his longtime colleague Nelson Fuson told contributor T. A. Heppenheimer in a telephone interview on May 19, 1998. He worked for NASA for nearly 20 years before finally retiring. He died of colon cancer in the fall of 1996.

Lawson married Lillian Arceneaux on June 10, 1940. They had four children: Ronald, Daryl, James, and Elizabeth. He was a highly capable tennis player and a golf enthusiast; at Fisk he also strongly supported the school's varsity sports teams. He served on the board of directors of the Urban League of Nashville. He also served on the board of Oak Ridge Associated Universities, which arranged for students and faculty members to conduct research at Oak Ridge National Laboratory, a leading center for nuclear physics.

FURTHER READING:

Books

Collins, L. M. *One Hundred Years of Fisk University Presidents 1875-1975.* Nashville, Tennessee: Hemphill's Creative Printing, 1989.

—Sketch by T. A. Heppenheimer

Carroll Moton Leevy
1920-

Physician and medical researcher

Carroll Moton Leevy

Carroll Moton Leevy is an internationally recognized researcher on liver disease. He has increased our understanding of how alcoholism damages the liver. He has also done much to help people with alcoholism by starting the first clinic in the world for alcoholics with liver disease, and by developing technology which greatly simplified the detection of liver disease. He is also a teacher and administrator, and remains active in all arenas as the Science Director at the Sammy Davis, Jr. National Liver Center in Newark, New Jersey.

Carroll Moton Leevy was born on October 13, 1920, in Columbia, South Carolina. Although his grandparents were freed slaves, Leevy's father, Isaac, and mother, Mary, had graduated from college. They both taught school, but later started a department store in Columbia. Early experiences with sickness and death gave Leevy a strong desire to become a physician. When four years old, he had a serious case of pneumonia, but gradually recovered under the careful watch of physicians. This incident gave him much respect for the medical community.

However, a few months later, his aunt, suffering from stomach cancer, moved in with his family. She had come to the city in search of medical care which was unavailable in her rural home. After she died, Leevy realized there were still many ways medical care could be improved. His father started an undertaking business when Leevy was in high school. He saw the bodies of many young black men, and believed many of their deaths could have been prevented if they had had better health care. His younger sister died of tuberculosis. In the sanatorium (a type of hospital) where she was care for, Leevy again saw the need for better medical care in his community. He decided to make a difference by becoming a physician.

Leevy worked hard in high school so that he could become a doctor. He graduated at the top of his class, and attended Fisk University in Nashville, Tennessee. While studying the sciences, Leevy was also active in the Student Christian Association. An important event was the racially integrated Young Men's Christian Association conference he attended in 1940. This showed Leevy, for the first time, how people of different races and cultures could work well together.

Leevy graduated from Fisk University with an A.B. degree, *summa cum laude* (1941), and enrolled in the medical school at the University of Michigan in Ann Arbor, Michigan. The United States had just entered World War II, and there was a shortage of physicians. Leevy entered the Army Specialized Training Program, which provided financial support for his medical education. Leevy obtained his M.D. degree in 1944 and moved to Jersey City Medical Center to complete his training as an intern and then resident.

Interest in Liver Disease Develops

While a resident in Jersey City, New Jersey, Leevy saw huge numbers of people with liver problems, many of them alcoholics. Little at the time was available to help them, or even to diagnose the extent of their problems. His teachers and mentors recognized Leevy's research and teaching skills and encouraged him to pursue those areas. Leevy developed a new and simple method of diagnosing liver disease, for which he holds the patent. He also developed an almost painless method for obtaining liver biopsy samples for microscopic analysis.

By the time Leevy completed his residency (1948), World War II was over and he did not have to immediately fulfill his military service. He continued his liver research at Jersey City, and also began training other physicians. In 1954 Leevy was assigned to the U.S. Naval Hospital in St. Albans, New York. Again, many people there had liver disease. Within two years, Leevy turned the Naval Hospital into a center for research on liver disease. During this time, Leevy also wrote his first textbook on liver disease (published in 1957). In 1956, Leevy married Ruth Secora Barboza, a chemist who also later helped Leevy with some of his research. They now have a daughter, Maria, and a son, Carroll Barboza Leevy, M.D., who is also a liver researcher at the Sammy Davis, Jr. National Liver Center.

Leevy had studied with other liver experts at the University of Toronto in 1952 thanks to a post doctoral fellowship. He now obtained another grant from the National Institutes of Health to do research at Harvard Medical School (1958-1959). His research examined the role of diet and environmental toxins in liver damage. There, he also learned about the administration of a large, highly successful medical school. He brought these experiences back to New Jersey with him, where a new medical school was being formed.

While Leevy was at the Naval Hospital, Jersey City Medical Center began discussions to start a new medical school. In 1956, Seton Hall College of Medicine and Dentistry, located in Jersey City Medical Center, admitted its first students. However, Seton Hall is a private, Roman Catholic institution, while the Medical Center is a government institution, which created problems regarding the separation of church and state. Leevy joined the faculty in 1957, and played an important role is helping resolve those problems. In 1965, the state purchased the medical school, renaming it the New Jersey Medical School, and forming the larger New Jersey College of Medicine and Dentistry. The school grew, and in 1970 it moved to Newark, New Jersey, being renamed the College of Medicine and Dentistry of New Jersey. Throughout this time, Leevy rose to the rank of full professor, and continued to publish widely. He served as chair of the department of medicine and physician-in-chief (1975-91) and in 1990 became director of the New Jersey Medical School Liver Center, a position he still holds. His concurrent position as scientific director of the Sammy Davis, Jr. National Liver Center began in 1984.

Carroll M. Leevy's contribution to the present knowledge of liver disease has been enormous. He has written four major textbooks and over 500 articles on the subject. He has served on national and international advisory panels, and received numerous awards. He received the Distinguished Achievement Award from the magazine Modern Medicine (1972), the Achievement Award from the National Medical Association (1987), and the Distinguished Service Award from the American Association for the Study of Liver Disease (1991). He was elected president of the International Association for the Study of the Liver (1971), and has honorary degrees from the New Jersey Institute of Technology (1973), Fisk University (1981), and the University of Nebraska (1989). Throughout his career he has also brought attention to the important work of African American scientists.

SELECTED WRITINGS BY LEEVY:

Books

Practical Diagnosis and Treatment of Liver Disease, New York: Hoeber-Harper, 1957.
Liver Regeneration in Man, Springfield: Charles C. Thomas, 1973.

Periodicals

(With C. B. Leevy) "Alcoholic Liver Disease," *Comprehensive Therapy,* Vol. 20, (1994): 6-9.
(With O. Frank, C. B. Leevy & H. Baker) "Nutritional Factors in Liver Disease of the Alcoholic," *Acta Medica Scandinavica. Supplement,* Vol. 703, (1985): 67-79.

FURTHER READING:

Books

American Men & Women of Science 1998-99, New Providence, NJ: R. R. Bowker. 20th Edition. Volume 4, p. 832.

Kessler, James H., et. al. *Distinguished African American Scientists of the 20th Century,* Phoenix, AZ: Oryx Press, 1996, pp. 224-228.

Periodicals

Journal of the National Medical Association, Vol. 63, (November 1971): 499.

Journal of the National Medical Association, Vol. 65, (May 1973): 259.

—Sketch by Dónal P. O'Mathúna

Lasalle D. Leffall, Jr.

LaSalle D. Leffall, Jr.
1930-
Surgical oncologist

Surgical oncologist LaSalle D. Leffall, Jr. has worked to focus attention on the problem of high cancer death rates among minorities, especially African Americans. As the first black president of the American Cancer Society, first black president of the American College of Surgeons, and as an educator at Howard University, Leffall has dedicated his career to educating both the medical profession and the lay public about cancer risks for minorities.

Leffall, the son of Martha (Jordan) Lefall and LaSalle Leffall, Sr., was born in Tallahassee, Florida, on May 22, 1930. He attended public school and was the valedictorian of his high school class, graduating in 1945. In 1948, he received a B.S., *summa cum laude*, from Florida A & M University. From there, Leffall enrolled in Howard University College of Medicine. Again, he achieved academic excellence, graduating first in his class and receiving his M.D. degree in 1952. Leffall's formal medical education continued for the next seven years. He was an intern at Homer G. Phillips Hospital in St. Louis and assistant resident in surgery at D.C. General Hospital and Freedmen's Hospital, both in Washington, D.C. From 1957 to 1959, Leffall was a senior fellow in cancer surgery at Memorial Sloan-Kettering Cancer Center in New York. He decided to study at Sloan-Kettering because of the new frontiers posed by cancer surgery, Leffall stated in an interview with contributor Devera Pine. "I thought surgery was the most

dynamic field," he recalled. "Memorial Sloan-Kettering was using some of the most exciting techniques."

After one year as Chief of General Surgery in the U.S. Army Hospital in Munich (1960 to 1961), Leffall turned to a career in education, becoming an assistant professor at Howard University in 1962. Leffall continued at Howard, serving as assistant dean of the College of Medicine from 1964 to 1970. In 1970, he was appointed professor and chair of the Department of Surgery. "I have a very strong feeling for Howard University. If I had not been accepted there, I wouldn't be a physician and surgeon today," he said in his interview. "When I came along in 1948, predominantly white medical schools rarely accepted blacks." As a researcher, Leffall has focused on clinical studies of cancer of the breast, colorectum, head, and neck. He has published more than 116 articles in various professional journals and forums.

In addition to his careers in medicine and education, Leffall has led an active professional life. Leffall became a diplomate of the American Board of Surgery in 1958 and a fellow of the American College of Surgeons in 1964. He was a consultant to the National Cancer Institute beginning in 1972 and a consultant to Walter Reed Army Medical Center beginning in 1971. In 1978 he became the first black president of the American Cancer Society. He used this national forum to emphasize the problems of cancer in minorities, holding the first conference on cancer among black Americans in February of 1979. "I have tried to point out the problems of lack of access to care and the increased death rate," he told Pine. In 1980, President Carter appointed him to a six-year term as a member of the National Cancer Advisory Board.

Leffall has lectured extensively and has served as visiting professor at more than 200 medical institutions. He has received many awards, including the St. George Medal and Citation, the highest divisional award of the American Cancer Society, and the Distinguished Volunteer Service Award from the Secretary of the U.S. Department of Health and Human Services. In 1987, M.D. Anderson Hospital and Tumor Institute in Houston established the Biennial LaSalle D. Leffall Jr. Award. In 1996 Howard University honored Leffall by establishing an endowed Chair in Surgery in his name. At the 1995 Clinical Congress in New Orleans, Leffall was instated as the president of the American College of Surgeons.

Though Leffall told Pine that he was grateful for all the awards, he said he considers the ones he received from his students over the years "first among equals." In fact, along with his medical career, Leffall considers his teaching one of his most important accomplishments. The role of a teacher, he said, is "to inspire, to instruct, to stimulate, to stretch the imagination and to expand the aspirations of others. It's an honor to be a teacher."

Leffall married Ruth McWilliams in 1956; the couple has one son, LaSalle III.

SELECTED WRITINGS BY LEFFALL:

Books

"Claude H. Organ, Jr., M.D.," "The Howard University Department of Surgery and Freedman's Hospital," "Surgical Leaders and Role Models," *A Century of Black Surgeons, The U.S.A. Experience,* Transcript Press, 1987.

Periodicals

"Alarming Increase of the Cancer Mortality in the U.S. Black Population (1950–1967)," *Cancer,* (April 1973): 736–768.

"Health Status of Black Americans," *The State of Black America,* National Urban League, Inc., 1990, p. 121.

"Access to Surgical Care in the Inner Cities: One Provider's Perspective," *Bulletin, American College of Surgeons,* (April 1993): 15–19.

FURTHER READING:

Other

Leffall, LaSalle D., Jr., *Interview with Devera Pine for conducted February 3,* 1994.

—*Sketch by Devera Pine*

H. Ralph Lewis
1931-
Theoretical physicist

H. Ralph Lewis spent nearly 30 years as a researcher at the famed Los Alamos National Laboratory in New Mexico. But his research took him to colleges and universities throughout the U.S., as well as Europe and Africa. Fluent in German, he co-translated several volumes of the works of the Austrian physicist Wolfgang Pauli.

Harold Ralph Lewis was born in Chicago on June 7, 1931. His father, Harold Lewis, was an electrical engineer; his mother, Lena Lewis, was a schoolteacher. Not surprisingly, they placed great emphasis on the importance of education—which was fine with young Ralph, who was naturally curious and an avid reader.

Lewis was a good student and decided in high school that he wanted to study physics. He graduated high school a semester early and went on to Wilson Junior College in Chicago. While there, he was offered a scholarship to attend the University of Chicago. He received a bachelor of arts degree after only three years, but stayed on to get a bachelor of science degree after two additional years. From there, he went on to the University of Illinois at Champaign-Urbana, where he received his master's in science in 1955. He remained at the university for his doctoral work, in which he measured the magnetic fields of superconductors using nuclear radiation. He received his Ph.D. in 1958.

Initially interested in experimental physics, Lewis had become intrigued by theoretical physics, and chose to do postdoctoral work in Germany at Heidelberg's famed Institute for Theoretical Physics. He spent two years there and then returned to the United States to join Princeton's physics department. While at Princeton, Lewis became interested in plasma physics, a new discipline that studied ionized gases. He also explored the possibilities of harnessing thermonuclear energy for such useful purposes as generating electricity.

His interests led Lewis to the thermonuclear fusion project at Los Alamos in 1963. While there, he collaborated with scientists and researchers at a number of institutions, including the University of Wisconsin, the U.S. Department of Energy, and the Witwatersrand University in Johannesburg, South Africa. Lewis left Los Alamos in 1990 but remained briefly in New Mexico to teach for one semester at St. John's College in Santa Fe. In 1991 he became a professor of physics at Dartmouth College in Hanover, New Hampshire.

FURTHER READING:

Books

Kessler, James H., et al. *Distinguished African American Scientists of the Twentieth Century.* Phoenix: Oryx Press, 1996.

—Sketch by George A. Milite

Julian Herman Lewis
1891-1989
Physiologist and pathologist

Julian Herman Lewis was the first African American to receive a Ph.D. in physiology at the University of Chicago. His early research in immunology was followed by investigations into a wide range of scientific fields, among them anthropology, pathology, physiology, tuberculosis research, and psychology. In addition, he became interested in the biological status of African Americans and made a detailed study of their ancestry in Africa, which he published in his book *The Biology of the Negro.*

Lewis was born in Shawneetown, Illinois, on May 26, 1891, to John Calhoun Lewis and Cordelia O. Scott Lewis, both of whom were public school teachers. His father had been born into slavery and had later attended Berea College, where he had met his wife. Although the college had been set up to educate newly freed slaves after the Civil War, by the time young Julian was ready to enter a new state law had been passed excluding Negroes, and he was sent to the University of Illinois instead. Here, as one of the few blacks at the college, he had to deal with a degree of discrimination and social exclusion; Richard Bardolph relates in his book *The Negro Vanguard* that when Lewis was elected captain of his ROTC unit, the dean had him transferred to a specially created ceremonial office to "prevent possible trouble." He nevertheless excelled in his classes and graduated Phi Beta Kappa in 1911. A year later, he received an M.A., and then studied at the University of Chicago, where he was awarded a Ph.D. in physiology in 1915. The same year, his dissertation on the role of lipids in immunity was published in the *Journal of Infectious Diseases,* for which he received the Ricketts Prize. In 1917, Lewis received his medical degree from Rush Medical College and obtained an appointment to the department of pathology at the University of Chicago. He would rise the position of associate professor, serving there until 1943.

In 1926, Lewis was among the first to be awarded the new John Simon Guggenheim Fellowship for study abroad and conducted research at the University of Basel, Switzerland. Throughout the years, he presented papers at many scientific conferences, and his work received coverage in such publications as *Life* and *Time.* During World War II, he participated in a government-sponsored research project to investigate the possibility of using beef plasma as a substitute for human blood.

Combining his interests in his field and in his ancestry, Lewis delved into the history of African Americans in relationship to their anatomy, their physiological characteristics, and their responses to a variety of diseases. In 1942, he published the results of his investigations in *The Biology of the Negro,* which he wrote with a grant-in-aid from the Julius Rosenwald Fund. So well documented was the book's objective analysis of the subject that it cited well over a thousand references in the scientific literature. A book review in the *Journal of the National Medical Association* called it "a fair, impartial, scientific and masterly study and analysis of racial characteristics, likenesses and differences, with special reference to the Negro," and added: "It is noteworthy that the author has failed to discover any fundamental evidence to show that the Negro is biologically inferior to other groups in the genus *Homo.*"

Lewis married Eva Overton in 1918, and they had three children, Gloria Julienne, Julian Herman, Jr., and John Overton. Lewis was a member of many scientific societies, including the Society for Experimental Pathology, the American Association of Immunologists, and the American Association of Pathologists and Bacteriologists. In recognition of his outstanding career, he was awarded the Benjamin Rush Medal in 1971. In his later years, he served as director of the pathology department at Our Lady of Mercy Hospital in Dyer, Indiana, a position he held until his death on March 6, 1989, just short of his 98th birthday.

SELECTED WRITINGS BY LEWIS:

Books

The Biology of the Negro. University of Chicago Press, 1942.

Periodicals

"Lipids in Immunity. The Absorption of Substances Injected Subcutaneously and the Inhibitory Action of Heterologous Protein Mixtures on Anaphylaxis," *Journal of Infectious Diseases,* (July 1915).

"The Racial Distribution of Isohemagglutinin Groups," *Journal of the American Medical Association,* (October 21, 1922).

"Studies of Psychosomatics," *Psychosomatic Medicine,* (April 1943).

FURTHER READING:

Books

Bardolph, Richard. *The Negro Vanguard.* Negro Universities Press, 1959, p. 188.

Sammons, Vivian O. *Blacks in Science and Medicine.* Hemisphere Publishing, 1990, p. 153.

Periodicals

Sammons, Vivian O. "Age Regression," *Life Magazine,* (November 30, 1942): 86, 88.
Review of *The Biology of the Negro, Journal of the National Medical Association,* (July 1942).

Other

Correspondence and telephone conversations with son, Julian H. Lewis, Jr., January, 1994.

—*Sketch by Maurice Bleifeld*

Ruth Smith Lloyd
1917-
Anatomist

R uth Smith Lloyd was the first African American woman to earn a Ph.D. in anatomy. Lloyd, who spent a large portion of her teaching career at Howard University, specialized in issues surrounding fertility as well as research on the female sex cycle and the relation of sex hormones to growth.

Ruth Smith Lloyd was born in Washington, D.C., on January 25, 1917. The youngest of three girls born to Mary Elizabeth Smith and Bradley Donald Smith, Lloyd graduated from Dunbar High School in Washington and went on to receive her A.B. from Mt. Holyoke College in 1937. At this point, Lloyd planned to study zoology and then begin teaching at the high school level. However, after she attained her master's degree at Howard University, her professors encouraged her to work towards an advanced degree in anatomy. Her mentor at Howard recommended specifically that she study at Western Reserve University, and it was there that she began her serious studies in anatomy. In 1941 Lloyd earned her Ph.D. in anatomy, thus becoming the first African American woman to achieve that goal.

While studying at Western Reserve, Lloyd worked in the school's fertility laboratories, which kept colonies of monkeys. Lloyd would eventually concentrate her research and teaching efforts in the field of endocrinology and medical genetics. In 1941 she took a position at the Howard University college of medicine as an assistant in physiology. After a brief period, during which she taught zoology at Hampton Institute, Lloyd took time to begin raising her family. In 1939 she married a physician, Sterling M. Lloyd, with whom she would have three children.

In 1942, Lloyd returned to Howard University, where she remained for the rest of her professional career. That same year she was promoted to an instructor, and by 1958 she was an assistant professor of anatomy. Soon afterward, she became an associate professor at Howard's graduate school, where she remained until her retirement. Lloyd, who now lives in her native Washington, D.C., said in an interview with contributor Leonard C. Bruno that even upon reflection, she is unimpressed with her unique accomplishments. She sees little that is unusual or remarkable about her story, and described herself to Bruno as an average person with a normal life.

FURTHER READING:

Other

Lloyd, Ruth S., *Interview with Leonard C. Bruno,* conducted January 6, 1994.

—*Sketch by Leonard C. Bruno*

Joseph Granville Logan, Jr.
1920-
Physicist and inventor

J oseph Granville Logan, Jr.'s most notable scientific contribution was his invention of a small jet engine. His engine, which featured lower fuel consumption compared to previous similar models, could be used on helicopters and guided missiles. Logan has done much research over his long career in the areas of high temperature gas dynamics, hypersonic aerodynamics, chemical kinetics, re-entry aerodynamics, and new energy systems. Logan also holds a patent on a non-steady engine.

Logan was born in Washington, D.C., on June 8, 1920, to Joseph Granville Logan, Sr. and Lula (nee Briggs) Logan. Logan's father was the school principal at a junior high in Washington, D.C. Logan received his B.S. from the District of Columbia-based Miner Teachers College in 1941. Upon graduation, Logan worked as a math teacher in Baltimore for one year, 1941, before returning to Washington, D.C. There he was employed as a math and science teacher until 1945. In 1943, Logan began a concurrent position at the United States Bureau of Standards. He worked as a physicist in the aerodynamics department there until 1946. While working in Washington, Logan married Esther M. Taylor in 1944, and together they had two children, Joseph Michael and Eileen Cecile.

In 1946, Logan and his family moved to Buffalo, New York, where he worked as a research physicist at the Cornell Aeronautical Laboratories in Buffalo. It was while working here, in 1950, that Logan developed his new engine, the valveless pulse jet engine. He also was instrumental in the development of a new form of gas turbine. While employed at the aeronautical lab, Logan completed his graduate work. Logan had done some work at Howard University and Cornell University before earning his Ph.D. at the University of Buffalo. In 1955, Logan earned his physics doctorate with a dissertation titled "The Effect of Isotopic Substitution on Vibrational Wave Functions and Dissociation Probability of Diatomic and Linear Tratomic Molecules."

In 1957, Logan left the Cornell lab. He worked as the head of the aerophysics laboratory for Space Technological Labs, Inc., from 1957-59, then manager of the propulsion research department for one year, 1959-60. In 1960, Logan became the Director of the Aerodynamic and Propulsion Laboratory, at the Aerospace Corporation in El Segundo, California. He held this position until 1967, when he was hired by the western division of McDonnell Douglas Astronaut Company as a special assistant to the director of research and development. Logan held several more positions in this company. He was the manager of vulnerability and hardening development engineering from 1969-72, and the chief engineer of nuclear weapons effects, 1972-74.

In 1974, Logan became president of Apple Energy Sciences, Inc., a position he held until 1978. In 1978, Logan became the vice president of research and development at the West Coast Research Corporation. Logan also worked in higher education. He became the director of the physics department at California Polytechnic University, in Pomona, from 1978-79, then the director of the Urban University Center at the University of Southern California, from 1979 until 1989, when he retired.

As a scientist Logan maintained membership in several relevant scientific organizations: the Physics Society, the Institute of Aeronautical Scientists, the Federation of American Scientists, the New York Academy of Sciences, and the National Technical Association.

FURTHER READING:

Periodicals

"Former D.C. Teacher a Ph.D. in Physics," *The Negro History Bulletin,* (April 1955): 158.

—*Sketch by A. Petrusso*

Miles Vandahurst Lynk
1871-1956
Physician and medical educator

In a long and distinguished career, Miles Vandahurst Lynk not only helped to create a medical school that trained hundreds of African Americans, but also founded, edited, and published the first black medical journal and served as one of the prime movers in creating the National Medical Association for black physicians. Fine accomplishments for anyone, they seem all the more amazing when it is realized that Lynk was born to former slaves and was self-educated until the age of 13.

Lynk was born on June 3, 1871, in Brownsville, Tennessee, the son of John Henry and Mary Louise Lynk. Former slaves, Lynk's parents were farmers leading a basic life close to the land. But Lynk wanted, from an early age, to become a doctor. He was largely self-educated throughout his early years. As he reports in his autobiography, *Sixty Years of Medicine,* "I cultivated home study [and] literally attended 'Pine Knot College.'" So successful were his independent studies, that at age 13 he passed his county's teacher's examination, but was too young to use the certificate he earned. He apprenticed for a time with a local Brownsville physician, J. C. Hairston, and then attended Meharry Medical College, graduating second in a class of 13 in 1891. He practiced medicine in Jackson, Tennessee, until 1901.

Pursues Career as Publisher and Medical Educator

In 1892, fresh out of medical school, he began publishing *The Medical and Surgical Observer,* the first black medical journal in the nation. One of the first editions of that journal carried a plea for "an Association of medical men of color, national in character," to parallel the then all-white American Medical Association. In 1895, Lynk, along with Robert F. Boyd, was instrumental in starting the National Medical Association (NMA) in Atlanta, Georgia, an organization with thousands of members today and a well-respected journal.

Private practice, helping to found the NMA, and publishing a medical journal were not enough for Lynk. He pursued his studies even while practicing medicine, earning an M.S. from Walden University in Nashville in 1900, and a Bachelor of Laws degree from the University of West Tennessee in 1901. Around 1900, he and his wife, Beebe Steven (a chemist and pharmacist), mortgaged their house to follow another dream: establishing a medical college for African Americans at the University of West Tennessee, located first in Jackson and then in Memphis, Tennessee. Lynk served as its president and his wife taught pharmacy and chemistry. Always under-funded, the school finally closed in 1923, but not before graduating 266 students, 98 of whom passed the state boards.

Lynk did not confine his activities solely to medical matters. A prolific writer, he also authored a how-to for public speaking and a history of African American soldiers in the Spanish-American War, as well as his own autobiography. Lynk married a second time, in 1949, to Ola Herin Moore, and in 1952 the NMA awarded him its Distinguished Service Medal for a lifetime of work in medicine and the advancement of African Americans. He died on December 29, 1956, in Memphis, Tennessee.

SELECTED WRITINGS BY LYNK:

Books

The Afro-American School Speaker and Gems of Literature for School Commencements Literary Circles, Debating Clubs, and Rhetoricals Generally. University of West Tennessee Press, 1911.

Sixty Years of Medicine: or, The Life and Times of Miles V. Lynk. Twentieth Century Press, 1951.

Black Troopers, or Daring Deeds of Negro Soldiers in the Spanish-American War. AMS Press, 1971.

FURTHER READING:

Books

Dictionary of American Medical Biography. Greenwood Press, 1984, p. 466.

Morais, Herbert M. *The History of the Negro in Medicine.* Publishers Co., 1967, pp. 63–68.

Sammons, Vivian Ovelton. *Blacks in Science and Medicine,* Hemisphere Publishing, 1990, pp. 157–58.

Periodicals

Sammons, Vivian Ovelton. *Journal of the National Medical Association,* (January 1941): 46–47; (November 1943): 205–06; (November 1952): 475–76; (December 1981): 1219–25.

—Sketch by J. Sydney Jones

John W. Macklin
1939-
Analytical chemist

Even as a young child, John W. Macklin was curious. His curiosity led him into many kinds of experiments, and these his investigations led to discovery on the small scale of a small boy. Objects of interest included any kind of mechanical object, a chemical reaction, or even living organisms.

Macklin was born on December 11, 1939, in Fort Worth, Texas and for his first few years lived with his grandmother. She encouraged his experimentation, and this nurturing laid the foundation for his scientific achievements. In 1946, Macklin moved to Seattle with his mother, stepfather, and sister. In grade school he did what most boys do—designed and built model boats and model airplanes, took on a newspaper route to help pay for his hobbies, experimented with chemistry sets, did woodwork, participated in the marching band, and played football for his school.

His interest in science never waned during his educational years. He majored in math and chemistry in high school and that, combined with his athletic ability, earned him a spot as an undergraduate student at Linfield College in McMinnville, Oregon. The small liberal-arts college was run by the Baptist church, and at that time only had an enrollment of 1,500 students. His high school activities of chemistry, music, and football carried over into college. Macklin majored in chemistry, minored in music, played the saxophone and clarinet, and sang in the school choir. He also played on the football team. He graduated from Linfield College in 1962 and was promptly accepted into the doctoral program at Cornell University. Like most doctoral students, Macklin worked as a teaching assistant. As he became more familiar with the program, he worked as a research assistant at the university.

Macklin's research at Cornell focused on the structural identification of objects through spectrometry, the field that studies the measurement of wavelengths of light. Simply stated, all materials absorb light radiation to varying extents, depending on the molecular structure of the material. Since visible light is made up of the colors of the spectrum, each material absorbs different colors of that spectrum. Studies of the colors that materials absorb can help identify not only the material, but also its molecular structure.

The research process was long and complicated, but his dissertation was finally completed in 1968, and Macklin was awarded his doctorate in organic chemistry with minors in physical and analytical chemistry. He was asked to join the faculty of the University of Washington after his graduation and further develop his research on Raman spectrometry. This method of spectrometry uses a laser, and Macklin further refined it to be able to test very small sample sizes. Macklin's techniques found use in the research that attempts to answer evolutionary questions of the origins of carbon-based life on Earth. Macklin has also been using Raman spectrometry to investigate environmental pollution.

Macklin's community service projects include his work helping minority students at the University of Washington. He also champions the effort to improve the science education curriculum in the schools in the state of Washington.

FURTHER READING:

Books

Phelps, Shirelle. *Who's Who Among African Americans, 1998-99.* Gale Research, 1998, p. 729.

Kessler, James H., et.al. *Distinguished African American Scientists of the 20th Century.* Oryx Press, 1996, pp. 174-177.

—Sketch by Roger Jaffe

Monroe Alpheus Majors
1864-1960
Physician and surgeon

Monroe Alpheus Majors was the first African American doctor to pass the California Medical Boards, as well as the first to practice medicine west of the Rocky Mountains. He is credited with adding the term "paralysis diabetes" to medical parlance. Majors was also key in the development of several hospitals in his hometown of Waco, Texas. Additionally, Majors helped in the formation of

Monroe Alpheus Majors

several medical societies in Texas and Chicago, when the American Medical Association was closed to black members. One of them, the Lone Star Medical Association, was the first for black physicians in the United States. Majors was an accomplished author and editor whose writings often focused on racial issues. He wrote one of the first books specifically intended for black children, 1921's *First Steps and Nursery Rhymes*.

Majors was born in Waco, Texas on October 12, 1864, to Andrew Jackson and Jane (nee Barringer) Majors, and was the youngest of three. Majors was reared primarily in Austin, where he attended public schools. He worked as a page in the Texas state legislature at the age of ten to help pay for his education. His political consciousness was raised by this early experience, and Majors spent much of his life as an racial activist and writer. He began his undergraduate education in Austin's Tillotson College and Normal School and West Texas College. (The former institution was later known as Huston-Tillotson College). Majors earned his B.S. from Central Tennessee College in 1886. He earned his M.D. in the same year from Meharry Medical College, Nashville, Tennessee.

Upon graduation, in 1886, Majors returned to Texas, where he practiced medicine in Austin, Brenham, Calvert (where he was the first black doctor), and Dallas, Texas. He organized the Lone Star Medical Association, the first black medical society in the United States. (It was later known as the Lone Star State Medical, Dental and Pharmaceutical Society.) The Association had its first meeting in Galveston,

Texas. Majors also taught school for a year, from 1887 to 1888.

Majors was threatened with lynching by segregationist supporters in 1888, and that year he moved to Los Angles, California, and continued to practice medicine. There he was also a lecturer at the Los Angeles Medical College and editor of the *Los Angeles Western News*. Majors became involved in local politics, where he helped get the first black men appointed to the local police force. On January 26, 1889, Majors became the first black man to pass the California medical boards. He married Georgia Groom (some sources say Green) in 1889, and had one daughter, Grace, with her. They divorced in 1904.

By 1890, Majors returned to Texas and resettled in Waco. Upon his return, Majors again practiced medicine. He also founded the Southwest's first black drugstore, as well as the Colored Hospital. From 1891 until 1894, Majors was a lecturer at Waco's Paul Quinn College, teaching sanitation and hygiene. The year 1893 was a significant one for Majors. He published a biographical dictionary entitled *Noted Negro Women,* a publication that was unprecedented at the time. He began his tenure as editor of Waco's *Texas Searchlight*, a post he held until 1895. Majors also spent several months in Chicago, working with Frederick Douglass and at Provident Hospital. In 1894, Majors became president of the Lone Star State Medical Society, which he had helped found several years earlier, and served as chair of the board of directors of the Texas Cotton Palace Exposition.

In 1896 or 1897, Majors spent a short time living in Decateur, Illinois, until his life was again threatened for his outspoken political activities and his success as a doctor. He then moved to Indianapolis, Indiana. Though he only lived in Indiana from about 1897 to 1899, Majors worked on the prestigious publication *Indiana Freeman*, as a columnist, writer, and editor from 1898-99. His column was entitled "Majors Melange." In addition to his political and race improvement articles, Majors published some poetry. In 1899, Majors returned to Waco, where he was the superintendent of the Colored Hospital, which he founded a few years earlier. He held this post until 1901, when he was again forced out of the area. This time Majors went to Chicago, and never returned to Texas.

In Chicago, Majors continued his medical practice, as well as his journalistic activities. He was involved in the organization of a society for medical practitioners and became a charter member of this organization. Majors was an editor here as well, of the *Broad Ax* and the *Chicago Conservator,* the latter from 1908-11. His involvement with the *Chicago Conservator* was at the behest of Booker T. Washington. In 1908, Majors was also involved with Chicago's Lincoln Day celebrations. Majors also remarried in 1909, to Estelle C. Bond, a musician. He had another daughter with her, Margaret Jeanette Bonds Majors.

Majors increased his writing output in Chicago. He published some poems, including 1917's "An Ode to Frederick Douglass," and a children's book, *First Steps to*

Nursery Rhymes. Majors also befriended famous black poet Paul Lawrence Dunbar.

In 1923 (or 1933, according to some sources), Majors returned to California, where he remained for the rest of his life. In 1925, Majors suddenly lost most of his eyesight. Two operations were unsuccessful in repairing this disability. Despite this, he continued to practice medicine for several years. Majors died on December 10, 1960, in Los Angeles after four years of poor health.

SELECTED WRITINGS BY MAJORS:

Books

First Steps and Nursery Rhymes. McElray and Clark, 1921.
Noted Negro Women: Their Triumphs and Activities. Donohue & Henneberry, 1893, reprinted Books for Libraries Press, 1971.

FURTHER READING:

Periodicals

Cobb, W. Montague, "Monroe Alpheus Majors, 1864-," *Journal of the National Medical Association,* (March 1955): 139-41.

—*Sketch by A. Petrusso*

Arnold Hamilton Maloney
1888-1955
Pharmacologist and physician

Arnold Hamilton Maloney hailed from the island of Trinidad and had humble beginnings. After coming to the United States to complete his education, he became the second black person to obtain both an M.D. and a Ph.D. in the United States, and went on to become the first black professor of pharmacology. However, Maloney was first a minister, and at one point he was the youngest ordained priest in the Episcopal Church. He was later a Bishop in the African Orthodox Church, but eventually left church ministry to pursue a career in medicine. He is best known for discovering an antidote for barbiturate poisoning.

Arnold Hamilton Maloney was born on July 4, 1888, in Cocoye Village, Trinidad, British West Indies. He was the oldest of the ten children born to Lewis Albert Maloney and Estelle Evetta (Bonas) Maloney. His father was a building contractor and owned a number of grocery stores, which his mother helped to run, while also teaching needlework. Maloney greatly respected his father, describing him in his book on race leadership as "a race champion who fought right nobly and well in his day." Maloney showed great aptitude for learning, and won numerous awards as a student. He also revealed a flair for writing and speaking, both of which he actively pursued throughout his life.

The first degree Maloney obtained was a bachelor of arts, or A.B., degree (1909), from Naparima College in Trinidad, which was affiliated with Cambridge University in England. He had planned to run a drug store, but a letter from an uncle in the United States changed his plans. His uncle suggested there were better opportunities in the United States, and Maloney emigrated in 1909. His early experiences did not live up to his expectations. A friend suggested he enroll in Lincoln University, Pennsylvania, which he did for a year. While there, his speaking skills were noted, and he was encouraged to become a pastor. He left Lincoln to attend the General Theological Seminary in New York.

Spends Time as a Minister

The General Theological Seminary had a reciprocal agreement with Columbia University from which Maloney obtain a master's degree, majoring in philosophy (1910). He was ordained a priest in the Episcopal Church (1911), the youngest priest in that church at the time. He was pastor of a church in Annapolis, Maryland, and completed his bachelor of science in theology degree from General Theological Seminary (1912). He became pastor of another church in Syracuse, New York (1915-1917), and considering leaving the ministry for a career in the forestry service. During this time, Maloney married Beatrice Pocahontas Johnston, who had grown up in Louisville, Kentucky. Together they had one daughter, Beatrice Louise, and one son, Arnold H. Maloney, Jr., who later became a physician.

Despite his misgivings, Maloney remained a pastor, and moved to Indianapolis, Indiana. However, relations with his authorities were strained, and he resigned his position in the church. A friend invited him to join the African Orthodox Church, and he eventually became a Bishop in that church. Again, relations became strained, however, and Maloney left church ministry completely in 1920.

The Move to Medicine

Maloney's next position was as professor of psychology at Wilberforce University, Ohio (1920-25). He enjoyed teaching very much, and decided to pursue his own education further. He entered medical school at Indiana University School of Medicine, in Indianapolis, Indiana. During this time he wrote a regular newspaper column, "The Indianapolis Negro," for the *Indianapolis Recorder*. He graduated with his M.D. degree in 1929.

After graduating, Maloney began an internship in Provident Hospital, Baltimore, Maryland. At the time, however, Howard University in Washington, D.C. was actively recruiting well-trained physicians for its medical school. Maloney was asked to join the faculty, but before starting to teach he was given a fellowship to enter the graduate program in pharmacology at the University of Wisconsin in Madison, Wisconsin. His research focused on how drugs (like morphine) act to either stimulate or depress breathing by acting on certain parts of the brain. He obtained his Ph.D. in 1931, along with **Joseph L. Johnson**. Maloney and Johnson were jointly the second and third blacks to obtain both M.D. and Ph.D. degrees in the United States. Together they joined the faculty at Howard University, with Johnson becoming head of the Department of Physiology, and Maloney head of the Department of Pharmacology. Maloney thus became the first black professor of pharmacology in the United States.

Maloney served on the faculty at Howard University from 1931 to 1953. In addition to teaching and administration, he continued his research into the effects of various drugs on breathing. His most notable discovery related to the use of barbiturates. These drugs are used as sedatives, but overdoses can depress breathing to such as extent that they can cause death. Maloney discovered that picrotoxin, a compound obtained from the seeds of a particular scrub (*Anamirta cocculus*), can reverse these effects and protect animals and humans from barbiturate poisoning.

While Maloney is most widely remembered for his picrotoxin discovery, he also published over 50 other scientific articles. He was awarded honorary degrees from Morris Brown University in Atlanta, Georgia (1918) and Wilberforce University (1937). He was actively involved in various scientific and medical organizations, such as the American Association for the Advancement of Science, the New York Academy of Sciences, and the National Medical Association. He has also made contributions in other fields. His list of books include one on Christian ethics, one on leadership on race issues within the church, and one on democracy (written with his brother and son). Maloney died in Washington, D.C. on August 8, 1955.

SELECTED WRITINGS BY MALONEY:

Books

The Adequate Norm: An Essay on Christian Ethics, Indianapolis, IN: C. E. Pauley, 1914.
Some Essentials of Race Leadership, Xenia, OH: Aldine, 1924.
(With C. McD. Maloney and A. H. Maloney, Jr.) *Pathways to Democracy,* Boston: Meador, 1945.
Amber Gold: An Adventure in Autobiography, Boston: Meador, 1946.

Periodicals

(With R. H. Fitch and A. L. Tatum) "Picrotoxin as an Antidote in Acute Poisoning by the Shorter Acting Barbiturates," *Journal of Pharmacology and Experimental Therapeutics,* Vol. 41, (April 1931): 465-482.
(With A. L. Tatum) "Picrotoxin as an Antidote in Acute Poisoning by the Longer Acting Barbiturates," *Journal of Pharmacology and Experimental Therapeutics,* Vol. 44, (March 1932): 337-352.

FURTHER READING:

Books

McMurray, Emily J., ed. *Notable Twentieth-Century Scientists,* Vol. 3. Detroit: Gale Research, 1995, p. 1305-1306.
Sammons, Vivian Ovelton. *Blacks in Science and Medicine.* Taylor & Francis, 1990, p. 160.

Periodicals

Journal of the National Medical Association, Vol. 47, (November 1955): 424-426.

—*Sketch by Dónal P. O'Mathúna*

Vance H. Marchbanks, Jr.
1905-1988
Flight surgeon

Vance H. Marchbanks, Jr. was a much-decorated Air Force flight surgeon who served in the military for 23 years. His combat mission work and bravery earned him several medals, including the Bronze Star and Air Force Commendation Medals. Marchbanks was one of the project physicians for Project *Mercury,* the United States' first manned space craft mission. He and 10 other physicians monitored the health of the astronauts by collecting medical flight data from them as they orbited Earth. This data enabled Marchbanks and others to determine the impact that space flight has on humans.

Marchbanks, the second of two children, was born on January 12, 1905, at Fort Washikie, Wyoming, to Vance H. Marchbanks, Sr. (a cavalry sergeant) and Callie Hatton. He received his baccalaureate degree from the University of Arizona in 1931, and his medical degree from Howard University, Washington, D.C., in 1937. After graduation, Marchbanks worked for the Veterans Administration Hospital in Tuskegee, Alabama, until April 1941, when he entered the Army Air Corps as a First Lieutenant. (At the time, medical officers who were in the Army Air Corps were considered part of the Army.) Marchbanks was awarded the Bronze Star for his heroism while fighting in Italy in World War II. He advanced in the Air Force ranks and was assigned to the Air Force Hospital in Nagoya, Japan, as the deputy commander and chief of the professional service; a year later, in 1955, his work there earned him a promotion to full Colonel in the Medical Corps.

Marchbanks wrote several papers about stress related to flying and combat fatigue, published in research journals and military manuals. While participating in a marathon 10,600-mile (16,960 km), 22.5-hour non-stop flight from Florida to Argentina to New York, he discovered a marker for identifying fatigue in flight crew members. During the flight, Marchbanks measured the amount of adrenal hormone in blood and tissue samples taken from the crew members. He determined that a certain level indicated physical fatigue, a condition which often presages a fatal crash. Marchbanks received an Air Force Commendation Medal in November 1957 for this research. He also received a medal for developing an oxygen mask tester, a device that reminds Air Force flight crew members to clean their oxygen masks frequently. His military record earned him two Commendation Medals, one in 1950 and another in 1958.

Selected as Project Physician for Project *Mercury*

By 1960, Marchbanks's work, his rating of Chief Flight Surgeon (with its prerequisite 1,500 flying hours and 15 years of flying status), and his research in aviation medicine qualified him as one of the eleven Air Force surgeons assigned to Project *Mercury*, the first manned space craft launched by the United States. Assigned a position as a project physician, Marchbanks was stationed in Kano, Nigeria, at one of the 18 tracking stations utilized on February 20, 1962, when Colonel John Glenn and the other astronauts circled Earth three times. Marchbanks's role in the mission was to monitor the astronauts' physical well-being by looking at readings of respiration rate, temperature, and heart reaction for the few minutes that they passed overhead. To determine whether they were having heart problems or not, Marchbanks compared their electrocardiograms (ECG) during spaceflight to a set of similar tests taken earlier at the Johnson Space Center while the astronauts were under both normal and stressed conditions. Prior to leaving for Nigeria, Marchbanks had spent more than a year studying Colonel Glenn's various ECG readings. Each time the *Mercury* passed, Marchbanks recorded normal ECG readings for the astronaut, indicating that the flight was not causing any physiological problems. After this assignment, Marchbanks helped to design the space suits and the monitoring systems the astronauts used for the *Apollo* moon shot. As Chief of Environmental Health Services at Hamilton Standard, a division of United Aircraft Corporation in Connecticut, Marchbanks was responsible

for the human safety aspects of the simulated training for the backpack being built for the Apollo astronauts.

Marchbanks spent much of his career studying the sickle-cell trait, which differs from the disease sickle cell anemia. In 1983 he was recognized by Howard University in Washington, D.C., for pioneering the initiative that resulted in the Department of Defense rescinding restrictions on the admission of persons with this trait to the Air Force Academy and to the Department of Defense.

Marchbanks married Lois Gilkey and they had two daughters. He was a member of the AeroMedical Association and the Society of Flight Surgeons. He died in 1988 of complications from Alzheimer's disease.

SELECTED WRITINGS BY MARCHBANKS:

Periodicals

"The Black Physician and the USAF," *Journal of the National Medical Association,* (January 1972): 73–74.
"The Sickle Trait and the Black Airman," *Aviation, Space, and Environmental Medicine,* (March 1980): 299–300.

FURTHER READING:

Periodicals

Ebony, (April 1962): 36–40.

—*Sketch by Barbara Proujan*

Alfred E. Martin
1911-
Physicist

Alfred E. Martin was an optical physicist who contributed to the development of the television picture tube. A private industry researcher, he also taught at the collegiate level throughout his career.

Martin was born in New York City on September 15, 1911. Upon graduation from high school, he enrolled in the College of the City of New York. The school granted him a bachelor of science degree in 1932. His high grades and recommendations secured him enrollment in the University of Michigan graduate program. In just a year, he earned his master of science degree from the school. Martin then joined the physics department at Shaw University, where he taught until 1936. It was then he became a member of the

Fisk University faculty. He stayed there until 1942, when he began a career in private industry.

Martin's career in industry began with the Signal Corps Laboratory in Eatontown, New Jersey. In 1944, he left this laboratory for the A.D. Cardwell Manufacturing Corporation in Brooklyn, New York. At this time, he began a long association with Hunter College in New York City as a lecturer. In 1946, the Sylvania Electric Products company in Bayside, New York, recruited Martin. He went to work there as an optical physicist and head of the photonics section of their physics laboratories. It was at Sylvania that he made his contribution to the television picture tube; he helped develop an innovation called the HaloLite principle, which reduced eye strain. This accomplishment was noted in the April 1954 edition of *Ebony* magazine, which noted that he supervised a staff of 12 people, all white.

Martin's next career move was in 1957; he joined the publishing company McGraw-Hill as a technical editor. He stayed there until 1959, when he accepted an offer from the Polaroid Electronics Corporation to become its director of engineering training. In 1961, he moved on to new challenges at the Arinc Research Corporation, where he worked as an engineer until 1964. This experience led him to the Grumman Aircraft Engineering Corporation, which he joined as a senior reliability engineer. In 1967, he resigned his position to return to academic life as an assistant professor at Manhattan Community College. His research efforts while there included work in radiometry and the luminescence of inorganic phosors.

Martin is a member and recipient of awards from the American Physical Society, American Association of Physics Teachers, Institute of Radio Engineers, Optical Society of America, Electrochemical Society of Colorimetry, and the Scientific Research Society of America. Martin is now retired.

FURTHER READING

Books

Sammons, Vivian. *Blacks in Science and Medicine.* New York: Hemisphere Publishing, 1990.

Periodicals

"Laboratory Supervisor." *Ebony* (April 1954): 5.

—Sketch by Patrick J. Longe

Walter E. Massey
1938-
Physicist

A respected physicist, Walter E. Massey has had an extensive career as an educator, administrator, and researcher. He was also nominated by President George Bush to be director of the National Science Foundation and became the second African American to hold this post. In the early 1990s, after his tenure as the director of the National Science Foundation, he accepted an appointment as senior vice president for academic affairs and provost at the University of California. Since 1995 he has served as the ninth president of the historically black Morehouse College. Massey also distinguished himself during his directorship of Argonne National Laboratory.

Walter Eugene Massey was born in Hattiesburg, Mississippi, on April 5, 1938. His parents were Almar and Essie Nelson Massey. He became interested in mathematics early in his childhood, and in an interview for *Scientific American* he explained that "there was just something about sitting down and working through problems" that intrigued him. Massey attended the Royal Street High School in Hattiesburg but left at the end of the tenth grade to accept a scholarship at Morehouse College in Atlanta, one of the premier black colleges in the nation. His early departure from high school meant that he entered Morehouse with no background in advanced mathematics, physics, or chemistry. As a result, he became discouraged during his first few weeks at Morehouse and wanted to return home. Massey's mother insisted that he remain, however, and four years later he graduated with a bachelor's degree in physics. Massey credits physicist Sabinus H. Christensen for his survival at Morehouse. Since he was the only physics major in his class at Morehouse, Massey received one-on-one tutorials from Christensen in many of his courses.

Establishes Himself in the Academic and Research Fields

Massey stayed on at Morehouse as an instructor for one year after graduation and then enrolled as a graduate student in physics at Washington University in St. Louis. Again, he was fortunate enough to encounter a concerned and inspiring teacher, the theoretical physicist Eugene Feenberg. "If he [Feenberg] had not taken extraordinary care," Massey told *Scientific American,* "I would have quit." Instead, he remained at Washington to complete his doctoral degree in physics in 1966.

Massey's research interests have included solid-state theory (study of properties of solid material) and theories of quantum liquids and solids. While still a graduate student, he studied the behavior of both solid and liquid helium–3 and helium–4, publishing a series of papers on this work in the early 1970s. Massey began his professional career as a research fellow at the Argonne National Laboratory in Batavia, Illinois, in 1966. Over the next two years he became a staff physicist and soon thereafter, he was appointed assistant professor of physics at the University of Illinois. But he stayed at this post only a year before moving to Brown University as associate professor of physics. He was promoted to full professor in 1975 and named dean of the college in the same year. Massey's best-known accomplishment at Brown was his development of the Inner City Teachers of Science (ICTOS) program, a program for the improvement of science instruction in inner city schools. He was awarded the American Association for the Advancement of Science's Distinguished Service Citation for his development of ICTOS.

In 1979 the University of Chicago invited Massey to become professor of physics and director of the Argonne National Laboratory, which the university operates for the U.S. Department of Energy. The latter appointment was a particular challenge, since the concept of national laboratories financed by federal tax funds was very much in question at the time. Massey made a concerted effort to see that Argonne research was made more readily available to private industry, and because of this, Charles E. Till, head of engineering research at Argonne, has credited Massey for the survival of the research facility.

Accepts Post at National Science Foundation

During his tenure at Brown, Massey's administrative adeptness led him to become involved in activities such as the Physics Review Committee of the National Academy of Sciences-National Research Council (1972–1975), the Advisory Panel of the Division of Physics for the National Science Foundation (1975–1977), and the Advisory Committee on Eastern Europe and the U.S.S.R. of the National Science Foundation (1973–1976). He also served on the National Science Board, the policy-making arm of the National Science Foundation, from 1978 to 1984.

In the fall of 1990, Massey was chosen by President George Bush to head the National Science Foundation (NSF), a position he held until 1993 when he was offered the post of provost and senior vice president for academic affairs at the University of California. The *New York Times* reported that Massey had hoped to complete his six-year term at NSF, but he said that the California offer was "an opportunity that I cannot pass up."

Massey was only in California two years when he took the position of president at Morehouse College, the prestigious black, all-male liberal arts college. The return to his alma mater demonstrated Massey's commitment to education and specifically his commitment to providing educational opportunity to black students.

Massey has received honorary degrees from a number of institutions, including Lake Forest College, Williams College, Elmhurst College, Atlanta University, Rutgers University, Marquette University, Boston College, as well as Morehouse College. He also served on the board of

directors of the American Association for the Advancement of Science from 1981 to 1985 and was elected the organization's president in 1988. Massey has also been appointed to the board of directors of various corporations, including Motorola and the (Chicago) Tribune Company. He married Shirley Streeter in 1969. The Masseys have two sons, Keith Anthony and Eric Eugene. Massey lists his hobbies as sailing, skiing, tennis, and jogging.

SELECTED WRITINGS BY MASSEY:

Periodicals

"Variational Calculations on Liquid Helium 4 and Helium 3," *Physical Review,* (December 5, 1967): 256.
"Training Science Teachers for the Inner City," *The Physics Teacher,* (February 1976).

FURTHER READING:

Periodicals

Beardsley, Tim. "Scientist, Administrator, Role Model," *Scientific American,* (June 1992): 40–41.
Bradburn, Norman M., and David Rosen. "Walter E. Massey: President-Elect of AAAS," *Science,* (December 18, 1987): 1657–1658.
Leary, Warren E. "Head of Science Education Will Take a University Post," *New York Times,* (January 28, 1993): A14.
Lepkowski, Wil. "Walter Massey Takes Over Helm of National Science Foundation," *Chemical & Engineering News,* (April 22, 1991): 22–24.

—*Sketch by David E. Newton*

Samuel P. Massie
1919-
Chemist

Samuel P. Massie's outstanding educational career as a chemistry professor has led him to be recognized as a leader in the field of chemical education. Massie was the first black faculty member at The Naval Academy in Annapolis.

Samuel Proctor Massie was born in North Little Rock, Arkansas, on July 3, 1919. An excellent student, Massie graduated from high school at the age of 13. He then attended Dunbar Junior College. When Massie graduated

Samuel P. Massie

from Dunbar he went to the Agricultural Mechanical and Normal College of Arkansas, where he received a bachelor of science degree in 1938. In 1939 he began working as a laboratory assistant in chemistry at Fisk University, where he also obtained his master of arts degree in 1940. Between 1940 and 1941 Massie was an associate professor of mathematics at the Agricultural Mechanical and Normal College of Arkansas. He was a research associate in chemistry at Iowa State University beginning in 1943 and received a doctorate in organic chemistry from that university in 1946. That same year he returned to Fisk University as an instructor. The year following, Massie married Gloria Tompkins. They have three sons.

Begins a Distinguished Teaching Career

During his long teaching career, Massie held several positions, including professor and chair of the chemistry department at Langston University from 1947 to 1953. From 1953 to 1960 he held a similar post at Fisk University. In addition to his regular teaching position at Fisk, Massie also served as Sigma Xi Lecturer at Swarthmore College. In 1960 Massie became associate program director at the National Science Foundation (NSF), an agency that works to support a national science policy by sponsoring research, science curriculum development, teacher training, and various other programs. In 1961 Massie went on to become chair of pharmaceutical chemistry at Howard University, a post he gave up in 1963 to become president of North Carolina College at Durham. In 1966 he joined the faculty

at the United States Naval Academy as a professor of chemistry, also serving as chair of the chemistry department from 1977 to 1981.

In addition to the award from the Chemical Manufacturers Association in 1961, Massie received an honorary doctorate from the University of Arkansas in 1970. In 1980 he was named Outstanding Professor by the National Organization of Black Chemists, and in 1981 he received a Distinguished Achievement Citation from Iowa State University. In 1994 The National Naval Officer's Association honored him by establishing an educational endowment in his name. In 1989 he was inducted into the National Black College Hall of Fame and he also received the White House Initiative Lifetime Achievement Award. Massie has been active outside academia as chair of the Maryland State Board for Community Colleges, and he has also served on the Governor's Science Advisory Council. He has contributed to his community in many capacities, including membership on the Board of Directors of the Red Cross, and distinguished service with United Fund.

FURTHER READING:

Books

Sammons, Vivian Ovelton. *Blacks in Science and Medicine.* Hemisphere, 1990, p. 164.

—*Sketch by M. C. Nagel*

Jan Earnst Matzeliger
1852-1889
Inventor

Jan Earnst Matzeliger was responsible for several industrial machine innovations. One of these—the shoe lasting machine—changed the shoe-making industry at its core. Though he had no substantive formal education and came to the United States as a non-English-speaking immigrant, he invented machines that changed the world. The one-time owner of several patents, Matzeliger died an early death. His inventions made his adopted home of Lynn, Massachusetts, the shoe capital of the world.

Matzeliger was born in Paramaribo, Dutch Guiana (also known as Surinam, a Dutch colony on the South American coast) on September 15, 1852. His father was a Holland-born engineer, and his mother was a black Surinamese woman. Some accounts claim she was a slave. After going to live an aunt, his father's sister, at age three,

Jan Earnst Matzeliger

Matzeliger began an apprenticeship in the government machine works run by his father at the age of 10. As a boy, Matzeliger received little or no formal education, but became interested in machines because of his work experience.

Emigrates to the United States

Matzeliger left his home in 1871 and spent the next two years as a sailor working aboard an East Indian freighter. He left his ship's employ and settled in Philadelphia. There, he worked in a shoe factory and other machine shops. By 1877, after a short stint in Boston, Matzeliger had moved to Lynn, Massachusetts, where he spent the rest of his short life.

When he first settled in Lynn, Matzeliger was treated as an outsider. First, he learned the English language, and then he studied science and mechanics on his own. Matzeliger also spent some of his spare time painting, and he was apparently accomplished enough to give others lessons in the art. He sought a spiritual community, but was rejected by Roman Catholic, Episcopalian, and Unitarian congregations because of his race. He was accepted at the North Congregational Church in 1884, where he often attended church and took part in church functions, but never became a formal member on his own accord. Matzeliger never forget their kindness and rewarded them financially upon this death.

Devises Machines in Spare Time

As he had done in Philadelphia, Matzeliger worked in a shoe factory in Lynn, owned by M. H. Harvey. He primarily worked on the McKay sole-sewing machine for turned shoe. But he also operated a number of other machines while employed there, including a sole-sewing machine, heel-burnishing machine, and a button-hold machine. Matzeliger began inventing machines at home on his own time. He was not immediately successful. He tried to make a machine that could wrap oranges, but it did not work. Matzeliger found success in the industry in which he was most familiar, the shoe industry.

Before Matzeliger, the Industrial Revolution had affected the shoe industry in several ways. Machines had been invented that could cut, sew, and tack shoes, but none could "last" them. It had to be done by hand by skilled laborers. In lasting a shoe, the leather uppers of a shoe are stretched over the last, which is foot-shaped model. After the leather is correctly lasted, it is sewn to the inner sole. The varying thicknesses and types of leather made it hard to invent a machine that could last properly. Hoxever, the labor required in the lasting process added significantly to the cost of a shoe.

Conquers "Lasting" Problem

Matzeliger was inspired to solve this problem after overhearing co-workers claim without a doubt that there would be never be a machine that could last shoes as well as humans. Matzeliger spent much of his free time, alone after work, designing such a machine. Initially he was forced to use crude materials like cigar and packing boxes, wood, and wire to create a first prototype. By the fall of 1880, Matzeliger felt confident enough in his machine that he looked for and found financial backers, C.H. Delnow and M.S. Nichols. With their financial support—for which they each got one-third ownership of the device—he made two more models with scrapped pieces of castings and iron parts. He assembled his machine in an empty corner of the plant that employed him. He took a patent (number 274,207) out on the second of these on March 20, 1883. The plans for his proposed patent proved so intricate that the government patent office sent an official to Lynn to inspect the machine in person.

Develops a Working Model

By 1885, Matzeliger had a fourth and final model that was appropriate for factory condition testing. It was this machine, which took Matzeliger about five years to develop, that could last the leather, arrange it over the sole, and drive in the nails, finishing the shoe in about one minute's time. In his first public demonstration, on May 29, 1885, Matzeliger's lasting machine made about 75 pairs of shoes in a 10-hour work day period. Before Matzeliger's lasting machine, an average skilled worker could last about 35-50 shoes per day. With adjustments, Matzeliger's machine could make between 150 to 700 pairs a day, depending on the leather's quality.

There were many benefits to Matzeliger's invention. The cost of shoes was cut in half. Unskilled shoe workers saw their wages doubled and their working conditions advanced considerably. However, their skilled counterparts, whose work was previously a well-paid craft, were not so impressed. Perhaps their attitude, combined with the era's racism, led to Matzeliger's invention being called "the niggerhead laster."

Falls Ill and Sells His Patent

Matzeliger had financial aspirations of his own. He wanted to market his invention and make his own fortune. He and his backers had formed a company, The Consolidated Hand Method Lasting Machine Company, in 1883, but could not totally finance production. Two more investors were brought in, George A. Brown and Sydney W. Winslow, and manufacture began. Because Matzeliger's illness, which began with a misdiagnosed cold in the summer of 1886, left him unable to continue working, the patents, and thereby the company, were sold to Winslow in exchange for stock. Winslow, with his own partners, merged with several other companies to form the United Shoe Machine Company, which built lasting machines based on Matzeliger's patent. Within 12 years, 98% of the shoe industry was using their machine; in 20 years, the company had earned over $50 million. Matzeliger's lasting machine became the standard for the shoe industry.

Matzeliger had also made other related inventions over the years, including an 1888 patent for "Mechanism for Distributing Tacks, Nails, etc." (patent no. 415,726). Most were issued posthumously: the nailing machine (patent no. 423,937, issued February 25, 1890); "Tack Separating and Distributing Mechanism" (patent no. 423,937, March 25, 1890); and another Lasting Machine (no. 459,899, September 22, 1891).

The inventor died on August 24, 1889, from tuberculosis in Lynn Hospital. Matzeliger spent his last days bedridden, working on designs for machines and painting. He never married, and, according to some sources, was homosexual. Matzeliger never saw the profound impact of his invention on the world. In his will, he left the bulk of his estate, his stock, to the North Congregational Church to benefit "the Christian poor," but specifying that the money was not to benefit anyone from the other churches in Lynn who had turned him away. Recognition of Matzeliger for his invention did not come until the Pan-American Exposition of 1901, when he was awarded the Gold Medal and Diploma. Matzeliger was honored with his own United States postage stamp in 1992.

FURTHER READING:

Books

Karwatka, Dennis. *Technology's Past: America's Industrial Revolution and the People Who Delivered the Goods.* Prakken Publishers, 1996, pp. 115-17.

Mitchell, Barbara. *Shoes for Everyone.* Minneapolis: Carolrhoda Books, 1986.

Robinson, Gary W. "Jan Earnst Matzeliger and the Last Machine," in *No Race of Imitators: Lynn and Her People, An Anthology.* Lynn, MA: Lynn Historical Society, 1992.

Periodicals

Kaplan, Sydney. "Jan Earnst Matzeliger and the Making of the Shoe," *Journal of Negro History.* (January 1955): 8-33.

Other

A Lasting Impression: The Jan Matzeliger Story. Lynn Historical Society.

—*Sketch by A. Petrusso*

Vivienne Malone Mayes
1932-1995
Mathematician

Vivienne Malone Mayes, the fifth African American woman to earn a doctoral degree in mathematics, spent much of her life struggling to create new opportunities for both blacks and women in the often insular world of mathematics. Despite opposition that ran through much of her career, she achieved a standing in the mathematics community that led to acceptance by institutions that initially barred her on the basis of her race. Mayes said later in her life that, like many early African American trailblazers, she held herself to high standards because she knew that white colleagues and administrators of the era would judge other blacks by her performance. Her field of research was asymptotic analysis and summability theory.

Mayes was born in Waco, Texas, on February 10, 1932. She attended the segregated A. J. Moore High School in Waco, graduating when she was only 16. She continued her education at Fisk University in Nashville, one of the finest African American universities of the day. There, she earned a bachelor's degree in 1952 and a master's degree in 1954. One of Mayes's professors at Fisk was **Evelyn Boyd Granville**, one of the first two African American women to receive a mathematics doctorate. Granville's teaching and encouragement inspired Mayes to pursue her master's degree and later proved crucial in her long, lonely struggle to earn a doctorate. "I believe it was her presence and influence [that] account for my pursuit of advanced degrees in mathematics," Mayes wrote later of Granville.

The Struggle Toward a Doctorate

From Fisk, Mayes returned home to Waco to chair the mathematics department at Paul Quinn College, an African Methodist Episcopal Church school. By 1961 she felt that she needed more challenges to continue her development as a mathematician. So she decided to apply to Baylor University in Waco to take a few mathematics classes. Baylor's response to her application was humiliating. They sent her a letter outlining their policy of not accepting African American students, a letter she kept for many years afterward. But Baylor's rejection was in some sense fortunate. That university did not offer doctorates in mathematics, and if she had attended Baylor she most likely would have taken only a few courses and then returned to work. Instead, in 1962, Mayes went to the University of Texas, which had recently been integrated by federal law and did offer a doctoral program in mathematics.

Graduate school proved a long, lonely road for Mayes. Many students find doctoral programs isolating; but for Mayes, the only black and the only woman in the department, the isolation was profound. Despite her teaching background, she was denied the income of a teaching assistantship. Classmates largely ignored her, and some would abruptly end their conversations when she approached. One professor openly forbid her from enrolling in his course because of her race.

"I could not join my advisor and other classmates to discuss mathematics over coffee at Hilsberg's cafe," she said, because that establishment did not serve African Americans. The closest she ever came to these discussions were overheard snatches of conversation as she and other African Americans picketed the restaurant. In an article in the *Association for Women in Mathematics Newsletter,* Mayes later wrote: ". . . it took a faith in scholarship almost beyond measure to endure the stress of earning a Ph.D. as a black, female graduate student." Even colleagues who were friendly to her goals often did not understand her struggle. One professor, complaining about a civil rights demonstration, said that there would not be race problems if the demonstrators were as hard-working and studious as Mayes. She answered him, "If it hadn't been for those hell-raisers out there, you wouldn't even know me." Church proved one of Mayes' few refuges. In 1960 she had become organist and director of the Youth Choir at New Hope Baptist Church. She would serve in this capacity until 1975.

Despite the isolation, the rigors of study, and the time required by her involvement in church and the civil rights movement, Mayes succeeded as a mathematician. In 1966 she became the second African American and the first African American woman to earn a mathematics doctorate at the University of Texas. Her dissertation was entitled "A Structure Problem in Asymptotic Analysis."

In that same year, came one of the most unexpected twists in Mayes's career. Under pressure from the federal government, Baylor was now not only accepting black students, it was ready to hire Mayes in a tenure-track professorship. Mayes would teach at Baylor for 28 years.

There, she published a number of mathematics papers and began experimenting with using audiovisual techniques to teach precalculus—a subject on which she also published. But Mayes felt that her Baylor years were not completely free of prejudice. Through much of her career, federal investigators kept a close eye on the school's hiring and promotion practices, with the aim of ensuring fair treatment for minority scholars. During this period, Mayes felt that she was treated fairly by the university. Beginning in the 1980s, however, the federal government cut funding for such inspections, and Mayes said that she noted a significant shift in administrators' attitudes.

In 1971, Baylor was named Outstanding Faculty Member of the Year by the Baylor Student Congress. She was the first African American to serve on the Association for Women in Mathematics' executive committee, and she also served on the board of directors for the National Association of Mathematics, an organization for black mathematicians. In 1985, the Women's Issues Forum of the Young Women's Christian Association presented her with one of its Pathfinder awards.

Mayes retired from Baylor in 1994 because of poor health. She died on June 9, 1995, survived by daughter Patsyanne Mayes Wheeler. Friends attributed her early death in part to the stress of the prejudice she faced during her life. Indeed, she herself felt that her pathbreaking status, and the fact that people would judge all African Americans based on her performance, placed a great burden on her: "When I made a low grade, I felt I'd let down 11 million people," she said. "You felt like you had no choice but to excel."

SELECTED WRITINGS BY MAYES:

Periodicals

"Some Steady State Properties of [Int(f(t),t,0 tox)]/f(x)." *Proceedings of the American Mathematics Society* 22 (1969): 672-677.
"Black and Female." *Association for Women in Mathematics Newsletter* 5 (1975): 4-6.
(with others) "Student Attitudes Toward an Audio-Visual Presentation of Pre-Caclulus." *Math Teacher* 70 (1977).
(with Rhoades, B.E.) "Some Properties of the Leininger Generalized Hausdorf Matrix." *Houston Journal of Mathematics* 6 (1980): 287-299.

FURTHER READING:

Periodicals

Cantwell, Catherine. "BU Math Professor's Life Filled with Firsts." *Waco Tribune-Herald* (February 26, 1986).

Falconer, Etta, and Lorch, Lee. "Vivienne Malone Mayes: In Memoriam." *Association for Women in Mathematics Newsletter* (November-December 1995).

Other

Williams, Scott W. "Vivienne Malone Mayes." *Mathematicians of the African Diaspora* http://www.math.buffalo.edu/mad/mayesviviennemalone.html (May 4, 1998).

—*Sketch by Kenneth B. Chiacchia*

Walter S. McAfee

Walter S. McAfee
1914-1995
Astrophysicist

Walter S. McAfee is best known as the mathematician for the U.S. Army's Project Diana. As mathematician for the project, he was responsible for making the essential calculations that led to the first human contact with the moon: a radar signal sent in January 1946.

Walter Samuel McAfee was born in Ore City, Texas, on September 2, 1914. He was the second of nine children born to Luther F. McAfee, a carpenter, and Susie A. Johnson McAfee. He received a bachelor's degree from Wiley College in 1934 and earned an M.S. from Ohio State in 1937. Unable to afford further graduate work, McAfee turned to teaching, and from 1939 to 1942 he taught physics at Champion Junior High School in Columbus, Ohio. There, he met Viola Winston, a French teacher, whom he married in 1941; they had two daughters. In 1946, McAfee was awarded a Rosenwald fellowship and enrolled in the doctoral program at Cornell University. There, he studied with theoretical physicist Hans Bethe, receiving a doctorate in physics from Cornell in 1949.

In May 1942, McAfee joined the theoretical studies unit of the Electronics Research Command, part of the U.S. Army's Signal Corps at Fort Monmouth, New Jersey. A civilian physicist, he remained with the group in various capacities for more than 40 years, studying and experimenting in theoretical nuclear physics and electromagnetic theory, quantum optics, and laser holography. From 1958 to 1975 he also taught graduate and undergraduate courses at nearby Monmouth College as a lecturer in nuclear physics and electronics. He retired in 1985.

Project Diana Pioneers Space Communications

Project Diana was an effort to bounce a radar signal off the moon's surface. It was not known at the time if a high-frequency radio signal could penetrate the Earth's ionosphere or stratosphere. Early experiments with low- and medium-frequency radio waves had failed. In sending a signal, Project Diana scientists needed to account accurately for the moon's speed, which varies from 750 miles per hour (1,200 km per hour) slower than the earth's rotation to 750 miles per hour faster. As mathematician for the project, McAfee made the necessary calculations. On January 10, 1946, a radar pulse was sent through a special 40-foot square (37 sq km) antenna toward the moon. Two and a half seconds later, a faint radar echo was heard, and Project Diana was recorded a success. Made public two weeks later by the Signal Corps, the experiment provided an important breakthrough in space exploration, establishing that communication was possible across the enormous distances of outer space.

The official news report of the accomplishment did not include McAfee's name, nor give any hint of the role he had played. Public recognition did not come until 25 years later, at the anniversary of Project Diana in 1971. Subsequently, however, he was honored by the Stevens Institute of Technology and by Wiley College, which in 1982 inducted McAfee into its Science Hall of Fame, founded to inspire students to excel in the sciences. In an interview at the time, quoted in *ERADCOM Currents,* he said, "If the [Hall of Fame] program bears fruit, and if my presence helped in some small way, then that shall have been reward enough." McAfee subsequently established a math and physical science fellowship at Wiley College to encourage minority students in math and science. He was member of the

American Association for the Advancement of Science, the American Astronomy Society, the American Physical Society, the American Association of Physics Teachers, and is a senior member of the Institute of Electrical and Electronics Engineers. McAfee died on February 18, 1995, at his home in South Belmar, New Jersey.

SELECTED WRITINGS BY MCAFEE:

Periodicals

"Determination of Energy Spectra of Backscattered Electrons by Use of Everhart's Theory." *Journal of Applied Physics* 47, no. 3 (1976): 1179-84.
"Electron Backscattering from Solids and Double Layers." *Journal of Vacuum Science Technology* 13, no 4 (1976): 843-47.

FURTHER READING:

Periodicals

Accardo, Carl A. "Walter S. McAfee" (obituary). *Physics Today* (June 1995): 72; 74.
Gould, Jack. "Contact with Moon Achieved by Radar in Test by the Army." *New York Times* (25 January 1946): 1; 19.
———. "McAfee Named to Wiley's Science Hall of Fame." *ERADCOM Currents* (May 1982).
———. "Original Participants Mark Diana's 25th Anniversary." *Army Research and Development Newsmagazine* (January-February 1971).

Other

McAfee, Walter S. Interview by F. C. Nicholson. February 9 1994.

—Sketch by F. C. Nicholson

Henry C. McBay
1914-
Organic chemist

For more than half a century, Henry McBay conducted ground-breaking chemical research and imparted his knowledge to many aspiring chemists. As a doctoral student in Chicago during the Second World War, he was offered the chance to join the atomic bomb research team. He turned down the offer to concentrate on his own research—research that ultimately resulted in the development of important chemical compounds. During the course of his long career, McBay won awards both for his research and for his teaching.

Henry Cecil Ransom McBay, the oldest of four children, was born in the town of Mexia, Texas, on May 29, 1914. His father was an undertaker who later ran a drugstore with his brother; his mother was a seamstress. Whether young Henry's initial interest in science stemmed from his father's business ventures is unclear, but he proved to be a good student from an early age.

Teachers Encourage Interest in Science

While McBay was growing up, oil was discovered in Mexia, which made the small town quite wealthy. Among the amenities the oil boom provided was a top-notch high school for the community's black students. Schools were still segregated in Texas in the 1920s, and the town's old black school only ran up to the seventh grade. But the new school offered a full program and attracted excellent teachers from around the country. Young McBay excelled in science and mathematics, and he also found the time to play on the school's football team.

Graduating from high school at the age of 16, McBay entered Wiley College in Marshall, Texas, where he received his bachelor's degree in chemistry in 1934. He went on to Atlanta University in Georgia for his master's in organic chemistry. McBay had worked his way through school while at Wiley, and although Atlanta University awarded him a scholarship, money was still tight. Fortunately, his faculty advisor, K. A. Huggins, was able to get McBay a job in the school's chemistry lab.

Huggins enlisted McBay's help in research on the chemical properties of certain plastics and whether they could be used as substitutes for rubber. At the time, Huggins was working on his doctorate at the University of Chicago. Huggins got his Ph.D. from Chicago in 1936—the same year that McBay received his master's from Atlanta.

McBay wanted to continue his studies, but with money is short supply he instead accepted a teaching position back at Wiley. He remained there for two years and then took a position at a junior college near Kansas City, Kansas. When the position was eliminated, he got a job teaching high school chemistry in Huntsville, Alabama. While there, he was invited to serve on a research team at the Tuskegee Institute's Carver Foundation. During this time he had also managed to take summer courses at the University of Chicago, where his old mentor K. A. Huggins had gotten his doctorate. In 1942, McBay enrolled full-time at the University of Chicago.

It was during this time that McBay was approached about serving on the research team that was developing the atomic bomb. McBay turned down the offer, attractive as it was, wanting instead to focus on getting his doctorate and working on his own research. Actually, his research at the time was probably more dangerous to him physically than working on the bomb. McBay worked with volatile chemical compounds that were so explosive he was provided with a private laboratory. His work involved creating new compounds from simple peroxides that could be used in chemical reactions. Later, it proved to be integral in the production of useful substances, such as an artificial hormone used in medicines. McBay's research won him the Elizabeth Norton Award in 1944 and again in 1945, as well as his doctorate from Chicago in 1945.

Commitment to Improving Science Education

After receiving his doctorate, McBay accepted a teaching post at Morehouse College in Atlanta. (Morehouse, Spelman, and McBay's alma mater Atlanta are all part of the Atlanta University system.) He taught at all three campuses over the next 36 years. A marriage during this time produced two sons but ended in divorce. In addition to conducting research, McBay also worked to make the instruction of chemistry more comprehensive. He believed strongly that students needed more time to devote to science and mathematics research, and he structured courses to provide for this extra time. In 1951, the United Nations Educational, Scientific, and Cultural Organization (UNESCO) invited McBay to help create a comprehensive chemistry education program in Liberia. Throughout his career, he was often asked to serve as a chemical consultant both for government organizations (notably the Canadian government laboratory in Ottawa) and for private industry.

McBay has won numerous education awards, including the Outstanding Teaching Award of the National Association for Black Chemists and Chemical Engineers in 1976. He was appointed Fuller E. Callaway professor of chemistry at Atlanta University in 1981 and retired in 1986. In 1991 he was Martin Luther King, Jr. Visiting Scholar at MIT, and in 1992 he was awarded an honorary doctorate by Emory University. A teaching award and a scholarship fund have been established in his name at Atlanta University.

FURTHER READING:

Books

Kessler, James, et al. *Distinguished African American Scientists of the Twentieth Century.* Oryx Press, 1996.

Sammons, Vivian O. *Blacks in Science and Education.* Hemisphere Publishing Co., 1990.

Who's Who Among Black Americans, second ed. Who's Who Among Black Americans Publishing Co. 1978.

World Who's Who Among Black Americans, 1985. Who's Who Among Black Americans Publishing Co., 1985.

Periodicals

Ebony, (December 1978): 110.
Ebony, (May 1961): 27.

—*Sketch by George A. Milite*

Caldwell McCoy, Jr.
1933-1990
Electrical engineer

Caldwell McCoy, Jr. contributed to the United States defense and technology industries as a project manager at the Naval Research Laboratory, the Department of Energy, and the National Aeronautics and Space Administration (NASA). A recipient of advanced degrees, he placed great emphasis on the recruitment of minority students to the sciences.

Caldwell McCoy, Jr. was born June 27, 1933, in Hartford, Connecticut. He attended Weaver High School in that city. After graduating, he entered the University of Connecticut, where he received a bachelor of science degree in electrical engineering. From 1956-59, McCoy served in the United States Air Force. Upon his discharge, he began a graduate program at George Washington University in Washington, D.C. He earned a master of science degree in mathematics and a doctoral degree in telecommunications. His dissertation was entitled "Improvements in Routing for Packet-Switched Networks."

Caldwell then joined the Naval Research Laboratory in Washington, D.C. As an engineer participating in research on antisubmarine-warfare, he designed, tested, and evaluated systems for detecting and tracking submarines. For his contribution to this effort, he was granted the Naval Research Laboratory's Thomas Edison Fellowship in 1968.

In 1976, McCoy joined the United States Department of Energy. There, he studied the possibility of achieving usable energy from magnetic energy. As part of his research, he managed the National Magnetic Fusion Energy Computer Network. This huge computer network maintained and distributed experimental data to hundreds of users across the country. His expertise eventually caught the attention of officials at NASA, who recruited him to manage their information systems. He went to work for the country's space program in 1983 and remained with NASA until his death in 1990.

His family has established a foundation, in his memory, to assist minority students who aspire to a career in the sciences. The Caldwell McCoy, Jr., Foundation, based near Hartford in Bloomfield, Connecticut, awards annual scholarships to minority students. In addition, the foundation has established a partnership with the Bloomfield school system to promote the involvement of minorities in science and mathematics.

SELECTED WRITINGS BY MCCOY:

Periodicals

"Effects of a Priority Discipline in the Routing for Packet-Switched Networks." *IEEE Transactions on Communications COM-24(5)* (May 1976): 505-516.

Elijah McCoy

FURTHER READING

Sammons, Vivian. *Blacks in Science and Medicine.*
    New York: Hemisphere Publishing, p.168.
Dee, Jane Ellen. "Town Takes Time to Celebrate
    Man's Life, Contributions." *Hartford Courant* (Feb-
    ruary 25, 1995): B2.

              —Sketch by Patrick J. Longe

Elijah McCoy
1843-1929
Engineer and inventor

Elijah McCoy made important contributions to the design of railroad locomotives and similar heavy industrial equipment by means of patented inventions that provided for automatic lubrication of moving parts. His initial work involved the steam locomotives that were in use following the Civil War, which were modest in size, in horsepower, and in their technical demands. But he kept pace with the progress of locomotive design, devising new lubricating systems that served the steam engines of the early twentieth century. These were demanding indeed, for they operated at high temperatures and pressures.

The date of McCoy's birth is not known; various sources give it as March 27, 1843; May 2, 1843; and May 2, 1844. His parents, George McCoy and the former Mildred Goins, were fugitive slaves who had escaped to Canada from Kentucky. George McCoy was a farmer. Canada at the time was part of the British Empire, which had abolished slavery by act of Parliament in 1833. When the Canadian leader Louis Riel launched a rebellion in 1837, the British government used troops to defeat the rebels. George McCoy enlisted with the British force, and in return for his loyal service, he received 160 acres (42.4 ha) of farmland near Colchester, Ontario. Here Elijah McCoy was born, as one of 12 children.

His father's ties to Britain proved useful as young McCoy pursued his education. As a boy, he was fascinated with tools and machines. At the age of 16, he traveled to Edinburgh, Scotland, to serve an apprenticeship in mechanical engineering. Scotland already was a center for shipbuilding and heavy industry, whereas Canada was largely rural. He therefore received opportunities for education and training that were unavailable at home.

In Edinburgh McCoy won the credentials of a master mechanic and engineer. He then rejoined his family. Following the Civil War, which ended in 1865, the McCoys returned to the United States and settled near Ypsilanti, Michigan, outside of Detroit. Young McCoy sought work as an engineer, but met defeat due to racial prejudice. Nevertheless, he obtained a job as a fireman and oiler on the Michigan Central Railroad in 1870. This was a responsible position, for service as a fireman was a customary prelude to promotion to the post of locomotive driver, which was prestigious indeed. But work as a fireman was a far cry from engineering, and it demanded much manual toil. As a fireman, McCoy had to shovel coal into the firebox of his locomotive, at the rate of two tons per hour. He also had to walk around the locomotive and lubricate its moving parts using an oilcan during frequent stops, while it took on water.

Pioneer in Automatic Lubrication

Locomotives were heavy, and subjected their moving parts to considerable wear. Lubrication was essential, or these parts—many of which were costly—would require frequent replacement. The railroad industry therefore held a strong interest in automatic lubrication, which was already being applied to railroad axles. These axles carried the full weight of locomotives and railroad cars, and were particularly subject to wear. But engineers had arranged for them to rotate within oil-filled chambers. The rotation of the axle carried oil into its bearing, and the oiled bearing allowed the axle to turn freely while reducing wear to a minimum.

But the direct use of oil-filled chambers did not apply to a locomotive's steam engine, which provided its power. Many parts of this engine operated under the pressure of steam, which acted to push oil away from the moving parts. This made it necessary to stop the engine when oiling it. But McCoy saw that he could keep the engine running by using steam pressure to pump the oil where it was needed.

Working within a homebuilt machine shop in Ypsilanti, he devised an invention that became known as the lubricating cup. It relied on a piston set within an oil-filled container; steam pressure pushed on the piston and thereby drove the oil into channels that carried this oil to the engine's operating parts. He sought and received a United States patent for this device, number 129,843. It was granted on June 23, 1872. McCoy took his invention to officials of the Michigan Central, and received their support. Installed on operating locomotives, it provided lubrication that was more regular and even than could be achieved by the old method of using an oilcan during intermittent stops. This gave the railroad a useful advantage, for its locomotives now lasted longer and needed less maintenance.

Even before receiving his first patent, McCoy was working on improvements that would lead to other patents as well. In addition, his lubricating cup proved adaptable to other types of steam engines which were used in factories and at sea. Versions of this cup became standard components on many types of heavy machinery, entering service on railways of the West, on Great Lakes steamships, and even on transatlantic liners.

New Lubricators Serve Powerful Engines

McCoy left the Michigan Central in 1882 and moved to Detroit, where he proceeded to devote all his time to his new career as an inventor. He also worked as an industrial consultant, assisting the Detroit Lubricator Company and other firms. The technical demands of railroads soon provided him with further challenges.

Amid the growth of industry and of passenger travel, railroad companies needed larger locomotives. James J. Hill, builder of the Great Northern Railroad, introduced monsters that were up to four times larger than their predecessors, along with large-capacity freight cars. But such locomotives burned coal in large amounts, and brought a demand for new designs that could achieve very high horsepower while using less coal. The solution lay in the use of superheated steam, with high temperature and pressure. Superheating boosted the engines' efficiency, allowing a locomotive to get more miles per ton of coal. It also brought new problems in lubrication.

The author Robert C. Hayden, in his book *Eight Black American Inventors*, quotes an article in the *Engineer's Journal*: "There is no denying the fact that our present experience in lubricating the cylinders of engines using superheated steam is anything but satisfactory ... If the oil feed was made regular so the steam would distribute it over the bearing surface of cylinder while the engine was

working, these bearing surfaces would be better protected than is now otherwise possible."

Rather than use oil alone as a lubricant, designers preferred to mix the oil with powdered graphite, a form of carbon. Powdered graphite is soft and greasy, and easily withstands high temperatures. However, because it is a powder rather than a liquid, it can clog an engine. In April 1915 McCoy received U.S. patent no. 1,136,689, for what he called a "Locomotive Lubricator." Within his patent application, he claimed that this invention would permit the use of graphite "without danger of clogging."

Hayden cites a letter from a railroad superintendent: "We have found the McCoy Graphite Lubricator to be of considerable assistance in lubrication of locomotives equipped with superheaters. . . . There is a decided advantage in better lubrication and reduction in wear in valves and piston rings, and as a well lubricated engine is more economical in the use of fuel, there is unquestionably a saving in fuel."

The Real McCoy?

In reviewing the life of this inventor, writers and essayists often note that railroad purchasing agents commonly insisted on buying "the real McCoy." Other inventors were offering lubricators that competed with those of McCoy, but these agents would accept no substitutes. Many of these authors assert that the phrase "real McCoy" passed out of the specialized world of railroad engineering and entered general usage, where it came to mean "the genuine article."

William and Mary Morris, in their *Morris Dictionary of Word and Phrase Origins*, disagree. They find the origin of this expression in the career of a welterweight boxing champion, Kid McCoy, who distinguished himself from imitators by billing himself as "the Real McCoy." He held the world championship in his weight class from 1890 to 1900, during years when McCoy lubricators were entering widespread use. The expression "real McCoy," coming into general use amid the popularity of boxing, then could have taken on a specialized meaning among railroad men.

But while McCoy's inventions made millions of dollars, little of this money reached his pockets. Lacking the capital with which to build his lubricators in large numbers, he sold many of his patent rights to well-heeled investors, receiving in return only the modest sums that allowed him to continue his work. He received at least 72 patents during his lifetime, most of which dealt with lubricating devices, but he retained ownership of only a few of them.

In 1868 he married Ann Elizabeth Stewart; she died in 1872, at age 25. A year later he remarried, to Mary Eleanora Delaney. This marriage lasted half a century, but neither of his marriages produced children.

In 1920, at age 77, he joined with investors and founded the Elijah McCoy Manufacturing Company in Detroit, serving as vice-president. The firm manufactured and sold his graphite lubricators, including an advanced version that also lubricated a railroad train's air brakes. But soon afterward, he and his wife Mary had a traffic accident. Mary received injuries from which she never fully recovered, and which hastened her death. She died in 1923.

For Elijah, the end now approached as well. He became very lonely and sad. His health deteriorated, and in 1928 he entered the Eloise Infirmary in Eloise, Michigan. Suffering from hypertension and from senile dementia, he died there on October 10, 1929.

McCoy was venerated in Detroit long after his death. In 1975 the city celebrated Elijah McCoy Day, as officials placed an historic marker at the site of his home. The city also named a street for him: Elijah McCoy Drive. These posthumous honors were modest. But they came a century after his invention of the lubricating cup, and showed that he had left an enduring legacy in his work.

FURTHER READING:

Books

Haber, Louis. *Black Pioneers of Science and Invention.* New York: Harcourt Brace Jovanovich, 1970.

Haskens, Jim. *Outward Dreams.* New York: Walker, 1991.

Hayden, Robert C. *Eight Black American Inventors.* Reading, MA: Addison-Wesley, 1972.

Klein, Aaron E. *The Hidden Contributors.* New York: Doubleday, 1971.

Towle, Wendy. *The Real McCoy.* New York: Scholastic, 1993.

—Sketch by T. A. Heppenheimer

Roscoe Lewis McKinney
1900-1978
Anatomist

In 1930, Roscoe Lewis McKinney became the first African American to earn a doctorate in anatomy. He established the anatomy department within the Medical College of Howard University, and served as its chairman for seventeen years. For a half-century, McKinney continued at Howard, and served abroad in stints as an instructor in Iraq, India, and Vietnam.

First African American to Earn Doctorate in Anatomy

Roscoe Lewis McKinney was born on February 8, 1900, in Washington, D.C., the son of Lewis and Blanche Hunt McKinney. Lewis McKinney worked for the United States Government Printing Office, and the McKinneys sent their son to public schools in the area.

During World War I, McKinney served in the U.S. Army. Later he earned his B.S. degree from Bates College in Lewiston, Maine, in 1921. For the two years following, from 1921 to 1923, he taught biology at Morehouse College in Atlanta; then in 1923 he returned to his native city to become an instructor in zoology at Howard University. Thus began an involvement with Howard that would continue until his death 55 years later.

Late in the 1920s, McKinney began his doctoral work at the University of Chicago on a Rockefeller Foundation fellowship. He earned his degree in 1930 with a dissertation entitled *Studies on Fibers in Tissue Culture III: The Development of Reticulum into Collagenous Fibers in Cultures of Adult Rabbit Lymph Nodes.* A reticulum is a network of cells in an organ; "collagenous" refers to collagen, a type of protein in the tissue connecting bones; "culture" in this context refers to living cells that have been cultivated for scientific study; and lymph nodes filter lymph, a plasma-like fluid that bathes the tissues and is ultimately discharged into the blood. McKinney was the first African American to earn a Ph.D. in anatomy.

Assignments to India, Iraq, and Vietnam

Having completed his doctoral work, McKinney in 1930 became a professor of anatomy at Howard. In fact, he established the anatomy department within the College of Medicine, and served as its chairman from 1930 to 1947. In 1931 he became vice-dean of the College of Medicine, a position he held concurrent with his departmental chairmanship until 1946.

From 1955 to 1956, McKinney served as a Fulbright fellow in Baghdad, Iraq. At Baghdad's Royal College of Medicine, McKinney worked as a professor of microscopic anatomy, and he impressed the Iraqi government so much that they invited him back to teach for another year, from 1956 to 1957. (During this era, Iraq was ruled by a king, and the United States counted it as an ally. A year after McKinney's departure, however, an army coup deposed the king.)

McKinney returned to Howard, but in 1960, the United States Department of State asked him to take another overseas assignment. This time he would be working as an instructor at the Osmania Medical College of Hyderabad, in south-central India. Once again McKinney was given a post to an exotic locale—Hyderabad had been the site of an ancient Hindu civilization until the Muslim empire of the Moguls overran it in the seventeenth century—and he served there for nearly three years, until 1962.

After spending most of the 1960s at Howard, McKinney in 1969 received an appointment to an even more easterly venue, this one fraught with greater possibilities of danger: Vietnam. The American military involvement in that country was near its height, but life in the capital of

Saigon continued with some semblance of order. From 1969 to 1971, McKinney served as a consultant in anatomy at the University of Saigon.

Recognition Among Anatomists

After stepping down as chairman of the anatomy department in 1947, McKinney continued as a professor at Howard for another 21 years, until 1968. In that year, he retired and became an emeritus professor, but in 1971—after his return from Vietnam—he went back to active teaching. McKinney continued teaching until 1976, just two years before his death.

In 1952, the editors of the *Textbook of Histology* incorporated McKinney's 1930 doctoral work on reticulum development in their textbook. Two tissue samples of his were included in *Gray's Anatomy*, the foremost text for anatomists, for many years. Within the community of black American scientists, McKinney was recognized not only for founding the anatomy department at Howard, but for establishing there the first tissue-culture laboratory in the Washington area. Numerous investigators in tissue-culture technique came to the lab for help and advice.

Other areas of McKinney's research included tissue-culture cytology, the study of cells; and microcinematography, the use of motion-picture cameras at the microscopic level to capture cell movements. He was also interested in the use of radioactive isotopes (a combination of atoms with differing physical properties but nearly identical behavior) in cell and tissue work. In addition, McKinney studied the development of connective tissue, such as ligaments, in vitro—that is, in an artificially maintained environment outside the living body.

McKinney married Ethel James in Upper Marlboro, Maryland, on August 1, 1937. The couple had four children: Roscoe, Arthur, Frances, and Jacqueline. McKinney's professional memberships included the American Association for the Advancement of Science, the American Association of Anatomists, Beta Kappa Chi, Omega Psi Phi, Phi Beta Kappa, Sigma Xi, and the Tissue Culture Association. His civic involvements included the PTA (Parent-Teacher's Association) and the Civil Air Patrol, in which he was an officer. McKinney belonged to the Congregationalist Church, and his interests included reading, camping, swimming, and photography. He died in Washington on September 30, 1978.

SELECTED WRITINGS BY MCKINNEY:

Books

Studies on Fibers in Tissue Culture III: The Development of Reticulum into Collagenous Fibers in Cultures of Adult Rabbit Lymph Nodes. University of Chicago, 1930.

FURTHER READING:

Books

American Men & Women of Science, 12th edition. R. R. Bowker, 1971-73.
The National Cyclopedia of American Biography, vol. 62. James T. White & Co., 1984.
Sammons, Vivian Ovelton. *Blacks in Science and Medicine.* Hemisphere Publishing, 1990.

Periodicals

"The Earliest Ph.D. Awards to Blacks in the Natural Sciences," *Journal of Blacks in Higher Education,* (March 31, 1997).
"Roscoe Lewis McKinney," *National Medical Association Journal,* (May 1979): 518.

—Sketch by Judson Knight

Ronald Erwin McNair
1950-1986
Astronaut and physicist

Ronald Erwin McNair earned the mournful distinction of being the first black astronaut to die during a space mission. A physicist and a mission specialist, McNair was one of the seven astronauts killed in the explosion of the space shuttle *Challenger* on January 28, 1986.

McNair was born October 21, 1950, in Lake City, South Carolina. His father, Carl, was an auto mechanic; his mother, Pearl, was a teacher. McNair attended Carver High School, which in 1962 was still segregated. He became a saxophone player of some ability there and graduated in 1967. When McNair enrolled at the North Carolina Agricultural and Technical University, he initially selected music as his major. A college counselor urged McNair to consider science, and in his freshman year he switched his major to physics.

McNair earned a bachelor of science degree in 1971 and then enrolled in the graduate program in physics at the Massachusetts Institute of Technology. He completed a doctorate in 1976; his dissertation focused on the generation of laser beams. Shortly after receiving his degree, McNair married Cheryl Moore, and then he accepted a position with Hughes Research Laboratories in Malibu, California. There, he worked on the use of lasers in satellite communications, and it was this work that attracted the attention of NASA.

Ronald Erwin McNair

His application to the astronaut training program was accepted, and in 1978 he and his wife moved to the Johnson Space Flight Center near Houston, Texas, so McNair could begin the six-year training program required for space shuttle crew members.

In February 1984, McNair was mission specialist aboard a successful flight of the space shuttle *Challenger*. During this mission, McNair monitored space gases and tested solar cells and a mechanical retrieval unit. He also brought his saxophone on board and became, as NASA notes, the first person to play a saxophone in orbit. Another flight was scheduled for 1986. McNair's scientific duties for his second mission were to have included deployment of a telescopic camera to study Haley's comet. That flight ended in tragedy. Rubber gaskets failed, and *Challenger* exploded less than two minutes after lift-off. McNair, six other crew members, and NASA's first civilian passenger, schoolteacher Christa McAuliffe, all died. After his death, Lake City renamed Carver High School for Ronald McNair.

FURTHER READING:

Books

Cassutt, Michael. *Who's Who in Space.* New York: MacMillan Publishing Company, 1987.

Hawkins, Walter L. *African American Biographies: Profiles of 558 Current Men and Women.* Jefferson, North Carolina: McFarland & Company, Inc., 1992.

Hawthorne, Douglas B. *Men and Women of Space.* San Diego, California: Univelt, Inc. Publishers, 1992.

Kessler, James H. *Distinguished African American Scientists of the 20th Century.* Phoenix, Arizona: Oryx Press, 1996.

Sammons, Vivian O. *Blacks in Science and Medicine.* New York: Hemisphere Publishing Corporation, 1990.

—Sketch by A. Mullig

Ronald Elbert Mickens
1943-
Physicist

Ronald Elbert Mickens is a physicist who has advanced the general understanding of the role that pure mathematics can play in science. He is perhaps best known for his work on difference equations—a type of equation that is now considered fundamental to the development of chaos theory, a relatively new field of research that deals mainly in mathematics. He has also written textbooks on advanced mathematics, as well as studies of scientific specialities.

Ronald Mickens was born in Petersburg, Virginia, on February 7, 1943. His parents were Joseph and Daisy Brown (Williamson) Mickens. An excellent high school student who showed an aptitude for science, Mickens earned a full scholarship to Fisk University in Nashville, Tennessee. He began his college studies as a chemistry major and then switched to mathematics before finally settling on physics. He graduated from Fisk in 1964 and enrolled in the graduate program in physics at Vanderbilt University in Nashville.

Mickens taught undergraduate physics courses at Fisk while completing the work required for a doctorate at Vanderbilt. As a graduate student, he was elected to Sigma Chi and Phi Beta Kappa and was awarded Woodrow Wilson and Danforth fellowships. He received his doctoral degree in 1968. He was then awarded a National Science Foundation Postdoctoral Fellowship, which supported his work at the Massachusetts Institute of Technology. There, he spent two years studying elementary particle physics.

In 1970, Mickens was appointed professor of physics at Fisk University, a post he held until 1982. He then accepted a position as a professor of physics at Clark Atlanta University and in 1985 was named Fuller E. Callaway Professor of Physics there. Mickens also held concurrent appointments as a visiting professor at Howard University, Massachusetts Institute of Technology, and Vanderbilt.

Mickens has devoted considerable energy to research. Grants from the National Science Foundation, the National Aeronautics and Space Administration, the Department of Energy, and the Army Research Office have enabled him to study a broad range of topics that includes nonlinear equations, numerical analysis, mathematical biology, and the history and sociology of science. Mickens has conducted research at the Los Alamos National Laboratory in New Mexico, the Stanford Linear Accelerator Center, the Aspen Center for Physics, the Joint Institute for Laboratory Astrophysics at Boulder, and the European Organization for Nuclear Research in Geneva, Switzerland.

The author of more than 170 published papers, Mickens has written five books on advanced mathematics. He also served as editor for *Mathematical Analysis of Physical Systems* (1985) and *Mathematics and Science* (1990). The latter book explores the philosophy underlying the work of 19 scientific leaders in a variety of specialties. His current research focuses on nonlinear difference and differential equations, differential equation modeling, the properties of nonlinear singular oscillator systems, and model construction for the electromagnetic form factors of the nucleon.

SELECTED WRITINGS BY MICKENS:

Books

Difference Equations. Van Nostrand Reinhold, 1987.
Difference Equations: Theory and Applications. Chapman and Hall, 1990.
Nonlinear Oscillations in Planar Dynamical Systems. World Scientific, 1996.
(Editor) *Mathematical Analysis of Physical Systems.* Van Nostrand Reinhold, 1985.
(Editor) *Mathematics and Science.* World Scientific, 1990.

Periodicals

"Relation Between the Time and Space Step-Sizes in Nonstandard Finite-Difference Schemes for the Fisher Equation." *Numerical Methods for Partial Differential Equations,* 13 (1997): 51.
"Exact Finite Difference Schemes for the Wave Equation with Spherical Symmetry." *Journal of Difference Equations and Applications,* 2 (1996): 263.
"A Discrete-Time Model for the Spread of Periodic Diseases Without Immunity." *BioSystems,* 26 (1992): 193.

FURTHER READING:

Books

Kessler, James H. *Distinguished African American Scientists of the 20th Century.* Phoenix, AZ: Oryx Press, 1996.

Sammons, Vivian O. *Blacks in Science and Medicine.* New York: Hemisphere Publishing Corporation, 1990.
Torpie, Stephen L., ed. *American Men and Women of Science.* Providence, NJ: R. R. Bowker, 1992.

—*Sketch by A. Mullig*

Dolphus Edward Milligan
1928-
Chemist

Dolphus Edward Milligan is a researcher and educator in the field of physical chemistry. His specialty is the spectroscopic study of free radicals and reactive molecules. In addition, for many years he served in government with the National Bureau of Standards.

Dolphus Milligan was born on June 17, 1928, in Brighton, Alabama. He enrolled at Morehouse College and received his bachelor of science degree in 1949. He then began work in the graduate program at Atlanta University, earning his master of science degree in 1951. Milligan then took his first teaching position as a chemistry instructor at Fort Valley State College. In 1954, he moved to California to join the faculty of California University as a chemistry instructor. While there, Milligan began his doctoral studies. His doctorate in chemistry was awarded in 1958. The topic of his dissertation was the spectroscopic study of reaction intermediates at extremely low temperatures.

After completing his education, Milligan went to work as a fundamental researcher for the Mellon Institute. In 1963, he joined the National Bureau of Standard as a physical chemist. In 1970, while continuing to work for the National Bureau of Standards, he accepted a position as an adjunct resident professor at Howard University. His accomplishments as a physical chemist resulted in Milligan being named the chief of the photochemistry section at the National Bureau of Standards in 1971.

Milligan received three important awards for his advances in physical chemistry: the Arturo Miolati Prize for Free Radical Research from the University of Padua in 1965, the Washington Academy of Sciences Award in Physical Science in 1968, and the Gold Medal for Distinguished Service from the United States Department of Commerce in 1970. He is a member of the American Chemical Society and the American Physical Society.

Dolphus Milligan married his wife in 1952; together they raised two children. He is now retired.

FURTHER READING:

Books

Sammons, Vivian. *Blacks in Science and Medicine.*
New York: Hemisphere Publishing, 1990.

Cattell, Jaques. *American Men and Women of Science.*
New Providence, NJ: R.R. Bowker Company, 1972,
p. 4295.

—Sketch by Patrick J. Longe

James E. Millington
1930-
Chemist

James E. Millington is an organic chemist, a scientist working in the branch of chemistry that deals with carbon compounds. Born in America and educated in Canada, he attained prominence in 1964, when he developed a special type of electrical insulating paper for Allis-Chalmers. Millington worked with that company for nearly 25 years, then joined the Hoechst Corporation, a large European chemical producer.

Works on Canadian Defense Projects

Millington was born in New York City on March 13, 1930. He attended Lincoln University in Pennsylvania, where he obtained his bachelor's degree in 1951. Immediately after graduating, he enrolled at the University of Western Ontario, and in 1953 earned his M.S. degree. Remaining at the Canadian university, the American chemistry student went on to obtain his Ph.D. in that field in 1956.

From 1953 to 1955, while undergoing the work for his graduate degrees, Millington worked as an assistant with the Defence Research Board of Canada at the University of Western Ontario. After obtaining his doctorate, he went to work as a research chemist with Allis-Chalmers Manufacturing Company, a producer of heavy industrial equipment and other products, in 1956.

Invents Insulating Paper, Wins Prize

Millington continued in the research chemist's position until 1961, at which point he became a project leader. In 1963, he moved up to the role of section head. During this time, he made a name for himself when he won the 1964 Allis-Chalmers Science and Engineering Award—which carried with it a $5,000 prize—for his development of a new product. Electrical transformers and regulators create hazards because of the great amounts of current that pass

through them, hazards which are greatly heightened if there are charged wires; Millington's achievement was to develop a new type of paper to insulate wires and thus keep them from coming into contact with each other.

In 1967, Millington moved on to the job of manager of organic chemistry, and in 1969 became section head in that area. He stayed in this position for eleven years, then in 1980 left Allis-Chalmers after nearly a quarter-century with the company. He took a position as manager with the Hoechst (pronounced "Hehrxt") Corporation, a Frankfurt, Germany-based chemical giant.

Millington's research work has chiefly involved polymers, the product of a chemical process whereby molecules combine to form larger units that contain repeating structural characteristics. Polymerization is an important function, for instance, in the making of plastics. As an organic chemist—a chemist who deals with compounds containing carbon—his research has concerned the structure and properties of polymers, as well as their characterization.

Married in 1947, Millington has two children. He is a member of the American Chemical Society, and as of the early 1990s was residing in the town of Breda in The Netherlands.

FURTHER READING:

Books

American Men and Women of Science, 17th ed. R. R.
Bowker, 1989.

Sammons, Vivian Ovelton. *Blacks in Science and Medicine.* Hemisphere Publishing, 1990.

Periodicals

Jet, (June 18, 1964): 27.

—Sketch by Judson Knight

Luna Isaac Mishoe
1917-1989
Mathematician

Luna I. Mishoe made a name for himself in both theoretical and applied mathematics, creating new mathematical tools and helping to solve some of the initial problems faced by the United States' satellite development program. Today Mishoe is better known for his 27-year tenure as president of Delaware State College (now

Luna Isaac Mishoe

Delaware State University), during which he transformed the institution from a struggling black college into one of the two major university systems in the state of Delaware.

Like many African American scientists of his generation, Luna I. Mishoe began life in poverty. Mishoe was born on January 15, 1917, to Henry Mishoe and Martha (Oliver) Mishoe of Bucksport, South Carolina. His father saw no future in the farming jobs available to black men in South Carolina, and so he traveled to New York to make a living while his family stayed behind. His mother had no desire to see her children become farm workers either; from an early age, she encouraged Luna and his five brothers to seek an education.

The family had no money to spare for Mishoe's education, and so he worked to put himself through school, taking any odd job he could find. In 1938, Mishoe graduated from Allen University, South Carolina, with a bachelor's degree in mathematics and chemistry. He then taught mathematics and physics at Kittrell College, North Carolina. During this period, he took summer courses at the University of Michigan toward his master's degree in mathematics and physics, which he earned in 1942. At Michigan, Mishoe met Hattie Bernice Dabney, a nurse from New York who was also taking summer classes at the university. The two were married in 1944.

In 1942, Mishoe joined the U.S. Army Air Corps. He served through World War II as a photographic intelligence and communications officer in the 99th Squadron. This all-black fighter squadron was also known as the "Tuskegee

Airmen," in which African American pilots first served combat missions. He left the service in 1946 to become a professor of mathematics and physics at Delaware State College in Dover, Delaware.

In 1948, Mishoe moved to Morgan State University in Baltimore, where he was a physics professor until 1960. From 1956-60, he was chairman of the Division of Natural Science at Morgan. Between 1952-60, while still at Morgan, he also served as a consultant at the U.S. Army's Aberdeen Proving Grounds, where he developed mathematical equations to support the country's missile and satellite research programs.

At the Helm of Delaware State College

In 1960, Mishoe faced the greatest challenge in his career when he accepted an appointment as president of Delaware State College. The move placed new burdens on Mishoe. It took him away from the mathematics that he loved. Also, as his son, Luna I. Mishoe II, suggested in a telephone interview with contributor Kenneth Chiacchia, "he felt lonely, because . . . he didn't have anyone to talk to and relate to at his level." Delaware State, a small black college with fewer than 400 students and paltry state support, needed a firm and diplomatic leader to prevent fiscal ruin. Mishoe filled this role.

Mishoe's first priority was finding the funds that Delaware State needed to keep running. He began a dialogue with the governor and state legislators; they were initially resistant, but Mishoe ultimately convinced them to invest money in the institution. With these funds, he began a building program that expanded the college into one of the two biggest university systems in the state. Under his leadership, the student body increased more than five-fold and the college became an integrated institution.

"He didn't get much help from the board of trustees," recalls son Luna, but Hattie's support and advice often inspired him to push harder for the school's benefit. "In one instance he wanted to ask the governor . . . for three buildings at once. The trustees told him not to; she told him to go for it. He did and obtained all three." As the first family at Delaware State, the Mishoes and their children were deeply involved in the lives of the college's students. Many of the students were very poor, and the Mishoes helped them make ends meet by inviting them for dinner. Since hotels in Delaware would not initially admit African Americans, the family also hosted many visiting guests of the college.

During his time at Delaware State, Mishoe served on a number of state committees and task forces on education. By the 1980s, his responsibilities as president had awakened his interests in business administration. Mishoe went back to school, first obtaining a bachelor's degree in business administration in 1981 from Delaware State college, and then an master's of business administration degree from the Wharton School of the University of Pennsylvania in 1985.

Business training served Mishoe in good stead as a university president. It served him especially well after his retirement in 1987, when he took on a new challenge: the construction of housing for low-income and handicapped tenants in Dover. Once again, financial backing was not easy to obtain. Federal agencies, church groups, and black fraternities and sororities were all unwilling to fund the project. Mishoe worked with son Luna, a city planner, to find a way to make the project happen. "If he decided he was going to do something, nothing was going to stop him," says his son. In the end, a political connection from his tenure at Delaware State payed off: a state senator sponsored a bill to provide a bond, which Mishoe then had to persuade a bank to purchase. But he succeeded in getting the funding.

Sadly, Mishoe died of cancer in 1989 before the project, Mishoe Towers, reached completion. But he died knowing that it was underway, and he left an enduring legacy at Delaware State College. Today Hattie Mishoe notes with pride that their children, Bernellyn Mishoe Carey, Luna Mishoe II, Wilma Mishoe, and Rita Mishoe Paige, all received both a college education and a graduate degree.

SELECTED WRITINGS BY MISHOE:

Books

Eigenfunction Expansions Associated with Non-Self-Adjoint Differential Equations. Dover: Delaware State College, 1964.

Periodicals

"On the Gibbs Phenomenon in a Certain Eigenfunction Series." *Proceedings of the American Mathematics Society* 9. no. 1 (February 1958).
"A Comparitive Study of Two Systems of Differential Equations for the Motion of a Guided Missile." *Ballistic Research Labs* (Summer 1957).

FURTHER READING:

Books

Newell, Virginia K. et al., eds. *Black Mathematicians and Their Works.* Ardmore, PA: Dorrance & Company, 1980.
Augustus, W. Low, and Clift, Virgil A. *Encyclopedia of Black America.* New York: McGraw-Hill, Inc., 1981.
Dr. Luna Isaac Mishoe: A Tribute Dinner-Dance Saluting the Dedicated Tenure of Dr. Luna Isaac Mishoe as President of Delaware State College, 1960 to 1987. Dover: Delaware State College, 1987.

—*Sketch by Kenneth B. Chiacchia*

Earl D. Mitchell, Jr.
1938-
Biochemist

As both a researcher and administrator, Earl Mitchell has worked hard during his career to open doors for minority students. A longtime member of the Oklahoma State Advisory Committee to the U.S. Commission on Civil Rights, he has worked tirelessly to create new and better opportunities for minority students to enter science programs in college.

Earl Mitchell was born in New Orleans on May 16, 1938. His family was not wealthy, but his parents worked hard and instilled in young Earl a strong work ethic that would serve him well later in life. He was a good student, and he did particularly well in chemistry. He enrolled at Xavier University in New Orleans in 1956.

Even though he lived at home during his Xavier years, Mitchell had to work his way through school. During the summers, he worked in a local hospital and later for the city recreation department. Every December he would work the night shift at the local Post Office during the busy holiday season; between school and work his day was 17 hours long—not counting time spent studying for exams. But he showed a flair for research and, encouraged by his professors, he decided to pursue a career in chemical research.

Mitchell graduated from Xavier in 1960 and went on to Michigan State University for his master's degree. In addition to his research, he also served as a teaching assistant in Michigan State's chemistry department. He was also a family man; he had married Bernice Compton while at Xavier, and their first child had been born in 1960. In 1961 Mitchell became a technician at the school's Plant Analysis laboratory, which allowed him to further develop his research skills. He received his master's degree in 1963, and remained at Michigan State to complete his doctorate.

As a doctoral student, Mitchell studied biochemical reactions in certain naturally occurring substances. He received his doctorate in 1966 and accepted a position as research associate at Oklahoma State University in Stillwater, Oklahoma. He was part of the research team that isolated the chemical in catnip that attracts cats, and discovered how it affects their nervous systems. In later research, Mitchell found that a substance similar to this chemical occurs naturally in humans and may play a role in cholesterol production.

Mitchell became assistant professor in 1969 and associate professor in 1972. He was also named assistant dean of the graduate college, but despite his new administrative duties he remained active in research. His role as assistant dean, however, afforded him the opportunity to take a more active role in developing research programs. He chaired the committee that created Oklahoma State's Black

Studies program in the mid 1980s. He also chaired the Oklahoma Alliance for Minority Participation in Science, Engineering, and Mathematics. In addition to his work at Oklahoma State, Mitchell has been an integral force in improving science education and research opportunities throughout the state. Through his involvement, the Oklahoma School of Science and Mathematics opened in Oklahoma City in 1990.

FURTHER READING:

Books

Kessler, James, et al. *Distinguished African American Scientists of the Twentieth Century.* Oryx Press, 1996.

—*Sketch by George A. Milite*

James W. Mitchell
1943-
Analytical chemist

Some people might wonder what analytical chemistry has to do with optical fibers. In fact, the relationship is extremely important; optical fibers (which carry information at very high speeds) cannot function properly if they are exposed to chemical contamination. The work of scientists such as James Mitchell has resulted in a number of effective techniques for removing chemicals from raw chemicals used in optical fiber manufacture.

James Mitchell was born in Durham, North Carolina on November 16, 1943, the oldest of five children. His parents, Willie Lee and Eunice Hester Mitchell, divorced when James was a boy, and finances were often strained. James saw education as an opportunity to prevent his own financial difficulties, and he excelled in school—particularly in science.

While in high school, he took a summer course in chemistry at North Carolina State University, sponsored by the National Science Foundation. He enjoyed it so much that he decided chemistry would be his major when he entered North Carolina A & T University in 1961.

During his undergraduate years, Mitchell became interested in analytical chemistry—which explores not just the "hows" of chemical reactions but the "whys." His research included work on the chemical makeup of proteins present in animals, and measuring the effects of radioactive materials on various chemical compounds. Mitchell also met Alice Jean Kea, who became his lab partner and, in 1964, his wife. The couple later had a daughter, Veronica.

Upon graduation from North Carolina A & T in 1965, the Mitchells went to Iowa State University for their graduate work. Before entering graduate school, they accepted summer internships at the U.S. Department of Energy's prestigious Oak Ridge National Laboratory in Tennessee. At Iowa State, while Alice Mitchell pursued her master's in nutrition, James Mitchell continued his studies in analytical chemistry. He was also given a research assistantship and a summer job at the school's laboratory. Mitchell received his Ph.D. in 1970 and took a position at Bell Labs in New Jersey.

At Bell Labs, Mitchell became part of the team that was developing optical wave guides, glasslike fibers that could transmit information via light pulses. Light pulse transmissions were much faster even than radio or microwaves, but the core materials of the optical wave guides had to be completely free of contamination. Mitchell worked to find new ways to eliminate contamination, using radioactive rays and manipulating the substances by changing their temperatures.

Mitchell's techniques were so successful that he became head of Bell Labs' analytical chemistry department in 1975 and received a patent for his chemical purification methods in 1976. He has won numerous awards, including the **Percy L. Julian** Research Award in 1981 and the Bell Laboratories Research Award in 1985. In addition to his research at Bell Labs, Mitchell is a frequent lecturer in the United States and overseas on scientific research.

FURTHER READING:

Books

Kessler, James, et al., eds. *Distinguished African American Scientists of the Twentieth Century.* Oryx Press, 1996.

—*Sketch by George A. Milite*

Mildred Mitchell-Bateman
1922-
Psychiatrist

The director of the West Virginia Department of Mental Health, Mildred Mitchell-Bateman was the first African American executive director in West Virginia. She was also the first black graduate of the Women's Medical College of Pennsylvania. Throughout her career, Mitchell-Bateman was influential in increasing the availability and quality of mental health services in West Virginia. She also held a professorship in psychiatry at Marshall University.

Mitchell-Bateman was born on March 22, 1922, in Cordele, Georgia. She earned her bachelor's degree from Johnson C. Smith University in 1941 and then attended Women's Medical College in Pennsylvania. She was awarded her medical degree in 1946, the first African American to graduate from Women's Medical College. Mitchell-Bateman interned at Harlem Hospital for a year after graduation, and then in 1947-48 she worked as staff physician at Larkin State Hospital in West Virginia. In 1951-52, she worked at Larkin as a clinic director. In this time period, she also had a private practice in Philadelphia and studied psychiatry. Mitchell-Bateman completed a three-year residency and fellowship in psychiatry at the Menninger School of Psychiatry in Topeka, Kansas, and she was certified for psychiatric practice in 1957.

In 1955, Mitchell-Bateman returned to Larkin, again as clinic director. She became superintendent of the clinic in 1958. Two years later, in 1960, she was given the position of superintendent of professional services for the West Virginia Department of Mental Health, a position she held until 1962. After a short stint as acting director of this department, Mitchell-Bateman was given the directorship outright by the end of 1962, a position she held until 1977. She was the first African American to hold such a position in the state of West Virginia.

As director, Mitchell-Bateman was in charge of services for the mentally ill as well as the development of mental health treatment and education in West Virginia. She also directed five state hospitals. During her tenure as director, local mental health programs increased in number from four to 54. Federal spending for mental health in West Virginia also increased as a result of her work. In 1958, federal funds totaled $268,000; by 1968 the total was $6 million. Mitchell-Bateman served on committees and commissions related to this position within the state of West Virginia. They included the Commission on Aging and the Commission on Mental Illness and Mental Retardation.

When Mitchell-Bateman left her directorship in 1977, she joined Marshall University's school of medicine as professor and chairman of the department of psychiatry. In 1982, she stepped down as department head but retained her professorship. In 1986, she concurrently held a position as a staff psychiatrist at the Huntington Medical Center in Virginia.

Mitchell-Bateman was a diplomate of the American Board of Psychiatry, and her undergraduate alma mater, Johnson C. Smith University, awarded her an honorary doctorate of science. In 1991, she was honored with the Warren Williams Distinguished Award by the American Psychiatric Association. She also received a special award from the West Virginia Medical Society. Mitchell-Bateman was a trustee of the Menninger Foundation, and a member of the Institute of Medicine of the National Academy of Sciences, the American Medical Association, and the American Psychiatric Association. She was vice-president of the American Psychiatric Association in 1973. Mitchell-

Bateman married William L. Bateman and had two daughters with him.

FURTHER READING:

Books

Sammons, Vivian Ovelton. *Blacks in Science and Medicine.* New York: Hemisphere Publishing, 1990.

Periodicals

"West Virginia's Director of Mental Health." *Ebony* (January 1964): 63-68.

—*Sketch by A. Petrusso*

Ruth Moore
1903-
Bacteriologist

Ruth Moore achieved distinction when she became the first African American woman to earn a Ph.D. in bacteriology from Ohio State in 1933. Her entire teaching career was spent at Howard University in Washington, D.C., where she remained an associate professor emeritus of microbiology until 1990.

Ruth Ella Moore was born in Columbus, Ohio, on May 19, 1903. After receiving her B.S. from Ohio State in 1926, she continued at that university and received her M.A. the following year. In 1933 she earned her Ph.D. in bacteriology from Ohio State, becoming the first African American woman to do so. Her achievement was doubly significant considering that her minority status was combined with that era's prejudices against women in professional fields. During her graduate school years (1927–1930), Moore was an instructor of both hygiene and English at Tennessee State College. Upon completing her dissertation at Ohio State—where she focused on the bacteriological aspects of tuberculosis (a major national health problem in the 1930s)—she received her Ph.D. in 1933.

That same year she took a position at the Howard University College of Medicine as an instructor of bacteriology. In 1939 she became an assistant professor of bacteriology, and in 1948 she was named acting head of the university's department of bacteriology, preventive medicine, and public health. In 1955 she became head of the department of bacteriology and remained in that position until 1960 when she became an associate professor of microbiology at Howard. She remained in that department until her retirement in 1973, whereupon she became an associate professor emeritus of microbiology. Throughout her career, Moore has been concerned with public health issues, and as such is a member of the American Public Health Association and the American Society of Microbiologists.

FURTHER READING:

Books

Sammons, Vivian O. *Blacks in Science and Medicine*, Hemisphere, 1990, p. 176.

—*Sketch by Leonard C. Bruno*

Garrett A. Morgan
1877-1963
Inventor

Garrett A. Morgan

A pioneer inventor, Garrett A. Morgan was responsible for the creation of such life-saving inventions as the gas mask and traffic lights. In a long and productive career that spanned over 40 years, Morgan worked diligently to create new products and services to enhance safety in modern-day living. His creations, for many of which he held patents, brought him much fame and prosperity in his lifetime, and he was nationally honored by many organizations, including the Emancipation Centennial in 1963.

Garrett Augustus Morgan was born in Paris, Kentucky, on March 4, 1877. He was the seventh of 11 children born to Sydney Morgan, a former slave who was freed in 1863, and Elizabeth (Reed) Morgan. Leaving home at age 14 with only an elementary school education, Morgan eventually settled in Cleveland. He taught himself to repair sewing machines, working with a number of companies before opening his own business specializing in sewing machine sales and repair in 1907. The venture was successful, enabling Morgan to set up house in Cleveland, and in 1908, he married Mary Anne Hassek. Together they had three sons.

Eventually, Morgan opened his own tailoring shop, and it was here that he developed his first unique product. Like other people in the clothing industry, Morgan was trying to solve a prevalent problem inherent in sewing woolen material: the sewing machine needle operated at such high speed that it often scorched the material. Morgan, who was working with a chemical solution to reduce this friction, noticed that the solution he was developing caused hairs on a pony-fur cloth to straighten instead. Intrigued, he tried it on a neighbor's dog, and when it straightened the

hair on the dog's coat, Morgan finally tried the new solution on his own hair. The success of the solution led Morgan to form G. A. Morgan Refining Company, the first producers of hair refining cream.

Invents Two Life-Saving Devices

During his lifetime, Morgan continued to experiment with new products, inventing such things as hat and belt fasteners and a friction drive clutch. His most significant invention, however, came in 1912, when he developed the "safety hood," the precursor to the modern-day gas mask. Morgan's patent application for the contraption referred to it as a "Breathing Device." Granted a patent in 1914, the device, which consisted of a hood with an inlet for fresh air and an outlet for exhaled air, drew a number of awards, including the First Grand Prize from the Second International Exposition of Safety and Sanitation in New York City. Although Morgan tested and demonstrated the use of the safety hood over the next few years, its most critical test occurred on July 24, 1916, during a tunnel explosion at the Cleveland Waterworks. The whole area was filled with noxious fumes and smoke, trapping workers in a tunnel under Lake Erie. Aided by his Breathing Device, Morgan went into the tunnel and carried workers out on his back, saving a number of men from an underground death. For this act of heroism, Morgan received the Carnegie Medal and a Medal of Bravery from the city, and the International Association of Fire Engineers made Morgan an honorary member. Not much later, Morgan established a company to manufacture and sell the Breathing Device in response to numerous orders from fire and police departments and mining industries. Fire fighters came to rely upon the gas mask in rescue attempts, and the invention helped save thousands from chlorine gas and other noxious fumes during World War I.

Next Morgan created the three-way traffic signal, a device responsible for saving thousands of lives over the years. The idea to build the warning and regulatory signal system came to him after he witnessed a carriage accident at a four-way street crossing. Once again, Morgan made sure to acquire a patent for his product, this time in Britain as well as the United States and Canada. Eventually, Morgan sold the rights to his invention to the General Electric Company for $40,000.

In addition to inventing new and unique products Morgan was actively involved in promoting the welfare of African Americans. In 1920, therefore, he began publishing the *Cleveland Call,* a newspaper devoted to publishing local and national black news. Additionally, Morgan served as an officer of the Cleveland Association of Colored Men, remaining an active member after it merged with the National Association for the Advancement of Colored People (NAACP). He developed glaucoma in 1943, losing most of his sight, and died in 1963.

FURTHER READING:

Books

Haber, Louis. *Black Pioneers of Science and Invention.* Harcourt, 1970, pp. 61–72.

Sammons, Vivian Ovelton. *Blacks in Science and Medicine.* Hemisphere Publishing, 1990, p. 176.

—*Sketch by Sharon F. Suer*

Kelso Bronson Morris
1909-1982
Chemist

Kelso Bronson Morris was a distinguished physical and inorganic chemist. His primary research areas concerned electrochemistry and the chemistry of hydroxylamine (a nitrogenous reducing agent); metal ions and their special bonding tendencies; and the chemistry of fused salts. Morris spent his teaching career first at his alma mater, Wiley College, and then at Howard University.

Morris was born on February 6, 1909, in Beaumont, Texas, to Isaiah H. and Frances (Kelso) Morris. He received his undergraduate education at Wiley College in Marshall,

Texas, where he earned his bachelor's degree in 1930. After graduation, Morris spent six years working at Wiley as an instructor in chemistry and mathematics. Morris also began his graduate work during this period; he held a General Education Board Fellowship from 1936-37. He was awarded his master of science degree from Cornell University in 1937. Wiley College then promoted him to an associate professor of chemistry. Morris continued his graduate work and received his doctoral degree in inorganic chemistry from Cornell in 1940. His dissertation was entitled *The Action of the Complex Delectronator, Potassium Permanganate, upon Hydroxylamine in Sulfuric Acid Solution.* In 1942, Morris became a full professor and head of the chemistry department at Wiley.

In 1946, Morris moved to Howard University as an associate professor in the chemistry department. While working at Howard, Morris held several visiting professorships. He was a visiting lecturer at Atlanta University in 1946, 1949, and 1951, and he did similar work at the National Science Foundation's Science Institute at North Carolina College during the summers of 1957-59. In 1959, Morris became affiliated with the Air Force Institute of Technology (AFIT), at Wright Patterson Air Force Base, Ohio, as an associate professor. He held this position concurrently with his Howard appointment and by the time he left the AFIT in 1961, he was the head of the chemistry section there.

In 1961, Morris became a full professor at Howard. He also married Marlene Isabella Cook in that year. This was his second marriage; Morris had also been married to Talitha Long, with whom he had one son, Kenneth Bruce. Together, Morris and Marlene would have three children: Gregory Alfred, Karen Denise, and Lisa Frances. By 1965, Morris was head of the chemistry department at Howard, a position he held until 1969. Wiley College honored Morris in 1972 with a Distinguished Alumni Achievement Award. He continued to lecture outside of Howard in the 1970s, appearing in the United Negro College Fund Dreyfus Foundation's Distinguished Lecture series each year from 1974-78. He retired from Howard in 1977 but retained professor emeritus status.

Morris was active in numerous professional and civic societies. He was a member of the Washington Academy of Science, which bestowed on him the Distinguished Teaching Award in 1968. Morris also served as president of the D.C. Insitute of Chemists in 1974-79, and he was given their Honor Scroll Award in 1979. He was a fellow of the Texas Academy of Science, the American Association for the Advancement of Science, and the American Institute of Chemistry. Morris was a member of the American Chemical Society, the Electrochemistry Society, the American Associaton of University Professors, the National Association of Reserch Science Teaching, and the National Institute of Science.

Morris died of pnemonia on August 26, 1982, in Washington Hospital Center, Washington, D.C.

SELECTED WRITINGS BY MORRIS:

Books

Principles of Chemical Equilibrium. London: Chapman and Hall, 1966.

Fundamental Chemical Equilibria: Nonionic-Ionic. New York: Gordand and Breach, 1971.

—*Sketch by A. Petrusso*

Harry L. Morrison
1932-
Theoretical physicist

Harry Morrison is a professor of physics at the University of California, Berkeley, where he studies quantum physics and its application to fluid dynamics. He directs the Lawrence Hall of Science, where he works to improve science instruction in grades K through 12, and is co-founder of the Mathematics, Engineering and Science Achievement (MESA) program, which helps prepare minority high school students for college science courses.

Harry Morrison was born on October 7, 1932, in Hall's Hill, Virginia. Harry's parents, Ethel and Charles Morrison, worked as servants on a nearby estate. Charles Morrison had a life-long interest in machinery, and shared this interest with Harry by working with him in his home workshop, and also visiting airfields in Virginia to learn about aircraft engines.

Morrison attended John M. Langston Elementary School, a segregated school with only six grades. The school was not able to provide a very good education, but his parents supplemented the lessons with assignments at home. When he was 10, his father started an auto repair shop, and Harry was able to learn more about machinery by watching his father work.

Morrison continued his education after sixth grade at a school for African American students near Washington National Airport in Virginia, and then transferred to Armstrong Technical High School in Washington, D.C. He did not do well at first. During his second year he began to lose interest in his studies and received a failing grade in geometry. The failure became a turning point for Morrison, shocking him into applying himself more seriously to his schoolwork. He retook the geometry class and earned an A-plus, and continued to do well in other classes as well.

Morrison's parents could not afford to send him to college, so after high school he started working. He worked as a janitor, but soon got a much better job at the Library of

Congress. Shortly thereafter, he applied and was accepted to Catholic University in Washington, D.C.

Morrison joined the Reserve Officers Training Corps (ROTC) to help finance his education. He graduated in 1955 with a degree in chemistry, mathematics, and philosophy, and was allowed to defer his military service by working at the National Institute of Health (NIH) in Bethesda, Maryland. The research he conducted, concerning chemical transport through living cells, could also be applied to the requirements for an advanced degree at Catholic University.

After 15 months at NIH, Morrison decided to return to school full-time. He earned his doctoral degree in 1960, performing research on the interactions between individual atoms involving the theoretical mathematical concepts of quantum physics.

In 1961, the U.S. Air Force called Morrison into active duty. He was assigned to the Air Force Academy in Colorado, where he was an assistant professor of physics until 1964. Around this time he married Harriet Brock.

After finishing his tour of duty, Morrison joined the Lawrence Radiation Laboratory (now the Lawrence Livermore National Laboratory, in Berkeley, California, where he studied how substances interact at very low temperatures. The laboratory is administered by the University of California, and in 1972 he transferred to the Berkeley campus to join the Physics Department Faculty.

At U.C. Berkely, Morrison has continued his studies of quantum theory. His broad educational background has allowed him to expand his roles in other areas as well. As director of the Lawrence Hall of Science, he has developed a series of hands-on laboratory exercises for elementary and middle school students, and as assistant dean for the College of Letters and Science, he oversees courses in literature and philosophy.

FURTHER READING:

Kessler, James H., J. S. Kidd, Renée A. Kidd, and Katherine A. Morin. "Harry L. Morrison" In *Distinguished African American Scientists of the 20th Century.* Phoenix: The Oryx Press, 1996.

—*Sketch by David E. Fontes*

Nathan Francis Mossell
1856-1946
Physician

Largely through his own efforts, Nathan Francis Mossell established Frederick Douglass Memorial Hospital, Philadelphia's first health-care facility for black patients. He also co-founded the National Medical Association

(NMA), the country's leading professional organization for black physicians, in 1895. A tireless activist, Mossell worked with civil rights pioneer W. E. B. Du Bois and initiated an effort to help black students gain admittance to Girard College in Philadelphia.

Turns Down Offer From American Colonization Society

Nathan Francis Mossell was born on July 27, 1856, in Hamilton, Ontario, Canada. His parents, Aaron and Eliza Bowers Mossell, had come from Baltimore, Maryland, and although slavery still existed in the southern United States at that time, they had been born free. Nonetheless, they had endured enormous troubles in America, and one day they simply loaded everything they owned into a cart and headed north. The Mossells had five children, of which Nathan was the third; his cousin through his mother's sister was Paul Robeson, who would eventually earn a name for himself as a performer and activist. Aaron built a lucrative business as a brick manufacturer, but troubles still dogged the family in Canada. After a dispute involving some land he owned, Mossell's father in 1865 moved his family back to the United States, where they settled in Lockport, New York.

In 1873, when he was 17 years old, Mossell went to Philadelphia. He and his older brother Charles got jobs at that city's Lincoln University, where in 1875 he enrolled as a student. After he earned his B.A. degree there in 1879, Mossell planned to enter medical school, but he lacked the funds to do so. At that time he was presented with what might have seemed a good opportunity to other young men in his situation: a position with the American Colonization Society, which was in the process of helping former slaves relocate to the west African nation of Liberia. Mossell, however, rejected the offer. In a bold letter to the Society, he questioned their motives: "The fact that the presence of the freed colored people [in Africa] increased the slaves' restlessness and dissatisfaction," he wrote, "had more to do with the American Colonization Society's interest in the deportation of free colored people to Liberia, than any interest on the Society's part in Liberia *itself*. This accounts for the disfavor of the colored people as a whole for the American Colonization Society. I decline your offer of assistance."

Somehow Mossell found the money to continue his education, and he entered the Medical School of the University of Pennsylvania. In 1882 he became the first African American to graduate from the university—and he did so with highest honors. His younger brother Aaron would become the first black graduate from the university's law school, and Aaron's daughter Sadie would become its first black female graduate 40 years later.

Establishes Frederick Douglass Memorial Hospital

Now that he had become a physician, Mossell attempted to join the Philadelphia County Medical Society. The latter group tried to keep him out, and only with the help of

his former professors at the medical school did he gain admittance. In 1885, he studied at Guy's and St. Thomas hospitals in London, England, where segregationist attitudes were not nearly as strong as they were in the United States.

His return to Philadelphia, however, confronted him with the realities of life in his homeland. Of the city's almost 30 hospitals, he discovered, none would accept black interns or nurse trainees. Several local medical colleges offered him a proposal: they would assist him in setting up a hospital to treat black patients, but only black patients. Leaders in the black community rejected this offer, whereupon Mossell—using what little savings he had, along with money raised by his wife—began efforts to establish a facility that would serve patients of all races. This was the Frederick Douglass Memorial Hospital and Training School for Nurses, which he opened in a three-story building on October 31, 1895.

Mossell's role as superintendent of the hospital was not an easy one. Money was always an issue, in spite of contributions from supporters and a yearly grant of $6,000 from the state legislature. In 1908, under his direction, the hospital built a $100,000 facility, but did not manage to pay for it until 1915, and then only through an extensive fund-raising effort on Mossell's part. (Later he wrote a pamphlet entitled "Hospital Construction, Organization, and Management.") He managed to assemble a talented staff, including several white doctors, but by 1907 Philadelphia had a "rival" health-care facility for black patients, Mercy Hospital. Officials at Mercy continually pressured him to allow a merger of the two in order to better serve the needs of the black community, and eventually he would agree to the creation of Mercy-Douglass Hospital.

Mossell continued at the hospital, and in his private practice, until 1933. He was also active in other areas. From 1907 to 1908, he served as president of the National Medical Association (NMA), the nation's leading professional organization for black physicians, which he had helped establish in 1895. In 1905 he became involved with W. E. B. Du Bois and the Niagara Movement, a civil-rights organization which in 1910 became the National Association for the Advancement of Colored People (NAACP). Mossell in 1915 he led marches to protest the showing of D. W. Griffith's *Birth of a Nation*, a film which presented the Ku Klux Klan as heroes and freed slaves as shiftless fools or dangerous rapists. (The film's popularity led directly to the establishment of the modern version of the Klan in Stone Mountain, Georgia, later that year.) Even after his retirement, Mossell led efforts to help blacks gain admittance to Philadelphia's Girard College. He died on October 27, 1946, in Philadelphia, leaving behind a wife and two daughters.

FURTHER READING:

Books

Kaufman, Martin, Stuart Galishoff, and Michael R. Winston, eds. *Dictionary of American Medical Biography.* Greenwood Press, 1984.

Logan, Rayford W. and Michael R. Winston, eds. *Dictionary of American Negro Biography*. Norton, 1982.

Sammons, Vivian Ovelton. *Blacks in Science and Medicine*. Hemisphere Publishing, 1990.

Treadwell, Thomas. *The Birth of the Black Medical Profession in Philadelphia*. West Chester State College, 1970.

Periodicals

Cobb, W. Montague, "Nathan Francis Mossell, M.D., 1856-1946," *Journal of the National Medical Association*, (March 1954).

—Sketch by Judson Knight

George Washington Murray
1853-1926
Inventor

George Washington Murray worked as a farmer and devised at least eight patented inventions related to agricultural implements. Murray's farming and local school teaching careers were overshadowed by his accomplishments in the realm of politics. At the height of his political career, Murray served in the United States House of Representatives for South Carolina. Murray was also an ardent supporter of black civil rights.

Murray was born into slavery on September 24, 1853, in Rembert, South Carolina. By the time slaves were emancipated, Murray was an orphan and apparently self-educated. Despite his desperate situation, Murray attended South Carolina University from 1874 until 1876, when it was closed to African Americans. Murray also attended the State Normal Institute in Columbia, South Carolina.

After 1876, Murray worked as a full-time farmer, public school teacher, and lecturer for the Colored Farmers Alliance. His activities as a farmer led to many of his patents. Murray received patents for a furrow opener, stalk-knocker-cultivator, and marker on April 10, 1894. Two months later, on June 5, 1894, Murray received patents on a planter, a fertilizer distributor, and a planter-fertilizer-distributor-reaper. Another item patented on that day was a cotton chopper, which was issued patent number 520,888.

In the late 1880s, Murray became interested in politics. His first position was as the chairman of the Republican Party in Sumpter County, in 1888. Then President Harrison appointed Murray to the position of customs inspector for the Port of Charleston in South Carolina.

In 1892, Murray was elected to the first of his two Congressional terms. Murray was the only black representative in the 53rd Congress, and an ardent supporter of free silver. During his next term, Murray became especially concerned with the rights of black Americans. He wanted to increase support for the education of black Americans and made a proposal to Congress to print a list of 92 inventions patented by African Americans. Murray did not mention that at least eight of them were owned by him. In 1897, Murray retired from politics, in part because of a nasty split in the Republican Party in South Carolina.

Murray returned to Sumpter County after his retirement. In addition to resuming his farming, Murray became involved in a real estate plan initiated to help local African Americans. However, something went wrong, and Murray was convicted of fraud in 1904. He and his family left for Chicago, Illinois, where he remained free. Murray spent the rest of his life writing and lecturing. Two of his books on race improvement were privately published, *Race Ideals* (1914) and *Light in Dark Places* (1925). He died in Chicago on April 21, 1926. He left behind his widow, Cornelia, and their two children.

SELECTED WRITINGS BY MURRAY:

Books

Race Ideals: Effects, Cause and Remedy for the Afro-American Race Troubles. 1910, rev. ed., Smith & Sons, 1914.

Light in Dark Places. 1925.

FURTHER READING:

Books

Tindall, George Brown. *South Carolina Negroes, 1877-1900*. University of South Carolina Press, 1952, pp. 57-58.

Periodicals

Gaboury, William. "George Washington Murray and the Fight for Political Democracy in South Carolina," *Journal of Negro History*, (July 1977): 258-69.

Other

http://www.usbol.com/ctjournal/Gwmurraybio.html

—Sketch by A. Petrusso

Peter Marshall Murray
1888-1969
Physician

Peter Marshall Murray was a physician and surgeon whose specialty was gynecology and obstetrics. With his extensive clinical experience, Murray's primary area of interests were gynecological surgery, pelvic inflammation and infection, uterine fibroids complicating pregnancy, and milk injections. As a talented doctor, Murray achieved a number of firsts for blacks in medical associations and societies. He also used his prestige to support access to quality medical care in hospitals for African Americans.

Murray was born on June 9, 1888, in Houma, Louisiana, one of four children of John and Louvinia (nee Smith) Murray. His father worked as a longshoreman, while his mother was a laundress. The family moved to New Orleans, in part to seek better educational opportunities for their children, when Murray was 12 or 13. In New Orleans, his father found work as a stevedore and his mother became employed as a practical nurse in New Orleans Women's Hospital and Infirmary. Her experiences there led her to inspire her son to become a doctor. Murray earned his B.A. from New Orleans University (later known as Dillard University) in 1910. While in medical school at Howard University, Murray had to work to send money home to support his ailing mother. He found a job as a security guard and studied as much as he could on duty while his co-workers covered for him. Murray graduated with his M.D. with honors from Howard Medical School in 1914.

Upon graduation until 1920, Murray worked in Washington, D.C. area, in addition to establishing his own private practice. For the first year, 1914-15, Murray was an intern at Bellevue Medical School at Freedman's Hospital. In 1915, Murray began work as an assistant to the dean and a professor of surgery at Howard University. From 1915-20, Murray was a clinical instructor in surgery at Howard. He also spent a year as the medical inspector for Washington, D.C., public schools, from 1917-18. In 1918, Murray was named assistant surgeon-in-chief at Freedman's Hospital, another post he retained until 1920. Murray married during this period. On July 2, 1917, he wed Charlotte Wallace, a music teacher and concert singer, and they had one child together, John Wallace Murray.

In 1920, Murray and his family moved to New York City, where he spent the rest of his life. Murray did some post-graduate work at the New York Post Graduate School and Hospital, Columbia University. By 1921, Murray had established a medical practice in the city, and while he was immediately successful financially, it took some years to develop professional respectability. For the first 15 or so years of Murray's career in New York, Murray performed surgery at a private institution, the Wiley Wilson Sanitar-

ium, operated by his friend Dr. Wilson, because many hospitals were closed to blacks.

Murray began his association with Harlem Hospital in 1925. (Some sources say 1928.) He rose through the ranks at Harlem Hospital beginning as an assistant adjunct visiting physician to the director of gynecology, then a member of the surgical staff, and was director of gynecology when he retired in 1953, after 25 years of service. Murray also was associated with a number of other hospitals during the period of 1924-64, including St. Clare's Hospital and Sydenham Hospital, New York City, and Beth Israel Hospital, Newark, New Jersey. At one point in 1953, Murray was the director of obstetrics and gynecology at Sydenham. He was also one of the first African American doctors appointed to Syndenham's executive committee in 1944.

While in New York City, Murray remained loyal to Howard University. He formed an informal local alumni society and medical reading club, and he was a Trustee of the university from 1924-58. Murray was also a Trustee for the State University of New York from 1954-59. Then-New York Governor Thomas Dewey appointed him as Trustee, and Murray served as chairman of its Committee on Medical Education. Murray also held a membership in the President's National Medical Advisory Committee on Health Resources.

Throughout the 1930s, Murray garnered many honors. In 1931, Murray was the first African American to be certified in gynecology by the American Board of Obstetrics and Gynecology. He served as President of the National Medical Association, the African American physician organization, from 1932-33, after serving as president of the North Harlem Medical Society in 1930. Murray also served the National Medical Association as chairman of the publications committee from 1942-57. In 1954, he was awarded a Distinguished Service Medal by the group.

Murray remained active in the medical community upon his retirement. He was president of the New York County Medical Society from 1954-57, the first African American to serve in that capacity. He was named a member of the Board of Hospitals in New York City in 1958. This was a considerably prestigious position, because in that capacity, he directed the 29 hospitals of New York City. Murray was also the first African American on the House of Delegates of the American Medical Association, from 1949-61. He used his position to advocate for an end to segregation in the American Medical Association's component societies. In 1969, the New York Academy of Medicine awarded him a plaque for distinguished service. He was a member of numerous other professional organizations, including the American College of Surgeons and the International College of Surgeons.

Murray was awarded several honorary degrees throughout his career: D.Sc. degrees from Dillard University in 1935, Lincoln University, Pennsylvania, in 1944, and Central State College, Ohio, 1962. In addition to all his clinical and societal work, Murray managed to publish regularly from 1922 and 1965. He died on December 19, 1969, in at St. Clare's Hospital, New York City.

SELECTED WRITINGS BY MURRAY:

Periodicals

"Gastric and Duodenal Ulcers, with Report of Two Cases," *Journal of the National Medical Association,*(1922): 143-46.

"Gynecological Morbidity and Mortality Analysis at Harlem Hospital," *New York State Journal of Medicine,* (1938): 361-64.

FURTHER READING:

Books

Germs Have No Color Line: Blacks and American Medicine, 1900-40. Garland Publishing, 1989.

Organ, Claude H., Jr., and Margaret M. Kosiba. *A Century of Black Surgeons: The U.S.A. Experience, Volume II.* Norman, OK: Transcript Press, 1987, pp. 497-500.

Periodicals

Cobb, W. Montague. "Peter Marshall Murray," *Journal of the National Medical Association,* (January 1970): 70.

—*Sketch by A. Petrusso*

Sandra Murray
1947-
Cell biologist

As a high school student, Sandra Murray was told by a guidance counselor that science was no career for someone who was black and female. Rather than becoming discouraged, she continued to pursue her interest in biology and attained success as a researcher and educator.

Sandra Murray was born on October 7, 1947, in Chicago, as the second of three children. Her parents, Charles and Muggy Wise Murray, owned a moving company. Often, families would leave odds and ends behind when they moved; Charles Murray would take these odds and ends and fashion toys for his children. This sparked an interest in Sandra as to how things worked. When she was older, her interest extended to how the human body functioned. Forced to spend three months in a hospital while recovering from corrective surgery on her shoulder, she asked the doctors countless questions about her condition and insisted on seeing her x-rays.

Murray did well enough in high school that she was chosen for a special biomedical research program that allowed high school students to take special weekend classes at the University of Chicago. It was during this time that Sandra's counselor admonished her for aiming too high in her career aspirations. For a while, Sandra's confidence was shaken; what if she *did* try to pursue a science career but failed? Fortunately, she decided not to give up. She worked after school in the anatomy laboratory of the University of Illinois School of Medicine, and in 1964 she enrolled there as a student.

Murray was still not completely sure she could succeed at science, and she put off choosing a major. She also had to work her way through school, and it took her six years to get her degree. After she took her first biology course in college during her sophomore year, though, she knew that biology was what she wanted to study.

After graduating from Illinois in 1970, she went on to the graduate biology program at Texas Southern University in Houston. She completed her master's in 1973 and went to the University of Iowa for her doctorate. A Ford Foundation Fellowship allowed her to devote most of her time to her research, which focused on how glandular hormones affected the growth of cancer cells. She was awarded her Ph.D. in 1980.

Shortly thereafter, Murray took a postdoctoral position at the University of California at Riverside. There, she continued her research on hormones, primarily the effects of deoxyribonucleic acid (DNA) and ribonucleic acid (RNA) on the glands that produce the various hormones. Eventually, Murray was offered a position on the medical school faculty at the University of Pittsburgh. During her career, her research has taken her to the Marine Biological Laboratory at Woods Hole, Massachusetts, and the Scripps Research Institute on Molecular Biology at La Jolla, California. Mindful of the difficulties in recruiting minorities for the sciences, she has also made time to visit a number of colleges with high minority enrollments, such as Morgan State University in Baltimore and Spelman College in Atlanta, to offer both instruction and encouragement.

FURTHER READING:

Books

Kessler, James H., et al. *Distinguished Aftican-American Scientists of the Twentieth Century.* Oryx Press, 1996.

—*Sketch by George A. Milite*

Samuel Milton Nabrit

Samuel Milton Nabrit
1905-
Biologist

Samuel Milton Nabrit is known for his research into animal regeneration, the ability of body parts to regrow or repair themselves after injury, and for his academic career as a promoter of science instruction among young African Americans. The first black Ph.D. from Brown University, Nabrit served as chairman of the biology department and as dean of the graduate school of arts and sciences at Atlanta University, and as president of Texas Southern University.

Born in Macon, Georgia, February 21, 1905, to James M. Nabrit, a Baptist minister and teacher, and Augusta Gertrude West Nabrit, Nabrit studied at Morehouse College, where he received his bachelor's degree in 1925. Taking to

heart the desire to teach inherited from his father, Nabrit returned to Morehouse College as a professor of biology from 1925–31, while he attended Brown University, working towards his advanced degrees. He obtained his M.S. in 1928 and his Ph.D. in biology in 1932.

While teaching during the school year at Morehouse, Nabrit conducted research at the Marine Biological Laboratory in Woods Hole, Massachusetts, every summer from 1927 to 1932. His specialty was the regenerative abilities of fish, particularly studying their ability to regrow tail fins. He found that the size of the fin rays on fishes' fins determined the rate of regeneration. The results of his research were published in the *Biological Bulletin.* A citation presented to Nabrit on April 30, 1982, by the Beta Kappa Chi Scientific Honor Society to which Nabrit belonged, noted that a study published by Nabrit in 1928 was still being quoted in studies of animal regeneration as late as the 1980s.

After earning his doctorate in 1932, Nabrit was appointed chairman of Atlanta University's biology department, a position he held until 1947. He continued his regenerative research at Atlanta University, focusing on fish embryo regeneration in particular. His work was described in articles appearing in such scientific publications as the *Anatomical Record, Journal of Parasitology,* and the *Journal of Experimental Zoology.* In 1947, Nabrit became dean of Atlanta University's graduate school of arts and sciences. In 1955 he was appointed president of Texas Southern University, where he served until 1966. During his tenure as president, Nabrit also served as president of the Association of Colleges and Secondary Schools and as a member of the board of directors of the American Council on Education. He also joined several committees for the Departments of State and Health and Human Services, and was appointed by President Eisenhower to a six-year term on the National Science Board in 1956. In 1966 President Johnson selected Nabrit for a term on the Atomic Energy Commission. The following year Nabrit became director of the Southern Fellowships Fund, an operating agency of the Council of Southern Universities, where he stayed until his retirement in 1981.

Nabrit was one of the founders of Upward Bound, a program designed to increase the numbers of qualified youth staying in college beyond one year. While a guest speaker at Kashmere Gardens High School, Nabrit was told that most of the scholarship winners would drop out during their first year in college. Nabrit decided to do something about this problem. In 1957, scholarship winners and other high potential students were invited to Texas Southern for the summer, essentially enrolling in the college for 11 weeks. Three nationally established specialists in reading, logical thinking, and mathematics were recruited to hold classes daily, and the students were paired with volunteers who stayed with them in the dormitories and tutored them every night. The number of students remaining in college was greatly increased by the program.

Speaking to contributor Sharon F. Suer in a phone interview, Nabrit recalled that when he began his academic career the "leading scientist in our field . . . produced only one or two biology students. All of his students he steered into medicine. My notion was that we needed to increase the number of young people who would be able to get the Ph.D. in biology and all the other sciences. At Brown, where I was the first Negro to graduate with a Ph.D. in Biology, I made sure that the next four black Ph.D.s were all out of my lab."

Throughout his college career, Nabrit played baseball and football. The game he loved playing the most, though, and continued playing into the 1940s was bridge; he and his foursome became expert enough to advance to a national bridge championship. Nabrit married Constance T. Crocker in 1927; she passed away in 1984. They had no children. Dr. Nabrit is retired and still lives in Georgia.

SELECTED WRITINGS BY NABRIT:

Periodicals

"The Role of the Fin Rays in Tailfins of Fishes Fundulus and Goldfish," *Biological Bulletin.* (April 1929).

"The Role of the Basal Plate of the Tail in Regeneration of Fishes Fundulus," *Biological Bulletin.* (February 1931).

"Human Ecology in Georgia," *Science Education,* (October 1944).

"The Negro in Science," *Negro History Bulletin,* (January 1957).

FURTHER READING:

Books

Sammons, Vivian O. *Blacks in Science and Technology.* Hemisphere Publishing Corp. p. 179, 1990.

Other

Beta Kappa Chi, text of citation, April 30, 1982.
Nabrit, Samuel Milton, *Interview with Sharon F. Suer conducted January 18, 1994.*

—*Sketch by Sharon F. Suer*

Onesimus
1600s-1700s
Slave

Onesimus was a slave in Boston, Massachusetts, during the early 1700s. He had grown up in Africa, a member of the Garamantes tribe, but was enslaved and brought to America. In 1706, the parishioners of a Bostonian church gave Onesimus to their pastor, Cotton Mather. A leading theologian at the time, Mather was also an avid natural scientist. He frequently wrote letters about his observations to the leading scientific journal of the time, the *Philosophical Transactions of the Royal Society of London.*

One of the dreaded diseases of that time was smallpox. The practice of inoculation was being experimented with as a way to make people immune to the disease. People were inoculated at that time by scratching their arms until they just started to bleed. A small amount of pus from an infected person would be rubbed into this incision. The hope was that the resulting infection would produce only a very mild case of the disease. However, there was no guarantee that would occur. Although the details of what was happening were not known then, today it is known that inoculation places a small amount of infectious material into people, and gives their immune system time to build up resistance to the disease. Methods are now available to insure that today's inoculating fluids cannot cause the full-blown disease.

Mather was reading one of his own letters in the July 12, 1716, issue of *Philosophical Transactions.* Immediately following his letter was an article by Emanuel Timonius describing the practice of inoculation in Turkey. Mather was struck by how closely this practice resembled what Onesimus had told him about what was done to him in Africa. Mather's description of what Onesimus had told him is reprinted in the *Yale Journal of Biology and Medicine* from a letter he wrote to the Royal Society (capitalization and spelling are in the older English format):

"Enquiring of my Negro-man Onesimus, who is a pretty Intelligent Fellow, Whether he ever had the Small-Pox; he answered, both, Yes, and, No; and then told me, that he had undergone an Operation, which had given him something of the Small-Pox, & would forever praeserve him from it; adding, That it was often used among the Guramantese, & whoever had the Courage to use it, was forever free from the fear of the Contagion. He described

the Operation to me, and shew'd me in his Arm the Scar, which it had left upon him; and his Description of it, made it the same, that afterwards I found related unto you by your Timonius."

Mather urged further investigation into inoculation, but nothing occurred for five years. In April 1721, the HMS Seahorse arrived in Boston Harbor from the West Indies. Unknowingly, it was carrying smallpox, which resulted in an epidemic in Boston and surrounding areas. Within a year, half of Boston's 12,000 inhabitants got the disease, and 900 died. Mather vigorously pleaded for widespread inoculation, but he was not a physician, and the medical community of the time was not convinced the procedure was safe (certainly reasonable given the knowledge of the time).

Spurred on by ravages of the epidemic around him, and remembering what Onesimus had told him, Mather wrote to Zabdiel Boylston, a self-educated country doctor who did not have a medical degree. On June 26, 1721, Boylston inoculated his six-year-old son, Thomas, and two of his slaves. All three were successfully inoculated. The controversy became more heated, but Boylston continued to safely inoculate more and more people. The epidemic gradually abated, and Boylston kept careful record of what happened the people he inoculated. Of the 286 people he inoculated, 2.1 percent died, compared to 14.9 percent of those who acquired smallpox naturally. Boylston reported his findings to the Royal Society, and the medical community became convinced of the value of inoculation. It gradually spread throughout the world, and Boylston was honored by being made a Fellow of the Royal Society on July 7, 1726, when Sir Isaac Newton was president.

Through the accurate recounting of the procedure carried out on him, Onesimus helped bring knowledge of inoculation to the Western World. This would remain the primary way of protecting people from the ravages of smallpox until the introduction of Jennerian cowpox vaccination in 1798.

FURTHER READING:

Periodicals

Breen, Louise A. "Cotton Mather, the 'Angelical Ministry,' and Inoculation." *Journal of the History of Medicine and Allied Sciences,* Vol. 46, (July 1991): 333-357.

Kilgour, Frederick G. "The Rise of Scientific Activity in Colonial New England." *Bulletin of the History of Medicine,* Vol. 22 (December 1949): 123-138.

Joan Murrell Owens

Viets, Henry R. "Zabdiel Boylston (1679-1766): Remarks at His Grave." *Bulletin of the History of Medicine,* Vol. 24, (November-December 1950): 539-540.

Viets, Henry R. "The African Slave, Onesimus, Introduced Inoculation to the Western World." *Journal of the National Medical Association,* Vol. 44 (May 1952): p. 219.

—Sketch by Dónal P. O'Mathúna

Joan Murrell Owens
1933-

Paleontologist and marine biologist

The first African American woman in the United States to receive a doctorate in geology, Joan Murrell Owens's career is a classic story of a woman's perseverance in holding on to her dreams. Born and raised near the ocean, she developed a fascination for the sea very early in life and began to dream of a career in marine biology while still in high school. But as things turned out, she was not to realize this dream for a few decades.

Owens was born on June 30, 1933, in Miami, Florida to Dr. William H. Murrell, a dentist, and Leola Peterson Murrell, a former school teacher. In 1950 she entered Fisk University in Nashville, Tennessee hoping to purse her chosen field, but found that neither women nor African Americans were encouraged to pursue careers in the marine sciences. This lack of peer support led her to try to follow her mother's suggestion to pursue a career in teaching, and she graduated in 1954 with a major in fine art, and a double minor in mathematics and psychology. She then joined a master's program in commercial art at the University of Michigan at Ann Arbor but was soon disillusioned with the field and switched to education. Before her graduation in 1956, she had already redirected her talents and began her work with brain damaged and emotionally disturbed children at the university's Children's Psychiatric Hospital. After working there for two years, she was appointed as a teacher in the English department at Howard University in Washington D.C., where she stayed until 1964. She then moved with her husband Frank A. Owens, a program analyst for the United States Postal Service, to Massachusetts, where she worked at the Institute for Services to Education in developing programs for teaching various educationally disadvantaged students.

In 1970, Owens returned to Washington D.C., where she reassessed her career and started to seriously consider re-entering school to study marine biology. None of the many institutions in the area had an undergraduate program in the field at that time, and upon the advice of an old friend, Owens re-enrolled herself in an undergraduate program—this time at George Washington University with a major in geology and a minor in zoology. She graduated in 1973 and immediately began graduate work in the geology department, opting to specialize in the area of paleontology. She received a Master's in 1976 and continued to study there for her doctoral degree. While searching for a dissertation topic she met with Dr. Stephen Cairns at the nearby Smithsonian Institute. He encouraged her to study a unique group of deep-sea corals, called "button corals," about which very little was known. When she completed her Ph.D. in 1984 she had already been teaching in the geology and geography department at Howard University for eight years. She remained there for the duration of her career, moving to the biology department after the geology department was eliminated, and retiring from active work in 1995.

In her years as a researcher, Owens contributed an immense amount of new information about her group of deep-sea corals. She redefined the classification of these creatures and discovered completely new organisms, one of which she named *Letepsammia franki* after her husband. Reminiscing about her career in a recent conversation with contributor Neeraja Sankaran, she remarked, "Scientifically, it was always very exiting to discover and describe a whole new genus or species and thus extend our knowledge of deep-sea corals. But I have also gotten a lot of satisfaction as a teacher—interacting with fresh minds and opening them up to possibilities."

She added that she was especially gratified by the response of the students in freshman level courses for non-science majors. "Suddenly they tell themselves, 'Hey! This is something I can do!' There is a great deal of satisfaction in helping students overcome their fear of science."

—Sketch by Neeraja Sankaran

Frederick Douglass Patterson

Frederick Douglass Patterson
1901-1988
Veterinarian

Founder of the United Negro College Fund (UNCF), Frederick Douglass Patterson was known for his visionary and pioneering efforts in promoting higher education for African American higher education. Under his guidance, the UNCF became the nation's largest independent source of monetary aid to educational institutions that were traditionally African American. Patterson also went on to establish the College Endowment Funding Plan, and he was the founder of the first African American school of veterinary medicine in the United States at Tuskegee Institute. All through his life, Patterson acted on his conviction that education was the best means to achieve African American mobility. For his lifelong efforts in promoting education, Patterson was awarded the Presiden-

tial Medal of Freedom, the nation's highest civilian honor, in 1987.

Born to William Ross Patterson and Mamie Lucille (Brooks) Patterson in Washington, D.C., on October 10, 1901, Patterson was named after the African American journalist and antislavery leader, Frederick Douglass. Patterson, who was orphaned at the age of two, was raised in Texas by his sister, Wilhelmina, who was a schoolteacher there. After attending Prairie View State College in Texas from 1915 to 1919, he attended Iowa State College in Ames, Iowa, and received his doctorate in veterinary medicine in 1923. In 1927 he earned his M.S. degree at that same school and later entered Cornell University at Ithaca, New York. He was awarded a Ph.D. in veterinary medicine from Cornell in 1932.

Begins a Teaching Career

Patterson also began teaching as an instructor in veterinary science at Virginia State College in Petersburg, Virginia, while he was still a student. Later, from 1927 to 1928, Patterson was appointed director of agriculture at Virginia State. In 1928 he was invited to join the Tuskegee Normal and Industrial Institute, an organization he remained affiliated with for the next 25 years. Patterson held various positions at Tuskegee, including serving as the first head of the school's new veterinary division and later as director of the School of Agriculture. From 1935 to 1953, he served as the Institute's third president, raising the school to new heights of achievement and national recognition. Tuskegee had been founded by Booker T. Washington, a black American educator, who believed that African Americans should receive vocational training. Patterson's ideas went beyond that, and he stressed the importance of both job training as well as the need to develop confident leadership skills. After he retired as president of the Tuskegee Institute in 1953, Patterson remained president emeritus until his death.

The Founding of the United Negro College Fund

In 1943, a few years after he had become president of Tuskegee, Patterson proposed that a group of African American colleges form a consortium to raise funds for their mutual benefit. Called the United Negro College Fund (UNCF), the organization had 27 original members who amassed an endowment of $765,000. Thirty-five years later, the Fund had grown to include 42 members with a combined monetary legacy of $42 million. The UNCF provided money for scholarships, staff salaries, library resources, and laboratories, and their motto, "A mind is a terrible thing to waste," became a well-known slogan. In addition to establishing the UNCF, Patterson was also instrumental in creating the College Endowment Funding Plan, which would encourage private businesses to donate funds by matching their gifts with federal funds.

Patterson also served as president and trustee of the Phelps-Stokes Fund, which worked for the improvement of the status of blacks in Africa and the United States, the welfare of the Native American, and the improvement of low-income housing in New York City. In 1987, Patterson was honored by the White House, along with actor Danny Kaye and composer Meredith Wilson, when former President Ronald Reagan named him a recipient of the Presidential Medal of Freedom for his life's work. When Patterson died of a heart attack on April 26, 1988, at his home in New Rochelle, New York, he was survived by his wife of 53 years, Catherine Elizabeth (Moton), and his son, Frederick Patterson.

SELECTED WRITINGS BY PATTERSON:

Books

College Endowment Funding Plan. American Council on Education, 1976.

FURTHER READING:

Periodicals

New York Times, (April 27, 1988): D27.
Washington Post, (April 28, 1988): D4.

—*Sketch by Leonard C. Bruno*

Georgia Esther Lee Patton

Georgia Esther Lee Patton
1864-1900
Physician

Georgia Esther Lee Patton was the first African American woman to be licensed to practice medicine, including surgery, in the state of Tennessee. She was also one of the first women to graduate from Meharry Medical College, a traditionally black medical school located in Nashville.

Georgia Esther Lee Patton was born on April 15, 1864, in Grundy County, Tennessee. By some accounts, she was born a slave, though she received an education from missionary teachers. This experience perhaps influenced

Patton's desire to become a missionary herself. After her mother, a widow, died in the late 1880s, Patton's siblings helped send her through college. Patton began her college education at Central Tennessee College (later known as Fisk University), completing the "normal course." When she graduated in 1890, she enrolled in Central Tennessee College's Meharry Medical Department. (This department eventually became a separate institution, known as Meharry Medical College.) In February 1893, after only two and a half years, Patton earned her medical degree and subsequently her medical license.

In April or May 1893, Patton boarded a ship to sail to Liberia, where she worked as a medical missionary. She had originally sought support for her missionary work from her church, the Centenary Methodist Episcopal Church, but was unable to secure it. So she supported herself while she was there, working in primitive surroundings and lacking supplies. Still, she treated patients, with apparent success, until her lack of funding and ill health brought her back to the United States in 1895.

Patton settled in Memphis, Tennessee, where she opened a medical practice in the downtown area. She was immediately successful, and her practice grew quite large. Patton shared her newfound wealth, sending regular checks, ten dollars monthly, to the Freedmen's Aid Society. The group dubbed her "the gold lady" for her generous contributions.

On December 29, 1897, Patton married David W. Washington, a businessman who was one of the first black letter carriers in Memphis. She practiced under his name, but ill health forced her to retire, perhaps as early as 1899, when she was no longer listed in Memphis's directory of physicians. She suffered from tuberculosis, which she had probably contracted in Africa. Patton also had two sons, neither of whom survived infancy. Willie Patton Washington died shortly after his birth on February 14, 1899. David W. Washington was born on July 11, 1900; his mother died on November 8, 1900. David W. only survived her by 13 days.

FURTHER READING:

Books

Sterling, Dorothy, ed. *We Are Your Sisters: Black Women in the Nineteenth Century,* New York: W.W. Norton & Company, 1984, pp. 445-46.

Summerville, James. *Educating Black Doctors: A History of Meharry Medical College.* The University of Alabama Press, 1983, pp. 31-32.

—Sketch by A. Petrusso

Benjamin Franklin Peery, Jr.
1922-
Astronomer and physicist

Benjamin Franklin Peery, Jr., one of the first African Americans to enter the field of astronomy, is an expert on stellar atmospheres. He has enjoyed a successful career as a researcher and has devoted much of his life to teaching and to recruiting minority students to enter the field of astronomy.

Benjamin Peery was born in Minnesota, where his father worked as a railway mail clerk. The family needed to move several times throughout Benjamin's childhood, as his father became employed by different railroads throughout southeastern Minnesota. One thing that remained constant through all the moves, however, was the night sky. At an early age, Peery developed a fascination for star-gazing, and he learned the names for all the different constellations.

His interest in the stars went far beyond just looking at them, however. He was fascinated by questions about how the world works, and in particular he became unquenchably curious about what it was that makes the stars shine. He discovered a book on astronomy and was thrilled with what he learned, but also tantalized by how much was still unknown.

Peery had other interests as a youngster as well. One of his favorite hobbies was building and flying model airplanes. When he graduated from high school in 1940, it was this interest which seemed most likely to lead to an employable career, so he enrolled in the University of Minnesota to pursue a degree in aeronautical engineering.

While at the university, Peery discovered that he enjoyed the theoretical aspects of science more than the applied practice of engineering, so he decided to change his major to physics. As a senior, he began to wonder more deeply about the physical properties of the stars that had so fascinated him throughout his life. He resolved to continue his studies, and enrolled in the graduate program at the University of Michigan to study astrophysics.

Peery's research, both at Michigan and after receiving his doctorate as a member of the astronomy faculty at Indiana University, concerned the interiors of stars and how they generate energy. Specifically, Peery concentrated on stars that are part of "close binary star systems," in which two stars are close enough that they will have noticeable affects upon each other.

During two decades at Indiana University, Peery made several important contributions to astronomical research. Then he decided to channel his love of astronomy in a different direction. Peery had noticed that of the thousands of members of the American Astronomical Society, fewer than a dozen were African Americans. He wanted to do something to fix this racial imbalance in astronomy and in all the sciences.

The opportunity to address these problems arose when Peery was offered a position at Howard University in Washington, D.C. Howard is one of the most prestigious and best-known educational institutions with a primarily black student body. Here, Peery would be able to convince minority students that science in general, and astronomy in particular, are not only fascinating subjects in school, but also offer excellent career opportunities.

Peery accepted the position at Howard, where he taught until his retirement. In addition to reaching out to his college students, Peery branched out to bring his message to students of younger ages as well. Through a grant from the National Science Foundation, he led a team of educators who taught elementary school teachers how to stimulate their students and foster an enthusiasm for science.

Peery was able to reach an even larger audience when he was profiled on the 1991 PBS series "The Astronomers." He is now retired from his position at Howard University, but continues to be fascinated by the stars, and, as ever, enjoys sharing this fascination with others.

FURTHER READING:

Goldsmith, Donald. *The Astronomers.* New York: St. Martin's Press, 1991.

Burns, Khephra. "Benjamin Peery: star doctor." *Essence* 22, no 1 (May 1991): 48.

—*Sketch by David E. Fontes*

Waverly J. Person
1927-
Geophysicist

W averly J. Person is the first black American to hold the prominent position of Director of the United States Geological Survey's National Earthquake Information Center. A respected geophysicist and seismologist, he was also one of the first black Americans in his field. Today, in addition to fielding inquiries from news organizations around the globe, he spends much of his time encouraging minority students to consider the earth sciences as a career.

Waverly J. Person was born on May 1, 1927, in Blackridge, Virginia, to the former Bessie Butts and Santee Person, who was a farmer. After completing high school, Person enrolled at St. Paul's College in his hometown of Lawrenceville, Virginia. In 1949, he obtained a Bachelor of Science degree from the school. His areas of study were general science and industrial education. Shortly thereafter, he joined the United States Army. His tour of duty included being stationed in Korea, where the conflict with communist forces had begun over control of the island. Person left the Army in 1952 as a First Sergeant and recipient of Good Conduct and Asian Pacific medals. Waverly J. Person and Sarah Walker Person were married on November 6, 1954.

Upon his discharge from the Army, Person found that no funds were available to continue his education. He chose to relocate to Washington, D.C., where a relative had offered him working managing a construction company. Several odd jobs followed until the summer of 1962, when he was offered a job as a technician with the U.S. Department of Commerce. The work that followed ignited a passion in Person that still persists. He was assigned to maintain the drum rolls recording earthquake readings at the National Earthquake Information Center—which was part of the Department of Commerce at the time. Because he was curious about what the wiggly lines on the machines meant, he was compelled to take up earthquake studies.

Realizing that career prospects were limited as a technician, Person took up graduate studies while continuing his technical duties at the National Information Earthquake Center. From 1962 to 1973, he held that position and simultaneously completed graduate work at American University and George Washington University. His supervisors increasingly assigned him more challenging tasks that he performed well, gaining notice among his peers at work. Soon he was qualified as a geophysicist and transferred to the United States Geological Survey's National Earthquake Information Center in Colorado. In 1977, Waverly J. Person was named director of the Colorado National Earthquake Information Center—a position he still holds.

As his career progressed, Person was not immune to the skeptics who questioned why, as a black man, he chose a field not traditionally associated with African Americans. A scholar who regularly publishes in academic journals and is out in the field, he bases his reputation on the ability to get the job done. Following are comments by Person regarding his rise to prominence as published in *Contemporary Black Biography*: "Any time you're breaking new ground, you've got to take a lot, do a lot. People were always asking, 'Why do you want to get into this field?' They wondered how I would do as their colleague—on the same level as they were. Anything I did that was professional or scientific, I was always expected to do better, or more. But I was one that never gave up. No matter what anyone would say, I had my goals set as to what I was going to do. Nothing was going to stop me. Once you get to respectability, people don't see your color anymore. They see you as an individual who knows what you're doing, and they accept you for that."

The National Earthquake Information Center monitors earthquakes all over the world in order to locate the tremor, determine its size, and pass that information along to emergency crews. The immediacy of this operation is enhanced by a connection with the North American Air Defense Command, which alerts state officials, who in turn contact local communities. As Director of the Center, Person often appears in the national and international media as the scientific expert presenting background information and what to expect after an earthquake occurs. He also performs the managerial functions of budgeting, staffing, and overseeing the numerous publications the National Earthquake Information Center issues.

Person has been honored with many distinguished awards throughout his professional life. They include an Honorary Doctorate in Science from St. Paul's College in 1988, Outstanding Government Communicator in 1988, Meritorious Service Award—United States Department Interior in 1989, and in 1990 the Annual Minority Award from the Community Services Department in Boulder, Colorado. His work at the National Earthquake Information Center has been praised by United States Department of the Interior with an Outstanding Performance Rating in the years 1990, 1991, 1992, 1993, and 1994.

A member of the Seismological Society of American since 1965, he has served as Treasurer of the Eastern Section since 1968. He is also been a member of the American Geophysical Union since 1975. The Colorado School of Mines admitted Person as an honorary member in 1991. In his hometown of Boulder, Colorado, he is well known through his association (since 1972) with the Flatirons Kiwanis Club, including serving as a past president. And, as a member of the Board of Directors of Boulder County Crimestoppers, which he joined in 1986.

Since 1962, Waverly J. Person has been monitoring earthquakes and is still fascinated by the subject. As he commented in *Emerge* magazine: "No two earthquakes are alike. It's never a dull moment because earthquakes are occurring all over the world and we are working to find out where all the different seismic zones are. It's something you just love to do because you continue to learn."

SELECTED WRITINGS BY PERSON:

Books

Significant earthquakes of the world 1985-1989. United States Department of the Interior, United States Geological Survey.

FURTHER READING:

Books

Mabunda, L. Mpho. *Contemporary Black Biography,* Detroit: Gale Research, 1995, p. 168.
Phelps, Shirelle. *Who's Who Among Black Americans,* Detroit: Gale Research, 1994, p. 1158.

—*Sketch by Patrick J. Longe*

Hildrus A. Poindexter
1901-1987
Physician and bacteriologist

Hildrus A. Poindexter had a distinguished career as a medical school professor and a physician in the United States Army and Public Health Service. His careful scientific observations in many countries, including Africa, Asia, Europe, and South America, provided the basis for much medical research and discovery by others. In the preface to his autobiography *My World of Reality,* Poindexter wrote: "My major interest in life is the physical world, the physical aspects of man and the effects of environment on a human life."

Hildrus Augustus Poindexter, the sixth of 11 children, was born on May 10, 1901, on a farm near Memphis, Tennessee, the son of Fred Poindexter, a tenant farmer, and Luvenia Gilberta Clarke. Poindexter worked on the farm at a very early age and later recalled that he had announced his intention of becoming a physician at about the age of five.

He attended the local segregated elementary school from age seven to 15, which was considered normal at the time. Poindexter furthered his own education, however, by learning Latin, Greek, and algebra. In 1916, he sold the horse and chickens his parents had given him to start in farm life and went off to Swift Memorial Academy, a secondary school located in eastern Tennessee. He worked his way through school, graduated in 1920, and then enrolled at Lincoln University. He graduated with honors in 1924, the same year he married Ruth Viola Grier, with whom he had one daughter, Patchechole Barbara.

After teaching for a year in a private secondary school in Oxford, North Carolina, and working as a Pullman porter to earn additional money, Poindexter entered the two-year program of the Dartmouth College Medical School in Hanover, New Hampshire. He did well enough there to be accepted for the third-year class at Harvard University Medical School in 1927, from which he received his M.D. in 1929. It was while at Dartmouth and Harvard that he decided to specialize in tropical medicine, the study and treatment of diseases and public health problems found in tropical lands. In late 1929, he entered Columbia University to do graduate work in bacteriology and parasitology; he received his Ph.D. in microbiology and immunology in 1932. Poindexter taught bacteriology, preventive medicine, and public health at the Howard University College of Medicine in Washington, D.C., from 1931 to 1943.

It was during this period that he did much of his scientific research, though he soon found himself preoccupied with administrative duties. From 1943 to 1946 he served as a physician in the U.S. Army in the South Pacific, New Guinea, the Philippines, and later in occupied Japan. In 1947, he became a physician in the U.S. Public Health Service. He served tours of duty in Liberia, Vietnam, Surinam, Iraq, Libya, Somali, Jamaica, and Sierra Leone. In all of these assignments, he used his knowledge of tropical medicine in efforts to improve the poor health situation of the citizens of these countries. In 1977, Poindexter retired from the Public Health Service as medical director and returned to the Howard University College of Medicine as a professor of community health practice.

Poindexter's importance as a medical researcher lies in his careful scientific observations of the many tropical diseases he encountered in his foreign duty posts and the very extensive reports he wrote concerning his findings. He often suggested possible medications to eliminate or alleviate the diseases, which were sometimes based upon his own field experiments. These reports served as valuable raw data upon which other scientists and public health physicians could base their own research. Poindexter received honorary doctorates from Lincoln University, Dartmouth College, and Howard University, and also was awarded the National Civil Service League Career Award in 1963 and the U.S. Public Health Service Meritorious Award in 1965. After a heart attack, Poindexter died in a Maryland suburb of Washington, D.C., on April 21, 1987.

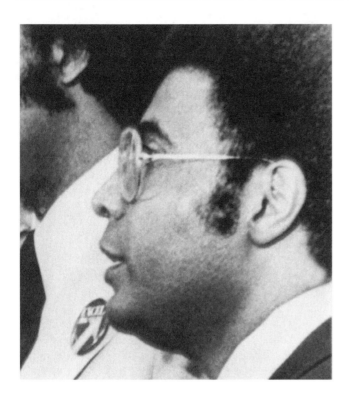

Alvin Francis Poussaint

SELECTED WRITINGS BY POINDEXTER:

Books

My World of Reality: An Autobiography. Balamp Publishing, 1973.

—*Sketch by John E. Little*

Alvin Francis Poussaint
1934-
Physician and psychiatrist

Alvin Francis Poussaint has had a distinguished career as a professor, academic administrator, social activist, and writer. He has made important contributions to changing public perceptions about the emotional behavior and social accomplishments of blacks in the United States.

The seventh of eight children, Poussaint was born on May 15, 1934, in East Harlem, New York City. His father, Christopher, was a descendant of Haitians and worked as a printer and typographer. His mother, Harriet, stayed home and devoted herself to her children. When Poussaint was nine, he came down with rheumatic fever, was hospitalized for three months, and then had to spend three months at a convalescent home. His stay in the hospital planted the seed of his future ambition to become a medical doctor. Because he was not allowed much physical activity during and after his illness, he read voraciously. He discovered that he had an aptitude for mathematics and science, and he was accepted to the highly competitive and prestigious Peter Stuyvesant High School in Manhattan. A gifted all-around student, he learned several musical instruments and won the school literary writing award when he graduated in 1952.

Although he was admitted to Yale, Poussaint's father wanted him to stay closer to home, so he attended Columbia University in New York City, where he graduated in 1956. He was admitted to Cornell University Medical School, and was the only black person in his class. He received his M.D. in 1960. While in medical school, he heard stories of professors who would not consider black interns to work for them. Because of these stories and many other racial situations, Poussaint grew curious about the emotional traumas that all people, black or white, suffered because of racial problems. He applied for an internship at UCLA's Neuropsychiatric Institute and was admitted. He received his master's degree from UCLA in 1964, and rose to the position of chief resident in the intern training program at his hospital in Los Angeles.

Racial relations had turned violent during the 1960s in the United States, and after Poussaint graduated from UCLA in 1964, he joined his sister and an old classmate from Stuyvesant High School in Jackson, Mississippi. In Jackson, he worked as the director of the Medical Committee for Human Rights for the Student Non-Violent Coordinating Committee. In 1966, he took a position at Tufts University, first as a senior clinical instructor, and then as an assistant professor. In 1969, he moved to Harvard Medical School as an associate dean of students and associate professor of psychiatry. In November 1973, Poussaint married Ann Ashmore, a social worker. They had one son, Alan. They were divorced in 1988.

Redefining Racial Emotions

While other psychologists have successfully attacked ideas that blacks are intellectually inferior to other races, Poussaint has focused on explaining the highly contradictory emotions that black people develop in response to racism. Some block out their aggressive feelings about racism and appear submissive, while some are quick to explode in rage. Some of Poussaint's thoughts began to crystalize while he was working in Jackson, Mississippi in 1964. One day he left his office with his black secretary. A white policeman yelled "Hey boy!" at him, and when Poussaint replied that he was no boy, he was a medical doctor named Dr. Poussaint, the policeman became threatening and ordered Poussaint to tell him his first name. Aware that no Mississippi jury would convict if the policeman beat him up, Poussaint meekly gave up his first name. Then the policeman ordered him to come running if he ever called him again, to which Poussaint responded, "Yes sir." Profoundly humiliated and angered by this confrontation, Poussaint began to reflect more on the effects of self-hate.

Poussaint realized that the self-hatred that some black people felt for themselves was a direct outcome of the self-hatred that white people themselves felt. The white policeman who felt he had to humiliate Poussaint was also full of self-hatred. Why else would he have gone out of his way to degrade Poussaint, who had done nothing wrong? Poussaint also recognized that white psychiatrists and white academics created self-serving theories that viewed blacks as emotionally handicapped, while portraying whites as mentally healthy. But white racism was a clear example of the mental instability of many white people. As Poussaint said in *Why Blacks Kill Blacks*, "blacks do not have the characteristics of a paranoid people. We have been patient; we have been generous. With a few historical exceptions, black men have been non-violent and have not attempted to assassinate even the most criminal, out-spoken white racist."

Challenging False Images of Black People

Poussaint had long been aware that stereotypes were a key ingredient of racism, and he had the chance to undermine misleading impressions of black people when he signed on in 1984 as a script consultant to Bill Cosby's enormously popular family comedy *The Cosby Show*. Before *The Cosby Show*, blacks had been portrayed in television and radio shows in many demeaning roles: clowns, buffoons, servants, junkyard proprietors, and custodial workers. Many Americans did not know that black people were also successful doctors, attorneys, business executives, scientists, engineers, accountants, and so on. Cliff and Claire Huxtable were, respectively, a physician and an attorney, and they and their five children represented life in an upper-middle class black family.

As a consultant, Poussaint checked scripts for negative racial stereotypes and for any details that would perpetuate racial tensions. Poussaint and Cosby were also aware of the power of details to suggest positive images, and they worked to include subtle touches that would give a more comprehensive and positive image of black American culture. To that end, *The Cosby Show* used such details as Cliff Huxtable's sweatshirts to introduce television viewers to historically black colleges and universities, and the program included references to black authors, artists, dancers, and composers to show the contributions that black professionals have made to American culture. The revolution in racial perceptions created by *The Cosby Show* made possible such later television programs as *A Different World*, *In Living Color*, *The Fresh Prince of Bel Air*, and others.

Poussaint continued working on *The Cosby Show* until it closed production in 1992. From 1986 to 1993, he also reviewed scripts for *A Different World*. In 1993, he married Tina Young, and he was promoted to full professor of psychiatry at Harvard Medical School. Poussaint has served as a consultant or member of many boards of directors, won many awards and honorary degrees, and has published prolifically in his long and distinguished career.

SELECTED WRITINGS BY POUSSAINT:

Books

Why Blacks Kill Blacks. New York: Emerson Hall Publishers, 1972.
(With James P. Comer) *Raising Black Children.* New York: Plume, 1992.

FURTHER READING:

Books

Bigelow, Barbara Carlisle, ed. *Contemporary Black Biography.* Volume 5. Detroit: Gale Research, 1993.
Kinsman, Clare D., ed. *Contemporary Authors, Vols. 53-56.* Detroit: Gale Research, 1975.
Metcalf, George R. *Up From Within: Today's New Black Leaders.* New York: McGraw-Hill, 1971.
Phelps, Shirelle, ed. *Who's Who Among African Americans, 9th edition.* Detroit: Gale Research, 1997.
Salzman, Jack, David L. Smith, and Cornel West, eds. *Encyclopedia of African-American Culture and History.* New York: Simon & Schuster Macmillan, 1996.

Other

Crenshaw, Anthony. "The Cosby Show Changes the way Blacks are Viewed." http:// www.engl.virginia.edu/~enwr1016/amc2d/cosby.html. (May 2, 1998).

—Sketch by Patrick Moore

Charles Burleigh Purvis
1842-1929
Physician

Practicing medicine at a time when segregation and prejudice severely limited opportunities for blacks in the medical field, Charles Burleigh Purvis made extraordinary contributions on behalf of black doctors in three areas. Over the course of a 60-year involvement with the medical college at Howard University in Washington, D.C., he helped to establish it as one of the only institutions in which a black medical student could be trained, and twice he literally saved the college from having to close its doors. As a surgeon at the Freedmen's Hospital in Washington, he greatly improved conditions in the District of Columbia's only medical facility for black patients. He also treated President James A. Garfield after the latter was shot. Finally, Purvis helped establish the National Medical Society of the District of Columbia, a professional organization for black doctors founded as a response to their exclusion by the American Medical Association.

Upholding a Great Legacy

Charles Burleigh Purvis was born on April 14, 1842, to a distinguished Philadelphia family. His grandfather, William Purvis, was an English cotton broker; his grandmother, Harriet Judah, was the daughter of a slave kidnapped from Morocco who, after gaining her freedom, had married a German baron. Purvis's father, Robert Purvis, Sr., became a wealthy benefactor and well-known abolitionist. His mother, whose name was also Harriet, came from a prestigious family as well. Her father, James Forten, had been a prominent Philadelphia sailmaker and community leader. Like her husband, Harriet Forten Purvis was a leader in the abolitionist movement, a co-founder of the Female Anti-Slavery Society. The Purvises had eight children, and raised them on an estate in Byberry, Pennsylvania, after moving from Philadelphia in 1844.

Through his parents, Purvis gained exposure to many of the great civil-rights leaders of his day, and their example—combined with his family's outstanding legacy—would prove a great influence on Purvis's development. He enrolled at Pennsylvania's Oberlin College in 1860, and in 1863 entered Wooster Medical School (later renamed Western Reserve Medical School) in Cleveland, Ohio.

Purvis would graduate from medical school in 1865, but the massive upheaval created by the Civil War took him from his studies in the summer of 1864. During that time, Purvis worked as a military nurse at a Washington, D.C. center for contraband relief. ("Contraband" was the name given to slaves who had either been freed by Union soldiers in the South, or had escaped their masters.) The relief center, located in the Camp Barker barracks, served as a prototype for the later Freedmen's Hospital, where Purvis would spend 25 years as a surgeon. While at the relief center, Purvis succumbed to typhoid fever, but after recovering in 1865, he joined the Union Army as an acting assistant surgeon. He continued to serve in that capacity until 1869.

Puts Salary on the Line to Save Medical School

In seven years between 1860 and 1867, the black population of Washington had grown from some 14,000 to nearly 39,000, yet the city had only six black physicians. The founding of Howard University in 1867, however, offered new opportunities. Established as an institution dedicated to the educational needs of African Americans,

Howard set up a small medical college next to the Freedmen's Hospital. Purvis, meanwhile, had been appointed assistant surgeon at the latter facility in 1869. On March 15 of that year, Howard appointed him to its medical faculty, making him only the second black man in the nation to become a university medical instructor.

Over the course of the next 60 years, Purvis would have an enormous impact on the development of the medical school at Howard University. During his first four years there, from 1869 to 1873, he taught courses on a variety of subjects, including materia medica (a branch of medical science dealing with the use of drugs to treat illnesses), therapeutics, botany, and medical jurisprudence, and from 1871 to 1873 he held the college's Thaddeus Stevens Chair. In 1873 he became a professor of obstetrics, and what would later be called family medicine. He continued to teach these subjects until 1888.

The aftermath of the Civil War had helped to create the medical school at Howard, but in the year Purvis began teaching obstetrics, a crisis of a different kind threatened its extinction. The Panic of 1873, a smaller version of the large-scale panic that would precipitate the Great Depression in 1929, hit the university hard. The law school closed, and Howard's trustees informed the faculty of the medical school that it could no longer pay their salaries. Instructors could continue in their positions, but to do so, they would have to resign and be reappointed without any guaranteed salary. Three men chose to do so: **Alexander T. Augusta**, Gideon S. Palmer, and Purvis.

It is not an exaggeration to say that Purvis, along with his two colleagues, saved the medical school—one of the only institutions in the country offering an education to prospective black physicians—from closing. In a June 16, 1873, letter to the university's namesake, General Oliver O. Howard, head of the Freedmen's Bureau which assisted slaves in making the transition to freedom, Purvis wrote: "While I regret [that] the University will not be able to pay me for my services, I feel the importance of every effort being made to carry forward the institution and make it a success." With its purse strings cut off, the medical school was attached to Howard University in name only, making its leadership a crucial issue. Purvis was elected to the key position of medical faculty secretary, an office he would hold until 1896. But for 33 years, from 1873 until 1906, he would collect no salary for his services.

First Physician to Treat Assassinated President

During much of his time at Howard, Purvis worked at the Freedmen's Hospital, first as an assistant surgeon from 1869 to 1881, and later as surgeon-in-chief. The latter appointment came as a result of an extraordinary incident in which Purvis was given a responsibility seldom accorded to any physician, let alone a black doctor of that era. On July 2, 1881, a disappointed office-seeker named Charles Guiteau shot President James A. Garfield at a Washington railroad station. Purvis was the first physician to treat the President, and though Garfield's wounds proved too severe to save him, Garfield's successor, Chester A. Arthur, recognized Purvis's efforts by appointing him to the head surgical position at the Freedmen's Hospital. He thus became the first black physician to head a civilian hospital, his colleague Augusta having been appointed earlier to head a military facility.

Purvis would continue in the head surgeon role until 1894, and during his tenure, the hospital grew quickly. By 1896 it was treating some 5,000 patients a year, many of them unable to gain admission to any other Washington hospital because they were black. Purvis greatly improved the facility's standards, and his removal from his position in 1894 resulted from political rather than professional causes. As the son of abolitionists, Purvis had been associated with the Republican Party; but in 1894 a Democrat, Grover Cleveland, became President. Hoke Smith of Georgia, Cleveland's Secretary of the Interior, replaced Purvis with a Democrat from Chicago, **Daniel Hale Williams**.

His removal did not end Purvis's role on behalf of the Freedmen's Hospital, which he continued to support from the outside. With the help of friends in Congress, he successfully defeated a 1903 District of Columbia proposal to shut down the facility and replace it with one that had no connection to Howard University. Had the District's plan succeeded, students at Howard—who had depended on the Freedmen's Hospital as a place in which to gain practical experience—would have been prevented from working at the new facility, and the medical school would probably have had to shut down. Thus once again Purvis saved the Howard medical school. Around the same time that he helped defeat the proposed municipal hospital plan, Purvis was able to influence Congress to appropriate $600,000—a vast sum at the time—for a new building to house the Freedmen's Hospital.

A Pioneer for Black Doctors

Purvis made many extraordinary contributions in addition to his work with Howard and the Freedmen's Hospital, the most notable of which was his role in founding the National Medical Society of the District of Columbia in 1870. Purvis, Augusta, and another black doctor had tried without success to join the Medical Society of the District of Columbia, which was affiliated with the American Medical Association (AMA). The Medical Society defended its segregationist policies by stating that it granted membership for social and personal, rather than professional, reasons. In other words, it was a private club, and blacks were not invited to join. After the defeat of a bill by Senator Charles Sumner to revoke the Medical Society's charter, in 1870 Purvis and his colleagues established the National Medical Society of the District of Columbia. The AMA responded, at its annual meeting that year, by refusing to recognize the new organization.

Purvis took a role in a number of civic groups, including the District of Columbia's Boards of Education, Health, and Medical Examiners. He also became one of the few black members of the powerful Washington Board of

Trade. With regard to his role as a leading black figure, however, Purvis had some ambivalence. "I have always resented the expression 'leading colored doctor or lawyer,'" he said. "A colored doctor means half a doctor." But he insisted on obtaining for himself and others the rights accorded in the Constitution: "We are all Americans," he said, "white, black, and colored. . . . As Negroes nothing is demanded, as American citizens every enjoyment of opportunity is demanded."

Described by contemporaries as physically imposing, Purvis was in many respects a man almost larger than life who more than proved his statement that "American manhood must know of no color." He had come from a background more distinguished than that of most white Americans, and his achievements exceeded those of all but a handful within the medical community or the nation as a whole. In his personal life, too, he was extraordinary for his time, or indeed for any age. He maintained a keen interest in international affairs, and after World War I, he made several predictions: Japan would become "a second Germany" that would "challenge the white nations of the world," and the European colonial empires of Africa and Asia would be dissolved. These predictions, which at the time seemed far-fetched, would come true in subsequent decades.

Purvis's wife Ann Hathaway, who he married in April 13, 1871, was white—a marriage which must undoubtedly have subjected the couple to great scorn from many quarters of society. They had two children, a boy and a girl, both of whom grew up to be doctors: Alice, a physician; and Robert, a dentist. In 1905, the Purvises moved to Boston, where Purvis began practicing medicine. Though he resigned from the medical school at Howard in 1907, his commitment to it continued when he became a member of the Howard Board of Trustees in 1908. He would remain on that body until 1926. Purvis died in Los Angeles on January 30, 1929.

FURTHER READING:

Books

Dyson, Walter. *Howard University, The Capstone of Negro Education, a History: 1867-1940.* Howard University, 1941.

Holt, Thomas, Cassandra Smith-Parker, Rosalyn Terborg-Penn. *A Special Mission: The Story of Freedmen's Hospital, 1862-1962.* Howard University, 1975.

Kaufman, Martin, Stuart Galishoff, and Michael R. Winston, eds. *Dictionary of American Medical Biography.* Greenwood Press, 1984.

Logan, Rayford W. *Howard University: The First Hundred Years, 1867-1967.*

Logan, Rayford W. and Michael R. Winston, eds. *Dictionary of American Negro Biography.* Norton, 1982.

Morais, Herbert. *The History of the Negro in Medicine.* Publishers Co., 1967.

Sammons, Vivian Ovelton. *Blacks in Science and Medicine.* Hemisphere Publishing, 1990.

Other

"The Long Walk: The Placemaking Legacy of Howard University." http://www.howard.edu/HU-HomePages/Howard/Past.htm (16 May 1998).

—Sketch by Judson Knight

Lloyd Albert Quarterman
1918-1982
Chemist

Lloyd Albert Quarterman was one of only a handful of African Americans to work on the "Manhattan Project," the team that developed the first atom bomb in the 1940s. He was also noted as a research chemist who specialized in fluoride chemistry, producing some of the first compounds using inert gases and developing the "diamond window" for the study of compounds using corrosive hydrogen fluoride gas. In addition, later in his career, Quarterman initiated work on synthetic blood.

Quarterman was born May 31, 1918, in Philadelphia. He attended St. Augustine's College in Raleigh, North Carolina, where he continued the interest in chemistry he had demonstrated from an early age. Just after he completed his bachelor's degree in 1943, he was hired by the U.S. War Department to work on the production of the atomic bomb, an assignment code-named the Manhattan Project. Originally hired as a junior chemist, he worked at both the secret underground facility at the University of Chicago and at the Columbia University laboratory in New York City; the project was spread across the country in various locations. It was the team of scientists at Columbia which first split the atom. To do this, scientists participated in trying to isolate an isotope of uranium necessary for nuclear fission; this was Quarterman's main task during his time in New York.

Quarterman was one of only six African American scientists who worked on the development of atomic bomb. At the secret Chicago facility, where the unused football stadium had been converted into an enormous, hidden laboratory for the "plutonium program," Quarterman studied quantum mechanics under renowned Italian physicist Enrico Fermi. When the Manhattan Project ended in 1946, the Chicago facilities were converted to become Argonne National Laboratories, and Quarterman was one of the scientists who stayed on. Although his contributions included work on the first nuclear power plant, he was predominantly a fluoride and nuclear chemist, creating new chemical compounds and new molecules from fluoride solutions. Dr. Larry Stein, who worked at Argonne at the same time as Quarterman, told interviewer Marianne Fedunkiw that Quarterman was very good at purifying hydrogen fluoride. "He helped build a still to purify it, which he ran." This was part of the research which led to the production of the compound xenon tetrafluoride at Argonne. Xenon is one of the "inert" gases and was thought to be unable to react with other molecules, so Quarterman's work in producing a xenon compound was a pioneering effort.

After a number of years at Argonne National Laboratories, Quarterman returned to school and received his master's of science from Northwestern University in 1952. In addition to his fluoride chemistry work, Quarterman was a spectroscopist researching interactions between radiation and matter. He developed a corrosion resistant "window" of diamonds with which to view hydrogen fluoride. He described this to Ivan Van Sertima, who interviewed him in 1979: "It was a very small window—one-eighth of an inch. The reason why they were one-eighth of an inch was because I couldn't get the money to buy bigger windows. These small diamonds cost one thousand dollars apiece and I needed two for a window." Diamonds were necessary because hydrogen fluoride was so corrosive it would eat up glass or any other known container material. Quarterman was able to study the x ray, ultraviolet, and Raman spectra of a given compound by dissolving it in hydrogen fluoride, making a cell, and shining an electromagnetic beam through the solution to see the vibrations of the molecules. His first successful trial was run in 1967.

Quarterman also began research into "synthetic blood" late in his career, but he was thwarted by what he described as "socio-political problems" and later fell ill and died before he could complete it. Besides holding memberships in the American Chemical Society, American Association for the Advancement of Science, and Scientific Research Society of America, Quarterman was an officer of the Society of Applied Spectroscopy. He also encouraged African American students interested in science by visiting public schools in Chicago, and was a member of the National Association for the Advancement of Colored People. In recognition for his contributions to science, Quarterman's alma mater, St. Augustine's College, departed from 102 years of tradition to award him an honorary Ph.D. in chemistry in 1971 for a lifetime of achievement. He was also cited for his research on the Manhattan project in a certificate, dated August 6, 1945, by the Secretary of War for "work essential to the production of the Atomic Bomb thereby contributing to the successful conclusion of World War II."

Quarterman was also a renowned athlete. During his university days at St. Augustine's College he was an avid football player. Van Sertima, who interviewed Quarterman three years before his death, later wrote, "As he spoke, the shock of his voice and his occasional laughter seemed to contradict his illness and I began to see before me, not an aging scientist, but the champion footballer." Quarterman died at the Billings Hospital in Chicago in the late summer of 1982. He donated his body to science.

FURTHER READING:

Books

Le Blanc, Ondine E. "Lloyd Albert Quarterman." In *Contemporary Black Biography,* Volume 4, Gale, 1993, pp. 199–201.

Sammons, Vivian O. *Blacks in Science and Medicine.* Hemisphere Publishing, 1990, p. 196.

Van Sertima, Ivan, ed. *Blacks in Science: Ancient and Modern.* Transaction Books, 1983, pp. 266–272.

Periodicals

Ebony, (September 1949): 28.
Jet, (August 9, 1982).

Other

Stein, Larry, *Interview with Marianne Fedunkiw,* conducted April 7, 1994.

                                        —Sketch by Marianne Fedunkiw

William Samuel Quinland
1885-1953
Pathologist

William Samuel Quinland was a distinguished pathologist and educator who contributed 28 studies to medical journals, including pioneering research on pathology in African Americans. His medical career spanned from Panama, to Brazil, to several regions of the United States, including Alaska. He was the first black member to be elected to the American Association of Pathologists and Bacteriologists, an appointment he received in 1920; the American Board of Pathology in 1937; and the College of American Pathologists in 1947.

Quinland was born on October 12, 1885, in All Saints, Antigua, in what was then the British West Indies, the son of William Thomas and Floretta Victoria (Williams) Quinland. After completing his secondary education in the West Indies, Quinland taught in public schools. He then embarked on his medical career, working for three years as a laboratory assistant in the Ancon Hospital in the Canal Zone, Panama, followed by four years as a laboratory worker at the Candelaria Hospital in Brazil.

After making his way to the United States, Quinland attended Howard University in Washington, D.C. from 1914 to 1915 and earned his B.S. degree from Oskaloosa College in Iowa in 1918. In 1919, he earned his medical degree, with an outstanding record, from Meharry Medical College in Nashville, Tennessee. Quinland was then awarded the first Rosenwald fellowship in pathology and bacteriology for study at Harvard Medical School, which he held from 1919 to 1922. In 1921, Quinland earned his certificate in pathology and bacteriology from Harvard, and also published his first professional article, a study of carcinoma, or malignant tumors. In 1922, Quinland's final year under the Rosenwald fellowship, he worked as an assistant in pathology at the Peter Bent Brigham Hospital in Boston.

Returns to Meharry Medical College

Although Harvard offered him a professorship in its Medical College, Quinland felt that Meharry, a groundbreaking institution for African-American medical practitioners, needed him more. In 1922, he accepted a post at Meharry as professor and head of the pathology department, a position he held until 1947. In 1923, he married Sadie Lee Watson; they had two children. In addition to his professorship at Meharry Medical College, Quinland worked as a pathologist at Meharry's George W. Hubbard Hospital, where he served as associate medical director from 1931 to 1937, and at the Millie E. Hale Hospital. In 1941 and 1942, he undertook post-graduate studies as a fellow of the University of Chicago.

During these years, Quinland published studies on tuberculosis, syphilis, heart disease, and carcinoma, among other subjects. Much of this research was particularly valuable for its focus on black patients; Quinland noted in his study on "Primary Carcinoma in the Negro," for example, that "while social differences in cancer have long been recognized," little research had been conducted on its occurrence among African Americans. That study looked at 300 cases of carcinoma and documented which types of cancers were found in samples from African American men and women of various ages. In addition, Quinland served on the editorial board of the *Journal of the National Medical Association* and of the *Punjab Medical Journal,* held a post as a reserve surgeon for the United State Public Health Service, and directed public health clinics in Virginia, South Carolina, and Georgia.

In 1947, Quinland left Meharry Medical College for a post as pathologist and chief of laboratory service at the Veterans Administration Hospital in Tuskegee, Alaska. His publications in this final phase of his career included a study of tumors. Quinland served at the Veterans Administration Hospital until his death on April 6, 1953.

SELECTED WRITINGS BY QUINLAND:

Periodicals

"Tuberculosis from the Standpoint of Pathology," *Journal of the National Medical Association,* 15, (1923): 1–5.

"Primary Carcinoma of Prostrate," *Meharry News,* 1928.

"Syphilis in Combination with Certain Diseases," *Journal of the National Medical Association,* 31, (1939): 199–205.

"Primary Carcinoma in the Negro: Anatomic Distribution of Three Hundred Cases," *Archives of Pathology,* 30, (1940): 393–402.

"Bronchogenic Carcinoma—Report of Three Cases in Negroes," *Southern Medical Journal,* 35, (1942): 729–732.

"Cancer of the Prostrate: A Clinico-pathologic Study of 34 Cases in Negroes," *Journal of Urology,* 50, No. 2, (1943).

"Histologic and Clinical Response of Human Cancer to Irradiation," *Journal of the National Medical Association,* 38, (1946): 171–178.

FURTHER READING:

Books

Blacks in Science and Medicine. Hemisphere, 1990, pp. 196–197.

Dictionary of American Medical Biography. Greenwood, 1984, pp. 618–619.

Periodicals

The Crisis, (December 1919): 64–65.

Journal of the American Medical Association, (July 1953): 298–300.

—*Sketch by Miyoko Chu*

Norbert Rillieux
1806-1894
Chemist and inventor

Norbert Rillieux was an engineer whose creativity transformed the sugar industry. By devising a mechanism for controlling how sugar was extracted from beet and cane juice, he was able to cut labor and fuel costs and make high-quality sugar readily available. Before his invention, sugar production was a slow, laborious, and expensive process that yielded unimpressive results. More than 150 years later, Rillieux's design remains the basis for today's sugar manufacturing techniques.

The life Rillieux led was markedly different from that of other blacks in nineteenth-century Louisiana. The son of a wealthy plantation owner, he was educated in Paris and lived a life of privilege and material comfort. Nevertheless, in his native Louisiana he constantly faced prejudice, and despite all his accomplishments he was still a second-class citizen.

Early Life

Norbert Rillieux was born on March 17, 1806, on the plantation of Vincent Rillieux, a wealthy French native. Vincent was Norbert's father, but his mother was Constance Vivant, a slave. Vincent Rillieux had been trained as an engineer; he invented a steam-powered cotton-baling press. Young Norbert displayed intelligence and mechanical aptitude at an early age, and his father determined that he should receive the best education possible. Unfortunately, blacks in New Orleans—even free blacks or those of mixed race—were not allowed to attend school. Fortunately for Norbert, his father was able to send him to school in Paris.

The young Rillieux studied at L'Ecole Centrale, where he excelled in his studies and showed a particular talent for engineering. By 1830 he had completed his education and was offered a position as instructor of applied mechanics. Over the next decade, he experimented with steam engines and steam evaporation—which would eventually form the basis for his most important invention.

Rillieux returned to New Orleans in the 1830s and found a chance to put his experiments with evaporation to practical use. On the family plantation, he watched how slaves refined sugar from beets and cane. The painstakingly slow process, known as the "Jamaica Train," involved boiling cane or beet juice and ladling it from one kettle to another until it had boiled down into a crude, molasses-like substance.

What Rillieux set out to do was devise a way that would not only refine sugar more quickly and efficiently, but also produce a finer sugar. He saw one possible answer in the evaporating pan—essentially a vacuum pan with condensing coils that could boil liquid at a controlled temperature. Since sugar caramelizes at high temperatures, this control was critical.

A Revolutionary Invention

Earlier scientists had understood the concept of the evaporating pan, but their attempts were crude and not particularly efficient. Rillieux studied the problem and hit on the solution. By enclosing the condensing coils in vacuum chambers, the vapors from one chamber could heat and evaporate the juice under a higher vacuum—the higher the vacuum, the lower the temperature needed to be. Rillieux worked for more than a decade until he perfected his design, which was first used at the plantation of Theodore Packwood (who encouraged Rillieux's efforts), just outside New Orleans.

The results of Rillieux's invention were several-fold. Because the liquid could be boiled at lower temperatures, less fuel was needed. The process was so efficient that it cut back significantly on labor. And the remaining sugar product was far superior in quality to that produced by the Jamaica Train method.

Rillieux received two patents (in 1843 and 1846) for this evaporation mechanism. The "Rillieux system" revolutionized the production of sugar and was used in the United States, Cuba, Mexico, and the West Indies. Eventually, the system was adapted for the manufacture of such diverse products as glue, soap, condensed milk, and paper. Although the machinery today is considerably more advanced, it is still essentially based on Rillieux's initial design.

Later Activities

Despite Rillieux's success, he was still the victim of prejudice. In the eyes of Louisiana law, he was a colored man, and subject to the restrictions on all colored individuals. Neither his education nor his accomplishments could change the fact that he was born to a black mother. Free blacks in New Orleans were required to pay school taxes just like whites, but they could not send their children to public schools. Rillieux put up with numerous restrictions and indignities, but when a new law enacted in 1854 required all colored individuals (slave or free) to carry a pass, he decided that he could tolerate no more. He left his home and returned to Paris, where he remained for the rest of his life.

In later years he became interested in Egyptology and spent a great deal of time deciphering hieroglyphic symbols. But he also continued his engineering, working to perfect his evaporation technique and continuing to patent his inventions. It is known that at some point in his life he married a woman named Emily Cuckow, who was 21 years his junior. Rillieux died in Paris on October 8, 1894, and was buried in the famed Pere Lachaise Cemetery. Mrs. Rillieux died 18 years later. In the 1930s, a bronze plaque honoring Rillieux was placed in the Louisiana State Museum.

FURTHER READING:

Books

Haber, Louis. *Black Pioneers of Science and Invention.* Harcourt Brace Jovanovich, 1970.

Robinson, Wilhelmina S. *Historical Negro Biographies.* Publishers Co., 1968.

Sammons, Vivian O. *Blacks in Science and Medicine.* Hemisphere Publishing, 1990.

Williams, James C. *At Last Recognition in America: A Reference Handbook of Unknown Black Inventors and Their Contribution to America,* vol. 1. B. C. A. Publishing Corp., 1978.

—*Sketch by George A. Milite*

Carl Glennis Roberts
1886-1950
Surgeon

Carl Glennis Roberts accomplished several firsts as an African American doctor. He was the first black to graduate from Valparaiso's medical program, in 1911, and he was the first black gynecologist at Provident Hospital, in 1916. Roberts was responsible for organizing the first surgical training program for African American doctors approved by the American College of Surgeons and the American Medical Association (AMA). Roberts coordinated the organization of the first black sanitary corps in the Chicago Red Cross during World War I. He was also the first black Commandant in the Chicago chapter. Roberts was also a pioneer in the American College of Surgeons, one of the first four African Americans to be admitted. Roberts was one of three doctors who successfully appealed

to the AMA to have the "colored" designation removed from the *AMA Directory.* Throughout Roberts's long career, he was involved in numerous professional societies as well as important civic activities, often related to racial justice.

Roberts was born on December 15, 1886, in Roberts's Settlement, Hamilton County, Indiana, to John A. and Nancy E. (maiden name, Simpson) Roberts. He attended high school at the Fairmont (Indiana) High School and Academy from 1901 until he graduated in 1905. In 1907, Roberts entered Valparaiso University's Chicago College of Medicine and Surgery. He was the first black to graduate from the program when he was awarded his M.D. in 1911. While he was a student, Roberts married Lucille Eleanor Williams on January 1, 1908. They eventually had two children, Beverly Yvonne and Carl Glennis, Jr.

After graduation, during 1911, Roberts began an affiliation with the German American Hospital and opened his own private practice. At German American, Roberts was a gynecologist as well as an instructor of nurses. Roberts was affiliated with this hospital until 1917. In 1916, Roberts became the first black gynecologist at Chicago's Provident Hospital, a position he held until 1930. Roberts also was a gynecologist at Diversey Parkway Hospital from 1917 until 1923.

Roberts was named chairman of Provident's gynecology department from 1918, a position he held until 1923. The year 1918 was a busy one for Roberts. That year he also reestablished his affiliation with the German American Hospital, a relationship that lasted four years. Roberts began serving as Commandant of the Sanitary Corps of the Chicago Red Cross in 1918. He left that post in 1920. Also in 1918, Roberts did some post-graduate work, studying at the Laboratory of Surgical Technique. In 1920, Roberts did further study at the Illinois Post-Graduate School of Surgery, and a year later at the Chicago Institute of Surgery.

By 1922, Roberts was the senior surgeon on the attending staff at the Chicago General Hospital. During this time period, in 1928, Roberts traveled in Europe, observing medical techniques. He left Chicago General in 1929, and in 1930, became a courtesy staff member at St. Elizabeth Hospital, also in Chicago. In 1930, Roberts was also named the senior attending surgeon at Provident Hospital, where he was also involved in teaching.

Roberts continued to increase his medical knowledge through education, first at Cook County Hospital from 1933-34, and then at the University of Chicago Medical School, from 1934-35. In 1935, Roberts became the chairman of the department of general surgery at Provident Hospital, a post he held until 1941. In 1936, Roberts became the a member of the senior attending surgical staff at Walter Memorial Hospital, a position he maintained until 1940. Roberts was also awarded the distinguished service medallion from the National Medical Association in 1936, for his surgical work. In 1936, Roberts also was responsible for the organization of a five-year graduate training course in surgery for African Americans at Provident, the first recognized of its kind.

Roberts maintained a high level of activity in professional organizations throughout his career. From 1926 until 1937, Roberts was president of the National Medical Association. He represented the National Medical Association when he appeared before the Senate Committee on the Wagner Bill in 1940, and was a contributing editor to the Association's *Journal.* He contributed articles to his and other professional journals. Roberts was also a diplomate to the American Board of Surgery and president of the Cook County Physician's Association. Roberts was a member of the International College of Surgeons, American Medical Association, the Illinois Medical Association, the Chicago Medical Society, and several similar organizations. In 1948, Lincoln University (Pennsylvania) bestowed an honorary degree on Roberts, a Sc.D.

Roberts participated a similarly high volume of civic work. He was president of the Chicago Branch of the National Association for the Advancement of Colored People (NAACP) in 1925. Roberts was a member of the Inter-racial Committee of Illinois, and lectured in white Protestant churches on race-related subjects. Roberts also worked on the Chicago Assembly as a member of the Board of Governors. His medical and civic interests intersected when Roberts was the chairman of the Southside Commission on Tuberculosis from 1940 until 1941.

Roberts's career spanned beyond medicine. He was a member of the board of directors for the Chicago Mortgage and Finance Company as well as the Chicago Radium Corporation.

In 1941, Roberts suffered a heart attack from which he never fully recovered and which limited his activities. He retired from St. Elizabeth's Hospital in that year, but maintained an emeritus position there from 1945 until his death. Roberts retired from Provident Hospital as senior attending surgeon in 1946, maintaining an emeritus position after that date as well. Roberts, a gifted public speaker, died on January 15, 1950, after addressing a dinner meeting of Provident Hospital's staff and Board of Trustees.

FURTHER READING:

Books

Organ, Claude H., Jr., and Margaret M. Kosiba, eds. *A Century of Black Surgeons—The U.S.A. Experience,*Vol 1. Transcript Press, 1987, pp. 273-76.

Periodicals

Drew, Charles R. "Carl Glennis Roberts, M.D.," *Journal of the National Medical Association,* (March 1950): 189-90.
Cobb, W. Montague. "Carl Glennis Roberts, M.D., 1886-1950," *Journal of the National Medical Association,* (March 1960): 146-47.

—Sketch by A. Petrusso

Eslanda Goode Robeson

Eslanda Goode Robeson
1896-1965
Anthropologist and chemist

Eslanda Goode Robeson had a varied career as a scientist, social activist, and wife of one of the most powerful black voices in the twentieth century, Paul Robeson. As a chemist, Robeson was, according to most accounts, the first African American staff member of the Presbyterian Hospital of New York. Robeson left this position in the mid-1920s to manage her husband's career as an actor, singer, and activist. Paul Robeson's career took the family to Europe and beyond, where his wife became interested in anthropology, especially as it related to Africa. Robeson went on to earn her Ph.D in the subject. Robeson herself was also an activist in causes related to civil rights and colonialism, especially in Africa.

Robeson was born on December 15, 1896, in Washington, D.C., one of three children and the only daughter born to John and Eslanda (nee Cardozo) Goode. John Goode worked as a clerk in the United States government's War Department. Eslanda Cardozo Goode came from a prominent free black South Carolina family. Her father was

Francis Lewis Cardozo, a Congregational pastor and noted black politician. Robeson's father died from the effects of alcoholism in 1902 when she was six, and her mother moved the family to New York City soon after. The move was made in part so Robeson and her brothers could attended non-segregated schools.

Robeson lived in Harlem and saw the beginnings of its Renaissance. After spending two years at the University of Illinois, Robeson returned home to earn her B.S. in chemistry from Columbia University in 1918. She also attended Columbia's medical school for one year. From 1918-25, Robeson worked as a chemist and surgical technician, running Presbyterian Hospital's surgical pathological laboratory.

While working at the hospital in 1921, Robeson met her future husband, then a Columbia University law student who was hospitalized with a football injury. They were married on August 17, 1921, and eventually had one child, Paul, Jr., born on November 17, 1927. Robeson persuaded her husband to take a role in a YMCA theatrical production soon after they were married. Paul Robeson's rich voice and acting prowess lead to his career as a singer and actor, and the couple's world travels. By 1925, Paul Robeson was engaged to appear in London, and Eslanda Robeson left her position at the hospital to become his manager.

In 1928, the Robesons made London their primary residence, a situation which lasted until 1939. She wrote a biography of her husband in 1930, entitled *Paul Robeson, Negro.* The Robeson's marriage was somewhat rocky, and they spent several years separated after 1932. Robeson became interested in anthropology in this time period, and began graduate studies at London University (1935-37) and the London School of Economics (1938). She eventually earned her Ph.D. in 1945, from the Hartford (Connecticut) Seminary.

Robeson's primary interest, as an activist and anthropologist, was people living under colonial rule, especially in Africa. In part because of her husband's work, Robeson's world travels allowed her to see first-hand the effects of such a system on its native peoples. Robeson was outspoken in her belief that independence was the only right and just government for Africans.

Robeson made her first trip to Africa in 1936 to do six months of anthropological field work, with her young son in tow. In 1945, Robeson published a book about the trip *African Journey,* written in diary form. Though it was more personal than anthropological, it nonetheless descriptively catalogued the customs of several tribes, covered a scope of economic and social classes, and was generally praised by reviewers. In 1941, Robeson was one of the founders of the Council on African Affairs, a organization intending to garner support of national independence in Africa. The group lobbied against colonizing Africa, and hoped the continent would be decolonized at the end of World War II. Though this was not accomplished then, Robeson was the group's representative observer when the United Nations' founding convention was held in 1945.

Robeson also believed in fighting fascism in every form. In 1938, Robeson and her husband were in Spain, were they observed and supported those fighting dictator Franco's fascist government. Indeed, Robeson and her husband were staunchly left-wing in their politics, vocally supporting such socialist countries as the Soviet Union and China. These sympathies led to problems for Robeson and her husband, and she was called before the House of Representatives Un-American Activities Committee (HUAC), led by Senator Joseph McCarthy, in 1953. She disavowed the Committee and its agenda, earning her a reprimand. Robeson and her husband were labeled subversives and Communist sympathizers.

Because of HUAC, Robeson and her husband were denied passports for several years. In 1958, when they were finally allowed to leave the United States, they moved to the Soviet Union, a country they had first visited in 1934. During this time period, Robeson continued her work, noting events in America and abroad. For example, in 1958, she attended a conference in Ghana, an African nation that had recently gained its independence. Robeson went to the All-African Peoples Conference as the Council of African Affairs' representative.

While living in the Soviet Union, Robeson developed cancer and underwent at least one operation in that country. In 1963, the couple decided to return to the United States. On their trip back, they stopped in East Germany, where she received the only accolades of her career, the Peace Medal and the Clara Zetkin Medal, awarded by the East German government. The latter was an honor specifically for women engaged in the struggle for world peace. After Robeson and her husband returned to the States, she continued to be politically active despite the cancer's recurrence. Robeson died of the disease on December 13, 1965.

SELECTED WRITINGS BY ROBESON:

Books

African Journey, 1945, reprinted Greenwood Press, 1972.
Paul Robeson, Negro, Harper and Brothers, 1930.

Periodicals

"Re the Assassination of Harry T. Moore and His Wife at Mims, Florida, Christmas, 1951," *Freedomways,* (Fourth Quarter 1966): 22.

FURTHER READING:

Periodicals

Golden, Lillie, "Remembrances of Eslanda," *Freedomways,* (Fourth Quarter 1966): 330-32.

Ransby, Barbara, "Eslanda Goode Robeson, Pan-Africanist," *Sage,* (Fall 1986): 22-26.

—*Sketch by A. Petrusso*

Hilyard R. Robinson
1899-1986
Architect

H ilyard R. Robinson was one of the preeminent black architects of the early and mid-twentieth century. Best known for his public-housing designs in Virginia, Maryland, and the District of Columbia, Robinson created a number of projects with historical significance, including the Army Air Force base in Tuskegee, Alabama. He taught architecture at Howard University for 13 years in the 1920s and 1930s.

Travels in Europe, Establishes Reputation

Hilyard R. Robinson was born in 1899. He attended the University of Pennsylvania and later the Columbia University School of Architecture in New York City, where in 1924 he earned his bachelors of arts degree. Following completion of his studies at Columbia, Robinson studied urban planning at the University of Berlin in Germany. It was an era of great flowering in German art: the destruction of World War I had begun to heal, and Hitler's ascension to power still lay in the future. This period saw the rise of such pivotal figures as the architect Walter Gropius, the filmmaker Fritz Lang, and many others; his experience in Berlin no doubt had a great influence on Robinson's future.

In 1926, Robinson designed the Henry Hudson Hotel in Troy, New York. Five years later, in 1931, he earned his M.S. in architecture at Columbia. During this time, he began teaching at Howard University, and later became the chairman of the Department of Architecture there. In all he served for 13 years as a professor of architecture at Howard.

By 1937, his reputation was sufficient to earn Robinson mention by Benjamin Brawley in the latter's *Negro Builders and Heroes*, as a prominent figure in "A field of effort [that is] comparatively new [for African Americans] . . . architecture." Brawley referred to Robinson alongside other greats such as Paul R. Williams and Albert I. Cassell. Brawley, noting that Robinson had traveled widely and competed with distinction in several national competitions, reported that he had been awarded a contract to design a federal housing project that would cost over a million dollars.

Designs Historic Resettlement Project

In the 1930s, housing projects were viewed as symbols of progress which offered the poor a much more humane environment than what they had experienced in the slums of the past. Under the "New Deal" of President Franklin D. Roosevelt, the federal government relocated thousands of needy families to settlements such as Aberdeen Gardens in Virginia. Designed by Robinson for families of black workers in the nearby shipbuilding towns of Hampton and Newport News, Aberdeen Gardens was funded largely by a $245,000 grant from the federal Resettlement Administration. Volunteers, however, cleared the 440-acre (176 ha) site, drained an adjacent swamp, and contributed some $35,000 for the project's completion.

In his design, Robinson was influenced by the work of "utopian" city planners, including Ebenezer Howard, Clarence Stein, and Henry Wright. Howard had begun the "garden city movement," which introduced greenery and plant life in urban areas formerly characterized only by concrete and steel. Stein and Wright were planners known for their creative manipulation of space through cul-de-sacs, walkways, and underpasses. Robinson's idea was to build the project along the corridor made by Aberdeen Road, and he conceived the homes as "gardenhouses." The first model homes opened on November 26, 1936, in spite of objections from some local whites. The project soon gained the support of First Lady Eleanor Roosevelt.

Aberdeen Gardens consisted of some 158 homes, which Robinson designed to be consistent with the local "Colonial Revival" style. Made of red brick, the houses were typically two stories, with a foyer, living room, dining room, kitchen, bathroom, and closet on the first floor; and two bedrooms and two closets on the second. Lots generally measured some 75 feet (22.5 m) in width and as much as 290 feet (87 m) in depth, the extra space to be used for a large garden to assist the family in supporting itself. Around the yards were numerous trees, and Robinson surrounded the project with a "greenbelt" of woodland to keep out noise.

The original plan for Aberdeen Gardens called for an elementary school, a church, a shopping center, and a community area. The church and community center were never built, but the elementary school—which was rebuilt in the 1970s as a larger structure—took on some of the functions of a community center. On March 10, 1994, the state designated Aberdeen Gardens as a Virginia Landmark, and on May 26 of that year, it was placed in the *National Register of Historic Places.*

Honored Along with Frederick Douglass and Others

Aberdeen Gardens was only one of many public designs by Robinson in a career that included the million-dollar project referred to by Brawley, which became the subject of a 1989 Public Broadcasting System (PBS) documentary, *Home: The Langston Terrace Dwellings.* Robinson designed it as "a planned utopia for the reclamation of human lives"; and more than a half-century later, when many such projects had become disasters of poverty, crime, and unfulfilled hopes, Langston Terrace could be described as not only one of America's oldest, but also one of its most successful, housing projects. The Langston Terrace design would have tremendous impact on public architecture in urban America. Robinson, along with McKissack & McKissack Construction Company, would also be awarded a contract for the design and construction of an Army Air Force base in Tuskegee, Alabama. It was here that the famed "Tuskegee Airmen" were trained during World War II.

Robinson himself lived in the historic Brookland neighborhood of Washington, D.C. The area, bounded by South Dakota Avenue, Michigan Avenue, North Carolina Street, and Franklin Street, contains Catholic University and the National Shrine of the Immaculate Conception. Brookland was home to singer Pearl Bailey and fellow architect Howard Mackey; Robinson, like Mackey, was commissioned to design houses for the neighborhood.

Robinson died in 1985, after a long and distinguished career. On March 16, 1994, the Washington Urban League recognized Robinson, along with such great figures from African American history as abolitionist Frederick Douglass and Supreme Court Justice Thurgood Marshall. The ceremony, attended by some 1,500 guests, honored great local personages of the past, and organizers presented Robinson's descendants with an award.

SELECTED WRITINGS BY ROBINSON:

Books

Presenting the Liberian Centennial and Victory Exposition, 1947-1949, in Monrovia, Republic of Liberia, West Africa. H. K. Press, 1946.

FURTHER READING:

Books

Brawley, Benjamin. *Negro Builders and Heroes.* University of North Carolina Press, 1937.
Brawley, Benjamin. *The Negro Genius.* Dodd, Mead, 1937.
Cederholm, Theresa Dickason, ed. *Afro-American Artists.* Boston Public Library, 1973.
The Negro Almanac, fifth edition. Gale, 1989.
Sammons, Vivian Ovelton. *Blacks in Science and Medicine.* Hemisphere Publishing, 1990.

Periodicals

Bond, Max, "Still Here: Work by Julian Abele, Hilyard Robinson, Paul Williams," *Harvard Design Magazine*, (Summer 1997).

Rackley, Lurma, "The Washington Urban League—Living Our Legacy," *Washington Afro-American*, (February 12, 1994).
Wright, James, "League Honors 30 Families with Legacy Awards," *Washington Afro-American*, (March 26, 1994).

Other

"Historic Aberdeen Gardens, Hampton, Virginia." http://www.preservenet.cornell.edu/aahpf/aberdeen.htm (May 11, 1998).
Home: The Langston Terrace Dwellings (videocassette), Public Broadcasting Corporation, 1989, 57 minutes.

—*Sketch by Judson Knight*

John Sweat Rock
1825-1866
Physician, dentist, and lawyer

John Sweat Rock was one of the first black men to earn an M.D. in the United States. He apprenticed with two doctors and a dentist before he was allowed to enter medical school to earn his medical degrees. Because of poor health, Rock was forced to abandon his medical practices, and he began to study law. Upon earning his law degree, he passed the bar and became a justice of the peace. Before his early death, Rock also became the first African American lawyer able to argue cases before the United States Supreme court. Throughout his life, he was active in many causes related to the civil rights of African Americans.

Rock was born in Salem, New Jersey, on October 13, 1825, to parents who were both free blacks. Young John was an enthusiastic learner, and his parents encouraged him to receive a formal education through his eighteenth year in Salem's public schools. He was an accomplished scholar, and he eventually learned to speak and read both French and German. After this phase of his education ended, Rock passed the exams to become a school teacher.

Rock initially decided to study medicine, but he was not admitted to any medical schools because of his color. While Rock worked as a teacher and a private tutor from 1844 until 1848, he also became an apprentice to two Salem-based white medical doctors, Dr. Shaw and Dr. Gibson. A few years later, from 1848-49, Rock had a similar learning arrangement with a dentist, Dr. U. Hubbard, though he had ceased to teach school simultaneously. Rock opened his own dentistry practice in 1850 in Philadelphia. He was skilled at making dentures and won a silver medal for his accomplishments in this area in 1851. Shortly thereafter, Rock was admitted to the American Medical College, a short-lived institution based in Philadelphia. While he attended medical school, Rock maintained his practice and became involved with a local high school. He was awarded his M.D. in 1852 or 1853.

Moves to Boston and Becomes an Activist

After earning his M.D., Rock moved to Boston, where he had both a medical and a dental practice. Rock believed in being available day and night for his patients, an attitude which undoubtedly contributed to his ill health. Rock was given the honor of being one of the first African Americans admitted to the Massachusetts Medical Society, though its records are incomplete on this matter and the exact year is unknown. Rock gave medical aid to fugitive slaves as they passed through Boston on the Underground Railroad. Indeed, while living in Boston, Rock became a leader in the abolitionist movement and the fight for blacks' rights. He was also involved in the temperance movement. Rock became associated with Lewis Hayden, a local abolitionist, and was part of the 1855 fight to desegregate the public schools in Boston. This fight was successful. Rock spent the rest of his life arguing for equality, and became a famous orator on the subject.

Rock maintained his practice until late 1850s, when he had to give up his career because of his declining health. Rock's illness began as a sore throat, for which he had an operation in the United States. Then, Rock wanted to go to France for what he considered to be a better operation, but the United States government refused to give him a passport. In their refusal, the government pointed out that a passport had never been issued to a black man before. Finally, in 1858, the state of Massachusetts gave him a passport that was acceptable to French officials. Rock was able to obtain the operation, but the man who operated on him in Paris, a Professor Auguse Nélaton, recommended that Rock cease practicing medicine and his public speaking activities. After spending eight months in France, Rock returned to the United States and gave up his practices. He continued his civil rights activities and public speaking engagements.

Becomes a Lawyer

Indeed, upon his return, inspired by his experiences in the civil rights movement, Rock began a study of law. On September 14, 1861, Rock passed the bar in Massachusetts. He then became justice of the peace in two communities, Boston and Suffolk. He practiced law in Massachusetts and in Washington, D.C., while continuing to be an activist. In 1862, Rock argued against resettling blacks in other countries, as the American Colonization Society wanted. During the beginning of the Civil War, Rock fought for equal pay for black soldiers fighting in the Union Army. A year later, in 1864, Rock served as a delegate to the National Convention of Colored Men, and continued to argue for equality of opportunity and legal rights for blacks.

On February 1, 1865, Rock was granted admittance to argue cases in front of the Supreme Court, the first African American to receive this honor. (Lawyers must receive a special bar certification to appear before the Supreme Court as legal representatives.) During the same trip, Rock was invited and received on the floor of the House of Representatives, again one of the first African Americans to do so. However, when Rock tried to board the train home, he was arrested for not having the pass black Americans were required to carry at the time. This incident contributed to the revoking of the law that required such passes. However, Rock's illness continued to affect him and he never actually argued a case before the Supreme Court. Rock finally died from tuberculosis on December 3, 1866 in Boston at the age of 41. (Some sources say Washington, D.C.) A son survived him.

FURTHER READING:

Books

Brown, William Wells. *The Black Man: His Antecedents, His Genius and His Achievement.* James Redpath, 1863, reprinted Kraus, 1969, pp. 266-70.

Periodicals

Contee, Clarence G., "John Sweat Rock, M.D., Esq., 1825-66," *Journal of the National Medical Association,* (May 1976): 237-42.

Link, Eugene P., "The Civil Rights Activities of Three Great Physicians," *Journal of Negro History,* (July 1967): 169-84.

—Sketch by A. Petrusso

Carl A. Rouse
1926-
Astrophysicist

Carl Rouse is a pioneering and controversial researcher whose goal is to solve the mysteries of the sun's atmosphere. He is the founder of Rouse Research, Inc. in Del Mar, California.

Carl Rouse was born on July 14, 1926, in Youngstown, Ohio. He lived with a large family, including two older brothers, four younger sisters, and two young cousins. His father, a talented mechanic, owned and operated an auto repair shop.

Rouse led an active childhood. He learned photography and woodworking at a neighborhood recreation center and enjoyed building model airplanes. He also learned to swim, play basketball, football, and baseball, but most of all enjoyed boxing, at which he excelled. In high school, he won the regional Golden Gloves championship in his weight class. Rouse had an early introduction to science through his photography and model airplane building and gained practical engineering knowledge by helping out at his father's auto repair shop.

Rouse received excellent grades in high school, and was encouraged by his chemistry teacher to consider a career in science. He graduated a semester early, in February, 1944, a time of intense U.S. involvement in World War II. The U.S. Army recognized Rouse's abilities, and rather than send him into combat duty, they had him trained as an engineer at Howard University in Washington, D.C., Pennsylvania State College (now University), and New York University. By the time he finished these programs, the war was over. He was discharged from the Army in July 1946.

After a year working as an engineering draftsman for the county government back home in Ohio, Rouse enrolled in the physics department at Case Institute of Technology (now Case Western Reserve University). His talent in physics and mathematics was quickly recognized, and he was elected to two national honor societies, Tau Beta Pi and Sigma Xi, and awarded the Physics Prize upon graduation for his excellent grades.

Rouse went on to graduate school at the California Institute of Technology in Pasadena, where he conducted research on subatomic particles. He helped develop a machine that allowed different particles to be characterized and identified by the patterns they create when interacting with different materials. He was awarded a doctoral degree in June 1956. Also while at CIT, Rouse met and married Lorraine Moxley.

Not long after graduating, Rouse accepted a position at the Lawrence Livermore National Laboratory, where he studied the effects of the high temperatures generated by the detonation of the atomic bomb. This led to an interest in the hot gases that make up the sun and other stars. After studying the writings of other physicists, Rouse realized that some of the accepted ideas about these gases were wrong.

Rouse discovered new techniques for measuring the sun's atmosphere and developed new theories about the interactions of its gases. His theories were opposed by many influential physicists whose ideas he was challenging, and Rouse was not given much support at Livermore Labs. He decided to transfer to the General Atomic Company of San Diego in 1968, where his main studies concerned the practical applications of atomic energy. Here, he developed an improved shielding material for use in nuclear power plants, for which he was awarded a U.S. patent.

In 1986, Rouse was granted access to the company's supercomputer for use in personal projects, enabling him to greatly increase his progress towards an understanding of stellar gases. In 1992, he founded his own research company

in Del Mar, California, through which he hopes to someday solve the mysteries of the solar atmosphere.

FURTHER READING:

Kessler, James H., J. S. Kidd, Renée A. Kidd, and Katherine A. Morin. "Carl A. Rouse" In *Distinguished African American Scientists of the 20th Century*. Phoenix: The Oryx Press, 1996.

—Sketch by David E. Fontes

Edwin Roberts Russell
1913-
Chemist and inventor

Edwin Roberts Russell is a chemist and inventor who holds 11 patents related to atomic energy and its processes. His research focused on bioassay (a test frequently used on medicinal drugs), radioactive tracers (used in medical testing), gas absorption, ion exchange absorption, monomolecular films, and radioactive waste treatment.

Russell was born on June 19, 1913, in Columbia, South Carolina. He earned his bachelor's degree from Benedict College in 1935. He then entered the graduate program in chemistry at Howard University, where he was awarded his master of science degree in 1937. While still a graduate student, Russell began teaching at Howard as an assistant. In 1938, he became an instructor in the chemistry department. He left Howard in 1942 and moved to the University of Chicago, where he spent the next five years as an assistant in the metallurgical laboratories. While there, Russell was involved with the Manhattan Project—the program that developed the atomic bomb during World War II. Russell also worked in the Argonne National Laboratory from 1943-47 as a group leader and associate chemist. Upon leaving, Russell remained a consultant with Argonne.

From 1947-49, Russell worked as a consultant in chemistry. During this time, he also joined Allen University as chair of the science division and professor of chemistry. These would be the last positions he held at a university. In 1953, Russell went to work at E. I. DuPont de Nemours & Company as a research chemist, and here he spent the rest of his career. He worked primarily in the atomic energy processes development area at the Savannah River Plant, located in Aiken, in his home state of South Carolina.

Russell was a member of several professional societies, including the American Association for the Advancement of Science and the American Chemical Society. In

1974, Russell received an honorary doctoral degree from his alma mater, Benedict College. Russell also has served as the chairman of the board of trustees of the Aiken County Service Council and as trustee of both the Friendship Junior College and the New Ellenton Building Commission.

Russell was honored with a special service award by the Manpower Commission. He married the former Dorothy Nance, and with her he has two children, Vivian and Martin. Russell is now retired.

—Sketch by A. Petrusso

S

Juanita Simons Scott
1936-
Developmental biologist

Juanita Simons Scott has done important research during her career as a biologist. But more far-reaching is her work as an educator. In addition to planning courses of study for students at the university level, she has actively worked with grade-school science teachers to ensure the highest level of skills and knowledge.

Juanita Simons was born on June 13, 1936, on a small farm in Eastover, South Carolina. She was one of 15 children, and the family had no electricity or running water in their farmhouse. But Juanita's parents knew the value of education and encouraged their children to study and work hard.

A good student, Simons had no strong leanings toward science. Upon graduation from high school, she enrolled in Clinton Junior College in Rock Hill, South Carolina. She found an affinity for biology—in part from her experience with plant and animal life on the family farm. Upon graduating, she transferred to Livingstone College in Salisbury, North Carolina, where she majored in biology. She also took teaching certification courses because she thought she might want to be a biology teacher.

Simons graduated from Livingstone in 1958 and took a job as a high school science teacher in Hopkins, South Carolina. A year later, she married her high school sweetheart, Robert Scott, and the couple eventually had three children. In 1960, she decided to enroll in Atlanta University for graduate work in biology. She was particularly intrigued by how certain animals, such as frogs, can regenerate lost limbs. Her master's research was centered around the connection between some species' ability to regenerate and organ transplantation in humans. She was awarded her master's degree in 1962.

A year after receiving her master's degree, Scott was offered a position on the faculty of Benedict College in Columbia, South Carolina. Her third child was born the following spring, and in the fall she took a position at Morris College in Sumpter, North Carolina (not far from her hometown of Eastover). Morris was a small school, and Scott was the only biologist on the faculty.

Scott returned to Benedict College in 1968 as an assistant professor of biology. For the next several years she taught and also conducted research on the effects of toxic waste on local waterways. But in the mid-1970s, she decided to switch gears and devote more time to education. Scott felt that many science teachers at the high school and even the college level were often ill prepared in actual teaching techniques. For this reason, she decided to take her doctorate in education rather than biology. She received her Ph.D. from South Carolina State College in 1979.

Scott continued her work as a researcher at Benedict, but devoted more and more time to curriculum development. By the 1980s she was involved in programs that provided better training for science teachers in grade school and high school, and that provided ideas to students for science projects that might motivate them to explore science more thoroughly. In 1987 she won financial support from the National Science Foundation for her work with fifth- and sixth-grade teachers.

Scott was named Dean of Arts and Sciences at Benedict in 1994, expanding her administrative responsibilities to 10 academic departments.

FURTHER READING:

Books

Kessler, James H., et al. *Distinguished African American Scientists of the Twentieth Century.* Phoenix: Oryx Press, 1996.

—*Sketch by George A. Milite*

Earl D. Shaw
1937-
Physicist and inventor

Earl D. Shaw, sometimes called "the Henry Ford of laser research," is best known as the co-inventor of the spin-flip tunable laser, a device that has been described as placing a dimmer switch on a laser beam. This invention makes it easier for experimenters and technicians to perform

Earl D. Shaw

intricate and complex procedures with lasers, which can be especially useful in biology and materials science.

The son of sharecroppers, Earl Shaw was born in Clarksdale, Mississippi in 1937. His father was shot to death when Earl, an only child, was six, and he was raised by his mother, Augusta. Earl spent his childhood living on the Hopson Plantation, and he attended a three-room school. This gave the young student an unexpected opportunity; because several grades had to be taught together, he was actually able to pick up and absorb course material from upper grades.

When he was 12 years old, Shaw and his mother moved to Chicago. There he attended Crane Technical High School. The neighborhood in which he lived was poor, and there was a strong gang element, but Shaw ignored those negative influences. He worked hard and excelled in school. He was admitted to the University of Illinois, where he received his bachelor of science degree in physics in 1960. From there, he went to Dartmouth College, where he received his master's degree in 1964. For his doctoral studies he went to the University of California, Berkeley, where he received his Ph.D. in physics in 1969.

After getting his degree, Shaw went to Bell Labs in Murray Hill, New Jersey. It was there that he developed, with fellow scientist Chandra K. N. Patel, the spin-flip tunable laser. In the late 1920s, the Indian physicist Sir C. V. Raman had done experimentation with light wavelengths. Shaw and Patel drew in part on Raman's work; hence one type of spin-flip laser is know as the Raman laser.

The practical application of the spin-flip laser is that it can be adjusted by the user. For example, biologists who are studying a cell but know that the laser frequency they need to explore the interior of that cell would destroy the cell wall can alter the adjustments to modify the laser's strength. A patent for the spin-flip laser was issued in 1971.

Shaw continued his work at Bell Labs until accepting a position as professor of physics at Rutgers University in 1991. Later, he was named head of the physics department of the Rutgers-New Jersey Institute of Technology program in Newark. He is a member of the National Society of Black Physicists. His first marriage, from which he has three children, ended in divorce; he and his second wife, Erin, live in Morris County, New Jersey.

FURTHER READING:

Books

Sammons, Vivian O. *Blacks in Science and Medicine.* Hemisphere Publishing, 1990.

Van Sertima, Ivan, ed. *Blacks in Science, Ancient and Modern.* Journal of African Civilizations, Ltd., 1984.

Periodicals

Alex, Patricia. "In Line for a Nobel? Scientist's Laser Helps Solve New jersey's Mysteries." *The Record* (Northern New Jersey), (September 5, 1995): A1.

—Sketch by George A. Milite

Jeanne Craig Sinkford
1933-
Dentist

Jeanne Craig Sinkford has ventured into an arena of science traditionally reserved for men, in the United States at least. When Sinkford entered the dental profession, only 2% of dentists were female. Through hard work and diligence, she rose to the top of her profession, becoming the first woman dean of a dental school in the United States. Along the way, she became a respected dental researcher and an able administrator, receiving the highest accolades her peers could grant. She played an important role in increasing female enrollment in dental schools, and today, 36% of dental students are women.

Yet with all her successes, she remains at heart a woman committed to helping others. As she wrote in

Jeanne Craig Sinkford

"Choose the High Road," an autobiographical essay, "Being a minority and a woman required a strong work ethic, a sense of morality and decency, a willingness to 'turn the other cheek' and a sincere motivation to help those who are less fortunate and underprivileged." Being the only woman doing what she did was difficult at times, but she has thoroughly enjoyed her career and the opportunities it has provided her.

Jeanne Craig Sinkford was born January 30, 1933, in Washington, D.C. She was one of four daughters born to Richard E. Craig and Geneva Jefferson Craig. Her family was loving and supportive, which helped her work towards her goals. Her mother taught her to be her best, and not to accept that being a woman should limit her opportunities. Her parents instilled in her a responsibility to give back to others once you have achieved. As an example of how this worked in their family, when her sisters graduated from college, each would help the next in line through college.

Encouragement from her family dentist interested Sinkford in dental school. She enrolled at Howard University in Washington, D.C., and graduated in 1953 with a B.S. degree, majoring in psychology and chemistry. While at Howard, she married Stanley M. Sinkford, who was then a medical student and later became a pediatrician. Reluctant to compete with her husband in medical school, she chose to enter Howard University College of Dentistry. She graduated as valedictorian with her D.D.S. degree in 1958. She became an instructor in the dental school at Howard (1958-1960), teaching crown and bridge prosthodontics. After her

husband completed his military service in 1960, they moved to Chicago. Sinkford attended the dental school at Northwestern University in Evanston, Illinois, from which she obtained an M.S. (1962) and Ph.D. in physiology (1963).

Sinkford taught at Northwestern University for one year while her husband studied at the University of Chicago. The Sinkfords alternated supporting one another in furthering their education. In a telephone interview with contributor Dónal O'Mathúna, conducted May 13, 1998, Sinkford stated that having a supportive spouse has been very important to her. She sees dentistry as a perfect career for women because of its blend of aesthetics and art, and the advantage of having small hands to work delicately within the restricted area of the mouth. But dentistry is also amenable to flexible scheduling whereby the many requirements of being a parent, spouse, and professional can be balanced satisfactorily. This has been important to the Sinkfords in raising their two daughters and one son.

In 1964 Sinkford returned to Howard University as associate professor and chair of the department of prosthodontics. Sinkford was the first female head of such a department, the largest in the dental college. Recognition of her leadership skills led to her appointment as associate dean of Howard University College of Dentistry (1967-1974). She was the first woman to hold such a position. In 1975 she became the Dean of the College of Dentistry, again the first woman to serve as dean of a dental school in the United States. Sinkford served as Dean until 1991.

After sixteen years as Dean, Sinkford was named professor and dean emeritus of Howard University College of Dentistry. Later that year (1991) she became director of the Office of Women and Minority Affairs at the American Association of Dental Schools in Washington, D.C. She remains at this same organization, now Assistant Executive Director, Division of Women and Minority Affairs.

As a dental educator, Sinkford's contributions have been numerous. She has served on a number of national committees examining dental education. The American Dental Association, along with the American Association of Dental Schools, commissioned her to write the background document for the Graduate Education Workshop, which received national acclaim and remains her most significant contribution to dental education. She is also author over 70 professional publications, and has written a *Manual for Crown and Bridge Prosthodontics.*

Sinkford's abilities have led to wider recognition. Among many organizations availing of her expertise, she was asked in 1972 to join a nine-member panel investigating the infamous Tuskegee Syphilis Study. This project began in 1932 as an attempt to understand the progression of syphilis. However, the 400 African American men enrolled in the project went untreated for 40 years, even though penicillin was accepted as standard, effective treatment by the 1940s. Sinkford had been very interested in research, but this project exposed her to the misuses of human research subjects, especially in research involving ethnic groups, children, and prisoners. She wrote the minority report criticizing the training of the U.S. Public Health Service researchers and the way the research was monitored and reported.

Sinkford has received many awards, including induction into the International College of Dentists in 1974. She was also named a fellow of the American College of Dentists. Foremost of all these awards, however, is the Candace Award, granted by the National Coalition of One Hundred Black Women. This award not only recognizes Sinkford's accomplishments, but is particularly significant because of its requirement to demonstrate a sustained commitment to serve others. Sinkford notes that it is vital to "stay focused because there are so many things that can distract individuals from their goals." When she gets derailed from her goals, as inevitably happens, Sinkford regroups and rechannels her efforts to prevent the setbacks from winning. Her career reveals what can happen when someone adopts this as his or her personal philosophy.

SELECTED WRITINGS BY SINKFORD:

Books

"Choose the High Road," in *Legacy, The Dental Profession,* Bakersfield, CA: Loader/Kishi, 1990, pp. 168-169.

FURTHER READING:

Books

American Men & Women of Science 1998-99, New Providence, NJ: R. R. Bowker. 20th Edition. Volume 6, p. 960.

Sammons, Vivian Ovelton, *Blacks in Science and Medicine,* Taylor & Francis, 1990, p. 213.

Smith, Jessie Carney, ed. *Powerful Black Women,* Detroit: Visible Ink Press, 1996, pp. 301-6.

—*Sketch by Dónal P. O'Mathúna*

John Brooks Slaughter
1934-
Physicist

As an engineer performing early work in the field of computer science, John Brooks Slaughter made important contributions to computerized control systems. He has also held a number of administrative posts, most notably as the first black Director of the National Science Foundation.

Resists Attempts to Discourage His Dream

John Brooks Slaughter was born in Topeka, Kansas, on March 16, 1934. His ancestors had come to Kansas following the Civil War, when that state became a refuge for freed slaves. Slaughter's father sold used furniture and worked as a janitor at the Meninger Clinic, a well-known medical institute. The oldest of three children, Slaughter decided at an early age that he wanted to become an engineer, to design and build great structures.

Educational opportunities for black children in Topeka, however, were not great. The famous Supreme Court case of *Brown v. Board of Education* (1954), which integrated Topeka's schools and thus led to the integration of public schools throughout the nation, lay well in the future. When Slaughter attended high school, he found that teachers and other potential role models often tried to discourage him from his aspirations. His coaches—Slaughter was an outstanding baseball pitcher, and he lettered in track—laughed at his notion that one day he would become an engineer. Teachers tried to encourage him to take vocational courses that would put him on a path to becoming a technician or mechanic. These educators, many of them no doubt well-meaning, saw the lack of opportunities for blacks in the sciences, and tried to prevent Slaughter from experiencing what they must have considered inevitable disappointment.

However, Slaughter was not to be so easily dissuaded. Because his teachers thought they knew what was best for him, he was discouraged from taking science classes, so he had to teach himself. In high school he received some technical education—which again was directed toward a skilled vocation, rather than the professional role of an engineer—and he supplemented this with outside learning by teaching himself how to repair radios. This hands-on experience taught him the rudiments of electronics, and he began what would become a life-long appreciation for the relationship between theory and practical experience.

Slaughter entered Topeka's Washburn University in 1951. Largely putting himself through school with his radio-repair business, he gained at Washburn the basic scientific and mathematical education that his high school counselors had discouraged him from receiving. By 1953 he had exhausted the school's limited educational resources in the engineering field, and enrolled at Kansas State University in the town of Manhattan. In 1956 he earned his B.S. degree there, and soon afterward moved to San Diego, California.

A Pioneer in Computer Control Systems

In San Diego, Slaughter went to work for the General Dynamics Corporation, a major defense contractor involved in development of aerospace systems including aircraft, rockets, and missiles. During this time, Slaughter continued his education through night classes at the University of California at Los Angeles (UCLA), studying electronics and control systems. The latter was a relatively new field of endeavor which was developing hand in hand with nascent computer technology. Among the more well-known examples of electronic control systems are the "automatic pilot" function on an airplane, or "cruise control" on an automobile. In each case, the control system augments human intelligence by performing routine functions—keeping a plane on course, maintaining a car's speed—at the guidance of a human operator.

The United States Navy had a significant presence in San Diego, and Slaughter left General Dynamics to work at the Naval Electronics Laboratory. He earned his M.S. degree in 1961, and this opened up new opportunities for him. During the next few years, Slaughter and others made great strides in the development of computerized control systems, and under his direction, a research team at the lab began building and testing a variety of such systems. In 1965, he earned the title "Scientist of the Year" for the Naval Electronics Laboratory.

Returning to college part-time at the University of California at San Diego in 1967, Slaughter moved from the practical work of the naval laboratory to the more theoretical research work involved in earning his doctorate. In 1971, he received his Ph.D. degree in engineering sciences. Throughout this time, he continued to work for the Navy; but four years later, in 1975, he was ready for a change.

Becomes First Black Director of the National Science Foundation

Slaughter moved to Seattle, Washington, in 1975, to become director of the University of Washington's Applied Physics Laboratory. This was in some ways a transitional post: he continued his connection with the Navy, which sponsored much of the laboratory's work, and he left the university after only two years. In 1977, President Jimmy Carter appointed him assistant director of the National Science Foundation (NSF), where he was responsible for coordinating studies in astronomy, geology, meteorology, and related subjects.

With this valuable administrative experience under his belt, Slaughter in 1979 returned to the Pacific Northwest to take a position as provost and academic vice president at Washington State University in Pullman. But his responsibilities in Washington D.C. were not over. In 1979, he was asked to become NSF Director, an invitation he initially declined. But when President Carter himself personally asked him to take the job, Slaughter agreed and was soon approved by the Senate. He needed time to finish up affairs at home, however, and by the time he arrived in the nation's capital, in November 1980, Carter had been voted out of office and Ronald Reagan was set to assume the presidency.

During his period as Director of the NSF, from 1980 to 1982, Slaughter dealt with a recurring theme in his career: theory versus practice. Though he had devoted much of his work to practical applications, he proved a friend of theoretical work as well, and encouraged the federal government to fund research at universities—particularly African American institutions. Slaughter resigned from the

NSF in 1982, and took a position as chancellor at the University of Maryland in College Park.

It was a time of great opportunity and challenge at the university. On the one hand, the local community was growing, which meant an increase in state funds to support the school; also, enrollment by black students was growing, since the surrounding area had a large number of African Americans. But when Maryland's star basketball player Len Bias succumbed to a cocaine overdose in June of 1986, the school entered a rocky period of negative national exposure.

Slaughter ended up replacing Maryland's head basketball coach, and it was during this time that he became an outspoken opponent of the policy of emphasizing athletics over academics in higher education. (Slaughter has been quoted in news stories such as a 1989 *Time* magazine exposé on the subject of "How the National Obsession with Winning and Moneymaking Is Turning Big-Time College Sports into an Educational Scandal. . . .") In 1988, Slaughter accepted an appointment as president of Occidental College in Los Angeles, California. In that capacity, he has worked for greater integration between races, educational disciplines, and between theoretical and practical studies.

During his career, Slaughter has held a number of positions concurrent with his primary work. These include stints as an instructor in engineering at California Western University (1961-63) and UCLA (1963), as a lecturer at San Diego State University (1964-66), and as editor of *The International Journal of Computers and Electrical Engineering* (1977). He has served on the boards of the American Cancer Society (1974), the Minority Committee of the Institute for Electrical & Electronics Engineers (chair, 1976-80), the Maryland Governor's Task Force on Teen Pregnancy (1984-85), the Prince George's County Public Schools Advisory Committee (1985-86), the National College Athletics Association (1986-88), the National Science Board (1980-83), the Maryland State Chamber of Commerce (1983-88), the Prince George's Chamber of Commerce (1984-88), and IBM (1990s). He is a member of the National Academy of Engineers, and a fellow of the Institute of Electrical & Electronics Engineers and the American Academy of Arts & Sciences. He has received some 10 honorary doctorates.

In 1956, Slaughter married Bernice Johnson of Kansas City. They have two children and reside in Los Angeles.

SELECTED WRITINGS BY SLAUGHTER:

Books

Interim Report: Governor's Task Force on Teen Pregnancy. Maryland Social Services Administration, 1984.
Goals, Objectives, and Initiatives: Fall 1984. University of Maryland, 1984.

Periodicals

(With Harold M. Williams) "Perspectives on Education: Renew the Master Plan Promise," *Los Angeles Times,* (March 8, 1998).

FURTHER READING:

Books

American Men & Women of Science. R. R. Bowker, 1994.

Kessler, James H., et al. *Distinguished African American Scientists of the 20th Century.* Oryx Press, 1996.

Spradling, Mary Mace, ed. *In Black and White.* Gale, 1980.

Periodicals

Brewington, Peter, "Schools Must Stress Priority for Academic Success," *USA Today,* (March 29, 1995).

Pyle, Amy, "Group Seeks to Draw Blacks into Academia," *Los Angeles Times,* (May 25, 1996).

Other

"John Brooks Slaughter." *Louisiana State University Chemistry Library.* 1998. http://www.lib.lsu.edu/lib/chem/display/slaughter.html (May 11, 1998).

—*Sketch by Judson Knight*

James McCune Smith
1813-1865
Physician

The first African American to practice medicine with a medical degree in the United States, James McCune Smith was also the first black person to own and operate a pharmacy. He was best known, however, as an essayist and an orator. Throughout his career, he lectured in support of the abolition of slavery and produced medical evidence against misleading information on the physical, mental, and intellectual traits of blacks.

Smith was born during the era of slavery on April 18, 1813, in New York City. His father was a former slave, freed by New York's Emancipation Act, and his mother was a self-emancipated bondswoman. The country's first black physician began his education at the African Free School in New York City. Unable to pursue a college education in the United States, Smith attended the University of Glasgow in Scotland, where prejudice based on color was comparatively

unknown. There, he received his bachelor's degree in 1835, his master's degree in 1836, and his medical degree in 1837.

Upon his return to the United States, Smith received a triumphant welcome from New York's black residents. About the event, William C. Nell wrote in *Colored Patriots of the American Revolution*: "Ransom F. Wake, in their behalf, congratulated [Smith] on having passed five years in a land where 'a man's a man,' without regard to his complexion—where the gentleman, the scholar, the Christian and the patriot did not restrict their benevolence to geographic limits, nor to the mean, degrading, illiberal, detestable and unholy distinction of color which prevails in our otherwise happy land." In response, Smith told the crowd: "I have striven to obtain education, at every sacrifice and every hazard, and to apply such education to the good of our common country." He began practicing medicine in New York in 1838 after studying in the clinics of the Paris Hospital in France. A short time later, Smith opened a pharmacy on West Broadway—considered to be the first pharmacy in the nation owned and operated by an African American.

Smith spent 25 years as a physician, mainly as a staff member of the Free Negro Orphan Asylum. Although his practice was successful, he is better known for his essays and his antislavery activities. Smith frequently spoke and wrote against slavery as well as the American Colonization Society, which was formed to repatriate blacks in Africa. He was prominently involved in the New York connection of the Underground Railroad, which helped escaped slaves from the South gain freedom in the North and Canada. His writings and lectures against slavery were often controversial but scientifically sound. One of his first reported speeches was delivered at the annual meeting of the American Anti-Slavery Society in 1838, which included a summary of abolition activities in England and France.

Smith was a contributor to antislavery publications, including the *Emancipator* and the *Liberator*. In an 1844 essay, "Freedom and Slavery," originally published in the *New York Tribune,* he responded to claims made by the Reverend O. Dewey that the slaves of the South were happier than the free Negroes of the North. Smith provided statistics to disprove Dewey's theory. In another well-known incident, John C. Calhoun and others made assertions about black health and insanity. Their claims were based in part on an 1840 census report that noted a high rate of black lunacy, but Smith used his knowledge of medicine to refute these accusations in a reply entitled "The Influence of Climate upon Longevity." He also proved that arguments regarding the small size and weight of the Negro brain were false.

Equality for blacks was a recurring theme in many of his essays and speeches. In 1849, he wrote on the equal school rights question in Boston: "It has ever been my solemn conviction, that separate organizations of all kinds, based upon the color of the skin, keep alive prejudice against color, and that no organizations do this more effectually than colored schools." Smith wrote the introduction to Frederick Douglass's second autobiographical work, *My Bondage and My Freedom,* which was published in 1855. In the introduction, Smith stated: "It is an American book, for Americans, in the fullest sense of the idea. It shows that the worst of our institutions, in its worst aspect, cannot keep down energy, truthfulness, and earnest struggle for the right. It proves the justice and practicability of Immediate Emancipation." Smith also wrote a more than 60-page introduction to Henry Highland Garnet's *A Memorial Discourse; Delivered in the House of Representatives,* which was published in 1865.

Smith received an appointment as professor of anthropology at Wilberforce University in 1863. However, poor health kept him from teaching. Suffering from heart disease, Smith died at his home in Williamsburg, New York, on November 17, 1865. He was survived by his wife and five children.

SELECTED WRITINGS BY SMITH:

Periodicals

"The Influence of Climate on Longevity: With Special Reference to Life Insurance." *Hunt's Merchants' Magazine* 14 (1846): 319-29.

FURTHER READING:

Books

Kaufman, Martin, Galishoff, Stuart, and Savitt, Todd L. *Dictionary of American Medical Biography* vol. II. Greenwood Press, p. 693.
Malone, Dumas. *Dictionary of American Biography.* New York: Charles Scribner's Sons, 1935, p. 288-89.
Nell, William C. *The Colored Patriots of the American Revolution.* Arno Press and The New York Times, 1968, p. 353-354.

—Sketch by Rose M. Estioco

Jeanne Spurlock
1921-
Physician and psychiatrist

Jeanne Spurlock has made significant contributions to understanding and treating the psychological stresses of poverty, racism, and sexism that impact women, children, minorities, and gays in the United States.

Spurlock was born on July 21, 1921, in Sandusky, Ohio. Her mother, Godene (Anthony) Spurlock, and her father, Frank Spurlock, had seven children of whom she was the eldest. She grew up in Detroit, Michigan where her family moved six months after she was born. Like many other Americans who grew up with phrases like "liberty, equality, and justice for all" ringing in their ears, Spurlock had an early conflict with a powerful public institution that made her stop and think. She broke her leg when she was nine years old, and the hospital handled her case badly. Later in her own career, she would do things differently.

In 1940, after she graduated from high school, Spurlock enrolled at Spelman College. Although she had a scholarship to pay for her tuition, she had to work almost 40 hours a week to cover her living expenses. After several years, she dropped out of Spelman. She moved to Chicago and enrolled at Roosevelt University until the spring of 1943, when she moved to Howard University in Washington D.C. In the early 1940s, Howard University had a special accelerated program leading to the degree of doctor of medicine. In the spring of 1943, Spurlock abandoned her plans to get a bachelor's degree at Roosevelt University and transferred into the M.D. program at Howard. She graduated with her M.D. from Howard in 1947.

Spurlock had decided to pursue a career in psychiatry, and after an internship from 1947 to 1948 at Provident Hospital in Chicago, she became a resident in general psychiatry at Chicago's Cook County Hospital from 1948 to 1950. During the next year, she was a fellow in child psychiatry at the Institute for Juvenile Research in Chicago. From 1951 to 1953, she held several positions in Chicago. She was a psychiatrist at the Institute for Juvenile Research and at the Mental Hygiene Clinic of the Women's and Children's Hospital. She also started her own private practice in psychiatry. From 1953 to 1962, Spurlock studied psychoanalysis part-time at the Chicago Institute for Psychoanalysis. While attending the Institute, she directed the Children's Pychosomatic Unit at the Neuropsychiatric Institute in Chicago, and she was an assistant professor of psychiatry at the University of Illinois College of Medicine. She was a clinical assistant professor of psychiatry at the Illinois College of Medicine from 1960 to 1968, and she worked concurrently at the Michael Reese Hospital as chief of the Child Psychiatry Clinic and as an attending psychiatrist. Through all of these years, she continued her private practice in psychiatry.

Spurlock was chair of the Meharry Medical College department of Psychiatry from 1968 to 1973. Then she moved to Washington D.C. to work at the National Institute of Mental Health as a visiting scientist for a year. Beginning in 1974 and continuing until her resignation in December 1991, Spurlock was the deputy medical director of the American Psychiatric Association, and she was a clinical professor of psychiatry at the medical schools of George Washington University and Howard University.

Spreading Resources to All Americans

If one adds the members of all the subcultures with few resources in America, the result is a majority of Americans. Jeanne Spurlock has recognized this truth, and she has been a powerful advocate for tens of millions of Americans with few social and community resources. Throughout her career, she has helped women, minorities, children, and gays gain more resources and advocates by focusing on the special situations and needs of important American subcultures: single women, children with absent fathers, women who must play several social roles in a family, African Americans with survival guilt, children whose parents suffer from work-related stress, people with different sexual lifestyles, the never-married woman, and others. Spurlock has worked to understand the different stresses and situations of these subcultures so she can develop the appropriate therapies to help them with their problems.

For many of her ideas, Spurlock drew from her own experiences. She grew up black and poor, yet she became a prominent, successful woman who never married or had children. As a result of these experiences, Spurlock was to study, among other subjects, poor black children, successful black Americans who felt guilty about their success, single women, and the myths about women who never married.

Helping Successful Blacks Cope with Survival Guilt

One example of Spurlock's work is her attempt to help successful African Americans cope with the alienation they feel when they leave their peer groups behind and become successful in another culture. One African American automobile executive became desperate when he was caught between two conflicting groups at his workplace. When he was younger, he had been a Black Muslim and had worked with the Equal Employment Opportunity Administration of the U.S. government. Then, as an auto company executive, he had to cope with a disagreement between his company's management and black workers who were protesting discrimination in hiring practices. The pressure became too much and he committed suicide. Although this is an extreme case, Spurlock wanted to develop psychiatric therapies to reduce the stress for African Americans who are high achievers. Two of her therapies were to help her patients sort out their priorities and to suggest alternative behaviors. In one case, a patient decided that he was better off not climbing the corporate ladder.

Spurlock has also helped high-achieving African Americans cope with the guilt that some feel when they become successful in another culture. Some high-achieving African Americans feel that they have abandoned people who have helped them out, or they feel guilty because their families become defensive about being left behind. Spurlock's therapies have included helping her patients to verbalize their concerns and connect them with past experiences, and she has helped her patients refrain from becoming involved in conflicts with family members about differences in attitudes and lifestyles.

In honor of Spurlock's many contributions to improving conditions for minorities and women, an important fellowship for minority medical students has been named after her. The Jeanne Spurlock Research Fellowship in Drug Abuse and Addiction for Minority Medical Students is sponsored by the American Academy of Child and Adolescent Psychiatry and the National Institute on Drug Abuse. After she resigned in 1991 from the American Psychiatric Association (APA), she served as a consultant to APA's Council on International Affairs and its Council on National Affairs.

SELECTED WRITINGS BY SPURLOCK:

Books

(With Ian A. Canino) *Culturally Diverse Children and Adolescents: Assessment, Diagnosis, and Treatment.* New York: The Guilford Press, 1994.
(With Alice F. Coner-Edwards) *Black Families in Crisis: The Middle Class.* New York: Brunner Mazel, 1988.

Periodicals

"Survival Guilt and the Afro-American of Achievement." *Journal of the National Medical Association.* Vol. 77, No. 1 (January, 1985): 29-32.

FURTHER READING:

Books

Salzman, Jack, David L. Smith, and Cornel West, eds. *Encyclopedia of African-American Culture and History.* New York: Simon & Schuster Macmillan, 1996.
Smith, Jessie Carney, ed. *Notable Black American Women.* Detroit: Gale Research, 1991.

—Sketch by Patrick Moore

Claude Mason Steele
1946-
Psychologist

Claude M. Steele is a social psychologist who became nationally known because of his controversial theory of "stereotype threat"—a cultural force that, he argues, adversely affects the academic performance of African

Claude Mason Steele

Americans and women. He has also conducted ground-breaking research on the social and psychological aspects of alcohol addiction.

Claude Mason Steele was born January 1, 1946, to Ruth and Shelby Steele in Chicago, Illinois. His mother, a medical social worker, and his father, a truck driver, were deeply involved in the civil rights movement. Both Steele and his twin brother, Shelby, grew up in the midst of conversations about racial equality, individual versus group rights, and the nature of prejudice. According to Steele in a telephone interview with contributor Ellen Cothran, he was drawn to social psychology because he wanted to study these same topics scientifically; he was particularly interested in their effects on the quality of life and relationships. He attended Hiram College and graduated in 1967 with honors in psychology. He then entered the graduate program in psychology at Ohio State University. He completed his doctoral degree in 1971 and was granted a Dissertation Year Fellowship.

Steele began teaching psychology at the University of Utah that same year. In 1973, he joined the faculty at the University of Washington in Seattle. His research interest was in self-evaluation: how what we are told about ourselves and our behavior actually leads us to fulfill these impressions. At the University of Washington, he focused on the social and psychological causes of alcohol addiction. With several colleagues, he developed a theory of what he called "alcohol myopia," in which alcohol hinders a person's ability to perceive and think about his or her

surroundings. According to this theory, it is exactly this narrowed functioning to which people become addicted; this "myopia" reduces stress and makes social situations easier to handle. The National Institute on Alcohol Abuse and Alcoholism considered this research an important contribution to helping Americans overcome alcohol addiction. This governmental organization supported Steele's work from 1972-79.

In 1987, Steele joined the University of Michigan, and it was here that he turned to examining self-evaluation in the face of group stereotypes. While studying the dropout rates of African American undergraduates, Steele first saw evidence of what he would later call the stereotype threat. At first, Steele referred to this phenomenon as "stereotype vulnerability"; later he changed the phrase to reflect his conviction that the locus of the problem is completely outside the individual. As Alex Kerry notes in his article "Twins Divided By Race," Steele "deduced that poverty, innercity travails, and discrimination . . . did not entirely account for the dropout phenomenon affecting black college students." Steele attributed such failure instead to crippling anxiety and self-doubt based on the negative academic stereotype of themselves which these students had unconsciously accepted. Steele argued that these negative stereotypes prevent students from thinking of themselves as academic successes; they see failure not as an obstacle to be overcome but as independent confirmation of the prejudices they have internalized.

In the *Stanford Observer*, Steele argued that his research showed how "affirmative action policies as they exist are reasonable and modest gestures to correct" the inequality of opportunity for minorities and women. His theories about "stereotype threat" sparked a national debate. Many believed that he had offered a new and unique argument for preserving affirmative action laws. In this debate, however, one of his most visible opponents was his twin brother, Shelby Steele.

In 1997, Steele moved to Stanford University, where he served as chair of the psychology department. In 1991, he joined the board of directors of the American Psychological Society; from 1995-96, he served as president of the Western Psychological Association. In 1987, he was named consulting editor for the *Journal of Experimental Social Psychology*. Married for 30 years, Steele has two grown children and lives in Stanford, California.

SELECTED WRITINGS BY STEELE:

Periodicals

"Faculty Forum: Focus on Affirmative Action." *Stanford Observer* (Spring, 1995).
"Heaven Can Wait: The Effects of Restrained and Unrestrained Drinking Styles on the Ability to Delay Drinking Gratification." *Cognitive Therapy and Research* 2 (1988): 261-278.

"The Psychology of Drunken Excess." *Psychology Today* (January 1986).

"Race and the Schooling of Black Americans." *The Atlantic Monthly* (April 1992).

"A Threat in the Air: How Stereotypes Shape the Intellectual Identities and Performance of Women and African Americans." *American Psychologist* (June 1997).

FURTHER READING:

Periodicals

Gose, Ben. "Test Scores and Stereotypes: Psychologist Finds That Blacks, Females are Vulnerable to Lowered Expectations." *The Chronicle of Higher Education.* (August 18, 1995).

Kerry, Alex. "Twins Divided by Race." *The College Hill Independent* (1995).

Leslie, Connie. "You Can't High-Jump if the Bar is Set Low: A New Prescription to Help Black Kids Succeed." *Newsweek* (November 6, 1995).

Watters, Ethan. "Claude Steele Has Scores to Settle."*The New York Times Magazine* (September 17, 1995).

—Sketch by Ellen E. Cothran

Clarence Francis Stephens
1917-
Mathematician

Clarence Francis Stephens is a mathematician known for his problem-solving ability and his efforts to improve the teaching of mathematics. He has also made concentrated efforts to help minorities and women establish themselves in mathematical careers.

Stephens was born in Gaffney, South Carolina, on July 24, 1917, to Sam and Jeannette (Morehead) Stephens. Stephen's childhood was a difficult one. His mother died when he was just two years old, and his father died a few years later. Along with his youngest siblings, Stephens went to live with his grandmother, but she died when Stephens was ten years old. Stephens then went to live with a great aunt in a three-room farmhouse without electricity or running water. At that time, many rural areas in the South did not offer a high school education to blacks. Stephens actually thought about running away to a city in the North, until an older sister paid for his first year at the Harbison Institute in Irmo, South Carolina. After his first year at the boarding school, Stephens worked the rest of his way

through Harbison and went on to study math at the Johnson C. Smith University on a scholarship.

Stephens earned a bachelor of science degree from Johnson C. Smith University in 1938 and continued his study of math at the University of Michigan. Although Stephens had to work part-time to pay for his tuition and living costs, he earned a master's degree in just one year. He began work toward his doctorate at the University of Michigan, but lack of funding forced him to leave. In 1940, he accepted a position teaching math at Prairie View A & M College in Texas.

By 1941 Stephens was able to return to the University of Michigan to study for his doctorate in math. There, Stephens married Harriette Josephine Briscoe on December 21, 1942. The couple eventually had two children, a daughter named Harriette Jeannette, and a son named Clarence Francis, Jr. He received his doctoral degree from the University of Michigan in 1943.

Stephens postponed his academic career while he served in the U.S. Naval Reserve, from 1943 until the end of World War II. In 1946, he returned to Prairie View A & M College to teach. Stephens moved on to Morgan State College in 1947, and in 1948 he published an article in the *Transactions of the American Mathematical Society.* In 1953, Stephens won a prestigious Ford Foundation fellowship and spent the next year at the Institute for Advanced Study at Princeton University. The following year, Johnson C. Smith University presented him with an honorary degree. Stephens served as a math professor and head of the department at Morgan State until 1962.

From 1962-69, Stephens taught at the State University of New York at Geneseo. He then became a professor and chairman in the mathematics department at the State University of New York College in Potsdam. Stephens retired in 1987, becoming a professor emeritus. Chicago State University awarded Stephens an honorary degree in 1990, and he earned the Distinguished Teacher Award from the State University of New York College in Potsdam in 1991. Stephens lives in Conesus, New York.

SELECTED WRITINGS BY STEPHENS:

Periodicals

"Nonlinear Difference Equations Analytic in a Parameter." *Transactions of the American Mathematical Society* 64, no. 2 (September 1948): 268-282. Also published in *Black Mathematicians and Their Works.* V.K. Newell, J.H. Gipson, L. W. Rich, and B. Stubblefield, eds. Ardmore, PA: Dorrance & Company, 1980. pp. 195-209, 294.

FURTHER READING:

Books

American Men & Women of Science. 19th edition. New Providence, NJ: R.R. Bowker Company, 1994. p. 1245.

Kessler, James H., et al. *Distinguished African American Scientists of the 20th Century.* Phoenix, AZ: Oryx Press, 1996. pp. 296-301.

Sammons, Vivian Ovelton. *Blacks in Science and Medicine.* New York: Hemisphere, 1990, p. 221.

Taylor, Julius H. *The Negro in Science.* Baltimore: Morgan State College Press, 1955, p. 189.

—*Sketch by R. Garcia-Johnson*

Susan Smith McKinney Steward
1847-1918
Physician

Susan McKinney Steward was the first black female doctor in the state of New York, and only the third in the United States. She had a successful private practice in New York City (Brooklyn and Manhattan), and was regarded as especially knowledgeable about curing the effects of malnutrition in children. Steward was one of the founders of the Women's Hospital and Dispensary in Brooklyn. She was also active in the community, participating in the temperance, suffrage, and civil rights movements.

Steward was born in 1847 to Sylvanus and Anne Eliza (nee Springsteel) Smith, activists who lived among the black elite in Brooklyn, New York. Her father was a prosperous hog farmer in then-rural Brooklyn. As a young person, Steward studied the organ with two of the most prestigious teachers in Brooklyn, John Zundel and Henry Eyre Brown. Steward retained this interest throughout her life, and while she lived in Brooklyn, she played in churches. Before becoming a doctor, Steward taught music in the District of Columbia's public schools for two years.

Steward received her medical education at the New York Medical College and Hospital for Women. The reasons for her career choice are unclear—perhaps related to the deaths of two of her brothers in 1966 from cholera—but it was unusual for a woman at that time. Indeed, women who aspired to be doctors were basically restricted to the study of homeopathic medicine, which is what Steward was educated in at her medical school. She proudly paid for her own education, though her father could have provided the funding for her. After three years of dogged study, Steward graduated in 1870, and was valedictorian of her class. After graduation, Steward married the Reverend William G. McKinney, an itinerant preacher. They eventually had two children together, a daughter, Anna, and a son, William S.

It took several years for Steward's career to flourish. When it did, her private practice attracted people of all races, ages, and incomes. In 1881, Steward was a founder of the Women's Hospital and Dispensary in Brooklyn, where she served as a staff member until 1896. (The institution later became known as Memorial Hospital for Women and Children.) In 1882, she became associated with the Brooklyn Home for Aged Colored People, where she was a manager and on the attending medical staff. She served on the Home's board of directors from 1892-95. In 1882, Steward also became a staff member at the New York Medical College and Hospital for Women, her alma mater.

Steward retained several memberships in professional associations, including the Kings County Homeopathic Society and the New York State Medical Society. She presented a paper before the former in 1883. It was a case study of one of her patients, a woman exposed to carbolic acid during pregnancy, resulting in her death and that of her baby. Three years later, Steward delivered a paper related to her specialty, childhood diseases, especially related to malnutrition.

While her career prospered, Steward remained active in social causes. She and her sister Sarah were important members of the Equal Suffrage League. Steward herself was one of the founders of the New York Women's Loyal Union. She was active in the temperance movement, and served as president of a local chapter of the Women's Christian Temperance Union. Steward attended the Bridge Street A.M.E. Church and participated in its missionary activities. Steward also maintained her organ playing and was active in the Brooklyn Literary Union.

In 1887-88, Steward took a year of post-graduate courses at Long Island Medical College, where she was the only woman in the school. Two years later, in 1890, Steward's husband fell ill with a cerebral hemorrhage. He was disabled for the rest of his life, and died on November 25, 1895.

In 1896, Steward was remarried to the Reverend Theophilus Gould Steward, who worked as a chaplain in the United States Army and as a writer. Upon their marriage, Steward left Brooklyn to move with her new husband to Fort Missoula, Montana, where he was stationed. Steward became licensed to practice medicine there. Two years later, Steward moved to Ohio, to become the college doctor and an instructor at Wilberforce University. She remained there until 1902, when her husband returned from his assignments as chaplain in Cuba and the Phillipines. Then Steward and her husband moved to his post in Fort Niobrara, Nebraska. In Nebraska, Steward also became licensed to practice medicine and was associated with a chapter of the Women's Christian Temperance Movement.

After a brief stint in Fort McIntosh, Texas, the couple returned to Wilberforce in 1906, after Steward's husband retired from the army. There, Steward resumed her former duties, while her husband became a faculty member in the department of history. Steward remained active in both her professional and social interests. In 1911, she and her husband went to Europe, where she delivered a paper titled *Colored Women in America* to the first Interracial Conference in London. Steward delivered a paper titled *Women in*

Medicine to the Colored Women's Club in Wilberforce. This paper was reproduced in pamphlet form and circulated widely, perhaps because it was one of the most complete studies of black women and their contributions to medicine. Steward also served with the Red Cross at the beginning of World War I.

Steward died suddenly at Wilberforce on March 7, 1918. Her body was transferred back to Brooklyn for burial, where W.E.B. DuBois gave the eulogy. After her death, Steward was twice honored. Black female doctors in New York, Connecticut, and New Jersey named their society after her. In 1975, Steward's grandson lobbied to have his grandmother honored by renaming a junior high school in Brooklyn for her, and it became known as the Susan Smith McKinney Junior High.

SELECTED WRITINGS BY STEWARD:

Periodicals

"Colored American Women," *The Crisis III,* (November 1911): 33-34.
"Marasmus Intantum," *Transaction of the Homeopathic Medical Society of the State of New York,* (1887): 150.

FURTHER READING:

Books

Lyons, Maritcha R. "Dr. Susan S. (McKinney) Steward," in *Homespun Heroes and Other Women of Distinction,* Hallie Quinn Brown, ed., Oxford University Press, 1988, pp. 160-64.

Periodicals

Alexander, Leslie A., "Susan Smith McKinney, M.D., 1846-1918: First Afro-American Physician in New York State," *National Medical Association Journal,* (March 1975): 173-75.
Seraile, William, "Susan McKinney Steward: New York State's First African-American Woman Physician," *Afro-Americans in N.Y. Life and History,* (July 1985): 27-44, reprinted in *Black Women in American History: From Colonial Times Through the Nineteenth Century,* Volume IV, Darlene Clark Hine, ed., Carlson Publishing, 1990, pp. 1217-34.

—Sketch by A. Petrusso

Albert Clifton Stewart
1919-
Chemist

During the early 1950s, Albert Clifton Stewart held a prominent role as a chemist at the Oak Ridge National Laboratory, a key nuclear research facility in eastern Tennessee. He later went to work for Union Carbide, a large chemical producer. Over the course of three decades, he held a number of significant positions with that company, most notably as its first black director of sales for the Chemical and Plastics Division. Stewart has also participated in a number of civic organizations, including the Oak Ridge Town Council, where he was the first black member.

Hardworking Student and Chemist

Albert Clifton Stewart was born in Detroit, Michigan on November 25, 1919, the son of Albert and Jeanne Kaiser Stewart. He attended the University of Chicago, where he obtained his B.S. degree in 1942. During the next decade, Stewart would intersperse periods of full-time employment with periods of progress on his postgraduate work, sometimes working while continuing his education. From 1943 to 1944, he worked as a chemist with the Sherwin-Williams Paint Company in Chicago; and in 1944, as the nation entered its third year of war with Germany and Japan, he joined the United States Naval Reserve as an officer. He would remain with the Reserve for the next 12 years.

In the mid-1940s, Stewart returned to the University of Chicago to pursue his master of science degree. From 1947 to 1949, he worked as an assistant in the university's inorganic chemistry department, and in 1948 received his degree. The following year, he married Colleen M. Hyland, and the couple moved to St. Louis, Missouri. There he began work on his doctorate in inorganic chemistry—that is, the area of chemistry dealing with compounds that do not contain carbon—at the University of St. Louis. During this time, he also taught chemistry courses and served as a research associate.

Stewart earned his Ph.D. degree in 1951 with a dissertation entitled *Reactions of Sodium Borohydride, Lithium-Aluminum-Hydride, and Lithium-Borohydride with Metal Ions.* An ion is an atom or group of atoms which has a net positive or negative charge, which it takes on by gaining or losing negatively charged electrons or positively charged protons. Stewart's doctoral work tested the response created by the use of ions with a variety of lightweight metallic compounds, several of them "reducing agents" used to negatively charge other compounds by adding electrons to them.

Senior Chemist at a Key Atomic Laboratory

After the completion of his doctoral studies, Stewart moved to Knoxville, Tennessee. The city is near Oak Ridge, a center for nuclear testing and research under the federal government's Atomic Energy Commission (AEC). In 1951 he became senior chemist at Oak Ridge National Laboratory, and though the AEC had other African American employees, Stewart was the first black Ph.D. to serve on its staff. He would continue to direct chemistry operations at the Oak Ridge lab for the next five years, until 1956.

During this period, Stewart found time for a number of activities outside his regular work. Starting in 1948 with *How to Invest in the Stock Market Successfully,* published while he was still in graduate school, Stewart presented a series of books on investment and the stock market, all published by a Detroit publishing house called Market Trend Survey. In 1951, he followed the first book with *Magic of Making Money in the Stock Market,* and in 1953 with *How Fortunes Are Made in Oil Stocks.*

Stewart also participated in the civic affairs of Oak Ridge, becoming in 1953 the first black member of its town council. It was an important post, given the unique situation of Oak Ridge—a town created by the federal government for its nuclear scientists during World War II—and the extremely high educational level of its average resident. He remained on the council until 1957.

While working as senior chemist at Oak Ridge, Stewart also taught chemistry and physics at Knoxville College from 1953 to 1956. In 1956, when a change of jobs took him north, he began lecturing at John Carroll University in Cleveland, Ohio, where he would continue for the next seven years.

Increasing Responsibilities and Honors

In 1956, Stewart took a job with Union Carbide, a large chemical firm. He started as group leader at its National Carbon Company Division Research Lab in Ohio, the first of many positions as he moved up within the company. His promotion to assistant director of research over the Consumer Products Division in 1960 gave him enormous responsibility over a wide array of household items produced by the company.

Stewart in 1963 became assistant development director, and during the mid-1960s his emphasis shifted from behind-the-scenes research to an increasing role in marketing. Thus in 1965 he switched to a position as planning manager in new market development, and in 1966 was placed in the position of market development management for the Chemical and Plastics Development Division.

While he was moving up the ladder at Union Carbide, Stewart also became involved in a number of significant outside activities, as he had done at Oak Ridge. He served as a consultant for the Ford Foundation, a prominent charitable organization, in 1963; and in the mid-1960s held two important consulting positions with the federal government, as administrative officer with the National Aeronautics and Space Administration (NASA) in 1963, and in the same role with the Agency for International Development (AID), which assists developing nations, from 1964 to 1969.

He also served with the Cleveland and New York Rotary clubs, as well as with the Urban League—as president of its Cleveland chapter—during the 1960s.

As the decade ended, Stewart took the role of market manager for rubber chemicals in Union Carbide's Market Area, and in 1971 was assigned as market manager for chemical coatings solvents. The mercurial Stewart made another shift in 1973, to international business manager for the Chemical and Plastics Division. Thus he held a high position within Union Carbide, a particularly notable fact given that he was a member of a minority group. In 1977 he became the first black director of sales for the Chemicals and Plastics Division, and in 1979 took the role of national sales manager over the Solvents and Intermediates Division. The year 1982 saw the last change of title in Stewart's quarter-century with Union Carbide, when he took a position as corporate director for university relations.

The university relations work led to a job switch in 1984, when Stewart left Union Carbide to become associate dean and professor of marketing at Western Connecticut State University. He continued, however, to consult with Union Carbide. In addition, his concerns over apartheid, a policy of institutionalized racism that prevailed in South Africa during the 1980s, led to his involvement with the Foundation for Social Justice in South Africa. He served as that organization's vice president from 1986 to 1993.

Stewart is a member of the American Academy of Arts and Sciences and the American Chemical Society, and from 1975 to 1980 served on the board of trustees for the New York Philharmonic. Among the awards he has received are alumni citations from St. Louis University in 1958 and from the University of Chicago in 1966. He received the Certificate of Merit from the Society of Chemical Professions in Cleveland in 1962, and holds two United States patents. He resides in Danbury, Connecticut.

SELECTED WRITINGS BY STEWART:

Books

How to Invest in the Stock Market Successfully. Detroit: Market Trend Survey, 1948.
Magic of Making Money in the Stock Market. Detroit: Market Trend Survey, 1951.
How Fortunes Are Made in Oil Stocks. Detroit: Market Trend Survey, 1953.

FURTHER READING:

Books

American Men & Women of Science, 20th edition. R. R. Bowker, 1994.
Spradling, Mary Mace, ed. *In Black and White.* Gale, 1980.

Sammons, Vivian Ovelton. *Blacks in Science and Medicine.* Hemisphere Publishing, 1990.

Who's Who Among African Americans, Ninth edition, 1996-1997. Gale, 1996.

Periodicals

Ebony, (July 1959): 7.
Jet, (September 9, 1965): 11.

—*Sketch by Judson Knight*

Gerald V. Stokes
1943-
Microbiologist

Gerald Stokes has been and continues to be a productive researcher in the fields of microbiology and immunology. His primary interest is in the study of the microbe *Chlamydia*, the organism responsible for many serious medical conditions including venereal diseases, eye infections, and some forms of pneumonia. Stokes hopes his research will lead to the discovery of an effective vaccine against these diseases.

Gerald was born on March 25, 1943, in Chicago, Illinois. He grew up in the small suburb of Argo, an industrial community with a large starch factory, but which also had farmlands and wooded areas where Gerald could explore the natural world.

Although his parents divorced when he was young, Gerald remained part of a closely knit extended family including both sets of grandparents, his mother and her second husband, and six younger brothers and sisters. Although none of the adult family members had finished high school, Gerald's family instilled in him the importance of education and encouraged him to obtain as much schooling as possible. He began at Argo Elementary School, where he soon developed an interest in science thanks to fascinating science projects at school, science programs on television, and explorations of nature near his home.

Gerald went to Graves Junior High School in Argo, where he was forced to sit in the back rows with the other African American students. He had problems seeing the blackboard, and began to fall behind in his classwork. Finally, the school nurse had his eyesight examined, and discovered that he needed glasses. Once he got glasses, he began to do well in classes.

Gerald's interest in science continued through high school, where imaginative and enthusiastic teachers helped convince him to go to college. He received excellent grades, and became a member of the National Honor Society. He earned money to pay for college by working at the local grocery store while in high school.

Stokes enrolled in the University of Illinois in Urbana, but did not like the university's large classes and impersonal conditions. After less than a year he returned home to work at the starch factory, saving his money for another try at college. After a year of working and saving, he enrolled at Wilson Junior High School in Chicago, where he earned an associate of arts degree. He then enrolled in Southern Illinois University in Carbondale, which had a smaller enrollment than the Urbana campus. He did well at SIU and received a degree in chemistry in 1967.

Stokes was offered a job at the Clinical Microbiology Laboratory at the University of Chicago. Thanks to this connection with the university, he was asked to apply to the graduate program in microbiology and was given a full scholarship. Here he began his study of the *Chlamydia* microbe. He discovered a way to detect early growth of *Chlamydia* colonies, enabling scientists everywhere to more easily grow the organism in laboratories for scientific studies. He received his Ph.D in 1973, the same year he married Charlotte Eubanks, a history graduate student at the university.

After a three year post-doctoral appointment at the University of Colorado, Stokes joined the faculty at Meharry Medical College in Nashville, Tennessee. In 1978, he accepted a position as assistant professor at the George Washington University School of Medicine in Washington, D.C., where he continues his study of *Chlamydia.*

In addition to his research, Stokes actively recruits African American students to the study of microbiology. He has launched a nationwide outreach program to these students through the American Society for Microbiology. Thus, his work has been beneficial not only to the scientific community, but to the African American community as well.

FURTHER READING:

Kessler, James H., J. S. Kidd, Renée A. Kidd, and Katherine A. Morin. "Gerald V. Stokes" In *Distinguished African American Scientists of the 20th Century.* Phoenix: The Oryx Press, 1996.

—*Sketch by David E. Fontes*

Beauregard Stubblefield
1923-
Mathematician

Beauregard Stubblefield has focused his research in mathematics on topology—the study of the transformation of geometric figures. He has written textbooks on geometry, trigonometry, and computer programming. While teaching at colleges in the United States and Liberia, Stubblefield has also worked to inspire and educate black mathematicians.

Stubblefield was born in Navasota, Texas, on July 31, 1923. He earned a bachelor of science degree from Prairie View A & M College in 1943 and a master's degree there in 1945. Stubblefield then entered the graduate program at the University of Michigan, earning a master of science degree in 1951. While still a doctoral student, he became a U.S. Department of State exchange professor, and in 1952 he went to work as professor and head of the mathematics department at the University of Liberia, in Monrovia, Liberia. He taught in West Africa for four years. Stubblefield returned to the United States, and in 1957 he began work as a research mathematician at the Detroit Arsenal. Stubblefield studied at the University of Michigan as he worked, and he earned a doctoral degree in mathematics in 1959. His dissertation was entitled, "Some Compact Product Spaces Which Cannot Be Imbedded in Euclidean n-Space."

That same year, Stubblefield won a prestigious National Science Foundation fellowship. He stayed at the University of Michigan until 1960, when he became an assistant professor at the Stevens Institute of Technology. In 1961, he went on to work as an associate professor at Oakland University, in Rochester, Michigan. Stubblefield taught at Oakland University until he took a leave in 1967 to return to Prairie View A & M College as a senior national teaching fellow. From 1968-69 he was a visiting professor and scholar at Texas Southern University. During the 1960s, Stubblefield produced a number of books and articles on geometric subjects. He published a book on computer programming in 1969. In 1971, Stubblefield began an appointment at Appalachian State University as a professor of mathematics. From 1976-85, he worked as a mathematician at the National Oceanic and Atmospheric Administration Environmental Research Laboratory.

Stubblefield demonstrated an interest in the process and the goals of education throughout his career. He worked as the director of the mathematics portion of the Thirteen-College Curriculum Program from 1969-71. Stubblefield served as a member of various educational committees, including a national committee for the training of elementary school teachers in mathematics. He wrote *An Intuitive Approach to Elementary Geometry,* published in 1969. He was also very active in the Mathematical Association of America's Michigan section. He served on the North

Carolina Council of Teachers of Mathematics in 1972. In 1972, he was named Outstanding Educator of America for 1972. By 1980, he had worked with Virginia K. Newell, Joella H. Gipson, and L. Waldo Rich to edit *Black Mathematicians and Their Works,* a book which allows young people a look at the careers and contributions of black math scholars.

SELECTED WRITINGS BY STUBBLEFIELD:

Books

An Intuitive Approach to Elementary Geometry. Cole Company, The Books, 1969.
Base Numeration Systems and Introduction to Computer Programming 1. Newton, MA: Curriculum Resources Group, 1969.
Number Systems and Elements of Geometry. Belmont, CA: Wadsworth, 1971.
(with Virginia K. Newell, Joella H. Gipson, and L. Waldo Rich, eds.) *Black Mathematicians and Their Works.* Ardmore, PA: Dorrance & Company, 1980.

Periodicals

"Primitive Skew Curves as Factors of Certain Compact Product Spaces in n-Manifolds." *Notices* (April, 1961).
"The Number of Topologies on a Set of Eight Elements."*Communications of the Association for Computing Machinery* (1973).

FURTHER READING:

Books

American Men & Women of Science. 19th edition. New Providence, NJ: R.R. Bowker Company, 1994, p. 1350.
Sammons, Vivian Ovelton. *Blacks in Science and Medicine.* New York: Hemisphere, 1990, p. 222.

—*Sketch by R. Garcia-Johnson*

Niara Sudarkasa
1938-
Anthropologist

Niara Sudarkasa is a renowned anthropologist who has devoted much of her career to comparative studies of traditions among Africans and the descendants of Africans in the New World. In 1987, she became the first female president of Lincoln University in Pennsylvania, one of the nation's oldest black institutions of higher learning.

Turning Point in Africa

Niara Sudarkasa was born Gloria Marshall in Fort Lauderdale, Florida, on August 14, 1938. Her grandparents, who raised her, came from the Bahamas, and she grew up thinking of herself as a West Indian rather than an American. Extremely precocious, she enrolled at Fisk University in 1953, when she was just 15 years old. Three years later, in 1956, she switched to Oberlin College, and in 1957—still only 19—she earned her bachelor's degree in sociology.

Many years later, Sudarkasa told *Ebony* magazine, which was interviewing a number of luminaries about "The Turning Point" in their lives, that her experience at these two schools was pivotal: "I didn't even know what anthropology was before I went to Fisk," she said, "and had never studied it very much at all until I went to Oberlin." Her time at Fisk, she said, contributed much to her later career as president of Lincoln University because it gave her a first-hand awareness of the value of attending a predominantly black college.

Other pivotal experiences were to follow. At Oberlin, she had discovered a link between customs among the Yoruba people of Africa, and savings and lending practices employed by her Caribbean relatives. This inspired in her a fascination with comparative cultures that would eventually take her to Africa, but before that could happen, she earned her doctorate at Columbia University in New York City in 1964. A teaching position at New York University followed, then in 1967 she became a member of the University of Michigan faculty.

During the 1970s Sudarkasa, who up to that time still went by the name of Gloria Marshall, visited Africa. Her experience there was another turning point, and she found herself captivated by the similarities between the customs of the Yoruba and those of the Afro-Caribbean community in which she had grown up. Africa offered to her a sense of ethnic rootedness, of cultural identity, and she resolved to take an African name. It was then that she became Niara (which means "woman of high purposes" in Swahili) Sudarkasa.

First Female President of Lincoln University

Sudarkasa became the first black woman to receive tenure—that is, a contract guaranteeing a long-term commitment of employment—from the University of Michigan. In the late 1970s, she was appointed associate vice president for academic affairs. Then in 1987, Lincoln University in Pennsylvania selected her as its eleventh president.

Lincoln, one of the oldest African American institutions of higher learning, had an extremely distinguished record, counting among its graduates a head of state, Kwame Nkrumah of Ghana; a Supreme Court Justice,

Thurgood Marshall; and a renowned poet, Langston Hughes. For much of its history, Lincoln had been a males-only school, which made Sudarkasa's selection as president a particular distinction.

Sudarkasa has proven a popular administrator with students, who have nicknamed her "Madame President." In 1991, she established her independence from the African American mainstream when she supported the nomination of Clarence Thomas—a controversial figure because of his conservative views—to take a seat on the Supreme Court. As for her role at Lincoln, Sudarkasa has worked to make it an outstanding institution not merely in comparison to other predominantly black schools, but to the top liberal arts institutions in the country. "Unless a sense of service and duty is instilled," she once told *Essence* magazine, "our upward mobility [as African Americans] will only be measured by cars and styling."

Among the professional groups to which Sudarkasa belongs are the African Studies Association, the American Anthropology Association (of which she is a fellow), the Association of Black Anthropologists, and the American Association for Higher Education. A member of the Council on Foreign Relations as well as 20 state and national boards, in the late 1990s she was one of five Americans appointed by President Bill Clinton to represent the United States on the 15-member Trilateral Task Force on Educational Collaboration that included representatives from Mexico and Canada.

Sudarkasa's awards include a Ford Foundation scholarship for early college admission (1953-57), a John Hay Whitney Opportunities fellowship (1959-60), a Ford Foundation Foreign Area Training fellowship (1960-63), a Carnegie Foundation Study of New Nation fellowship (1963-64), a Social Science Research Council fellowship (1973-74), a senior Fulbright research scholarship (1982-83), 12 honorary degrees, and awards from Alpha Kappa Alpha, Zeta Phi Beta, the Elks Club, Links, and the City of Fort Lauderdale, Florida. She has published numerous books and articles.

Sudarkasa is married to John L. Clark, an inventor, sculptor, and contractor. Their son Michael has followed somewhat in his mother's career path, at least as regards her interest in African affairs. After earning a law degree from Harvard University, he took an internship with the African Development Bank of the Ivory Coast.

SELECTED WRITINGS BY SUDARKASA:

Books

Where Women Work: A Study of Yoruba Women in the Marketplace and in the Home. University of Michigan, 1973.

(Guest editor) *Migrants and Strangers in Africa.* Michigan State University, 1975.

Can We Afford Equity and Excellence? Can We Afford Less? Lincoln University, 1989.

Success Speaks for Itself: The Legacy and Promise of Historically Black Colleges and Universities. Bethune-DuBois Foundation, 1991.

Quality Teaching Is Judged By What We Teach, Not Just How Well. Teaching Education, 1991.

(Editor, with others) *Exploring the African-American Experience.* HarperCollins, 1994.

The Strength of Our Mothers: African and American Women and Families: Essays and Speeches. Africa World Press, 1996.

Periodicals

"Racial and Cultural Diversity Is a Key Part of the Pursuit of Excellence in the University," *Chronicle of Higher Education,* (February 25, 1987): 42.

"All 117 Black Colleges and Universities Require Dramatic New Levels of Philanthropic Support," *Chronicle of Higher Education,* (March 28, 1990): B1-B3.

"Don't Write off Thomas," *Black Scholar,* (Winter 1991): 99-102.

"Absent! Black Men on Campus," *Essence,* (November 1991): 140.

FURTHER READING:

Books

African American Biography, vol. 4, S-Z. UXL, 1994.

Contemporary Black Biography, vol. 4. Gale, 1993.

Hine, Darlene Clark, ed. *Black Women in America.* Carlson Publishing, 1993.

Smith, Jessie Carnie. *Notable Black American Women,* Book I. Gale, 1992.

Periodicals

McKinney, Rhoda E., "Lincoln University Appoints First Female President," *Ebony,* (February 1988): 86.

"The Turning Point: Notables Talk About Events That Changed Their Lives," *Ebony,* (May 1996): 83-86.

Washington, Elsie B., "Niara Sudarkasa: Educator for the 1990s," *Essence,* (May 1989): 106-108.

Other

"Niara Sudarkasa." *AED.* http://www.aed.org/more/sudarkasa.html (11 May 1998).

—*Sketch by Judson Knight*

Louis Wade Sullivan

Louis Wade Sullivan
1933-
Hematologist

Louis Wade Sullivan is most widely known as the Secretary of the Department of Health and Human Services of President George Bush's cabinet (1989-92). His term in office was only the most visible part of a career dedicated to the health of all people, especially that of African Americans. As a physician, a researcher of blood disorders, and as president of Morehouse Medical School in Atlanta, Georgia, Sullivan has sought to improve the health of minorities and the poor both in the United States and abroad.

Louis Wade Sullivan was born on November 3, 1933, in Atlanta, Georgia. His father, Walter Wade Sullivan, was an insurance salesman and undertaker, and his mother, Lubirda Elizabeth Priester Sullivan, was a school teacher. Because of the difficult economic times during the Great Depression, his parents moved to a farming community in rural Georgia. Educational opportunities for African Americans were very limited there, so Sullivan attended school through fifth grade while staying with relatives in Savannah, Georgia. He and his brother then lived in a rooming house in Atlanta to complete high school. Sullivan graduated at the top of his class.

These early years were very influential on Sullivan. His eighth grade teacher, Laura Woods, was one of many teachers who encouraged and challenged Sullivan to pursue his interest in science. His parents were a tremendous support and always encouraged his ideas. They were role models, giving him a strong sense of self-discipline. They taught him to treat others fairly and to always strive for personal integrity. He stated in a telephone interview with Dónal O'Mathúna, conducted May 9, 1998, that "Shortcuts only cheat yourself; they don't allow you to develop all your capabilities."

After high school, Sullivan remained in Atlanta to attend Morehouse College. Benjamin E. Mays was the President at the time, and became an important mentor for Sullivan, as he has been for many others who attended Morehouse. Sullivan graduated with a B.S. from the premedical program (1954) and received a scholarship to attend medical school at Boston University. Being the only African American in his class, and one of only three at the university, Sullivan was apprehensive about attending this integrated college, especially because of negative experiences he had in the segregated south. However, he was warmly received and treated very well, which left a lasting impression on him of how society could be truly integrated. He married Eva Williamson in 1955, and they later became parents to two boys and one girl. Sullivan was awarded the M.D. degree (*cum laude*) in 1958, third in his class.

Sullivan completed his three years of internship and residency at Cornell University Medical Center in New York City, where he developed his interest in pathology, the study of the causes of diseases. He focused on diseases of the blood, in particular, anemia and the role of vitamin B_{12} in the production of blood platelets. He discovered that alcohol in the blood interferes with this process, leading to lower red blood cell levels. Heavy drinkers are thus at higher risk for acute anemia, but Sullivan also found that this can be reversed by stopping alcohol consumption and taking vitamin B_{12}.

This early research was conducted by Sullivan at Massachusetts General Hospital in Boston (1960-1961) and at Harvard Medical School (1961-1963). He joined the faculty at New Jersey College of Medicine in Newark (1964-1966) and later moved to Boston University (1966-1977). In the midst of a very successful career as teacher and researcher, Sullivan was asked to join a committee investigating the possibility of starting a medical school at Morehouse College. He became intrigued by the project, initiated in response to the poorer health of the African American community in Georgia. There was also a significant shortage of African American physicians serving their communities. Sullivan remembered his father's example of always trying to find ways to improve life for his black community. In 1977, Sullivan became the Dean and President of Morehouse Medical School, a position he still holds.

A Scientist Moves into Politics

Sullivan's fund-raising activities for Morehouse Medical School brought him into contact with many politicians. The school did not have a major foundation funding it, so significant funds were raised from the state and federal governments. In 1982, Sullivan invited then Vice-President George Bush and his wife, Barbara, to the dedication ceremony of a building funded to a large extent by federal funds. Mrs. Bush was so impressed by the medical school that she became one of its trustees. Later that year, Vice-President Bush invited Sullivan to accompany him on a trip to Africa to examine health-care needs there. Over the years, Sullivan and Bush became friends, with Sullivan acting as an unofficial advisor on health matters.

When George Bush was elected President in 1988, he nominated Sullivan to be Secretary of the Department of Health and Human Services. Upon confirmation, Sullivan took office at a time when AIDS (acquired immune deficiency syndrome) was on the increase, as was the incidence of tuberculosis among the poor. He also worked diligently to try to ban smoking in all federal facilities. Although he never achieved this goal, he is encouraged to see recent developments aimed at reducing smoking.

While few scientists involve themselves deeply in politics, Sullivan sees this as a potential problem. Public understanding of science is often lacking, leading to questions about levels of public investment. Scientists themselves are best able to explain the significance of scientific discoveries so that the public can appreciate the benefits of science. They can also ensure that legislation appropriately benefits and protects science and society. While science has been strongly supported by the public and the government, its costs and the ethical quandaries it generates (such as with human cloning or medical research) make it imperative that some scientists become politicians. As Sullivan stated, "If scientists don't get involved in the political process, it will be to the detriment of science."

Sullivan's career in medical research and education has focused on issues particularly relevant to the African American community. Many areas remain to be addressed more fully. One of the most important issues needing attention is the improved understanding of human behavior and habits. While biomedical research has made great strides in recent decades, much remains to be learned, especially in areas related to how people make health-related decisions. In spite of everything known about the adverse effects of tobacco, drugs, and high-speed driving, many people still choose those high-risk behaviors. Although much is known about the benefits of prenatal care and proper nutrition, many do not choose to take advantage of them. Learning more about how to appropriately influence people's decisions could dramatically improve people's health. The high incidence of preventable injuries and deaths among minorities and the poor makes these issues especially relevant to African Americans. While Sullivan has contributed greatly to progress in these areas, much remains to be done.

SELECTED WRITINGS BY SULLIVAN:

Books

The Education of Black Health Professionals, 1977.
*Healing America's Wounds: One Man's Journey
    Through Race Health,* Rowman Littlefield, 1997.

Periodicals

"Minority Student Recruitment: The Challenge and the
    Obligation," *Journal of Dental Education,* Vol. 59,
    (June 1995): 641-644.
"Health Promotion and Disease Prevention," *Medical
    Education,* Vol. 26, (May 1992): 175-177.

FURTHER READING:

Books

American Men and Women of Science 1998-99. New
    Providence, NJ: R. R. Bowker. 20th Edition. Vol-
    ume 6, p. 1366.
Kessler, James H., J. S. Kidd, Renée A. Kidd, Kathe-
    rine A. Morin. *Distinguished African American Sci-
    entists of the 20th Century.* Phoenix, AZ: Oryx
    Press, 1996, pp. 304-307.
Sammons, Vivian Ovelton. *Blacks in Science and Medi-
    cine.* Taylor and Francis, 1990, p. 224.

Other

Who Shall Be Healed? The Fred Friendly Seminars,
    Graduate School of Journalism, Columbia Universi-
    ty, 1994. PBS Videocassette.

—Sketch by Dónal P. O'Mathúna

Julius Henry Taylor
1914-
Physicist

Physicist Julius H. Taylor has taught and done research at a number of institutions, including the University of Pennsylvania and Morgan State College (later University) in Baltimore, Maryland. In addition to his work as an educator, he is known for his research in solid-state physics, his efforts in space-flight development for NASA, and for the 1955 book *The Negro in Science*, which he edited.

Wartime Solid-State Research

Julius Henry Taylor was born on February 15, 1914, in Cape May, New Jersey. He earned his B.A. degree at Lincoln University in Pennsylvania in 1939, when he was 25 years old. Two years later, in 1941, he received his M.S. from the University of Pennsylvania in Philadelphia.

During World War II, Taylor worked as a research assistant at the University of Pennsylvania, a position he held until 1945. The term for Taylor's area of specialty, solid-state physics, would not even be coined until 1951; as for the name itself, it describes a branch of science dealing with the properties of solid metals with regard to conducting electricity. Solid-state physicists study the structure and reactivity of a solid material, especially the behavior of ions, molecules, nucleons, and electrons within it. They work with crystals and explore the effects of imperfections on solid substances.

While he was at the University of Pennsylvania, during the year from 1943 to 1944, Taylor held a Rosenwald fellowship. In 1945 he became a physics professor at West Virginia State College in Institute, West Virginia. From 1947 to 1949, he returned to the University of Pennsylvania as a research physicist. Meanwhile, he continued to work on his Ph.D. degree, which he would earn from Pennsylvania in 1950. Taylor's dissertation concerned the properties of germanium, a semi-metallic element with qualities similar to those of silicon. First isolated in 1886, germanium would later be used for optical instruments, and as a semiconductor in transistors.

Work in Explosives and Rocketry

In 1949, Taylor became a professor of physics at Morgan State College (later renamed Morgan State Univer-

sity) in Baltimore, Maryland. The following year, he was named chairman of the department, a position he would hold for the next quarter-century. In 1953, he received a research award from the Army's Office of Ordnance Research, which explored developments in explosives. Taylor continued to receive the research award for each year through 1957.

In 1955, Taylor served as editor for a notable historical work on African-American contributions to scientific knowledge, *The Negro in Science*. Twenty-four years after his graduation from college, in 1963, Lincoln University made him its Alumnus of the Year. Taylor left Morgan University in 1978, when NASA, the National Aeronautics and Space Administration, awarded him a contract at their Goddard Space Flight Center.

Taylor is married to Patricia Spaulding, and they have two children, Dwight and Trena. The Taylors live in Baltimore. He is or has been a member of the American Physical Society, the American Institute of Physics, Beta Kappa Chi, the Chesapeake American Association of Physics Teachers (president, 1962-63), the Governor's Science Advisory Council, the National Committee of Physics in Secondary Education of the American Association of Physics Teachers, the National Institute of Science, the National Science Foundation, Sigma Chi, the Society of Physics Students (zone councillor), and the Travelers Aid Society.

SELECTED WRITINGS BY TAYLOR:

Books

(Editor) *The Negro in Science*. Morgan State College Press, 1955.

FURTHER READING:

Books

American Men & Women of Science. R. R. Bowker, 1979.

Spradling, Mary Mace, ed. *In Black and White*. Gale, 1980.

Sammons, Vivian Ovelton. *Blacks in Science and Medicine*. Hemisphere Publishing, 1990.

—Sketch by Judson Knight

Moddie Taylor
1912-1976
Chemist

Moddie Taylor gained distinction early in his career as an associate chemist on the U.S. Manhattan Project, which led to the development of the atomic bomb during World War II. A chemistry professor at Lincoln and later Howard universities, Taylor published a chemistry textbook in 1960 and served as head of the chemistry department at Howard from 1969 to 1976.

Moddie Daniel Taylor was born in Nymph, Alabama, on March 3, 1912, the son of Herbert L. Taylor and Celeste (Oliver) Taylor. His father worked as a postal clerk in St. Louis, Missouri, and it was there that Taylor went to school, graduating from the Charles H. Sumner High School in 1931. He then attended Lincoln University in Jefferson City, Missouri, and graduated with a B.S. in chemistry in 1935 as valedictorian and as a *summa cum laude* student. He began his teaching career in 1935, working as an instructor until 1939 and then as an assistant professor from 1939 to 1941 at Lincoln University, while also enrolled in the University of Chicago's graduate program in chemistry. He received his M.S. in 1939 and his Ph.D. in 1943. Taylor married Vivian Ellis on September 8, 1937, and they had one son, Herbert Moddie Taylor.

Joins Manhattan Project Team

It was during 1945 that Taylor began his two years as an associate chemist for the top-secret Manhattan Project based at the University of Chicago. Taylor's research interest was in rare earth metals (elements which are the products of oxidized metals and which have special properties and several important industrial uses); his chemical contributions to the nation's atomic energy research earned him a Certificate of Merit from the Secretary of War. After the war, he returned to Lincoln University until 1948 when he joined Howard University as an associate professor of chemistry, becoming a full professor in 1959 and head of the chemistry department in 1969.

In 1960, Taylor's *First Principles of Chemistry* was published; also in that year he was selected by the Manufacturing Chemists Association as one of the nation's six top college chemistry teachers. In 1972, Taylor was also awarded an Honor Scroll from the Washington Institute of Chemists for his contributions to research and teaching. Taylor was a member of the American Chemical Society, the American Association for the Advancement of Science, the National Institute of Science, the American Society for Testing Materials, the New York Academy of Sciences, Sigma Xi, and Beta Kappa Chi, and was a fellow of the American Institute of Chemists and the Washington Academy for the Advancement of Science. Taylor retired as a professor emeritus of chemistry from Howard University on April 1, 1976, and died of cancer in Washington, D.C., on September 15, 1976.

SELECTED WRITINGS BY TAYLOR:

Books

First Principles of Chemistry. Van Nostrand, 1960, revised edition, 1976.

FURTHER READING:

Books

Sammons, Vivian O. *Blacks in Science and Medicine.* Hemisphere, 1990, p. 227.

Periodicals

Jet, (May 26, 1960): 19.
Washington Post, (obituary), (September 18, 1976): D6.

—*Sketch by Leonard C. Bruno*

Welton Ivan Taylor
1919-
Microbiologist

The detection of diseases in the food supply and the treatment of food-borne infections have made great strides in the last century thanks to Welton Ivan Taylor. His scientific contributions have helped ensure the safety of America's foods.

Taylor was born November 12, 1919, in Birmingham, Alabama, to Cora Lee Brewer and Frederick Enslen Taylor. Soon after he was born, his family moved to Chicago. His interest in biology was sparked when, in the late 1920s, a neighbor friend found some snakes in the yard. Taylor was the only boy who didn't run—snakes were a curiosity, not creatures to be feared. Thus began his lifelong interest in biology and living creatures.

The stock market crash of 1929 and the ensuing economic depression left little hope of employment in Chicago, so in 1930 the Taylor family moved to Peoria, Illinois. It was here that Taylor's curiosity about living things blossomed. He found and learned about fossils, insects, butterflies, and moths. He captured and observed many different creatures. Particularly interesting were the butterflies—he learned about their entire life cycle by observing the transformation from caterpillars to chrysalis and finally to adults.

In 1936 the Taylor family moved back to Chicago to enjoy the improved economic times. He graduated from high school at the top of his class. Because of his excellence in school, he was sponsored by some successful Chicago-area African Americans; they helped pay for Taylor's college education at the University of Illinois. Although the sponsorship covered most of Taylor's financial responsibilities, he still had to work. One of his unique employment opportunities was the classification and preservation of poison ivy. Taylor was uniquely qualified for this, since he was lucky enough to be immune to the plant's effects on human skin.

Taylor graduated from the University of Illinois in 1941 with a degree in bacteriology. He joined the U.S. Army Reserve Officer Training Program at the university, so after graduation, he was sent to active military duty at Fort Sill, Oklahoma. At this time, the United States was getting involved in the war in Europe and the Pacific war was about to begin.

Although his poor eyesight disqualified Taylor serving as a pilot when he entered the Army in 1941, the regulations were relaxed in 1943 due to the pilot shortage. Since his eyesight was fully correctable with glasses, he became an Army spotter pilot, and was part of the first all-black division in combat in the war. When he was off-duty, the jungles around the army bases in the Pacific provided superb opportunities for studying a variety of insects.

After the war, Taylor took advantage of the GI Bill to earn his master's degree in 1947 and his doctorate degree in 1948 from the University of Illinois. It was during his doctoral research that he focused on the study of microbes that cause food-borne illnesses, particularly botulism, one of the most deadly causes of food poisoning.

He found a position with the University of Illinois Medical School in Chicago as a bacteriology instructor in 1948 and was promoted to assistant professor in 1950. In this position he was able to direct students working toward their advanced degrees in bacteriology. He developed new treatments for tetanus and gangrene, combining conventional treatment methods with new antibiotics and analgesics.

Because of his work with food-borne pathogens, Taylor was asked to join Swift and Company, a meat packing firm, as a microbiologist to help keep their products safe for humans. He worked there for five years before going back into academics at the Children's Memorial Hospital in Chicago. He also took positions at Northwestern University's School of Medicine, the World Health Organization, the Pasteur Institute in France, and the Colindale Central Public Health Laboratories in England. To fulfill his many obligations, he was able to take many overseas trips, oftentimes taking his family with him.

In 1964 he returned to the University of Illinois as a professor, and in 1965 Taylor developed a revolutionary method to detect various bacteria that cause food-borne illnesses. As the 1970s approached, Taylor's detection methods became standard practice in the Food and Drug Administration's food inspection process. Today these tests have become standard all across the globe. Because of his expertise, Taylor found himself doing work as a consultant and expert witness, dealing with microbiological and bacteriological issues.

Taylor is a member in many organizations, including the American Association of Bioanalysts and the Chicago Medical Mycological Society. In 1961 Taylor was the founding chairman of the Chicago Chapter of the Episcopal Society for Cultural and Racial Equality. He has been honored with numerous awards related to his research, including the Alumni Achievement Award given by the University of Illinois and the Pasteur Award from the Illinois Microbiology Society. In 1985 a new species of bacterium was named *Enterobacter taylorae* in honor of Taylor's achievements in bacteriology.

Taylor married Jayne Rowena Kemp in 1945 and has two children, Karyn and Shelley.

FURTHER READING:

Jaques Cattell Press, ed. *American Men & Women of Science, Physical and Biological Sciences*, 15th Edition, Volume VII. New York: R.R. Bowker Company, 1982, p. 47.

Kessler, James H., et.al. *Distinguished African American Scientists of the 20th Century.* Oryx Press, 1996, pp. 307-311.

Phelps, Shirelle. *Who's Who Among African Americans, 1998-99.* Gale Research, 1998, p. 1,462.

—Sketch by Roger Jaffe

Lewis Temple
1800-1854
Inventor

Lewis Temple, an illiterate metalsmith in Massachusetts, improved the whaling harpoon. His invention, called the "Temple Toggle," revolutionized the whaling industry, since there had been no harpoon refinements in several centuries before him. Temple never patented his invention, and it was immediately copied by other smiths. Though his financial benefit was indirect, Temple's fortunes did improve because of his toggle.

Temple was born in Richmond, Virginia, in 1800. There is little information on his early life until he came to New Bedford, Massachusetts, a significant port for whaling in the United States. While living in New Bedford in 1829, he married Mary Clark, and subsequently had three children with her, Lewis, Jr., Nancy, and Mary.

Temple worked as a blacksmith and metalsmith, and was apparently somewhat prosperous even before his invention. He ran a whalecraft shop in New Bedford on Coffins Wharf by 1836. Within nine years, Temple owned his own smithy on the Walnut Street Wharf. It was here that he invented the Temple Toggle, also known as the Temple Iron or Temple's Iron, in 1848.

Before Temple's invention, whaling harpoons had small arrow-shaped heads, from which the animals could easily free themselves. Temple improved the harpoon used to spear whales by adding a toggle to its head with lines that would stay attached and hinder the animal's escape. Temple's toggle had a barbed head that could pivot and a pin that broke upon entering the whale's body, securing the harpoon within it. Temple's invention was apparently responsible for doubling the number of whales caught in the United States and became the standard around the world.

Temple prospered for several years after his invention, though because the invention went unpatented, he was not its only manufacturer. Indeed, between 1848 and 1868, one of Temple's business rivals, one James Durfee, made 13,000 of them. By 1852, Temple opened a larger smithy next to his home. There is also record of Temple's civic activity in this period, as he signed a petition supporting temperance in 1853. However, in the fall of 1853, Temple suffered an accident, tripping on a plank left by a careless city employee who was building a sewer. Temple sued the city, and $2000 was promised to him as compensation in March 1854.

By 1854, Temple began building an even larger blacksmith shop in New Bedford's Steamboat Wharf. However, this smithy went unfinished because Temple died in May 1854 from complications related to the accident. His family never received the compensation promised to him by the city. The city of New Bedford eventually built a statue honoring Temple, which stands outside the Public Library.

FURTHER READING:

Books

Hayden, Robert. *Eight Black American Inventors,* Addison-Wesley, 1972, pp. 32-43.

Periodicals

Kaplan, Sidney, "Lewis Temple and the Hunting of the Whale," *Negro History Bulletin,* (October 1953): 7-10.

—Sketch by A. Petrusso

Hubert Mach Thaxton
1912-1974
Theoretical physicist

Hubert Thaxton did pioneering work in theoretical nuclear physics, performing research that helped explain the forces that hold atomic nuclei together. A teacher of both physics and mathematics, he also did applied research in acoustics and electronics.

Hubert Mach Thaxton was born in Virginia on December 28, 1912. He attended Howard University, earning his bachelor of science degree in 1931, when he was only 18 years old. He earned an master of science degree from Howard in 1933, for a thesis entitled "The Reflecting Power of Mercury." Thaxton then entered the graduate program in physics at the University of Wisconsin, where he earned an master's degree in 1936 and a doctoral degree in 1939. His dissertation was entitled "Scattering of Protons by Protons."

Performs Research in Nuclear Physics

Thaxton's doctoral dissertation and the majority of his early scientific work was in the area of theoretical nuclear physics. His work addressed an important question about how nuclear forces bind protons and neutrons into the nucleus of the atom. Electrical forces between positively charged protons should cause them to repel each other; yet in the atomic nucleus, protons exist very close together. At the very close range of the atomic nucleus, the strong nuclear force that attracts protons is more powerful than this repulsive electrical force. Yet over a distance larger than the size of the nucleus, this strong nuclear force must be insignificant—otherwise, atoms would be overcome by the strong nuclear attraction and crunch into each other. Electrical and gravitational forces have a simple mathematical dependence on distance, that is, the force decreases with the square of the distance. Nuclear forces, on the other hand, have a much more complex dependence on distance and other factors. Thaxton addressed this problem of dependence.

To find this dependence, nuclear physicists perform scattering experiments. They accelerate subatomic particles, protons in the case of Thaxton's work, to a high energy and aim them at target particles. In Thaxton's work, the targets were either protons or neutrons. By studying the scattering of the particles after the collisions, physicists can deduce the forces acting between the particles. The collisions are actually near misses, in which the distance of closest approach is related to the type of interaction and to the energy, and therefore speed, of the incoming particle. Hence, the work must be done for a wide range of different interactions and energies. Because this work requires both elaborate experiments and difficult mathematical calculations, there is a division of labor between theoretical and experimental physicists. Thaxton did the theoretical work. He performed the detailed calculations needed to deduce the nature of the strong nuclear forces. Comparing the results of experiments and calculations for a wide variety of energies and possible strong nuclear-force laws provides insight into the nature of the strong nuclear forces. Thaxton's work with proton-proton and with proton-neutron scattering contributed to our current understanding of the strong nuclear force that binds the nuclei of atoms together.

Works in Industry and Struggles Against Discrimination

After earning his doctorate, Thaxton became professor of physics and head of the physics department at the Agricultural and Technical College of North Carolina (now North Carolina Agricultural and Technical State University) in Greensboro. In 1945, he left North Carolina for New York City, where he was hired as a lecturer in mathematics in the evening division of the City College of New York. Thaxton worked concurrently for various companies, performing physics research with industrial applications. His employers included International Electronics, the Solar Manufacturing Company, Sperry Gyroscope Company, Tube Deutschmann Corporation, Sylvania Electronic Company, and various divisions of Englehard Hanover Incorporated and Englehard Industries Incorporated. Thaxton also taught at Walter Henry Junior College.

Thaxton held his position the City College of New York until 1969, when he was denied tenure. He charged the college with denying him tenure because of his race. According to *The New York Times,* a hearing on this issue was held at the New York State Division of Human Rights on September 23, 1969. Thaxton's lawyer stated that in 1945 Thaxton had been hired as a lecturer, which is generally a low academic rank, and that he had not been promoted in over 20 years. City College claimed that Thaxton was not qualified to teach advanced mathematics courses. The college then offered to grant him tenure if he would take a mathematics competency exam. Thaxton refused. He argued that he should not be required to take a competency exam unless all the other faculty in the department were also required to take a similar exam. He felt that his advanced degrees and his original publications should be considered evidence of his competence.

Thaxton's work in nuclear physics came to an end after the mid-1940s. Much of his later work was of a directly applied nature. This applied work included research in optics, acoustics, and electronics. D.A. Edwards, a colleague of Thaxton's during the 1940s, recalled that Thaxton had designed a type of circular slide rule, which would have been a valuable computational aid in the days before calculators. Thaxton authored a number of publications, including one with A. S. Eddington, the prominent British astrophysicist. It is not known whether Thaxton was ever married.

SELECTED WRITINGS BY THAXTON:

Periodicals

(with G. Breit and L. Eisenbud) "Analysis of Experiments on the Scattering of Protons by Protons." *The Physical Review* 55 (June 1, 1939): 1018.

(with O.L. Gallagher) "Increasing Bandwidth of Ultrasonic Radiators." *Electronics* 35 (July 6, 1962): 60.

(with A.S. Eddington) "On the Interaction Potential in the Scattering of Protons by Protons." *Physica* 7 (February, 1940): 122.

(with G. Breit and C. Kittel) "Note on p-Wave Anomalies in Proton-Proton Scattering." *The Physical Review* 57 (February 15, 1940): 255.

FURTHER READING:

Books

Carwell, Hattie. *Blacks In Science: Astrophysicist to Zoologist.* Exposition Press, 1977, p. 61.

Greene, Harry Washington. *Holders of Doctorates among American Negroes.* Meador Publishing, 1946, p. 157.

Sammons, Vivian Ovelton. *Blacks In Science And Medicine.* New York: Hemisphere Publishing, 1990 p. 229.

Periodicals

New York Times (September 24, 1969): 33.

—*Sketch by Paul A. Heckert*

Emmanuel Bandele Thompson
1928-
Pharmacologist

Emmanuel B. Thompson is a pharmacologist and educator known for his research regarding treatments for high blood pressure and sickle-cell anemia. Both diseases, particularly the latter, have a high rate of incidence among African Americans, and Thompson has published numerous studies of these conditions. In addition, he has conducted important research on drug screening, and published a textbook on the subject. Raised in Nigeria, Thompson was inspired by a visit from **George Washington Carver** to his school, and came to the United States to study pharmacology when he was in his mid-twenties.

Inspired by George Washington Carver

Emmanuel B. Thompson was born on March 15, 1928, in the town of Zaria in the northern part of Nigeria, when that country was under British rule. His father ran an all-purpose store in the town for the United Africa Company, which purchased the agricultural products of the area and sold manufactured goods from outside to the locals. It was a lucrative line of work, and Thompson's father was a successful merchant.

Thompson, the oldest of five children, attended a Roman Catholic school. Throughout his early life, churches would have an influence on his education. In the elementary school, the Irish priests and the Nigerian instructors used heavy doses of discipline along with their teaching. Nonetheless, Thompson was inspired to learn, and took an early interest in biology.

This interest was piqued when the legendary African American scientist George Washington Carver visited the school. The latter taught students a variety of novel processes for turning the products of indigenous plants into end-products such as perfume. Given the size of the school—there were some 200 students—and the impact of the Carver's reputation (he was in his seventies at the time, having long before made the discoveries which would assure him a place among the greatest American scientists), it is almost certain that the encounter had a great influence on Thompson's later career.

Restless Years After High School

For his secondary education, Thompson attended St. Gregory's College, a boarding school in the Nigerian capital, Lagos, some 800 miles (1,280 km) southwest of Zaria. Given the time, the place, and the traveling conditions, this put him several days' journey away from his family; but with his father's successful business and the emphasis both his parents placed on education, it seemed the proper course for the young man's studies. Just as Carver had influenced him before, several teachers at the school would have a profound impact on him. One of these was a Brazilian priest who encouraged his scientific curiosity; another was a Nigerian physics instructor who taught him the rudiments of electricity and magnetism.

The conclusion of high school began a restless period in Thompson's life. He first went to work for the United Africa Company, his father's employer, as a bookkeeper in its Lagos offices. But his mind thrilled to the challenges of science, and he found his work tedious. Soon he sought other employment, and obtained a job working for the government at a research laboratory in a northern village, studying diseases that affected cattle in the region.

The new position seemed like a good choice, given his interests, but after some friction with the director, Thompson left within three months of being hired. He moved to the town of Koduna, where he began teaching science and geography at a Catholic high school, St. John's College. At this point he was in his early twenties, and realizing that he

would have to further his education if he intended to reach his goals, he entered Lagos's Yaba School of Pharmacy at the beginning of 1951. Almost two years later, in the latter part of 1952, he received a diploma as a technician. At that point, an exciting and unexpected opportunity opened up for him.

Comes to America with the Help of a Concerned Missionary

Dr. Desmond Bittinger, a Quaker, had been a missionary in Nigeria for a decade, and when he returned to the United States, had become president of Rockhurst College in McPherson, Kansas. Concerned about the futures of the young people he had encountered in Africa, Bittinger had set up a scholarship to assist promising Nigerian students in gaining a higher education in America. The scholarship trustees invited Thompson to come to America, and the young man readily accepted the invitation.

Thompson finished his biology degree in three years, earning his room and board by working late each night. After graduating from Rockhurst with a B.S. in 1955, he entered the University of Missouri in Kansas City. There he met and married Nova Garner, who was from Kansas, and the couple would eventually have two daughters. In 1959 he earned his pharmacy certification, and was thus qualified to work as a pharmacist anywhere in the United States. However, driven by a desire to understand the use of drugs from a theoretical as well as a purely practical standpoint, he opted to continue his education.

Therefore in 1961, Thompson enrolled at the University of Nebraska in Lincoln, where he began work on his M.S. in pharmacology. For the two years prior to entering the university, he put away money for his schooling, first by working at the University of Kansas Medical Center, where he was employed as a hospital pharmacist from 1959 to 1960, and later at the Queen of the World Hospital in Kansas City. During this period, he also moonlighted as a drugstore pharmacist at Cundiff Drug Store in Kansas City.

During his two years at the University of Nebraska, Thompson focused his attention on studying the use of garlic extracts to control high blood pressure, a type of treatment that would become popular in the 1980s and 1990s with over-the-counter sales of garlic tablets as diet supplements. Earning his M.S. in 1963, he went on to the University of Washington in Seattle, where he entered the Ph.D. program in pharmacology. He earned his degree in 1966 with a dissertation entitled *The Action of a Beta-Receptor Antagonist on the Positive Chronotropic Response to Nerve Stimulation and Applied Catecholamine in Isolated Rabbit Atria*. In his writing he discussed new ways of treating high blood pressure, in this case through the use of synthetic compounds which would inhibit nerve messages to the heart.

Continuing Concerns for High Blood Pressure and Sickle-Cell Anemia

Having obtained his doctorate, Thompson went to work as a senior research pharmacist at Baxter Laboratories in Morton Grove, Illinois, near Chicago. In this capacity he developed a variety of general anesthetics, one of which gained use among surgeons in Japan. Following a three-year stint with Baxter, Thompson became an assistant professor at the University of Illinois Medical Center's College of Pharmacy, where the Class of 1971 voted him "Teacher of the Year." Also in 1971, he began working part-time at West Side Veteran's Administration Hospital in Chicago as its principal researcher and consultant.

His work at the University of Illinois, however, would continue to be his primary occupation for the next quarter-century. In 1973, Thompson became an associate professor, and though his base remained in the College of Pharmacy, he also taught classes in the schools of Public Health and Associated Medical Sciences, and in the College of Nursing. An occasional lecturer at the Illinois College of Pediatric Medicine and the Chicago State University School of Nursing, he published a textbook called *Drug Bioscreening* in 1985. A revised edition saw print in 1990.

In addition to his work on high blood pressure, Thompson in the 1980s and 1990s continued to research treatments for sickle-cell anemia. As of the late 1990s there was no cure for the disease, which primarily affects African Americans, but in literally dozens of papers on this and high blood pressure, Thompson suggested methods of treating it. Perhaps harkening back to the example of Dr. Carver, he has also conducted vital research in the area of screening tropical plants for their medicinal uses.

Thompson retired from teaching in 1997, but continues to consult with hospitals. He is a member of the New York Academy of Science, the American Association of Colleges of Pharmacy, and the American Pharmaceutical Association. He lives in Chicago.

SELECTED WRITINGS BY THOMPSON:

Books

Drug Bioscreening: Drug Evaluation Techniques in Pharmacology. Graceway, 1985; VCH, 1990.

FURTHER READING:

Books

American Men & Women of Science, 20th edition. R. R. Bowker, 1998.
Kessler, James H., et al. *Distinguished African American Scientists of the 20th Century.* Oryx Press, 1996.
Sammons, Vivian Ovelton. *Blacks in Science and Medicine.* Hemisphere Publishing, 1990.

—*Sketch by Judson Knight*

Margaret E. M. Tolbert
1943-
Analytical chemist

Throughout her career as a researcher and a manager, Margaret E. Mayo Tolbert has been intrigued both by how chemical reactions happen and by how her own actions can promote positive change. Inspired at an early age by such scientists as **George Washington Carver** and Madame Curie, she has performed important research on the biochemistry of the liver and has assumed management positions at the United States Department of Energy and the National Science Foundation, as well as in private industry.

Tolbert was born on November 24, 1943, to J. Clifton Mayo and Martha Artis Mayo in Suffolk, Virginia. Her father, a World War II veteran, worked as a landscape gardener; her mother was a domestic worker. The third of six children, Tolbert was still young when her parents separated and, shortly thereafter, her mother died. For a short period, the children were cared for by various neighbors and friends; then they moved in with their paternal grandmother, Fannie Mae Johnson Mayo. As a teenager, Tolbert contributed to the family's income by working as a babysitter and a maid but kept up with her studies well enough to be at the top of her class. When her father died and her grandmother became ill, the youngest four children moved in with an older sister. Tolbert continued to work as a maid and became close with one of her employers—the Simon Cook family. The Cooks encouraged her to attend college and helped her research possible schools.

Tolbert studied in chemistry at Tuskegee University in Tuskegee, Alabama, with a small scholarship from the school. By the time she graduated in 1967, she had served as a research assistant on a project to identify how various chemicals conduct electricity when placed in water and faced with different degrees of resistance. She had also completed summer internships at Central State College in Durham, North Carolina, and the Argonne National Laboratories in Illinois. She went on to Wayne State University in Detroit, Michigan to obtain her master's degree in analytical chemistry in just one year. For the next three years, she returned to Tuskegee, where she supervised the research projects she had worked on as an undergraduate and taught in the mathematics department.

In 1970, Tolbert was recruited to join the doctoral program in chemistry at Brown University in Providence, Rhode Island. Her research on biochemical reactions in liver cells was partially funded by a scholarship from the Southern Fellowship Fund. At the same time, she taught science and math to adults at the Opportunities Industrialization Center in Providence. She was awarded her doctoral degree in 1974, a year after she returned to Tuskegee University as assistant professor in chemistry. She continued her research on liver cells at the Carver Research Foundation laboratories. She moved on to associate professor at the College of Pharmacy and Pharmaceutical Sciences at Florida A&M University in 1977. There, she was promoted twice over a two-year period; the last promotion was to associate dean of the school of pharmacy.

In 1979, Tolbert spent five months in Brussels, Belgium, studying how different drugs are metabolized in rat liver cells at the International Institute of Cellular and Molecular Pathology. The effort was funded through a faculty scholarship provided by the National Institute of General Medical Sciences. She continued this research as a visiting associate professor at Brown University upon her return to the United States and published two reports on the biochemistry of the liver.

Heads Carver Research Foundation

Tuskegee beckoned again in 1979, and Tolbert returned for the final time to head the Carver Research Foundation. As director, she organized research in the agricultural, behavioral, and natural sciences, and she coordinated several domestic and international outreach programs. During her tenure, Tolbert was able to bring several large scientific research contracts to the university from the federal government—contracts which expanded the research capabilities of the entire school. Many of these contracts provided the opportunity for the university to develop vital connections with large federal laboratories such as Battelle, Oak Ridge, and the Lawrence Livermore National Laboratory.

At Tuskegee, Tolbert had also served as the university's associate provost of research and development, and in this position she traveled extensively to identify possible summer research opportunities for students. Through these travels, she was recruited to take a sabbatical at Standard Oil to develop science education programs; when the company was sold to British Petroleum soon after, she was asked to become the senior planner and senior budget and control analyst for the company's research center at Warrensville, Ohio. Tolbert remained with British Petroleum from 1987-90.

From 1990-93, Tolbert directed the Research Improvement in Minority Institutions Program for the National Science Foundation (NSF), which works to strengthen the infrastructure of research programs at minority colleges and universities. She coordinated the review of grant proposals from several topic areas, and her efforts paid off at several institutions. During part of her tenure at NSF, she also served as interim executive secretary of the Committee on Education and Training, a cooperative program established by the White House under the federal coordinating council for science, engineering, and technology. The committee coordinated the education and training programs of 16 federal agencies.

In 1994, Tolbert spent three months as a consultant at the Howard Hughes Medical Institute, where she reviewed hundreds of proposals for international scientific research from Eastern European countries. In that same year, she joined the Argonne National Laboratories as director of its division of educational programs. In this position, she used her previous experiences to coordinate educational and training research between the laboratory and universities, colleges, and other national and international organizations. Two years later, Tolbert was appointed the director of the New Brunswick Laboratory at Argonne National Laboratories.

As a facility owned and operated by the U.S. Department of Energy, the New Brunswick Laboratory is the federal government's central authority for nuclear material measurement, evaluation, auditing, and validation. Tolbert oversees approximately 40 scientists who create and maintain reference materials for nuclear accountability and nuclear safeguards; they certify all other nuclear reference materials for the government. As only the third director in the laboratory's almost 50-year history, Tolbert believes her position allows her to help the entire country by enhancing nuclear security nationally as well as support international nonproliferation efforts.

Tolbert continues creating educational opportunities at the laboratory to motivate young students to join the sciences. This includes sponsorship of the Boy Scout Explorer Science and Engineering post at Argonne National Laboratories and the creation of an explorer program for Boy Scouts and Girl Scouts from local high schools. She also serves as a mentor to the student chosen annually to intern at Argonne, an experience she herself had in 1966 as an undergraduate.

Tolbert was elected a fellow in 1998 of the American Association for the Advancement of Science, and she is a member of Sigma Xi, the American Chemical Society, the Organization of Black Scientists, and the American Association of University Women. She organized the U.S. Department of Energy's Science Education Directors Council in 1994 and served as the council's chair in 1995-96. She also served on the advisory committee for training in nuclear power and nuclear safety of the International Atomic Energy Agency in Vienna, Austria, and she served as team leader for several duty tours to Liberia, Senegal, Ghana, South Africa, Libya, and Sudan. Tolbert has been divorced since 1978; she has one son, Lawson Kwia Tolbert, and one grandchild.

SELECTED WRITINGS BY TOLBERT:

Periodicals

(with M.I. Spaletto) "A Safeguards Measurement Evaluation Program with International Significance," *Proceedings of the Symposium on International Safeguards, International Atomic Energy Agency, Vienna, Austria.* (October 14, 1997).

"Minority Women in Science and Engineering: A Review of Progress." *Journal of College Science Teaching* (September/October 1996).

(with J.N. Fain) "Studies on the Regulation of Gluconeogenesis in Isolated Rat Liver Cells by Epinephrine and Glucagon." *Journal of Biological Chemistry* (1974).

Other

(with W.E. McHenry) "Resource Guide to Selected Undergraduate Programs of 10 Federal Agencies 1993-1994." *National Science Foundation* (October 1993).

FURTHER READING:

Books

Kessler, James, et. al. *Distinguished African American Scientists of the 20th Century.* Phoenix, AZ: Oryx Press, 1996, pp. 317-320.

Sammons, Vivian Ovelton. *Blacks in Science and Medicine.* New York: Hemisphere Publishing Corporation, 1990.

Periodicals

Pietri, Charles E. "JNMM Interview with Margaret Tolbert," *Journal of Nuclear Materials Management* (Fall 1997).

Flanagan, Brenda. "Essence Women." *Essence* (August 1980).

—*Sketch by Sally Cole-Misch*

Charles Henry Turner
1867-1923
Zoologist and entomologist

Charles Henry Turner's primary research area was insects, and he was the first to prove demonstrate insects have hearing, and further, could discern pitch. Turner was also the first to describe a particular ant movement that was named the "Turner's circling" in his honor. Turner conducted many kinds of experiments on various insects, including ants, roaches, spiders, and bees, investigating how they learn. He was regarded in the United States and Europe as an authority on spiders and ants, and their patterns of behavior. Turner also had an interest in smaller crustaceans, especially crawfish.

Turner spent the majority of his career as a secondary school teacher, which gave him a certain freedom to conduct research without the demands of tenure and university teaching loads. However, this also meant he worked unfunded, alone without assistants, and only with equipment purchased by himself. Still, he managed to publish nearly 50 articles in his lifetime and contribute to important books on related topics. Turner was also a civil rights activist.

Turner was born on February 3, 1867, in Cincinnati, Ohio, to Thomas and Addie (nee Campbell) Turner. Thomas Turner worked as a church janitor, and had been born a freeman as he was a native of Alberta, Canada. Addie Turner worked as a practical nurse and had been born in slavery in Kentucky. Both of Turner's parents had an enthusiasm for learning, and encouraged their son's education by purchasing as many books as they could manage to on their small salaries. Turner displayed interest in insects and their behaviors from a very young age.

After graduating from a local high school, Turner began studying at the University of Cincinnati. While an undergraduate student, Turner married Leontine Troy. He earned his B.S. from the University of Cincinnati in 1891, and his M.S. a year later from the same institution. While working on his Masters degree, Turner was employed as an assistant instructor in the University's biology laboratory.

Throughout his career, Turner worked as a teacher and professor. From 1892-95, he was a biology professor at Clark College in Atlanta, Georgia. In 1895, Turner's wife died, leaving him a widower with five children. He eventually remarried. After his job at Clark, Turner bounced between several high school teaching positions. Between 1895 and 1905, Turner taught in Evansville, Indiana, and in his hometown of Cincinnati, before moving to Cleveland, Tennessee, where he served as principal of College Hill High School. In 1906, Turner went back to Georgia where he again worked as a biology professor, this time at Augusta's Haines Normal and Industrial Institute. During these years, Turner began his experiments into insect behavior and began publishing his observations.

Enters the University of Chicago

Because of his research and publishing activities, Turner was accepted into the doctoral program at the University of Chicago. This was a big honor for him at the time, for few black Americans were accepted into such kinds of programs, and the University of Chicago was one of the best. In 1907, Turner earned his Ph.D. in zoology from the University of Chicago, graduating *summa cum laude*. (Some sources say *magna cum laude*). His dissertation was titled *The Homing of Ants: An Experimental Study in Ant Behavior.*

Experiments with Ants

In one of Turner's significant ant experiments, he wanted to determine how ants find their way back home. To find out if they used smell, light, landmarks, or even their own trails, Turner set up some clever trials. To determine if light was a factor, he put an ant nest equidistant from two ramps, each with their own heat-filtered light bulb, attached to a platform, with a mirror underneath. After putting some ants, with ant eggs and larvae, on the platform, Turner turned one of the lights on and kept the other off, then switched sides. The ants always used the lighted side to carry the eggs and larvae to their nests, though it took them a bit to reorganize after the lighted sides switched. Thus Turner determined that light was at least one factor in directing this action.

Turner was the first to describe a movement made by certain kinds of ants upon return to their nests. The ants moved towards the nest in a turning, circling pattern, and this was dubbed "Turner's circling" by his French scientific colleagues.

Teaches High School Biology

After earning his Ph.D., Turner decided that being a high school teacher would best suit his research needs. He worked as a biology teacher at St. Louis, Missouri's, Sumner High School, from 1908 until his death in 1923. (The school was also known as Sumner Teachers College, and Turner also taught psychology there.). It was here that Turner conducted the majority of his experiments that led to publications in numerous prestigious journals of the time, including the *Journal of Animal Behavior*.

Turner conducted his experiments alone, without outside aid—monetary or otherwise, and paid for equipment himself. Turner's experiments were primarily concerned with the behavior of insects: their psychology, their vision and hearing abilities, how they hunt, and if they had the ability to learn.

Conducts Conditioning Experiments with Cockroaches and Moths

Turner discovered that cockroaches could learn by running them through mazes. Turner set up a maze with food at one end. Though it took the cockroaches a whole day to learn to go through the maze to the food without error, they did indeed learn from their mistakes. If a cockroach took a path to a dead end, Turner observed that they did not go the same route again. Similarly, Turner discovered that moths could be taught to adapt. Working from the knowledge that a certain moth species reacted only to high pitches, Turner trained them to equate low pitch sounds with food. These kind of experiments proved that insects, like other animals, could be trained by experience, where previously scientists thought they functioned only instinctual behavior.

In Turner's work on bees, he learned that they could distinguish colors, as well as a single color's different geometric patterns. In another experiment, Turner studied the nesting habits of a certain kind of bee. Unlike most bees that live in hives, this species lives alone in its own underground nest. To test how the bees find the hole that leads to their nest, Turner tried to camouflage the hole with a piece of paper, then a piece of watermelon rind. Through trials, Turner surmised that the bee remembered where the hole was by the features around it, as long as the hole was in the same place.

Turner's prestige in scientific circles meant that he was often quoted by his scientific colleagues. He also received several honors. For example, for three straight years, he was invited to write an article for a significant journal about the progress made in the field of biology for the past year.

Though Turner's teaching career was unprestigious, his enthusiasm for the subject led his students to become interested in biology, including Phil Rau, who later became an expert on bees and wasps. Turner also was interested in writing, and before his death, he was working on juvenile nature stories and a novel. He had earlier written 32 poems. Turner died on February 18, 1923, in Chicago. In 1925, St. Louis honored Turner by naming a newly built school after him. Turner's work has remained highly regarded long after his death.

SELECTED WRITINGS BY TURNER:

Periodicals

"The Homing of Ants: An Experimental Study in Ant Behavior," *Journal of Comparative Neurology and Psychology,* (1907): 367-434.
"Morphology of the Avaian Brain," *'Journal of Comparative Neurology,* (1891).

FURTHER READING:

Books

Robert C. Hayden. *Seven Black American Scientists.* Addison-Wesley, 1970, pp. 70-91.

Periodicals

The Crisis, (June 1923): 71-72.
"The Negro in the Beginnings of Science," *The Negro History Bulletin,* (May 1939): 68.

—*Sketch by A. Petrusso*

Thomas Wyatt Turner
1877-1978
Botanist

Thomas Wyatt Turner was an accomplished scientist and social activist. As a well-respected botanist and biologist, his areas of interest as a well-respected researcher were plant physiology and pathology; physiological effects of mineral nutrients on root growth in seed plants; and physiological effects of nitrogen and phosphorus on plants. Turner was the first black man to present a paper to the Virginia Academy of Science, and for many years, was the organization's only black member from south of Philadelphia. But Turner's work as an activist overshadowed his many scientific accomplishments. He was a leader in the movement to fight racism in the Catholic Church, of which he was a staunch member. He also participated in the founding of the NAACP (National Association for the Advancement of Colored People), and worked to increase opportunities for blacks in the sciences and higher education in general.

Turner was born in Hughsville, Maryland, on March 16, 1877. (Some sources claim November 16 is his correct birthdate.) He was one of nine children born to Eli and Linnie (nee Gross) Turner, both former slaves. His father worked as a sharecropper until his death, when Turner was only eight years old. Turner attended local schools—some of them Episcopalian since the Catholic ones would not admit him—until he was accepted at Howard University Preparatory School. To attend this prep school, Turner walked the 50 mile (80 km) distance between his hometown and Washington, D.C. He went on to earn his B.A. from Howard University in 1901. He subsequently was awarded his graduate degrees from Cornell: his M.A. in 1905, and his Ph.D. in Botany in 1921.

Teaches High School

After acquiring his undergraduate degree, Turner became employed as an educator. From 1901 until 1914, Turner taught biology in several high schools successively. He spent a year at Tuskegee Institute in Alabama (1901-02), as a favor to his friend Booker T. Washington. Then Turner taught at Baltimore High and Training School (1902-10) and spent a year at a high school in St. Louis, Missouri, before finally returning to Baltimore, where he finished his high school teaching career in 1914. While employed as a teacher, in 1907, he married Laura Miller. She died in the 1920s.

Turner spent his spare time learning in the years between his graduate degrees. He attended graduate classes at several universities and related institutions. Among them were Johns Hopkins, Columbia, the University of Rochester, and the Cold Spring Harbor Laboratory. Though he wanted to attend Catholic University of America, it was segregated at the time and he was not granted admittance.

Helps Found the NAACP

Turner was an activist from early in his career. He was a founding member of the NAACP when it formed in 1909, served as secretary in the Baltimore branch in 1910, and also was the chairman for the organization's first membership drive in Washington, D.C., in 1915. Turner also was elected president of the NAACP's Phoebus, Virginia, branch at one time. The NAACP honored his contributions

by making him a life member. Turner's activism also crossed over into patriotic concerns. During World War I, from 1916-17, he acted as an agent of the New York's National Security League, promoting patriotism, loyalty, and thrift during the war.

Turner moved up to the university level of teaching in the mid-1910s, serving as a professor of botany and applied biology at Howard University from about 1914 until 1924. He was also Acting Dean at the School of Education from 1914-20. During that time, from 1916 through 1921, he completed his Ph.D. from Cornell. His dissertation was entitled "Studies of the Mechanism of the Physiological Effects of Certain Mineral Salts in Altering the Ratio of Top Growth to Root Growth in Seed Plants." His thesis was eventually published in the *American Journal of Botany*.

While working on his dissertation, Turner spent parts of 1918-19 working for the United States Department of Agriculture as a cytologist (a cell biologist) and special investigator in Maine. There he examined potato fields. Throughout his career, Turner would be consulted by the American government about agricultural problems. Indeed, Turner worked as a collaborator of Virginia's plant diseases under the auspices of the United States Secretary of Agriculture at one point.

In 1924, Turner became associated with the Hampton Institute, Virginia, as a biology professor. (The Institute later became Hampton University.) After serving for a time as head of the Department, Turner was forced to retire in 1945 because of the effects of glaucoma. He held emeritus professor status at Hampton until his death in 1978. While at Hampton, Turner was a key figure in advancing the institution's natural science curriculum. In 1977, the school honored him by renaming its science building Turner Hall.

Founds the Federation of Colored Catholics

The year 1924 was also significant for Turner as an activist. That year he established the Federation of Colored Catholics to fight racism and segregation in the Catholic Church and promote racial harmony. (This group had existed in several forms since 1917.) Turner and others from his parish organized it to promote African American solidarity within the Church, and Turner himself served as the Federation's president several times until 1934. Against his protests, his organization was forcibly made part of the Catholic Interracial Council in 1933. Though the Federation retained its own identity until 1958, the group lacked focus and power after the mid-1930s. Turner was against this integration because he thought the Council was racist and passive, as well as being dominated by whites. Still, Turner, remained a loyal member of the Catholic Church. Throughout the 1920s, Turner was also active in the black voter registration movement.

Turner had long been interested in science education, especially in traditionally black colleges. He organized the Virginia Conference of College Science Teachers in 1931, and served as president of that group for two terms. He was motivated to form the group because he noted that historically black colleges were involved only minimally in the advancement of science and its education. During 1942-43, Turner studied science teaching at 32 black colleges, most of them land grant colleges, and he produced several papers on the topic. He noted that science was still not being taught for its own sake, but to prepare students for other careers. His work was key in the founding of The National Institute of Science, of which he was the first president.

After his retirement from Hampton, Turner continued to work in the collegiate science community. He was a consultant at Florida Normal College from 1947-48. He also spent a year, from 1949 to 1950, working at Texas Southern University. Turner organized their biology department, served as a consultant to the University's president, and was himself a professor of biology.

Though he had many conflicts with the Catholic Church, in 1976, the Secretariat of Washington D.C.'s Black Catholics named its highest award for Turner. The Turner Award has become an annual honor. The same year Turner was also awarded an honorary science doctorate from the Catholic University, the very institution that would not admit him earlier in the century.

Turner died on April 21, 1978, at the age of 101 in a Washington, D.C., hospital. While Turner was survived by his second wife, Louise Wright, whom he married in 1936; they had no children. Throughout his career, Turner held memberships in numerous scientific organizations, among them the American Association for the Advancement of Science and the American Society of Horticultural Science.

SELECTED WRITINGS BY TURNER:

Periodicals

"Mineral Nutrition of Plants," *American Journal of Botany,* (October 1922): 415-55.
"Science Teaching in Negro Colleges," *Journal of Negro Education,* 1946.
"The Spirit of the Federated Colored Catholics," *Chronicle,* (May 1932): 92.

FURTHER READING:

Books

Nickels, Marilyn Wenzke. *Black Catholic Protest and the Federated Colored Catholics, 1917-33.* Garland Publishing, 1988.

Periodicals

"Hubert Branch Crouch and the Origins of the National Institute of Science," *Journal of Negro History,* (Winter 1994): 18-33.
The New York Times. (April 25, 1978).

"NOBC Pioneer Dies in 102nd Year," *Impact!,* (April-May 1978): 2-3.

—*Sketch by A. Petrusso*

Neil de Grasse Tyson
1958-
Astronomer and astrophysicist

Neil de Grasse Tyson is an astrophysicist whose research has included such varied areas as dwarf galaxies, the nucleus of our own galaxy, explosions of massive stars known as supernovae, and star formation. He has also done much work to make astronomy accessible to the average person. Tyson teaches, serves as director of Hayden Planetarium in New York, and writes many columns and books aimed at a general audience.

Tyson was born in New York City in 1958 and grew up in the Bronx. His father, Cyril de Grasse Tyson, is a retired sociologist who worked as a commisioner in the administration of New York's Mayor Lindsay. His mother, Sunchita Feliciano Tyson, is a gerontologist for the department of Health and Human Services.

Tyson's interest in astronomy began in the sixth grade, when he saw details on the Moon's surface through a friend's binoculars. Tyson soon started voraciously reading astronomy books. His parents supported his interest by finding astronomy books and helping him attend events that increased his knowledge. He took courses and attended shows at New York's Hayden Planetarium. At age 13, Tyson experienced the very dark skies of the Mohave desert at a summer astronomy camp. Without interference from city lights, he was able to see more stars than he had ever seen before. To earn the money needed for his first telescope, Tyson walked dogs for neighbors in his apartment complex. In 1973, Tyson took this telescope along on an eclipse expedition to Africa. He was the youngest person on this trip. The following year, he visited Stonehenge. To pay for these expeditions, Tyson won scholarships. These experiences, combined with the positive support of his parents and teachers, reinforced Tyson's ambition to become an astronomer.

Tyson attended the Bronx High School of Science. There, he was surrounded by other students who were also interested in science, and he was able to immerse himself in astronomy, as well as physics and related subjects. He graduated in 1976. Moving to Boston, Tyson earned his bachelor's degree in physics from Harvard University in 1980. For his master's degree, Tyson moved to Austin to study at the University of Texas. Returning to New York, he earned a doctoral degree in astrophysics from Columbia University in 1991. Earning his doctorate fulfilled Tyson's major life goal; for this reason, he says, delivering the doctoral convocation address at Columbia is the accomplishment of which he is most proud.

After completing his doctorate, Tyson joined the faculty at Princeton University in Princeton, New Jersey. His duties included both teaching and research. Many students found Tyson to be a particularly inspiring professor. In May of 1996, Tyson was appointed the Frederick P. Rose Director of the Hayden Planetarium. Directing the planetarium helps Tyson insure that the next generation will have the same chance he had to be inspired by astronomy. In addition to his duties at Hayden Planetarium, Tyson serves simultaneously as a visiting research scientist at Princeton University.

Tyson's research centers around observational astronomy. He has made astronomical observations with telescopes at McDonald Observatory in Texas, Cerro Tololo InterAmerican Observatory in Chili, and Las Campanas Observatory also in Chili. His research concentrates on supernovae and stars in the nucleus of our own galaxy. Supernovae are huge explosions representing the death throes of massive stars that release as much energy in a year as the sun does in ten billion years. Tyson's studies of stars in the nucleus provide clues to the structure of our galaxy. He has also studied the formation of stars and dwarf galaxies that are much smaller than our own Milky Way Galaxy.

In addition to his scientific research, Tyson does considerable writing for the general public. While at the University of Texas, Tyson started writing a regular column for *Stardate* magazine, which accompanies a popular show by the same name on public radio. In this column, Tyson answers questions about astronomy by posing as Merlin, the magician. Two of Tyson's books have resulted from collections of these columns. Tyson also writes a regular column for *Natural History* magazine. Using his teaching experience, Tyson wrote *The Universe Down to Earth* to explain astrophysics to nonastronomers.

Tyson was the captain of his high school wrestling team and a member of the varsity wrestling team in college. He continued wrestling into adulthood by occasionally working out with the Princeton team. In addition to his earned degrees, Tyson was awarded an honorary doctor of science degree from York College of the City University of New York in 1997.

SELECTED WRITINGS BY TYSON:

Books

Just Visiting This Planet. New York: Doubleday, 1998.
Merlin's Tour of the Universe. New York: Columbia Press, 1989.
Universe Down to Earth. New York: Columbia Press, 1994.

FURTHER READING:

Books

Caines, Bruce. *Our Common Ground.* Crown Publishers, 1994.

—Sketch by Paul A. Heckert

After showing promise in mathematics as a girl, Velez-Rodriguez earned a bachelor's degree in 1955 from the Marianao Institute of Cuba and a Ph.D. in 1960 from the University of Havana. Her doctoral dissertation concerned the use of differential equations in figuring astronomical orbits. Her father, Pedro Velez, had worked in the Cuban Congress under Fulgencio Batista, the leader ousted by Fidel Castro in 1959.

Velez-Rodriguez's first teaching position in the United States was at Texas College, where she began teaching mathematics and physics in 1962. In 1972, she became a professor of math and served as the department's chair at Bishop College in Dallas. Velez-Rodriguez's research at the time focused on differential equations and classical analysis. After leaving Bishop in 1979, she was hired by the NSF to work on the Minority Science Improvement Program. Velez-Rodriguez has also studied teaching strategies, with a particular focus on helping minorities and disadvantaged students learn mathematics. She directed and coordinated several NSF programs for high school and junior high school mathematics teachers.

Velez-Rodriquez was married to Raul Rodriguez in 1954 in Cuba, and they had two young children when the family fled the country in 1962. "I had just finished my Ph.D.," she told contributor Karl Bates in an interview. Her son is now a surgeon, and her daughter is an industrial engineer with a Harvard MBA. She and Rodriguez are divorced, and she is a naturalized citizen of the United States.

Argelia Velez-Rodriguez

Argelia Velez-Rodriguez
1936-
Mathematics educator

Since leaving her native Cuba shortly after completing her Ph.D., Argelia Velez-Rodriguez has devoted her career to mathematics and physics education. She has been involved with math education programs of the National Science Foundation (NSF) since 1970 and became director of the Minority Science Improvement Program at the U.S. Department of Education in 1980.

FURTHER READING:

"Argelia Velez-Rodriguez." *Biographies of Women Mathematicians.* June 1997. http://www.scottlan.edu/lriddle/women/chronol.htm (July 22, 1997).

Other

Velez-Rodriguez, Argelia, interview with Karl Leif Bates, conducted June 17, 1997.

—Sketch by Karl Leif Bates

William James Lord Wallace
1908-1997
Chemist

William James Lord Wallace began his career as a chemistry instructor and worked his way up the ranks of academic administration to become president of West Virginia State College. During Wallace's 20 years as president, he was also very active in community service. He received numerous awards for his professional and volunteer work.

Wallace was born in Salisbury, North Carolina, on January 13, 1908, to Thomas Walker and Lauretta Julia (Lawson) Lord. He was educated at the University of Pittsburgh, where he received a bachelor of science degree in 1927. That same year, Wallace began work as a science instructor at Livingstone College. He married Louise Eleanor Taylor on December 7, 1929; the couple eventually had one child, a daughter named after her mother.

When Wallace entered the graduate program at Columbia University, he retained his position at Livingstone College. He received a master's degree from that institution in 1931, and the journal *Crisis* reported the event. Wallace began work as an instructor at Lincoln University in 1932. He left in 1933 to became an instructor at West Virginia State College; by the following year, he was an assistant professor there. While teaching, Wallace pursued a doctorate in physical chemistry. He earned a Sage Fellowship at Cornell University and wrote a dissertation entitled "The Freezing Points of Aqueous Solutions of Alpha Amino Acids." He was awarded a doctoral degree in physical chemistry from Cornell University in 1937. That same year, he was promoted to associate professor at West Virginia State College.

In addition to his research, Wallace studied and wrote about education. In 1940, he published *Chemistry in Negro Colleges*. Wallace was full professor at West Virginia State College by 1943. In 1944, he became the acting administrative assistant to the president and began a career in educational administration. He was named administrative assistant to the president in 1945. In 1952, he became the acting president. Then for 20 years, from 1953 until he retired in 1973, he served as president of the college. He also served in the West Virginia Association of Colleges and Universities, the American Association of State Colleges and Universities, and the National Education Association.

Wallace was active in public service. He served his community on its library board and on its parks and recreation committee; he was a member of the Mason and Lion groups and gave time to the Boy Scouts of America. At the state level, he served on the Governor's Committee on the Employment of the Physically Handicapped and the West Virginia Crime and Delinquency Council. He was also a member of the West Virginia Advisory Commission to the U.S. Commission on Civil Rights from 1960-74. Wallace served in various roles in the AME Zion Church of West Virginia for decades. He was affiliated with several fraternities, including Sigma Xi, Alpha Phi Alpha, and Kappa Delta Pi. In 1973, he retired as president of West Virginia State College but continued to serve organizations as diverse as the Herbert H. Thomas Memorial Hospital Association and the West Virginia State Bar Legal Ethics Committee. He also served on the board of advisors of West Virginia State College.

During the later years of his life, Wallace was awarded honorary degrees from various colleges, including West Virginia State College and Marshall University. Wallace received an Outstanding Civilian Service medal from the Army in 1972 and a Distinguished Service medal from the State of West Virginia in 1973. In 1986, he won a Washington Carver Award for Outstanding Service to the Citizens of West Virginia by the State Department of Culture and History; that same year Wallace won recognition from the West Virginia State Bar. In 1987, he won a Martin Luther King Jr. "Living the Dream" Award for Scholarship. Wallace died in 1997.

SELECTED WRITINGS BY WALLACE:

Books

Chemistry in Negro Colleges. Institute, West Virginia: West Virginia State College Press, Bulletin Series No. 2, April, 1940.

FURTHER READING

Books

American Men & Women of Science. 19th edition. New Providence, NJ: R.R. Bowker Company, 1994, p. 492.

Green, Harry Washington. *Holders of Doctorates Among American Negroes.* Boston: Meador Publishing Company, 1946, pp. 158-59.

Alyce Faye Wattleton

Phelps, Shirelle, ed. *Who's Who Among African Americans.* Detroit: Gale Research, 1996, p. 1544.

Sammons, Vivian Ovelton. *Blacks in Science and Medicine.* New York: Hemisphere Publishing, 1990, p. 241.

Taylor, Julius H. *The Negro in Science.* Baltimore: Morgan State College Press, 1955, p. 187.

Periodicals

Crisis (May 1931): 164.

—*Sketch by R. Garcia-Johnson*

Alyce Faye Wattleton
1943-
Nurse, public health executive

Alyce Faye Wattleton began her health care career as a nurse, but she is best known for her role as an advocate for women's reproductive rights. In 1978, she became the first African American to head the Planned Parenthood Federation of America—a position she held for 14 years.

Wattleton was born on July 8, 1943, in St. Louis, Missouri, to George and Ozie (Garret) Wattleton. Her mother was a preacher in the fundamentalist Church of God, and Wattleton spent the summers of her childhood traveling to evangelical tent meetings. She notes in her autobiography, *Life on the Line,* that she inherited her strength from a long line of family members who fought against racism. Her great-grandmother, Mariah Williams, "faced down a white straw boss who had tried to take away her son to work in the fields." Wattleton's mother was from a sharecropping family, and she had faced prejudice and opposition in her quest to become a preacher.

In 1964, Wattleton earned a bachelor's degree in nursing from Ohio State University. Three years later, she received a master's degree in maternal and infant health care from Columbia University. Wattleton began her health care career as an instructor at Miami Valley School of Nursing in Dayton, Ohio. From 1967-70, she was assistant director of nursing at the Dayton Public Health Nursing Association.

During her years in nursing, Wattleton cared for women and girls who were dealing with the consequences of unintended pregnancies and illegal abortions. In 1970, when she became executive director of the Planned Parenthood Association of Miami Valley, Dayton, Ohio, Wattleton was at the forefront of the fight to legalize abortion. In 1973, the United States Supreme Court decided *Roe v. Wade* and provided women with the legal right to obtain an abortion. After the decision, Wattleton worked to prevent the erosion of the right.

At the Helm of Planned Parenthood

Wattleton headed the Dayton-based Planned Parenthood Association for eight years. In 1978, she became the first African American president of the Planned Parenthood Federation of America. At that time, the organization was a network of 191 affiliates in 43 states and the District of Columbia. Planned Parenthood served more than one million people annually, with a staff of 3,000 workers and 20,000 volunteers. One of the nation's largest health care organizations, Planned Parenthood's primary function at the time was to provide contraceptive services and education in family planning.

At the organization, Wattleton continued the fight to keep abortion legal. In *Life on the Line,* Wattleton recounts her numerous battles with political conservatives, anti-abortion activists, and the religious right. Just three weeks before she was to take office, coordinated anti-abortion actions took place across the nation. Demonstrators forced their way into abortion clinics and disrupted medical services.

Two of Wattleton's biggest struggles during her 14 years at Planned Parenthood focused on Title X in 1981 and a United States Supreme Court case, *Webster v. Reproductive Health Services* in 1989. Title X provided federal support for family planning. Then-President Ronald Reagan proposed returning such health care funding decisions to the states, which would mean that states did not have to spend the funds on family planning. In March 1981, the Senate Committee on Labor and Human Resources held a hearing on Title X. Wattleton appeared before the committee to testify. Of the experience, she wrote in *Life on the Line:* "Seeing Title X buffeted in the Senate and House committees, I felt even more strongly that we had to become more politically forceful." In the end, the federal government, rather than the states, retained control over this funding. In *Webster v. Reproductive Health Services,* the justices decided how far states could go in restricting abortion. Concerning this decision, Wattleton told the media: "Our anticipation is that we will fight on to make certain that all women in this country continue to have access to safe abortion. We are not daunted by this Supreme Court decision."

Wattleton's desire to make Planned Parenthood a more political organization met with opposition from some colleagues who did not want to be crusaders for abortion rights. She also discovered many years later that her mother, who had preached against abortion in her sermons, was deeply hurt by her daughter's work. Wattleton commented in her autobiography, "I'd even been told that Mama had publicly requested prayers for my salvation after I'd taken the job at the Planned Parenthood Federation of America. Still, she'd always seemed to take a measure of pride in the advances of my career. It never occurred to me that her pride had its roots in such a profound sense of loss."

After resigning as head of Planned Parenthood in 1992, Wattleton turned her attention to hosting a television talk show and developing the Center for Gender Equity. About her life after turning 50, Wattleton said in a 1997 *Time* magazine article: "I had not expected to be as settled down and as peaceful about myself as I believe I am now. Things sort of fall into place. Those qualities and strengths that carried us through our 20s, 30s and 40s are even better, they're even stronger."

Throughout her career, Wattleton has been honored and applauded by women's groups and others for her courage and determination in the face of great opposition. She won the Dean's Distinguished Service award from the Columbia School of Public Health in 1992; the Jefferson Public Service award in 1992; the Margaret Sanger award in 1992; the Spirit of Achievement award from the Albert Einstein College of Medicine, Yeshiva University in 1991; the 20th Anniversary Advocacy award from the National Family Planning and Reproductive Health Association in 1991; the Pioneer of Civil Rights and Human Rights award from the National Conference of Black Lawyers in 1990; and numerous others.

Wattleton was married to Franklin Gordon in the 1970s. The couple divorced in 1981. They have one daughter, Felicia.

SELECTED WRITINGS BY WATTLETON:

Books

Life on the Line. New York: Random House, Inc., 1996.

FURTHER READING:

Periodicals

Powell, Joanna. "A Preacher's Daughter Finds Her Calling." *Good Housekeeping* (November 1996) : 24.

Freedman, Samuel G. *The New York Times Book Review* (November 17, 1996): 30-1.

—Sketch by Rose M. Estioco

Harold Dadford West
1904-1974
Biochemist

For 47 years Harold Dadford West was involved in biochemical research and education at Meharry Medical College. For 13 of those years, he was president of the institution. He was selected to be the first honorary member of the National Medical Association, and the Science Center at Meharry was named for him.

Born in Flemington, New Jersey, on July 16, 1904, West was the son of George H. West and the former Mary Ann Toney. He attended the University of Illinois, where he received a bachelor of arts degree in 1925. He was an associate professor and head of the science department at Morris Brown College in Atlanta from 1925 to 1927. On December 27, 1927, West married Jessie Juanita Penn. They eventually had one daughter and one son.

In 1927 West joined the faculty of Meharry Medical College in Nashville, Tennessee, as an associate professor of physiological chemistry. Meharry Medical College had become an independent institution in 1915. Prior to that it was part of Central Tennessee College, established by the Freedmen's Aid Society of the Methodist Episcopal Church after the American Civil War in 1866. During his early years on the faculty of Meharry Medical College, West completed a master of arts degree and a doctorate. He was a recipient of a fellowship from the Julius Rosenwald Fund at the University of Illinois while he earned a master of arts degree in 1930. Following that he was a Rockefeller Foundation Fellow, receiving a doctorate degree from the

Harold Dadford West

same university in 1937. The title of his dissertation was "The Chemistry and Nutritive Value of Essential Amino Acids." In 1938 West became professor of biochemistry and chairperson of the department.

West's work in biochemical research was vast, including studies of tuberculosis and other bacilli, the antibiotic biocerin, and aromatic hydrocarbons. He worked with amino acids, becoming the first to synthesize threonine. As noted in the *Journal of the National Medical Association,* among his other investigations were "the role of sulfur in biological detoxification mechanisms; blood serum calcium levels in the Negro in relation to possible significance in tuberculosis; relation of B-vitamins, especially pantothenic acid, to detoxification of sulfa-drugs and susceptibility to bacillary disease."

West's studies were supported by the John and Mary R. Markle Foundation, the Nutrition Foundation, the National Institutes of Health, and the American Medical Association. His research papers were published in a number of professional journals, including the *American Journal of Physiology, Southern Medical Journal,* and *Journal of Biological Chemistry.*

In 1952 West was named the fifth president of Meharry Medical College, its first African American president. In 1963 he was the first black American to serve on the State Board of Education. West retired as president in 1965, returning to the position of professor of biochemistry. When he retired from Meharry in 1973 he became a trustee

of the college. In his final years he worked on a complete history of the college. West died on March 5, 1974.

During his career, West was awarded two honorary degrees. In 1955 he received a doctor of laws from Morris Brown College, and in 1970 a doctor of science from Meharry Medical College. He was a member of many honorary and professional societies, including the American Chemical Society, the Society of Experimental Biology and Medicine, and the American Society of Biological Chemists. He was also elected to Sigma Xi, the scientific research society, which describes itself "as an honor society for scientists and engineers. . . . Its goals are to foster interaction among science, technology and society."

FURTHER READING:

Books

Sammons, Vivian Ovelton. *Blacks in Science and Medicine.* Hemisphere, 1990, p. 246.

Periodicals

Journal of the National Medical Association, (September 1974): 448–449.

—*Sketch by M. C. Nagel*

Doris L. Wethers
1927-
Pediatrician

Doris Wethers was a major force in developing and expanding programs to help professionals and the public deal with sickle-cell disease in children. The second black woman to graduate from Yale University School of Medicine, Wethers went on to become founder and director of the Comprehensive Sickle Cell Program at St. Luke's/Roosevelt Hospital Center in New York and a professor of clinical pediatrics in the College of Physicians and Surgeons at Columbia University. Throughout her career, Wethers served on advisory boards, participated in educational and service networks, and worked directly with inner-city patients to encourage infant screening and treatment for sickle-cell disease.

Doris L. Wethers was born in Pasaic, New Jersey to Lilian (Wilkenson) Wethers, a school teacher, and William Wethers, a physician with a family practice. After World War II, her family moved from New Jersey to New York City, just outside central Harlem. Her father's office was on the ground floor of their home, and Wethers was exposed to her father's medical practice throughout her childhood.

According to Wethers in a telephone interview with contributor Ellen Cothran, she and her sister, Agnes, accompanied their father on his house calls. A compassionate and much-loved physician, William Wethers set an example of professional service which young Doris mimicked by setting up her dolls in sick wards around her room. She always wanted to be a doctor. In 1948, Wethers graduated from Queens College with a major in premedical biology; she completed medical school at Yale in 1952 and was granted her New York State License to practice medicine in 1953. By 1955 she was chief resident of pediatrics at King's County Hospital in Brooklyn, New York.

Wethers spent the first 10 years of her career caring for children in her father's office. During this time, she treated many diseases that stem from poverty, including lead poisoning, tuberculosis, drug dependency passed from mother to baby, and premature births due to poor prenatal care. At the end of this period, she developed a particular interest in children with sickle-cell disease. According to the Sickle-Cell Disease Guideline Panel, on which Wethers served in 1993, sickle-cell anemia is a potentially fatal genetic condition which affects about one of every 375 African American infants. Wethers left private practice in 1965 to join a health maintence organization, a move that allowed her to continue seeing patients directly while branching out into administrative and educational work aimed at her special interest. Between 1965-79, she acted as director of pediatrics at three New York hospitals consecutively: Knickerbocker Hospital, Sydenham Hospital, and St. Luke's/Roosevelt Hospital Center. Beginning in 1979, she began to concentrate more on sickle-cell research; she founded the Comprehensive Sickle Cell Program at St. Luke's/Roosevelt Hospital Center and became its director. During this period she also began teaching, and in 1987 she was made professor of clinical pediatrics in the College of Physicians and Surgeons at Columbia University.

Wethers was also a consultant to numerous organizations around the country. She served as director of pediatrics for the Manhattan Medical Group (1983-92), as chair of the GENES Sickle-Cell Advisory Committee (1978-92), and as reviewer for the *American Journal of Pediatric Hematology/Oncology*. She was a member of the Sickle-Cell Advisory Committee of the Department of Health and Human Services Agency (1982-86), the American Academy of Pediatrics Committee on Careers and Opportunities (1989-95), and the Council of Regional Networks for Genetic Services beginning in 1993. In recognition of her extensive clinical and research work, she received the St. Luke's/Roosevelt Hospital Center Community Service Award (1993), the Charles Drew Memorial Award from Columbia University College of Physicians and Surgeons (1984). She was also named Preceptor of the Year by the New York Health Research Training Program (1991).

Wethers's work has touched the lives of many patients whose economic circumstances would have prevented them from receiving comprehensive care for a disease as dangerous as sickle-cell anemia. She inherited the compassion she

so much admired in her father and carried it through her long and distinguished career, balancing her administrative duties with hands-on care for patients from newborn to teenage years and serving as a mentor and role model for patients and students alike. Married in 1953 to Garval H. Booker, a dentist, Wethers raised three sons. She lives in New York City.

SELECTED WRITINGS BY WETHERS:

Periodicals

"Pediatrics: The Adaptable Specialty Fact Sheet." *Journal of the SNMA* (Summer 1991).

(with Grover, R.) "Management of Acute Splenic Sequestration Crisis in Sickle-Cell Disease." *Journal of American Association of Minority Physicians* 2 (1991): 80-83.

(with others) "Consensus Conference Report: Newborn Screening for Sickle Cell Disease, and Other Hemoglobinopathies." *Journal of American Medical Association* 258 (1988): 1205-1209.

(with Grover, R., Newman, S., Yeboa, K.A., and Pass, K.) "Newborn Screening for Hemoglobinopathies: The Benefit Beyond the Target." *American Journal of Pediatric Hematology/Oncology* 76 (1986): 1236-1287.

—Sketch by Ellen E. Cothran

Albert Harold Wheeler
1915-
Bacteriologist and public health specialist

Albert Harold Wheeler is a successful bacteriologist and public health specialist who also pursued a career in politics. In the early 1950s, he became the first full-time African American faculty member at the University of Michigan, and during the 1970s, he was the first African American mayor of the city of Ann Arbor, Michigan.

Wheeler was born on December 11, 1915, in St. Louis, Missouri, to Harold William and Elizabeth Theora (Massey) Wheeler. He received a bachelor's degree in 1936 from Lincoln University, an institution founded in 1854 to provide a higher education in the arts and sciences for youth of African descent. He earned a master of science degree from Iowa State College in 1937, before entering the graduate program at the University of Michigan. There, he received a master of science and public health degree in 1938 and a doctorate in 1944. His dissertation was entitled, "A Study of Certain Factors in Attempts to Alter Resistance of Animals to Virus Infections of the Respiratory Tract."

Wheeler began his scientific career in 1938 as a medical technologist at the Howard University College of Medicine. He was a research associate at the University of Michigan University Hospital Serology Laboratory from 1944-52. In 1952, he was appointed assistant professor in the department of microbiology and immunology, becoming the first full-time black faculty member at the University of Michigan. Wheeler received a promotion to associate professor in 1959 and eventually became a full professor.

Wheeler's research projects centered around serology, a science dealing with the reactions and properties of serums. From 1944-46, he studied the serology of malaria, an infectious disease transmitted by the anopheles mosquito; from 1944-49, he studied syphilis, an infectious venereal disease; and from 1952-70, he focused primarily on cancer.

During the 1960s, Wheeler became increasingly involved in politics. He was a member of the Committee to Study Racial Imbalance in Ann Arbor schools in 1965 and vice chair of that city's planning commission. From 1965-69, he was president of the Michigan Conference of NAACP Branches, and from 1967-75, he was a member of the Michigan Advisory Committee to the U.S. Civil Rights Commission. During the 1968 National Democratic Convention in Chicago, Wheeler served as a delegate.

In 1968-69, Wheeler was a World Health Organization (WHO) grantee. He was a member of the steering committee of the Michigan Democratic Black Caucus from 1968-71 and director of the Department of Christian Service, Archdiocese of Detroit from 1970-74. In 1970, Wheeler became the first president of the National Commission for Campaign for Human Development—a post he held for four years. He was also a member of the National League of Cities Human Resources Steering Committee and the Michigan Advisory Committee to Study Financing of Public Schools. In addition, he served on commissions to study the problems of the aging and the problems of youth.

A democrat, Wheeler became the first African American mayor of Ann Arbor, Michigan, in 1975. Running for a second term in 1976, Wheeler defeated opponent Louis Belcher by one vote, but his victory was marred by controversy. Election officials discovered that 20 nonresidents had voted in the election. Two of those voters faced the possibility of jail for refusing to reveal how they had cast their votes. The case eventually went before the Michigan Supreme Court, where the secrecy of a voter's ballot was upheld. During his second administration, Wheeler served on the Mayors' Advisory Council to the White House Office of Drug Abuse in 1977. In 1978, however, Belcher narrowly defeated Wheeler by 178 votes in a special election.

Wheeler received the Community Service Award from the National Association of Black Social Workers in 1973, an Alumni Award from Lincoln University in 1961, the Martin Luther King Dream Keepers Award from the University of Michigan in 1990, and the Development of People Award from the National Conference of Catholic Bishops in 1991. He is a member of the American

Association of Immunologists; Sigma Xi, the international honor society for scientists and engineers; and Kappa Alpha Psi.

Wheeler married Emma Watson Monteith on April 15, 1939. They have three children: Mary Evelyn Wheeler McDade, Alma Monteith Wheeler Smith, and Nancy Cornelia Wheeler Walker.

FURTHER READING:

Books

Who's Who in America, 1978-1979 Vol. 2, Marquis Who's Who Inc., p. 3444.

Periodicals

The Detroit News. (October 22, 1977): 11A.
The Detroit News. (April 4, 1978): 1A.

—*Sketch by Rose M. Estioco*

Emma Rochelle Wheeler
1882-1957
Physician

Emma Rochelle Wheeler was the founder, owner, and superintendent of the first hospital to be run by an African American in Chattanooga, Tennessee. She also introduced a prepaid plan covering the costs of hospitalization that was unique for its time. In addition to her medical practice, Wheeler supported the education of young blacks and founded a nursing school. A leading black citizen of Chattanooga, she was also active in civic matters.

Wheeler was born in Gainesville, Florida, on February 8, 1882. Her father worked as a farmer and veterinarian. Wheeler apparently became interested in medicine as early as age six, when her father took her to a physician who was a white woman. Befriending Wheeler, this doctor supported her ambitions. Wheeler attended the Cookman Institute in Jacksonville and graduated in 1899. The next year she married a teacher, Joseph R. Howard. In 1901, while Wheeler was pregnant, Howard died of typhoid. Their son, Joseph Howard, Jr., was born shortly after his death.

Wheeler then enrolled at Walden University in Nashville, Tennessee. In 1905, she graduated from that university's medical program, the Meharry Medical, Dental, and Pharmaceutical College. That same year, Wheeler married again, to John N. Wheeler. Her husband was also a

Emma Rochelle Wheeler

physician, and in 1905, they moved to Chattanooga where they set up a joint practice. Eventually, the couple had two daughters together, Thelma and Bette, and they adopted Wheeler's nephew George.

By 1915, Wheeler had saved enough money to open Walden Hospital in Chattanooga to serve the needs of African American patients requiring more intensive care. Before this time there was no such facility, and the state of black health care in the city was relatively poor. This project was entirely Wheeler's, and though her husband was an attending physician there, she managed the hospital herself and served as its superintendent. Wheeler also used Walden as a training school for nurses for approximately 20 years, and both the Wheelers were engaged in teaching.

In 1925, Wheeler began her new plan for prepaid hospitalization. Called the Nurse Service Club, people joined the organization and as members were entitled to two weeks of hospitalization at no charge and the care of a nurse at home afterwards. In that same year, Wheeler and several other prominent black women organized Chattanooga's first Alpha Kappa Alpha sorority chapter, Pi Omega. Wheeler was also a member of the Mountain City Medical Society and the Volunteer State Medical Association.

Wheeler's support of local young people led the local branch of the National Association for the Advancement of Colored People (NAACP) to name her "Negro Mother of the Year" in 1949. Beginning in 1951, Wheeler's heath began to fail; she retired from the hospital two years later, though she continued to practice medicine privately on an

intermittent basis. In 1953, Walden Hospital closed, failing without Wheeler's leadership. Wheeler died on September 12, 1957, in Nashville, and she was buried in Chattanooga. In 1958, the city of Chattanooga named a new housing project after Wheeler, dubbing it the Emma Wheeler Homes.

FURTHER READING:

Books

Wynn, Linda T. "Emma Rochelle Wheeler." *Profiles of African Americans in Tennessee*. Nashville, TN: Annual Local Conference on Afro-American Culture and History, 1996.

—Sketch by A. Petrusso

William Rodney Wiley
1931-1996
Microbiologist and biochemist

William Rodney Wiley was a talented researcher and an effective administrator, as well as a respected teacher. He spent his entire scientific career at Pacific Northwest National Laboratory in Washington state, where he earned numerous honors. He was about to assume the presidency of Sigma Xi, the international honor society for scientists and engineers, when he died suddenly in June 1996.

Wiley was born in Oxford, Mississippi, on September 5, 1931. His father, William Russell Wiley, owned a shoe repair shop, and his mother, Edna (Threlkeld) Wiley, managed a small restaurant. Wiley's family valued education, and his mother and aunt encouraged his interest in science. During those early years, Wiley considered a career in medicine, particularly after seeing his sister treated for poisoning by a local doctor.

In high school, Wiley showed both academic and athletic promise. He received a scholarship to Tougaloo College near Jackson—in part due to his talent on the football field. During the 1950s, Tougaloo was known for its premedical program, and Wiley received a great deal of personal attention from the faculty. His chemistry professor, St. Elmo Brady, was a role model, and Wiley began considering a career in research instead of medicine. Graduating with honors, he received his bachelor's degree in chemistry in 1954. Wiley served in the U.S. Army from 1954-56 and then worked as a civilian instructor in electronics for two years before continuing his education.

In 1958, Wiley received a scholarship from the Rockefeller Foundation and began his graduate studies at the University of Illinois in Champaign-Urbana. While there, he studied under James Watson, who was part of the scientific team that discovered the structure of deoxyribonucleic acid (DNA). Wiley also worked with Salvador Luria, who in 1969 would win a Nobel Prize for research that made the development of genetic engineering possible. Wiley received his master's degree in microbiology in 1960. He went on to earn a doctoral degree in bacteriology from Washington State University in 1965.

A Career in Research and Administration

After receiving his doctorate, Wiley joined the Pacific Northwest National Laboratory in Richland, Washington. This research center is an independent scientific organization managed by the Battelle Memorial Institute for the United States Department of Energy. During his early years there, Wiley studied yeast and related organisms, showing that yeast can ingest materials for the assembly of proteins within its cells. Later, he would focus on methods to remove the sugarlike molecules that make up the outer shell of yeast cells. Wiley studied the development of brain cells and the growth of cancer cells.

In 1974, Wiley was promoted to manager of the biology department at Pacific Northwest National Laboratory. He now supervised more than 200 research scientists. In 1979, he was appointed director of research, with a staff of 1,500 scientists and engineers. Six years later, Wiley was named director of Pacific Northwest Laboratories and senior vice president of Battelle Memorial Institute. In 1994, he became senior vice president for science and technology policy.

Wiley actively encouraged minority students to pursue careers in science, and he promoted afterschool science activities as well as summer internships at Pacific Northwest National Laboratory. Peter Blair, executive director of Sigma Xi, discussed Wiley's commitment to young people in the society's publication *American Scientist:* "Bill had a deep and abiding commitment to making the world a better place and setting an example young people would want to emulate." Blair also wrote that Wiley ". . . saw scientific research and development as the catalyst for economic growth, and during his tenure as director of the Pacific Northwest National Laboratory his vision and commitment to the objective were the driving forces behind establishment of PNNL's Environmental Molecular Science Lab."

Wiley won numerous awards, including one of the U.S. Department of Energy's highest honors, the Distinguished Associate Award, in 1994. He was also awarded the Alumni Achievement Award from Washington State University in 1986, an honorary doctor of law degree from Gonzaga University in 1988, an honorary doctor of science degree from Whitman College in 1990, and in 1994 the Black Engineer of the Year Award from *Black Engineer Magazine.* Wiley was a member of several professional and academic organizations, including the Board of Regents of

Gonzaga University, the Advisory Committee for Advanced Studies in Biomedical Sciences at the University of Washington, the Washington State Governor's Economic Development and Environmental Enhancement Task Force, the American Society of Biological Chemists, the American Society of Microbiology, and the Society for Experimental Biology and Medicine.

Expecting to assume the presidency of Sigma Xi, Wiley was quoted in the July-August 1996 issue of *American Scientist:* "Sigma Xi must continue to be more than a honor society. I believe the scientific community, though organizations such as Sigma Xi, is obliged to bring its collective wisdom to bear on current decision-making processes that will affect the future of science well into the 21st century." Wiley was just one day away from taking the helm at Sigma Xi when he died on June 30, 1996.

Wiley had been married to Myrtle Louise (Smith) Wiley, whom he had met at Tougaloo College, since 1953. They had one child, Johari.

SELECTED WRITINGS BY WILEY:

Periodicals

"Everyone Wants Quality R&D, But How Do You Measure It?" *Research & Development* 36, no.14 (March 1994).

FURTHER READING:

Books

Sammons, Vivian. *Blacks in Science and Medicine.* New York: Hemisphere Publishing, 1990, p. 249-50.

Periodicals

American Scientist 5, no. 4 (July-August 1996): 413.
American Scientist 84 (September-October 1996): 420.

—*Sketch by Rose M. Estioco*

J. Ernest Wilkins, Jr.
1923-
Mathematician and physicist

A distinguished applied mathematician and nuclear engineer, J. Ernest Wilkins, Jr., has enjoyed a diverse career spanning governmental, industrial, and academic positions. He was involved in the Manhattan Project—the

J. Ernest Wilkins, Jr.

top-secret quest to construct a nuclear bomb during the 1940s—and was a pioneer in nuclear reactor design. He served as President of the American Nuclear Society, and contributed to the mathematical theory of Bessel functions, differential and integral equations, the calculus of variations, and to optical instruments for space.

Jesse Ernest Wilkins, Jr. was born in Chicago on November 27, 1923, the son of J. Ernest Wilkins, Sr., and Lucile Beatrice Robinson Wilkins. The senior Wilkins was a prominent lawyer who was president of the Cook County Bar Association in 1941–42, and an Assistant Secretary of Labor in the Eisenhower administration. Wilkins's mother was a schoolteacher with a master's degree. Both parents remained active in the Methodist church. Wilkins's two brothers became lawyers, but Wilkins preferred mathematics, entering the University of Chicago at the age of 13, and becoming the youngest student ever admitted to that institution. He completed his baccalaureate in 1940, his master's in 1941, and, by the age of 19, had earned his doctoral degree.

Wilkins went to the Institute for Advanced Study on a Rosenwald scholarship in 1942, then taught at Tuskegee Institute in 1943–44. He returned to the University of Chicago, where he worked on the Manhattan Project at the Metallurgical Laboratory from 1944 to 1946. Wilkins spent the bulk of his career in industry, however, starting with a position as Mathematician at the American Optical Company in Buffalo, New York, in 1946. He left to become a Senior Mathematician at the Nuclear Development Corpora-

tion of America (NDA), later United Nuclear Corporation, in White Plains, New York, in 1950. There he became Manager of the Physics and Mathematics Department in 1955 and later Manager of Research and Development. While he was at NDA, Wilkins earned a B.M.E. degree in 1957, and an M.M.E. in 1960, from New York University.

Beginning in the 1960s, Wilkins held various offices in the American Nuclear Society, becoming President of the organization during 1974–75. In the early sixties, Wilkins moved to the General Atomic Division of General Dynamics Corporation in San Diego, where he remained until 1970. Wilkins next took an academic position as Distinguished Professor of Applied Mathematical Physics at Howard University in Washington, D.C., remaining in that position for the next seven years.

In 1977 Wilkins went to EG&G Idaho in Idaho Falls, where he was Associate General Manager and then Deputy General Manager. Leaving in 1984, Wilkins was an Argonne Fellow at Argonne National Laboratory in 1984 and 1985, and although retired beginning in 1985, he remained active as a consultant. In 1990, Wilkins joined Clark Atlanta University as Distinguished Professor of Applied Mathematics and Mathematical Physics.

Completes Gamma Ray Research

During his career Wilkins published roughly a hundred papers and reports on pure and applied mathematics, nuclear engineering, and optics. He is best-known for studies with Herbert Goldstein on gamma-ray penetration, the results of which are used for the design of nuclear reactor and radiation shielding, and of neutron absorption, which produced the Wigner-Wilkins approach to estimating the distribution of neutron energies in nuclear reactors. Wilkins also wrote papers on reactor operation and design and heat transfer. In addition, Wilkins continued to write on optical optimization problems and did interesting work on the estimation of the number of real roots of polynomials with random coefficients.

Wilkins served on advisory committees on scientific and engineering education for the National Academy of Engineering, the National Research Council, and other organizations and universities. Wilkins married Gloria Stewart in 1947. They had two children, Sharon and J. Ernest III. Wilkins was remarried in 1984, to Maxine Grundy. He is retired.

SELECTED WRITINGS BY WILKINS:

Books

"Status of Experimental and Theoretical Information on Neutron Slowing-Down Distributions in Hydrogenous Media," *Proceedings of the International Conference on the Peaceful Uses of Atomic Energy,* Volume 5, United Nations, 1956, pp. 62–76.

"The Landau Constants," *Progress in Approximation Theory,* Academic Press, 1991, pp. 829–842.

"Mean Number of Real Zeroes of a Random Trigonometric Polynomial, II," *Topics in Polynomials and Their Applications,* World, 1993, pp. 581–594.

Periodicals

"Systematic Calculations of Gamma-Ray Penetration," *Physical Review,* 89, (1953): 1150.

"Steady-state Heat Conduction in Slabs, Cylindrical and Spherical Shell with Non-uniform Heat Generation," *Nuclear Engineering and Design,* 24, (1973): 62–77.

"Minimum Critical Mass Nuclear Reactors, Part I and Part II," *Nuclear Science and Engineering,* 82, (1982): 307–315, 316–324.

"Apodization for Maximum Central Irradiance and Specified Large Rayleigh Limit of Resolution, II," *Journal of the Optical Society of America A, Optics and Image Science,* 1, (1984): 337–343.

FURTHER READING:

Books

Glasstone, Samuel and Alexander Sesonske. *Nuclear Engineering.* Van Nostrand, 1955.

In Black and White, A Guide to Magazine Articles, Newspaper Articles and Books Concerning more than 15,000 Black Individuals and Groups, Volume 2, 3rd edition, Gale, 1980, p. 1040.

Periodicals

Ebony, (February 1958): 60–67.

—*Sketch by Sally M. Moite*

Daniel Hale Williams
1858-1931
Surgeon

Arguably the most prominent black physician of his time, Daniel Hale Williams performed the first recorded successful heart surgery; founded Provident Hospital in Chicago; reorganized Freedmen's Hospital in Washington, D.C.; instituted policies and programs that made Meharry Medical College in Nashville a first-class institution for the training of black medical practitioners; and helped found the National Medical Association, the black

Daniel Hale Williams

counterpart to the segregated American Medical Association. Williams's distinguished career was recognized in 1913 when he was asked to become a charter member of the American College of Surgeons, the only black doctor so honored.

Williams was born January 18, 1858, in Hollidaysburg, Pennsylvania. He was the fifth child of Daniel Williams, a barber, and Sara (Price) Williams. After his father's death, his mother moved the family to Rockford, Illinois, and later to Janesville, Wisconsin, where Williams completed his secondary education. In 1878, he began an apprenticeship under Henry Palmer, a physician who had served as Wisconsin's surgeon general. His training under Palmer enabled him to enter Chicago Medical College, an affiliate of Northwestern University, where he received his medical degree in 1883. After serving an internship at Mercy Hospital in Chicago, Williams opened his practice in an integrated neighborhood on the south side of Chicago.

These early years saw Williams successful in his new practice, where he was meticulous in observing the sterilization and antiseptic procedures (newly advanced by the English surgeon Joseph Lister, based on the germ theory of French microbiologist Louis Pasteur) in the domestic locales of his surgeries. In 1884, he became a surgeon for the South Side Dispensary and an attending physician at the Protestant Orphan Asylum. He began instructing in anatomy at Chicago Medical College in 1885 and also served during this time as surgeon to the City Railway Company. In 1889, he was appointed to a four-year term on the Illinois State

Board of Health, where he played a role in drafting important public health regulations.

Founding of Provident Hospital

In spite of his many medical commitments, "Doctor Dan," as he was affectionately called, was determined to establish a progressive interracial hospital that would focus on offering internships to black doctors and training for black nurses. Williams realized this dream in 1891 with the opening of Provident Hospital. It was here that he performed the first recorded heart surgery by suturing a tear in a stabbing victim's pericardium (the membrane that encloses the heart); the patient completely recovered from the risky operation. Williams was subsequently to perfect a suture for spleen hemorrhage.

In 1894, President Cleveland appointed Williams as surgeon-in-chief of Freedmen's Hospital in Washington, D.C. At Freedmen's, Williams used his administrative skills to reorganize and upgrade what was essentially a collection of decrepit Army buildings that had been converted to civilian medical use. Under his guidance, Freedmen's hospital was divided into seven departments: dermatological, genito-urinary, gynecological, medical, obstetrical, surgical, and throat and chest. The number of internships was increased, the nurses training program was strengthened, and a horse-drawn ambulance was put into service. During his tenure, the hospital saw a significant decrease from its former 10% mortality rate. Williams's administrative achievement at Freedmen's was substantial, although he did not realize all of his far-reaching plans for the institution. In 1895, Williams helped found the Medico-Chirurgical Society of Washington. Ultimately discouraged by political infighting, he resigned from Freedmen's in 1897 and returned to Chicago.

In Chicago, Williams resumed his affiliation with Provident, and also began practicing at other hospitals. In 1899, in addition, Williams accepted a professorship of clinical surgery at Meharry Medical College in Nashville, Tennessee, where he began holding annual surgery clinics. In 1900, Williams presented research to the Chicago Medical Society refuting the myth that black women were not at risk for ovarian cysts. His association with the white-clientele St. Luke's Hospital, beginning in 1913, was instrumental in building one of the largest gynecological practices in Chicago. Over this period, Williams also helped establish 40 hospitals in 20 states to serve black communities.

Although Williams retained his affiliation with Provident for many years, his return to Chicago and the hospital came at a time of dissension: it was said that jealous and powerful associates, among them Dr. George C. Hall, looked unfavorably on Williams's advancements within the white medical establishment. The rivalry between Williams and George C. Hall eventually forced Williams to cut his ties to the hospital he had founded. In 1925, Williams invited Leon Tancil to assist him in his practice. Tancil remained for a few years, but then left to establish his own

office. Shortly thereafter, Williams's failing health forced him to end his long and distinguished practice.

Williams married Alice Johnson, a school teacher, in 1898; their only child died during birth a year later. Williams's favorite hobby was music; he often played his bass viol for charitable affairs. In 1926, two years after the death of his wife, Williams suffered a stroke and remained in ill health. He died at his summer home in Idlewild, Michigan, on August 4, 1931, and was buried in Chicago's Graceland Cemetery.

SELECTED WRITINGS BY WILLIAMS:

Periodicals

"Stab Wound of the Heart and Pericardium, Suture of the Pericardium. Recovery. Patient Alive Three Years Afterward," *New York Medical Record,* (March 27, 1897): 437–439.
"The Need of Hospitals and Training Schools for the Colored People of the South," *National Hospital Record,* Detroit (Reprint of paper read before the Phillis Wheatley Club, Nashville, Tennessee, January 23, 1900).

FURTHER READING:

Books

The African American Encyclopedia. Marshall Cavendish, 1993, pp. 1705–1707.
Blacks in Medicine and Science. Hemisphere, 1990, pp. 251–252.
Buckler, Helen. *Daniel Hale Williams, Negro Surgeon.* Pitman, 1968.
Doctor Dan, Pioneer in American Surgery. Little, Brown, 1954.
Fenderson, Lewis R. *Daniel Hale Williams: Open-Heart Doctor.* McGraw-Hill, 1971.
Patterson, Lillie. *Sure Hands, Strong Heart: The Life of Daniel Hale Williams.* Abingdon, 1981.
Scientists in the Black Perspective. The Lincoln Foundation, 1974, pp. 101–103.

—*Sketch by Jane Stewart Cook*

O. S. Williams
1921-
Aeronautical engineer

The second African American to receive a degree in aeronautical engineering, O. S. Williams headed the team that originated the first experimental airborne radio beacon for tracking crashed aircraft. Williams also managed the development of the control rocket systems that successfully guided the *Apollo* lunar landers.

Oswald S. "Ozzie" Williams was born on September 2, 1921 in Washington, D.C., to Oswald S. Williams, a postal worker, and Marie (Madden) Williams, a housewife. He grew up in New York, graduating from Boys High School in Brooklyn in 1938. Williams became interested in engineering as a teenager. He loved to make model airplanes and decided to become an engineer after a family friend described an engineer as a person who designs things.

When Williams went to New York University, he was discouraged by a dean. As he recounted in an interview with contributor Terrie M. Romano, the dean told him that "people of your race are not ready for engineering, and engineering is not ready for you. I warn you not to waste your ambition and training where you cannot get a job." Despite such advice, Williams completed his bachelor's degree in aeronautical engineering at New York University in 1943; he received his master's degree in aeronautical engineering from the same institution in 1947.

Aids in Design of War Planes

During World War II, Williams was a senior aerodynamicist with the Republic Aviation Corporation. He helped to design the P47 Thunderbolt, which was pivotal in the war effort. The P47 was the escort plane that protected the American high-altitude bombers. As an aerodynamicist, he was responsible for estimating and calculating, from wind tunnel testing, the lift of the plane's wings, its propelling forces, and its drag in order to determine how well the airplane would fly and its overall stability.

In 1947 Williams moved to the Babcock and Wilcox company, where he was a design draftsman. He then spent two years as a technical writer with the United States Navy Material Catalog Office, leaving in 1950 to take an engineering position at Greer Hydraulics, Inc. At Greer, as a group project leader, he was responsible for the development of the first experimental airborne radio beacon, which was used to locate crashed airplanes. The project was very challenging since the beacon had to operate equally well wherever it landed and whatever the weather conditions. The beacon would be fired by catapult and parachute to the ground as the airplane disintegrated, potentially landing anywhere: in water, in a tree, on level ground, or on a mountainside. Williams's team developed a beacon that could recognize where it had landed and transmit its position, but unfortunately, it was never produced commercially.

In 1956, Williams moved to the Reaction Motors Division of Thiokol Chemical Corporation, where he was responsible for pioneering work on small rocket engines. Williams was hired as a propulsion engineer by Grumman International in 1961 because of his expertise on liquid-fuel rockets. He had published several papers on the subject, one of which, "On the feasibility of liquid bipropellant rockets for spacecraft attitude control," was translated into Russian

by Dr. Leonid Sedov, the president of the Soviet Space Academy.

Helps Develop *Apollo* Lunar Module

At Grumman, Williams managed the development of the *Apollo* Lunar Module reaction control subsystem. Williams was fully responsible for the $42 million effort for eight years. He managed the three engineering groups that developed the small rocket motors—which used 100 pounds of thrust in comparison to the 10,500 pounds of thrust of the lunar module's main engine—that guided the lunar module, the part of the *Apollo* spacecraft that actually landed on the moon.

Williams went on to a career in marketing at Grumman, culminating in his election as a company vice president in 1974. After leaving Grumman he became a marketing professor at St. John's University in Queens, New York, where he had completed an M.B.A. in 1981. Williams was a member of the American Institute of Aeronautics and Astronautics, as well as an associate fellow and past chair of its Liquid Rockets Technical Committee. His varied career was profiled on Queens Public Television in the one-hour program, *O.S. Williams, A Man of Three Careers*.

In 1993, O. S. and Doris Reid Williams celebrated their fiftieth wedding anniversary. They had three children: Gregory (who died in 1982), Bruce, and Meredith.

FURTHER READING:

Other

Biography provided by Grumman International Inc., dated August, 1985.
O. S. Williams, interviews with Terrie M. Romano, conducted March 18 and 21, 1994.

—Sketch by Terrie M. Romano

Paul Revere Williams
1894-1980
Architect

Architect Paul R. Williams designed some 2,000 structures throughout California, as well as the rest of the nation and the world. Many of these were private homes, and he is most remembered for the houses which earned him the nickname "Architect to the Stars." At a time when African American actors were relegated to stereotypical roles, Williams acquired a client list of celebrities that would eventually include Frank Sinatra, Lucille Ball, Bill "Bojangles" Robinson, and Anthony Quinn. He also designed numerous commercial, non-profit, and government structures, including parts of the Los Angeles International Airport, the Pearl Harbor Memorial in Hawaii, Saks Fifth Avenue in Beverly Hills, the MCA Building, and an addition to the famous Beverly Hills Hotel.

Applying a Unique Strategy

Paul R. Williams was born in Los Angeles, California, the son of Chester and Lila Wright Williams. His parents died when he was four years old, however, and Williams spent his childhood in a series of orphanages. This experience exposed him to children of various racial and ethnic backgrounds, and no doubt contributed to the characteristics of adaptability and lack of self-consciousness that he would display throughout his life. Because of the ethnic variety in his environment, he was hardly aware of the fact that he was "different" as a black child, he later recalled. As a student at Sentous Avenue Grammar School, his drawings attracted the attention of a local builder, whose praise for his work inspired in him the dream of becoming an architect. Because he did not "know" that an African American in early twentieth-century America should not aspire to such a dignified profession, he continued to dream—and to draw.

But in 1912, when he was in high school, a teacher asked him a discouraging question: "Whoever heard of a Negro being an architect?" It was at that point that he confronted the issue of race, and the barriers it might pose to his career. Williams resolved to succeed as an individual rather than as a member of a group, and to let adversity become an inspiration rather than a discouragement. "Without having the wish to 'show them,'" he later said, "I developed a fierce desire to 'show myself.' I wanted to vindicate every ability I had. I wanted to acquire new abilities. I wanted to prove that I, *as an individual*, deserved a place in the world." With such powerful aspirations, there was no room for self-doubt or self-pity. "If I allow the fact that I am a Negro to checkmate my will to do, now," he wrote on another occasion, "I will inevitably form the habit of being defeated."

After high school, Williams enrolled in the Los Angeles School of Arts, where he won the prestigious Beaux-Arts Medal from the Beaux-Arts Institute of Design in New York City. At the age of 20 in 1914, he won a design prize for a Pasadena, California, civic center, in a contest that put him up against architects from all over the country. And that was before he had even graduated from architecture school; but when he did, in 1919, he again faced the reality that very few white architects would hire him. One by one, he went through the architects in the Los Angeles phone book until he found one who would take him on as a draftsman. Eventually he became chief draftsman at the firm, and the Society of Architects in Los Angeles invited him to join their organization. By 1922, he was ready to open his own office.

As the head of his own firm, Williams yet again had to confront the likelihood that many of his prospective clients would see his skin color rather than his work. In order to counteract this, he developed a unique strategy involving techniques he labeled "attention-getters." A white prospect might come to his office and, suddenly realizing that Williams was black, say something to the effect that he was "just shopping around"—meaning that he would leave and never come back. Williams, already a dapper gentleman with a graceful manner, would engage the prospect in conversation. Once he had ascertained the amount of money the client intended to invest in the project, he would name a figure higher than that and say that he never designed buildings that cost any less. But, he would add, "perhaps I might be able to offer some suggestions about the design. . . ." Often this led to a lengthy discussion of the project, and Williams would end up with a client. Another "attention-getter" was his ability to draw upside-down: with a prospective client sitting across the desk from him, Williams would begin sketching out a plan which was right-side-up from the perspective of the viewer. In both his attitudes and his talents, Williams was proving himself to be unique, and soon his efforts would meet with success.

"Architect to the Stars"

Despite the bluffing tactic he used with reluctant white prospects, in his early days as an architect Williams took any project he could find, no matter how small. From working with limited budgets, the man who would later design multimillion-dollar homes and public buildings learned how to figure costs precisely. Gradually he began to acquire a reputation for good work, and took on more substantial commissions, such as one from a senator to whom Williams had delivered papers as a boy. In 1931, automobile manufacturer E. L. Cord came to him with a request that Williams present him with a design for a house costing $100,000.

At a time when $5,000 would build a comfortable middle-class home, this represented a tremendous architect's commission, and Williams was not about to miss this opportunity. Cord was choosing between several architects, and he asked Williams how soon he could present a design. When Williams said he would have it ready by four o'clock the next afternoon, Cord was incredulous; the other architects had requested a minimum of two weeks' time. But Williams made good on his promise, working for 22 hours straight, and Cord gave him the job.

This experience was a turning point for Williams. During the next decades, he would earn the title "Architect to the Stars" for the many celebrities' homes he designed. His client list began to grow as he took on Hollywood figures, many of this famous from the early days of film: silent film star Corinne Griffith; singer and actress Grace Moore; starlet Zasu Pitts, whose style of fluttering her hands and speaking in a nervous, high-pitched voice inspired the character of Olive Oyl in the *Popeye* cartoons; and the film censor Will Hays. Bill "Bojangles" Robinson, famous for his roles opposite Shirley Temple, was a rare African American film star of the era, and he too became a client.

In fact, as Robert Arthur King would later point out in *Quarterly Black Review of Books,* "In a time when African-American actors in Hollywood were relegated to the predominantly restrictive roles of servants, dimwitted comedians, musicians and dancers, Williams enjoyed celebrity status as one of the most sought-after architects." This was ironic; so, too, was the fact that Williams designed a home for Charles Cottrell, who played Andy on *Amos 'n' Andy,* a radio show often criticized for its racist overtones. In his personal life, Williams still had to confront the prejudice he was overcoming in his career: only in 1951, long after he could afford to do so financially, was he able to build a home in one of the prestigious L.A. neighborhoods where so many of his houses were located.

A Concrete Legacy

Eventually Williams's client list would read like a *Who's Who of Hollywood.* He designed homes for Frank Sinatra, Lucille Ball and Desi Arnaz, Zsa Zsa Gabor, Anthony Quinn, Lon Chaney, and Tyrone Power. Gabor, Pilar Viladas later wrote in *Town and Country,* "got closets the size of a master bedroom." As for Sinatra's house, it was "a veritable push-button heaven." The beauty of Williams's comfortable designs, Viladas pointed out, passed easily from generation to generation: hence at the time of her 1994 article, actors Don Johnson and Melanie Griffith lived in the home Williams had designed for Bert Lahr, the "Cowardly Lion" in *The Wizard of Oz.*

Williams's style has often been described as "gracious" in accordance with his principle that "Good architecture should reduce human tension by creating a restful environment and changing social patterns." He did not create homes only for the wealthy, however, and he addressed his two books, *The Small Home of Tomorrow* (1945) and *New Homes for Today* (1946), to the needs of middle-class families. Williams designed the nation's first public-housing project in 1936, at a time when such facilities were viewed with optimism as a means of providing better housing for the poor.

Williams's many public designs include parts of the Los Angeles International Airport, as well as the Los Angeles County Court House, the Hollywood and 28th Street YMCAs in Los Angeles, the Pearl Harbor Memorial in Hawaii, St. Judge Hospital in Tennessee, and buildings for Howard University in Washington, D.C. Among his well-known commercial designs in the Los Angeles area are the Beverly Hills Saks Fifth Avenue Store, an addition to the Beverly Hills Hotel, the MCA Building, and the Al Jolson Memorial Shrine. His international projects include buildings in Colombia, Ecuador, and Liberia.

In the course of his career, Williams earned a number of awards, including the Omega Phi Psi Man of the Year Award in 1951, the NAACP Spingarn Medal in 1953, and honorary doctorates from Howard University, Lincoln University, and the Tuskegee Institute. Williams was one of the first blacks to become a member of the American Institute of Architects (AIA), which in 1957 elected him to its College of Fellows, making him the first African American to be accorded this, the AIA's highest honor.

Williams and his wife Della had two children. He died in 1980, leaving a vast and quite literally "concrete" legacy in the form of some 2,000 homes and public structures throughout California and elsewhere. It was ironic, then, that one of the first buildings to burn during the 1992 Los Angeles riots was his Broadway Federal Savings and Loan, which contained much of his archives. His granddaughter Karen Hudson, who in coming years would publish two books about Williams (including one, *The Will and the Way,* for children), said of the rioters, "If those young people knew that a black person had designed that building, would they have burned it down?" But as the riots subsided, another structure in South Central L.A. became a symbol of calm: the First African Methodist Episcopal Church. It, too, had been designed by Williams.

SELECTED WRITINGS BY WILLIAMS:

Books

The Small Home of Tomorrow. Murray & Gee, 1945.
New Homes for Today. Murray & Gee, 1946.

FURTHER READING:

Books

Hudson, Karen. *Paul R. Williams, Architect: A Legacy of Style.* Rizzoli, 1993.
Hudson, Karen. *The Will and the Way: Paul R. Williams, Architect.* Rizzoli, 1994.

Periodicals

King, Robert Arthur, "*Paul R. Williams, Architect: A Legacy of Style,*" *Quarterly Black Review of Books,* (November 30, 1994).
Viladas, Pilar, "Breaking New Ground (Architect Paul Williams)," *Town and Country,* (January 1, 1994): 76-91.

Other

"Architect Paul R. Williams." http://www.usc.edu/Library/Ref/Ethnic/williamsmain.html (May 11, 1998).
Paul Williams: Architect to the Stars (television special), HGTV, 1998.

—Sketch by Judson Knight

Theodore R. Williams

Theodore R. Williams, Jr.
1930-
Analytical chemist

Theodore R. Williams Jr., was born during on October 23, 1930, in Washington, D.C. His father, Theodore Williams, Sr., was a pharmacist who worked as a laboratory technician in a laboratory in the research arm of the U.S. Health Services (which later became the National Institutes of Health) and his mother was a school teacher. Williams developed his interest in chemistry while still in high school, due to an exceptionally dedicated teacher. He majored in chemistry at Howard University and graduated with a B.S. in 1952 with an award from the American Chemical Society for the best student in his class. He went on to Pennsylvania State University at State College and graduated in 1954 with a masters degree, having conducted independent research on the reactions of organic chemicals in water. During this time he met another student, Wyonne Carter. They got married in 1954 and then started graduate school at the University of Connecticut in Storrs, where he continued to pursue chemistry and she studied public policy.

Williams completed his Ph.D. in 1960 with a dissertation on the electrical properties of organic compounds. A year before he graduated, though, he had already begun to teach at the College of Wooster at Ohio, which remained his principal base for the duration of his career. One of the main reasons he was attracted to this college was its emphasis on teaching students at a one-on-one level, through independent projects at the undergraduate level.

"My frustration has often been that when Americans think of higher education, they seem to assume that the quality of teaching is in direct proportion to other, more easily quantifiable statistics—like the publications of the faculty or the national ranking of the football team . . . " he wrote once in an editorial for the *The Daily Record*. His dedication to teaching was recognized time and again during the course of his career, including a national award for Excellence in Teaching from the American Chemical Society in 1988. In 1991 Williams was named to a National Science Foundation advisory committee on undergraduate science education. Time and again he has assumed a leadership role in outreach programs to make science accessible and fun to young people and minorities. Always looking for ways to broaden the experience of students, Williams coordinated a program at Wooster that brings world-class classical musicians to perform at the college.

In addition to teaching, Williams remained active on the research front. An enduring source of pleasure has been the investigation of new instruments for analytical research. In an interview with contributor Neeraja Sankaran, he mentioned that on occasion he was led to his problems by the research interests of his students. Over the course of his tenure at Wooster he took sabbaticals to visit other institutions and collaborate on research projects. One such visit was to the University of Connecticut's medical school where he became conversant with chemistry of eye-lens chemistry. This was an area to which he says an enthusiastic undergraduate student literally, "dragged me along!" Williams subsequent work in this area has proven valuable in the effective treatment of conditions such as cataracts.

SELECTED WRITINGS BY WILLIAMS:

Periodicals

"Open the doors for black scientists." *The Philadelphia Inquirer* (August 6, 1990).
"A lesson in how not to take teaching for granted." *The Daily Record* (May 3, 1998).

—Sketch by Neeraja Sankaran

Geraldine Pittman Woods
1921-
Embryologist

Geraldine Pittman Woods had a rather brief career as a scientist. It is her actions as an administrator, directing the actions of the federal government towards improving the research capabilities of minority institutions and the educational opportunities for minority students, for which she is best known.

Geraldine Pittman was born on January 29, 1921, in West Palm Beach, Florida. Her parents, Susie King Pittman and Oscar Pittman, were comfortably established in the farming and lumber industries of central Florida, and also owned several properties in West Palm Beach.

Jerry began her schooling at a private Episcopal school, but in the fourth grade transferred to Industrial High School. At that time, the school was the only public school in West Palm Beach that allowed African American students. Jerry was not an outstanding student in these early years, and occasionally required tutors to keep her from falling behind her classmates. Despite an early interest in science, she received little encouragement from her teachers or family, who did not consider science a realistic career choice for an African American woman.

Jerry led a comfortable, but busy, life through grade and high school. She participated in church activities, learned to play the piano, and was an avid reader. The relatively care-free life of a Palm Beach teenager was, however, saddened by the death of her father.

After graduating from Industrial High School in 1938, Pittman attended Talladega College in Talladega, Alabama. The college had been established to serve the African American community, and provided an environment not much different from her high school. Uninspired, Pittman made only mediocre progress.

In 1940, her mother became seriously ill, and was admitted to Johns Hopkins Hospital in Baltimore, Maryland. Pittman left Talladega at this time, transferring to Howard University in Washington, D.C., to be closer to her mother. At Howard, she concentrated much harder on her studies, perhaps because of a concern for her mother's health. The faculty at Howard were impressed with Pittman's performance and supportive of her interest in science. One professor in particular, Dr. Louis Hansborough in the Department of Biology/Zoology, was instrumental in her decision to apply to, and her acceptance in, the graduate biology program at Radcliffe College and Harvard University in Cambridge, Massachusetts.

Fortunately, her mother recovered from her illness, and Pittman moved to Cambridge to join top students from throughout the country. It was a great challenge for her to compete with these students, most of whom came from

much stronger academic backgrounds. Still, Pittman was totally committed to excelling at Harvard, and became so focused on her work that she earned two graduate degrees in only three years and was elected to Phi Beta Kappa, the national scholastic honor society.

Pittman's doctoral research involved studying the development of nerves in the spinal chord. In the early stages of the development of embryos, the cells that will become nerves are not much different from all the other cells. As the embryo grows, however, the cells become differentiated. Pittman hoped to determine whether this process was controlled by factors within the cell itself or by stimulation from other, adjacent cells. She discovered that both effects are important, and also that the number of nerve cells produced is at least partly dependent on the number of muscle cells present.

Pittman returned to Howard University as an instructor after receiving her doctorate from Harvard in 1945. Shortly thereafter, she married Robert Woods, a student of dentistry at Meharry Medical School in Tennessee. The two commuted between Washington, D.C. and Nashville until Robert graduated. They then moved to California, where, Robert Woods set up a dental practice. Geraldine Pittman Woods temporarily put aside her career to raise a family.

Years later, when all three of her children were teenagers, Woods began the administrative career which was to yield some of her most important accomplishments. At first, she volunteered for local social services and civil rights organizations near Los Angeles, then branched out to statewide activities. Her strong support and advocacy of minority interests earned her an invitation to the White House in 1965, where she helped to launch Project Head Start, a federal program established to help children from low-income families gain preschool experience.

Woods continued her activism through serving on governing boards for many institutes of higher education, philanthropic organizations, and government bodies. Her main goal was to establish programs to get minority students, professors, and institutions involved in research training. In 1969 she was asked to be a special consultant at the National Institute of Health, where she helped develop the Minority Biomedical Research Support (MBRS) program and the Minority Access to Research Careers (MARC) program.

The MBRS program helped minority institutions to better compete for government and philanthropic grants by giving the applicants an understanding of the requirements and organization of grant proposals. Woods herself traveled throughout the country to give seminars at minority institutions on the preparation of grant applications, and gradually, the rate of grant approvals at these institutions improved.

The MARC program was designed to increase the recruitment and retention of minority students in scientific fields. Not only did this program establish scholarships for students at all levels of higher education, but it also provided funding for visiting scholars programs. These programs enabled faculty members from minority institutions to work with colleagues at some of the nation's most prestigious universities, and led to an overall improvement in teaching quality.

Woods is now retired from her position with the National Institute of Health. Her accomplishments have directly led to an increase in the number of professors involved in scientific research training at minority institutions, and an increase in the number of minority students able to enter graduate and professional schools. Her tireless efforts in support of minority interests have helped countless numbers of budding scientists realize their goals.

FURTHER READING:

Kessler, James H., J. S. Kidd, Renée A. Kidd, and Katherine A. Morin. "Geraldine Pittman Woods," In *Distinguished African American Scientists of the 20th Century.* Phoenix: The Oryx Press, 1996.

Smith, Carol Hobson. "Black Female Achievers in Academe," *Journal of Negro Education* 51, no. 3 (1982): 318-341.

—*Sketch by David E. Fontes*

Granville T. Woods

Granville T. Woods
1856-1910
Engineer and inventor

Granville T. Woods was a contemporary of Thomas Edison, and in fact was known in his lifetime as the "Black Edison." Interestingly, there were many parallels between the two mens' lives. Both were born in Ohio, and both left school at an early age. Both worked on the railroads, and both possessed an insatiable curiosity about machines and electricity. More important, Woods, like Edison, became a prolific inventor. Between 1884 and his death in 1910, he was awarded more than 60 patents; he contributed significantly to railway speed, efficiency, and safety.

Early Life

Woods was born in Columbus, Ohio, on April 23, 1856. Not much is known about his family; one source suggests that his parents immigrated from Australia. It is known that he had a brother and a sister—and it is also known that family circumstances forced him to leave school at the age of 10. Although in later years he did briefly attend night school and eventually took a course in electrical and mechanical engineering, he was essentially self-taught.

His first job was as an apprentice in a machine shop, where he learned both the machinist's and the blacksmith's trade (in the nineteenth century, blacksmithing was a state-of-the-art skill). The knowledge Woods gained in this position helped him later in life when he designed his own machines.

At 16, Woods went to Missouri, where his skills and training helped him land a job as an engineer on the Danville and Southern Railroad. Around this time, he became fascinated with electricity. He read voraciously on the subject, taking books out of public libraries and borrowing books from friends and acquaintances. (Some libraries would not allow blacks to borrow books; Woods would enlist the aid of friends in getting him the books he needed.)

Two years later, Woods moved to Springfield, Illinois, where he worked for a time at a rolling mill. By 1876, when he was 20, he had decided to head east, hoping to find more opportunities to put his skills and interests to work for him. Upon his arrival, he took a part-time job in a machine shop. This was also the time when he took the engineering course. In 1878, Woods took a slightly different path, landing a job as an engineer on the British steamer H.M.S. *Ironsides.* Within two years he had been promoted to chief engineer.

First Inventions

By 1881, Woods was back in Ohio, having settled in Cincinnati. His experience in the railways and aboard ship had given him a number of ideas; coupling this experience with his natural creativity, he began to put his ideas to the test.

Woods had become intrigued by thermal power and steam-driven engines. Convinced that steam power could be harnessed more effectively, he set about designing an improved steam-boiler furnace. He submitted his design to the U.S. patent Office in 1884, and the patent was granted.

His next invention, patented the same year, was a telephone transmitter. The telephone had been invented by Alexander Graham Bell nearly a decade earlier, but Woods's invention improved on the quality of transmitted sound. Woods employed an alternating electrical current, which was better able to differentiate between strong and weak voice signals, and thus carry the voice over longer distances.

In 1885, Woods invented a device that combined the telephone with the telegraph—a process he referred to as "telegraphony." This "apparatus for transmission of messages by electricity," as he called it, dramatically altered the way was messages were sent. Until Woods created his new invention, messages were sent either by telegraph or telephone. At the time, telegraph was the more common method—but only trained telegraphers, skilled in Morse code, could send messages or understand any messages that were received. Woods's machine allowed the user to switch between telegraph and telephone. A message could either be sent via Morse code as with a telegraph, or via actual speech as with a phone. This invention was so important that the American Bell Telephone Company purchased it from Woods. In fact, Bell telephone became one of several companies that would purchase his inventions.

In 1887, Woods brought forth what is arguably his most important invention, the induction telegraph, patented as the "Synchronous Multiplex Railway Telegraph." This invention was truly revolutionary. It allowed messages to be sent between moving trains, or from moving trains to railroad stations. Before the induction telegraph existed, there was no way for railroad stations and trains to contact each other. As a result, rail travel could be extremely dangerous. A railroad engineer would have no idea whether there was a stalled train on the track or a washed-out bridge, until he came across the obstacle. There was also no guarantee that he could stop the train in time. Woods's invention relied on existing telegraph lines, many of which ran parallel to railroad tracks. By harnessing static electricity, the induction telegraph could conduct messages to those wires; because the messages were sent via static electricity, regular messages could be sent simultaneously over the wires.

Later Inventions

By now Woods had earned a reputation as a gifted inventor. He also earned the ire of his competitors. The Phelps Company, which was working on a machine similar to the induction telegraph, challenged Woods's patent, but the courts ruled that Woods was unquestionably the inventor. Thomas Edison also challenged Woods—but it was obvious that Edison had great respect for his fellow inventor. At one point, Edison offered Woods the chance to become a partner in his business. Woods declined, preferring to work independently. In 1887 he organized the Woods Electric Company, which he moved to New York City in 1890. Around that time, he did take on a partner of his own—his brother Lyates, who was also an engineer and inventor.

Woods's later inventions put electricity to safer and more efficient use. He discovered that theater lights were dimmed by use of a single resistor that operated all the other electrical equipment in the theater. This wasted a great deal of electricity and was potentially dangerous if circuits got overloaded. Woods invented a circuit-breaker type of apparatus to allow the lights to function on their own current. Theater owners were quite pleased at the improved performance—and at the 40 percent savings on their electric bills.

Woods was also a key figure in railroad electrification. His overhead conducting system, designed in 1888, allowed rail and trolley cars to run via electric current instead of steam power. Not only were the electric cars more efficient, they were cleaner to operate. Woods also created the "third rail" that is still common on many electrified rail lines. The third rail carries electricity by means of electromagnetic switches, and essentially pulls the train along. General Electric bought the patent from Woods in 1901. His improvements to the automatic air brake for railroad cars further added to the safety of rail travel; the Westinghouse Air Brake Company bought his brake inventions because they were a considerable improvement over the brakes then in existence.

Not all of Woods's inventions involved trains or telegraphs. In 1890 he invented an electrically heated egg incubator, which worked by means of a thermostatic control similar to the ones currently found in buildings.

Woods continued to invent for the remainder of his life. In his 50s he began to suffer from poor health; he was only 53 when he died in Harlem Hospital in New York on January 30, 1910.

FURTHER READING:

Books

Haber, Louis. *Black Pioneers of Science and Invention.* Harcourt Brace Jovanovich, 1970.

Logan, Rayford W. and Michael R. Winston. *Dictionary of American Negro Biography.* Norton, 1982.

Robinson, Wilhelmina S. *Historical Afro-American Biographies.* Publishers Company, 1969.

Sammons, Vivian O. *Blacks in Science and Medicine.* Hemisphere Publishing, 1990.

Jane Cooke Wright

Van Sertima, Ivan, ed. *Blacks in Science, Ancient and Modern*. Journal of African Civilizations, Ltd., 1984.

—Sketch by George A. Milite

Jane Cooke Wright
1919-

Physician

J ane Cooke Wright has carried on the medical legacy of her prominent family through a career in internal medicine, cancer research, and medical education. She has served as director of the Cancer Research Foundation of Harlem Hospital in New York City, faculty member and director of cancer chemotherapy at the New York University Medical Center, and professor of surgery and associate dean at New York Medical College and its affiliate hospitals. Wright has also devoted her efforts to educating fellow practitioners about advances in chemotherapy, a service she performed in her 1983 convention lecture to the National Medical Association entitled "Cancer Chemotherapy: Past, Present, and Future."

Wright was born in New York City on November 20, 1919, to Louis Tompkins and Corinne (Cooke) Wright. Her paternal grandfather was one of the first graduates of Tennessee's Meharry Medical College, an institution founded to give former slaves professional training. Another relative, **Harold D. West**, was Meharry's first black president. Her step-grandfather, William Penn, was the first black person to earn a medical degree from Yale. Her father, **Louis Tompkins Wright**—one of the first black graduates of Harvard medical college—was the first black physician to be appointed to the staff of a New York City hospital; he was also a pioneer in cancer chemotherapy and New York City's first black police surgeon. Jane Cooke Wright was the first of two daughters; her sister, Barbara, also became a physician.

Wright was educated in private elementary and secondary schools and won a four-year scholarship to Smith College in Massachusetts, where she set records as a varsity swimmer. Graduating in 1942, Wright entered New York Medical College, again on a four-year scholarship, and received her medical degree with honors in 1945. An internship and assistant residency followed at Bellevue Hospital in New York City. After leaving Bellevue Hospital, she completed her training with a two-year residency in internal medicine at Harlem Hospital.

Wright's first position after residency was as a school and visiting physician at Harlem Hospital in 1949. She became a clinician later that year at the hospital's Cancer Foundation, which was then headed by her father. There she studied the response of tumors and growths to drugs and the application of chemotherapy in the treatment of cancer. She explored the complex relationships and variations between test animal and patient, tissue sample and patient, and individual patient responses to various chemotherapeutic agents. Upon her father's death in 1952, she became the Cancer Foundation's director.

In 1955, Wright joined the New York University Medical Center to direct the cancer chemotherapy research department and teach research surgery. Her continuing research explored animal and human responses to chemotherapeutic agents (such as triethylene thiophosphoromide, CB 1348 and Dihydro E. 73) and isolation perfusion and regional perfusion chemotherapy techniques. In 1961, Wright became adjunct professor of research surgery at the medical center and also served as vice-president of the African Research Foundation, a position which took her on a medical mission to East Africa. In 1964, she was appointed to the President's Commission on Heart Disease, Cancer, and Stroke; the commission's work resulted in a nationwide network of treatment centers for these diseases. The Albert Einstein College of Medicine presented Wright with its Spirit of Achievement Award in 1965.

Wright became associate dean and professor of surgery at New York Medical College in 1967, where she was also responsible for administrating the medical school and developing a program for the study of cancer, heart disease, and stroke. She was awarded the Hadassah Myrtle Wreath in 1967, and the Smith College medal in 1968. In December, 1975, Wright was one of eight scientists saluted by *Cancer Research* in its observation of International Women's Year, and in 1980 was featured on an Exceptional Black Scientists poster by Ciba Geigy. Since 1987, she has been emerita professor of surgery at New York Medical College.

Wright has served on the editorial board of the *Journal of the National Medical Association* and as a trustee of Smith College and of the New York City division of the American Cancer Association. She married David D. Jones, Jr., a graduate of Harvard Law School, on July 27, 1947; the couple have two daughters, Jane and Alison. Her hobbies include sailing, painting, and reading mystery novels.

SELECTED WRITINGS BY WRIGHT:

Periodicals

"Cancer Chemotherapy: Past, Present, and Future," *Journal of the National Medical Association,* (August 1984): 773–784; (September 1984): 865–876.

FURTHER READING:

Books

Blacks in Medicine and Science. Hemisphere, 1990, p. 258.
Notable Black American Women. Gale, 1992, pp. 1283–1285.

—*Sketch by Jane Stewart Cook*

Louis Tompkins Wright
1891-1952

Surgeon and hospital administrator

Louis Tompkins Wright, one of the first black graduates of the Harvard Medical School, was a distinguished surgeon, hospital administrator, and civil rights activist. His talents and determination as a black leader improved access to quality health care for black people and the professional prospects of his fellow African American medical practitioners. During Wright's prolonged affiliation with Harlem Hospital in New York City, he became the hospital's surgical director and founded its Cancer Research Center. An active member of the New York City chapter of the National Association for the Advancement of Colored

People (NAACP), Wright ultimately chaired its national board of directors, holding that position from 1934 until his death.

Wright was born on July 23, 1891, in La Grange, Georgia. He was the younger son of Ceah Ketcham and Lula Tompkins Wright. His father, a doctor who practiced for only a short period before becoming a clergyman, died in 1895; in 1899, his mother married William Fletcher Penn, also a physician. Wright enrolled in Clark University in Atlanta, where he was valedictorian of the class of 1911. After being subjected to a special examination, Wright was accepted by the Harvard Medical School, where he was to graduate *cum laude* and fourth in his class in 1915. After a two-year internship at Freedmen's Hospital in Washington, D.C., he briefly joined his stepfather's practice in Atlanta.

In 1917, in the midst of World War I, Wright entered the U.S. Army Medical Corps, and was eventually appointed director of surgical wards for an Army field hospital in France. While in France, he was exposed to phosgene gas, which caused him permanent lung damage. For his military service, Wright was awarded the Purple Heart and discharged at the rank of captain, later achieving the rank of lieutenant-colonel in the U.S. Medical Reserve Corps through examination. When Wright returned from France in the spring of 1919, he settled into private practice in New York City.

Association with Harlem Hospital

Shortly thereafter, the Medical Board of Harlem Hospital was persuaded by Civil Service Commissioner Ferdinand Q. Morton to admit Wright and some other black physicians as provisional adjunct surgeons. A few white doctors on the staff of the hospital (whose clientele was then a prosperous white community) resigned in protest, but Wright quickly established himself professionally. In 1926, he was granted a permanent appointment at the hospital. A few years later, in addition to his hospital commitments, he began his service as surgeon for the New York City Police Department, a post he held for more than 20 years. In 1943, he was named director of Harlem Hospital's Department of Surgery. In 1948, he became president of the medical staff board and director of the hospital's Cancer Research Foundation, and founded the *Harlem Hospital Bulletin.*

Wright's contributions to medicine were various. Early in his career, while an intern at Freedmen's Hospital, he was critical of the medical establishment's belief that the Schick test for diphtheria (which, for diphtheria susceptible individuals, reddens the skin where injected) was not useful on black patients; his research proved this supposition to be without basis. He originated an intradermal smallpox vaccination method that minimized undesirable side effects. Wright directed the research team that first tested the antibiotic aureomycin for the treatment of venereal disease and also conducted research with the antibiotic terramycin; he was to publish over 30 papers on aureomycin and eight papers on terramycin. Wright invented several surgical devices, including a brace for cervical fractures and a plate used in repairing fractures of the knee. His research into skull and brain injuries led to the first authoritative publication in this area by a black doctor. His cancer research, which led to 15 publications, focused on the use of teropterin, triethylene melamine, folic acid, and hormones in chemotherapy. Throughout his career, moreover, Wright opposed various forms of medical discrimination, such as efforts to establish segregated medical facilities (including a segregated Veterans Hospital) in New York. Another achievement was fostering solidarity and harmony among Harlem Hospital's ethnically diverse medical staff.

In 1934, Wright became the second black doctor to be admitted to the American College of Surgeons. He received an honorary doctorate from Clark University in 1938, and was awarded the NAACP's Spingarn Medal in 1940. In 1952, he was honored by the John A. Andrews Memorial Hospital of the Tuskegee Institute in Alabama. Wright held membership in numerous professional associations in addition to the American College of Surgeons, including the American Medical Association, the National Medical Association, and the American Board of Surgery; he was also a founding member of the American Academy of Compensation Medicine. In connection with his civil rights activism, he served as president of the Crisis Publishing Company, printers of the *Crisis,* which was to become the official organ of the NAACP.

Wright married Corinne Cooke in 1918. They had two daughters: **Jane Cooke Wright**, a physician who became director of the Cancer Research Foundation on her father's death; and Barbara Penn Wright, also a physician. Wright died of a heart attack on October 8, 1952. The Louis T. Wright Medical Library at Harlem Hospital had been established in his honor that same year; in 1969, the Louis T. Wright Surgical Building at Harlem Hospital was dedicated in his memory.

SELECTED WRITINGS BY WRIGHT:

Books

"Head Injuries," Chapter 22 of *The Treatment of Fractures,* (11th edition), edited by Charles L. Scudder, W. B. Saunders, 1938.

FURTHER READING:

Books

Blacks in Medicine and Science. Hemisphere, 1990, p. 259.
Dictionary of American Negro Biography. W. W. Norton, 1982, pp. 670–671.
Scientists in the Black Perspective. The Lincoln Foundation, 1974, pp. 105–107.

James Howard Wyche

Periodicals

New York Times, (October 9, 1952): 31.

—Sketch by Jane Stewart Cook

James Howard Wyche
1942-
Cell biologist

James Wyche has studied bacterial genetics and the generation of hormones, as well as the workings of the pancreas and pituitary glands. As professor of medical science at Brown University, his current research is contributing to the search for long-term solutions to cancer and leukemia. As associate provost at Brown and executive director of the multi-university Leadership Alliance, Wyche is also working to include a larger percentage of minorities among tomorrow's scientists and scholars.

James Howard Wyche was born on November 14, 1942, in Greenport, New York, to William and Fannie (Harris) Wyche. His father worked as a house painter, and his mother was a physician's technician. Greenport is on the northeastern tip of Long Island, and Wyche spent his early years exploring the plants and animals living in what was then a rural environment. His parents and his teachers encouraged these explorations, and by the end of high school he had decided to study agricultural sciences.

In 1960, Wyche entered the two-year food-science program at the State University of New York at Morrisville. He studied the causes of bacterial contamination in food and earned an associate of art and science degree in 1962. Wyche continued his focus on bacteriology at Cornell University in Ithaca, New York, graduating with a bachelor of science degree in 1965. Wyche performed excellent work at Cornell, despite several race-related incidents, and he quickly received a job offer from Brookhaven National Laboratory. After only a year, he entered the doctoral program in bacterial genetics at Johns Hopkins University on a fellowship provided by the National Institutes of Health. Before his degree was awarded in 1972, he participated in two research projects in cell biology at the University of California at Berkeley. One of the fellowships took him to the medical school of the University of Naples in Italy. These experiences, as well a postdoctoral fellowship at the University of California at San Diego, began his fascination with the mechanisms by which a cell can produce chemicals that impact the health of the entire body.

From 1974-80, Wyche taught as assistant and later associate professor of biology at the University of Missouri-Columbia. He continued his research on how the glands produce hormones. In 1981, he moved to the City University of New York. Appointed program coordinator and then director of the Minority Biomedical Research Program at the university's Hunter College, here Wyche began his dual role of professor and mentor for minority students. In 1988, he became associate professor of medical science and associate dean of biology and medicine for minority affairs at Brown University in Providence, Rhode Island.

At Brown University, Wyche has combined his two priorities—researching cell biology and increasing minority participation in scientific careers. He is currently studying cell apoptosis, or programmed cell death, and the role that proteins and genes play in cueing or suppressing this process. Wyche has established that certain unique proteins can grow in cancerous cells that have survived initial treatments such as chemotherapy and radiation and continue to resist further treatment. Through these studies, he has identified a new chemical that will initiate apoptosis in these cells; although too toxic for human use, Wyche is investigating natural plants and other sources that replicate this chemical.

At the same time, Wyche leads an academic consortium of 23 institutions of higher learning called the Leadership Alliance, which encourages minorities to attend graduate school and become part of the broader research and faculty community. Increasing the available fellowships and grants is key to the alliance's efforts, and their efforts, Wyche says, are essential to progress: "As a nation we face

a tremendous challenge, if we close off our educational opportunities, we put ourselves at risk." Despite all he has accomplished in the field of cell biology, Wyche is most proud of his efforts to diversify the population of scientists and scholars.

Wyche has received numerous awards, fellowships and scholarships. He received fellowships from the American Cancer Society in 1974 and the Ford Foundation in 1987. He has accepted awards for achievements in science and minority medical education from the National Council of Negro Women (1991) and the National Association of Medical Minority Educators (1990); he was also the recipient of the 1996 Howard University Outstanding Achievement Award. He has been a visiting scholar and speaker at various universities and colleges and has organized several national and international conferences on cell biology and science education. Wyche has served on committees for the National Academy of Sciences, the National Institutes of Health, the Department of Energy, the National Research Council, and the American Society for Cell Biology.

Wyche is married and the father of three sons. He lives in Providence, Rhode Island.

SELECTED WRITINGS BY WYCHE:

Books

(With D. Allensworth, E. Lawson, L. Nicholson, eds.) *Schools and Health: Our Nation's Investment.* National Academy Press, 1997.

Periodicals

(with D. Chatterjee, Z. Han, J. Mendoza, L.A. Goodglick, E.A. Hendrickson, P. Pantazis) "Monocytic Differentiation of HL-60 Promyelocytic Leukemia Cells Correlates with the Induction of Bcl-xL1." *Cell Growth & Differentiation* 8 (October 1997): 111083-1089.

(with Z. Han, N. Malik, T. Carter, W.H. Reeves, E.A. Hendrickson) "DNA-dependent Protein Kinase Is a Target for a CPP32-like Apoptotic Protease." *The Journal of Biological Chemistry* 271, no. 40 (October 4, 1996): 25035-25040.

(with C. Johnson) "The Leadership Alliance: A Coordinated Effort in Mentoring." *NESPA News* 4 (1995): 2-8.

(with H. Frierson) "Increasing Minority Biomedical Scientists Through the Physician-Scientist Route." *Journal of National Institutes for Health Research* 6 (1994): 16.

FURTHER READING:

Books

Kessler, James, et al. *Distinguished African American*

Scientists of the 20th Century. Phoenix, AZ: Oryx Press, 1996.

—Sketch by Sally Cole-Misch

Gender Index

Field of Specialization Index

Embryology
- Alexander, Lloyd E.   7
- Graves, Artis P.   135
- Woods, Geraldine Pittman   324

Endocrinology
- Henry, Walter Lester, Jr.   156

Engineering
- Bluford, Guion S.   30
- Boykin, Otis   39
- Crosthwait, David Nelson, Jr.   85
- Davis, Stephen Smith   92
- Gourdine, Meredith Charles   131
- Kornegay, Wade M.   192
- Latimer, Lewis H.   196
- McCoy, Elijah   225
- Woods, Granville T.   325

Entomology
- Chambers, Vivian Murray   62
- Turner, Charles Henry   301

Genetics
- Harris, Mary Styles   148

Geology
- Bromery, Randolph W.   43
- Gipson, Mack, Jr.   130

Geophysics
- Bromery, Randolph W.   43
- Person, Waverly J.   252

Invention
- Banneker, Benjamin   18
- Barnes, William Harry   20
- Beard, Andrew Jackson   21
- Blair, Henry   29
- Boykin, Otis   39
- Croslin, Michael   84
- Gourdine, Meredith Charles   131
- Latimer, Lewis H.   196
- Logan, Joseph G., Jr.   208
- Matzeliger, Jan Earnst   218
- McCoy, Elijah   225
- Morgan, Garrett A.   236
- Murray, George Washington   240
- Rillieux, Norbert   263
- Russell, Edwin Roberts   270
- Shaw, Earl D.   273
- Temple, Lewis   295
- Woods, Granville T.   325

Marine biology
- Jearld, Ambrose, Jr.   176
- Just, Ernest Everett   185
- Owens, Joan Murrell   246

Mathematics
- Bharuca-Reid, Albert Turner   24
- Blackwell, David H.   27
- Browne, Marjorie Lee   49
- Cox, Elbert Frank   83
- Granville, Evelyn Boyd   133
- Hrabowski, Freeman A. III   162
- Jones, Eleanor Green Dawley   182
- King, John Quill Taylor   190
- Mayes, Vivienne Malone   220
- Mishoe, Luna Isaac   231
- Stephens, Clarence F.   282
- Stubblefield, Beauregard   287
- Velez-Rodriguez, Argelia   307
- Wilkins, J. Ernest, Jr.   316

Medicine
- Adams, Numa Pompilius Garfield   1
- Alexander, Leslie Luther   6
- Allen, William E., Jr.   9
- Anderson, Caroline Still   11
- Augusta, Alexander Thomas   14
- Barnes, William Harry   20
- Berry, Leonidas Harris   23
- Black, Keith   26
- Bousfield, Midian Othello   37
- Brown, Arthur McKimmon   46
- Brown, Dorothy Lavinia   47
- Callender, Clive O.   53
- Calloway, Nathaniel Oglesby   54
- Cole, Rebecca J.   75
- Cooper, Edward S.   79
- Cornely, Paul Bertau   80
- Crumpler, Rebecca Lee   86
- Dailey, Ulysses Grant   89
- Drew, Charles R.   96
- Durham (Derham), James   100
- Elders, M. Joycelyn   105
- Ellis, Effie O'Neal   108
- Evans, Matilda Arabella   111
- Ferebee, Dorothy Boulding   115
- Ferguson, Angella D.   116
- Garvin, Charles Herbert   125
- Giles, Roscoe Conkling   127
- Grigsby, Margaret E.   139
- Gunning, Lucille C.   140
- Harrison, Robert Walker III   151
- Henry, Walter Lester, Jr.   156
- Hinton, William Augustus   160
- Jason, Robert S.   172
- Jemison, Mae C.   177
- Johnson, Halle Tanner Dillon   178
- Johnson, John Beauregard, Jr.   179
- Johnson, Joseph Lealand   180
- Jones, Edith Mae Irby   181
- Kountz, Samuel L., Jr.   193
- Leevy, Carroll Moton   203
- Leffall, LaSalle D., Jr.   205
- Lynk, Miles Vandahurst   209

- Majors, Monroe Alpheus   211
- Maloney, Arnold Hamilton   213
- Marchbanks, Vance H.   214
- Mossell, Nathan Francis   238
- Murray, Peter Marshall   241
- Patton, Georgia Esther Lee   250
- Poindexter, Hildrus A.   253
- Poussaint, Alvin Francis   254
- Purvis, Charles Burleigh   255
- Roberts, Carl Glennis   264
- Rock, John Sweat   268
- Smith, James McCune   278
- Spurlock, Jeanne   279
- Steward, Susan Smith McKinney   283
- Sullivan, Louis Wade   289
- Wattleton, Alyce Faye   310
- Wethers, Doris L.   312
- Wheeler, Emma Rochelle   314
- Williams, Daniel Hale   318
- Wright, Jane Cooke   327
- Wright, Louis Tompkins   328

Meteorology
- Anderson, Charles Edward   12
- Bacon-Bercey, June   17

Microbiology
- Amos, Harold   10
- Brooks, Carolyn Branch   45
- Brown, Russell Wilfred   48
- Fuller, A. Oveta   121
- Hammond, Benjamin Franklin   144
- Jay, James M.   174
- Stokes, Gerald V.   286
- Taylor, Welton I.   294
- Wiley, William R.   315

Neurology
- Black, Keith   26
- Fuller, Solomon Carter   122
- Hudson, Roy Davage   165

Nuclear engineering
- Bishop, Alfred A.   25

Nutrition
- Edwards, Cecile Hoover   103
- Kittrell, Flemmie Pansy   190

Oceanography
- Forde, Evan B.   119

Organic chemistry
- Alexander, Benjamin H.   4
- Barnes, Robert Percy   20
- Calloway, Nathaniel Oglesby   54
- Dorman, Linneaus C.   95
- Elliot, Irvin Wesley, Jr.   106

Subject Index

Page numbers in *italics* indicate photos; those in **boldface** refer to the full biography for a scientist.

physician to pass to the California
Medical Boards 211

physician to practice medicine west of
the Rocky Mountains 211

physicians commissioned as a First
Lieutenant in the U.S. Army 125

physicians to practice in the U.S. 100

police surgeon in New York City 327

president of Meharry Medical College
312, 327

president of the American Cancer
Society 205

president of the American College of
Surgeons 205, 206

president of the American Heart
Association 80

president of the American Public Health
Association 80, 82

president of the New York County
Medical Society 241

presidential appointee 18

professional teacher of physical
education in Washington, D.C. 154

professor at Harvard Medical School
160

professor of pharmacology 213

psychiatrist of note 123

recipient of the American College of
Physician's Master Award 156

Regent of the American College of
Physicians 156

space shuttle pilot 138

student at Yale University 36

student to attend mixed university
classes in the South 181

surgeon commissioned with the U.S.
Army (regular army) 46

surgeon to speak on an international
medical panel 90

tenured full professor in the
Massachusetts Institute of Technology,
Physics Department 170

tenured professor at the University of
Iowa 164

tenured professor of medicine at the
University of Pennsylvania School of
Medicine 79

test pilot to be selected for astronaut
training 200

to earn entry into Phi Beta Kappa 36

to hold a faculty position in a U.S.
medical school 15

to own and operate a pharmacy in the
United States 278

to practice medicine with a medical
degree in the United States 278

to present a paper to the Virginia
Academy of Science 303

winner, University of Pennsylvania
Medical School scholarship 20

woman administrator for the American
Medical Association 108, 109

woman admitted to the American
College of Surgeons 47

woman admitted to the astronaut
training program 177

woman anthropologist 94

woman doctor in the state of New York
283

woman elected to the Tennessee State
Legislature 47

woman mathematician to receive an
honorary degree 135

woman meteorologist 17

woman Ph.D. from the Massachusetts
Institute of Technology 170

woman Ph.D. in anatomy 208

woman Ph.D. in geology in the United
States 246

woman president of Spelman College
73, 74

woman surgeon in the South 47

woman to attend the University of
Arkansas Medical School 105

woman to earn a Ph.D. in bacteriology
from Ohio State University 235

woman to earn a Ph.D. in chemistry 91

woman to earn a Ph.D. in mathematics
at the University of Texas 221

woman to earn the doctor of dental
surgery degree in the U.S. 136

woman to graduate from the Female
Medical College 75

woman to practice dentistry in Chicago
136

woman to receive tenure at the
University of Michigan 288

woman to serve in the Tennessee State
Legislature 47

woman to sit for Alabama's medical
boards 178

women Ph.D.s in mathematics in the
United States 182

women to receive a medical degree in
the U.S. 86

women to receive doctoral degrees in
mathematics 49, 133

First Principles of Chemistry 294

First Steps and Nursery Rhymes 212

Fisk University

    Infrared Research Laboratory 202

    Infrared Spectroscopy Institute 202

    Physics Department 166

    presidents 202

Flash-drying 143

Flow distributor 25, 26

Fluid dynamics 163

Fluoride chemistry 259

Fluorine chemistry 12

Fluorine compounds 12

Fluorine-19 chemistry 13

Flying Black Medics 23

Food technology 143

Food-borne pathogens 295

Foods, bacterial contamination in 330

Forde, Evan B. **119**, *119*

Forten, James 30

Francisco, Joseph **120**

Frand, Joseph 135

Franklin, Renty Benjamin **120–21**

Frederick Douglass Memorial Hospital 238,
239

Freedom (space station) 3

Fuller, A. Oveta **121–22**

Fuller, Solomon Carter **122–24**

Furnaces, steam-boiler 326

G. A. Morgan Refining Company 236

Galatis, George 171

Game theory 27

    Kuratowski Reduction Theorem 29

Gamma-ray penetration 317

Gangrene 295

Garfield, James A. 256

Garlic extracts 298

Garnet, Henry Highland 279

Garvin, Charles Herbert **125–26**

Gas masks 236

Gas turbines 209

Gastrobiopsyscope 23

Gastrointestinal Panendoscopy 23

Gathings, Joseph Gouverneur **126–27**

GE 197

Gendell, Julien 42

General Dynamics 137

General Theological Seminary 213

Geological Society of America 44

Geoscience Engineering Corporation 44

Gibbs, Josiah Willard 36

Gibson, William 14

Giles, Roscoe Conkling **127–28**

Gillam, Isaac Thomas, IV **128–29**

Gillyard, Cornelia Denson **129–30**

Gipson, Joella H. 287

Gipson, Mack, Jr. **130–31**

Girshick, Abe 28

Glaucoma 183

Glidden Company 184

The Glory and the Dream 202

Glucocorticoids 152

Glut-1 transporter 10

Goldstein, Herbert 317

Goudsmit, Samuel 202

Gourdine Systems 132

Gourdine, Meredith Charles **131–33**, *132*